# Jonathan Swift

A Literary Reference to His Life and Works

PAUL J. DEGATEGNO

R. JAY STUBBLEFIELD

An imprint of Infobase Publishing

Critical Companion to Jonathan Swift: A Literary Reference to
His Life and Work

Facts On File, Inc.
An imprint of Infobase Publishing
132 West 31st Street
New York NY 10001

**Library of Congress Cataloging-in-Publication Data**

DeGategno, Paul J.
Critical companion to Jonathan Swift: a literary reference to his life and
works / Paul J. DeGategno, R. Jay Stubblefield.
p.   cm.
Includes bibliographical references and index.
ISBN 0-8160-5093-7 (acid-free paper)
1. Swift, Jonathan, 1667–1745—Encyclopedias. 2. Swift, Jonathan,
1667–1745—Handbooks, manuals, etc. 3. Satire, English—History and
criticism—Handbooks, manuals, etc. 4. Authors, Irish—18th century—
Biography—Handbooks, manuals, etc. 5. Church of Ireland—Clergy—
Biography—Handbooks, manuals, etc. I. Stubblefield, R. Jay.  II. Title.
PR3726.A24 2006
828'.509—dc22      2005025470

Text design by Erika K. Arroyo
Cover design by Cathy Rincon

Printed in the United States of America

VB Hermitage 10 9 8 7 6 5 4 3 2 1

This book is printed on acid-free paper.

# CONTENTS

# INTRODUCTION

Jonathan Swift engages scholars and students alike with the outstanding range of his writing. Whether one reads his political pamphlets, journalistic pieces, allusive satires on religious and political topics, intimate and direct letters, or entertaining and pungently ironic poetry, his intelligence, wit, and creativity shine clearly through. The memorable prose pieces of *Gulliver's Travels*, "A Tale of a Tub," "Battle of the Books," and "A Modest Proposal" remain at the forefront of any discussion concerning satire, irony, the mock-epic, the errors of human nature, the value of classical traditions, and literary portraits of starvation and poverty. While his works provide important insights on the events, persons, and society of his own day, they also offer artful commentaries on enduring issues.

During the 19th century, many readers believed Swift crossed over into uncontrolled anger for the sake of being outrageous, embraced a rebelliousness that was dangerous to the common good, and exhibited "an incipient disorder of the mind" (as Sir Walter Scott described it) in writing his so-called scatological poems. But in our time, readers and critics alike have come to realize and accept that Swift's powerful imagination places him in the ranks of Rabelais, Sterne, Joyce, and even Borges. His allusiveness and inventiveness remain the hallmarks of his work and must be interpreted in the fullest range possible. *Critical Companion to Jonathan Swift* is a guide to Swift's works and to the images, events, and people surrounding them, as well as to the critics and biographers who have commented on his writing.

## Swift's Poetry and Prose

Each of the 280 poems and nearly every one of Swift's 150 prose works are discussed in Part II. These entries provide the reader with publication information as well as the context, content, and narrative structure of the prose work or poem. Many entries, especially those on the most important or most anthologized works, contain a synopsis, followed by a separate commentary section that considers the content and characteristics of each work. For some of Swift's writings, it was impossible to provide commentary without going into extensive detail about the plot. In such cases, we have combined the synopsis and commentary entries into a single discussion. Entries on many major works also feature a separate section in which characters are individually listed and discussed. Finally, entries on the most important topics end in a further reading list. However, the bibliography in Part IV lists many more works of criticism relating to these and other writings.

## People, Places, and Topics
## Related to Swift's Work

Understanding many of Swift's works requires knowledge of the individuals who were associated with his life: his literary peers, his ecclesiastical colleagues and superiors, his political friends and enemies, his printers and publishers, his friends both intimate and occasional, and his relatives. Part III provides a variety of entries on these individuals, focusing on their relationship with Swift. In addition, it contains a number of entries on important topics and places of biographical or literary significance in Swift's writing.

## Cross-references

Any reference to a work by Swift that is the subject of an entry in Part II and any reference to a person, place, or topic that is the subject of an entry in Part III is rendered partly or entirely in SMALL CAPITAL LETTERS the first time it appears in a particular entry.

## Scholarship and Criticism

Many Swift scholars who have focused on his writing, his life, or both are mentioned throughout this book. We have been heavily dependent on the work of these critics and biographers, in addition to many others. There are, for example, plentiful references throughout the text to well-known studies, such as the biographies of Swift by Irvin Ehrenpreis and David Nokes; books on Swift's poems by Nora Crow Jaffe, John Irwin Fischer, and Louise K. Barnett; Herbert Davis's edition of Swift's prose works; and Kathleen Williams's collection of 18th- and 19th-century criticism on Swift's writing. While these and numerous other secondary works are noted in the entries, it was impossible to provide references to them all. The extensive bibliography in Part IV lists the references we relied on in bringing clarity to the readings of Swift's works, as well as information on numerous other secondary sources analyzing Swift's work. Works of criticism or biography cited in parenthetical references within an entry are listed in the Works Cited appendix in Part IV.

## Sources and Terms

The list below contains sources we used for certain texts and for terms, common to Swift scholars, we employed.

"Battle of the Books" and "A Tale of a Tub": All quotations in the text from "The Battle of the Books" are from the Oxford World's Classics edition of *A Tale of a Tub and Other Works*, edited by Angus Ross and David Woolley (Oxford: Oxford University Press, 1984).

*Gulliver's Travels:* All quotations in the text from *Gulliver's Travels* are from the revised Penguin Classics edition, edited by Robert Demaria (New York: Penguin, 2003).

*Miscellanies:* Unless otherwise noted, this term refers to the four volumes of *Miscellanies* published in London between 1727 and 1732, which contained works by Swift, Alexander Pope (who edited and compiled the volumes), and others.

*OED:* This abbreviation refers to the *Oxford English Dictionary.*

*Poems:* Unless otherwise noted, this term in italics refers to the edition of Swift's poems edited by Harold Williams (3 vols. Oxford: Clarendon Press, 1958). We have cited many of Williams's notes. However, quotations of Swift's poetry in the text are from the Penguin Classics edition, *Complete Poems,* edited by Pat Rogers (New York: Penguin, 1983).

*Prose Works:* This refers to the 14-volume *Prose Works of Jonathan Swift,* edited by Herbert Davis et al. (Oxford, England: Blackwell/Shakespeare Head, 1939–74).

## Acknowledgments

Completing a book-length project of this size and scope would not have been possible without the assistance and support of many people and institutions. We are especially grateful to Jeff Soloway, our editor at Facts On File, whose careful reading and thoughtful criticism have saved us from many errors. The early and continuous support of the North Carolina Wesleyan College administration, faculty, and library staff was an essential part of our bringing this project to completion. In 2004 Paul deGategno's new institution, Wesley College of Dover, Delaware, was willing to have a new dean of arts and sciences continue with this project and encouraged his work in this field.

Several research libraries, including the University of North Carolina at Chapel Hill, North Carolina State University, and Duke University, provided research materials. We are especially grateful to Dianne Taylor of the Pearsall Library at North Carolina Wesleyan College for her help in accessing numerous materials through Interlibrary Loan. Wesleyan College Trustee Dewey Clark, a good friend and former student, provided financial support that permitted us to add further books to our research materials and purchase necessary computing equipment. His faith in our efforts at a critical time in our work made an important difference.

Finally, our wives and families deserve our warmest appreciation for their patience, support, and encouragement at every stage of the work.

# PART I

# *Biography*

# Swift, Jonathan

(1667–1745)

Anglo-Irish satirist, poet, and political writer; dean of St. Patrick's Cathedral, Dublin. Swift was born November 30, 1667, at 7 Hoey's Court in Dublin, Ireland. His father, also named Jonathan SWIFT, was "the seventh or eighth son of the Mr. Thomas SWIFT," vicar of Goodrich ("FAMILY OF SWIFT" 191). Swift's mother, Abigail Erick SWIFT, came from a well-established family of modest means in Leicester. Born in Ireland to parents who had migrated there from England, she was a distant relative of Sir William TEMPLE. She and the elder Jonathan Swift were married in 1664.

Thomas Swift and his family resided in Yorkshire, England, and he owned a great deal of land there. He was married to Elizabeth Dryden (SWIFT) of Northamptonshire. Her great-uncle was Erasmus

Jonathan Swift, from an engraving by E. Scriven, based on a portrait by Francis Bindon

Dryden—John DRYDEN's grandfather—and this connection made the younger Jonathan Swift and John Dryden distant cousins. Thomas Swift's unwavering support of King Charles I during the Puritan Revolution cost him his position in the church (and later became a source of great pride for his grandson). After his death in 1658, his family was left to its own devices. Godwin SWIFT, the eldest of Thomas Swift's sons, was (like several of his brothers) trained in the law and migrated to Ireland after his father's death. He became wealthy, and most of his brothers—including the elder Jonathan Swift in 1660—eventually followed him to Ireland. Jonathan practiced law in Dublin and was named steward of the King's Inn but died in 1667 at the age of 27. Abigail Swift was left with a one-year-old daughter (Jane SWIFT) and gave birth to the younger Jonathan Swift seven months after her husband's death.

With no viable means of support at her disposal, Abigail Swift depended on other members of Swift's family for support. Soon after the elder Jonathan Swift's death, his brother Godwin took Abigail, Jane, and the younger Jonathan into his home. Less than a year after Jonathan's birth, however, his mother returned to her family's home in Leicester and left him with a nurse. In 1669 the nurse traveled to Whitehaven to visit an ill relative and took Swift with her. They remained there for three years, and Swift later wrote that under her care he learned to "read any chapter in the Bible" by the time he was three years old ("Family of Swift" 192). He was eventually brought back to Dublin, and was sent by his uncle Godwin to attend Kilkenny Grammar School from 1673 to 1682. In 1682 he began his studies at Trinity College, Dublin, and received his B.A. *speciali gratia* (by special grace) in February of 1686. College documents indicate that he did well in Latin and Greek but struggled in other subjects. Records also show that he was officially chastised during his years at Trinity College for offenses such as "neglect of duties and frequenting the town." In the autobiographical "Family Life of Swift," he blames these academic struggles on "the ill Treatment of his nearest Relations" (192). Swift remained in residence at Trinity College even after receiving his degree and was frequently censored and fined for causing trouble and breaking college rules. After beginning work on his M.A., Swift left for England in 1689 amid the turmoil surrounding the Glorious Revolution, in which King JAMES II—a Catholic— was eventually deposed and replaced by the Protestant WILLIAM III. Swift visited his mother in Leicester and soon moved to Moor Park in Surrey to become secretary to Sir William TEMPLE. His duties included tutoring eight-year-old Esther JOHNSON (whom he later called Stella), who was a member of Temple's household.

Within six months of taking up residence at Moor Park, Swift developed the first symptoms of what is now termed Ménière's disease (idiopathic endolymphatic hydrops). Sometimes referred to as "labyrinthine vertigo," this is an inner ear disorder characterized by headaches, dizziness, nausea, and deafness. He blamed his health problem on eating too much fruit, and based on the advice of physi-

Jonathan Swift portrait, by Charles Jervas, c. 1718
*(Library of Congress)*

cians he returned to Ireland in 1690 in an attempt to regain his health. When this failed, he resumed his duties as Temple's secretary in 1691, anticipating preferment in the form of an appointed position in the church or government. He received his M.A. from Oxford in 1692. Between 1691 and 1694, Swift wrote a number of odes including his first surviving poem ("ODE TO THE KING"), the first poem he published ("ODE TO THE ATHENIAN SOCIETY," which appeared in the *Athenian Mercury*), and three others. He became an Anglican deacon in October 1694 and was ordained as a Church of Ireland priest the following year. To Swift's dismay, he was assigned to the small parish of Kilroot (near Belfast). This was not what he had hoped for: Kilroot was surrounded by Presbyterians (known then as Dissenters), the church was in disrepair, and the congregation had been so badly ignored by Swift's predecessor that many of its members had begun to attend the Dissenters' services. Swift spent a disappointing year in Kilroot before accepting Temple's invitation to come back to Moor Park in May 1696. He proposed marriage to Jane WARING (Varina) in a letter written that same month. Swift remained at Moor Park until August 1699, and it was during this time that he began work on "A TALE OF A TUB" and "The BATTLE OF THE BOOKS"—the latter being his entry in the ongoing debate on whether ancient learning was superior to modern. Temple had argued in favor of the ancients in his essay *Ancient and Modern Learning* (1690), and Swift's "Battle" defended Temple's views against the criticism of Richard BENTLEY and William WOTTON. Seven months after Temple's death in January 1699, Swift returned to Dublin as chaplain to the earl of BERKELEY, lord justice of Ireland.

In February 1700, Swift became vicar of Laracor (about 30 miles outside Dublin) and eight months later was appointed prebend of St. Patrick's Cathedral in Dublin. When the earl of Berkeley returned to England in April of 1701 following his dismissal as lord justice, Swift accompanied him. In August Esther Johnson and her companion Rebecca DINGLEY moved to Dublin in order to be closer to Swift, and he returned there himself one month later. Before the year had ended, he published his edition of volume 3 of Temple's *Miscellanea* along with his

St. Patrick's Cathedral, Dublin *(Library of Congress)*

own "DISCOURSE OF THE CONTESTS AND DISSEN-
SIONS IN ATHENS AND ROME."

Swift received his doctor of divinity degree from
Trinity College, Dublin, in February 1702. He
remained in Ireland until November of the following year, when he returned to England and published "A Tale of a Tub" and "The Battle of the
Books." Between 1706 and 1709, he worked as a
Church of Ireland representative in London, lobbying to have Irish clergymen—like their brethren in
England—exempted from having to pay the "first
fruits and twentieth parts" (a tax normally levied
on clergymen). During this period Swift met 20-
year-old Esther VANHOMRIGH (whom he later
called Vanessa), along with Joseph ADDISON and
Richard STEELE. Swift also published the "Bickerstaff Papers" (1708) and began writing for Steele's
*Tatler* (the periodical in which Swift's "DESCRIPTION

OF THE MORNING" was first printed in 1709). He
returned to Ireland at the end of 1709.

Early on in his work as a Church of Ireland commissioner, Swift had found himself aligned with the
Whigs, but by late 1710 (after having returned for
another visit to London) he had become more
closely associated with the Tories (see TORY and
WHIG). This shift was the result of at least two factors: Swift's having failed to secure preferment
among the Whigs, and that party's increasing
friendliness with religious Dissenters (a group Swift
passionately opposed). The fall of the Whig ministry, led by Lord Treasurer Sidney GODOLPHIN,
paved the way for the Tories' rapid rise to power
under Robert HARLEY, and Swift began writing in
support of that party in the pro-Tory *EXAMINER*
(which he edited from late 1710 through June
1711). This shift in Swift's allegiances led to a grad-

ual change in his companions, and (as relations with Steele became strained) he gained friends including Alexander POPE and John ARBUTHNOT. His visit to England in September of 1710 also marked the beginning of what eventually became known as *The JOURNAL TO STELLA*—a collection of letters Swift wrote to Esther Johnson and Rebecca Dingley, who were back in Dublin.

The year 1711 marked the publication of Swift's *Miscellanies in Prose and Verse*, the first authorized collection of his works, and the printing of his "CONDUCT OF THE ALLIES." In this work, Swift argued against England's further involvement (spearheaded by the Whigs) in the War of the Spanish Succession. In 1712 he published his "Proposal for Correcting, Improving and Ascertaining the English Tongue," in which he argued for estab-

Jonathan Swift, from an engraving by C. Fritsch: "a fair likeness" *(Library of Congress)*

lishing an academy dedicated to that purpose. During a brief visit to Ireland in June of the following year, Swift was made dean of St. Paul's Cathedral, Dublin, but returned to London in September to continue lobbying for Irish clergy to be exempt from the first fruits tax. Soon after, he began meeting regularly with Arbuthnot, Pope, and other members of the SCRIBLERUS CLUB, working together on the *Memoirs of Martin Scriblerus*, a satire dedicated to exposing and ridiculing what Pope called "false tastes in learning." The first fruits negotiations went well, and after Robert Harley assured him that his wishes would certainly be granted, Swift (only two months after his arrival in London) wrote to William KING, archbishop of Dublin, that the matter had been resolved.

Swift's controversial "PUBLIC SPIRIT OF THE WHIGS" appeared in early 1714, and in June he retired to the rectory at Letcombe Bassett, Berkshire. Roughly two weeks after Queen ANNE's death on August 1 (with the inevitable fall of the Tories soon to follow), Swift reluctantly returned to Dublin to assume his post as dean of St. Patrick's Cathedral. A letter he wrote to Vanessa before leaving suggests that he did not expect to stay there for long. His arrival in Ireland began the period he would thereafter refer to unhappily as his exile from England. Miserable and bored, he sorely missed his London friends and the bustling environment in which they lived. Only two months after his departure from London, Vanessa followed Swift to Dublin and took up residence in nearby Celbridge—having ignored his attempt to dismiss her quietly before leaving London and still clinging to the hope that they might one day be married. As David Nokes explains in his biography, having Vanessa and Stella in such close proximity put Swift in an awkward position and compelled him to decide between them. He halfheartedly (but consistently) rebuffed Vanessa's attempts to rekindle their relationship, and she became increasingly despondent.

As matters continued to worsen for the Tories in England, Henry BOLINGBROKE (one of the few Tories who remained in power) left unexpectedly for France in March 1715, and Harley was impeached. The Hanoverian GEORGE I was increasingly anxious to expose Jacobite sympathizers and quell the rebellion they had undertaken. In this climate of rampant suspicion, two letters addressed to Swift were intercepted in May by suspicious authorities. Archbishop King entertained the notion that a charge might be made against Swift for treason, but it never materialized. For his part, Swift seems to have felt incredibly isolated in his "vast unfurnished house" in Dublin and completely alienated from the political upheavals taking place in London (*Corr.* II.276).

As Swift discharged his duties as dean of St. Patrick's, throughout the next year he was forced to deal with ongoing suspicion that he was a Jacobite sympathizer. Whigs received church appointments in increasing numbers, and he found himself constantly having to assert his authority among his ecclesiastical associates in Dublin. His alleged secret marriage to Stella supposedly took place in 1716 after—according to Nokes—Swift had returned to Laracor in the spring, but sometime before early October (234). If the marriage did actually occur, it did not prevent Swift from resuming contact with Vanessa before the year was out.

In 1718 Swift had begun to cultivate friendships with Thomas SHERIDAN and Patrick DELANY and seems to have started thinking of Ireland as something more than a place of temporary exile. His subsequent involvement in Irish political affairs shows that this was a lasting change in his perspective. By 1720 he had come to look upon the Irish as victims of English and Whig oppression. Despite suffering more frequent and pronounced onsets of dizziness and deafness, Swift entered the fray over Anglo-Irish relations with the publication of his "PROPOSAL FOR THE UNIVERSAL USE OF IRISH MANUFACTURE," in which he urged the Irish to resist English trade policies. As Swift's first work on Irish affairs, the piece caused Chief Justice William WHITSHED to have Swift's printer—Edward WATERS—prosecuted for his involvement in its distribution. Whitshed's reaction, however, reflected his Whig allegiances more than anything else, and the Dublin jury refused to find Waters guilty even after Whitshed sent them back into deliberations nine times. By 1721 Swift had also begun to write GULLIVER'S TRAVELS.

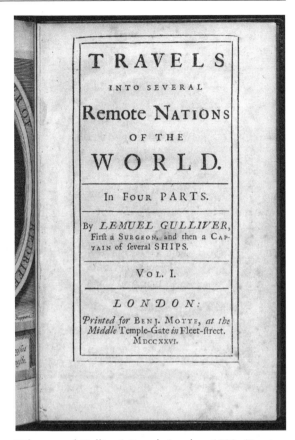

Title page of *Gulliver's Travels*, London, 1726 *(Courtesy of University of Pennsylvania Libraries)*

Swift's activities as an advocate for Ireland did not end there. In 1722 William WOOD (an English ironmaster) received a patent to introduce copper coinage in Ireland. The Irish were never consulted on the matter, and it was taken for granted that they would accept and circulate the new coins, even though Wood stood to make incredible profits at Ireland's expense. Both houses of the Irish Parliament opposed the arrangement, and in March 1724 Swift joined them in doing so by anonymously publishing the first of his DRAPIER'S LETTERS. The fourth letter of the series ("To the Whole People of Ireland," which appeared on October 22, 1724) led Lord CARTERET to prosecute John HARDING for having printed it and to offer a reward for divulging the author. In November Swift wrote a letter from the Drapier to the grand jury, however, and the case against Harding was dropped (see "SEASONABLE ADVICE TO THE GRAND JURY"). He was also successful in rallying the Irish into refusing to accept Wood's coinage, and the patent was ultimately revoked. As the Drapier, Swift had gained remarkable popularity with the public and had achieved the status of an Irish patriot (rather than an Englishman exiled in Ireland).

After five full years in Ireland, Swift returned to England in March 1726. He stayed with Alexander Pope at his villa near Twickenham (on the Thames about 10 miles west of London), and the two worked together in preparing *Gulliver's Travels* for publication. The first edition came out in London on October 28 and was greeted with immediate popularity. "CADENUS AND VANESSA" was published in Dublin that same year (without Swift's approval). Largely because of reports of Stella's poor health, Swift had returned to Dublin in September 1726, where he received a hero's welcome. He visited England once again in April the following year, where he and Pope worked for several months on compiling materials for more volumes of *Miscellanies*. When further reports of Stella's failing health arrived in September, Swift immediately left Twickenham for what was to be the final time. His trouble-filled journey back to Dublin was made even worse by his own health problems and became the subject of his "HOLYHEAD JOURNAL" and several poems (see, for example, "The POWER OF TIME"). Stella died on January 28, 1728. That same year, Swift collaborated with Sheridan on several issues of the *Intelligencer,* a weekly newspaper.

Despite health issues, Swift continued to write prolifically—especially on issues concerning Anglo-Irish relations and the church. He decried what he viewed as England's oppression of Ireland in "A MODEST PROPOSAL" (1729) and his "ANSWER TO THE CRAFTSMAN" (1730), and sought to protect the Irish clergy from unfavorable legislation in "CONSIDERATIONS UPON TWO BILLS . . . RELATING TO THE CLERGY OF IRELAND" (1731). He also wrote some of his most famous poetry during this period, including "VERSES ON THE DEATH OF DR. SWIFT," "The LADY'S DRESSING ROOM," "A BEAUTIFUL YOUNG NYMPH GOING TO BED," and "STREPHON AND

CHLOE." In "ADVANTAGES PROPOSED BY REPEALING THE SACRAMENTAL TEST ACT" (1732), he opposed granting Dissenters the right to hold office, and another volume of *Miscellanies* (a joint effort with Pope) appeared the same year. "ON POETRY: A RHAPSODY" was published in 1733. In 1734–35 Dublin printer George FAULKNER issued four volumes of Swift's collected works, including a revised version of *Gulliver's Travels* in volume 3. When, in December of 1735, Ireland's House of Commons agreed to hear the petitions of Irish landowners seeking exemption from paying tithes, Swift bitterly responded with his "CHARACTER, PANEGYRIC, AND DESCRIPTION OF THE LEGION CLUB" (1736)—a verse satire against what he viewed as the parliamentary majority's hypocrisy and stupidity.

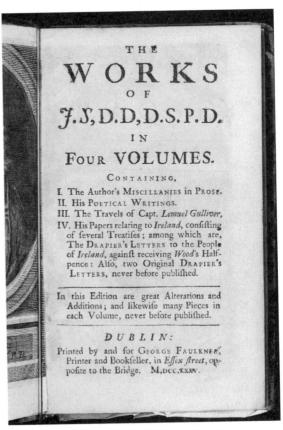

Title page of Swift's *Works*, Dublin, 1735 *(Courtesy of University of Pennsylvania Libraries)*

By 1738 the symptoms of Ménière's disease were becoming more pronounced and debilitating for Swift. His COMPLETE COLLECTION OF GENTEEL AND INGENIOUS CONVERSATION (also known as *Polite Conversation*) was published that year, but memory loss, dizziness, and constant anxiety made it increasingly difficult for him to work. His cousin Martha WHITEWAY took over the management of his affairs. Rev. Francis Wilson (a prebend of St. Patrick's Cathedral) moved into the deanery and allegedly mistreated Swift by stealing his books and money, and perhaps even physically assaulting him. Nokes cites Swift's last extant correspondence to Mrs. Whiteway to sum up his condition in 1740: "I have been very miserable all night, and today extremely deaf and full of pain. . . . I hardly understand one word I write. I am sure my days will be very few; few and miserable they must be" (quoted in Nokes 410). There are numerous tales surrounding Swift's final "miserable" years, many suggesting flashes of clarity, most describing him as having lapsed into a state of utter incoherence. In August 1742 Rev. Wilson called for a Commission of Lunacy to assess Swift's mental state. At the age of 75, he was declared to be of "unsound mind and memory" and "incapable of transacting any business" or caring for himself. He died in the deanery on October 19, 1745, and was buried next to Stella in St. Patrick's Cathedral. In his will, Swift designated part of his estate to be used for the construction of a hospital for the mentally ill in Dublin (eventually St. Patrick's Hospital). The Latin epitaph he wrote for himself was later translated by

Jonathan Swift bust in St. Patrick's Cathedral

William Butler Yeats in *The Winding Stair and Other Poems* (1933): "Swift has sailed into his rest; / Savage indignation there / Cannot lacerate his breast. / Imitate him if you dare, / World-besotted traveller; he / Served human liberty."

# Part II

# Works A–Z

# "Abstract of the History of England"

First printed from Swift's manuscript by Deane SWIFT in his edition of Swift's *Works* (London, 1765) and again in Dublin the same year. It did not appear in his lifetime, and some do not consider it a literary work. Swift wrote the piece in 1697 at Moor Park, after returning the second time to work for Sir William TEMPLE. As he edited the first two volumes of Temple's *Works* (1702), Swift was also preparing "A TALE OF A TUB," as well as, in the opinion of some critics, making these notes for a projected continuation of Temple's *Introduction to the History of England* (1695).

## SYNOPSIS

Britain's population was divided into small kingdoms across the island, and the Britons themselves were pagans. The males painted their bodies "sky-colored blue" in preparation for battle. Their religion had a strong oral tradition, maintained by illiterate priests, known as Druids, who lived "in hollow trees." About 50 B.C., Julius Caesar invaded Britain to add to his reputation but chose not to remain, though the Romans returned, during the reigns of Claudius and Nero, to establish a colony governed by Roman civil and military rulers, "as Ireland is now by deputies from England." The Romans held the island and its borders against Caledonians and Picts, building a wall in the north against their intrusions.

Once the Romans left, the Britons invited the fierce Saxons to live with them as protection against more frequent attacks from the Picts, but rather soon the Saxons forced the Britons into Wales and established the Saxon Heptarchy of seven kingdoms. King Arthur emerged during this period, which suggests "the whole story be not a fable," and repulsed the Saxons in several places. As for religion, the Britons were early converts to Christianity, though the Saxons were not and did not accept conversion until Pope Gregory's mission had success with the arrival of St. Augustine.

With the settlement of the Saxons, a form of English became the dominant language, and they created the present names of villages, cities, and shires. With thoughts of plunder foremost, the Danes began their years of raiding the English coast, and as a response to these constant ravages King Edgar of Albion formed the first English navy, and in time the Danes mixed with the English and even lived under Saxon government. The inevitable conflict continued after the massacre of the Danes in A.D. 978 (Swift's date is wrong, actually A.D. 1002), and the Danes' and Saxons' control of the country shifted back and forth until the emergence of Edward the Confessor, who first introduced common law.

Edward, who died without an heir, appointed the grandson of his brother to succeed him, but the boy's governor took the crown for himself. King Harold then had to face the demands of William, duke of Normandy, who threatened invasion; and after refusing to surrender, Harold lost his final battle as William became king of England.

## COMMENTARY

Swift agreed with his mentor Temple's philosophy regarding the writing of history, which extolled the aesthetic and imaginative delights of reviewing the great spectacle of progress. He understood, though his "Abstract" is not the best evidence, that history is not a parade of events but a process governed by large, environmental, social, and cultural forces that must be described and analyzed with confidence. This curious essay shows that Swift was developing, as critics have said, a gratifying consciousness of what mattered in English history. Swift is loyal to Temple's method on the whole but without its egregious qualities. His first accomplishment was in escaping a few of Temple's hypothetical digressions and reducing the praise of Edgar to a line. Adding to the oddness of the piece is its purposeful simple-mindedness, as one critic reminds us, a kind of grave foolishness where Swift refers to the Britons as heathens "as all the world was before Christ," the Druids living in hollow trees, the English language as quite different now, and other curiosities. The "Abstract" more than likely does not represent his preparation for writing his own history, but a teaching aid for a young Stella (Esther JOHNSON) or some other student.

# "Accomplishment of the First of Mr. Bickerstaff's Predictions"

This four-page essay, written as a letter "to a person of honor," was printed in London in 1708, and all the Bickerstaff papers were reprinted in *Miscellanies,* 1711; 1713; 1727; and in the *Works* in 1735. In this text, Swift carries on the joke precipitated in the "PREDICTIONS FOR THE YEAR 1708," where he reports John PARTRIDGE's painful death on March 29 "about eleven at night, of a raging fever." The "Accomplishment" was published on March 30, the day following the "death."

## SYNOPSIS

An "independent" observer writes of Bickerstaff's predictions, which include an account of the upcoming death of Mr. Partridge, the almanac maker, on March 29. He has been checking regularly to determine whether Partridge is still alive, trying to assess the accuracy of Bickerstaff's foresight. Having known Partridge for a number of years when he was selling almanacs, the witness notes the man's health becoming progressively worse, though his closest friends did not take notice. As he progresses toward his inevitable death, Partridge droops and languishes, grows ill, and ends up in his bed, where Dr. Case and Mr. Kirleus—two famous London quacks—provide care. After questioning Partridge, the observer determines that Bickerstaff's so-called fictitious reports of his death have worked on his imagination, and he has come to believe them himself to the point of becoming delusional. Partridge provides a form of deathbed confession, pleading in the clearest terms that Bickerstaff could not have predicted his death, since astrology and predictions are only for fools, the ignorant, and the poor. He begs the mercy of his listener, explaining that as a former cobbler, he had no other options in making ready money. He supposes that as a quack practicing medicine he could have done as well. Finally, combining lunacy with a revelation of his Nonconformist principles, he invites a "fanatick preacher" to be his final spiritual guide. The independent witness withdraws to a coffeehouse for the inevitable death, which comes only four hours earlier than predicted. This result would seem to confirm the accuracy of Bickerstaff's predictions, but the observer intends to await the death of another person, one Cardinal de Noailles, a papist who the astrologer determines will be next.

## COMMENTARY

This playful, taunting answer to Partridge—who had become the classic embodiment of everything Swift scorned—punishes the almanac maker for his regular attacks on the Church of England. The balancing act Swift manages between fact and fiction, relying on impersonation and disguise, provided him the ultimate success—drawing out Partridge himself, who was fooled into denouncing Bickerstaff as someone who actually existed. Falling into Swift's ornate trap, Partridge revealed how he took his own astrological speculations seriously and proved himself a superstitious pedant and a nervous charlatan. "Accomplishment" clearly out-Partridged Partridge in its predictions, and in the process it casually foretold his death. The hit was amazingly accurate and direct, so much so that Partridge's name was struck from the rolls of the Company of Stationers, and he thereby lost his right to publish his almanac.

# "Account of the Court and Empire of Japan, An"

According to Deane SWIFT, Swift wrote this essay in 1728, but it was first published by this cousin in the *Works* in 1765, and later in the same year in Dublin, when printer George FAULKNER reprinted the essay in *Works*. In his biography of Swift, Irvin Ehrenpreis convincingly suggests the composition date as mid-1727, when GEORGE II had met with Robert WALPOLE shortly after the king's accession (III.529).

## SYNOPSIS

This fragment provides the history of the past two years in the Empire of Japan, focusing on the death of one emperor and the accession of another, the initiation and functioning of its two political parties, and the actions of its chief minister, Lelop-Aw.

As the name (an anagram of *Walpole*) suggests, the character satirizes Robert Walpole. This essay is a thinly disguised satire on the political environment in England in 1727–28 with the Japanese emperors as George I and George II, and the political parties, Husige (WHIG) and Yortes (TORY). The minister writes a long letter to the king, justifying and describing the importance of his work to the proper running of the government, using bribes "to grease the wheels" and advocating nepotism. Lelop-Aw makes clear the damage the Yortes have done to the nation, educating the new monarch in the realities. All will be improved, states the minister: for the sum of a million pounds sterling, new senators can be purchased who will suit the king's desires.

## COMMENTARY

From April to September 1727, Swift was in England hoping to consult with the son and friends of the earl of OXFORD for his "History" and to discuss with Alexander POPE a volume of *Miscellanies,* their first project together. His dislike for Walpole and the Whigs was palpable, and their distrust of him even more pronounced than before. Swift joined the Opposition against Walpole, but due to his own sickness and Stella's (Esther JOHNSON's) final illness, he left for Ireland abruptly. If this fragment offers the contemporary reader a point of reference, it reflects the corruption of the Walpole second administration; these ministers are "furious intriguers." Swift hoped his essay would be published and serve as advice to the new king, and he subscribed to the idea that self-interest would urge these ministers to act in the best interests of the nation. If these men would reform themselves, then all would prosper, as would the nation. This view did not prove practical or accurate.

## "Ad Amicum Eruditum Thomam Sheridan"

Poem by Swift; first published 1735, written 1717. It is a Latin eulogy praising Dr. Thomas SHERIDAN for his learning and other admirable qualities. The title translates "To My Learned Friend Thomas Sheridan."

## "Addenda Quaedam"

Verses Swift included in a June 5, 1736, letter to Dr. Thomas SHERIDAN. The title means "a certain addition." The poem answers lines Sheridan had written in two earlier letters he sent to Swift describing County Cavan, Ireland, where Sheridan had established a school.

## "Advantages Proposed by Repealing the Sacramental Test, Impartially Considered, The"

This pamphlet was first printed in Dublin on February 8, 1732, and reprinted in London for J. Roberts at the Oxford Arms in Warwick Lane during March 1732. It was advertised in the *Grub Street Journal,* March 9, 1732. Dublin printer George FAULKNER added it to the *Works* in 1735.

## SYNOPSIS

The anonymous author of this pamphlet projects an air of objectivity and impartiality on the issues of whether Dissenters in Ireland should be permitted civic, military, and judicial posts. His impartial tone disguises the predominant undercurrent of the whole piece—pervasive irony. Under the Sacramental Test Act, nonconforming Protestants, especially Presbyterians, could not hold public office unless they agreed, using occasional conformity, with the supreme authority of the Established Church of England, or Ireland in this case. Writing against toleration was a simple choice for Swift, who viewed dissent as a dangerous form of religious insanity that violated political and clerical integrity.

Focusing on the need for one religion, the author describes how other nations who have one religion have found it beneficial, whereas those who have permitted diversity have realized "horrible destructive events." He predicts that repealing the Test Act would produce a clashing of wills and interests. The Presbyterians are above morality, and in every respect he feels that if the law allowed them their share of employments they would still not be satisfied. He imagines that a Presbyterian army officer could want to become a preacher too, and then begin teaching as well. In a cool, straightforward manner, the author imagines the most outrageous situations to be possible.

## COMMENTARY

Swift clearly advances what could have been a minor irritation about Dissenters into a major fixation of his writing career, in both the early and late periods. He fears the damage they can do to the stability of the nation and the Established Church, and he remains unapologetic about his intolerance for their existence and actions. Repealing the Test Act would be a major mistake, one that would not be in the national interest. If the Established Church has corrupt elements within it, then he supports reform, but no scattering of religious interests can have any positive effect. Swift distrusts Presbyterians, who are the largest and most powerful body of Irish Dissenters, realizing that if they gained a preeminent position in the country, the Episcopal faith would soon suffer attacks. One can compare this pamphlet to the earlier "LETTER FROM A MEMBER OF THE HOUSE OF COMMONS IN IRELAND" (1708), though critics point to the difference in tone between the two essays. The later piece seems bleak and hopeless, even angry, reflecting Swift's displeasure with Hugh BOULTER's connivance to remove the test, as well as the government's general contempt for the clergy's condition. Swift wrote three other essays in opposition: "Queries Relating to the Sacramental Test," "Reasons Humbly Offered to the Parliament of Ireland, for Repealing the Sacramental Test, in Favour of the Catholics," and "The Presbyterians' Plea of Merit." See also the poem "ON THE WORDS 'BROTHER PROTESTANTS AND FELLOW CHRISTIANS.'"

# "Advertisement by Dr. Swift, in His Defence against Joshua, Lord Allen"

This 300-word paragraph was first printed by John Nichols in *Works*, in 1801. Herbert Davis does not think the advertisement was ever published in a Dublin newspaper, and can find no evidence to support any other conclusion.

## SYNOPSIS

Swift announces that he has learned that on February 13 [1730] a certain person (Viscount Joshua ALLEN) had complained to the lord mayor of Dublin in public about Swift's having been awarded a gold box. The unhappy citizen supposedly asked the mayor how the city could waste money giving a gold box to someone who had libeled the government. Swift makes it clear that if such a statement had been made, it was scandalous and malicious, particularly since the city had unanimously granted him this freedom of Dublin for services rendered. In addition, the person who reportedly made these comments had professed friendship for him (the dean) and had affirmed his affection for him by sending an intermediary to renew this friendship. Swift believes he has been lied to, and when he discovers the lie the next day, explains the conspiracy to his true friends.

## COMMENTARY

The distinction of receiving the freedom of the city in a gold box from the lord mayor and the Common Council meant a great deal to Swift, who had earnestly sought such a commendation. When Allen tried to repair the damage from his outburst, the insult had already gone too far, and Swift responded with this piece, dated February 18. Allen, taking the opportunity from his bench in the House of Lords, denounced Swift again, without naming him, and asked that the writer of "A LIBEL ON THE REVEREND DR. DELANY AND HIS EXCELLENCY JOHN, LORD CARTERET" should be prosecuted as a Jacobite libeler. Swift proceeded to attack him without mercy. See also "A CHARACTER, PANEGYRIC, AND DESCRIPTION OF THE LEGION CLUB," "TRAULUS," "A PANEGYRIC ON THE REVEREND DEAN SWIFT," and "An EPISTLE UPON AN EPISTLE."

# "Advertisement" in the *Dublin News Letter*

Swift signed this one-paragraph notice, which appeared in early January 1737 and was reprinted two weeks later in the *Dublin News Letter,* also referred to as the *Dublin Weekly Newsletter.*

During the mid-1720s, John HARDING published the *News Letter* and printed the first five pamphlets of *The DRAPIER'S LETTERS,* until he was arrested and died in prison the week after Swift had all but secured his release when a grand jury refused to charge him. Swift had relied on the *News Letter* as a tool in the publicity campaign against William WOOD's patent. His solicitation here 13 years later invokes that period abstractly, reminding his readers that he "is never last in encouraging the honest and industrious trader of Ireland." Swift asks for contributions to assist two men and their families from his parish who had lost their goods and possessions in the St. Mary's Abbey fire.

Herbert Davis includes this piece in his miscellaneous volume, Swift's *Prose Works* (containing mostly material never before collected in any previous editions). The manner and argument are normal for Swift: treating the request for funds as a natural responsibility of those neighbors of "Godfrey and Green" who might themselves face "a calamity from which no family can promise themselves to be secure." His bullying tone works well, announcing that as their dean he has done his part and now they must act charitably, too. His values here are reasonable and appropriate, though colored with an impatience for those who forget or refuse to act properly within the community.

# "Advice Humbly Offer'd to the Members of the October Club"

This pamphlet was printed on January 22, 1712, in London and advertised two days earlier in *The Post Boy.* George FAULKNER reprinted it in *Works,* 1738. Swift calls upon the membership of the club to remain loyal to Robert HARLEY (first earl of Oxford) and refrain from petty complaining. The October Club, as Swift explains in *The JOURNAL TO STELLA,* "is a set of above a hundred parliamentmen of the country who drink October beer at home, and meet every evening at a tavern near the parliament, to consult affairs, and drive things on

to extreams against the Whigs." These high-flier TORY squires met to talk politics at Bell Tavern in King Street, Westminster, and became a source of concern to the ministry due to their radical attitudes, so much so that Swift fretted that they might become an independent party.

## SYNOPSIS

Sympathy and trust are the watchwords of the essay. The writer, in the spirit of letting one friend confidentially explain a critical issue to another, describes how "the Enemy" has been intriguing lately and their spirit of revenge remains stronger than ever. Knowing this, the club should refrain from further demands for wholesale removal of all WHIG officials who remain in the new government, especially since the new ministry has already accomplished a great deal because of one great person. He assures the club that the current chief minister serves the best interests of the nation, and if they consider themselves patriots, then they should act accordingly and support the minister as he does the nation's work. Though Oxford is never mentioned by name, his moderate policies will have the best chance of success.

## COMMENTARY

This pamphlet emerged as an insider piece with an argument designed to redirect the supposed faults from Oxford to the duke of Somerset. Swift argues convincingly that the October Club must leave Lord Treasurer Oxford alone, or all the Tories will be lost and their government defunct. Swift received suggestions from the duchess of Shrewsbury (see SHREWSBURY, CHARLES TALBOT) that the queen could be persuaded to turn out Somerset, and with his departure from Court would go the most significant member of the Whig junto, giving the Tories the firmest hold on the government they would have had to date. Also, the continuing divisiveness between Henry St. John (Viscount BOLINGBROKE) and Oxford caused Swift frequent concern, and though he followed Oxford's directions and placed some blame for the present difficulties on St. John, critics feel the decision to write anonymously was in part due to Swift's not wanting this minister to know his authorship. As an occasional piece, a modern reader finds the political moment hard to grasp but not the facility of language, the wit, the control of information on people and events, the appropriate tone of the wise counsellor who has the best interests of the club members at heart—all these virtues and others make this a memorable pamphlet. See also *The* JOURNAL TO STELLA.

# *"Advice to a Parson"*

Poem by Swift; first published in 1732, written the same year. Along with the "EPIGRAM (ON SEEING A WORTHY PRELATE GO OUT OF CHURCH)" this poem was originally printed by James Roberts in his first edition of "The LADY'S DRESSING ROOM." Sarcastic in tone, it is a set of mock instructions on how to "rise in the church." Referencing (without naming) clergymen such as Hugh BOULTER and Josiah HORT, Swift offers a scathing commentary on the worldly self-centeredness he saw among bishops promoting English interests in Ireland. The poem was prompted by Parliament's consideration in late 1731 and early 1732 of the Bill of Residence and the Bill of Division. The first gave bishops the power to force clergymen who earned more than £100 per year to build a home near their church, while the second divided parishes worth more than that amount in half. See also "CONSIDERATIONS UPON TWO BILLS . . . RELATING TO THE CLERGY OF IRELAND," "ON THE IRISH BISHOPS," and "JUDAS."

# *"Advice to the Freemen of the City of Dublin"*

This essay was printed as a broadside in September 1733 and reprinted in Dublin by George FAULKNER in his editions of Swift's *Works* (1746 and 1751) and in London in *Miscellanies* (1746).

## SYNOPSIS

Dubliners have great respect for Swift's words, and Lord Lieutenant CARTERET complains in a letter that when the dean speaks Dubliners will comply—clearly Carteret knows the power Swift can wield in a pamphlet or advertisement. With the upcoming parliamentary election, the dean argues that only two parties exist in Ireland: the Anglo-Irish and the English who are sent to govern the Irish. Every election should be taken seriously, every citizen has a responsibility to vote with intelligence and discretion, particularly when one considers "the state of our unfortunate country." In order to do so, the writer will analyze each candidate's general character and experience. Before proceeding further with these encouragements to proper action, the writer focuses on his main theme: a dysfunctional government that prevents independent thought and deprives the Irish of their personal freedoms. If English politicians serving in Ireland have only their country's national interests in their view, and those interests seem more about gaining power and riches, then Ireland will never take its proper place as a free country. The writer urges that Dubliners vote for the lord mayor, Humphrey French, since he has shown more virtue, skill, and activity than anyone in recent memory.

### COMMENTARY

Swift had been active in parliamentary elections over the past year beginning in 1732, and had come out in favor of the lord mayor, not only because he respected French but also because the office of mayor was not controlled by the British Crown. Since the English government cannot exert direct influence on the mayor, he will have more freedom to act in the best interest of the Dublin freemen. Swift also could make clear once again his deep distrust of the English representatives in Ireland. This annoyed Lord Lieutenant DORSET, who apparently was about to take steps to prosecute the pamphlet's printer and its author. Though he considered Dorset and Carteret his friends, they did not believe Swift's statement that the men he recommended were presented without regard to party. Swift's goal was to wrest some justice from the English government for the Irish. If direct action was necessary, whether confronting one's enemy in a straightforward manner or using an anonymous pamphlet to create defiance, then he was willing to take either approach.

# "Advice to the Grub Street Verse-Writers"

Poem by Swift; first published in *Works* (1735), written in 1726. Addressed to the "ragged and forlorn" poets of GRUB STREET, it suggests that the only way they will ever "thrive" is to lend their poems—printed with wide margins—to "paper-sparing" Alexander POPE in the hope that he will fill the margins with his own verses. They should then "recall" the "loan" and try to pass Pope's work off as their own. In his edition of Swift's verse, Pat Rogers suggests that Swift may have written the poem during his stay with Pope at Twickenham in the summer of 1726.

# "Anglo-Latin Verses"

Poems by Swift written in a language he contrived called "Latino-Anglicus," which appears to be Latin but is actually made up of phonetic versions of English words ("Molli dii vinis" = "Molly divine is"). Harold Williams notes that "Swift and his Irish friends were in the habit of exchanging *jeux d'esprit* in disguised English or disguised Latin" (*Poems* III.1038). Like other poems such as "TO DR. HELSHAM," the "Anglo-Latin Verses" reflect Swift's love of various word games he played in correspondence with his friends.

# "Another Reply by the Dean"

Poem by Swift; first published 1735, written c. 1718. Subtitled "In Dan Jackson's Name," it is a supposed response to the series of poems by George ROCHFORT, Dr. Thomas SHERIDAN, and Swift making fun of Daniel JACKSON's large nose. Here Jackson declares himself victorious, having silenced the other writers, and he offers some consolation in their defeat. See also "TO MR. DELANEY," "ON DAN JACKSON'S PICTURE," "DAN JACKSON'S REPLY," and "SHERIDAN'S SUBMISSION."

# "Answer of the Right Honourable William Pulteney, Esq; to the Right Honourable Sir Robert Walpole, The"

This essay was written in October 1730 but first printed in 1768 by Deane SWIFT in his edition of Swift's letters in the *Works*. Later, Dublin printer George FAULKNER published the piece in the *Works* in the same year. Herbert Davis believes the probability of Swift's having written this essay is strong though not conclusive.

## SYNOPSIS

Swift adopts the persona of William PULTENEY and begins with reference to corruption in politics and how this type of fraud causes particular damage to a freeborn Englishman. No "corporation of pamphleteers" can defend a corrupt politician since the facts are obvious to anyone who has sense. He proceeds to a listing of some of Robert WALPOLE's more impudent decisions in foreign affairs and then to his favorite theme: the damage to the national church from tolerating Dissenters. He touches upon the importance of maintaining the principles of the constitution, which ensure that all serving government officials should remain subject to inquiries of Parliament. Pulteney had worked with Henry BOLINGBROKE to begin the *Craftsman*, a journal offering a coherent opposition to the Walpole administration. Alluding to the articles in this publication, he suggests any group of citizens of wisdom, virtue, and generous nature who point out to the public the actions of avaricious ministers and cringing flatterers do the state a beneficial service. Finally, "Pulteney" assures Walpole that he has no responsibility nor should he assume any guilt for insults and comments against the king and his government. The writer knows the difference between a patriot and a plunderer, and all the libelous attacks on him (Pulteney) will not turn a loyal servant of his king into a disloyal traitor.

## COMMENTARY

Swift's resentment toward Walpole remained strong at the time this work was composed. Pulteney—who met Swift in London in 1726—urged the dean to join him and Bolingbroke in a sensible opposition to the Walpole administration. Swift felt politically and ethically sympathetic with their plans but could not join them and returned to Dublin. But for a time, Swift would join with Alexander POPE and John GAY in correcting the imbalance the power of the moneymen and stockjobbers had introduced into England and its government. This essay spoke to the essential issues of corruption, pride, vanity, and exploitation. Swift did urge Walpole in two separate interviews to respond to the grievances of Ireland, but with no success. Pulteney's antiministerial efforts, which would soon be realized in his journal, unfortunately proved to Swift the impossibility of reaching an accommodation with Walpole. Some have argued that Pulteney's and Bolingbroke's activities were nothing short of quixotic and smacked of pure nostalgia—why return to the notions of old landed capitalism when the new money-capitalism seemed essential in a healthy society? See also "ON MR. PULTENEY BEING PUT OUT OF THE COUNCIL."

# "Answer to a Paper, Called 'A Memorial of the Poor Inhabitants, Tradesmen, and Labourers of the Kingdom of Ireland,' An"

The essay was first printed by Sarah HARDING in Dublin, March 1728, and reprinted as an abstract in *Mist's Weekly Journal*, May 11, 1728 (though it was announced in the same journal on April 23, 1728). It later appeared in George FAULKNER's 1735 Dublin edition of Swift's *Works*.

## SYNOPSIS

A. B. (Swift's pseudonym) declares clearly his opposition to the *Memorial's* proposal, but proceeds with a history of Irish agriculture in recent times. His history seems more a list of accusations against all those responsible for the sorry state of tillage: landlords, graziers, and tenant farmers. Grazing sheep for the English woolen trade becomes a better use of the land with a higher profit margin than tilling it for grain.

The result is apparent, as tenant farmers lose their leases and end up as homeless beggars. Swift returns to the projector's suggestion for purchasing grain in the short term—"you . . . forget the twenty shillings for the price." Ireland is too poor to pay for importation of grain, and the destitute former Irish tenants, now starving, are too poor to purchase the grain should it become available. Instead of this "crude but pardonable" proposal, A. B. suggests creating a public charity to provide the poor with potatoes and buttermilk. In fact, if the English would contribute a small amount of the millions they gain from Ireland every year, the Irish might have a chance to survive. Then, Swift takes the final satiric step that he applies in "A MODEST PROPOSAL" and *GULLIVER'S TRAVELS*, proposing that the rest of the nation stop worrying about the poor and let them emigrate; as he would say later, people are the riches of a nation only if they can be sold as slaves. His harshness is meant to show the foolishness of the other writers whose projects have little chance of success.

## COMMENTARY

In the late 1720s Swift was developing the theme of Ireland's special circumstance in Europe. In nine separate essays he would argue for various methods for the Irish to escape (or at least reduce) English repression. Nearly every tract responds to proposals written by other writers concerned with Irish interests. "An Answer to a Paper" focuses on agriculture, and addresses Sir John BROWNE's earlier pamphlet, which suggested a plan for importing 100,000 barrels of wheat to lessen the effects of a bad harvest. Though Swift appreciated the sympathy of Browne's suggestions, as they showed concern for the Irish suffering, he could not approve of them. His answer combines a dose of truth about the origins of these agricultural failures, an analysis of Browne's projection with its flaws, and a final satiric jab at the English who have reduced the Irish to either emigration or starvation.

# "Answer to a Scandalous Poem, An"

Poem by Swift; first published in 1733, written in 1732. It is a reply to Dr. Thomas SHERIDAN's *A New*

*Simile,* a lengthy poem (according to Swift's subtitle) "Wherein the Author Most Audaciously Presumes to Cast an Indignity upon Their Highnesses the Clouds, by Comparing Them to a Woman." First printed with Sheridan's text, Swift's "Answer" is written in the voice of Dermot O'Nephely—a chief cloud—who expresses his indignity at being compared to women. The poem contains the famous final couplet, "We own, your verses are melodious, / But such comparisons are odious."

# "Answer to a Scurrilous Pamphlet, Lately Printed, Entitled, A Letter from Monsieur du Cros, An"

Swift wrote this essay at MOOR PARK in 1692–93, and it may be considered his first published prose work, which appeared in February 1693.

## SYNOPSIS

The anonymous writer suggests that "the author of the *Memoirs*" (Sir William TEMPLE) has nothing to worry about from the attack of du Cros but his friends expect him to answer these charges. He reports the facts of du Cros's biography, painting him as a papist and comparing him to an incompetent playwright whose hero appears and disappears haphazardly. After a case-by-case analysis of du Cros's comments regarding the *Memoirs,* the writer concludes that Temple's handling of the treaty met every diplomatic requirement, and "what occasion Monsieur du Cros had to publish so unjust and invidious a calumny, no body can tell but himself." His review of the *Letter* against Temple proceeds with care, alluding to John DRYDEN's statement about Ben Jonson that describing the traits of any character he would introduce was critical in a full understanding of the motives of these individuals—du Cros does not provide such detail. Also, Swift argues that the lack of information regarding who published du Cros's pamphlet reduces its credibility. Temple has no real interest in du Cros, "an enemy of so prostitute a character."

## COMMENTARY

The curious essay originates with Temple's mission to The Hague in 1678 when CHARLES II sent him to assist WILLIAM, prince of Orange, in resisting a peace initiative from the Dutch states to France. The Dutch hoped to end the war with France and resume free trade. William, however, insisted, as a condition of signing any treaty, on the establishment of a defensive barrier of towns between Holland and France. LOUIS XIV refused to agree without payment of restitution to his ally Sweden; in the meantime, Temple managed a bilateral military alliance—the Anglo-Dutch defensive treaty. Apparently, Charles had second thoughts, and without informing his ambassador, sent counterinstructions through Joseph August du Cros (c. 1640–1728), a Frenchman who came to England in the 1670s, married an Englishwoman, and served as a double agent working for both the Swedes and French. Du Cros's assignment depended on his convincing the Swedes to agree to release the towns in the Spanish Netherlands to Holland and Spain and secure France's compliance with this arrangement. Temple became furious, now realizing that he would be undercutting his efforts with William and the newly formed Anglo-Dutch treaty. Nonetheless, he had no choice but to pursue his king's wishes. Later, in letters and in his *Memoirs of What Passed in Christendom* (1691), Temple made du Cros the prime villain of his later diplomatic career, calling him "the Rogue." When du Cros discovered these statements, he responded sharply in a pamphlet, *Lettre de Monsieur du Cros à Mylord* (1692). Originally published with a Cologne imprint (but actually published in Holland), its English translation soon appeared in London.

Soon after, Temple or (more probably) Swift wrote and had published *An Answer.* This response only added fuel to the debate and two more pamphlets appeared that year exchanging blows. Since Swift would later write in support of Temple's ideas and concerns, in "The BATTLE OF THE BOOKS" (1697) and as an editor of Temple's *Miscellanea: Part Three* (1701), as well as numerous prose strategies and rhetorical modes, all these writings point toward Swift's composition of this energetic tract.

# "Answer to Bickerstaff, An"

Swift did not publish this work during his lifetime, and its first appearance was in Deane SWIFT's *Works*, 1765. Herbert Davis does not fully agree that this essay was Swift's work, though he does not conclusively argue either way. Irvin Ehrenpreis considers that Swift probably wrote this work in February 1708 (*Swift* II.199 n.6); Angus Ross and David Woolley find no reason to doubt that Swift in the first months of that year wrote four of the Bickerstaff papers, including "An Answer." He then followed this highly successful joke in February and April 1709 with two final pieces. Swift may have held off publishing "An Answer" because of the allusion, the direct autobiographical confession, connecting Bickerstaff with the author of "A TALE OF A TUB."

## SYNOPSIS

This amusing but densely constructed joke within a joke reveals Swift in an elaborate balancing act, as Irvin Ehrenpreis says, between self-concealment and self-revelation (*Swift* II.203). The anonymous writer, a man of quality, who has been the best kind of observer, now writes in an objective tone, having spotted Bickerstaff as a cheat, one huckster (Bickerstaff) seeing through another (PARTRIDGE). The writer sarcastically comments on Bickerstaff's having tricked thousands of readers into actually believing his *Predictions*, as they await the eventual results according to the timetable Bickerstaff set. The frequent references to this earlier work demand that the reader either refresh his memory by rereading his copy or purchase another. Twice the man of quality assures us of the carelessness of the composition and how easily the public "bites" when tempted with the least bit of strangeness, its members so dulled with daily life that they can hardly ignore opportunities like this. The first part of "An Answer" seems more concerned with how the author will compel himself to maintain his disguise, even when friends observe him closely, thinking he might be the author. He finishes with a combination of arrogance and irony, suggesting the accuracy of the "Predictions" but diminishing their importance with the announcement of Bickerstaff's having died.

## COMMENTARY

The astrologers, their tremendous profits, and the duping of a gullible public serve as the true impulse for these essays. Certainly, Partridge's frequent attacks, which were Low Church and anti-Tory, annoyed Swift and deserved a response. But he also intends this essay as a complement to the "Predictions," a way of illuminating that earlier, more complete statement. The pleasure in this piece radiates from our knowing the truth while watching as the author manages a complicated hoax.

# "Answer to Delany's Riddle, The"

Poem by Swift; first published along with Patrick DELANY's riddle as a broadside in 1726. Swift provides the actual answer to the riddle—"an eye"—in the very first line of the poem. In the remaining lines he disagrees with some of Delany's clues and adds his own commentary on the answer.

# "Answer to Dr. Delany, The"

Poem by Swift; first published 1735. It is Swift's response to a short poem Patrick DELANY sent to him in the summer of 1724, while Swift was suffering a long period of deafness. Delany complained that Swift had shut ears and doors to him, and expressed his desire to see Swift soon. Swift's "Answer" is chiefly devoted to explaining the difficulty of coping with hearing loss compared to dealing with the loss of one limb or one eye, in which case the other can help compensate. See also "ON HIS OWN DEAFNESS."

# "Answer to Dr. Delany's Fable of the Pheasant and the Lark, An"

Poem by Swift; first published 1730, written the same year. The fable mentioned in the title was

Rev. Patrick DELANY's attempt to remedy the embarrassment he had suffered due to his 1729 "Epistle to Lord Carteret" (see "EPISTLE UPON AN EPISTLE"). Delany also thanked Swift in the fable for the encouragement he had provided in "TO A FRIEND WHO HAD BEEN MUCH ABUSED IN MANY INVETERATE LIBELS." The fable itself outlines the jealousy of those who made fun of Delany in print upon seeing his letter to Carteret. Each of these authors—Thomas SHERIDAN, William DUNKIN, etc.—is cast as an inferior bird that envies the lark (Delany) because the pheasant (Carteret) has befriended him. Swift is cast as the nightingale who defends the lark and forces the other birds to "hide their heads, and hush their throats" (148). In his "Answer," Swift writes in the person of an English admirer of his enemy Joshua ALLEN and asserts that Delany made poor choices in choosing birds to represent his characters. He points out that the nightingale was a particularly inappropriate bird for Swift.

# "Answer to 'Paulus,' The"

Poem by Swift; first published 1754, probably written 1728. It first appeared in *The Dreamer,* an anonymous prose satire by Dr. William King (not Archbishop King). That text also contained the poem called "Paulus" that initiated Swift's response. Written by Robert LINDSAY in early September 1728, it makes fun of lawyers as driven to their hard livings by a love of wealth. Swift's "Answer" continues the satire against lawyers but also praises Lindsay for having distinguished himself as a virtuous attorney and legislator.

# "Answer to Several Letters from Unknown Persons"

This essay was first printed from Swift's original manuscripts by Deane SWIFT in *Works* in 1765, and reprinted in the same year by George FAULKNER in his Dublin edition of Swift's works. Swift wrote this essay in April 1729 but did not publish it during his lifetime. Deane Swift gave it the title and added a note, "To Messrs. Trueman and Layfield," pseudonyms of two correspondents who had inspired Swift's 19th *INTELLIGENCER.*

## SYNOPSIS

He begins by referring to a letter he received last summer from these concerned citizens, who had ordered an answer to be printed. He intends to deal with their second letter in the same way. Baffled as to why so many Irish are emigrating to America—a place of harsh weather and wild, untamed land—the writer would rather have them stay and fight their oppressors. If the Irish actually have evidence supporting their complaints, then they should bring those forward. He rambles to a discussion of the cruel, exacting landlords and the clergy who are excused for the small tithes they receive, and the plans for Ireland that will "encourage agriculture and home consumption, and utterly discard all importations which are not absolutely necessary for health or life." His final comments suggest a quiet desperation, based on the knowledge that only a few people will ever read these words and the poor will continue suffering.

## COMMENTARY

This essay and three others—"A LETTER TO THE ARCHBISHOP OF DUBLIN CONCERNING THE WEAVERS," "An ANSWER TO SEVERAL LETTERS SENT ME FROM UNKNOWN HANDS," and "A LETTER ON MACULLA'S PROJECT"—reveal Swift's despair over the continuing famine in Ireland. As emigration to America proceeded, Swift did what he could, from his perspective, to slow it down and improve conditions for the poor. He made a substantial contribution to a subscription for the poor for food and produced thoughtful writings designed to encourage or improve the debate over whether the government could do more to improve the dire circumstances. But he also amused himself with these pamphlets, commenting on various topics such as the balance of trade, landlords, emigration, the lack of hard currency, and women's remarkable extravagance for importing foreign luxuries. Swift has no specific solutions to these many problems, but often recommends attitudinal or behavioral changes in the Irish. Ironically, he comes around to the belief that if emigration could answer the constant suffering, then why should he persuade sufferers to stay in Ireland?

# "Answer to Several Letters Sent Me from Unknown Hands, An"

First printed by Deane SWIFT in *Works*, 1765, and reprinted in Dublin by George FAULKNER in the same year. Deane Swift had Swift's original manuscript.

## SYNOPSIS

Swift argues once again for economic self-sufficiency and outlines here various schemes for road construction, bog reclamation, and reforestation. He refreshes his audience's memory that he was the Drapier and had made a difference in that capacity. The time for governments who base their objections to these improvements on the laziness (codeword for *barbarism* or *savagery*) of the poor Irish has passed: Civilization will come by rewards at least as much as punishments. His irony deepens when he admits the necessity of abolishing the Irish language (Gaelic) though it would cost too much (though he had made a similar proposal for founding a school in every parish to teach native Irish children to speak and read the English language), and acknowledges that feeding the Irish has become exceedingly expensive, as the wealthy and the middle class who represent the tax base move in greater numbers to England. Good sense would argue for encouraging agriculture, and once again Swift mentions the necessity for an Irish coinage.

## COMMENTARY

With the clear and present danger of famine looming and emigration increasing, Swift returned from vacation at MARKET HILL to Dublin and began writing pamphlets in early 1729. His view was that if the English would not improve Ireland, then the Irish needed to take responsibility for saving their own country and its citizens. Swift is speaking directly to the Irish Parliament session that would convene in September 1729 and could take appropriate action if it would show courage against the English. The essay remains unfinished but his aim is clear, though he knew his chances of effecting substantial change were nonexistent.

# "Answer to the Ballyspellin Ballad, An"

Poem by Swift; first published 1728, written the same year during Swift's first visit to MARKET HILL. It is a response to the ballad Thomas SHERIDAN wrote and sent to Swift on the famous spring at Ballyspellin (now Ballyspellan) near Kilkenny. The spring was renowned for its medicinal properties. In a September 28, 1728, letter to John WORRALL, Swift wrote that Sheridan "had employed all the rhymes he could find" to the word *Ballyspellin*, but that "we [perhaps referring to Sir Arthur ACHESON] have found fifteen more, and employed them in abusing his ballad, and Ballyspellin too" (*Corr.* III.302).

# "Answer to the *Craftsman,* The"

This essay was published with the reprint of the original *Craftsman*, a new anti-WALPOLE periodical that William PULTENEY and Henry BOLINGBROKE had begun in 1726. Issue number 227 (dated November 7, 1730), which had inspired Swift, was first published by Dublin printer George FAULKNER in the 1758 collected *Works*, and later in the 1764 London edition.

## SYNOPSIS

Swift answers the *Craftsman* with his usual boldness: "I discover you to be as great an enemy of this country, as you are of your own." After a brief, but detailed review of the unhappy trade and economic situation for Ireland, he argues that sending thousands of healthy young Irishmen to fight for France and Spain makes good economic sense, saving food, clothes, and labor costs at home. He reviews the ironies of keeping 20,000 English soldiers in Ireland to force the natives into supporting English interests. In fact, if transporting thousands of Irish soldiers abroad is successful, why not convert all of Ireland into one great pasture, and a smaller number of Irish can serve as graziers and the English army can supervise them and collect taxes, too? He suggests the formation of this new Arcadia, where whenever a surplus of Irishmen occurs they can be shipped off to whoever can pay for them or as a defense between the English settlers and the Native Americans in the colonies.

## COMMENTARY

The idea of the French recruiting officers in Ireland trying to raise an army to fight on the continent for France seemed outrageous to the *Craftsman*. But Swift took up the issue, replying as a loyal WHIG defending Walpole's policy against the objections of this TORY paper. He answers the *Craftsman* as an economic projector, and this essay serves as his last major attack on England's treatment of Ireland. When Pulteney and Bolingbroke provoked Swift, they relied on an allusion to "A MODEST PROPOSAL" and charged him with cruelty, as opposed to the charity that seems to have been his true intention. Swift's use of irony and satire works very effectively in depicting in an exaggerated sense the prevalent notion of transporting all "the moveables" of Ireland and Scotland to the rest of Great Britain. The idea of refuting the principle of people as the riches of a nation who could be traded or used for whatever purpose a nation might intend became a critical issue for Swift. In *Swift and Ireland,* Oliver Ferguson also finds four other economic refutations in the essay: Exports should exceed imports; only raw goods should be imported; a surplus of gold and silver should be hoarded by the government; and the government should ensure sufficient agricultural activity to meet its needs (179–80). The condition of Ireland remains desperate and requires desperate action—Swift's rhetorical approach projects the annihilation of Ireland.

## "Answer to the Injured Lady, The"

See "STORY OF THE INJURED LADY, The."

## "Answer to Vanessa's Rebus, The"

Poem by Swift; first published as an undated broadside along with the rebus mentioned in the title, perhaps between 1714–20. The date of composition is uncertain. The original rebus was an 11-line poem, "something between a riddle and a verbal charade, spelling out the name Jo-nathan Swift" (Rogers, *Poems* 707n.). Swift's self-deprecating "Answer" praises the author, Esther VANHOMRIGH, for her wit.

## "Apollo: or, A Problem Solved"

Poem by Swift; first published in *Works* (1735), written in 1731 or earlier. The "problem" the poem considers is that with all Apollo's "beauty, wealth, and parts" he was more "unfortunate in love" than any other "vulgar deity." Even with "nine muses always waiting round him, / He left them virgins as he found 'em." After comparing Apollo to "Nicolini [Grimaldi]," a castrato famous in London between 1708 and 1714, Swift concludes: "At last, the point was fully cleared; / In short, Apollo had no beard." In *The Poet Swift*, Nora Crow Jaffe reads the poem as Swift's dramatization of all poets as "impotent observers in a decadent age" (46). See also Apollo in "Characters" under "The BATTLE OF THE BOOKS."

## "Apollo Outwitted"

Poem by Swift subtitled "To the Honourable Mrs. Finch (Since Countess of Winchilsea), Under the Name of Ardelia"; first published 1711, written

1709. Anne FINCH's *Miscellany Poems, Written by a Lady* (1713) contained poems written under the name "Ardelia." In a January 12, 1708/09, letter to Robert HUNTER, Swift wrote that he was in the habit of amusing himself by writing poems to her (*Corr.* I.121). This poem describes Apollo's failed attempt to woo Ardelia and the triumph of her superior wit. See also Apollo in "Characters" under "The BATTLE OF THE BOOKS."

# "Apollo's Edict"

Poem by Swift; first published in an undated quarto in Dublin, then in a 1734 edition of Mary BARBER's poems. It was probably written in 1721. The poem is generally accepted as Swift's, although Barber may have been coauthor. It is a reply to Patrick DELANY's "News from Parnassus" (1721), in which Apollo appoints Swift as his vice-regent in Ireland. In the "Edict" the same god outlaws a number of common poetic clichés and similes, encouraging poets to be original rather than merely imitative. See also Apollo in "Characters" under "The BATTLE OF THE BOOKS."

# "Apollo to the Dean"

Poem by Swift; first published 1724. It was part of an exchange of lighthearted poems between Swift and Patrick DELANY in January and February 1721. In one of the poems Delany—with Stella's (Esther JOHNSON's) input—claimed that Swift had chosen Apollo as host in his house, so guests who came expecting a meal left with nothing but wit and wine. "Apollo to the Dean" is Swift's response. In a lengthy speech, Apollo laments how men take advantage of his provisions (namely gold, food and drink, and poetic inspiration), citing Delany as specifically guilty of stealing his poems. In retribution for Delany's thievery, Apollo orders a vulture "in the shape of a spleen" to eat the mortal's liver and declares that Delany will no longer be able to claim any material as his own. Apollo decides that

time's ravages have already punished Stella sufficiently for her part in the scheme. See also "APOLLO'S EDICT," and Apollo under "Characters" in "The BATTLE OF THE BOOKS."

# "Apology to the Lady Carteret"

Poem by Swift subtitled "On Her Inviting Dean Swift to Dinner"; first published as a pamphlet in 1730, probably written in 1725. The poem is preceded by a prose explanation of the events surrounding its composition. The poem itself describes Swift being invited to dine with Frances, Lady CARTERET only to find her absent upon his arrival. He too quickly assumes that he has misunderstood the invitation and returns home. He visits the lady the following day to apologize, and she asks him to write a poem about the incident. She also agrees to visit him and see Naboth's Vineyard. Walking through the orchard tires her, and Swift concludes that just as she cannot be blamed for being out of place in such a rude scene, she should forgive his blunder since he is unaccustomed to the Court. See also "IN PITY TO THE EMPTY'NG TOWN."

# "Argument to Prove That the Abolishing of Christianity in England May . . . Be Attended with Some Inconveniencies"

The first printing of this famous tract in *Miscellanies in Prose and Verse* (1711) used the longer title "An Argument To Prove, that the Abolishing of Christianity in England, May, as Things now Stand, be attended with some Inconveniencies, and perhaps, not produce those many good effects proposed thereby," but in subsequent publications over the years the title has been shorted to "An Argument against Abolishing Christianity in England." Swift corrected this essay for George FAULKNER's 1735 edition of Swift's *Works*.

## SYNOPSIS

The earnest gentleman begins almost apologetically, saying that he cannot entirely see the necessity of abolishing the Christian faith. Certainly, the Gospels are old-fashioned, and the general public seem embarrassed to refer to them. But he makes clear his dedication to real Christianity, the primitive kind: If people had the courage to grasp the essential truths of real faith, it would force us to deconstruct "the entire frame and constitution of things." But why abolish Christianity when it scarcely exists now? The advantages of its present condition will provide deists and others plenty of opportunities for exploitation.

He lists eight advantages of abolishing Christianity: It would diminish the credibility of the clergy and extend the public's freedom; increase the importance of the deists by removing the Gospels; replace the majority of the clergy with men of wit and pleasure; restore Sunday as a day of work and trade; eliminate political parties and remove factional strife; oppose ridiculous customs and prohibitions; banish education and thereby encourage peace of mind; and unite all Protestants, without worry from any "spirit of opposition."

The speaker continues his playful exaggeration, even at points lapsing into bathos or rhetorical tricks as he proceeds to a listing of "a few inconveniencies." The unemployed clergy will be wandering about now without any duties, yet gentlemen of wit will have more examples to serve their comedic pleasure. Deists will suffer with the removal of Christianity because they will have no way of practicing their verbal attacks on religion, and the free-thinking writers, like Matthew TINDAL, will sink into silence. The Anglican Church and its institutional structure will likely disappear, as it seems we are proceeding toward a presbytery, or council of elders. Finally, the most dangerous consequence will be the resurgence of popery. But the last paragraph offers his most telling argument when he appeals to economic sense, fearing that the entire economic structure of the nation will suffer a significant loss if Christianity is abolished.

## COMMENTARY

Swift considered himself a WHIG when he wrote this in 1708, but he directed this powerful, ironical tract at Whigs and at all who favored the repeal of the Test Act, which made public office eligible only to Anglicans. He felt the Anglican Church needed the extra support, and one might regard this essay as the work of a political propagandist; but it transcends its immediate context and takes its place among his most universally relevant satires. His use of the false persona device became one of his most effective rhetorical methods. The pretended writer is a "man of the world," who blandly assumes a general unanimity favoring the abolition of Christianity. He cautiously explores with the reader some of the difficulties that would emerge if Christianity were abolished: deists and wits would have lost a favorite subject for their attacks.

In 1704 the Test Act was extended to Ireland, but Swift had supported the Test his whole life, even against many attempts by the Whigs to repeal it, first in Ireland and then in England, where legislation was being enacted. Extra pressure was being exerted on the Church of Ireland when the government made clear that the Crown's right to first fruits (Queen Anne's Bounty) would be maintained without relief, a favor the Irish bishops had sent Swift to negotiate in England. If the abolition of the Test Act in Ireland was not opposed, the government might consider a compromise with these payments. Swift expressed his concerns in the title with the phrase, "as Things now Stand," especially since he believed the state had the implicit right to require specific religious observances. In other essays, the "Maxims," he argues against the power of coercion to influence belief, suggesting the validity of "primitive Christianity," which he presents as an essential characteristic of English life. The irony of the speaker's talk of "abolishing" when faced with the truth of the Gospels sharpens the tone of the essay, as does his insistence on defending only "nominal Christianity." These strategies take for granted that asking readers to practice "Real Christianity" would seem too demanding. Swift's target is not only the freethinkers who would abolish Christianity as a separate faith but all individuals whose allegiance to God is superficial and contains only empty words.

## FURTHER READING

Curry, Judson B. "Arguing about the Project: Approaches to Swift's An Argument against Abolishing

Christianity and A Project for the Advancement of Religion." *Eighteenth-Century Life* 20 (1996): 67–79.

Lund, Roger D. "Swift's Argument and 'the Church in Danger.' " In *Critical Approaches to Teaching Swift*, edited by Peter Schakel, 239–254. New York: AMS, 1992.

Richardson, J. A. "Swift's Argument: Laughing Us into Religion." *Eighteenth-Century Life* 13 (1989): 35–45.

Seidel, Michael. "Crisis Rhetoric and Satiric Power." *New Literary History: A Journal of Theory and Interpretation* 20 (1988): 165–186.

Smith, Lisa Herb. " 'The Livery of Religion': Reconciling Swift's Argument and Project." *English Language Notes* 31 (1993): 27–33.

# "Atlas"

Poem by Swift; first published 1728, written 1712. Swift compares Robert HARLEY, first earl of Oxford, to the mythical Atlas, who temporarily persuaded Hercules to bear the weight of the spheres for him. In March of 1711 Swift had written to Stella (Esther JOHNSON) that the earl's great fault was his unwillingness to delegate responsibilities even when he could not accomplish everything himself (*The* JOURNAL TO STELLA 2.504).

# "Author's Manner of Living, The"

Poem by Swift; first published 1746, probably written during his early years as dean of St. Patrick's Cathedral in Dublin (in his edition of the *Poems,* Pat Rogers suggests 1718). The speaker gives a self-effacing account of his dining habits, suggesting they are dictated largely by the weather. See also "The AUTHOR UPON HIMSELF," in which Swift claims to despise extravagant food and drink (15).

# "Author upon Himself, The"

Poem by Swift; first published 1735, written 1714 after Swift left England following Queen ANNE's death and the fall of the Tories. Lavishly complimenting himself throughout, in a series of couplets Swift indicts the queen, the duchess of SOMERSET, Archbishop John SHARP, and others as having actively prevented his preferment in England. He comes across as a resentful victim whose noble efforts have gone mostly unappreciated, but who resolves to act virtuously despite the undeserved treatment he has received from the ingrates surrounding him.

Written in the third person, the poem provides a revealing perspective on the talents and powers Swift ascribed to himself as he looked back on his political career prior to the fall of the TORY ministry. He notes, for example, that he possessed wit and displayed it in everything he wrote—even in verse. He frugally avoided expensive food and drink, and yet enjoyed dining "at the tables of the great," including "lords" and those that regularly had an audience with Queen Anne. Significantly, Swift suggests that he was reluctant to get involved in politics, and that he turned his "dangerous wit" in that direction only at the urging of his friends. He makes it clear, however, that once he made that decision he immediately found favor with Robert HARLEY, who brought him to Court, and Henry BOLINGBROKE, who made sure everyone respected him once he arrived. The poem suggests that Swift took pride in the notoriety he gained among powerful figures as a "dangerous priest" who had managed to get "behind the curtain" and who played a primary role in important affairs of state. It also, however, illustrates his resentment at having become a victim of false charges (such as supporting the Pretender) and ungrateful leaders, including the queen herself. Even though he bravely stayed the course and was eventually vindicated, Swift ultimately asserts that he has grown weary of "faction" and—having done all he could to "reconcile" his "great contending friends"—has decided to retire. See also "HORACE, LIB. 2. SAT. 6."

## "Aye and No: A Fable"

Poem possibly by Swift; first published 1728, likely written during Sir William Yonge's tenure as lord commissioner of the treasury from 1724–27. This is not the same poem as "AYE AND NO (A TALE FROM DUBLIN)." Pat Rogers calls the "Fable" a very dubious item, noting that it has been attributed to John GAY. On their way to battle in Parliament, Aye and No stop to converse. They decide not to remain at odds since they do not gain any titles, offices, or money from the strife. They resolve to go and live on some "great man's tongue" and in the future to fight only for pay.

## "Aye and No (A Tale from Dublin)"

Poem possibly by Swift; first published 1776, written 1731. It portrays a conversation between Swift and Archbishop Hugh BOULTER about why the Irish are unhappy and increasingly bold. This is not the same poem as "AYE AND NO: A FABLE." Responding to the declining value of gold in Ireland, in 1727 Boulter had proposed devaluing the Irish guinea and importing a significant amount of copper halfpence. Swift was opposed to both measures, and told Boulter so at a 1737 banquet in honor of the outgoing lord mayor of Dublin (the "feast" mentioned in line 1). As the poem indicates, Swift blamed Boulter for unrest among the Irish, and threatened to unleash the mob upon the archbishop.

## "Ballad on the Game of Traffic, A"

Poem by Swift; first published 1746, written 1702 during his stay at Berkeley Castle. It pokes fun at various members of the BERKELEY household, outlining their habits when playing cards. The card game described is probably Commerce rather than Traffic. Lady Elizabeth GERMAIN added lines 25–28 (which lampoon Swift himself) after finding the unfinished poem in Swift's room. This led Swift to write "A BALLAD TO THE TUNE OF CUTPURSE," in which he reacts favorably to Lady Betty's unexpected collaboration.

## "Ballad to the Tune of Cutpurse, A"

Poem by Swift; first published 1711, written 1702. It was first printed with the title, "Lady B[etty] B[erkeley] finding in the author's room some verses unfinished, underwrit a stanza of her own, with raillery upon him, which gave occasion to this ballad." During Swift's stay at Berkeley Castle in 1702, Lady Elizabeth GERMAIN surprised him by completing his unfinished "BALLAD ON THE GAME OF TRAFFIC." He responded with this poem, casting himself as a friar who is pleasantly amazed to find his half-written verses secretly completed by a young spirit. "Cutpurse" refers to Nightingale's ballad in Ben Jonson's 1614 *Bartholomew Fair* (III.v).

## "Bank Thrown Down, The"

Poem possibly by Swift; first published as broadsides (one undated, one dated 1721), probably written 1721. Like "PART OF THE NINTH ODE OF THE FOURTH BOOK OF HORACE," it reflects Swift's opposition to establishing a bank of Ireland. See also "LAST SPEECH AND DYING WORDS OF THE BANK OF IRELAND."

## "Battle of the Books, The"

Prose satire by Swift. He began writing it about 1696 while living at Moor Park with Sir William TEMPLE, working as his secretary, editor, executor, and pupil. It was completed about 1698, and first published with "A TALE OF A TUB" as the secondary piece in 1704 by John Nutt in London. The full title is *A Full and True Account of the Battle Fought Last Friday, Between the Ancient and the Modern Books in St. James's Library.* Swift divides the essay into three sections: "The Bookseller to the Reader," "The Preface of the Author," and "A Full and True Account of the Battle Fought Last Friday." It was first included in Swift's collected works by Hawkesworth in 1755.

## SYNOPSIS

Swift begins with a historical introduction of the controversy over the superiority of ancient or modern learning, and then depicts the Moderns challenging the legal rights of the Ancients to the intellectual ground of Parnassus. The keeper of St. James's Library makes an appearance as Charles Boyle (who had been a fierce champion for the Moderns) but becomes confused for a time. This intermission provides time for the fable of the spider and the bee, followed by the mobilization of the Ancient and Modern writers. A second interlude traces the episode of Momus and Criticism and a number of battles between the writers, with an ending episode of Richard BENTLEY and William WOTTON meeting Temple and Boyle. Boyle defeats the two Moderns in a confident manner, leaving them pinned together with his spear so that even Charon the boatman could not distinguish between them. The ending promises sweetness and light (a phrase the poet Matthew Arnold would use effectively) and clarity of sense.

## COMMENTARY

Swift's work is a comic drama enacting what for many scholars and dilettantes was a serious issue in the intellectual history of late 17th-century Europe: whether modern or ancient scholars were superior. Modern critics typically accept the view that the "Battle" clearly demonstrates Swift's personal and cultural loyalty to Temple and the older man's support for the Ancients. In addition, one can see Swift digressing from his position in "A Tale of a Tub" and anticipating certain sections of GULLIVER'S TRAVELS. His satire defending Temple's *Essay upon Ancient and Modern Learning* against the

attacks of the scholars Wotton and Bentley becomes a lively mock-heroic piece. Temple had taken the side of the Ancients in the great debate but unfortunately had used spurious documents (Aesop and the *Epistles of Phalaris*) to defend his position against the modern gospel of progress. Wotton and Bentley, great textual critics, had quite rightly criticized the use of such documents, but Swift is much more interested in dealing with the profound question of the humanist and the pedant, polite learning and scholarship. The great question posed in the fable of the spider and the bee is a central point in the document: "Whether is the nobler Being of the two, That which by lazy contemplation . . . turns all into excrement and venom . . . or that, which, by an universal range, with long search, much study, true judgment, and distinction of things, brings home honey and wax." This interlude in which a pompous and ill-tempered Modern, the Spider, finds his Gothic cobweb invaded by a Bee reveals Swift granting the achievements of Gothic architecture and scholastic disputation to the Modern. But Horatian urbanity (the current model of style in the late 1690s) is the defining quality of his Ancients. This latter group represents those who keep the past alive in the present, encouraging the virtues of antiquity without embracing their worst vices. In their ambition to be self-sufficient, the Moderns risk parochial narrowness; their manners show a failure of humanity as well as of humanism.

In 1701 Swift arranged the publication of Temple's *Miscellanea: The Third Part,* which contains "Some Thoughts upon Reviewing the Essay of Ancient and Modern Learning," the answer to Wotton that he and Temple had written together. The "Battle" is Swift's satirical dialogue on Temple's original *Essay* and his later *Thoughts.* Using animal imagery again to declaim on man's often contemptible behavior, he compares the two chief Moderns to "mongrel curs, whom native greediness and domestic want provoke and join in partnership." His attack on pretense and false learning remains relevant today as each reader seeks out true learning's sweetness and light while casting aside sterile scholarship and learned pomposity.

## CHARACTERS

**Aesculapius** God of healing and medicine in Greek mythology, although in Homer's *Iliad* he is simply a great physician. In "Battle of the Books" he defends Sir Richard BLACKMORE during his clash with Lucan. The son of Apollo and Coronis, Aesculapius was raised by the centaur Chiron, who taught him the arts of healing and hunting. He eventually became physician to the Argonauts and was capable not only of healing the sick but of bringing the dead back to life. He married Epione and had two sons, Machaon and Podalirius, who both became well-known physicians in the Greek army. Their sister, Hygeia, was the Greek goddess of health. Fearing that the healing powers of Aesculapius might lead men to seek to escape death altogether, Jupiter killed him with a thunderbolt. At Apollo's request, however, he was given a place among the stars.

**Aesop (Aesopus)** Well-known ancient Greek author of the *Fables*. He lived about 570 B.C. Born a slave, Aesop eventually received his freedom and was sent to Delphi, where he was to distribute money in equal amounts (four minae) to each of the citizens. Due to a disagreement, he ultimately refused to give any money at all and was killed by the Delphians.

In his essay on *Ancient and Modern Learning* (1690), Sir William TEMPLE praised Aesop and Phalaris as ranking among the finest ancient authors. This evoked bitter criticism from William WOTTON and Richard BENTLEY, and (as indicated in the section "The Bookseller to the Reader") sparked the controversy that led to Swift's "Battle of the Books." The battle itself begins after Aesop offers a long-winded commentary on an altercation between a spider and a bee in St. James's Library. He argues that their conflict is remarkably parallel to the ongoing feud between the books by ancient authors and those by modern writers. On one hand, he claims, the spider is like the Moderns, who "spin" their works out of their own entrails. On the other, the bee is like the Ancients, whose work is the result of "infinite Labor," searching and ranging through "every Corner of Nature." When he finishes, "both parties" take the hint and imme-diately decide that their heightened animosities will be resolved in a battle. During the battle itself, Bentley happens upon Aesop and Phalaris (who are both asleep) and decides to kill them. The goddess Affright, however, causes the sleeping heroes to have frightening dreams and "turn at the same instant" (Aesop's nightmare involves a wild ass breaking loose and "dunging" the faces of the "Ancient Chiefs" during a meeting). The simultaneous movement of Aesop and Phalaris frightens Bentley and he runs off with their armor.

**Afra** See Behn, Aphra.

**Aldrovandus (Aldrovandi, Ulisse)** (1522–1605) Italian biologist and physician. In "Battle of the Books," BENTLEY and WOTTON pass by his grave during their night attack on the Ancients. During the Renaissance, Aldrovandi became well known for his meticulous observations in botany, mineralogy, and animal taxonomy. His most famous and influential work was the pharmacopoeia, *Antidotarii Bononiensis Epitome* (1574).

**Apollo** Greek god of prophecy, of musical and artistic inspiration, of archers and healing. Swift adapts myth and mythological figures to his own purpose, often to cast a satiric light on modern writers. Nora Crow Jaffe finds Swift using Apollo as the ruler of the poetic wits who often neglects the world below, resulting in poetic impotence (*The Poet Swift* 46). In "APOLLO'S EDICT," Swift refers to his friend Patrick DELANY who suggested earlier a contrasting view that Swift was Apollo's viceroy in Ireland, whose political intervention on behalf of the Irish was indispensable. See also "APOLLO OUTWITTED," "APOLLO TO THE DEAN," and "APOLLO: OR, A PROBLEM SOLVED." In "Battle of the Books," Apollo serves as a powerful symbol of balance and moderation in the so-called war between the Ancients and the Moderns. His presence in this prose mock-heroic marks Swift's pleasure in using classical epic techniques to puncture the complacency of modern writing.

**Aquinas, St. Thomas** (c. 1225–1274) Italian scholastic philosopher, theologian, and Dominican friar. In "Battle of the Books," he helps to lead the "confused multitude of moderns." His most famous work, the unfinished *Summa Theologica* (1265–1272), is a textbook of Scholasticism, or scholastic philosophy—the attempt to join faith and reason mainly by reconciling the Scriptures and the works of Aristotle.

**Aristotle** (384–322 B.C.)   Ancient Greek philosopher. In "Battle of the Books," his writings, along with those of Duns Scotus, successfully remove Plato from his place "among the Divines, where he had peaceably dwelt near Eight Hundred years." He also inadvertently kills Descartes with an arrow intended for Sir Francis Bacon. During Lemuel Gulliver's visit to Glubbdubdrib in Part III of GUL-LIVER'S TRAVELS, the governor summons Aristotle's spirit from the dead so that Gulliver can converse with him. Gulliver asks that Aristotle appear at the head of all of his commentators, but there are so many of them that they cannot fit in the governor's palace. In another gibe at these commentators (including Ramus and Duns Scotus), Swift has Gulliver add that neither Aristotle nor Homer—who has also been summoned—recognize any of them since the commentators stay as far away from their "principals" as possible, embarrassed by the extent to which they have "misrepresented the meaning of those Authors to Posterity."

Aristotle was born in Stagira, and his father Nicomachus was the royal physician of Amyntas II, king of Macedonia. In 367 B.C. he went to Athens where he became a student of Plato and remained there for 20 years, leaving after the death of his teacher. Philip of Macedonia later appointed Aristotle as a tutor to his son Alexander and (at Aristotle's request) rebuilt Stagira, which Philip's armies had earlier destroyed. Upon Alexander's accession in 335, Aristotle returned to Athens and began teaching at the Lyceum (a gymnasium sacred to Apollo Lyceus). In his "Character of Aristotle," Swift writes that his "followers were called *Peripateticks* from a Greek word which signifies *to walk*; because he taught his disciples walking." Aristotle wrote most of his well-known works during his 13-year tenure at the Lyceum.

After the death of Alexander in 323, Aristotle became the object of widespread political suspicion based on his ties to Macedonia. He was officially accused of impiety but left Athens before his trial to settle in Euboea, where he died at age 63. Best known for his greatly influential *Ethics*, *Poetics*, and *Politics*, Aristotle (in Swift's words) "writ upon *logick*, or the art of reasoning; upon *moral* and *natural philosophy*; upon *oratory*, *poetry*, &c.". In *Swiftiana*, Charles Henry Wilson wrote that Swift's "knowledge" was more like "that of Homer, Shakespeare, Addison, and Fielding, than that of Aristotle," since Swift "used to declare that he never could understand logic, physics, metaphysics, . . . or anything of that sort" (*Critical Heritage* 262). Swift, however, called Aristotle "a person of the most comprehensive genius that ever lived."

**Athena**   See PALLAS.

**Behn, Aphra** (1640–1689)   Playwright, TORY poet, novelist, translator, and professional writer. Best known for her play *The Rover* (1677) and her novel *Oroonoko* (1688), where the latter functions

Aphra Behn, by Sir Peter Lely *(Library of Congress)*

superficially as a travel narrative of encounters with foreign cultures. In "Battle of the Books," Swift has Pindar, the Greek lyric poet, slay "Afra the Amazon light of foot." This battle alludes to Virgil's *Aeneid* (XI) and the death of Camilla, the queen of the Volscians, who for a time is the equal of all the Trojan warriors. Swift notes in the JOURNAL that his cousin, Dryden Leach, had a small role in Thomas Southerne's tragedy *Oroonoko* (1695).

**Bellarmine, Roberto Francesco Romulo** (1542–1621) Italian theologian and cardinal who vigorously defended the Roman Catholic Church against Protestantism in his *Disputationes de Controversiis Christianae Fidei adversus hujus temporis haereticos* (1581–93). Dutch Protestants designed a drinking jug called the "Bellarmine" as a lampoon on the cardinal. The distinct features of the jug were its large belly and slender neck. In "Battle of the Books," Bellarmine helps to lead the "confused Multitude" of Moderns who, although mighty in "Bulk and Stature," lack weapons, courage, and discipline.

**Boileau, Nicolas** (1636–1711) French poet and critic who stated classical standards for poetry, and his criticisms gained him both friends and enemies. Based on the *Ars Poetica* of Horace, his didactic verse treatise *L'art Poetique* was highly regarded by Alexander POPE and John DRYDEN. It was also an important contribution to the ongoing Ancients-Moderns controversy that led to Swift's "Battle of the Books," in which Boileau (called "Despreaux") commands the Moderns' light cavalry with Abraham COWLEY. Boileau's mock-epic *Le Lutrin* (The Lectern; 1674–83) may have influenced Swift's heroic treatment of mundane events in "DESCRIPTION OF THE MORNING" (II.248). In addition to exemplifying mock-epic techniques, *Le Lutrin* was also an important precursor to Swift's "Battle." In Boileau's poem, a conflict between two churchmen over where to place a lectern leads to a bookshop battle in which the combatants assault one another with the works of their favorite Ancient and Modern authors.

**Creech, Thomas** (1659–1700) Translator of Lucretius and Horace. In "Battle of the Books," the goddess Dullness seeks to protect him during the battle by hiding him behind an image of Horace, but he is eventually killed by John OGLEBY. In the introduction to A COMPLETE COLLECTION OF GENTEEL AND INGENIOUS CONVERSATION, Simon Wagstaff calls Creech's translation of Horace "admirable."

**Criticism** Evil goddess called upon by Momus to aid the Moderns in "Battle of the Books." She lives "on the Top of a snowy Mountain in *Nova Zembla*" (the Russian island Novaya Zemblya), and Momus finds her lounging in her den atop the "numberless Volumes" she has devoured. Criticism has claws like a cat, but her "head, ears and voice" resemble those of an ass. Her teeth have all fallen out, and her eyes are "turned inward," as though she looks only upon herself. A "Crew of ugly Monsters" suck "greedily" on the "Excrescencies" protruding from her enlarged spleen, which is itself "so large, as to stand prominent like a Dug of the first Rate." Like the monsters crowding around her, the goddess lives on the gall her spleen produces.

Criticism is accompanied by several family members. Her father and husband Ignorance sits at her right hand, while at her left her mother Pride perpetually dresses her up in scraps of paper. Her sister Opinion is also there, described as "light of Foot, hoodwinkt, and headstrong, yet giddy and perpetually turning." Criticism's children Noise, Impudence, Dullness, Vanity, Positiveness, Pedantry, and Ill-Manners play at her feet. When Momus informs her of the impending battle between the books of the Ancients and Moderns, Criticism rises in a rage and (with her entourage in tow) drives her geese-drawn chariot to St. James's Library. Upon seeing her son William WOTTON among the Moderns, she disguises herself as Richard BENTLEY and asks that the battle begin immediately. Before vanishing, she orders Dullness and Ill-Manners to protect Wotton (her "Darling" son) during the battle.

In "The Female Monster in Augustan Satire," Susan Gubar has pointed out interesting similarities between the goddess Criticism as portrayed by Swift and "the repellent figure of Sin" in the second book of John MILTON's *Paradise Lost*: "Milton's version of the classical Gorgon suckles insatiable grotesques while barking hell hounds creep in and out of her womb." Gubar argues that, like Sin (and Errour in Edmund Spenser's *Faerie Queene*), the goddess Criticism threatens to "overwhelm" the poet with her "ceaseless production of deformities which will overrun civilization." Since her offspring are both her weapon and her food, Criticism embodies a self-enclosed and self-sustaining system that is both "cannibalistic and solipsistic."

The description of this bizarre goddess in "Battle of the Books" sums up Swift's frustrations with what he believed criticism had become by the 18th century. As the naïve narrator of "A TALE OF A TUB" happily declares in his "Digression Concerning Critics," the "true critic" is nothing more than a *"Discoverer and Collector of Writers Faults."* There were once critics who limited their tasks to aiding careful readers and restoring ancient learning, but they are "utterly extinct." For Swift, of course, this was nothing to celebrate. By associating Criticism with Momus (whom the other gods expelled from Olympus for his incessant nit-picking), Swift highlights abortive fault-finding as Criticism's primary characteristic.

**Davila, Enrico (or Arrigo) Caterino** (1576–1631)   Italian historian. In "Battle of the Books," he commands the Moderns' infantry. Beginning in 1583, Davila worked as a page in the household of King Henry II of France and fought in the French civil wars. His remarkably popular *Historia delle guerre civili di Francia* (1630) went through more than 200 editions.

**Despreaux**   See BOILEAU, Nicolas.

**Dryden, John**   See entry in Part III.

**Dullness (or Dulness)**   "Slowness or obtuseness of intellect; stupidity" (*Oxford English Dictionary*). In classical mythology—and in Alexander POPE's *Dunciad*—she is an early deity who ruled the world before the birth of Pallas. In "Battle of the Books," Dullness is one of Criticism's daughters. Along with Ill-Manners, she is ordered by her mother to protect Richard BENTLEY during the battle. She also lures Thomas Creech away from the battlefield with an image of Horace fashioned from a cloud.

Throughout his work, Swift alludes to dullness as a widespread problem, but a statement in "VERSES ON THE DEATH OF DR. SWIFT" best sums up his attitude toward it: "True genuine dullness moved his pity, / Unless it offered to be witty. / Those, who their ignorance confessed, / He ne'er offended with a jest; / But laughed to hear an idiot quote, / A verse from Horace, learnt by rote." This suggests that in Swift's view, dullness itself was less of a problem than what he saw as virtually ubiquitous posturing on the part of dullards—especially among GRUB STREET writers and politicians. Swift's sentiments echo those in the 1729 "Letter to the Publisher Occasioned by the First Correct Edition of [Pope's] *The Dunciad*." The author—supposedly Pope's friend William Cleland, but more likely Pope himself—writes, "Deformity becomes an object of Ridicule when a man sets up for being handsome; and so must Dulness when he sets up for a WIT." The objects of satire in *The Dunciad* (as in Swift's own work) "are not ridiculed because Ridicule in itself is, or ought to be, a pleasure; but because it is just to undeceive and vindicate the honest and unpretending part of mankind from imposition . . . and a great number who are not naturally Fools, ought never to be made so, in complaisance to a few who are."

Dullness was as common a topic as wit in the work of 18th-century English writers, and the two terms helped to define one another, since dullness came to mean an utter lack of wit. For Swift, Pope, and other members of the SCRIBLERUS CLUB, their writings were part of an ongoing campaign against dullness, which they viewed as a contagion of pretension and pedantry that had spread throughout all learning and art.

**Duns Scotus, John** (c. 1265?–1308)   Medieval Scottish philosopher and influential Franciscan. In "Battle of the Books," he joins Aristotle in successfully removing Plato from his place among the divine authors in St. James's Library. In Part III of GULLIVER'S TRAVELS, Gulliver explains Duns Scotus's views to Aristotle (whose spirit the governor of Glubbdubdrib has called up from the dead). In response, Aristotle loses his patience and asks "whether the rest of the Tribe" is made up of such "great Dunces."

Educated at Oxford, Duns Scotus became well known for his opposition to St. Thomas Aquinas in the medieval church, for his defense of the Immaculate Conception, and for his argument that the Incarnation was not a direct result of human sin. He argued against Aquinas's attempt to synthesize faith and reason (one of the basic principles of Scholasticism), asserting that it is impossible to provide rational proof for certain religious doctrines. Duns Scotus also claimed (in opposition to Aquinas) that the will was not necessarily subject to the reason. In the 16th century, his philosophy (and his followers, known as the Scotists) became the object of great scorn among humanists and Protestants. Those who supported Duns Scotus eventually became known as "Duns," from which the modern word *dunce* (a stupid, uneducable person) is derived.

**Euclid** (323–283 B.C.) Ancient Greek mathematician, best known for the *Elements*, his treatise on geometry. In "Battle of the Books," he is the chief engineer in the army of the ancients.

**Galen (Galenus Claudius)** (129–199) Ancient Roman physician, philosopher, and prolific author. In "Battle of the Books," he fights on the side of the Ancients and survives an attack from Paracelsus. Born at Pergamum, Galen served as attending physician to the joint emperors Lucius Verus and Marcus Aurelius. Of the more than 500 treatises he reportedly authored, more than 100 are extant.

**Gassendi, Pierre** (1592–1655) French philosopher and scientist; Roman Catholic priest. Gassendi was cited favorably in William WOTTON's *Reflections* and became well known for his efforts to refute Aristotle and DESCARTES and to promote materialistic atomism. An important topic in the works of Democritus, Epicurus, and Lucretius, atomism was the belief that all substance is made up of very small, indivisible particles. Along with Descartes and Thomas HOBBES, Gassendi commands the Moderns' archers in "Battle of the Books." In Part III of GULLIVER'S TRAVELS, Lemuel Gulliver has the governor of Glubbdubdrib call Gassendi and Descartes back from the dead to explain their materialist theories to Aristotle. The ancient philosopher readily admits "his own Mistakes in Natural Philosophy," but finds that although Gassendi "had made the doctrines of Epicurus as palatable as he could," his theories (like Descartes's Vortices) are passing fads that are easily "exploded."

**Gondibert** Title of an unfinished (but lengthy) epic poem of chivalry by Sir William DAVENANT, published in 1651. Made up of 1,700 quatrains, *Gondibert* is set in Lombardy at King Aribert's court. The plot details Duke Gondibert's love of Birtha, which blinds him to the affections of Princess Rhodalind. Oswald, one of Rhodalind's suitors, tries to kill Gondibert, but the poem ends abruptly due (by his own admission) to Davenant's boredom with his topic.

In "Battle of the Books," Swift personifies Gondibert as a cavalryman in the army of the Moderns. He is the first Modern to advance against Homer, and rides a "staid sober Gelding, not so famed for his Speed as his Docility in kneeling, whenever his Rider would mount or alight." The narrator explains that Gondibert had vowed to Pallas that he would never leave the field until after he had "spoiled Homer of his Armour." Homer nonetheless defeats this "Madman" quickly, leaving Gondibert (and his chivalrous gelding) "to be trampled and choak'd in the Dirt."

**Guicciardine (Guicciardini, Francesco)** (1483–1540) Florentine historian, author of the famous unfinished *Storia d'Italia* (*History of Italy*). In *Battle of the Books*, he commands the Moderns' heavily armed infantry.

**Herodotus** (c. 480–425 B.C.) Ancient Greek historian best known for his narrative *History* of the Greco-Persian wars. In *Battle of the Books*, he commands the Ancients' infantry. Swift was fond of quoting and alluding to Herodotus, and owned a copy of the 1618 Geneva edition of his *History*. In handwritten notes facing the title page of that volume, Swift refers to Herodotus as the "Father of History" and writes that despite his tendency toward digression and excessive detail, Herodotus ranks among those authors "who deserve the very highest praise."

**Hippocrates** (c. 460–357 B.C.) Greek physician. In *Battle of the Books,* he commands the Ancients' dragoons. In "THOUGHTS ON VARIOUS SUBJECTS" Swift cites Hippocrates' claim that "stuttering People are always subject to a looseness" and adds, "I wish Physicians had Power to remove the Profusion of Words in many People to the inferior Parts."

**Homer** See entry under "Characters," in GULLIVER'S TRAVELS.

**Ignorance** In "Battle of the Books," he is the father and husband of the evil goddess Criticism. Old and blind, Ignorance sits at the left hand of his wife and daughter. Such a close relationship between Criticism and Ignorance is echoed in the "Digression Concerning Critics" in "TALE OF A TUB," where the narrator claims that the work of "True Critics" is wholly devoted to "the Faults and Blemishes, and Oversights, and Mistakes of other Writers."

In his "LETTER TO A YOUNG GENTLEMAN, LATELY ENTERED INTO HOLY ORDERS," Swift personifies Ignorance differently: "Ignorance may, perhaps, be the Mother of Superstition; but Experience hath not proved it to be so of Devotion: For Christianity always made the most easy and quickest Progress in civilized Countries." Admitting that "the Clergy are in most Credit where Ignorance prevails," Swift argues that this has less to do with religion than with the wholesale corruption of education. Nowadays, he claims, "you will hardly find a young Person of Quality with the least Tincture of Knowledge; at the same Time that many of the Clergy were never more learned, or so scurvily treated."

**Ill-Manners** In "Battle of the Books," a child of the evil goddess Criticism. Along with Dullness, Ill-Manners is ordered by Criticism to offer protection and aid to their half brother William WOTTON during the battle.

**Impudence** In "Battle of the Books," a child of the evil goddess Criticism. The name *Impudence* alludes to the character's cockiness and excessive boldness. Along with Criticism's other children—Noise, Positiveness, Dullness, Vanity, Pedantry, and Ill-Manners—Impudence plays at the goddess's feet.

**Jupiter (Jove)** King of the gods in ancient Roman mythology, known as Zeus in Greek lore. In "Battle of the Books," the goddess Fame alerts Jupiter to the impending conflict between the Ancients and Moderns. In response, he summons a council of the gods "in the *Milky-Way*" but (after looking it up in the Book of Fate) refuses to reveal the eventual outcome of the battle. In "A DISCOURSE TO PROVE THE ANTIQUITY OF THE ENGLISH TONGUE," Swift wryly explains the origin of Jupiter's name. So many statues of St. Peter resemble those of "this pagan god," he writes, because "when the emperors had established Christianity, the Heathens were afraid of acknowledging their heathen idols of the chief God, and pretended it was only a statue of the *Jew Peter.* And thus the principal Heathen God came to be called by the ancient Romans, with very little alteration, *Jupiter.*"

**Lucan (Marcus Annaeus Lucanus)** (39–65 A.D.) Ancient epic poet. In "Battle of the Books," he fights for the Ancients "upon a fiery Horse, or admirable Shape." After Lucan slaughters a number of Moderns, Richard BLACKMORE attempts to defeat him but the two end up exchanging gifts. Lucan receives a bridle, and Blackmore gets a pair of spurs.

Lucan's only extant poem, *Pharsalia,* details in 10 books the fight for dominance between Julius Caesar and Pompey. Although it was never completed, the *Pharsalia* is unique among classical epic poems in that it does not include divine intervention as part of the action. Lucan's success and popularity aroused the jealousy of the notorious Roman emperor Nero, who prohibited Lucan's works from being read in public. In retaliation, Lucan participated in Piso's conspiracy against Nero, and committed suicide when the plot was discovered.

**Mercury** Cunning messenger of the gods and Jupiter's footman—a kind of servant—in Roman mythology. He is known as Hermes in Greek lore. As the god of trade and commerce, eloquence, and healing, he is also portrayed as the patron of thieves, travelers, and athletes. He is usually pictured holding a winged caduceus (the staff entwined with snakes that has become the symbol of medicine), wearing winged sandals and a winged cap. In "Battle of the Books," Mercury brings Jupiter the Book of Fate (in three folio volumes) so he can look up the outcome of the battle before it occurs. In "THOUGHTS ON VARIOUS SUBJECTS," Swift writes that "A Footman's Hat should fly off to every Body; and therefore *Mercury*, who was *Jupiter*'s Footman, had wings fastened to his Cap."

**Noise**   In "Battle of the Books," a child of the repulsive goddess Criticism. Along with the goddess's other children—Positiveness, Impudence, Dullness, Vanity, Pedantry, and Ill-Manners—Noise plays at Criticism's feet.

**Opinion**   In "Battle of the Books," sister of the goddess Criticism. Swift identifies Opinion primarily by her fickle vacillation: She is "light of Foot, hoodwinked, and headstrong, yet giddy and perpetually turning." He presents a similarly negative view of Opinion in his "ODE TO DR. WILLIAM SANCROFT," where he writes that "foolish man still judges what is best" by "Following opinion, dark, and blind, / That vagrant leader of the mind."

**Pallas (Athena)**   Greek goddess of wisdom, war, and handicraft; known as Minerva in Roman mythology. She was the oddly born daughter of Jupiter, having sprung from his head after he had swallowed a Titaness. In "Battle of the Books," Pallas is *Protectress of the* Ancients." After Jupiter calls a Council of the Gods to discuss the impending battle, Momus makes a speech in favor of the Moderns, and Pallas answers with an oration of her own, touting the virtues of the Ancients. See also "CADENUS AND VANESSA."

**Paracelsus**   See "TALE OF A TUB, A"

**Pedantry**   In "Battle of the Books," a child of the malignant goddess Criticism. In "HINTS TOWARDS AN ESSAY ON CONVERSATION," Swift defines pedantry as "the too frequent or unseasonable obtruding our own Knowledge in common Discourse, and placing too great a Value upon it." Similarly, in his "Treatise on Good-Manners and Good-Breeding," he writes that pedantry "is properly the overrating any kind of knowledge we pretend to. And if that kind of knowledge be a trifle in itself, the pedantry is the greater."

Along with Alexander POPE and other members of the SCRIBLERUS CLUB, Swift equated pedantry with dullness and regarded it as a widespread and particularly annoying character flaw: "There is a pedantry in manners, as in all arts and sciences; and sometimes in trades" (*Good-Manners*). It was especially prevalent among the Moderns, who in his view were overly proud of the patchy learning they possessed. In his "ODE TO THE ATHENIAN SOCIETY," for example, he laments that the face of Philosophy is so often "patched o'er with modern pedantry, / With a long sweeping train / Of comments and disputes, ridiculous and vain." As Part III of GULLIVER'S TRAVELS and "VERSES ON THE DEATH OF DR. SWIFT" indicate, pedantry as "pretended" learning was a favorite target of Swift's satire: "Those, who their ignorance confessed, / He ne'er offended with a jest; / But laughed to hear an idiot quote, / A verse from Horace, learnt by rote."

The close relationship between Criticism and Pedantry in "Battle of the Books" reflects Swift's conviction that most critics—and too many poets—were nothing more than pompous fakes whose devotion to pedantry led them to grossly overvalue their work and learning. In "Hints towards an Essay on Conversation," for example, he recalls "the worst Conversation" he ever heard, which took place in Will's Coffeehouse and involved so-called 'Wits' sharing their writings "as if they had been the noblest Efforts of human Nature." This display led those who witnessed it to leave with "their Heads filled with Trash, under the Name of Politeness, Criticism, and Belle Lettres." Likewise, in "ON POETRY: A RHAPSODY," he tells the aspiring poet that if writing verse proves too difficult, criticism would be a much easier occupation since pretended learning is really all it requires: "Get scraps of Horace from your friends, / And have them at your fingers' ends. / Learn Aristotle's rules by rote, / And at all hazards boldly quote."

**Phalaris**   Tyrant of ancient Agrigentum (in Sicily). He ruled from about 570 until his death around 554 B.C., when the people of Agrigentum revolted and murdered him. Phalaris was notorious for his cruelty. The most infamous evidence of his brutality was his habit of burning victims alive inside a bronze bull (so that their cries imitated the bellowing of a bull). Ironically, the first unfortunate subject to suffer this fate was Perillus—the maker of the bull. Sir William TEMPLE's praise of the *Epistles of Phalaris* in his essay *Ancient and Modern Learning* led to Richard BENTLEY's successful effort to prove that Phalaris was not the true author. This dispute was part of the broader controversy over ancient and modern learning involving Temple, Bentley, and William WOTTON, which led to "Battle of the Books." During the battle, Bentley happens upon the sleeping Phalaris and (after an unsuccessful attempt to kill him) steals his armor. See also Aesop.

**Pindar**   (c. 520–c. 440 B.C.)   Greek poet, famous for his odes. He was one of Horace's primary influences. Pindar's odes were written for special occasions such as sporting events like the Olympian games, and they were designed to be performed with musical accompaniment. Famous examples of Pindaric odes—characterized by their division into the strophe, antistrophe, and epode—include John DRYDEN's "Alexander's Feast" (1697) and Cowley's odes in *Poeticall Blossoms* (1656). Cowley's early reputation was built mainly upon his imitations of Pindar. In "Battle of the Books," Pindar commands the Ancients' light cavalry and kills John OLDHAM, Afra Behn (see above), and Cowley.

The remarkable fight between Pindar and Cowley in "Battle of the Books" is recorded in some detail, with Cowley (as he advances) "imitating" to the best of his ability his foe's "Address, and Pace, and Career, as well as the Vigour of his horse." The combatants finally draw close enough to fight with their swords, and Cowley eventually begs for mercy, addressing Pindar as *"God-like"* and offering (in exchange for his life) his horse, arms, and the ransom his friends will pay. In an act that poignantly illustrates what Swift thought of Cowley's Pindaric imitations, Pindar disdainfully rejects Cowley's

request and cleaves the Modern in two with his sword. What happens next is very similar to what becomes of John DENHAM's corpse after his death in the "Battle": One half of Cowley's body is left "panting on the Ground, to be trod in pieces by the Horses Feet" while Venus turns the other half into a dove, which she harnesses to her chariot.

**Positiveness**   In "Battle of the Books," a child of the repulsive goddess Criticism. Along with her other children—Noise, Impudence, Dullness, Vanity, Pedantry, and Ill-Manners—Positiveness plays at Criticism's feet. To Swift and his contemporaries, positiveness meant "subjective certainty; confidence, assurance; expression of assuredness; dogmatism, obstinacy" (*Oxford English Dictionary*). In "THOUGHTS ON VARIOUS SUBJECTS" Swift quips that, "Positiveness is a good quality for preachers and orators, because he that would obtrude his thoughts and reasons upon a multitude, will convince others the more, as he appears convinced himself." Later in the same work, he lists positiveness among the vices that are to blame for a widespread lack of quality conversation among the multitudes.

**Pride**   In "Battle of the Books," mother of the goddess Criticism. She sits at Criticism's left hand, constantly "dressing her up in the scraps of paper herself had torn." See PRIDE, SWIFT'S VIEW OF.

**Regiomontanus**   Latin name of Johann Mueller (1436–76), a German mathematician and astronomer. In "Battle of the Books," he and John WILKINS command the Moderns' engineers.

**Tasso, Torquato**   (1544–1595)   Italian epic poet of the late Renaissance. In "Battle of the Books," he is one of the many "private trooper[s]" who pretend to command the Moderns' cavalry. Tasso is best known for his romantic epic *Gerusalemme Liberata* (*Jerusalem Delivered*), published in 1581 and 1593 and subsequently translated into many European languages. This poem greatly influenced Edmund Spenser in writing *The Faerie Queene*. Tasso's many years at the court of Ferrara were marked by constant paranoia and anxiety. His overwhelming fear of others plotting against him affected him so profoundly that Duke Alfonso II d'Este had him locked up for insanity from 1579 to 1586.

**Vanity**   In "Battle of the Books," a child of the repulsive goddess Criticism. Along with her other children—Noise, Impudence, Dullness, Positiveness, Pedantry, and Ill-Manners—Vanity plays at Criticism's feet.

**Vergil (or Virgil), Polydore** (1470–1555)   Italian historian. A Roman Catholic priest, he arrived in England in 1502 as a subcollector of Peter's Pence (a payment to the pope). He then became archdeacon of Wells in 1508 and became friends with a number of English humanists, including Thomas More. In the service of King Henry VII and King Henry VIII of England, Vergil authored the famous Latin *Anglicae historia libri XXVI* (*Twenty-six Books of English History*), which was partially published in 1546 and became one of William Shakespeare's principal sources in the writing of his histories. In *Battle of the Books,* Vergil is one of several commanders of the Moderns' "heavy-armed" infantry.

**Vossius,  Gerard  John** (1577–1649)   Famous Dutch classical scholar and theologian; held various posts at Leiden (including professor of rhetoric, chronology, and Greek), and was a nonresident prebend at Canterbury. He was also a professor of history at Amsterdam's Athenaeum. In "Battle of the Books," Swift gives Vossius a place among the Ancients' allies alongside Sir William TEMPLE.

### FURTHER READING

Ehrenpreis, Irvin. *Swift: The Man, His Works and the Age.* 3 vols. Cambridge, Mass.: Harvard University Press, 1962–83.

Elias, A. C., Jr. *Swift at Moor Park: Problems in Biography and Criticism.* Philadelphia: University of Pennsylvania Press, 1982.

Fox, Christopher, ed. *The Cambridge Companion to Jonathan Swift.* Cambridge and New York: Cambridge University Press, 2003.

Ramsey, Richard N. "Swift's Strategy in *The Battle of the Books,*" PLL 20, no. 4 (1984): 382–389.

Tinkler, John F. "The Splitting of Humanism: Bentley, Swift, and the English Battle of the Books," *Journal of the History of Ideas* 49, no. 3 (1988): 453–472.

# "Baucis and Philemon"

Poem by Swift; first published in 1709, written in 1706, but revised with Joseph ADDISON's help in 1708–09. A satiric adaptation of a tale in Ovid's *Metamorphoses* I.8, it provides an account of an impoverished, elderly couple entertaining two hermits ("saints by trade") who are disguised as beggars. Having been treated inhospitably by the inhabitants of a nearby town, the hermits receive a meager but meticulously prepared meal at Baucis and Philemon's home. The "saints" promise to drown everyone in the town but reward the old couple by turning their hovel into a magnificent church with Philemon (a "good old honest yeoman") being "furbished up" as parson. In Swift's hands, Philemon's transformation becomes an opportunity to satirize unlearned clergymen. As soon as the change is complete, for example, Philemon talks constantly of "tithes and dues." He recycles old sermons and preaches them from memory, and (in the hope of gaining some free food) makes it his business to visit families whose sows have just given birth. He rails against "Dissenters" who question the authority and practices of the church, argues in favor of the divine right of kings, and (although he knows many systems of divinity) is completely ignorant of classical authors. As in Ovid's version, the two eventually turn into trees before their roughly simultaneous deaths. In Swift's adaptation, however, the tree that was once Baucis is unceremoniously cut down by the succeeding parson. In response, the other tree (formerly Philemon) becomes "scrubby" and unhealthy, and is ultimately cut down and burned by the parson.

In his 1804 *Letter to a Young Lady on a Course of English Poetry,* John Aikin praised "Baucis and Philemon" as "one of the happiest examples of that kind of humour which consists in modernizing an ancient subject in the way of parody" and suggested that reading the Ovidian original is helpful in appreciating Swift's version (Williams, *Critical Heritage* 268).

# "Beasts' Confession to the Priest, The"

Poem by Swift; first published 1738, written 1732. The subtitle is "On Observing How Most Men Mistake Their Own Talents." In a prose preface, Swift outlines the extent and degree of this folly and claims that it is far more widespread in London than in Dublin. Set in a time when beasts could talk, the poem begins with the lion directing his subjects to a priest for confession. After very defensive confessions from several animals, the narrator claims that his fable shows how humans acknowledge their sins only by vainly describing them as "virtues carried to excess" (76). The rest of the poem contains similar confessions from a lawyer, a politician, a chaplain, and others who claim that their only fault is being overly devoted to some moral principle. The statesman, for example, declares that his flaw is being too sincere, which causes him to offend his friends. In the last section of the poem, the narrator claims that Aesop was guilty of libel in assigning human characteristics to animals in his fables since beasts have far more sense than men.

# "Beau's Reply to the Five Ladies' Answer, The"

Poem by Swift; first published 1765, written about 1728. It is a response to Thomas SHERIDAN's "The Five Ladies Answer" (see "ON THE FIVE LADIES AT SOT'S HOLE, WITH THE DOCTOR AT THEIR HEAD"). The speaker suggests that fine ladies could never have written such "haggard lines" and blames Sheridan for having written the "Answer" himself.

# "Beautiful Young Nymph Going to Bed, A"

Poem by Swift, subtitled "Written for the Honour of the Fair Sex"; first published 1734 in a pamphlet with "STREPHON AND CHLOE" and "CASSINUS AND PETER," written about 1731. Swift's primary source may have been the very popular *Visions of . . . Quevedo . . . Burlesqu'd* (London, 1702), in which an old man uses gross details to convince an enamored young man not to be fooled by the apparent beauty of a woman who has just walked past. Swift's poem may also be a parody of John Donne's "To His Mistress Going to Bed," which describes each detail of a woman undressing before bed. The "beautiful nymph" in Swift's poem is actually a syphilitic Drury Lane prostitute named Corinna who strips her disease-ridden body of all its ornaments before turning in for the night. The poem provides a catalogue of her ailments and nightmares, along with all the items she uses to conceal her ugliness. When she awakes the next morning—"A dreadful sight!"—she finds that a number of her adornments have been ruined by vermin and her pets while she slept. Swift concludes that it is impossible to describe Corinna's appearance at daybreak, adding simply that "Who sees, will spew; who smells, be poisoned."

Using a technique similar to that in "The LADY'S DRESSING ROOM" and "Strephon and Chloe," Swift in this poem heartily discourages idealized views (so popular in pastorals and cavalier love lyrics) of women as anything more than mortal. In his 1755 edition of Swift's *Works*, John Hawkesworth—disagreeing with those who had condemned the poem—praised "On a Beautiful Young Nymph Going to Bed" as promoting public health: "This poem, for which some have thought no apology could be offered, deserves on the contrary great commendation, as it much more forcibly restrains the thoughtless and the young from the risk of health and life by picking up a prostitute, than the finest declamation on the sordidness of the appetite" (*Critical Heritage* 155).

## "Bec's Birthday"

Poem by Swift; first published 1765, written 1726. Addressed to Rebecca DINGLEY on what was probably her 60th birthday, the poem praises her longevity and gently mocks her unthinking self-centeredness.

## "Behold! A Proof of Irish Sense"

Poem possibly by Swift; first published in 1759, written after 1742. Rogers includes this item in his edition of Swift's poems but treats it as dubious. According to contemporary reports, Swift wrote this epigram "in his lunacy" to make fun of a new building in Dublin to house arms and gunpowder.

## "Billet to the Company of Players"

Poem by Swift; first published in 1765, written in 1722. It was his response to Edward HOPKINS's attempt to charge the acting company at Dublin's Theatre Royal an annual fee of £300. See also "EPILOGUE TO A PLAY FOR THE BENEFIT OF THE WEAVERS IN IRELAND."

## "Blunders, Deficiencies, Distresses, and Misfortunes of Quilca, The"

This short essay is dated April 20, 1724, but more than likely was written a year later when Swift was at Quilca from April to October 1725, writing GULLIVER'S TRAVELS. Often associated with "CHARACTER OF DOCTOR SHERIDAN," this essay was first printed in the Miscellanies in 1745 and reprinted in George FAULKNER's Dublin edition of the Works in 1763.

### SYNOPSIS

Promising that 20 volumes of deficiencies could be listed, Swift offers to begin with a weekly listing. Reviewing all of the broken furniture, damaged walls and floors, dysfunctional kitchen, and damaged chimney, Swift finally mentions how the house and environs have injured the servants' bodies and work ethic, his closest friends (Esther JOHNSON and Rebecca DINGLEY), and him. All of these issues pale before the possibilities of gaining peace.

### COMMENTARY

In County Cavan, Ireland, in the village of Quilca, Thomas SHERIDAN owned a small 17th-century country house where Swift spent four months in 1724, and again in 1725. For additional commentary from Swift on this country place, see "A RECEIPT TO RESTORE STELLA'S YOUTH," "TO QUILCA," and "VERSES FROM QUILCA." Swift willingly escaped from Dublin and his duties there to this distant thatched-roof house for peace and reflection. Though the setting clearly deprived him of the comforts of the deanery, he relished his time there, compiling this list with the same ironic tone in which he wrote a number of his letters and journals. This place is a parody of a gentleman's retreat, "a way of life that beggared civilized belief." His own health at this time remained uncertain, as he suffered bouts of vertigo and deafness, and Quilca provided the shelter he wanted from Dublin society.

## "Bon Mots de Stella"

This text was first printed in Miscellanies, 1745, and reprinted by George FAULKNER in Dublin in 1746 and afterward in London in Works, 1755, with the omission of the last witty comment about the Quaker apothecary, which was added in the London edition of 1779.

### SYNOPSIS

Swift recounts that Stella (Esther JOHNSON)—"a lady of [his] intimate acquaintance"—who lived in Ireland 26 years had the finest attributes of anyone he has ever known. Her skill in matching wits and a pleasant conversational style with some of best minds in Ireland reminds him that her remarks were never collected. He hopes this short list will partially correct this oversight. Their friends Thomas SHERIDAN and Charles JERVAS appear in the remarks, adding color and variety to her rapid-fire responses to various situations. Swift provides one piquant memory: "After she had been eating some sweet thing, a little of it happened to stick on her lips; a gentleman told her of it and offered to lick it off; she said, no sir, I thank you, I have a tongue of my own." In this essay, Stella becomes not some figure on a pedestal, but a living, almost sensuous woman whom Swift found especially attractive.

### COMMENTARY

His poem "TO STELLA, VISITING ME IN MY SICKNESS" compliments Stella's virtues, focusing on her courage, intelligence, and her "fund of wit and sense." After she dies, Swift continues to mourn her loss, and remembering and gathering these bon mots helps him deal with it. One of Stella's particular intellectual skills combines her quick, responsive language skills with her agile mind in a game known as "What is it like?" or Similitudes. The game requires one person to think of a subject, and the others try to guess it by naming similitudes. Swift remembers her sense and sensibility with obvious affection and respect.

## "Bounce to Fop"

Poem by Swift; first published in 1736, probably written the same year. It is subtitled "An Heroic Epistle from a Dog at Twickenham to a Dog at Court." There is some doubt surrounding authorship of the poem, which has been attributed to Swift, John GAY, and Alexander POPE. Bounce was Pope's dog, and Fop most likely belonged to Henry Herbert.

## "Bubble, The"

See "UPON THE SOUTH SEA PROJECT."

## "Cadenus and Vanessa"

Poem by Swift; it began to circulate in manuscript after the death of Vanessa—Esther VANHOMRIGH—in 1723, and was first published in 1726 without Swift's approval. Early popularity is evident: The poem went through seven printings that same year. It continues to be one of Swift's better-known works. Although there is some question surrounding the date of composition, it was most likely 1713. Swift was made dean of St. Patrick's Cathedral, Dublin, in June of that year, and it seems improbable that he would have referred to himself as "Cadenus" prior to that date, since the name is an anagram for "Decanus"—Latin for "dean." Swift coined "Vanessa" from Vanhomrigh and Essy, a

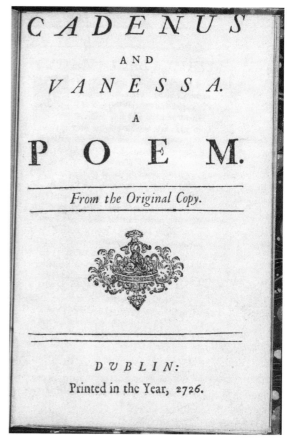

Title page of *Cadenus and Vanessa* (*Courtesy of University of Pennsylvania Libraries*)

nickname for Esther. By 1709 Swift was regularly visiting the Vanhomrighs' London home and corresponding with Esther from Ireland. Vanhomrigh expressed her love for Swift in 1712 and followed him to Ireland in 1714, hoping he would reciprocate. By the following year, the friendship had become uncomfortably passionate for Swift, who worried that it might compromise his attachment to Esther JOHNSON (Stella).

The poem was Swift's attempt to cool the relationship without insulting Vanhomrigh. The poem begins at the court of Venus, where the goddess listens as nymphs complain that men no longer marry for love, having become concerned with more superficial issues. In response, shepherds contend that women themselves are to blame for this, since they have forsaken rationality and given themselves up to passion and appetite. Rather than declaring one side or the other the winner of this debate, Venus decides to conduct an experiment designed to pacify both parties. She bestows numerous virtues upon the infant Vanessa and predicts that the child will grow up to be loved by men and imitated by women. Venus even tricks Pallas into equipping Vanessa with wisdom normally reserved for males. The experiment fails, however, because Vanessa turns out to be so wise and sensible that neither fops nor coquettes can effectively interact with her. The clergyman Cadenus (who is old enough to be her father) becomes Vanessa's only companion, and she eventually expresses her love for him. Cadenus, however, reacts with surprise and offers a rational explanation of why they should only be friends. Vanessa unsuccessfully offers to become his tutor and teach him to love. Frustrated with the results, Venus declares that men are a "senseless, stupid" lot and that if she had it to do again "She'd study to reform the *Men*" (872–873).

As what Louise K. Barnett calls "Swift's most comprehensive poetic treatment of the position of women," "Cadenus and Vanessa" has compelled many readers to compare Swift's relationship with Vanhomrigh and his bond with Esther Johnson (*Swift's Poetic Worlds* 161). In his biography of Swift, David Nokes points out that both ladies were sickly, fatherless, and surrounded by other women (159). Nora Crow Jaffe suggests that Swift "adopted

the same role of teacher, father, and quasi-lover" with both women, and notes a further analogue in Swift's interactions with Lady Anne ACHESON, to whom he was also a friend and tutor (*The Poet Swift* 140). Barnett, however, argues that Swift's relationships with Stella and Vanessa were very different— and so were his poems regarding each woman. She notes that the verses to Stella "describe a mutually satisfactory relationship threatened by external forces," while "Cadenus and Vanessa" focuses on Swift's "inability to love" and the "tension and disequilibrium inherent" in his relationship with Vanhomrigh (107).

In its treatment of wisdom and sense as "for manly Bosoms chiefly fit" and therefore particularly valuable virtues in women, the poem has been compared to the later "TO STELLA, VISITING ME IN MY SICKNESS," and Jaffe cites "TO LORD HARLEY, SINCE EARL OF OXFORD, ON HIS MARRIAGE" as its closest verse counterpart in this regard (*The Poet Swift* 138–139). As a commentary on feminine virtue, it is also similar to the "LETTER TO A VERY YOUNG LADY, ON HER MARRIAGE." Swift argues there that, while reason often requires more cultivation in women than in men, females are equally capable of acting upon reason and good sense. Swift also offers advice on how to choose a husband, suggesting (as he also does in "STREPHON AND CHLOE" and "Thoughts on Religion") that one's mate should be of good character and complementary intellect. As Barnett has pointed out, one of the chief ironies in "Cadenus and Vanessa" is that, although Vanessa seems to have chosen Cadenus based on those very criteria, she is nonetheless rejected (162). Despite its popularity, "Cadenus and Vanessa" has often been described as one of Swift's lesser poems. Patrick Delany, for example, found only "idle vanity" in what he called "these vile verses" (quoted in Glendinning 206). Negative responses generally take issue with Swift's cold, rational approach in pointing out the folly of Vanessa's love for him after he had encouraged that same devotion. In 1816, for example, Francis Jeffrey wrote that the poem is "complete proof that [Swift] had in him none of the elements of poetry. . . . All the return he makes to the warm-hearted creature who had put her destiny into his hands, consists in a frigid, mythological fiction" (Williams, *Critical Heritage* 321–322). John Irwin Fischer has called it a "fractured and contradictory poem," containing a grossly oversimplified caricature of Swift as a "silly pedant, incapable of passion" and an equally reductive portrayal of Vanessa as a "charming, but naïve schoolgirl" (*On Swift's Poetry* 111, 117). Nokes finds that Vanessa "emerges as the de-sexed, hygienic Swiftian ideal" in Swift's attempt to assert that she could never be more than a "truly rational companion" to the much older clergyman Cadenus (*Hypocrite Reversed* 161–162). And in response to feminist attempts to praise the poem for the "excellencies" it attributes to Vanessa, Jaffe writes that "they tend to forget that it is, at bottom, a brush-off" (*Dictionary of Literary Biography*).

## "Cantata, A"

Poem by Swift; first published in 1746 with a musical setting by Rev. John ECHLIN. The date of composition is uncertain. The poem is a parody of attempts to imitate everyday sounds in music. According to Nora Crow Jaffe, those guilty of this included George Frideric Handel, "the writers of opera, the silly [Ambrose] PHILIPS, and the poets of modern love and birthday songs" (*The Poet Swift* 54).

## "Can You Match with Me"

Poem by Swift; first published 1767, written 1731. Swift sent these lines to Dr. Richard HELSHAM as part of a rhyming game in which he and Swift engaged (through verse letters) during November of that year. See also "TO DR. HELSHAM," "TO DR. SHERIDAN," and "A RIDDLING LETTER."

## "Carberiae Rupes"

Latin poem by Swift; first published in 1735, written in 1723 during his long summer journey to the wilds of southwest Ireland following the death of Esther VANHOMRIGH. The poem describes the landscape as bleak and deadly. In his biography of Swift, Irvin Ehrenpreis calls it "a set of indifferent verses" (III.430). George FAULKNER included a translation of the poem by William DUNKIN.

## "Cassinus and Peter"

Poem by Swift, subtitled "A Tragical Elegy"; first published in 1734 in a pamphlet with "A BEAUTIFUL YOUNG NYMPH GOING TO BED" and "STREPHON AND CHLOE," probably written 1731. A student named Peter visits his friend Cassinus one morning to find him disheveled and upset. After a long discussion, Cassinus reveals that he is traumatized from having discovered that his lover CELIA has committed "A crime that shocks all humankind; / A deed unknown to female race." Her offense, he finally admits, is defecation. This scatological poem is closely related to "The LADY'S DRESSING ROOM" in its emphasis on the fact that "Celia shits," and the horror that arouses in her lover when he discovers that she does. The poem makes fun of Cassinus for his ludicrous idealization of Celia and, like the other scatological verses, illustrates Swift's characteristic disdain for viewing women as anything more than mortal.

## "Causes of the Wretched Condition of Ireland"

This sermon was probably composed sometime after 1715 or, as Herbert Davis suggests, after 1720. Swift took up residence in his deanery in August 1714 after the death of Queen ANNE and the disintegration of the ministry. He may have written the sermon at this time, or he may have composed it during the period when he had begun writing various Irish tracts, such as "A PROPOSAL FOR THE UNIVERSAL USE OF IRISH MANUFACTURE," and learned of William WOOD's patent for the manufacturing of copper coins in Ireland. See this sermon's companion, "ON FALSE WITNESS," probably composed sometime between 1715 and 1727. Both were first printed by George FAULKNER in July 1762 at Dublin for the collected *Works* and in the Hawkesworth edition in the same year in London. These sermons were part of the Glasgow edition of Swift's *Sermons* printed in 1763.

## SYNOPSIS

Swift argues for the potential of Ireland but says that poverty remains so ingrained that realizing this potential is impossible without serious reform. What are Ireland's disadvantages: increased servitude of its people; an increasing wave of emigration of its population and greedy absentee landlords; the pride and vanity of the Irish, especially of women, which leads to an increased importation of foreign goods and an imbalance of trade; and a weakening of the work ethic, causing laziness and crime. He urges a vigorous response from his parishioners, recommending the founding of charity schools in every parish across Ireland, improving the training and supervision of the servant class, reducing poverty in the cities, and using a registration method so alms will go only to those most in need.

## COMMENTARY

This sermon was in fact a political pamphlet delivered from his pulpit to an audience of tradesmen and artisans with their families, who were quite pleased at being rescued by a clergyman. Of course, Swift intended they should know this and understand that the Established Church and condition of Ireland were inextricably tied together for better or worse. His words would provide information, guidance, and a call to action—if not a physical response then at least intellectual and moral ones. Patriotism and religious salvation wedded to improved economic prosperity can serve both the material and spiritual needs of his parishioners.

He attacks English economic policy toward Ireland where what is best for the mother country reigns supreme while the colony must tolerate whatever others determine it shall have. His complaints about Ireland's suffering ring true for those American colonialists who would nearly 60 years later rebel against oppressive mercantilist policies

legislated in London. Swift objects to Ireland's dependent status and urges all to recognize the Irish as equal citizens in Great Britain, not a lesser people who must accept a denial of their basic common rights and privileges under a threat of force.

# "Certificate to a Discarded Servant"

Swift composed this memorandum on January 9, 1739, and it was printed by Laetitia PILKINGTON in the third volume of her *Memoirs*, 1754. She mentions that Alexander POPE hired the "discarded servant" after her recommendation that he take this certificate and apply for the position, where he remained until Pope's death.

## SYNOPSIS

This memo is published in modern editions with two other related documents: "LAWS FOR THE DEAN'S SERVANTS: DECEMBER 7, 1733" and "The DUTY OF SERVANTS AT INNS." Swift states that he had employed the servant for one year during which time he was "an idler and a drunkard." He fired the man, who subsequently enlisted in the British navy for five years, and may have, according to Swift, "mended his manners." Without further committing himself to whether this man will be a good servant in the future, he expects another employer will decide for himself.

## COMMENTARY

This statement contains the essential facts of this man's employment without glossing over his problems. But Swift also suggests the man is employable and acknowledges the possibility that his character has undergone a disciplined transformation while in military service. Though Swift had a reputation as a domestic tyrant the "Certificate" and other publications dealing with his attitude toward servants (as well as documented actions and comments of Swift and his friends) suggest a more complex response to the master-servant relationship: He often showed much care and concern for those who were loyal and honest, and though he had rigorous standards he responded in kind despite the difference in status. The "Certificate" contains an element of that dominance and also an understanding of a subordinate's position, which comes from his own background as well as his mindset of embracing the drama of a servant who searches for the right combination of actions for wreaking vengeance on his masters.

# "Character of Doctor Sheridan"

This short essay, written in 1738, was first printed by Deane SWIFT in *Works*, 1765, and reprinted by George FAULKNER in Dublin in the same year.

## SYNOPSIS

Thomas SHERIDAN was a superior teacher, especially of Greek and Latin, with an excellent imagination and a talent for poetry. Though Swift compliments the wit and humor of his verses, he finds the meter and rhythm often incorrect. Since Sheridan owned an excellent library, he should not have been so easily made a fool by a tradesman or someone who took pleasure in tricking an empty-headed man, but his indiscretions often caused him and his family harm. In the classroom, however, no one could outdo his skill in training and teaching young men.

His marriage was a mistake, bringing him little money, a mother-in-law, and poor relatives. His daughters were raised and dressed as if they were great ladies—a luxury he could ill afford with his small salary. His talented son could not finish school in England due to the father's lack of funds, and was forced to complete his education in Dublin. Sheridan's unwillingness in demanding his full salary from parishioners forced him to leave and seek other opportunities—all of which failed. Swift urges Sheridan's students to build a decent monument over their teacher's grave.

## COMMENTARY

Sheridan was Swift's closest friend in Ireland, and playfully sent Latin and English verse puns to the deanery, which were quickly answered in kind. The two argued and separated shortly before Sheridan's death on October 10, 1738. Though the source of this disagreement is not certain, Swift in writing this essay shows only the real friendship which was known to have existed since the end of 1717 between the two men. Sheridan's main troubles were his irresolution and a difficult wife, and though Swift nearly always liked the man, both of two short "Characters" he writes focus on these problems. The dean saw these as Sheridan's burden—his folly. Once again, Swift's difficult standards concerning women, especially wives who could become a misery for a clergyman, surface in what is apparently a celebration of his friend.

# "Character of Mrs. Howard"

Swift wrote this short essay on June 12, 1727, while on his last visit to England and staying at Alexander POPE's Twickenham home. The essay was first printed by Deane SWIFT in *Works*, 1765, and reprinted by George FAULKNER in Dublin in the same year in his edition of Swift's *Works*.

## SYNOPSIS

Swift readily acknowledges Henrietta HOWARD's beauty and wit, the first being transient and the second irrelevant in this character study. Biographical details were minimal since only her services at the Court of Hanover and becoming "the greatest favorite of the court at Leicester house" have significance. As an astute politician who could function well within the court and Parliament, she has no equal. However, her sophistication in manipulating those with whom she speaks could have a dangerous effect on her. Swift feels she may lose what sincerity she has: Her hold on the truth will become even more uncertain. Courtiers, for this is what she has become, often end up caught in their own web: "she may possibly be deceived when she thinks she deceiveth." In every other respect, Swift finds her just and generous, someone who could have become a friend no matter her status in society. Finally, he believes her virtues (morals) will be either severely tested as a courtier or simply irrelevant in court business.

## COMMENTARY

This "Character" is clearly an attack on Henrietta Howard, whom Swift had known since their first meetings at Leicester House, the London residence of GEORGE II as Prince of Wales in 1726. As the Prince's mistress, Mrs. Howard had been given land along the Thames at Twickenham, less than a mile from Richmond Lodge, the country house of the prince. Her house, Marble Hill, which was being built for her by the prince, became the meeting place for the Scriblerians. As a bright, sharp-witted woman, she had particularly well-honed political instincts, and could maintain her affections for the prince without alienating his wife, Princess Caroline. Though Alexander POPE and John GAY thought she would have influence with her royal lover, she proved incapable or at least unwilling to tamper with that relationship.

Swift introduced himself to her as "a wild dean from Ireland" whom she should appreciate since she had sent for "a wild boy from Germany." He intends to test her sincerity and wonders whether her kindness will be reflected in actions that will help her friends and gain their political wishes. Particularly, he still nurtures hope for English preferment from the new king. When no help is forthcoming, Swift decides she is good for nothing. See "VERSES ON THE DEATH OF DR. SWIFT, D.S.P.D."

# "Character of Primate Marsh, A"

This 300-word essay was first printed in *Miscellanies*, 1745, and reprinted in *Works*, London, 1755. Davis believes Swift wrote the "Character" sometime between 1703 and Marsh's death in 1713. Another likely date is when Marsh was seriously ill in 1710 and not expected to recover.

## SYNOPSIS

Though well educated and intelligent, Marsh became, in Swift's metaphor "an old rusty iron-chest in a banker's shop, strongly locked, and wonderfully heavy . . . and what is in it be wedged so close that it will not by any motion discover the metal by chinking." He is a man who enjoys doing good deeds for others but does these so awkwardly and hesitantly that the recipient does not appreciate them. For all his learning, he retains a provincial simplicity of manner, yet his pride and ambition have grown as he stolidly achieved one Church of Ireland promotion after another. His enjoyment in study and scholarly effort remains so obsessive that it has become a compulsion, and few, if any others, receive any pleasure from it. He has neither friend nor enemy, and even his servants who see him every day have no personal importance for him, since he is without passions or affections for anyone. His achievements have placed him above all temptation, "having nothing to get or lose; no posterity, relation, or friend to be solicitous about."

When he gives preferment to men of merit, they end up feeling less obliged to him and consider good luck a more likely reason for their success. With all his accomplishment, he cannot be considered a great man. For someone so concerned with his health, his lack of cleanliness is quite startling. He remains devoid of wit and idiosyncrasy because he sees no value in them, and will only respect an officious and outwardly pious superior who "knows how to manage and make the most of his fear." No one will mourn him at his death except his successor.

## COMMENTARY

During early 1694, Swift decided to leave Sir William TEMPLE and Moor Park to seek ordination in the Anglican Church, and accept a career as a clergyman. Archbishop Marsh of Dublin insisted on a full letter of reference from Temple before permitting Swift's ordination as a deacon and a priest in the Church of Ireland. This character study suggests rather coldly Marsh's difficult disposition and "elephantine regularity," alluding to the lack of confidence he had shown in Swift both as a student (1682–83) when the archbishop had been a provost of Trinity, and as a young candidate for church preferment. Later, when the Irish bishops had sent Swift to conduct the difficult job of managing the first fruits issue in London, Marsh ignored the arrangement Swift had achieved and removed his commission, deciding to appeal instead to the new lord lieutenant of Ireland. Though a learned churchman, Marsh did not appreciate Swift's intelligence and unusual talents. It seems possible, too, that Marsh did not intend to give Swift the prebend of Dunlavin in St. Patrick's Cathedral in 1700, and only after Lord BERKELEY's persuasive efforts did he change his mind.

## "Character of Sir Robert Walpole, The"

Poem by Swift; first published 1733. It was originally included with an October 26, 1731, letter Swift sent to Henrietta HOWARD, countess of Suffolk. The poem is a bitter attack upon Sir Robert WALPOLE, portraying him as a shallow, inept, greedy and conniving cur. One of several contemporary transcripts of the poem includes the heading, "A translation of a French lampoon on Cardinal Fleury." Swift's version was reprinted at least once, along with the French original, which attacks "the chief minister Cardinal André-Hercule de Fleury (1653–1743)" (Rogers, *Poems* 839n.).

## "Character, Panegyric, and Description of the Legion Club, A"

Poem by Swift; first published anonymously in 1736, written the same year. It is Swift's response to decisions by the Irish House of Commons in December 1735, and March of the following year to hear two petitions by landowners seeking exemption from tithe requirements. Irvin Ehrenpreis explains the background of the poem in his biography of Swift: "As landlords shifted from tillage to pasture, hardpressed clergymen who found their titles painfully reduced began to enforce title agistment, which was the title on pasturage, especially pasture grazed by dry and barren cattle" (III.827). Parliament (which consisted mainly of landowners) was receptive to petitions against this tithe, and the clergy feared that if this

tithe was overturned by lawmakers, it might be just the first of many. In late April 1736, Swift wrote to Thomas SHERIDAN regarding his "very masterly poem on the *Legion-Club*," but in a later letter to Sheridan and Mrs. Whiteway, he contributed to the controversy surrounding authorship of the poem: "Here is a cursed long Libel running about in Manuscript, on the *Legion-Club* . . . and the foolish Town imputes it to me" (*Corr.* IV.480, 487).

Louise K. Barnett calls the "Character" Swift's "longest and most celebrated piece of invective" in which he suggests "radical" punishments for "a group of powerful adversaries" (*Swift's Poetic Worlds* 190). In this especially bitter poem, Swift brutally attacks the parliamentary majority—"the Legion Club"—for what he viewed as their stupidity and hypocrisy in siding with the landowners to (as he put it in a letter to Charles WOGAN) "defraud us [the clergy] of our undoubted dues" (*Corr.* IV.469). He presents the lawmakers as meddling, self-important fools who have no respect for law, the church, or its representatives, and vows to ignore their decisions: "Let them, with their gosling quills, / Scribble senseless heads of bills; / We may, while they strain their throats, / Wipe our arses with their votes" (59–62). While anger at the club's audacity may explain some of the poems's remarkable vitriol, much of it must certainly have come from Swift's frustration at the clergy's utter inability to stop them. See also "ON NOISY TOM" and "ON A PRINTER'S BEING SENT TO NEWGATE."

## "Clad All in Brown"

Poem by Swift; first published 1728, written the same year. Dedicated to—and directed against—Richard TIGHE ("Dick"), it is a parody of Abraham COWLEY's "Clad All in White" from *The Mistress* (1647).

## "Clever Tom Clinch Going to Be Hanged"

Poem by Swift; first published 1735, written in the period 1726–27. This ballad describes the title character's final journey through London on his way to be executed at Tyburn for robbery. It centers on Tom's defiant last speech, part of which is devoted to thanking Jonathan WILD—a notorious criminal—for having given him an extra year of life.

# Complete Collection of Genteel and Ingenious Conversation, A

*Polite Conversation*, as it is commonly known, was published in London by Motte and Bathurst in March 1738, an octavo volume of 215 pages. George FAULKNER published the same edition under Swift's supervision in Dublin, and this piece is the last substantial work revealing his genius. The subtitle of the *Collection* is "According to the Most Polite Mode and Method Now Used at Court, and in the Best Companies of England." A project begun more than 30 years earlier as a satiric compendium of conversations gathered as well as collections of proverbs. This anthology displays the flexibility of the English language, its clichés, platitudes, proverbs, slang, and barbarisms. The structure follows a two-part form: three dialogues at the noble house of Lord and Lady Smart prefaced with an ironical introductory essay written by the "compiler" Simon Wagstaff, a fictional character.

## SYNOPSIS

*Introduction:* Wagstaff has spent more than 40 years observing, recording, and improving the speech of the nobility. He began his study in a scientific manner, focusing on 50 upper-class families, and carefully, pedantically recording the choicest expressions. Over a 12-year period he has conducted an exhaustive study with the hope of publishing it, though he worries it will be devoid of wit. In his opinion, England has achieved the highest artistic form of conversation, which is summed up perfectly in his work.

Certain of our approval, Wagstaff promises that his polite speech model contains no proverbs and not one witty phrase. If his work can be of use, the reader must memorize and learn every single sentence. All the advantages of teaching this material to various groups of people are discussed, and he

British cartoon depicting quote from *A Complete Collection of Genteel and Ingenious Conversation:* "Bachelors fare; bread and cheese, and kisses" *(Library of Congress)*

believes that books will become useless because of the certain success of this work. Only teachers and scholars may need books, since the nobility and the wealthy have no use for them now.

Meanwhile, the pleasure of living in a country where no new words or phrases of importance have been added in nearly 50 years seems beyond expression. The only competition or opportunity for cultivating conversation would occur in the clubs and coffeehouses. Also the philosophy of freethinking contains very little wit or humor in its vocabulary, probably because a group of fanatics introduced it.

Oaths and blasphemous expressions are missing from his study and must be considered a loss. Swearing, Wagstaff points out, adds so much to the flavor of artful speech, but the book would have become too long. After a careful arithmetic review, Wagstaff decides the collection will be sufficient for one year. The danger of the common people learning to swear and speak with such art should not be feared since they must acquire "hundreds of graces and motions and airs," qualities of voice, and facial contortions. The time required for this accomplishment would be beyond them.

A careful review of the design of the dialogues follows, with special emphasis given to character. The author assures us he is an illiterate man, unlearned, irreligious, and devoted to card playing. His crowning achievement remains his loyalty to his country above all else. With reference and encouragements from the Crown, the Parliament, and the ministry, a writer needs no other support, especially when he expects his fellow citizens to praise his name forever.

*Conversation One:* In St. James's Park (during Queen ANNE's reign), Lord Sparkish meets Colonel Atwit on the mall and Tom Neverout joins them on their way to Lady Smart's house for breakfast. After a few moments, the main character, Miss Notable, appears and greets the younger gentleman, Tom (a Derbyshire squire who has recently married), beginning a pattern of mutual teasing. The Lady Answerall seems a carbon copy of Lady Smart. This is also true of the two bachelors, Colonel Atwit and Lord Sparkish. The characters' lack of both depth and individuality helps make Swift's point that when everyone substitutes mindless clichés for original thoughts,

identity hardly matters since no one is very interesting. After tea, the group breaks up, except Lord Sparkish and the two gentlemen, who are invited to dinner beginning at 3 P.M. The topics of courtship and marriage dominate the conversation.

*Conversation Two:* The most interesting figure who now appears at the dinner is Sir John Linger, a rough-hewn Derbyshire squire, newly married, who anticipates Henry Fielding's Squire Western. Sir John peppers the conversation with dirty double entendres and coarse comments. The conversation at dinner ranges over such topics as the meats, wines, courtship, and marriage. With the dinner concluded, the ladies retreat to another room for tea while the gentlemen remain to drink another bottle of claret.

*Conversation Three:* The ladies are having their tea and enjoying the gossip about men and husbands, until the gentlemen decide to join them. Soon after, they begin to play quadrille (a popular card game), until the party breaks up about 3:00 A.M. when everyone goes home. All the dialogue reflects the witlessness of their choice of language: clichés, platitudes, slang, barbarisms, colloquialisms/minor contemporary references, inanities, and proverbs.

## COMMENTARY

*Polite Conversation* dramatizes what Swift saw as the lamentable and widespread substitution of cliché and repetition for clarity and originality among the upper classes of his society. It satirizes the modern writer Richard BENTLEY as a product of a culture of politeness in which pedantry, vanity, ill-mannered raillery, and hypocrisy often shape the political and social fabric. Swift had been working on this "perfection of folly" for three decades, and his experiences in London society had provided much of the material. The art of conversation had been satirized in the *Tatler,* and Swift appreciated William CONGREVE's technique for revealing the emptiness of moral and political speech. Swift writes a comedy of manners that explores linguistic abuse with the intention of banishing affectation. Using a catalogue of clichés, he has the courtly family exchange witless dialogue, proving the foolishness of the gentry. Swift manages quite effective social satire, showing the ruling families of the nation wasting their time and energy on empty ritual and excessive consumption, while those they command suffer from poverty, hunger, and the vulgar contempt of their supposed superiors.

Wagstaff, an idiotic projector of the likes of Bickerstaff, is convinced of his own significance but has no taste or judgment, and offers his stylish speech as a catalyst for wit. He is proud of his ignorance of language and literature and reads such pedestrian authors as Thomas Brown, Gildon, and Ward. Not unexpectedly, he mocks the talented authors of the period: "Let the Popes, the Gays, the Arbuthnots, the Youngs, and the rest of that snarling brood, burst with envy at the praises we receive from the court, and kingdom." Though readers often find Wagstaff to be Swift's funniest creation, the dialogues seem wooden and mechanical, and suggest Swift's strength really lay in writing characters, not dramatic comedy. In his "Notes on *A Collection of Genteel and Ingenious Conversation*" (1755), John Hawkesworth explains that it is "written with the same view, as *Tritical Essay on the Faculties of the Mind*, but upon a more general plan: the ridicule, which is there confined to literary composition, is here extended to conversation, but its object is the same in both; the repetition of quaint phrases picked up by rote either from the living or the dead, and applied upon every occasion to conceal ignorance or stupidity, or to prevent the labour of thoughts to produce native sentiment, and combine such words as will precisely express it" (Williams, *Critical Heritage* 155). In his 1758 *Life* of Swift, W. H. Dilworth calls the *Collection* "a ridiculous exposition of the quaint and absurd phrases that were in [Swift's] time practised by the unfurnished heads of both sexes, miscalled *high life*, or people of fashion; though, by their phraseology, which is here exhibited, it appears that none could be lower in understanding" (Williams, *Critical Heritage* 177).

## Complete Key to the "Tale of a Tub," A

In 1709, as the fifth edition of "A TALE" was in preparation to appear in London, the rogue publisher Edmund Curll published this pamphlet. Swift

was angry at Curll for having suggested that his first cousin, the Reverend Thomas Swift, had jointly written the "Tale." Certain critics credit Thomas Swift with the annotations to a copy of the "Tale" in his possession, which was given to Curll, though Curll does not confirm this. Swift calls it a "perfect Grubstreet piece," but his publisher Benjamin TOOKE only wanted to know whether Swift wants the key at the end of the work or at the bottom of each page.

## "Concerning That Universal Hatred Which Prevails against the Clergy"

Swift left an incomplete draft of this paper, which he began writing on May 24, 1736. The fragment was printed by Deane SWIFT in 1765 for the London edition of Swift's *Works*, and George FAULKNER reprinted it in Dublin in the same year. Swift had been particularly disturbed by the rise in anticlerical rhetoric among government ministers in England and Ireland. Recalling the government's suppression of Roman Catholicism during the Reformation, Swift suggests that similar oppression could occur once again.

### SYNOPSIS

Swift considers the recent anticlericalism, believing that conditions have never been worse, certainly not since the early 16th century in England. Henry VIII's actions against the church and the injustice he promoted because of his own ambitions and appetites imply the danger of absolute rule: "Among all the princes who ever reigned in the world there was never so infernal a beast as Henry the VIII in every vice of the most odious kind, without any one appearance of virtue: but cruelty, lust, rapine, and atheism, were his particular talents."

The Catholic Church had been wrong in acquiring extensive tracts of land and permitting, or even introducing, corruptions within its institution. But no one can deny the piety of the early Christians, and when the monasteries and other symbols of theological authority in the land evolved into examples of idleness and luxury (according to Swift), then the time came to check their wealth and power. Again he returns to the issue of church lands, which amounted to nearly one-third of the entire kingdom, which is clearly excessive, but King Henry's efforts to eliminate papal superstition was nothing more than a plundering to establish a war chest for the conflict with Catholic Europe that now seemed inevitable. The essay ends abruptly as Swift further condemns Henry's dexterity in selecting Thomas Cromwell, the earl of Essex, as his hatchet man for dissolving the monasteries and directing the Reformation in England.

## COMMENTARY

A consistent enemy of popery and the power of the Catholic Church, Swift did not pretend that the government, if given a chance, would not threaten the tithe system and Irish church lands. One can read this essay as his reaction to the threat, either real or imagined, of the landowners, or the government that represented them, who had conducted a long-standing campaign against the vitality and endurance of the Irish church. Swift's knowledge of and strong belief in the cyclical characteristics of history served as a warning to him of the likely possibility that the alienations of church property during the era of Henry VIII could occur in his own time. He had seen the Establishment's success in weakening the Church of Ireland during the 17th century, and these dangerous precedents had carried over into the 18th century, threatening the security of every clergyman. Critics have pointed out that Swift's attitudes toward King Henry VIII reveal a view widely held among contemporary Anglican clergymen. The misappropriation of ecclesiastical estates, titles, and tithes into lay hands remained a scandalous occurrence and was worsened when the current Establishment refused to restore to the parishes in Ireland the lands and tithes that had been held under Catholicism for the use of the monasteries.

Swift's tenacity of purpose in this case during 1736 was not caused under the pressure of current events. He had been reading and formulating his position on these matters since his days with William

TEMPLE, and a number of his writings address this issue. See also "A SERMON UPON THE MARTYRDOM OF KING CHARLES I," "The SENTIMENTS OF A CHURCH OF ENGLAND MAN," "An ARGUMENT TO PROVE THAT THE ABOLISHING OF CHRISTIANITY IN ENGLAND . . . ," The DRAPIER'S LETTERS, Marginalia, A COMPLETE COLLECTION OF GENTEEL AND INGENIOUS CONVERSATION, and "The CONTESTS AND DISSENSIONS IN ATHENS AND ROME."

# "Conduct of the Allies, The"

This very popular essay (which is nearly unread today) has as its full title "The Conduct of the Allies, and of the Late Ministry, in Beginning and Carrying On the Present War." This pamphlet was printed by John BARBER on November 27, 1711, and sold by the bookseller John Morphew. Two more editions appeared within five days, and three more editions within two months. Though critics argue Swift personally supervised through the fourth edition only, the sales continued, resulting finally in best-seller status with its eighth edition in 1715, which appeared also in Edinburgh and Dublin.

## SYNOPSIS

Angus Ross and David Woolley's *Tale of a Tub and Other Works* provides the best short description of the structure of the pamphlet, while *The* JOURNAL TO STELLA reveals a number of references to its composition and publication. Irvin Ehrenpreis suggests the title comes from William TEMPLE's *Memoirs*, in which he refers to WILLIAM of Orange (later William III) complaining of the conduct of his allies during the Dutch war in 1676 (*Swift* II.485n).

Beginning with a 500-word preface, Swift argues for certain principles that rise above party politics or individual interest. Ten years of war with victories will not replace a lasting, honorable peace. The main text of the essay falls into five sections:

1. A blueprint for the argument following historical references and political theory
2. A review in greater depth of the events leading to the War of the Spanish Succession, using

modern historical methods in citing existing state papers and data on military gains and losses

3. The central thesis and longest section containing his three main elements: England's irrational and imprudent role in the war, its poor conception and management of strategic and tactical military operations that led to poor results and greed, and dishonorable treatment of its allies, which brought greater burdens on the country

4. An explanation, after suggesting the need for a unilateral treaty with France, of why the Whigs brought the country into the war and why they lost their leadership role

5. A final section with five subsections arguing against the WHIG aim of conquering Spain, ensuring that Louis XIV's grandson would not become king of Spain; more effectively, his analysis of how England's economy will continue suffering if the war lasts addresses the immediate concerns of his readers.

In the fourth edition (December 1711), Swift added a 140-word postscript concerning the royal succession in England, with his hope that any change from the House of Stuart would be a distant prospect. He also responds to one of the replies to his pamphlet, something he would not do again.

## COMMENTARY

Vehemently disagreeing with Whig policies, Swift had shifted his support to the TORIES in 1710 and soon became their principal spokesman and propagandist, managing in October the editorship of their journal, the EXAMINER. Writing effectively for nine months, he then capped his efforts in support of the ministry with "Conduct of the Allies," which sought to expose the mercenary and selfish motives of the Whigs who had entered this War of the Spanish Succession (1701–13), and called for an end to this war. Since the intentions of discrediting the opposition and encouraging popular support for establishing a peace treaty with France were the main objectives of this essay, Swift's argument required a serious but engaging tone, one that would appeal to the intellect and emotions of his readers and listeners who were observing the Tories' handling of international affairs. Robert HARLEY and Henry

BOLINGBROKE decided their strategy would provide Swift with classified information on current diplomacy and the war's financial costs eight to 10 weeks before the opening of Parliament, giving him time to produce a strong propaganda pamphlet in favor of peace. His pamphlet went through a series of drafts and Bolingbroke provided comments and further facts and figures, until the piece was judged its most potent and published on deadline. Aside from the complete command of the facts and its plain style, Swift convinced readers through a clever manipulation of a rhetorical device which distinguished between the public or national interest of England versus the private greed and cunning of a few who would make money on the suffering of many.

# "Considerations about Maintaining the Poor"

This unfinished 900-word essay was probably started years before its eventual publication, possibly in September 1726, when Swift had also begun writing "A Proposal for Giving Badges to the Beggars in All the Parishes of Dublin" (published in April 1737). Deane SWIFT published both in Works, 1765, and George FAULKNER the same year.

## SYNOPSIS

For 30 years, Swift finds, a series of badly conceived schemes was presented for responding to the poor—each one worse than the other. Why Ireland apparently receives "the perpetual infelicity of false and foolish reasoning" remains a subject of continuous frustration.

The Irish constitution and its laws have created an absurd, dysfunctional state. Numerous examples exist, and a list of these mistakes may help those with the authority to change the future direction of the nation:

1. mismanagement of government contracts for building construction
2. mishandling of private funds
3. existence of fraudulent fire insurance
4. existence of deception by merchants (whom Swift repeatedly criticizes)

If the foreign beggars could be kept out of Dublin, we might improve the problem. But due to the laziness of the Irish, lack of available jobs, exorbitant rents for poor lodgings, early marriages resulting in an enormous birth rate, poor agricultural methods, and the hindrance of growth for trades and other occupations will damage opportunities for reducing the number of poor. The constant presence of beggars from other sections of the country upsets Swift, not because of the burden they present, but because their poverty can be blamed on the country landlords who have abandoned these tenants. The essay ends inconclusively on the contradiction that the poorhouse can manage about 425 persons, but the reality suggests that closer to 2,000 poor people are roaming the Dublin streets.

## COMMENTARY

Swift's attitude toward charity was legendary. His concern for the poor was demonstrated in a more practical manner, since he believed simple charity was demeaning. He supported self-help, hoping each individual's survival instincts would take hold. At times Swift could be harsh in his condemnation of the poor, blaming their economic situation on laziness and early marriage. However, the true enemies here remain a corrupt government and the wealthy, undoubtedly Anglo-Irish and English, who show less concern for the native Irish than for improving their own economic condition. In this work, Swift's harshness toward the poor is somewhat muted while he focuses on the social issues that (in his view) may have caused this intolerable situation.

# "Considerations upon Two Bills . . . Relating to the Clergy of Ireland"

This pamphlet was published in London in March 1732 and advertised in the *Dublin Journal* (March 21–25, 1732). This version may have come from a pirated edition set up from a manuscript copy, but the first authorized edition, corrected by Swift, and brought to England by Matthew PILKINGTON,

appeared in late August 1732. George FAULKNER later reprinted it in *Works*, 1738.

## SYNOPSIS

As a friend to the Irish clergy, the narrator assures his readers of his lack of resentment toward any who might attempt to control them. He reminds the bishops of when they were "inferior clergy" and provides a history of the background and tasks of most Irish clergy which remains appallingly different from those of bishops. He complains that the two bills were created and passed through committee without the opportunity for the clergy to make their position clear.

After a thorough explanation of each bill (see the commentary below for details), the writer cannot understand why either proposal would be useful legislation, since less than 100 clergy in the country possess sufficient wealth to qualify for building a home on the glebe lands. The House of Commons will, in their "great wisdom," realize that an educated clergyman may be an entertaining companion for the gentry. The clergy have value in the community as peace commissioners, better than the illiterates who are the only other choice. If the bills were passed, the clergy would become freeholders and capable of influencing parliamentary elections. If the bishops are concerned about nonresidence, let them choose clergy based on their merits, not on party affiliation, alliance, flattery, or personal favor. Dividing a valuable parish into thinly supported parishes would create chaos with "reduced" clergy, who would be forced to supplement their incomes with various unpleasant tasks. Men faced with such a future would refuse to enter divinity schools, and the entire institution would suffer. If the Commons passes these two bills, the dismantling of the Church of Ireland will begin in earnest.

## COMMENTARY

The Irish Parliament's session for 1731–32 introduced two bills—a Bill of Residence (requiring clergy to live at their assigned office with its fixed assets and build a manse house on the land associated with that office) and a Bill of Division (providing for the dividing of large parishes into two or more parts without permission of the incumbent). As Swift knew, the proposals addressed in this pamphlet originated with the bishops in the Irish House of Lords. Both were approved there, although they were ultimately defeated in the Commons in late February 1732. His sense of outrage at a further attempt to plunder the already vulnerable and ill-protected country clergy grew, until he decided to directly counter these coercive efforts. He had earlier been asked by some of the affected clergy for his help, and soon began writing a series of three pamphlets; after the bishops lost this attempt, he followed with three poems, "JUDAS," "ON THE IRISH BISHOPS," and "ADVICE TO A PARSON." The first essay, "On the Bill for the Clergy's Residing on Their Livings," and the third pamphlet, "A Proposal for an Act of Parliament to Pay Off the Debt of the Nation without Taxing the Subject," suggest the bishops should reconsider their position in this discussion, possibly giving up their exorbitant incomes for the welfare of Ireland. If nonresidence seemed a critical problem, let the bishops build the manse houses or split their bishoprics.

This second essay revealed Swift's bitterness toward the Church of Ireland's bishops, who should have had the interest of their clergy as a first priority, but instead these mostly English ecclesiastics allowed ambition and malevolence to guide their actions. Though Swift knew he would never have his own bishopric, his sense of moral outrage seems very much on target. He was not alone in complaining or supporting these actions, but when the House of Commons voted the legislation down, many felt Swift's arguments had been the most influential. The pamphlet appeared after the vote, but he got his concerns published in the *Dublin Journal* in response to "Some Queries" within four days before consideration.

# "Consultation of Four Physicians upon a Lord That Was Dying, A"

These exercises in Anglo-Latin (see "ANGLO-LATIN VERSES") with which Swift and Thomas SHERIDAN enjoyed testing each other's learning and wit were found by George FAULKNER after Swift's death and published in the *Works*. The probable date for composition is late 1735.

## SYNOPSIS

This extravagant parody of four learned men conversing in what Irvin Ehrenpreis calls polylingual punning vocabularies with Latin written as English and English written as Latin offers one of the most curious bits of prose in Swift (*Swift* III.821). Understanding these phrases and sentences can prove difficult, since the correct translation often depends on a code for certain mock-Latin phrases: "Nono Doctor I ne ver quo te aqua casu do" (No, no, Doctor, I do not spring for water as you do).

## COMMENTARY

The relationship between Sheridan and Swift has been reinterpreted in recent years, and the evidence shows that both men had strong links of temperament and background, age and rank, seriousness and serendipity. This period of punning for the two men was a dark, depressing time when issues of Swift's health and loss of friends and Sheridan's financial problems caused them both much concern. The facetiousness of their letters, poems, and other prose pieces provided humor and welcome distractions in the midst of these hardships.

# "Copy of Dr. Swift's Memorial to the Queen, A"

The 170-word text appeared in Hawkesworth's London edition of Swift's *Works*, 1765. Deane SWIFT prepared the text for publication, as he did for the companion piece "Some Considerations upon the Consequences Hoped and Feared from the Death of the Queen." George FAULKNER reprinted the "Memorial" in his edition of the *Works* in 1765. The unrecovered original was sent, after a three-month delay, to John ARBUTHNOT for passing on to Henry BOLINGBROKE, as it proved ineffective since the post had already been filled. In his edition of Swift's *Correspondence*, David Woolley treats this essay as a letter.

## SYNOPSIS

The date, April 15, 1714, serves as the subtitle to the three-paragraph memorial. Swift begins with a brief précis of the past four years from John MARLBOROUGH's dismissal to the signing of the Treaty of

Utrecht. He argues that more than likely the opposition party will do all they can to reject the TORY achievements. Swift proposes writing the official history of Queen ANNE's reign so that in the future the settlements that were made would be understood and the impending crisis averted, or at least resisted. Finally, Swift announces his willingness to begin this project and requests nomination to the post of royal historiographer. He assures the queen that he has no interest in the salary but only wishes to serve his country and needs the appointment to gain access to the relevant papers and records.

### COMMENTARY

Swift had begun writing his "HISTORY OF THE FOUR LAST YEARS OF THE QUEEN" in 1712 and continued until mid-1713, when he put the manuscript aside. Beyond his political motivations for writing this history, he was also exploring preferments outside the church and in 1710 had urged Joseph ADDISON to speak with John SOMERS and Charles HALIFAX about his becoming historiographer. Certainly he hoped to secure the achievements of this last ministry for posterity, and holding this post suggests he might add credibility to his account, though a realist could argue that a government job and the truth might not typically coexist. He had written to Bolingbroke, Mrs. MASHAM, and Robert HARLEY asking for their support, but all either ignored the memorial or found the timing unsuited for this request. By late July someone else had received the nomination, and Swift's petition became nothing more than a historical artifact. Swift wrote two other histories on the subject: "Memoirs, Relating to that Change Which Happened in the Year 1710," and "An ENQUIRY INTO THE BEHAVIOUR OF THE QUEEN'S LAST MINISTRY."

## "Copy of Verses upon Two Celebrated Modern Poets, A"

Poem possibly by Swift; first published 1734, written 1726. Comparing verse writers Edward Young and Ambrose PHILIPS to lumberjacks, it presents them as "laborers" of comparable skill.

## "Corinna"

Poem by Swift; first printed in *Miscellanies* (1727). Dating from 1711–12, it details the birth and career of a writer named Corinna. While she is still an infant, Cupid and "a satyr" argue over whether she will grow up to write about love or to satirize "the world." She soon does both, however, "laugh[ing] and squall[ing] in rhymes" that "lampoon" illicit affairs as she engages in some of her own. References throughout the poem point to Mary de la Rivière as the "Corinna" Swift had in mind. She was best known for her *New Atalantis* (1709), a popular and scandalous political allegory to which Swift alludes in line 31 of the poem. De la Rivière took Swift's place writing the *EXAMINER* in 1711, and in addition to having been acquaintances, they may have coauthored several pamphlets.

## "Dan Jackson's Reply"

Poem by Swift; first published in 1735, written c. 1718. Subtitled "Written by the Dean in the Name of Dan Jackson," it is a supposed response to the series of poems by George ROCHFORT, Dr. Thomas SHERIDAN, and Swift, making fun of Daniel JACKSON's large nose. "Jackson" petulantly dismisses Rochfort and Sheridan and berates them for rudeness and bad writing. See also "TO MR. DELANEY," "ON DAN JACKSON'S PICTURE," "ANOTHER REPLY BY THE DEAN," and "SHERIDAN'S SUBMISSION."

## "Daphne"

Poem by Swift; first published 1765. The title character is based on Lady Anne ACHESON. Swift likely wrote the poem during one of his visits with her and Sir Arthur ACHESON at MARKET HILL between 1728 and 1730. While there he "undertook the education of the lady" (Ehrenpreis III.601), and in this poem he goads her for being contrary, vowing "never more" to "advise" her. In Greek mythology, Daphne is the nymph whose father Peneus turned her into a laurel tree to save her from Apollo's pursuit. See also "Journal of a Modern Lady," "To a Lady," "Lady Acheson Weary of the Dean," "To Janus," "Death and Daphne," and "Twelve Articles."

# "Dean and the Duke, The"

Poem by Swift; first published 1765, written 1734–35. It reflects Swift's bitter dislike of James Brydges, first duke of CHANDOS, whose friendship with Swift— according to the poem—ended as soon as he was "beduked" (line 2). The poem also suggests that as paymaster to the forces, Chandos greedily misappropriated public funds, and that the only thing that kept him out of jail was his status as a duke.

# "Dean of St. Patrick's Petition to the House of Lords, against the Lord Blaney"

First printed by Sheridan in his *Life of Swift* in 1784, this short piece was probably written during the winter of 1715–16.

## SYNOPSIS

The petition is written in a formal style with the writer referring to himself throughout as the Petitioner, an individual who has ventured onto the public highway for his health, as directed by his physicians, and found not peace and exercise but instead violence and threats against his life. Two gentlemen tried to run him down—one a lord whom the writer remembers as "Blaney" (sic) and whom he had introduced to Joseph ADDISON in the earl of WHARTON's government and helped in other ways since "he was represented as a young man of some hopes and a broken fortune." When that failed, BLAYNEY pointed a gun at Swift and only the dean's quick thinking prevented a further mishap. Since there is no law permitting a nobleman to assault a citizen who is minding his own business, the Petitioner requests that the lords provide for the security of the public highways.

## COMMENTARY

Swift wrote this piece at a time when he was being accused of Jacobite sympathies during the Risings in Scotland and Ireland. Efforts to associate TORY politics with Jacobitism were increasing, and many landowners believed all Tories prayed for the Pretender's success (see James Francis Edward STUART). Lord Blayney's interfering with the safety of Swift, who was riding his horse, accompanied by two mounted servants, on a road one late afternoon between Dublin and Howth has more to do with the dean's reputation at that time than the inability of Blayney to control his coach horses. Swift had given up his WHIG connections (he even had introduced Blayney to Joseph Addison), and become a well-known "Hibernian patriot" through his Drapier essays and other writings. The new Whig majority in the Irish Parliament had little patience with the minority, even resorting to revenge and intimidation of the Tory members, among whom were friends of Swift. Not only did the dean become the object of this nobleman's road rage, but he also found that his mail had been intercepted earlier. He faced the possibility of arrest and may have come under attack from a stone-throwing, taunting mob. In *Swift's Landscape*, Carole Fabricant suggests the essay underscores the opposition on every level (in terms of social class, power, and outlook) between travelers in private coaches and journeyers on horseback (237). For more information on this episode, see the letter from Bolingbroke to Swift, July 28, 1721, in the *Correspondence*.

# "Dean of St. Patrick's to Thomas Sheridan, The"

Poem by Swift; first published 1808, written 1718. Along with other poems such as "A LEFT-HANDED LETTER TO DR. SHERIDAN" and "SHERIDAN, A GOOSE," it is one of a number of items in an extended series of trifles circulated among Swift, Dr. Thomas SHERIDAN, Rev. Patrick DELANY, Rev. Daniel JACKSON, and the ROCHFORT brothers. In this poem Swift makes fun of Sheridan (as he had in the earlier "DEAN SWIFT'S ANSWER TO THE REV-

EREND DR. SHERIDAN") for posing an illogical riddle and promises to "explain, or repay" in kind any further riddles Sheridan may send.

# "Dean's Answer to 'Upon Stealing a Crown', The"

Poem by Swift; first published 1745. The date of composition is uncertain, but Pat Rogers estimates that it was probably 1719. "Upon Stealing a Crown" was a short poem by Dr. Thomas SHERIDAN about an incident involving Swift being robbed during his sleep.

# "Dean Smedley Gone to Seek His Fortune"

Poem by Swift; first published in the INTELLIGENCER 20 (1729), written the same year. It is directed against Jonathan SMEDLEY, who in 1729 resigned his preferments (including his post as dean of Clogher) and sailed for India to seek riches.

# "Dean's Reasons for Not Building at Drapier's Hill, The"

Poem by Swift; first published 1765, written 1729–30. Swift explains his decision not to build near MARKET HILL at Drumlack on land he bought for that purpose from Sir Arthur ACHESON. His primary complaint is the treatment he receives from Acheson, who is aloof during conversation and who has isolated himself from his neighbors. In his biography of Swift, Irvin Ehrenpreis explains that the dean's decision was due in large part to "a rift between Lady Anne ACHESON and her husband" that "became so noticeable that it troubled the dean" (III.666). See also "DRAPIER'S HILL."

# "Dean Swift's Answer to the Reverend Dr. Sheridan"

Poem by Swift; first published 1735, written 1718. Along with other poems such as "A LEFT-HANDED LETTER TO DR. SHERIDAN" and "SHERIDAN, A GOOSE," it is one of a number of items in an extended series of trifles circulated among Swift, Dr. Thomas SHERIDAN, Rev. Patrick DELANY, Rev. Daniel JACKSON, and the ROCHFORT brothers. In this poem Swift questions the logic behind one of Sheridan's riddles and offers one of his own in return. Pat Rogers points out that "the two men were already fully engaged in a battle fought out with riddles, rebuses, and similar wordgames" (676).

# "Dean to Himself on St. Cecilia's Day, The"

Poem by Swift; first published 1765. The occasion for the poem may have been a 1730 St. Cecilia's Day festival held by the Dublin Music Society in St. Patrick's Cathedral. The dean asks himself in consternation why he would have allowed a group of musicians to come play in his cathedral.

# "Dean to Thomas Sheridan, The"

Poem by Swift; first published 1808, written 1718. Along with other poems such as "MARY THE COOK-MAID'S LETTER TO DR. SHERIDAN" and "SHERIDAN, A GOOSE," it is one of a number of items in an extended series of trifles circulated among Swift, Dr. Thomas SHERIDAN, Rev. Patrick DELANY, Rev. Daniel JACKSON, and the ROCHFORT brothers. In this poem Swift claims that he and Sheridan should call a truce to their verse quarrel since the Rochforts are enjoying it so much.

# "Death and Daphne"

Poem by Swift; first published in 1735, written in 1730 and subtitled "To an Agreeable Young Lady, But Extremely Lean." *Daphne* here refers to Lady Anne ACHESON, and Swift likely wrote this poem during his last long visit with her and her husband Sir Arthur ACHESON at MARKET HILL. The poem describes events following Pluto's order that Death must seek a wife. He "take[s] a house in Warwick Lane," and Daphne eventually takes note of him. She "freely" makes "the first advance" because his gaunt, pale appearance is so much like her own. Death flees, however, after placing his finger on her hand and finding it "dry and cold as lead." As he indicated in a December 9, 1712, letter to Charles FORD, Swift was concerned with Lady Acheson's leanness as the result of "sit[ting] up late" and "go[ing] to bed sick" (*Corr.* IV.92). One of Swift's nicknames for her was "Skinnibonia." In addition to goading Lady Acheson about her appearance, the poem makes fun of her as a "haughty nymph" for being prideful and ambitious enough to think that Death would choose her for a wife (89–91).

"Death and Daphne" is a good example of the numerous "libels" (as he termed them) Swift wrote against Lady Anne to pass the time during his visits to Market Hill. She evidently enjoyed his jokes, and regularly shared them with her friends. In her biography of Swift, Victoria Glendinning notes that Swift's friend Alexander POPE recognized these gibes at Lady Anne as a sign of true affection, and wrote that if Swift was "abusing" her regularly in libels, "then she must indeed be a 'valuable lady'" (157). See also "DAPHNE," "JOURNAL OF A MODERN LADY," "TO A LADY," "LADY ACHESON WEARY OF THE DEAN," "TO JANUS," and "TWELVE ARTICLES."

# "Decree for Concluding the Treaty between Dr. Swift and Mrs. Long, A"

Edmund Curll published this essay in a 1718 miscellany entitled *Letters, Poems, and Tales: Amorous, Satyrical, and Gallant . . . Now First Published from their respective Originals, found in the Cabinet of that Celebrated Toast Mrs. Anne Long, since her Decease.* The date of composition of the *Decree* is probably early 1709. See also the companion piece, "Death of Mrs. Anne Long," dated December 22, 1711.

## SYNOPSIS

The formal language of this mock decree begins with a signal that Dr. Swift of Leicester Fields and Mrs. Long of Albemarle Street have now acknowledged a treaty of acquaintance. Because of his undoubted merit and extraordinary qualities, Swift claims the right to meet whomever he wishes, no matter the law or custom. Mrs. Long agrees that Swift has the right, but she has her own demands, as the Lady of the Toast (she is one of the beauties the Kit-Cat Club would toast, and a few lines of Lord WHARTON's verses which allude to her are appended). As a member, she refuses to betray the others, as well as Mrs. VANHOMRIGH and her daughter, Hessy. The decree continues with its judgment on Mrs. Long's request that no matter her position, she must "make all advances to the said Doctor" since he is a man of great merit. Finally the Vanhomrighs shall not aid Long in her efforts to set aside this decree. She will instead be recognized in all company as a person who may speak with Swift without seeking license or leave.

## COMMENTARY

Mrs. Anne LONG's acquaintance with Swift probably began about January 1709 (though David Woolley is the only editor of Swift's *Correspondence* who does not believe the date was 1708). This mock-edict mentions the Vanhomrighs and Swift and is supposedly issued by Ginkel Vanhomrigh, a 14-year-old member of the family. Also, the pressures of living in Ireland seem to drop away while he is in London, and this burlesque shows his sense of humor, wit, and playfulness. Her beauty and amiability proved irresistible, and her early death deeply saddened him.

# "Description of a City Shower, A"

Poem by Swift; first published in the *Tatler*, number 238 (October 17, 1710). Set in London, it depicts signs around the city foreshadowing a rainstorm, dramatizes the deluge itself and its effects on Londoners, and finally describes the medley of refuse the storm washes through the city's open sewers. Soon after the "Shower" was published, Swift wrote to Stella (Esther JOHNSON) that "they say 'tis the best thing I ever writ, and I think so too" (JOURNAL TO STELLA 62). Nora Crow Jaffe finds the poem "less well integrated and coherent" than "DESCRIPTION OF THE MORNING," and suggests that Swift's primary concern in writing "City Shower" was to assert (in part by showing his firsthand knowledge of London) that he belonged among "some of the most famous and urbane Englishmen of his age" ("The Poet Swift" 78, 80).

"City Shower" can be read as a "mock" or "anti-" pastoral in which Swift applies conventions of pastoral poetry to an urban event. While pastorals generally provide an idealized and unrealistic view of rural life, in which even the most mundane happenings give pause to meditative shepherds, Swift presents the shower—along with its prelude and aftermath—in stylized language that mockingly elevates the significance of this commonplace occurrence, its disgusting results, and the more repulsive elements of city life. For example, the terms in which he describes changes in the sky as the shower approaches initially suggest that a marvel is underway: "Meanwhile the south, rising with dabbled wings, / A sable cloud athwart the welkin flings" (13–14). This grandiose image falls apart, however, when (in the very next lines) Swift compares the raincloud to a vomiting drunkard. Likewise, Swift's account of the rain settling clouds of dust mockingly presents this distinctively unimpressive event as a fascinating struggle for survival: "Nor yet the dust had shunned the unequal strife, / But aided by the wind, fought still for life; / And wafted with its foe by violent gust, / Twas doubtful which was rain, and which was dust" (23–26). While most of the "City Shower" is written in couplets, it ends with a famous triplet in which Swift parodies John DRYDEN and other Restoration poets who used this three-line sequence in their verses. In an April 12, 1735, letter to Thomas Beach, Swift called the triplet a "vicious way of rhyming, wherewith Dryden abounded, and was imitated by all the bad versifiers in Charles the Second's reign" (Corr. IV.321).

Analogues for the "Shower" include the first of Virgil's *Georgics* and the *Aeneid* 4.160–68. Edward Penny's 1764 painting *A City Shower* is based on Swift's poem.

# "Description of an Irish Feast, The"

Poem by Swift; first published in 1735, probably written 1720. Subtitled, "Translated Almost Literally Out of the Original Irish," it is based on a poem by the Irish poet Hugh MacGauran. The poem describes a feast honoring Brian O'Rourke, a 16th-century Gaelic chieftain. Nora Crow Jaffe characterizes this poem by its "swirling dimeter and wild rhymes" (*The Poet Swift* 33).

# "Description of a Salamander, The"

Poem by Swift; first published 1711, written 1706. It makes fun of John, first Baron CUTTS, by exploring the negative connotations of his nickname, "Salamander." Drawing on Pliny the Elder's notes on salamanders in his *Historia Naturalis*, Swift portrays Cutts as sneaky, lascivious, and repulsive.

# "Description of Mother Ludwell's Cave, A"

Poem possibly by Swift; first published in 1911, probably written between 1692–94, about a cave near MOOR PARK. Pat Rogers makes a strong case for accepting the attribution but notes that Joseph Horrell is the only other editor to treat the poem as Swift's (*Poems* 615).

# "Description of the Morning, A"

Poem by Swift; first published in the *Tatler*, number 9 (April 30, 1709). An early urban pastoral, it describes events in London's West End occurring as morning breaks. Introducing the poem in the *Tatler*, Richard STEELE refers to its author as Humphrey Wagstaff, who has "described Things exactly as they happen" without "form[ing] Fields, or Nymphs, or Groves where they are not, but makes the Incidents just as they really appear." Joseph Warton (an 18th-century literary critic) similarly suggests that this poem illustrates Swift's aptitude for "describing . . . objects as they really exist in life, . . . without heightening or enlarging them, and without adding any imaginary circumstances" (*Critical Heritage* 209).

Like "DESCRIPTION OF A CITY SHOWER," this poem is mainly concerned with the dreary elements of London life. While some—like promiscuous Betty—hurry to end their illicit nighttime activities, other characters (such as the inept and dirty "prentice") commence their "worn" and unrewarding routines at "the ruddy morn's approach." Carlton Clark has suggested that the image in line 15 of the "turnkey" awaiting his "flock" is the clearest evidence of the poem's character as an "anti-" or "mock" pastoral: "Here the pastoral shepherd becomes a jailer who releases inmates at night to steal money for bribes. [The poem] gives us an unromanticized, naturalistic vision of the working- and lower classes in the city, as opposed to the romanticized images of rural folk characteristic of the pastoral genre" ("Such a Vision"). As Louise K. Barnett notes, "the poem shows a smooth-running mechanism in which corrupt elements, indicative of societal disorder, contribute to the same superficial order of the morning routine that the honest and harmless are caught up in" (*Swift's Poetic Worlds* 130). In his "unromanticized" depiction of the morning as a time when one set of mundane activities simply gives way to another, Swift highlights this boring redundancy as the city's most distinctive characteristic.

# "Desire and Possession"

Poem by Swift; first published in 1735, written in 1727. Harold Williams suggests that Swift wrote it during his final visit to England (which was cut short by reports of Esther JOHNSON's failing health), but Pat Rogers notes that there is no evidence to support Williams's claim. Cast as a retelling of a tale first told by a wise moralist, it is a fable of two brothers—Possession and Desire—competing in a race. They are led astray by Envy, Slander, Sloth, and Doubt. Desire ("the swifter of the two") is further distracted by Power and Titles, all of which he casts aside as soon as he picks them up. Possession follows, gathering up all that Desire has left behind, but he soon slows due to the load he carries. When Desire finally reaches the end of the race (a tall tower with Fortune standing on top), Fortune knocks him headlong into an abyss. Possession sinks beneath the weight of his burden as ravenous birds pick him to pieces.

The moral of the poem seems to be that wanting more and actually getting it are equally harmful, but Swift also suggests that "man" (by expecting blessings from unworthy things) habitually sets himself up for disappointment. Swift makes a similar point in a sermon, "On the Poor Man's Contentment" (published in 1762). He argues there that the Bible is filled with illustrations of the "miserable Condition of Man," based in large part on "his unmeasurable Desires, and perpetual Disappointments." He also claims that no one gains real blessings—a quiet mind and healthy body—through wealth or power. In fact, "by multipllying our Desires, they . . . destroy our Health, Gall us with painful Diseases, and shorten our Life" (*Prose Works* 9.190, 195). Possession's miserable death at the end of the poem provides a memorably graphic affirmation of Swift's assertions throughout the sermon.

# "Dialogue between an Eminent Lawyer and Dr. Swift, Dean of St. Patrick's, A"

Poem by Swift; first published in 1755, written in 1729. Based loosely upon Horace's *Satura* II.i, it records a conversation between a satirist (Swift) and a lawyer (Robert LINDSAY). Alexander POPE's *Imitations of Horace* (1733) was based on the same Latin original. When Swift asks for advice on how to handle negative reactions to his satires, the lawyer encourages him to stop writing poetry altogether or at least to write on safer subjects. Swift rejects this advice, saying his conscience compels him to write against "stupid blasphemy and nonsense" (38).

barisms introduced into the vocabulary of English as it is spoken in Ireland serves as the basis of this dialogue. Swift writes to Alexander POPE in November 1734 about projects he is trying to complete, one being COMPLETE COLLECTION OF GENTEEL AND INGENIOUS CONVERSATION (1738) for which this "Dialogue" serves as an early set of notes. Though Swift diligently avoided impurities in his speech and written prose, he dealt with others daily who were far less meticulous in their use of language.

# "Dialogue between Captain Tom and Sir Henry Dutton Colt, A"

Poem by Swift; first published (anonymously) in 1710, written the same year. The poem depicts an argument between the TORY Thomas ("Captain Tom") MEDLYCOTT and Colt (M.P. for Newport and Westminster) over how the volatile parliamentary election of 1710 will turn out. Both men competed to represent Westminster in the election, which turned out to be a landslide TORY victory. In response to Colt's prediction of sure victory, Captain Tom delivers a stinging reply that sends Colt away saddened and speechless.

# "Dialogue in Hibernian Style, A"

Herbert Davis prints this conversation from the original manuscripts in the Huntington Library. The conversation between A and B consists of 23 short interrogative and declarative sentences. These Irishisms fascinated Swift, and he exhibits comic irony in exploring these linguistic abuses. For example, "Lord, I am boddered tother day with that prating fool Tom. Pray, how does he get his health?" The "Dialogue" was probably composed late in Swift's career, and shows his interest in linguistics and the evolution of the English language in particular. His curiosity about the Irish dialect and various bar-

# "Dialogue in the Castilian Language, A"

This and other trifles were apparently written during the winter of 1707, when Swift was in London, staying at Sir Andrew FOUNTAINE's home in Leicester Fields, but he may have begun it earlier in the same year in Dublin. Though the work is dated 1707 and was printed in 1710, some question remains regarding its origins, since Swift seems to have put it away in a notebook which he reviewed again in the early 1730s, handing over the manuscript to John Boyle, fifth earl of ORRERY in July 1737.

### SYNOPSIS

The interchange begins with Robert HOWARD asking Thomas PEMBROKE if he intends to dissolve Parliament or prorogue it. Pembroke ignores the question and offers Swift coffee, while "Captain" Thomas ASHE and William MOLYNEUX pun on a series of medicinal herbs, medicines, and cures for dissolving Parliament, while joking that coffee will not serve as a remedy. Howard complains about Ashe's talkativeness and says that if he had a medical instrument for shutting his mouth, he would use it. Fountaine enters the discussion with a pun on osculation/ostentation, which proceeds to Howard's long monologue on oysters. Without any transition, puns on aristocrats' last names being well-known English place names for counties, rivers, and towns goes on between Dillon ASHE and Milles. The punning continues with topics concerning cats, physicians, popes, beggars, lords, and rogues.

## COMMENTARY

These puns and linguistic oddities form the basis of an extended conversation among a small group of friends, including Swift. Thomas Ashe; the Lord Lieutenant Thomas, earl of PEMBROKE; Dr. Ralph Howard; Dr. Thomas Molyneux; Sir Andrew Fountaine; Reverend Dillon ASHE; Dr. Thomas Milles; and Bishop St. George ASHE of Clogher— all would gather at Dublin Castle during Pembroke's residence and, for entertainment purposes, play word games. This domestic circle offered relaxation and intellectual stimuli aside from their serious professional activities and became the setting for "extended logomachic exchanges" within the group.

# "Dick, a Maggot"

Poem by Swift; first published 1745, written c. 1728. Like a number of other Swift poems, it is directed against Richard TIGHE. See also, for example, "MAD MULLINIX AND TIMOTHY" and "CLAD ALL IN BROWN."

# "Dick's Variety"

Poem by Swift; first published in 1745, written c. 1728. Another of Swift's insulting verses against Richard TIGHE. See also, for example, "MAD MULLINIX AND TIMOTHY" and "CLAD ALL IN BROWN."

# "Dingley and Brent"

Poem by Swift; first published in 1765, written in 1724. It is subtitled "A Song to the Tune of 'Ye Commons and Peers.'" It is a gentle satire of Mrs. BRENT and Rebecca DINGLEY, portraying them as silly, carefree, and slow-witted.

# "Directions for a Birthday Song"

Poem by Swift; first published in 1765, written in 1729. Pat Rogers calls it Swift's "first 'mature' political poem" since it "exhibits a new directness in its anti-Hanoverian rhetoric, and clearly foreshadows poems such as "ON POETRY: A RHAPSODY" and "TO A LADY" (799). It was written for King GEORGE II's birthday (October 30) as a satire on Laurence EUSDEN, poet laureate who had written New Year's odes and birthday odes from 1719 to 1730. Swift addressed the poem to Matthew PILKINGTON, who was in the midst of writing an ode to the king in the hope of gaining preferment. Throughout the "Directions" Swift overtly suggests that Pilkington's poem will—like most odes of its kind—ascribe to the king and other nobles virtues they will never exhibit.

# "Directions to Servants"

Unfinished prose work by Swift, first published in 1745. In a June 12, 1732, letter to Alexander POPE, Swift claims to have begun work on "Directions" and *A COMPLETE COLLECTION OF GENTEEL AND INGENIOUS CONVERSATION* more than 28 years prior. In his 1758 *Life of Dr. Jonathan Swift,* W. H. Dilworth wrote that although "Directions" was not published until after Swift's death, it was "handed about" in manuscript "and applauded in his lifetime." Dilworth added that "the tract is written in so facetious a kind of low humour, that it must please many readers . . . by pointing out with an amazing exactness" the many "faults, tricks, blunders, lies, and various knaveries of domestic servants" (Williams, *Critical Heritage* 174).

## SYNOPSIS

Two sections form its structure, with the first ("Rules That Concern All Servants in General") establishing the theme in which master and servant interact across the spectrum of the human comedy. The second section comprises 16 chapters of varying length, each one entitled "Directions to the [occupational title]." Chapters 1 (Butler), 2 (Cook), 3 (Footman), 5 (Groom), 8 (Chamber-Maid), 9 (Waiting Maid), and 10 (House-Maid) seem well developed essays, but 4 (Coachman), 6 (House Steward and Land Steward), 7 (Porter), 11 (Dairy-Maid), 12 (Children's-Maid), 13 (Nurse), 14 (Laundress), 15 (House-Keeper), and 16 (Tutoress or Governess) are brief anecdotes, sometimes a sentence or two.

In Part I, the narrator adopts the persona of a former footman who provides straightforward advice (intelligence) to servants (inferiors) whose mental powers apparently equal or exceed their master's. The apparent ignorance of the upper classes whose follies will outrage and amuse becomes the focus of this section. "When your Master or Lady call a Servant by name, if that Servant be not in the way, none of you are to answer" or "when you have done a fault, be always pert and insolent, and behave your self as if you were the injured person; this will immediately put your Master or Lady off their mettle." This mixture of respect and contempt has a libertarian quality. (See Character entries below for synopses of each chapter in Part II.)

## COMMENTARY

Usually discussed as a less significant piece that Swift wrote mainly for his own amusement late in life, "Directions" offers advice to servants in various occupations. The humor of the work comes from the irony of the instructions, which are divided into several sections including a lengthy introduction, "To Servants in General," followed by individual segments addressed to the Butler, Cook, Footman, Groom, Chamber-Maid, Waiting-Maid, and House-Maid. "Directions" also contains nine fragments of similar unfinished segments, which are written from the perspective of a former footman who left his post after seven years.

In his biography of Swift, David Nokes calls "Directions" "a handbook for domestic guerrilla warfare" and "an anarchist's handbook compiled by the chief of police" (402–403). Its remarkable detail reflects Swift's years of observation of the duties and habits of domestic servants, along with his frustration at their annoying tendencies. Despite Swift's obvious familiarity with the servants' duties and the

tendencies he describes, several critics caution that "Directions to Servants" should not be read as a commentary based solely on Swift's experiences with his own household servants. The most compelling support for this claim is that "Directions" is set in the London household of a married couple and their children. Its scope, however, is even broader than that, providing an extensive portrayal of what Swift seems to have viewed as two fairly universal desires among servants. The first was to reduce their workloads by outwitting their masters, the second to subject their masters to a perpetual series of petty punishments for having overworked them in the past and continually seeking to do so in the present.

A further element of this work emphasizes the ugliness and squalor of servants' lives, particularly as they come in contact with their master's or mistress's habits, personal mannerisms, and contempt for those who attempt to lessen their physical discomforts. Swift refuses to present a sanitized view of his world, since regardless of one's social or economic class, excremental realities must be acknowledged. Those of the menial or servant class, however, face not only their own waste matter but also tend to that of the more privileged. In "Directions," a servant's household duties establish the structure of the existing society, with the menial class cleaning up the filth of the upper class, yet the satire cuts both groups. The Chamber-Maid may be ignorant and lazy, but the mistress who acts as if she has no responsibility for her daily physical acts exposes, as Carole Fabricant states, "her absurd priggishness and anality . . . relying instead on elaborate modes of concealment and . . . others hired specifically to mediate between themselves and reality" (*Swift's Landscape* 42). "THE LADY'S DRESSING ROOM," "A BEAUTIFUL YOUNG NYMPH GOING TO BED," and "STREPHON AND CHLOE" provide more insight into Swift's excremental universe, but "A PANEGYRIC ON THE DEAN" and "MRS. HARRIS'S PETITION" specifically mention the servants who function within this class society.

This was not the first time Swift had written in extensive detail of servants' duties. On December 7, 1733, he had presented his own staff with a quite serious set of "Laws for the Dean's Servants," including specific financial penalties for breaking them. One of these laws, for example, stipulated that, "Whatever servant shall be taken in a manifest lie, shall forfeit one shilling out of his or her board-wages." He had also written specifically on "The Duty of Servants at Inns," outlining what he required of grooms and footmen. These rules included such petty responsibilities as "Search under your Master's Bed when he is gone up, lest a Cat or something may be under it."

While the "Directions" are generally humorous in their portrayal of servants, there is an undertone of seriousness that sometimes suggests Swift regarded servants as sinister rather than simply crafty, dishonest, or annoyingly lazy. Perhaps the most poignant example appears in his advice to the Nurse, when the narrator counsels her never to confess if she happens "to let the Child fall, and lame it," and he adds, "if it dies, all is safe." David Nokes describes the serious side of "Directions" in terms of the "note of despair" he perceives "behind the comedy." In his view, when Swift wrote the "Directions" at such an advanced age, he had already begun to feel "increasingly helpless and besieged"—finding himself resentfully at the mercy of "these incompetent and careless yahoos" (*Hypocrite Reversed* 403).

Swift's use of irony throughout the completed essays and the fragments remains consistent, so it seems possible to conclude that Swift's recommendations for servant behavior actually stand as the opposite of what he approved in his servants. The book parodies various English and French conduct and morality books, such as *The Whole Duty of Mankind* (1658). But the verve and energy of the piece comes ironically from Swift's process of gathering these instances over the years with an interest toward both their comic sense and satiric values.

## CHARACTERS

**Butler**  A male head servant in a household, in charge of the plate, table, and liquors. Since he is "the principal party concerned," Swift mixes both respect and contempt for this servant while advising responsible behavior, yet the comic vein runs deeply throughout the text: "and to save your master's candles, never bring them up until half an hour after it be dark, although they be called for ever so often."

**Chamber-Maid**  She is addressed in chapter 8, following the instructions given to the Porter in the preceding chapter. The advice offered to the Chamber-Maid is lengthy in comparison to most of the other sections in "Directions." While the narrator admits that the nature of this servant's employment will differ greatly depending on "the Quality, the Pride, or the Wealth of the Lady" she serves, he addresses his advice to all chambermaids who work in households with a separate "House-Maid" (Housekeeper), who has different responsibilities.

The advice to the Chamber-Maid is similar to that offered to other servants, in terms of its ironic general suggestion that being a good servant requires doing precisely the opposite of what the master would want. For example, frolicking with her "favourite Footman" in the Lady's bed, breaking dishes, and sweeping dust into corners are (in the narrator's view) all strategies the Chamber-Maid should employ to please her master. In one section, however, this chapter is even more overtly Swiftian than other parts of "Directions," based upon its attention to chamberpots, waste, and the gross humanity of the "Lady" the Chamber-Maid serves. In this sense the advice recalls the "excremental" poems such as "The LADY'S DRESSING ROOM" and "STREPHON AND CHLOE," and presents (from a slightly different perspective) Swift's trademark tendency to debunk the false pretenses he abhorred and found so prevalent in his society's views of women. In a manner characteristic of Swift's satire, the narrator promotes precisely the airs Swift hated, telling the Chamber-Maid not to carry chamberpots downstairs to empty them since that would allow the "Fellows" to see them. Instead, she is to "empty them out of the Window" for the "Lady's credit." "It is highly improper," he explains, "for Men Servants to know that fine Ladies have Occasion for such Utensils; and do not scour the Chamber-pot, because the smell is wholesome." The instructions to the House-Maid in chapter 10 deal with similar issues.

**Children's-Maid**  She is addressed in chapter 12, following the instructions to the Dairy-Maid in the previous section. This segment is unfinished and brief in comparison to many other chapters in "Directions."

Like the instructions to the Nurse in chapter 13, the advice to the Children's-Maid illustrates the darker aspects of the "Directions" that are periodically evident amid their generally humorous irony. While much of the work deals with petty and annoying tendencies of specific servants, the chapters addressing these servants point out more troubling habits with potential consequences far beyond merely irritating the master. While the narrator advises the Nurse on what to do if she drops and injures, or even kills, one of the children, he suggests to the Children's-Maid that when a child is sick, she should "give it whatever it wants to eat or drink, although particularly forbid by the Doctor." She should then "throw the Physick out of the Window," which will cause the child to love her more, but she should be careful to "bid it not tell." He also warns that if the "Mistress" of the house ever "offers to whip a child," the Children's-Maid should snatch it violently from her hands ("in a Rage") and tell her "she is the cruellest Mother" alive.

**Coachman**    His instructions appear in chapter 4, following those addressed to the Footman. The narrator explains that this servant's only duty is "but to step into the Box [the carriage], and carry your Master or Lady." The advice offered to the Coachman is similar in its irony to that given to his fellow servants: he is told (for example) to train his horses to wait while he slips into a bar for a drink, to lie about the horses' ill condition if he does not feel like driving when his master wants to go out, and to drink as much as possible before driving. The narrator also advises the Coachman to have a new set of wheels bought for the coach as often as possible. If nothing else, he explains, this will be a "just Punishment on your Master's Covetousness."

**Cook**    She is addressed in chapter 2, following the long first chapter addressed to the Butler. The narrator begins by acknowledging that while many "People of Quality" have begun keeping male cooks, he is speaking to the "general Run" of upper-class citizens and will therefore speak of the Cook as a woman. It is only natural, he claims, to deal with her directly after his chapter on the Butler, since she and that character are "joined in Interest." With that in mind, he advises her to avoid quarrels with the Butler at all costs, since these are "very dangerous to you both, and will probably end in one of you being turned off."

The rest of the advice he offers is similar to the set of ironic suggestions he makes to servants in general in the introduction. For example, he exhorts the cook never to "send up a Leg of Fowl" at supper if there is some animal in the house she can blame for running off with it. He tells her she should never use a spoon to do something she could accomplish just as easily with her hands, and that she should never wash her hands until after all of her work is finished. Like other sections of "Directions," the chapter on the Cook is filled with a level of detail that could come only from having paid close attention to the annoying little habits—such as cutting up onions and apples with the same unwashed knife—that had come to typify the profession.

**Dairy-Maid**    Her instructions appear in chapter 11, and consist of only a few brief notes offering advice on what to do in order to avoid tiring out when churning butter. The notes suggest that she should put scalding hot water into the churn ("although in Summer") and churn week-old cream close to the kitchen fire.

**Footman**    The Footman is a servant who (as Swift's narrator says) performs "a great Variety of Business." The Footman was responsible for riding in front of his master's carriage, but also for answering the door at home, running errands and serving his master's table. In "Directions," the Footman is addressed in chapter 3, following the chapter dealing with the Cook. The narrator says he has a "true Veneration" for the Footman's occupation, since he "had once the Honour to be" one himself, until he "foolishly left by demeaning [him]self with accepting an employment in the Custom-house."

In terms of its irony and humor, the advice offered to the Footman is similar to that provided in other chapters and in the general introduction to "Directions." For example, the narrator tells the Footman that as he serves meals, he should take the largest dishes and "set them with one Hand" as a show of vigor and strength for the ladies. He must always do so, however, between two ladies. That way if the dish falls, "the Soup or Sauce may fall on their Cloaths," and not on the floor. The narrator further suggests that "while Grace is being said after Meat," the footman and his "brethren" should "take the Chairs from behind the Company, so that when they go to sit again, they may fall backwards, which will make them all merry."

While most of the chapter addressed to the Footman exemplifies the light irony that appears throughout "Directions," its conclusion is more like the less common, darker elements of this otherwise comic work. As in chapter 13 (where the narrator advises the Nurse to lie if she drops a child and injures or even kills it), it is difficult to tell whether Swift is joking or pointing out a serious problem by having the narrator advise the Footman on how he should conduct himself on his way to the gallows. This outcome is treated as a virtual certainty, as the Footman's punishment "either for robbing [his] Master, for House-breaking, or going upon the High-way, or in a drunken Quarrel, by killing the first Man [he] meet." Whether or not this is a somber commentary on the general character of men in this occupation, the narrator insists that the Footman must never confess, that he hold a book in his hand (despite his illiteracy), and kiss the hangman while making an unforgettable dying speech. This, he says, will ensure that the Footman's fame "shall continue until a Successor of equal Renown succeeds in your Place."

**Governess**   Chapter 16 is addressed "to the Tutoress, or Governess," and is intended for the servant who is primarily responsible for educating the children of the household. In this brief, unfinished chapter, the narrator first advises her to make excuses for the children to explain their lack of study: "Say the Children have sore Eyes; Miss *Betty* won't take to her Book, &c." He also offers suggestions on what to have the young girls read: "Make the Misses read French and English Novels, and French Romances, and all the Comedies writ in

King *Charles* II. And King *William*'s Reigns, to soften their Nature, and make them tender-hearted." In truth, Swift seems to have wished young ladies would read anything other than romances: In his notes or "Hints" on the "Education of Ladyes," he had written that there should be "No French Romances, and very few plays for young Ladyes" and that it was a "shame that not one in a million [women] can properly be said to read or write, or understand." Also, in I.5 of GULLIVER'S TRAVELS, the empress of Lilliput's apartment is set on fire "by the carelessness of a Maid of Honour, who fell asleep while she was reading a romance."

**Groom**   He is addressed in chapter 5, following the advice offered in chapter 4 to the Coachman. The Groom's section is lengthy in comparison to most of the others in the "Directions." The Groom was a manservant who (in some cases) was also in charge of caring for his master's horses. Swift's narrator focuses on the Groom's responsibilities as the servant who accompanies his master while traveling. The directions addressed to him provide various strategies for procuring ale and free time in places the master visits. For example, the narrator tells the groom, "Leave your Master to the Care of the Servants in the Inn, and your Horses to those in the Stable: Thus both he and they are left in the properest Hands; but you are to provide for yourself; therefore get your Supper, drink freely, and go to Bed without troubling your Master, who is in better Hands than yours." Like the advice offered to other servants in "Directions," the suggestions in this section are geared toward making life easier for the servant at the expense of his master.

**House-Keeper**   Her directions appear in chapter 15, following those addressed to the Laundress in the preceding section. Like many other chapters, this one is very brief and unfinished. The narrator advises the House-Keeper that she should "always have a favourite Footman" who can serve as a lookout for her while she steals food from the master's table: "order him to be very watchful when the Second Course is taken off, that it be brought to your Office, that you and the Steward may have a Tit-bit together."

**House-Maid** She is addressed in chapter 10. Like the instructions to the Chamber-Maid in chapter 8, this section of "Directions" is particularly Swiftian in its virtually pervasive concern with what the narrator calls "the worst Necessities" of the lady of the house. In this sense, this section of "Directions" recalls Swift's "excremental" poems, such as "The LADY'S DRESSING ROOM" and "STREPHON AND CHLOE." The bulk of what the narrator tells the House-Maid has to do with handling chamberpots and disposing of their contents in ways that will embarrass the lady of the house by highlighting her need to use something so crude. For example, he instructs the Maid to "leave [the] Lady's Chamber-pot in the Bed-chamber Window, all Day to air," and when making the lady's bed, to "put the Chamber-pot under it, but in such a manner, as to thrust the Valance along with it, that it may be full in Sight, and ready for [the] lady when she hath Occasion to use it." In other words, she should strive constantly to remind everyone—including the lady, herself— that despite her refinement, the lady of the house is bound by the same necessities as everyone else.

The narrator also explains that he is "very much offended" with ladies "who are so proud and lazy, that they will not be at the Pains of stepping into the garden to pluck a Rose, but keep an odious Implement sometimes in the Bed-chamber itself, or at least in a dark closet adjoining, which they make use of to ease their worst Necessities." To cure this habit, the narrator suggests that when this chamberpot gets full, the House-Maid should go out of her way to make a spectacle of emptying it. She should carry it "down the great Stairs, and in the presence of the Footmen; and, if any body knocks," she should "open the Street-door" with the evidence still in her hands. This, the narrator claims, will teach the lady of the house to "take the Pains of evacuating her Person in the proper Place," instead of "expos[ing] her Filthiness to all the Men Servants in the house." The rest of his advice in this section is similar to that offered to other servants in "Directions," encouraging the House-Maid to do all she can to make life easier for herself and annoy her master: If, for example, the lady insists that she take cleaning buckets downstairs to empty them rather than dumping their contents

out the upstairs windows, the House-Maid should be sure to carry the pail "so as to let the Water dribble on the Stairs all the way down."

**House Steward** This character and the Land Steward are addressed in chapter 6, an unfinished section of "Directions" containing only a few brief notes. These suggest that, in advising these servants, Swift intended to have the narrator cite the earl of PETERBOROUGH's steward as an example— he tore down his master's house, "sold the Materials, and charged my Lord with Repairs."

**Land Steward** See House Steward.

**Laundress** Her brief instructions appear in chapter 14, following those addressed to the Nurse in the preceding section. In keeping with the consistently ironic tone of the "Directions," in this chapter the narrator—who is ostensibly concerned with helping servants learn to please those for whom they work—advises the Laundress to do precisely what most masters would not want this type of servant to do: tear the linens to pieces and hang them all on "young Fruit Trees, especially in Blossom."

**Nurse** She is addressed in chapter 14, following the advice offered to the Children's-Maid in the preceding chapter. In Swift's day, the Nurse was "a woman employed to suckle, and otherwise attend to, an infant" (*Oxford English Dictionary*). The Nurse's directions are unfinished and very brief, consisting of only a few lines. Like the instructions to the Children's-Maid, this short chapter illustrates how, at times, "Directions" point out serious problems with certain types of servants in addition to making fun of their annoying little habits. The tone of this section suggests a disturbing disregard on the narrator's part (which he assumes the Nurse shares) for the children of the household. The Nurse is told that if she should happen to let one of the children fall and make it lame, she should "never confess it; and, if it dies, all is safe." She should also, the narrator warns, work to get pregnant as soon as possible while she is "giving Suck," so that she "may be ready for another Service" when the child she nurses "dies, or is weaned." The narrator's matter-of-fact treatment of both potential outcomes focuses entirely on the Nurse's well-being, and recalls the kind of callous indifference toward children that Swift parodied and criticized in "A MODEST PROPOSAL."

**Porter**   He is addressed in the very brief chapter 7, following the instructions offered to the House Steward and Land Steward in chapter 6. The Porter is a servant who answers his master's door and admits (or turns away) those who wish to enter. The narrator of "Directions" addresses his instructions to porters who work for "Ministers of State." He advises them to turn away everyone who seeks entry into the minister's house except for a select few, including—among others—his "pimp," "chief Flatterer," and "hired Spy."

**Tutoress**   See Governess.

**Waiting Maid**   She is addressed in chapter 9, following the instructions to the Chamber-Maid in the preceding section. The directions to the Waiting Maid are more developed than those aimed at her fellow servants and are distinctly coarse in comparison. The narrator repeatedly tells her that when dealing with men—her Lord or otherwise—she should try at every turn to increase her wealth. This quickly becomes a suggestion that she turn prostitute in her own household, which is something the narrator assumes she will do, anyway. For example, he explains to the Waiting Maid that if she serves "in a great Family" and the Lord likes her, she must "take Care to get as much out of him as you can; and never allow him the smallest liberty, not the squeezing of your Hand, unless he puts a Guinea into it." After all, he argues, "Five Guineas for handling your Breast is cheap Pennyworth, although you seem to resist with all your Might; but never allow him the least Favour under a hundred Guineas, or a Settlement of twenty Pounds a Year for Life."

In his advice regarding whom she should take as a lover, the narrator tells the Waiting Maid that she has three choices: "the Chaplain, the Steward, and my Lord's Gentleman." Although the Steward is her best choice, the narrator insists, she must take up with the Chaplain if she "happen[s] to be young

with Child by my Lord." She should use particular caution, he warns, in allowing the Lord's eldest son to take her as a lover. If he is a "Rake," in fact, she should "avoid him like *Satan*": "after ten thousand Promises, you will probably get nothing from him, but a big Belly, or a Clap, and probably both together." Aside from these particularly vulgar examples, the instructions addressed to the Waiting Maid are generally characteristic of "Directions." The narrator encourages her to annoy her mistress as often as possible through a variety of acts (such as waking her up from naps when she is ill), which he presents ironically as though they are guaranteed to endear this servant to the entire household.

# "Discourse Concerning the Fears from the Pretender, A"

The fragment is dated February 20 [1714], the year determined after it was preserved in the papers of Charles FORD and first printed in *The Letters of Jonathan Swift to Charles Ford*, edited by D. Nichol Smith (1935).

## SYNOPSIS

The TORIES and WHIGS have no reason for continuing their ongoing battle for political power since the critical issues of the War of the Spanish Succession have been resolved with the peace treaty signed at Utrecht. The war is over and cannot be renewed. The parties now have important issues to discuss concerning the commerce bill, the status of Sophia the electress of Hanover, and the future of the Old Pretender (the exiled Prince of Wales; see James Francis Edward STUART). The Pretender's future and current actions, according to Swift, are a minor concern for Parliament, and if only the Whigs could be sincerely convinced of that, they would leave the queen to choose her own administration without their interference.

## COMMENTARY

This fragment had its beginning after Swift finished "The Public Spirit of the Whigs," but before that piece was published on February 23, 1714. Swift knew the great weapon against Robert HARLEY and Henry BOLINGBROKE was the suspicion that the ministry was making overtures to the Pretender. Though he knew these suspicions were groundless, Swift found it necessary to assure Archbishop KING of the ministry's honesty as well as his own on this point. When Swift retreated to the English countryside, he was primarily concerned with his inability to reconcile Oxford and Bolingbroke, but when the latter left for the Pretender's court, it seemed to prove all the doubts. After the ministry's collapse, Swift intended on continuing the "Discourse" in its present form with this title, but finally dropped the title and redirected the discussion, the result being "Some Free Thoughts on the Present State of Affairs."

# "Discourse Concerning the Mechanical Operation of the Spirit, A"

This piece serves as the third independent essay in the miscellany volume entitled A TALE OF A TUB, which was composed in 1696 or 1697. The first edition was printed in 1704 for John Nutt in London; second and third editions appeared in the same year, a fourth in 1705, and an enlarged fifth edition with the apology and notes in 1710. John Hawkesworth published it in the *Works* in 1755.

## SYNOPSIS

The work has four parts, beginning with the opening letter to T. H. Esquire, who is probably Thomas HOBBES (Swift uses parallels from *Leviathan* throughout the work). Section I focuses on dissenting congregations and the hallmarks of Nonconformity; Section II discusses dissenting preachers, examining their mental activities, speech characteristics, and obnoxious voices; and the final part concludes with a mock "history of enthusiasm which concludes the origin of their beliefs depends on hidden lust." The "Bookseller's Advertisement" adds drama and mystery, indicating that this fragment came

into his hands years ago, and after editing, he can now present this piece to the public. The author is unknown, and the bookseller urges readers to make their own judgments about the writer's intentions.

He proposes to examine religious enthusiasm, "or launching out the soul, as an effect of artifice and mechanic operation." The report will be delivered by this pompous expert, or mechanic, as a parody of a Royal Academy session, but he uses objectivity and detail in describing how one mechanically produces the Spirit. Soon casting aside minimal objectivity for direct attack, the narrator criticizes Jack (of the "Tale") for his canting, zealous language and other various gross behaviors. Swift links religious zeal and enthusiasm with assertive sexuality and passion. As the fragment concludes, the narrator returns to his original story thread: Read this letter and then burn it. The key element is his satire on "the inward light," which serves as the first ingredient toward the art of canting.

## COMMENTARY

In 1704 Swift published in London a set of three highly influential satiric pieces that would pose the argument concerning how the divisions within Christianity were ultimately destroying the Church of England. "A Tale of a Tub," "The BATTLE OF THE BOOKS," and "Discourse Concerning the Mechanical Operation of the Spirit" all attack fanaticism, corruption, and extremism in all its forms, while using satire and irony. The publisher (John Nutt) who printed these works kept any mention of the writer hidden in the hope the mystery would add interest to the work, and the controversy over his ideas did promote its popularity so that four editions appeared within a year.

Using the familiar letter genre, Swift adopts the persona of a Fellow of the Royal Society who corresponds with "T. H. Esquire," a fellow of the fictional Academy of the Beaux Espirits. Esquire may be a caricature of the philosopher Thomas Hobbes, whose designation as a leading Modernist in the "Tale of a Tub" suggests the essay's contempt for new learning. Only a society of experts, like philosophers Hobbes or René DESCARTES, could appreciate the metaphysical terminology and vocabulary of scientific information and investigation. These "virtuosi" communicate in separating mind from matter, torturing the divine entity into a mechanical spirit, and reducing religion into a fanatical enthusiasm. Swift cannot tolerate the abuses existing in contemporary Christianity: the excesses and arrogance of the Roman Catholic Church, the presumption of Protestant Dissenters, and sectarian Enthusiasts who employ hypocrisy in creating their fantasies.

Critics believe the true enemies for Swift are the Nonconformists, or Dissenters, who have weakened the Anglican Church, especially dissenting preachers. But his distrust of science and the pseudo-scientists also becomes an important theme in this essay. Though well read in contemporary scientific investigation, he sees any departure from practical reality damaging. Fanaticism, a form of which is practiced by the mad scientists of Balnibarbi in GULLIVER'S TRAVELS, ends up deceiving not only the unaware but the individual under its control who imagines himself inspired when he is simply delusional. The mad scientist of the later work has the role of a Puritan preacher in "Mechanical Operation": "These are the men, who pretend to understand a book, by scouting thro' the Index, as if a Traveler should go about to describe a palace, when he had seen nothing but the privy."

In his biography of Swift, Irvin Ehrenpreis finds this essay a far weaker production when compared with the "Tale" or "Battle of the Books," too obsessional on characterizing fanatics and leading the reader away from the satiric point (I.241–42). But as the essay draws to a close, Swift does write without lapsing into sharp invective and employs a more balanced irony in analyzing the role of religion among Indians and English Christians. He finds Indians have maintained a harmonious stability between good and evil, never mixing the natures of the two principles: "I applaud their discretion in limiting their devotions and their deities." In contrast, the English have "most horribly confounded the frontiers of both," and in doing so, brought about war and dissent so complete that entire nations have been disturbed to their core. Irrationality, egotism, and zeal all corrupt the senses and discredit the imagination. These are the problems for which Swift blames the Puritans, accusing them of having created a kind of madness

similar to that described in the "Digression on Madness" in Section IX of "A Tale of a Tub." As Claude Rawson points out, however, for Swift "the term 'free-thinking' slides deliberately from its restricted or technical sense to that more literal and inclusive sense which covers the unregulated thoughts of every human being" (*Gulliver and the Gentle Reader* 128). In the "Discourse" and "Digression," Swift suggests that the temptation to give free rein to those "unregulated thoughts" is a form of madness that everyone—not just Puritans and projectors—must seek to avoid.

### FURTHER READING

Boyle, Frank T. "Profane and Debauched Deist: Swift and the Contemporary Response to *A Tale of a Tub*." *Eighteenth-Century Ireland* 3 (1988): 25–38.

Ehrenpreis, Irvin. *Swift: The Man, His Works and the Age.* 3 vols. Cambridge, Mass.: Harvard University Press, 1962–83.

Levine, Jay Arnold. "The Design of *A Tale of a Tub* (with a Digression on the Mad Modern Critic)." *ELH* 33 (1966): 198–227.

Smith, Frederik N. *Language and Reality in Swift's "A Tale of a Tub."* Columbus: Ohio State University Press, 1979.

Swift, Jonathan. *A Tale of a Tub.* Edited by A. C. Guthkelch and D. Nichol Smith. 2d ed. Oxford: Clarendon Press, 1958.

———. *A Tale of a Tub and Other Works.* Edited by Angus Ross and David Woolley. Oxford: Oxford University Press, 1984.

# "Discourse of the Contests and Dissensions in Athens and Rome, A"

Swift's first political tract, initially printed in October 1701 in London for John Nutt. The essay was reprinted in two *Miscellanies*, 1711 and 1727, and George FAULKNER's 1735 edition of Swift's *Works*. The latter edition shows corrections, probably made by Swift or his friends.

## SYNOPSIS

The essay is divided into five chapters, with chapters 1 through 4 focusing on the political battle going on in Parliament. Chapter 1 centers itself on the balance-of-power issue within a state. Chapter 2 reviews the instability and trouble surrounding impeachments, and relies on Athenian history for examples. Chapter 3 presents the critical argument as an ongoing struggle between nobles and commoners for power, illustrated with examples from Roman history. Chapter 4 concludes the argument, beginning with a discussion of impeachment as the panacea of the ancients, then revisiting the balance-of-power question, and ending with a reminder of how easily tyranny can supplant a free state. Chapter 5, clearly an addendum to the original four, sets aside the classical allegory for a spirited discussion of recent events (in June of 1701, the king prorogued Parliament and effectively quashed the impeachments of the WHIG lords.). The general discussion in this final chapter serves as a primer on political science, examining the flaws in the parliamentary and party systems, as well as the imminent danger facing the national constitution. The parallels in tone and argument regarding man's nature between this essay and "A TALE OF A TUB" are striking, and no confusion can exist as to who wrote both pieces.

## COMMENTARY

This pamphlet was written during Swift's WHIG period. It impressed the men he hoped it would, especially John SOMERS, William PORTLAND, Edward ORFORD, and Charles HALIFAX. Two years earlier, the Tories had begun gaining power in response to WILLIAM III's actions, particularly his large gifts of land in Ireland to his cronies and mistress. With the impeachments of the Whig lords over charges of political corruption, Swift began composing (in the summer of 1701) an explanation of deeply held political principles that he hoped would contribute to reestablishing order among the parliamentary chaos and constitutional instability. Also, as he finished editing Sir William TEMPLE's *Miscellanea: the Third Part*, he saw the need of escaping the Laracor parish assignment for better,

more significant church duties: He hoped "Contests and Dissensions" would advance his reputation and declare his loyalties.

As a political allegory, the essay relies on carefully chosen references to classical history and figures from Greece and Rome, which Swift uses as part of his discussion of tyranny and the dangers inherent in repeating history. Contemporary history offered Swift many examples of these dangers. During the time between the Peace of Ryswick (1697) and the emergence of a new war in 1702, the War of the Spanish Succession, politicians and journalists were determined to raise England's attention against LOUIS XIV's expansionist policies throughout Europe. Over a four-year period, a struggle for a balance of powers within the state resulted in fractional discontent, so much so that Swift feared that the specter of ancient tyranny had risen and would dominate political life in England. The Whig Junto was under severe attack and the House of Commons hoped to increase its powers within the state and deprive the king and the House of Lords of some of their sway. William's ministers had been negotiating further treaties with the French and the Dutch, which led Robert HARLEY and the Commons to seek relief through impeachment proceedings. In Swift's view, these issues (including matters of foreign policy and the national interest) called for a conservative and traditional statement, quite unlike what one might see in the popular press or in the work of Daniel DEFOE.

His studied calm and serenity belied a real fear of the restlessness of the mob, which can be seen in his use of beast imagery: The public were silkworms, the French king is a vulture, and party followers are sheep. Continued references to balance of power, the essay's most striking positive image, effectively means "mixed government," where the people retain true power but the administration functions as a troika with king, Lords, and Commons all held in balance. Maintaining a tone of reasonableness, Swift prefers using Temple's technique of finding historical examples to help explain contemporary social institutions. See also "TOLAND'S INVITATION TO DISMAL TO DINE WITH THE CALVES' HEAD CLUB" and "The STORM."

## FURTHER READING

Downie, J. A. *Jonathan Swift: Political Writer*. London: Routledge & Kegan Paul, 1984.

Ehrenpreis, Irvin. *Swift: The Man, His Works and the Age*. 3 vols. Cambridge, Mass.: Harvard University Press, 1962–83.

Fox, Christopher, ed. *The Cambridge Companion to Jonathan Swift*. Cambridge and New York: Cambridge University Press, 2003.

Fox, Christopher, and Brenda Tooley, eds. *Walking Naboth's Vineyard: New Studies of Swift*. South Bend, Ind.: University of Notre Dame Press, 1995.

Palmieri, Frank, ed. *Critical Essays on Jonathan Swift*. New York: G. K. Hall, 1993.

# "Discourse to Prove the Antiquity of the English Tongue, A"

The essay was first printed by Deane SWIFT in 1765 in the *Works*, London, and reprinted by George FAULKNER in *Works*, Dublin, in the same year.

## SYNOPSIS

The narrator sarcastically announces his ambition to study language with a passion similar to that of Richard BENTLEY and Isaac NEWTON. He intends to prove the antiquity of English in a far more successful manner than current etymologists. The key argument relies on the fact that English, as it is now spoken, is easily linked to Hebrew, Latin, and Greek. In typical fashion, Swift tortures the word *cloak* into *cloaca*, or "outhouse." Although many examples could be provided to prove his thesis, the narrator concentrates on proper names of persons, beginning with the Greek and Trojan heroes, gods, and wives from the *Iliad*. The absurd lengths of the joke seem stunning in "Andromache . . . her father was a Scotch gentleman. . . . Hector fell in love with his daughter, and the father's name was Andrew Mackay. The young lady was called by the same name, only a little softened to the Grecian accent." Swift repeats the pattern another 20 times.

## COMMENTARY

This piece has been called a learned joke, a parody of philological scholarship in which Swift tracks down the linguistic origins in Hebrew, Greek, and Latin of words in English. He may have intended to publish it in the INTELLIGENCER but set it aside instead. One key reference to the classical scholar and theologian Richard Bentley surfaces as Swift, who hated Bentley's "pert" style, satirizes him as an "illustrious modern star." He compares Bentley to Isaac Newton (an ironical reference) for whom he holds a longstanding aversion, especially since the scientist as Master of the Mint approved William WOOD's coinage. Etymologists' methods come under attack, and their science seems more like a game. The piece depends heavily on satirically reductive, homophonic puns: Achilles becomes "A kill-ease"; Diomede, "die-a-Maid"; and Ajax, "a Jakes." Throughout the piece, Swift uses sexual and scatological metaphors to reduce classical and heroic dignity.

# "Discovery, The"

Poem by Swift; first published in 1746, written in 1699. It is a satire directed against Arthur BUSHE and Charles, second earl of BERKELEY and lord justice of Ireland. In addition to resenting Berkeley's choice of Bushe as his secretary, Swift was convinced that Bushe had prevented him from becoming dean of Derry in favor of John BOLTON.

# "Dog and the Thief, The"

See "FABULA CANIS ET UMBRAE."

# "Doing Good: A Sermon, on the Occasion of Wood's Project"

This sermon was printed in Hawkesworth's edition of the *Works*, London, 1765, and George FAULKNER printed it the same year in Dublin. It was among the last of Swift's sermons to be printed. The dean preached this sermon between August 4 and October 26, 1724, at the same time that he was actively focused on writing The DRAPIER'S LETTERS.

## SYNOPSIS

The speaker addresses the moral issue of how an individual will typically do himself a good turn before helping someone else. The law of nature requires us to love our neighbors, but not to love them as well as ourselves. Yet if an individual can do a neighbor a kindness without causing himself harm or loss, the law of God requires him to love that neighbor as himself.

Extending this thought beyond the individual to the community of men and women (the commonwealth), Swift argues love of country is the great virtue. Neither loyalty to a king nor public spirit can get us what we need as a nation; instead we must recognize three issues:

- All men have the potential to be useful to their country.
- All men have the potential to cause harm to their country.
- God considers any willful harm to one's country a great sin.

The types of harm one can cause are grouped into four areas: (1) elevation of private advantage over public advantage, (2) use of false accusation and perjury, (3) the spreading of lies and false rumors so as to cause fear in the public, and (4) the use of reason and plausible argument in convincing the public to accept a damaging proposal.

Injuries to the commonwealth remain a sin in the eyes of God, especially since government and order are from God, and any effort to breed confusion among the public destroys God's creation. Though man may forgive a traitor, we cannot fully understand God's mercies, without which no salvation is assured. Being an enemy to one's country causes such harm that we are obliged to nurture our public spirit and avoid temporal evils.

## COMMENTARY

Ireland's economic problems serve as the central issue in this piece. Charity, wealth, and poverty had been the usual topics in Swift's sermons, but in 1724 he extended his philosophical study of the human condition. The argument suggests that even the poor and lower classes could influence the economic condition of the country. The real enemies, in his view, were those whose short-term interests demanded immediate profits, quick advantages, and the pleasure of spreading false rumors. He suggested punishment for anyone who would support William WOOD's coinage scheme, a program which was the equivalent of a cardinal sin. Crimes against a whole people deserve the same punishment given out to traitors.

Two years had passed since Wood's patent had been issued and the furor against it had grown into a wave of poems, pamphlets, broadsides, and public declarations. When Swift decided to introduce economic issues into his devotional efforts, he had already decided to speak directly for the cause of Irish equality. This essay marks his initial salvo as the champion of Irish grievances. He knew (and his readers soon learned) that the argument over Wood's copper coins had much broader implications.

# "Dorinda Dreams of Dress Abed"

Poem by Swift; first published in 1814, written in 1720. Swift included it (along with "Lines from 'CADENUS AND VANESSA'") in a letter to Esther VANHOMRIGH written in July of that year. He prefaces the poem with the statement, "Here is an epigram that concerns you not."

# "Drapier's Hill"

Poem by Swift; first published 1729, written the same year. It announces Swift's purchase of land at Drumlack near MARKET HILL and his plans to build there. He eventually decided against doing so. Drapier's Hill was to be the name of the mansion he planned to construct there, but he uses the term interchangeably with Drumlack. See also "DEAN'S REASONS FOR NOT BUILDING AT DRAPIER'S HILL."

# Drapier's Letters, The

The complete series of seven letters written in 1724–25 was printed for the first time as one volume by George FAULKNER in 1735. This Irish edition contained material printed earlier in *The Hibernian Patriot* (1725), including two broadsides and two unprinted letters, as well as corrections, omissions, and alterations in Swift's hand. He may have also provided the notes. The first five letters were published in the following manner, with the additional two added to complete the series:

- Letter 1: "A Letter to the Shopkeepers, Tradesmen, Farmers, and Common People of Ireland" (April 2, 1724)
- Letter 2: "A Letter to Mr. Harding the Printer" (August 6, 1724)
- Letter 3: "Some Observations upon . . . the Report of the Committee" (September 5, 1724)
- Letter 4: "A Letter to the Whole People of Ireland" (October 22, 1724)
- Letter 4a: "Seasonable Advice to the Grand Jury" (November 14, 1724)
- Letter 4b: "An Extract of a Book" (November 21, 1724)
- Letter 4c: "The Presentment of the Grand Jury of the County of the City of Dublin" (November 28, 1724)
- Letter 5: "A Letter to Lord Viscount Molesworth" (December 31, 1724)
- Letter 6: "A Letter to the Lord Chancellor Middleton" (1725)
- Letter 7: "An Humble Address to Both Houses of Parliament" (1725)

## COMMENTARY

The British government, apparently responding to a request from the king (though his ministers may have initiated this scheme) for a pension for his mistress, Ermengarde Melusina von der Schulenburg, now duchess of KENDAL and a naturalized British citizen, created a royal patent in 1720. The patent would grant permission for minting Irish copper halfpence and farthings, and the patent could be sold for the benefit of the duchess. The British often used the Irish establishment to maintain absentee pensioners, landlords, and government officials, and this further burden seemed an easy choice. William WOOD, who may have conspired in this plan, paid £10,000, and in 1722 the king signed the patent. Immediately, complaints from the commissioners of the Irish Revenue reached the lord lieutenant, the duke of GRAFTON, who maintained that the Irish government could not control the mint—the position English government had held for more than 200 years.

All too frequently the Irish were not consulted on proposals directly involving their economy; once again neither their Parliament nor commissioners of Revenue were asked if such an idea had merit. Certainly, the issue would cause concern since the quantity and quality of the new money suggested a devaluation of Irish currency. The English employed this method of subjugation and subordination in Scotland and the American colonies as well. The confused economic situation, aided by the poor circulation of money in Ireland, demonstrated the general mismanagement of the country. However, this fight over copper coins had much broader implications for both sides: The English government and its Dublin emissaries had to show strength, or their sway over the Irish would have weakened and concessions would have been required. After much debate, a cloud of pamphlets attacking English oppressiveness, and various minor government reviews and changes, the English withdrew the patent. Robert WALPOLE's government had suffered a major blow to its pride, and the Irish took pleasure in momentary relief.

Throughout the series of letters, Swift adopts the persona of a Dublin linen draper and tradesman, a member of the middle class, pleading for Irish equality in an informed manner. The dean finally agreed to become fully involved in this controversy (which had been brewing for two years) and after hearing numerous requests for assistance from colleagues, he wrote the most effective statement against Wood's manufacture of copper coinage. As the Irish champion, Swift found immediate response to his combination of fact and invective. After the fourth letter was published, his printer was prosecuted and a price placed on the author's head. Unintimidated, he continued writing and publishing so that in the summer of 1725 (when he had ready a seventh letter) public pressure compelled the government to relent, revoking the patent and compensating the embattled Wood.

M. B. Drapier may stand for Marcus Brutus, the Roman political figure and one of the principal assassins of Julius Caesar, while Caesar represents GEORGE I in this series. Throughout *The Drapier's Letters,* Swift consistently applied the strategic ideas of Archbishop William KING and Alan MIDDLETON, who had quickly realized the value of a boycott in which the Irish would simply refuse the halfpence. Convincing the ordinary middle-class Dubliner was essential: The tone had to be recognizable, and the economic damage that such coinage could produce in Ireland had to be understood. Using his typical downbeat ridicule, Swift created in the Drapier a perfect opponent for the English

Swift as the Drapier, from the frontispiece of Swift's *Works,* 1735 *(Courtesy of University of Pennsylvania Libraries)*

ironmonger Wood, assuring his Irish readers that they had no reason to fear this pirate. Of course, "the Drapier" and Wood were masks for the real antagonists in this fight: Swift and Walpole.

## Letter 1: "A Letter to the Shopkeepers, Tradesmen, Farmers, and Common People of Ireland"

### SYNOPSIS

In an opening exhortation, Swift declares the seriousness of this pamphlet's topic: "next to your duty to God, and the care of salvation, of the greatest concern to your selves, and your children; your bread and clothing, and every common necessary of life entirely depend upon it." He worries that human nature being what it is, even if someone tries to give good advice, it will be ignored. Reminding his readers of his earlier "PROPOSAL FOR THE UNIVERSAL USE OF IRISH MANUFACTURE," he recalls how a jury consisting at least partially of men whom the pamphlet sought to inform and protect found its printer guilty of sedition. Putting aside the reader's potential foolhardiness, Swift focuses on the "plain story of the fact." He recounts the unfortunate history of Wood's patent and the damage his coinage would cause to the Irish economy. The Irish customs apparently refused entrance to barrels of these coins, but this will not prevent their entry into the monetary system. What is worse, the Irish can expect that the English army, stationed in the country, will be paid in this coin. Based on the financial implications of this scheme upon them, the shopkeepers and tradesman can either accept this debased trash or raise the cost of all their goods, sending the entire economy into an unmanageable inflationary spiral. He predicts that farmers will be carting pounds of coins about to pay for their needs (modern readers will recall the reports of citizens in the post–World War I Weimar Republic pushing wheelbarrows full of nearly worthless currency about the streets). The socioeconomic chaos resulting from the use of this base coinage should not be underestimated, and as the Irish economy collapses from English pressure, they can expect their trading partners, the Dutch, will pay for Irish goods with the same worthless currency.

The last section reviews the laws which should protect the Irish citizen against such outrages. In 17 paragraphs, complete with earlier case precedents, Swift presents a series of constitutional protections that a free Irishman can employ in his favor. The conclusion states categorically what the law obliges each person to do and what it does not: Swift's reduction of the argument into three actions could not be clearer, no matter the education of his reader.

## COMMENTARY

Swift alerts his fellow Dubliners: Know the laws of your country and use them in protecting your interests. Their duty in this case becomes a sacred act, a Christian responsibility, and a matter of survival. In boycotting Wood's coinage, Dubliners avoid fraudulent behavior, and constitutional guarantees remain the only source of protection left to the ordinary man. If Swift can alarm his fellow citizens, he may possibly reach a populace so used to being manipulated and mistreated that his words might unite them in action against Wood's patent. He is not bound by objectivity and facts but easily inflates and expands its disastrous potential. As Irvin Ehrenpreis suggests in his biography of Swift, good propaganda requires a human subject, but the writer must avoid alienating his readers (III.214). The choice of Wood as a mercenary and deceitful charlatan, isolated and alone, suits the nature of this piece exactly. No sympathy can come from the reader for this figure, as he is simply another arrogant Englishman, hoping to take advantage of the Irish. Focusing on the legal means for defeating the patent, Swift proves, even to the unlettered reader, that sense is on his side.

## Letter 2: "A Letter to Mr. Harding the Printer. Upon Occasion of a Paragraph in His Newspaper of August 1st"

### SYNOPSIS

Swift responds to the British Privy Council's leak of Wood's proposal to limit the monetary amount of his issue of coins. Although the letter is addressed to only one person (John HARDING, the Drapier's printer) it indicates that all the Irish should hearken to his words.

The letter begins with a close analysis of the reprinted news report on the proposal's status. Who are those Irish merchants and traders supporting "Wood's Brass"? Swift decides they could only be traitors or confederates of Wood. That aside, he complains about the excessive amount of currency proposed in this scheme.

Swift deconstructs Wood's arguments in favor of his patent: Each proposition becomes another weapon turned against the ironmonger. Concluding this review, the writer suggests the Irish have been dealing with a traitor and, warming to this approach, proceeds to call Wood a highwayman, a housebreaker, and a devouring rat. How could the king willingly agree to having his image placed on Wood's coin? Associating the monarch at this stage with Wood will only diminish the English government and its legitimate ruler even further, especially if the king issues a proclamation commanding the Irish to accept the currency. Swift assures his readers no such outrage would occur since Ireland's revenues remain far too vital to England's national interests.

Assuming that Wood and his friends have nothing but contempt for the Irish (otherwise they would not have presumed to try this scam), Swift warns his readers about the persistence of such thieves. Finally, the greatest danger may exist with those Irish who use these coins: "let them be watched at markets and fairs[;] . . . let the first honest discoverer give the word about . . . and caution the poor innocent people not to receive them." To prevent such a desperate event, Swift proposes an advertisement making clear Wood's crime, signed by 300 principal men in the kingdom. Such a plan might give courage to them all.

### COMMENTARY

The key idea in this second letter concerns Swift's continuing effort at reminding his readers about Wood's scheme and the dangers it poses to the Irish economy. Working against apathy, ignorance, and misinformation, Swift speaks clearly and without ornamentation, hoping to have convinced those who doubt or remain uncertain about the problem. The time has come for boldness and courage in the face of such obvious lying and fraud.

Those so-called facts that Wood and his supporters have published remain unverified responses to legitimate questions. Using some rather amazing calculations, Swift has the Drapier "prove" the use of these debased coins will ruin each shopkeeper's business. Again, the true enemies are King GEORGE and Robert WALPOLE, who either ignored their responsibilities to protect their subjects against greed or failed to treat the people as free members of a self-governing country.

In *Jonathan Swift and Ireland,* Oliver Ferguson marks the important difference between the first of the *Drapier's Letters* and the letter to Harding, finding that the argument shifts from explaining the rights of the Irish to proposing a "collective boycott" (104). Swift expresses outrage at Wood's apparent power, which seems to have placed him above the king's wishes. If this proposal is not "perfect High Treason," then nothing can fit that definition. Anger moves the tone of this letter and becomes the natural outgrowth of the fear that Swift sought to produce in the earlier letter by leading the Irish to realize the dangers posed in Wood's scheme.

Though neither the Drapier nor Wood emerges as a full character in these letters, they clearly function as complementary devices. The Drapier balances the relative unimportance of Wood with the significance of the threat and clear damage proposed to the nation: If Wood seems insignificant, then his advisers must accept responsibility for the proposal. Neatly shifting the blame for the patent away from Wood to Walpole and George I takes courage on Swift's part, but the Drapier mask functions well in this dangerous game. Confidently asserting that the king would never exceed the limits of the law by issuing a proclamation to force the coinage on the Irish, Swift argues the Irish have no obligation to accept such a proclamation if one comes out by mistake. Returning to his final point, the Drapier believes anyone who accepts these halfpence is guilty of treason. With a general boycott, the Irish can protect fellow countrymen who might make such a mistake against themselves.

## Letter 3: "Some Observations upon a Paper, Called the Report of the Committee of the Most Honourable the Privy Council in England"

### SYNOPSIS

Addressing himself to the *"Nobility and Gentry"* of Ireland, Swift (as M. B. Drapier) indicates that he is writing in response to a report recently issued by the Privy Council of England regarding "Mr. Wood's *Half-pence and Farthings.*" He asserts that Wood had the report published without obtaining the council's permission and his sole intention was to vindicate himself while charging those who oppose his patent with "casting Rash and Groundless Aspersions upon him." As the Drapier, Swift identifies himself as a lowly and illiterate shopkeeper who is simply seeking to do what is right, adding that Wood—a simple *"Hard-ware-man"*—has managed to keep the entire kingdom at his mercy for almost two years. As evidence of Wood's dishonesty, the Drapier points to an experiment commissioned by Sir Isaac NEWTON that compared the weights of coins submitted by four men (including Wood) seeking a patent for Irish halfpence. Wood's coin was found to be lighter than all the others by "three Half-pence in a Pound."

With insulting disregard for the well-being of the Irish people, the English Crown has ignored the Irish Parliament's unified objection to Wood's patent as a "ruinous destructive *Project* of an *obscure, single, Undertaker.*" One major problem with the patent is that it lacks the limitations and conditions of those issued in the past. Other coiners, for example, had to agree to receive (on demand) their halfpence back "and pay Gold or Silver in Exchange for them," but Wood is subject to no such restriction. The Drapier argues that this would have never been allowed to happen in England, and asks whether or not the Irish were born as free as the English: "Am I a *Free-man* in *England,* and do I become a *Slave* . . . by crossing the Channel?"

The Drapier then summarizes and argues against each of the report's principal claims in favor of Wood's patent. In response to the report's assurance that Wood's copper coinage was found to exceed minimum requirements for *"Fineness, Weight, and*

*Value,"* the Drapier argues that the test was biased since Wood was allowed to pick out unusually good coins from several different "parcels." The weight of Wood's coins, he adds, is notoriously inconsistent. The poor quality of Wood's product is even more egregious when one considers the incredibly unreasonable profit he stands to make from the patent.

The Privy Council's report also claims that Wood's halfpence *"far exceed the like Coinage for* Ireland" produced in the past. The Drapier insists that this is patently false, but only because Wood misled the council by providing them with "the worst Patterns he could find." In response to the report's claim that the king of England has simply exercised his rightful royal prerogative in coining copper for Ireland and England, the Drapier concludes that it is a *"little extraordinary"* that the king has done so without consulting any Irish officials. There were no investigations into whether or not "the Grant were reasonable, and whether the People desired it or no" and the Irish Parliament's objections were summarily ignored. Moreover, he argues, the king's prerogative is supposed to be governed by his concern for the *"Good* and *Welfare* of his *People."* In this case, however, those concerns have been neglected and "Mr. Wood" has been awarded the "Power of Ruining a whole Nation, for his private Advantage." The kingdom of Ireland has undeservedly been "sacrificed to one *Single, Rapacious, Obscure, Ignominious* PROJECTOR."

As for the report's claims that Wood's patent will benefit Ireland, the Drapier asks whether or not £800 a year (the annual profit the Crown gains from the patent) is worth ruining the entire kingdom. It would be better, he asserts, for the Irish people simply to pay "Eight thousand Pounds a Year into His Majesty's Coffers, in the midst of all [their] taxes" than to submit themselves to Wood's shameless profiteering. Moreover, the £14,000 Wood has to pay for the patent is nothing more than a *"Small Circumstantial Charge."* The Drapier goes on to explain how the secrecy with which the patent was handled is particularly problematic. It was kept secret from the Irish people, who are the *"Only Sufferers"* because of it and yet the group best qualified "to advise in such an Affair." The people of Ireland

should have received "timely Notice," and the patent should not have been negotiated solely between Wood and the Crown since they are "to be the only Gainers by it."

Other arguments against Wood's patent follow: The Drapier questions its legality (especially in the power it gives Wood *"to break into Houses"* in search of counterfeit coins), argues that the absence of copper coins in Ireland would not have been a real problem for the Irish, and reaffirms his claim that it was wrong for the English Crown to make such a ruinous imposition on the Irish without even consulting them. He also questions the report's use of precedents to defend Wood's patent, arguing that none of the precedents cited have anything to do with "coining Money for *Ireland."* The Drapier dismisses the use of precedents altogether, claiming that they allow lawyers to "justify the Legality" of something "without ever considering the Motives and Circumstances" surrounding it.

After reviewing his objections to the patent and asserting that Wood himself (rather than the committee that wrote the report) deserves most of the blame, the Drapier encourages his audience to boycott Wood's coins: *"Wood* hath Liberty to *Offer* his Coin, and we have *Law, Reason, Liberty,* and *Necessity* to *Refuse* it." Throughout Ireland, he claims, no one should part with any goods or provide any services until they have been paid in silver or gold. Refusing to accept "this FATAL *Coin"* is the only way to save the kingdom from destruction. After apologizing for the poor quality of his "long undigested Paper," the Drapier compares himself to David and Wood to Goliath and calls on the Irish nobility to draw up a declaration resolving "never to receive or utter any of *Wood's* Half-pence or Farthings; and forbidding [their] Tenants to receive them."

## COMMENTARY

Called a systematic demolition of the Privy Council report, letter 3 addresses itself to the aristocracy of landholders and senior church leaders, answering the various points of the report with "high art propelled by moral energy." This letter is twice as long as the second piece, but Swift must recapitulate the essential points in the debate, as well as emphasizing Wood's fraudulent behavior. If he can convince the Irish reader that this behavior would never be tolerated in England, then the argument takes on an additional sharpness.

Swift presumes for the sake of his essay that Ireland remains an independent country, and that England's government cannot treat the Irish as colonists (no matter that the Declaratory Act of 1719 clearly stated that the British Parliament would make laws binding the Irish to Great Britain). Though he would not presume to declare a revolution, his reason and respect for tradition suggest that what England has demanded and urged upon the Irish was wrong. Royal prerogatives could become oppressive without boundaries and limits to protect the people. Swift assured his readers that the king would not force the Irish to accept this new currency: the House of Stuart had made this mistake, but the House of Hanover would not—especially if the king could ignore the greedy who would advise him differently.

For Irvin Ehrenpreis, the major theme of liberty in this letter takes the reader into another area of interest, away from the currency crisis to the issue of complete independence (*Swift* III.238). Swift clearly dismisses Irish political leaders who would fear an independence movement, and addresses the commoners instead. Focusing on prejudices he discovers in the English Privy Council, the lies and manipulations of Wood and his supporters, and the misleading information in the report, the Drapier dissects the pretensions and arrogance of a government that believes in oppression.

The rhetorical structure depends on dual conflict: Wood versus the Drapier, with both serving as foils for the principal actors, England versus Ireland. Swift's dominant concern throughout this letter is the burdens a powerful nation places on a weaker one. When the demands made on a free people exceed what humanity can bear and insult their faith and morality, then this burden becomes brutality.

## Letter 4: "A Letter to the Whole People of Ireland"

### SYNOPSIS

Addressing himself to his "dear Countrymen," the Drapier in this letter seeks to comfort and encourage the Irish in the face of rumors promising imminent punishment from England based on Ireland's refusal to accept Wood's coinage. He begins by explaining that the Irish, like other populations "long used to Hardships," have lost "by Degrees the very Notions of *Liberty*" and have come to "look upon themselves as Creatures" at the mercy of others. Wood and his "Impostors" have begun circulating pamphlets that equate the Irish refusal of his coins with disputing the king's royal prerogative. In response, the Drapier urges his audience to treat these rumors as nothing more than "the last Howls of a Dog dissected alive." The king's prerogative, he argues, is limited by law and cannot be used to force subjects to accept any currency "except it be Sterling, Gold or Silver."

The Drapier next reviews the events leading up to the current situation: (1) Wood was granted a patent to coin copper halfpence for Ireland, (2) the Irish Parliament requested that the king recall the patent, and (3) this request was refused, and an investigative committee was appointed from the English Privy Council, which reported that Wood had "performed the Conditions of his Patent." This leaves Wood to do the best he can, with "the King and his Ministry" entirely out of the picture, and (according to the Drapier) "the Matter is left to be disputed between" Wood and the people of Ireland.

There is also widespread fear in Ireland that England is about to send a lord lieutenant over to force the Irish to accept Wood's patent. Even if this occurs, the Drapier argues, Ireland's Parliament has already made up its mind regarding Wood's coinage and will not be persuaded to reverse its position. The opposition to Wood is universal, he claims, shared even among those officials who have been sent over from England to hold office in Ireland: "*Money,* the great *Divider* of the World, hath, by a strange Revolution, been the great *Uniter* of a most *divided* People." Wood's claim that the Irish are engaged in a papist-led attempt to "shake off" their dependence on the English Crown does nothing to detract from the virtue of their cause. And while the English tend to view Ireland as dependent upon them, the truth is that both realms are equally dependent upon the same monarch. The charge against Wood's imposition has nothing to do with

English ministers, and the Drapier concludes this section of his argument telling his audience, "by the Laws of GOD, of NATURE, and of NATIONS, and of your own Country, you ARE and OUGHT to be as FREE a People as your Brethren in *England.*"

The Drapier further asserts that English contempt for the Irish is based in part on the fact that they have heard only one side of the story regarding Wood's halfpence. The only documents being printed in England present the Irish in a negative light, asserting that only a vocal minority opposes the patent for self-serving reasons, and that the majority supported it until they were inflamed by these rabble-rousers. All of this shows, of course, that Wood and his hireling authors lie at every turn. However, while Wood strives to convince the English that the Irish should accept his patent, the Drapier promises to continue seeking to persuade all of Ireland that they should reject it. He concludes by chiding Wood for having dishonored Sir Robert WALPOLE by claiming that Walpole would "*cram*" Wood's brass down the throats of the Irish. Walpole, the Drapier asserts, is an honorable minister who is "against this Project of Mr. *Wood;* and is an entire Friend to *Ireland.*"

## COMMENTARY

Readers and critics alike consider this pamphlet the most provocative of the series, and it is the one that often represents *The Drapier's Letters* in modern anthologies and other collections of 18th-century prose. Swift appeals to the whole population of Ireland, which really means landowners, Anglicans, and the ethnically English. He perfectly timed the pamphlet's release to coincide with the arrival of the new lord lieutenant, John CARTERET, whom he knew from his London period and respected for his intelligence. The Walpole ministry, reacting to the furor caused by the two earlier letters, decided to send Carteret to this assignment nearly a year ahead of schedule. The effect on the Irish establishment caused an immediate weakening of their resolve, and Swift prepared a counterattack specifically against the lies emerging from London.

Instead of preaching resistance and discussing further opposition to Wood, the ministry, and "some weak People" (the Irish), Swift's major theme in this

segment is Irish liberty. Establishing his central point in the first paragraph, he encourages readers in considering that their liberty is a matter of their inalienable rights. Strengthened by this knowledge, his readers should not concern themselves with rumor and depend instead on their political status, not as colonists, but as citizens of a loyal, independent nation. Extending this point, critics suggest Swift was also referring to the members of a community who have, in Locke's political philosophy, rights and liberties as a society, distinct from government.

Cleverly suggesting that Carteret has no real power over the Irish, Swift can ambiguously show "utmost respect to the person and dignity of his Excellency" while simultaneously aligning him with that "sharper" Wood. Why fear a viceroy who cannot order the Irish into accepting brass money? How can Carteret bribe anyone when the English already hold all the lucrative Irish government posts? Balancing between outright sedition and impudence, Swift manages to avoid blatantly traitorous language, although the lord lieutenant and his Privy Council decided four days after its publication on the following response: Certain passages were treasonable, the printer John HARDING should be arrested, and a proclamation was issued offering a reward of £300 to whomever could identify the person posing as the Drapier.

When Swift decides to confront George I, he has taken a more dramatic and dangerous step: "he hath the power to give a patent to any man . . . [but] no body alive is obliged to take them." One of the best sections of the pamphlet examines the royal prerogative as an issue of law, not personality or force. Though English imperialism depended on the application of a powerful force (either its army or navy), Swift appeals to moral authority, arguing that the Irish were clearly victims of brutal oppression. Relying on support from constitutional history, he argues against the notion of Ireland as a "depending kingdom," where its citizens seem more like slaves than free people. This view was unacceptable to Walpole and the WHIG ministry, who expected the Irish to set aside such pretensions of freedom.

The entire piece addresses the nature of injustice, and Swift effectively argues that something is amiss when a forger is on a level plane with a minister, a lord lieutenant praised above his king, and "a nation sacrificed to the greed of a concubine." No other action is left to a people in this condition except resistance: "we have been rewarded with a worse climate, the privilege of being governed by laws to which we do not consent; a ruined trade, a House of Peers without jurisdiction . . . and the dread of Wood's half-pence." The moral remains one of facing these troubles boldly and denying the constant role of victim.

## Letter 4 (A): "Seasonable Advice to the Grand-Jury"

## (B): "An Extract of a Book"

## (C): "The Presentment of the Grand Jury of the County of the City of Dublin"

### SYNOPSIS

"Seasonable Advice to the Grand Jury" is addressed to the group of men charged with deciding the fate of printer John Harding for publishing *The Drapier's Letters* (see Commentary below). He begins by encouraging the jurors to recall that the other three "discourses" he wrote regarding Wood's patent were well received, and that if these pamphlets had not been written it is likely that Wood's coinage would have "over-run the Nation some months ago." He goes on to remind them that no one has ever doubted "the Innocence and Goodness" of the Drapier's motives: he is a loyal subject, "devoted to the *House* of *Hanover*" and vehemently opposed to the Pretender (James Francis Edward STUART). His only goal is (and always has been) "THE GOOD OF HIS COUNTRY," and none of his statements are as malicious as his detractors claim, nor do they insult the king or question royal authority.

The Drapier urges the grand jury to consider carefully what effect their ruling on printer John Harding will have on the people of Ireland. Since the Irish have found no fault with the Drapier's writings, a ruling against his printer will be viewed as a demoralizing measure "in favour of Wood's *Coin*," and as evidence that further resistance to it would be worthless. Members of the jury should also, he adds, consider their status as "Merchants, and principal Shop-keepers" who can lose nothing in the way of government "Employments" by "reject-

ing the Bill" against the printer. The Drapier asserts that it would be wrong to punish a "poor," "innocent" and "ignorant Printer" who simply did what he thought was right. He concludes with "a Fable, ascribed to *Demosthenes*" in which a group of wolves sought to make peace with some sheep on the single condition that the "*Shepherds* and *Mastiffs*" (the only "Cause of Strife") be taken away. Once this was done, the wolves immediately "made Havock of the *Sheep*."

Swift initiated the publication and distribution of "An Extract of a Book Entitled, An Exact Collection of the Debates of the House of Commons, Held at Westminster, Oct. 21, 1680," following Chief Justice William WHITSHED's angry dismissal of the grand jury on November 21, 1724. Whitshed was frustrated with the jurors because they refused to denounce "Seasonable Advice to the Grand Jury" as libelous. The "Extract" presents precedents against Whitshed's action, listing resolutions adopted by the House of Commons following "the Dismissing [in 1680] of a Grand-Jury in *Middlesex*." The resolutions declare, among other things, that "the Discharging of a Grand-Jury, by any Judge, before the End of the Term . . . [or] while Matters are under Consideration . . . is arbitrary, illegal, destructive to publick Justice, and a manifest Violation of his Oath[.]" See also SCROGGS, Sir William.

In "The Presentment of the Grand Jury of the County of the City of Dublin," Swift provides a categorical rejection of "*Wood*'s Half-pence" which was ultimately adopted and issued by the jury Whitshed had assembled to convict Harding. Dated November 28, 1724, the "Presentment" begins by explaining that Wood's coins have been brought into Dublin with the intention of circulating them "clandestinely," and that the king has left it up to the citizens to accept or reject the coins. With these facts in mind, the jury presents "all such Persons" who have sought (or will attempt) to "impose" Wood's halfpence on the Irish as "Enemies" to the government, "and to the Safety, Peace, and Welfare of all his Majesty's Subjects of this Kingdom." The proclamation stipulates, however, that King George himself is not to blame: The attempt to force Wood's coinage upon the Irish was undertaken "contrary to all his Majesty's most gracious Intentions," and while the jury is grateful to those *"Patriots"* who spoke out against Wood and "his base coin," they utterly detest any negative "Reflections" all this may have cast upon "his Majesty, and his Government" (which they are ready to defend with their lives).

## COMMENTARY

In November 1724 Lord CARTERET ordered the arrest and imprisonment of Swift's printer John Harding and his wife, Sarah, for their involvement in distributing the *Drapier's Letters*. Harding's willingness to print controversial materials had brought him to the attention of the dean in 1719, when Harding had been involved in publishing a proclamation in support of Jacobite efforts on behalf of the Pretender's claim to the English throne. As an experienced political operative/journalist, Harding took chances for the money and publicity these publications brought him, but now he would wait in jail while the grand jury decided the state's legal position. On his part, Harding told anyone who would listen that he could not identify the Drapier and nothing in the letters seemed dangerous or "exceptionable."

With this anonymous broadside, Swift (having sensed the restive mood of the Dublin public) seized the arrest of his friend as an opportunity for reminding the jury members and everyone else that Harding was innocent—actually ignorant—of these pamphlets' true message. Also he assured Dubliners of the Drapier's accuracy in interpreting the deviousness of the British government in this matter. While Carteret had managed to unite the Privy Council in voting for a proclamation, Swift argued that any true bill against Harding would be viewed as supporting the government in its manipulation, but a grand jury's vote against finding sufficient cause for a charge of sedition would do a great service for all of Ireland.

Through a combination of unexpected events, the case did not go to the jury for weeks and when it did, the jury refused to find "a presentment" for trial. The justices, led by the arbitrary Whitshed, who knew their duty to the Crown, were outraged, dismissing the first jury and impaneling a second. This tactic also failed when the second jury issued "The Presentment of the Grand Jury," written by Swift, condemning the government for the Wood affair and refusing any bill of charges against Harding.

During these weeks of debate, Swift also managed a second publication, "An Extract of a Book" on the English Parliamentary debates of 1680, which stated the illegality of discharging a grand jury before the end of its term. Using this precedent, he had accomplished much in a short time: alerting and encouraging the town to the dangers of Wood's coinage, convincing Dubliners of the value of a boycott, protecting his printer from prosecution as a matter of national interest, and weakening the new viceroy, Carteret, without losing his respect.

## Letter 5: "A Letter to the Right Honourable the Lord Viscount Molesworth"

### SYNOPSIS

In his "Directions to the Printer" preceding this letter, the Drapier assures John HARDING that he never intended any evil (or good) in asking him to publish his previous letters. He laments the reality that printers so frequently risk their lives and liberty for such a small profit. After alluding to Harding's arrest and imprisonment, the Drapier asserts that he never sent Harding anything that he thought would be viewed as seditious. He asks Harding to send the enclosed letter to Lord Viscount MOLESWORTH, but to kindly print it first in order to make it more legible *"for the Convenience of his Lordship's Reading."* The Drapier also warns Harding that should he be inclined to publish the letter, he should by all means have a lawyer peruse it carefully to guard against another arrest.

As the "Directions" suggest, the Drapier addresses this letter to Robert Molesworth, who had endeared himself to the dean by dedicating his controversial *Considerations for Promoting Agriculture* (1723) to the Irish House of Commons in appreciation for their stand against Wood's patent. After musing on the ironies of being held liable under human laws without having done anything to break divine ones, he outlines the reward offered to anyone who can identify him, and assesses his writing up to this point as "a weak Attempt to serve a Nation in Danger of Destruction, by a most wicked and malicious

Projector." Describing his writings as various pieces of clothing, he assures Molesworth that selling "all the several *Stuffs* [he has] contrived" has not made him any richer—not even "by the Value of one of Mr. *Wood's* Half-pence."

He claims that the current pamphlet (a "*Piece of Stuff* to be woven on purpose" for Molesworth) is particularly coarse, patched together from the "*Shreds and Remnants of the Wool employed in the Former.*" Alluding to his "Seasonable Advice to the Grand Jury" (see letter 4, above), the Drapier explains that the government's displeasure with him is based mainly on his assertion that King George's comments on Wood's halfpence have been distorted by his ministers, and his argument that the kingdom of Ireland is undoubtedly *not* dependent upon England. Regarding the first issue, he explains that he was simply pointing out (and seeking to explain) how different Wood's patent was from all others that had been issued before. As for his argument that Ireland cannot be viewed as a dependent kingdom, he says he will have to leave it up to "the World" to decide whether or not he was "mistaken" or "WENT TOO FAR in examining" the question. The Drapier apologizes for what he now recognizes as his excessive zeal in affirming his (and all of Ireland's) allegiance to the king. In the heat of making this declaration, he wrote that should the Pretender ever gain England's throne, he would lose "*the last Drop of* [his] *Blood*" before "*submit*[ting] *to him as King of* Ireland."

The Drapier goes on to explain that the "severe Treatment" he has received is mainly the result of his mistaken assumption that freedom is based on "*People being governed by Laws made with their own Consent; and Slavery in the Contrary.*" Nonetheless, he claims, the writings he produced would surely have done nothing more than expose him as a fool to an English audience, and pale in comparison to some of Molesworth's own writings. These were far worse than anything the Drapier ever penned, and were written with "infinitely more Wit and Learning, and stronger Arguments." All he wants, ultimately, is for Ireland to be rid of Wood's patent: "Let me have but Good City Security against this pestilent Coinage," he promises, "and I shall . . . *Renounce* every Syllable in my Four Letters, [and]

deliver them chearfully . . . [to] the common Hangman, to be burnt with no better Company" than Wood's "*Effigies.*"

Wood, the Drapier claims, deserves most of the blame anyway, since he is the one who "gave the first Provocation" and "struck the first Blow": "therefore I should humbly propose to have him first *Hanged,* and his *Dross* thrown into the Sea." The Drapier chides himself for having ignored the advice of "a certain *Dean,*" who warned him against placing too much faith in the people's goodwill and promised the Drapier that however benevolent his intentions, they would not save him from "*those who watched every Motion of* [his] *Pen.*" Even so, while the printer (Harding) has been prosecuted, the Drapier finds his own state far from "deplorable"—thanks to the unwavering impartiality of two grand juries. And while two recent "printed Papers" have been attributed to the Drapier, he argues that there is no evidence to justify attributing "Seasonable Advice" nor "An Extract of a Book" to him.

In an aside on the "Extract," he comments that the case of the Middlesex grand jury having been dissolved illegally does not really apply to Lord Lieutenant Carteret's dismissal of the grand jury assembled against the Drapier: Sir William SCROGGS, he notes, had dissolved the Middlesex jury in order to prevent them from "presenting," but Carteret dismissed the Dublin grand jury because they would *not* present against the Drapier. In any case, he claims, juries need a "short plain authentick Tract" to consult for directions before they deliberate. The Drapier laments what he sees as the sad case of any private citizen who would dare to "inform the People; even in an Affair," such as Wood's patent, "where the publick Interest and Safety are so highly concerned." These well-meaning individuals are paralyzed by a fear of being "entrapped" by the law simply for telling the truth. He adds that his printer, Harding, faces this very dilemma: "either to let my learned Works hang for ever a drying upon his Lines; or venture to publish them at the Hazard of being laid by the Heels."

As he concludes the letter, the Drapier explains that if the English ministers only understood the effects Wood's coin would have on Ireland, they would do all in their power to save this "*most loyal*

*Kingdom from Destruction."* In the meantime, however, he hopes the Irish will continue to refuse the coinage. Admitting that he is beginning to "grow Weary" of his "Office as a Writer," the Drapier claims that he has buried his copies of Molesworth's writings on liberty, and promises that should he (the Drapier) ever write anything else on the subject it will be completely banal and "without a Sting."

## COMMENTARY

Swift probably knew that his efforts at destroying Wood had been successful—Carteret had privately recommended before the release of this pamphlet in December that the Crown should rescind the patent. The pleasure of addressing the libertarian Whig, Viscount Molesworth, provided Swift with the perfect vehicle for celebrating his achievement over the authorities. No new arguments are introduced attacking Wood; in fact, Swift enjoys his victory over his enemies. His ploy with the Drapier persona depends on portraying him as weary and tired of the battle, caught in a web laid by the government and unable to extricate himself now. The Drapier turns for help to Molesworth, hoping to gain his sympathy since the shopkeeper's troubles were brought about through his patriotic efforts. Swift seems unconcerned about allusions which clearly identify him as the writer, but the pretense of the Drapier's trying to clear himself of any charges has more to do with the structure of this pamphlet.

Swift reviews the central charges against the Drapier—criticism of the king, the independence of Ireland, and a refusal to accept a pretender to the throne. In doing so, he can now illustrate at some length the ludicrousness of these charges, which goes to prove further the maliciousness and weakness of the government's lawyers. Oliver Ferguson suggests that Swift may have intended this letter to be the last, while Irvin Ehrenpreis echoes Herbert Davis's claim that it is the "best written of all" the *Drapier's Letters* (Ferguson 131; Ehrenpreis, *Swift* III.293).

The ironic pleading of this last letter to be published during the crisis reveals a typically Swiftian version of freedom, one where the free man seems more a prisoner released from his cell to the exercise yard. A freedom bound by walls of legal repression and limited possibility becomes the operative metaphor. Though using the fiction of the Drapier, Swift assures his reader of the empirical reality of the suffering Irish and the perverse nature of their confinement.

## Letter 6: "A Letter to the Lord Chancellor Middleton"

### SYNOPSIS

Unlike the other letters, this one is signed not by "M. B." (the Drapier) but by Swift, himself. Addressed to Alan Brodrick, Viscount MIDDLETON, it begins with an "Advertisement" from the printer, explaining that he obtained this letter from one of the author's friends and decided to print it based on the favorable public reaction to the Drapier's other writings.

At the beginning of the letter itself, Swift asks Middleton to regard him as a latecomer to the debate over Wood's patent. Recalling Middleton's own opposition to the patent, Swift outlines the widespread public opposition to it and explains that it is "every Man's duty, not only to refuse this Coin," but to "persuade others to do the like." Since the Drapier will (in all likelihood) never be heard from again, Swift's goal is to step in and take his place by rehearsing old arguments against Wood and adding some new ones along the way.

Swift lists two points on which he and Middleton must certainly be in agreement: that the Irish "are a most loyal People," and that the Irish "are a free People" living as subjects under "a limited Monarch." Since they are loyal, the Irish should rightly expect and receive all the benefits and protections a free people deserve "from so gracious a King"—and the primary, most immediate expectation is that Wood's coins "may never have Entrance into this Kingdom."

After lamenting the charges leveled against the Drapier and his writings (especially those involving his comments about King George), Swift asserts that the Drapier never actually encouraged the Irish to talk about Wood's patent and the king in the same conversation: "in many Discourses," he argues, "I do not remember His Majesty's Name to be so much as mentioned." The only ministers who were referred to in these debates were the duke of GRAFTON and Sir Robert WALPOLE. Walpole, Swift urges, brought calumnies upon himself by making negative comments about "the people of *Ireland.*" Moreover, Wood himself promoted a negative opinion of Walpole among the Irish by "boasting of his Favour with Mr. *Walpole.*" Ultimately, the Drapier's writings have not taught the Irish any "bad Lessons" in terms of the king and his ministers.

Another ill effect attributed to the Drapier's letters is that they have put the English and Irish at odds with one another. Swift argues that this accusation is not justified because these groups were alienated long before the Drapier began writing: For their part, the English know as much about Ireland as they do about Mexico—thinking only that it would be better for England if the whole of Ireland "were sunk into the Sea." They are also misinformed about Irish affairs, even to the point of thinking that Ireland embraced Wood's patent. As for the Irish, they are either papists (who have no more power than women and children) or Protestants, who love their kingdom and sometimes complain if they think it is being abused. In any case, Swift asks, how can the "personal Affections" of the English and Irish be of much consequence "while the Sea divides them; and while they continue in their Loyalty to the same Prince?" Swift proceeds to argue that since the Irish are a free people, they cannot be forced to accept any coin as payment other than silver or gold. And since that is the case, there can be no argument against "any Man"—including the Drapier—who would warn his countrymen "against this coin of *William Wood,*" who seeks to rob the Irish of the property "the Laws have secured."

Having argued that the Drapier has done no wrong in his writings, Swift begs leave to review the arguments against Wood's patent. After rehearsing these objections, he concludes that he regards it as his duty to urge his "Fellow-Subjects . . . never to admit this pernicious coin," even in small amounts. Based on the lies Wood and his associates told about the Irish being compelled by a royal proclamation to accept the halfpence, it was vital for the Drapier to clear up the confusion and explain that

"the King's Prerogative was not at all concerned in the Matter." As for the fourth letter—the one that evoked a proclamation against the Drapier—Swift wishes that everything objectionable could simply be removed from the letter. The Drapier's controversial comment in that letter, that he would shed his own blood in defending the throne from the Pretender, should be forgiven based on "the loyal Intention of the Writer." Anyone who finds anything else in the letter to be seditious should come forth and identify the Drapier, since this would yield the satisfaction of hearing judges and lawyers offer their arguments "upon this Case."

Swift adds that to avoid similar controversies in the future, it would be helpful if "some able Lawyers" would clearly define how far an individual citizen may go in expressing his opinions on public affairs. Questions he would like answered include, Is it illegal for "any Writer" even to mention the king's prerogative? How far does that prerogative go in forcing a particular form of currency on the subjects? What is the real significance of Ireland's status as a "depending Kingdom," and what does that dependence consist of? And finally, how do Ireland's rights pertaining to liberty and property differ from England's? The lack of sufficient clarity on these issues has caused all sorts of trouble, including the prosecution and conviction of one printer (by which Swift certainly means John Harding) who published a pamphlet by an author whose intentions "were as good and innocent, as those of a Martyr at his last Prayers."

Why should a private man like the Drapier speak out on a public issue such as Wood's patent? Swift's answer is that since the addresses against Wood from both houses of the Irish Parliament failed, it was left up to someone else to handle the threat. Had no one told the Irish how they could legally refuse Wood's coins and how dishonest and fraudulent Wood himself was, it is not likely that anyone "would ever have had the Courage or Sagacity to refuse it." After reminding Middleton that the Irish still have every right to reject the coins, Swift promises to carry on the important work that the Drapier began. After citing statistics to explain the fiduciary consequences of accepting Wood's inferior coinage, Swift thanks Middleton for opposing the patent. Should Wood's halfpence be accepted, it would ultimately remove all gold and silver from Ireland and force England to transmit money there to pay "the salaries at least of the principal Civil Officers."

As a final observation, Swift notes that within recent months myriad papers have been written in Ireland on "the Love of our Country." Authors have expressed themselves on this subject with no thought of "Profit, Favour, and Reputation"—all the motives that commonly drive writers to engage in their craft. This burst of nationalism leads Swift to conclude that he, the Drapier, and his "numerous Brethren" (the other writers) are "all true Patriots." He admits that compared to the Drapier's pamphlets, what he has written will seem "low and insipid," but he takes comfort in the possibility that it may help to preserve the unity the Irish have found in their opposition to Wood's "fatal project." A lawyer, moreover, has reviewed all that Swift has written and declared it to be utterly innocent and legal. From here on, Swift adds, no one will need to write any more on the subject if the "*Bell-man* of each *Parish*" will only cry out, "*Beware of* Wood's Half-Pence" every night after midnight.

## COMMENTARY

Swift began writing this letter in October 1724 soon after Carteret had urged the council to issue a proclamation rejecting the Drapier's comments and offering a reward to anyone who could identify the author of these letters. However, he chose not to publish it until 11 years later because Swift had certain knowledge that when he revealed himself as the true author, something he told Archbishop William KING was his intention, that Carteret would certainly have him arrested. He does sign this pamphlet, the only one of the *Letters* where he feels safe enough to do so, but ends up changing his decision.

The design of the pamphlet reflects the intellect and tone of a highly accomplished writer with sophisticated political sense—not a tradesman's voice. Addressing the letter to the powerful Middleton, the man who first signed the proclamation against the Drapier, Swift suggests the continued seriousness and willingness to confront the highest legal authorities in Ireland. In fact, he had reached a new stage of combativeness in this contest with the government, stating in the "Letter to Middleton" that he would willingly submit to arrest and trial, trusting that no Irish jury would convict him. When his printer Harding was arrested a couple of weeks later, however, Swift had made his point, as well as gained the full attention of the public once again. As stated earlier in these pamphlets, he offers his major thesis once again: "a true lover of his country may think it hard to be a quiet stander-by, and an indolent looker-on, while a public error prevails; by which a whole nation may be ruined."

Adding to the interest of this pamphlet was the fact that both Swift and Middleton held a common opposition to Wood's halfpence, which brought them closer, though the lord chancellor had no compunction about prosecuting the author and printer. They also agreed, with Swift a more vehement supporter, in the liberties involved in this protest, particularly the freedom of the press. Protection from constant harassment for writing and printing points of view in opposition to the government was a British citizen's right, but one that was under severe threat depending upon the issue and the ministry. Why, Swift would query in this letter, does a double standard exist between the English and Irish manner for discussing issues before Parliament? The nature of pamphlet wars serves the best interests of the nation where both sides air concerns that may influence the final vote, and the government would not threaten these authors. Theoretically this arrangement makes excellent sense, but in practice the British government often resorted to charging writers with whom they disagreed with sedition and libel. Liberal attitudes such as freedom of the press formed the core of debate between the Tories and the Whigs, and Swift would champion this point of view especially when trying to alleviate Ireland's domestic problems.

## Letter 7: "An Humble Address to Both Houses of Parliament"

### SYNOPSIS

The Drapier begins his address by claiming that the entire nation of Ireland wishes that Parliament would "strictly examine" the fraud perpetrated by

William Wood. Citizens who would object to such an inquiry constitute only a small, obscure minority. Some who favor Wood's patent do so only because they believe it will yield political gains, but they are like those who would set their houses ablaze simply to roast some eggs. The primary problem with Wood's patent is that it moves beyond the realm of everyday vices (which ruin only "*particular* Persons") and delivers the entire kingdom of Ireland over to "*certain* Destruction" solely for the profit of one dishonest individual.

Widespread opposition to Wood's patent is clear in recent judicial activities, particularly in the grand jury's refusal to condemn the Drapier's fourth letter as seditious (see above). However, Chief Justice Whitshed's angry dismissal of the grand jury because of that refusal is worrisome, since trial by jury is a vital aspect of the law. This incident has caused the Irish people to unite in wishing that Parliament would affirm the "Power and Privilege of *Juries*" and publicly censure those who violate those powers. This is the only way the people of Ireland can distinguish their enemies from their friends.

In all of his writings, the Drapier never sought to cast aspersions upon anyone but Wood himself. He has not targeted the king or any ministers, and his only intention has been to make Parliament aware of "the general Wishes of the Nation"—the most prevalent of which is that Parliament would subject Wood to a strict examination and do the same to other schemers. This would discourage profit-seekers from endangering the public good. It is best, at this point, to leave Ireland's currency in its present state and trust in the people's "general Aversion" to Wood's debased halfpence. It is remarkable that all the "unanimous Addresses" to the king against Wood's patent from both houses of the Irish Parliament (and from just about everyone else in Ireland, including the Drapier) have been brushed aside and the patent approved. This is especially puzzling when one remembers that not one of these arguments ever mentioned that the absence of halfpence in Ireland was a problem. At any rate, Ireland would have been ruined by this point if "God, in his Mercy, had not raised an universal Detestation of" Wood's coins and led the Irish to

resolve "never to receive them." Wood's project is, without a doubt, the most harmful scheme ever hatched in an attempt to "compleat the Slavery and Destruction of a poor innocent Country," and the entire kingdom is hopeful that Parliament will put a stop to it.

If the Drapier is guilty for having articulated Ireland's position on Wood's patent, all Parliament needs to do is order him to be silent. He would honor the request because he views the "unanimous *Voice*" of Parliament as the voice of the nation. As an alternative to Wood's patent, it would be best if the Irish were allowed to coin their own halfpence (in the same way that Scotland was). As history illustrates, the greatest danger of allowing Wood to debase the value of Irish currency is that no one will be able to say they own anything outright.

Besides the inherent dangers associated with Wood's patent, England owes the Irish the "indulgence" of refusing the measure because of all the gains Ireland provides. In terms of these benefits, Ireland is the perpetual loser and "*England* a Gainer." Ireland's provisions to the English include rents of land, the entire revenue from the post office, pensions "paid to Persons in *England*," pay for army officers who are "absent in *England*," numerous civil employments, students for the Inns of Court and universities, £80,000 per year for coal, £100,000 a year paid to England for corn, "the full profit" from Ireland's mines, and "many other articles," amounting to an annual profit of £700,000 for England. In reality, Ireland has become a source of pure profit for individuals who never set foot in the kingdom. Had these wealthy "Lords" been content to live among the Irish instead of spending all their time in England, Irish affairs would not be in such a sad state.

As a further benefit to England, Ireland also provides a "receptacle" for "Pretenders to Offices"—second-rate politicians who fail in England but come to Ireland to get rich. In spite of England's abuse of the Irish in pursuit of massive profits, Ireland does have "one great Advantage," which is its unity: "all the *Regular Seeds* of *Party* and *Faction*" have been "entirely rooted out." Issues that once caused great division in the kingdom are no longer of any consequence. This unity compensates somewhat for the power that has been stripped from the Irish. When this spirit of cooperation manifests itself in measures unanimously supported in the House of Commons (and at least partially affirmed in the House of Lords), the Drapier feels obligated to act in accordance with these measures. For example, if both Houses of Parliament declared it treason to accept brass coinage, the Drapier would view it as "a heinous Sin" to violate "such a Vote." Likewise, if both Houses made it illegal to wear garments made of imported wool, the Drapier would wholeheartedly comply and persuade others to do the same.

Unfortunately, some individuals who have proposed ways of advancing the public good have been accused of "FLYING IN THE KING'S FACE." The Drapier himself has been charged with doing so in his writings against Wood's patent, and his printer prosecuted because of the accusation (see HARDING, JOHN). This charge is patently false, however, because—the Drapier argues—the "vile Representation" of the king's face stamped on Wood's "adulterate Copper" is nowhere close to "his sacred Majesty's [actual] *Face*." The Drapier never intended to insult the king and was simply articulating the "*Wishes* of the Nation," which are that: (1) fears of Wood's patent be put to rest, (2) the Irish be allowed to coin their own halfpence, (3) Parliament make it illegal to wear imported wool, (4) some effort be made to "civilize the poorer Sort" of Ireland's "Natives," (5) more be done to encourage agriculture in Ireland, and (6) earlier laws "for planting Forest Trees" be revised and made more effective. The Irish need to work with particular diligence to improve their lands because they are "so strangely limited in every Branch of Trade" that might prove profitable for them. At this point in Ireland's history, one "*honest Farmer*" who could turn a fallow piece of land into a fertile and productive parcel would be more valuable than hordes of politicians.

## COMMENTARY

Unsure of whether Parliament would act on Carteret's request to withdraw Wood's patent and put an end to this unfortunate, if not dangerous, situation, Swift, who was visiting Thomas SHERIDAN at his country estate at Quilca, began writing

this essay in April 1725. With the Irish Parliament prorogued (closed on Carteret's order) until August, he intended to carry on the fight as soon as the two Houses gathered again. His thesis poses the question: What can Parliament do in reaffirming its value to the citizens, or alerting them to the ongoing importance of the present crisis and focusing their attention on Ireland's future, if its condition will permit a future?

In an unexpected turn of strategy, Swift exerts very little effort on the Drapier's character; instead, he addresses the leading Irish politicians rather than their constituencies, seeking a list of economic reforms. Critics find this seventh letter strongly reminiscent of the 1720 "PROPOSAL FOR THE UNIVERSAL USE OF IRISH MANUFACTURE," where he attacks absentee landlords for ruining the economy, hypocritical English bishops, and the Irish who purchase English goods to the detriment of their own countrymen's products. Now, in this last Drapier piece, he revives his "modest proposals" for self-reliance, improved land management, the boycott of irrelevant goods, and elimination or reduction of absentee landlords and officeholders.

After giving directions to his Dublin friends, Rev. John GRATTAN and Rev. John WORRALL, for editing the letter and arranging its printing, Swift learns in late August that the Irish Privy Council had officially announced the cancellation of Wood's patent. The Drapier's efforts had achieved an outstanding success, and the literary campaign celebrated the defiance against tyranny, as had its fictional hero in his initials M. B. for Marcus Brutus. This ancient figure represented in Swift's pantheon of heroes the height of moral virtue, and he brought the full weight of his classical learning against such corruption.

Since this letter has an evangelical spirit, it calls for reform in terms of actually achieving results from the proposals, assuming the government has already agreed to them. Put simply, Swift educates his readers to consider change and reform of existing community patterns as a natural part of existence. The impulse toward generating ideas and schemes is a healthy, productive behavior. No matter how miserably the English had treated the Irish, the people of the country still had within their intellectual, moral, and spiritual resources the power of securing an improved life for themselves.

The theme of moral energy always resonates strongly in Swift's work, and certainly in this final pamphlet he is referring to moral courage. The strength not of wielding weapons with skill in battle but the ability and spirit of ideas employed in benefiting the community can achieve lasting results, as well. When Swift agreed to George FAULKNER's request to publish the first edition of *The Drapier's Letters* in October 1725, the dean certainly assisted the younger man, especially by reintroducing words and phrases his Dublin friends had deleted earlier. The collaboration between the two men had lasting importance for Swift, since later Faulkner would be responsible for printing the first collected edition of Swift's *Works* in 1735 (this seventh letter was first printed in this edition).

### FURTHER READING

Baltes, Sabine, ed. *Jonathan Swift's Allies: The Wood's Halfpence Controversy in Ireland, 1722–25*. Frankfurt, Germany: Peter Lang, 2004.

Downie, J. A. *Jonathan Swift: Political Writer*. London: Routledge & Kegan Paul, 1984.

Ehrenpreis, Irvin. *Swift: The Man, His Works and the Age*. 3 vols. Cambridge, Mass.: Harvard University Press, 1962–83.

Fabricant, Carole. "Speaking for the Irish Nation: The Drapier, the Bishop, and the Problems of Colonial Representation," *ELH* 66 (1999): 337–372.

Kelly, James. "Jonathan Swift and the Irish Economy of the 1720s." *Eighteenth-Century Ireland/Iris an dá Chultúr* 6 (1991): 7–36.

Rawson, Claude. "The Injured Lady and the Drapier: A Reading of Swift's Irish Tracts," *Prose Studies* 3 (1980): 15–43.

Swift, Jonathan. *The Drapier's Letters to the People of Ireland against Receiving Wood's Halfpence*. Edited by Herbert Davis. Oxford: Clarendon Press, 1935.

# "Dr. Swift's Answer to Dr. Sheridan"

Poem by Swift; first published in 1765, written in 1719. Following "FROM DR. SWIFT TO DR. SHERIDAN" and "A Letter from Dr. Sheridan to Dr. Swift,"

this verse epistle was part of an exchange between the two men in December of that year.

# "Dr. Swift to Mr. Pope"

Poem by Swift; first published in 1732, written in 1726–27. The subtitle indicates that Swift penned the poem for his friend while Alexander POPE was writing the *Dunciad*. Joking that Swift and Pope cannot communicate because, while the dean is deaf, the other's "loudest voice is low and weak," the speaker suggests that Swift deserves all the credit for Pope's "wit," since "had our deaf divine / Been for your conversation fit, / You had not writ a line."

# "Dunkirk to be Let"

See "HUE AND CRY AFTER DISMAL."

# "Duty of Servants at Inns, The"

This short piece was not published until after Swift's death. Though it is undated in manuscript, George FAULKNER printed it first in 1746 in the *Works*, though one may associate it with two other trifles, "LAWS FOR THE DEAN'S SERVANTS" and "CERTIFICATE TO A DISCARDED SERVANT," dated in the 1730s. The connection to the longer "DIRECTIONS TO SERVANTS" is obvious, though his instructions in the latter suggest behavior that he despised and spoke of ironically.

### SYNOPSIS

In a series of commands addressed to servants directly, Swift outlines with great detail when, where, and what they should do for their masters. The list includes such things as being ready to ride before he is, making sure his horses are well fed and cared for, and not making him wait while the servant eats. He also stipulates that if the inn's employees "have not been civil," the servant should tell the master "before their Faces, when he is going to give them Money." The second section deals with duties "of the other Servant, where there are two." These responsibilities are similar but also include personally tasting all foods and wines before they are served to one's master. Swift also lists specifically the supplies that the groom should carry with him.

## COMMENTARY

"The Duty of Servants" contains specific instructions for the groom and footman, but what seem clearer are the expectations the master has for his own welfare. His dignity, respect for himself and his position, and the emphasis on the clear distinction between those who serve and those who are served make the impact for the reader. Swift calls for social decorum and an ordered society, as well as an appreciation for man's folly. Taken separately, the "Duty" has less of the black humor of its longer cousin, more light than the other's nightmare of domestic subversion and anarchy. Something of why Swift felt so strongly about providing exact instructions to his groom can be seen in his December 27, 1714, letter to Archdeacon WALLS: "I rode on, and found Tom did not come up, I stayed, he galloped up; I chid[ed] him, he answered foolishly, he was drunk as a dog, tottered on his horse, could not keep the way, sometimes into the sea, then back to me, swore he was not drunk, I bid him keep on, lasht him as well as I could, then he vowed he was drunk, fell a crying, came back every moment to me." The scene concludes when Bolingbroke, the horse, finding the behavior of his rider unacceptable (unreasonable) throws Tom—the Houyhnhnms of *GULLIVER'S TRAVELS* would reflect on such antics.

# "Dying Speech of Tom Ashe, The"

This fictional joke, which apparently was one of many Swift wrote for his friends, serves as a pleasant memorial of the time he spent within the domestic circle of the earl of PEMBROKE during the latter's short stay at Dublin Castle while lord-lieutenant of Ireland, 1707–08.

## SYNOPSIS

Dedicated to Thomas Herbert, earl of Pembroke, this piece "records" the oration Thomas ASHE delivered to friends who had gathered at his bedside on the night before he died. The narrator admits that it is "long, and a little incoherent" and adds at the end that although the speech contains some "false spellings here and there," such errors "must be pardoned in a dying man." The speech is filled with the kind of humorous puns Ashe loved, many of which depend (in part) upon the "false spellings" the narrator excuses. For example, Ashe claims that "I, that supported myself with good *wine*, must now be myself supported by a small *bier*." He later laments, "Little did I think you would so soon see poor *Tom stown* under a *tomb stone*," and ends the speech with, "Farewell: I have lived ad amicorum *fastidium*, and now behold how *fast I di um!*

## COMMENTARY

Swift's love of juxtaposing words and connecting two or more possible applications of a word or words found a ready audience among a few of his close friends and acquaintants. His use of verbal quips or puns was matched in the speech and entertainment of Captain Thomas Ashe, one of three brothers who had all become his friends (or in the case of St. George Ashe, his tutor at Trinity College, Dublin).

"The Dying Speech" manuscript was sent to Pembroke and, when printed half a century later, Faulkner added a long footnote explaining the origins of Ashe and suggesting how one pun of which he was the victim and which he often repeated offered insight to the man's whimsical character. This essay poses the "eternal punster" Ashe on his deathbed delivering a famously clever set of puns whose category changes depending on the person being addressed as each one crowds about the bed hoping for a final verbal nonsense jab. Ashe comments that "it is time for a man to look grave, when he has one foot there."

David Nokes and others have commented on Swift's manner of punning, especially his reducing polysyllabic or technical terms by a kind of physical enactment of their meaning: thus "di-arrhea, di-abetes, di-sentery" put us in mind of death as much as the medicines prescribed for these afflictions, like "di-acodium [or] di-apente" (Nokes, " 'Hack at Tom Poley's' "). Latin and Greek references become "Farewel: I have lived as amicorum fastid-ium, and now behold how fast I di um!" If Ashe addresses his brother Dillon, he uses puns dealing with medicated candy or sweetened elixir; when he turns to Dr. Ralph Howard, the puns focus on the names of diseases and medicines; Pembroke (also known as Montgomery) undergoes references to his position as "long live tenant to the Queen in Ire-land"; and Sir Andrew Fountain suffers 26 puns on water in 10 lines of prose.

These examples of verbal magic add further lights to our portrait of Swift: "performing the Scriblerian trick of revealing the interdependence of the bathos and the sublime." Aside from such aesthetic and rhetorical considerations, puns like these celebrate fellowship and good spirits.

## "Elegy on Demar"

See "ELEGY ON THE MUCH LAMENTED DEATH OF MR. DEMAR, THE FAMOUS RICH USURER."

## "Elegy on Dicky and Dolly, An"

Poem by Swift; first published in 1732 with "LADY ACHESON WEARY OF THE DEAN," written about 1728. It deals with the death of Dorothea Stop-ford ("Dolly") and the subsequent death of her husband, Lieutenant-General Richard Gorges ("Dicky"). The poem suggests that while Dicky died of grief, it may have been grief over the loss of his wife's wealth—rather than of his wife—that killed him.

## "Elegy on the Much Lamented Death of Mr. Demar, the Famous Rich Usurer, An"

Poem partly by Swift; first published in two Dublin broadsides in 1720, written the same year. Com-posed by Swift and some of his friends (including Esther JOHNSON), it mockingly eulogizes Joseph DAMER, emphasizing his well-known greed and miserly living.

## "Elegy on the Supposed Death of Mr. Partridge, the Almanac Maker, An"

Poem by Swift; first published as a broadside in 1708, written the same year. The term *elegy* in this case is used not in the classical sense (which has to do with the meter of the poem), but to describe verses that respectfully lament the death of an admired individ-ual. Not surprisingly, however, Swift's elegy makes John PARTRIDGE the target of satire rather than respect. Along with other works such as "PREDIC-TIONS FOR THE YEAR 1708" and "ACCOMPLISHMENT OF THE FIRST OF MR. BICKERSTAFF'S PREDICTIONS," this poem was part of Swift's ongoing lampoon of Partridge, who claimed to be a gifted astrologer. The elegy jokingly laments the completely fictional death of Partridge, claiming that it had come to pass just as Bickerstaff had predicted.

The speaker makes fun of Partridge throughout, jokingly explaining how easy it is to comprehend the supposedly natural connection between work-ing as a cobbler (as Partridge did) and an astrologer: "Thus Partridge, by his wit and parts, / At once did practise both these arts." Like a bat that "Steals from her private cell by night," Partridge "Creep[s] in the dark from his leathern cell [the cobbler's shop], / And in his fancy fl[ies] as far, / To peep upon a twinkling star" (47–56). The Epitaph scorn-fully ridicules those who were foolish enough to have taken any of the amateur astrologer's predictions seriously. In his 1758 biography of Swift, W. H. Dilworth wrote that this "Elegy"—along with all of Swift's other writings regarding Partridge—is filled with "genuine humour," and was "designed as a ridicule upon all that absurd tribe, who set up for astrologers, and, without the least ray of true learning, are mighty pretenders to science." He adds that readers cannot "sufficiently relish" the "Elegy" if they are "unacquainted with these whimsical facts" (Williams, *Critical Heritage* 159).

# "Elephant, The"

Poem possibly by Swift; first published 1728. The date of composition is uncertain. The subtitle reads, "Written Many Years Since, and Taken Out of [Sir Edward] Coke's Institutes." The speaker advises reading the *Institutes* before choosing a representative for Parliament. Coke, he says, compares a good Parliament member to an elephant: "free from gall," "stubborn," and of sound memory. In this poem, however, the comparison is revised to create an unfavorable picture of current members of Parliament.

# "Enquiry into the Behaviour of the Queen's Last Ministry, An"

During 1715, after hearing of Oxford's imprisonment in the Tower, Swift began "An Enquiry" as an elaborate defense of James ORMONDE, Henry BOLINGBROKE, and Robert HARLEY. Knowing the danger in which it would place him and the Church of Ireland, he refused to publish it during his lifetime but continued revising and correcting the work over the next 20 years.

## SYNOPSIS

Having explained that he retired from public life after the death of Queen ANNE, Swift asserts that (based on the little news he has heard since then) he has concluded that "all Amicable Commerce between

People of different Parties" has ended. Because of widespread misreporting, there are two points he feels compelled to make regarding the recently fallen TORY ministry. The first issue is the extent to which Harley, Bolingbroke and the duke of Ormonde deserve to be blamed "for their Neglect, Mismanagement, and mutuall Dissensions." The second is whether or not these ministers actually worked "to alter the Succession of the Crown, in favor of the Pretender," as their enemies have accused them of doing (see James Francis Edward STUART).

Before delving into his discussion of these issues, Swift engages in what he calls a "long digression" on the character of each minister couched in terms of a history of the affairs leading up to the fall of the Tory ministry. He first discusses the duke of Ormonde, who had been accused of high treason and stripped of his property and titles soon after the queen's death. Swift writes that the duke is a noble man characterized by "unspotted Loyalty," friendliness, "Generosity, and Sweetness of Nature." He is, however, prone to an "easyness of Temper" which sometimes causes him to follow the lead of others who possess inferior understandings. Swift claims to stop short of seeking to vindicate Ormonde against Parliament's ruling, but adds that if Ormonde did anything wrong it was only because he was following Queen Anne's orders.

Swift next writes of "the late Secretary" Bolingbroke, who—having descended from one of the greatest families in the kingdom—is characterized by "a sound Constitution, and a most gracefull, amiable" disposition. God had also blessed him with an extraordinary memory and other gifts. He is, Swift admits, "fond of mixing Pleasure and Business," but is adept at both. Many had accused him of "Affectation," but this "infirmity" in Bolingbroke is simply the inevitable result of one so young having taken on "half of the Business of the Nation."

The earl of Oxford, Swift asserts, is as virtuous as a man who loves power can be. He is the only person Swift knows who moved "from a private Life through severall Stages of Greatness" without any noticeable changes occurring in "his Temper or Behaviour." He especially enjoyed associating with men of great wit and learning (regardless of their party affiliation), and never entertained the possibility that some of them could be his enemies. As an absolute "Stranger to Fear," the earl always maintained his composure during "Emergencies." Among the many shortcomings of which others accused him, he was "heavily charged" with having a tendency to make many promises without following through on them. Swift admits that he cannot deny the charge, but adds that the earl's "Intentions were generally better than his disappointed Sollicitors would believe." He was, however, fairly inept at gaining friends and quite good at making enemies. Swift concludes the digression on these ministers by musing on how common it is for men of "exalted Abilities" to enter public life and find themselves troubled with "Inconveniences and Misfortunes" that others consistently avoid. He argues that this phenomenon must be the result of such men seeking to turn the "Art of Government" (which requires only honesty, hard work, and common sense) into a complex and difficult science.

Following this "long Digression," Swift describes what happened to him within about two weeks after the queen's death. Whigs and Tories alike sought him out at home, and while the Tories reproached him for "the Slowness and Inactivity" of his friends, the Whigs "directly asserted" that the entire Tory ministry consisted of nothing but traitors who—along with the queen herself—worked "to bring in the Pretender." He promises to examine the validity of each one of these charges, revealing some little-known information in the process. What follows is a lengthy history of recent events, described in a manner that casts most of the blame for the Tories' fall onto Queen Anne. Following the trial of Henry SACHEVERELL, for example, she replaced a number of her "Servants" because of personal animosities rather than a desire for general improvement. After the public outcry following the trial, the queen also dissolved Parliament—only to find that members of the new Parliament displayed "more Zeal" than she "expected or desired." Swift also describes the origins and results of the enduring animosity between Bolingbroke and Oxford. He attributes its beginnings to Bolingbroke's ambitious handling of affairs while Oxford was recovering from Antoine GUISCARD's attack: "some Things happened during Mr. Harley's Confinement, which bred a Coldness and Jealousy

between these two great Men; and these increasing by many subsequent Accidents could never be removed."

All the while, Swift claims, the queen grew increasingly stubborn and displayed an utter lack of interest in promoting a High Church ministry. In fact, for more than 20 years past, royal favor had fallen almost exclusively on "Low-Church" Whigs. In contrast, the vast majority of landowners maintained their allegiance to Tory principles (which put King WILLIAM in an awkward position). At the outset of Queen Anne's reign, those who supported the Tories hoped she would appoint High-Church noblemen to positions of power. She did so for a time, ultimately taking Oxford "into Her Councils." Eventually, however, he aroused the queen's suspicions by seeking too many appointments for his friends, and she became excessively "cautious and slow" in "dispensing her Favours." When he was passed over for promotion, Bolingbroke blamed Oxford and vowed never to "depend upon the Earl's friendship for as long as he lived." The ongoing enmity between these two men "split the Court into Parties," and (like Bolingbroke) the queen blamed Oxford for the whole dilemma. When Queen Anne fell ill in December 1713, she ceased her attempt to reconcile the factions that had formed. The quarrel between Oxford and Bolingbroke continued, and Swift regretfully comments that it never would have started had Oxford "dealt with less Reserve" and Bolingbroke placed more trust in his friend.

Having "with some Pains" outlined the "unaccountable Quarrels of the late Ministry," Swift concludes that the queen herself was the principal cause of them all. Having become exceptionally opinionated and fond of scheming, she paid attention to hints "that She had formerly been too much governed" and "grew very difficult to be advised." He assigns some of the blame to Oxford as well, who lost his ability "to influence the Queen" and accepted all the blame for her hesitancy and delays. Finally, he blames those who should have made it their business (especially since it would have been in their best interest) to heal the "unhappy breach" between Oxford and Bolingbroke.

In the second chapter of the "Enquiry" ("written above a year after" the first), Swift addresses the accusation that the former Tory ministry sought to bring in the Pretender. He had assumed it would be unnecessary to comment on this charge, but has decided to do so since the rumor of it is still circulating. Swift's argument is twofold: First, he asserts that neither Queen Anne nor any of her ministers "did ever entertain a Design of bringing in the Pretender during Her Majesty's Life, or that he should succeed after Her decease." Second, he claims that if they had ever "conceived such as Design," they would have had to begin putting it into action at least a year before the queen's death. Otherwise it would have been impossible to carry out. Swift cites several points of evidence to support his claim, most of which are based on his own interviews with "almost every Person in great Employment" during recent years. He also offers other evidence: (1) when Queen Anne decided "to change her Servants," she appointed a number of Whigs rather than Tories; (2) anyone who knew the queen's disposition would know she opposed the Pretender—she even got angry with Bolingbroke because he once attended an opera "under the same roof with that Person"; (3) the changes Queen Anne made in her ministry were based on personal animosity, and it was always difficult to persuade her "to dismiss any Person upon the Score of Party"; (4) the cause of the Pretender has become "stale" and obsolete; and (5) the Treaties of Utrecht were designed "directly against the Pretender." He also claims that those accused of having plotted to alter English succession simply do not have personalities that would support such a charge. The queen, especially, was so "little enterprising," "so much given to Delay," "so obstinate in her Opinions," and such a "Pursuer of Peace and Quiet" that she could never have engaged in such an effort. In the end, Swift decides, all of this shows that imperfect individuals make up imperfect governments, and the best remedy is a set of "good Fundamental Laws" that force those who break them to suffer the consequences of their infractions.

## COMMENTARY

With the Tory ministry of Robert Harley and Henry Bolingbroke disintegrating in 1714, Swift finished and published his attack on Richard STEELE, "The Public Spirit of the Whigs," and was threatened with arrest and trial. He retreated to Letcombe Bassett in June for a few weeks but decided rural England would not serve and arrived in Dublin in August, taking up his duties as dean. Though Swift states early in the "Enquiry," "I have not found the transition very difficult into a private life," he certainly was still heavily focused on the ministry's affairs and less so on Irish issues, also producing "Memoirs, Relating to that Change Which Happened in the Year 1704" (probably completed in 1717).

Both these works provide further evidence that Swift was living in the past, hoping the ministry could recover itself (a hope also shared by Bolingbroke who objected to any history of the ministry). If "An Enquiry" is history, Swift resists the objectivity of a historian, a characteristic that would have given the work a more balanced perspective. Instead, his argument depends on persuasion and piling up convincing evidence. Other critics argue for a different interpretation, however, seeing him explain the accomplishments of the ministry alongside the faults of Queen Anne and Robert Harley. His comment about avoiding malice as a historian does not actually seem accurate when he reviews various Whigs, but describing Oxford and Bolingbroke becomes a quite different effort. This essay reveals Swift's affection and respect for both without ignoring their talents and strengths as politicians, while honestly probing into why this ministry failed. If blame can be placed on any figure, Swift seems more disposed after mentioning Oxford's procrastination and Bolingbroke's vanity to blame the queen, or at least those in her domestic circle who too easily could manipulate her opinions and biases. Anne, who knew of the friction between these two ministers, had caused these difficulties through "her own dubious management" and willingness "to lay the blame upon her Treasurer [Harley]." Extending these comments, Swift blames "the variety of hands she had employed and reasonings she had heard since her coming to the crown[;] . . . she grew very difficult to be advised."

Ricardo Quintana suggests the ministry represented true national characteristics, those which would preserve the country (*Mind and Art of*

*Jonathan Swift* 199). The Whigs' political philosophy remained directly opposed to the tenets of Enlightenment thought since their self-interest guided nearly all their decisions. Swift's own ambition and hope of seeing the Tory ministry revived colored his comments in this essay, but he believed peace and the interests of the church should be preserved, and the Tories had shown dedication to this task. Swift searches for a champion of liberty, and finds two champions in Harley and Bolingbroke. This view, though heartening, remains far too simplistic for Swift, who recognized that the growth of factions within his party had become so severe that he could not blame the other party. The Tories, he finally concludes, must accept the responsibility of their errors, but his clarity on this issue does not set aside his own pessimism which he fully embraces, relieved only when he focused his fierce intelligence and moral vigor on Ireland's "singular condition."

## "Epigram, An"

Poem by Swift; first published 1767, written 1735–36. Like "ON DR. RUNDLE," it concerns Thomas RUNDLE, bishop of Derry. The epigram sarcastically portrays Archbishop Hugh BOULTER as "weighty and profound" (5).

## "Epigram, Inscribed to the Honourable Serjeant Kite, An"

Poem possibly by Swift; first published 1814, probably written 1734. Pat Rogers calls it a dubious item. "Serjeant Kite" is an insulting nickname for Richard BETTESWORTH, who was so offended by Swift's poem "ON THE WORDS 'BROTHER PROTESTANTS AND FELLOW CHRISTIANS'" that he had threatened to cut Swift's ears off. In this epigram, Swift claims that being forced to listen to Bettesworth's tirades would be an even worse torture—one that would likely drive him to sever his own ears. See also "ON THE ARCHBISHOP OF CASHEL AND BETTESWORTH" and "The YAHOO'S OVERTHROW."

## "Epigram on Fasting, An"

Poem by Swift; first published in 1735. It is written in French and followed by an English translation. Dating the composition of the poem is impossible, but Pat Rogers suggests 1730–34. Swift's short prose preface claims that the verses were written "extempore" by a French gentleman who had offended fellow diners by ordering bacon and eggs on a "fast-day." The speaker suggests that it is foolish to assume that God, "wrapped up in majesty divine," gives any regard to what foods we eat.

## "Epigram (on Seeing a Worthy Prelate Go Out of Church)"

Poem by Swift; first published 1732, written the same year. Along with "ADVICE TO A PARSON," this poem was originally printed by James Roberts in his first edition of "The LADY'S DRESSING ROOM." Like "Advice," it addresses the worldliness of bishops promoting English interests in Ireland—here epitomized when "Lord Pam" (representing Josiah HORT) stops praying and promptly leaves church when he hears that Lionel SACKVILLE, first duke of Dorset is in town: "To the court it was fitter to pay his devotion, / Since God had no hand in his Lordship's promotion."

## "Epigram on Wood's Brass Money, An"

Poem by Swift; first published 1746, written 1724. Another of Swift's statements against William WOOD and his patent for Irish coinage, it was occasioned by Lord CARTERET's arrival in Ireland on October 22, 1724, to calm violent reaction against the measure. The poem suggests that the outcry against "Wood's brass" drowns out the guns, trumpets, drums and bells welcoming Carteret to Ireland. See also *The DRAPIER'S LETTERS*, "DOING GOOD: A SERMON ON THE OCCASION OF WOOD'S PROJECT," "AN EXCELLENT NEW SONG UPON HIS GRACE OUR GOOD LORD ARCHBISHOP OF DUBLIN," "ON WOOD THE IRONMONGER," "PROMETHEUS," "A SERIOUS POEM UPON WILLIAM WOOD," "A SIMILE," and "WOOD, AN INSECT."

## "Epilogue to a Play for the Benefit of the Weavers in Ireland, An"

Poem by Swift; first published in 1721, written the same year. Swift wrote this poem for a performance of *Hamlet* on April 1, 1721, at the Theatre Royal, Smock Alley, in Dublin. Thomas SHERIDAN wrote a prologue (printed with Swift's epilogue) for the same performance. The play was one of several relief measures in response to the crippling recession of 1721 that left many Irish weavers unemployed.

## "Epistle upon an Epistle, An"

Poem by Swift; first published 1729, written the same year. It is Swift's response to Rev. Patrick DELANY's 1729 "Epistle to Lord Carteret," in which he requested more lucrative preferment in addition to the church offices he already held. Delany complained that "very wretched . . . is he, that's double, / In nothing, but his Titles, and his Trouble" (43–44). Swift's reply is keenly sarcastic, and suggests throughout that Delany's request to Carteret was inappropriate. Swift asks, for example, "If your expenses rise so high; / What income can your wants supply?" and he advises his friend to be less ambitious and more frugal (95–96, 113–16). Delany's "Epistle" elicited a number of other poems by Swift, including "LIBEL ON THE REVEREND DR. DELANY," "ON THE IRISH CLUB," "DIALOGUE BETWEEN AN EMINENT LAWYER AND DR. SWIFT," "TO DR. DELANY, ON THE LIBELS WRITTEN AGAINST HIM," and "TO A FRIEND WHO HAD BEEN MUCH ABUSED IN MANY INVETERATE LIBELS."

## Epitaph, Swift's

In addition to leaving specific instructions on where his body should be buried after his death, Swift, in his will dated May 3, 1740, penned his own epitaph and left a detailed description of how and where he wanted it engraved. He stipulated that three days after his death, his corpse should be buried in a private ceremony at midnight in the "great [ai]sle" of St. Patrick's Cathedral, Dublin, "on the South Side, under the Pillar next to the monument of Primate Narcissus Marsh." A slab of "Black Marble" was to be "erected" on the wall "seven Feet from the Ground," on which his epitaph was to be inscribed "in large Letters, deeply cut, and strongly gilded" (*Prose Works* 13.149).

The epitaph is written in what Victoria Glendinning has described as "elliptic" Latin (275). In it Swift asserts that he has now gone where "savage indignation" can no longer harm him. He challenges the reader—as a "*viator,*" or traveler—to imitate him "*si poteris*" ("if you can") as one who fought for the liberty of men (see Part I for a full translation). David Nokes calls it a "proud epitaph," which "stresses Roman courage rather than Christian humility" and stands as "the last of [Swift's] long line of self-assessments" (*Hypocrite Reversed* 412). As a final comment on his own life and career, the epitaph links Swift to the ancient Roman satirist Juvenal, who had claimed (in the first of his satires) that his indignation at the lunacy he saw all around him made it difficult to refrain from writing satire. Likewise, the *saeva indignatio* (savage indignation) Swift claims to have escaped in his final inscription is not that of others directed at him. Instead, it is the irresistible compulsion he felt to write satire as a means of exposing (and seeking to free his audience from) what he saw as rampant hypocrisy, pride, and injustice. William Butler Yeats translated the epitaph thus: "Swift has sailed into his rest; / Savage indignation there / Cannot lacerate his breast. / Imitate him if you dare, / World-besotted traveller; he / Served human liberty."

## Esquire, T. H.

See "DISCOURSE CONCERNING THE MECHANICAL OPERATION OF THE SPIRIT."

# "Examination of Certain Abuses, Corruptions, and Enormities in the City of Dublin"

In any discussion of Swift's so-called excremental vision, a phrase introduced by the psychoanalytic critic Norman Brown, this satiric essay published in Dublin in the spring of 1732 serves as an excellent example. When it was reprinted in London in the same year, a new primary title had been added to the existing one: "City Cries, Instrumental and Vocal: Or, An Examination . . ." Swift combines both vision and reality to shock and amuse the reader into recognizing the befouled and corrupt world he inhabited.

## SYNOPSIS

While Dublin has a number of excellent laws, they are poorly enforced and even more are needed. In this "Examination," Swift promises to outline "some of the greatest Enormities, Abuses, and Corruptions" and to propose solutions he hopes the legislature will approve. It was a wise notion to allow hawkers "of both sexes" to stroll the streets selling goods, but lawmakers should compel these "Traders" to "pronounce their Words in such Terms" as everyone can understand. As numerous examples illustrate, they currently use slang and jargon that only Dubliners can recognize. Many of the cries uttered by these peddlers even have subversive political slants.

Another enormity involves the "immense Number of human Excrements" polluting the city. Members of "the disaffected [TORY] Party" wrongly suggest that *British Fundaments* (anuses) secretly laid the feces all over Dublin to show that hunger in Ireland is only a myth promoted by "*Jacobites and Papists.*" The butchers of the city are engaged in another abuse involving the "cossing" of dogs. When a stray dog happens to wander through the meat market, a butcher cries out "Coss, Coss!" and everyone proceeds to chase the animal. The Jacobites claim that this is a form of persecution reserved for "*Dogs* of the *Tory* Principle," but the Whigs all know that their dogs were once treated just as badly.

The Tories have also hired chimneysweeps to call for a coach whenever they hear a WHIG M.P. do the same. They are particularly fond of doing this on days when important issues are to be debated in Parliament. The sneaky Tories—as "Enemies to the Government"—do all of this with the intention of doing what they can to bring in the Pretender (James Francis Edward STUART). Likewise, there are seemingly innocent signs hanging all over the city (particularly "over Houses, where *Punch* is to be sold") that contain veiled references to this ongoing plot against the government. The legislature should immediately do "away with these *Popish, Jacobite,* and idolatrous Gew-gaws."

Returning to the issue of subtly seditious cries being heard throughout the streets of Dublin, it turns out that many were devised "in the *worst of Times,* under the late Earl of *Oxford's* Administration, during the four last Years of Queen Anne's reign." A papist and a Jacobite, he adapted "several *London* Cries" to serve his subversive ends. All of these cries should be "rejected with Horror," or at least "trusted" only "in the Hands of *true Protestants*" who have sworn their allegiance to the government.

## COMMENTARY

Herbert Davis calls this essay a trifle, which Swift had been bothered about and finally decided to write as an amusing and sensitive portrait of the city, but with a distinctively satiric edge. The pamphlet offers a typical Swiftian beginning: a playful juxtaposition of words and phrases meant to bring attention to a particular occupation or create insinuations suggesting a political point of view. The idea of using hawkers, those peddlers who advertise their goods by shouting to passers-by in the streets, catches the true atmosphere of Dublin with its interplay of order and disorder. They have a role which should contribute to the ordering of their world. Traders offer the "many necessaries of life," whether it is farmers offering milk, fishermen selling herring or salmon, baker's assistants providing "sweet-hearts" (a small sugar cake), or garbage men who clean away the rubbish for a price.

While apparently preserving order, these figures are actually involved in disrupting it. For example, instead of communicating the availability of food for hungry "strangers, forced hither by business, who reside here but a short time" the farmer produces confusing sounds and no clear information. Fishwives call out "herrings alive . . . salmon alive, alive here," pretending their goods are fresh, but instead offer lies and stinking, dead fish to their neighbors. Ordinary speech can distort the facts for purposes of commerce or politics. Swift's irony embraces the lack of men in the town, so women must purchase sweethearts themselves (instead of expecting gifts from their lovers who serve in the English army in distant places). The impression of order really suggests a radical disorder as the cry of "sweet-hearts" reflects how Ireland's colonial status permits England's use of their men, creating instability at home.

Studying things as they are represents another approach Swift employs in this satiric essay. Excrement on the Dublin landscape was a literal and linguistic fact for him, and as he walks about the city he notes "the immense number of human excrements at the doors and steps of waste houses, and at the sides of every dead wall." Proceeding from this fact, Swift graphically applies scientific principles, calling upon an "eminent physician, who is well versed in such profound speculations," to compare "a British anus" to "a Hibernian," and determine further whether the resulting excrement belongs to one group or the other. This study will disprove, in the minds of some, that the Irish are poor and ill-fed, instead "our Irish vulgar do daily eat and drink." The comic absurdity of this satiric picture effectively conveys an impression of disorder, the excremental reality at war with a false science that attempts an understanding of the ongoing political disintegration between the two countries.

Swift continues his analysis of these abuses by suggesting how the mind refuses the facts before it, not deciding on factual evidence but reaching a conclusion first and interpreting the facts to fit it. As John Bullitt suggests, Swift believed one could understand the origins of much of religious and political fanaticism from this intellectual conversion. Satirizing the corruption of the senses in this essay, Swift interpreted the street cries, tavern signs, and other urban characteristics as being "code words of sedition" (Bullitt 137). If a person

holds such biases and possesses an inflexible and intolerant mind, then an eagle as the centerpiece of a tavern sign becomes a cross and a code for popery (with all the usual prejudice against Roman Catholicism and even Jacobites).

# Examiner, The

The *Examiner*, a paper sponsored by the government, was first published in August 1710. In this paper, Swift adopted the role of an anonymous and objective, yet critical, observer without party affiliation who believed honestly in the virtues of TORY rule. His first essay appeared in the paper in the first week of November 1710, and 33 weekly articles ran during the Tory Parliament's opening session until June 1711, when Swift was asked to conclude the series. Swift provided a running commentary on events in these fervently partisan political essays, which portrayed the WHIGS as mad for war and corrupt. These essays anticipated our contemporary op-ed pages of newspapers and the numerous cable news shows where the anchor meditates for a few minutes and delivers a modest opinion—though surely our modern examples of political commentary pale before Swift's.

Printed as a single 2,000-word essay on a folio half-sheet, the *Examiner* was influential in shaping public opinion toward the Robert HARLEY administration. It also became the vehicle for Swift establishing himself among numerous journalists, dramatists, and poets as a political writer with an unmistakably potent and attractive prose style. His audience would be the core Tory supporters: rural clergymen and country squires—the bedrock of English society.

His themes in each essay remained constant throughout: concern over increasing economic risk, extended credit, and godless capitalism. The Established Church and the constitution served as the twin pillars of his moral force, and often Swift easily achieved a moral victory against his critics. In becoming a widely popular columnist throughout Great Britain and Ireland, Swift realized the necessity to examine those great Whig figures, John

MARLBOROUGH, Thomas WHARTON, and Lord SOMERS, and found them avaricious, self-serving, and subversive.

Though Daniel DEFOE also wrote for Harley, his assignment differed in that his audience consisted of merchants and those who worked in connection with the various trades. The writers Joseph ADDISON and Richard STEELE in their periodicals—the *Tatler* and the *Spectator*—had in mind "to expose the false arts of life, to pull off the disguises of cunning." Swift certainly opposed vanity and affectation whenever he noted them in the characters he held up to public scrutiny, but Addison and Steele hoped to divert and amuse while providing their readers with a healthy dose of culture and learning. Swift's observer (or "Examiner") turned his attention to a government in need of nurturing and a political agenda requiring explanation and increasing levels of support and encouragement.

## SYNOPSIS

### Number 13: Thursday, November 2, 1710

[This paper first appeared as number 14, but most later editions of the *Examiner* follow John BARBER in omitting the original number 13, which was Francis ATTERBURY's defense of hereditary right (Ellis, *Swift vs. Mainwaring* lxx).] The writer begins by asserting that he has always made a habit of conversing freely with "deserving Men of both Parties." Because of recent events, however, he has had to change this practice. Specifically, many of his acquaintances in the "declining" Whig party have become unforgivably "peevish" and pessimistic, and he has decided to avoid them. In this paper, he intends to show that these Whigs' fears for the future are groundless and that all of the kingdom's problems are the result of "the very Counsels they so much admire." He also plans to argue that Queen ANNE's dismissal of Whig ministers was necessary to preserve the constitution.

Complaints against the queen's "late Revolutions at Court" include the charges that they were poorly timed (due to the ongoing War of the Spanish Succession) and were directed at affecting "the Settlement of the Crown, and call[ing] over the PRETENDER." These and other charges have been "plentifully scattered abroad, by the Malice of a ruined Party, to render the QUEEN and her Administration odious, and to inflame the Nation." It is truly a shame that continuing the war has become a means of profit for so many government officials, and if things continue it is likely that "a Landed Man will be little better than a Farmer at a rack Rent, to the Army, and to the publick Funds."

This desperate situation originated when "an under Sett of Men" convinced King WILLIAM that the principles of the Anglican Church were "inconsistent with the *Revolution*." Widespread "caressing" of the Dissenters followed, along with the disenfranchisement of universities and clergymen. At the same time, the costs of the ongoing war led the government to borrow large sums of money at "exorbitant Interest," and now the kingdom's wealth depends on rising and falling stocks rather than on the value of its land. The writer asks whether it is wise for a king to continue a war whose costs "perpetually exceed" what he is able to collect in the form of taxes from his subjects. What makes it even worse is that neither England's enemies nor her allies have placed themselves under such a burden, and will much more easily "recover themselves" after the war is over. Based on all of these factors, "it was the most prudent Course imaginable" for Queen Anne to enact "the Disposition of the people" by making sweeping changes in her ministry and in Parliament—freeing herself from the influence of those whose only interest lay in "perpetuating the War" for personal gains.

### Number 14: Thursday, November 9, 1710

In response to "the Importunity" of his friends, the writer in this paper discusses "the Art of *Political Lying*." Although the devil is undeniably the father of lies, his reputation (like that of all inventors) has diminished in light of "all the Improvements that have been made" on the lie as he originated it. Historically, lying has been associated with fallen political parties. Modern politicians, however, have turned it into a means of obtaining (and retaining) power and as a tool for taking revenge after that power is lost. Political lies, moreover, are slightly different from others: They are often the brainchild of a fallen politician, and are usually "delivered to be nursed and dandled by the *Rabble*." A lie is a type of monster that dies immediately after birth if it happens to be born without a sting. Lies can (among other things) overthrow kingdoms, offer and remove employments, make atheists into saints, and raise or ruin a nation's credit. If someone in London possessed the ability to see lies (just as the Scots can see ghosts), that individual would be much entertained by the varied hordes of lies buzzing around the city.

Unlike everyday liars, those of the political variety must have very short memories. This is vital because of the constant need to contradict oneself and "swear both Sides of a Contradiction." The earl of WHARTON has been remarkably successful because of his skill in this area, and his fame is based only on maintaining "an inexhaustible Fund of *Political Lyes*." He never concerns himself with the truth or falsehood of any "proposition" but only with whether or not it is expedient under the present circumstances.

Based on the widespread willingness among politicians to lie (and on the public's complementary tendency to believe them), the old adage that *"Truth will at last prevail"* seems questionable. However, after the Whigs exploited England for 20 years and made it impossible for the English to distinguish friends from foes, the people finally came to their senses and intervened. This shows that Truth will eventually win out, even if it sometimes takes a while.

### Number 15: Thursday, November 16, 1710

For many years, England has sorely needed a paper like the *Examiner*. The writer vows to produce the periodical "without entering into the Violences of either Party." Because persons and events are so widely misrepresented, the public needs some "impartial Hand" to set their opinions right. England, the writer reminds his readers, is a limited monarchy. However, the English are unfortunately divided into two parties and face manifold enemies in religion and government. Two fanatical "stupid illiterate Scribblers" have undertaken to direct English sentiments regarding these threats in a pair of rival papers: "the *Review* and *Observator*." While the majority of the population lacks the means to

talk and think on their own, it is sad that they must be led by such rags as these.

The writer claims that his goal is to show the "remote and unstructured Part of the Nation" that they have been led astray by wild extremists "on both Sides." He has heard that a recent *Observator* was filled with specific refutations of his statements in an earlier *Examiner*. He refuses to engage in this popular tactic, having decided that the author is not worthy of his concern. The greatest problem with this sort of propaganda is that it "inflames small Quarrels by a thousand Stories," deepening divisions among those of different parties and preventing those who disagree about an issue from ever understanding one another. In fact, the terms *Tory* and *Whig* simply do not mean much anymore and have been utterly transformed in recent years to mean the opposite of what they once denoted.

In an attempt to dismiss some of the more popular falsehoods scattered by alarmist "idiots" in the press, the writer examines two of their favorite "maxims." The first is that the church is in danger. This may be true, but "the Church and State may be both in Danger" at any time during any monarch's reign no matter how skilled any particular ruler may be. The second false maxim is that England stands to suffer from the Tories owing much of their greatness to "the young *Pretender* in *France*." The writer cites this claim as evidence that the rabble-rousing "scribblers" have made a habit of ascribing all causes to the Pretender (James Francis Edward STUART), whether a secretary resigns or the queen dismisses a Parliament. In this regard, they have become like the boy who cried wolf, having cried out against the Pretender so often that no one is listening anymore. The threat of the Pretender is contrived, since an act of Parliament has made it plain that "her present Majesty is Heir to the Survivor of the late King and Queen her Sister."

### Number 16: Thursday, November 23, 1710

The writer recalls that in an earlier paper (number 13), he mentioned that "one specious Objection" to Queen Anne's recent change of ministry was that it had created "uneasiness" on the part of "a General, who hath been long successful abroad."

This general (John Churchill, first duke of MARL-BOROUGH) has supposedly been treated with great ingratitude despite his remarkable service to queen and country. In reality, however, the only evidence of this ingratitude that the queen's detractors can produce is the fact that she "dissolved her Parliament" and significantly altered her ministry while Marlborough was abroad. These detractors further allege that it is not just the queen but the entire kingdom that is guilty of slighting Marlborough's service, since everyone participated in "*joining as one Man,* to wish" that the ministry be changed.

In fact, it is an embarrassment to the kingdom that the only thing that preserved the now-defunct ministry for so long was "a tender Regard" for Marlborough. It is also important to remember that even at the height of the controversy, nothing negative was ever stated or implied about "this great Commander." On the contrary, the entire citizenry "seemed Unanimous" in wanting him to remain in control of all "Confederate Forces."

There are, the writer argues, two types of ingratitude: one involves a monarch (or the public) repaying good with evil, while the other occurs when "good Services are not at all, or very meanly rewarded." Having already dispensed with the first in Marlborough's case, the writer now turns his attention to showing that the second type is equally inapplicable. The queen has handsomely rewarded Marlborough for his service to the kingdom. He has received valuable land and property, funds, and even pictures and jewels—all totaling "a good deal above half a Million" pounds, not even counting "what is *untold.*" The only reason for providing these details is to dismiss the comparisons some have drawn between the British and "the Greeks and Romans" who treated so many of their greatest generals with the utmost ingratitude. These figures (along with the table the writer provides to illustrate them) make it easy to see that the British at their worst are nowhere nearly as ungrateful as the "*Romans* were at *best.*" If the truth were known, most people who cry out against ingratitude would find that they themselves are indebted to those they accuse.

### Number 17: Thursday, November 30, 1710

Having resolved that the *Examiner* would deal exclusively "with Things, and not with Persons,"

the writer has discovered that the topics he addresses are inseparably linked with specific individuals. Writing is like building—one's plans are often cast aside once the project gets under way, and the writer finds himself having to use whatever materials he can just to keep things moving. In public affairs, especially, when matters have been handled badly it is impossible to discuss them without unintentionally identifying and casting blame on those responsible.

One technique that satirists have often used to avoid naming names is to choose and discuss a historical figure "bearing a Resemblance to the Person" they have in mind. The problem with this approach, however, is that the audience too often fails to recognize the actual object of the satire. In an attempt to avoid this confusion, the writer perused the works of Livy and Tacitus to find useful characters to whom he could compare the modern politician he wishes to satirize (the earl of WHARTON). He ultimately decided that drawing any parallels would only damage the reputations of the Romans, so he determined to imitate Cicero and use extracts from his "harangues" against Caius Verres (a corrupt governor of Sicily). Accordingly, the writer includes what he calls a "faithfully translated and abstracted" oration Cicero delivered against Verres in the senate.

The speech begins with Cicero reminding senators of the widespread suspicion (in Rome and surrounding nations) that the wealthy can get away with crimes simply because of their wealth. In "condemning" Verres as a "Robber of the Publick Treasure" and an "Overturner of Law and Justice," the senate can send a powerful signal to the public that this suspicion is false. He follows with a litany of reasons in favor of holding Verres accountable for the crimes he has committed, arguing that while Verres governed the Sicilians were robbed of their rights to law and property: "I believe there is no Man who ever heard his Name, that cannot relate his Enormities."

In his comments after the extract, the writer laments that "modern Corruptions" cannot accurately be compared to ancient ones. There is no precedent, for instance, to which he can compare a man (undoubtedly Wharton, although he is still unnamed) who manipulates the laws in order to excuse his own crimes.

### Number 18: Thursday, December 7, 1710

The writer admits that he is often tempted to reveal his identity as author of the *Examiner* so people will stop criticizing the papers in his presence. The criticism he finds in rival papers does not bother him so much because when he tires of it, he can simply fold it up or cast it aside. It would be "happy," he adds, if he possessed the same "Power over People's Tongues." That way he would not have to listen as his work is "rallied at and commended fifty Times a Day."

He has further realized that he made an unfortunate choice when he chose to side with the Tories in his writings. What point is there (he asks) in defending worthy causes that the queen and Parliament have already embraced? He finds himself utterly at the mercy of printers nowadays, and wonders how much longer his paper will last. He promises, however, to continue writing the *Examiner* " 'till either the World or my self grow weary of it." All along, his goal has been to "undeceive those well-meaning People, who have been drawn unaware into a wrong Sense of Things"—many having fallen victim to wrongheaded politicians and "the foul Misrepresentations that were constantly made of all who durst differ from them in the smallest Article." An overwhelming number of these false representations came on the heels of the queen's recent decision to change her ministry: it is not enough, the writer laments, to point out that a wise monarch should be allowed the freedom "to change his Ministers without giving a Reason to his Subjects."

If his statements thus far have reflected badly on any individuals, the writer admits that it was impossible to avoid. It would truly be better, in fact, if for posterity's sake the names of those responsible for misleading the public were listed along with the deeds he has described. While a contemporary audience (by virtue of his hints and insinuations) can easily figure out whom he means to chastise, it will not be so easy for his and his readers' grandchildren.

Nonetheless, he will continue to capitalize on every opportunity to show "the misled Part of the

People" just "how grosly they have been abused, and in what Particulars." Those who have spoken out most vocally against his paper never miss a chance to criticize the queen's decision to alter her ministry, but they ignore the fact that every branch of the government had become so corrupt that this was the only way to save the kingdom from ruin. Why else would the queen have taken so drastic a step? Based on all the negative backlash, it is remarkable that any of the new ministers agreed to step in. Their willingness to do so can be attributed only to their love for England and their strength of character. Sadly, they can expect nothing less than "the utmost Efforts of Malice from a Set of enraged domestick Adversaries" who are determined to cross them at every turn. In the end, however, the truth is plain: The queen made her intentions clear, the two houses of Parliament unanimously agreed with her, and the revolution in her ministry was absolutely necessary.

### Number 19: Thursday, December 14, 1710

When the printer recently came by to pick up his copy of the latest *Examiner* manuscript, he dropped off several papers that had been "swinged off the *Examiner*." Having read these for the first time, the writer finds himself convinced that "the Prejudice of Parties" best explains the current and pervasive lack of taste among the English. Neither party is entirely blameless in this regard, but Whig writers (in their responses to the *Examiner*) provide a particularly accurate portrayal of their party's "weak" and "ruined" condition. If "these People will not be quiet," the writer promises, he will be forced to begin answering his own papers—a tactic of which he has already been accused. Even supporters of the *Examiner* are causing him grief: while some complain that he has failed to deliver on his promise "to discover the Corruptions" of the now-defunct Whig ministry, others curse him for "discovering so many." Unable to please both sides, he has determined simply to proceed with his design, which in this paper is to outline some of the Whigs' tactics that "were no Hindrance to the [recent] Change of the ministry."

Their first practice was to introduce "new Phrases into the Court Style" of speaking, each of which threatened desertion unless certain conditions were met. Statements such as, *"Madam, I cannot serve you while such a One is in Employment"* became commonplace in their parlance. Another practice was their ongoing attempt to remove "the Obligation upon Fellows of Colleges in both Universities to enter upon Holy Orders." This strategy was designed to prevent students from being misled by clergymen, who (supposedly) "infused into their Pupils too great a Regard for the Church and the Monarchy." The Whigs also sought "to impeach" Lady Abigail MASHAM for nothing other than her "faithful and diligent Service to the Queen" and the favor she enjoyed because of it. Finally, when they were in power the Whigs placed a "cruel Tyranny" upon conscience in England. At every turn they absolutely refused to exercise "the least *Toleration* or *Indulgence*" in politics, and in their rigidity excluded 90 percent of the kingdom from "the Pale of their [political] Church."

The writer ends this paper with a story "from an old History of *Sarmatia*" about "a great King in *Scythia*," whose prime minister allowed a lord to build forts against an outside enemy, the *"Tartars."* The lord almost immediately began to "insist upon Terms" and threatened to unite with the Tartars against the king. Upon learning of this, the king's prime minister feared for his life and successfully urged the king to marry one of the lord's daughters. Afterward, the prime minister prided himself on having authored "a most glorious Union"—even though it was necessary only because of his own "Corruption." The writer explains that he has included this anecdote in order to confuse the "little smattering Remarkers" who so readily answer each of his papers, and to challenge them to find "an Application."

### Number 20: Thursday, December 21, 1710

Admitting that he is "at a loss how to proceed," the writer indicates that a recent occurrence has prompted him to write on the subject "of *Soldiers* and the *Army*." Despite numerous changes over the years in how wars are fought, there are several maxims (or "eternal Truths") that still apply. The armies of ancient Greece and Rome fought to defend their own interests, and never expected to be paid for their efforts. In modern Europe, however, the use of mercenary troops has become commonplace. These soldiers are nothing more than armed servants, hired "either to awe the *Children* at home; or else to defend from Invaders, the Family who are otherwise employed."

The practice of turning soldiers into paid tradesmen developed because of two factors. The first was usurpation, when "popular Men" robbed their peers of liberties "and seized power into their own Hands." In order to maintain their ill-gotten sovereignty, these usurpers had to hire "Guards" to keep the people under control. The other factor that popularized these "Mercenary Armies" was that large kingdoms frequently found themselves subduing distant "Provinces," and were compelled to hire soldiers to prevent rebellion on the natives' part. In a "free state" (including a monarchy), therefore, these hired armies are needed only for maintaining "Conquests" or for waging war in distant lands.

Since the latter case applies to England's current situation, it is important to recognize "certain maxims" that have always been observed by "wise Governments" engaged in military conflicts far from home. The first is that "no *private* Man" should ever be granted a commission making him a "*General for Life*." If any monarch is so foolish as to grant such a commission, he should go ahead and hand over his crown along with it. Requests for this type of appointment must be powerfully discouraged, and those who dare to make them should be put on record as criminals against the state. A second maxim that free states should observe when making war is that the military must remain separate from and subordinate to the civil power. The army, in other words, is a group of servants "hired by the Civil power to act as they are directed." As such, generals and their forces should be held in "absolute Subjection" to the government at home and must never be allowed to interfere with domestic affairs. Finally, armies are now more humane than they used to be, and it is vital for governments to encourage and preserve this civility in order to prevent soldiers from becoming "savages." One of the best ways to do so would be "to forbid that detestable Custom of *drinking to the Damnation or Confusion* of any Person whatsoever."

*Number 21: Thursday, December 28, 1710*
Those who revere England's constitution must be happy to witness its ongoing restoration, especially following the long period in which it was blatantly neglected. Having already outlined "some Abuses" during the previous ministry, the writer promises in this paper to "say something of the *Church.*"

Few in Europe have ever been so mistreated as the English clergy. The best arguments in favor of "*Revolution* against those many Invasions" of citizens' rights came from this group, who (unlike the Dissenters) refused to be swayed from the truth by attractive offers of preferment. The London clergy, moreover, provided "the best collection of arguments against *Popery* that ever appeared in the World." During the revolution (and even after JAMES II's coronation), a vocal minority took the clergy's call for reform to an extreme and promoted "a *thorow Reformation*" that would have destroyed both the church and the state. Ever since then, a "violent Humour" has run against English clergymen. They have been blamed for every sin committed by anyone in the realm. With their reputations ruined and unjustly assaulted from every side, the clergy finally found a friend in Queen Anne, who—acting as God's "Instrument"—turned the tide of public opinion in favor of these downtrodden churchmen. Not everyone, however, followed her lead. In particular, one group of men decided that English trade could never flourish until England became "a common Receptacle for all Nations, Religions, and languages." Such ridiculous politics have caused a number of problems, and were intended to turn worship (and God himself) into "a Creature of the State."

Ultimately the schemes of those malevolent men have failed. The queen wisely changed her ministry and quickly called for a convocation of the clergy. She also sent an important letter to the archbishop encouraging the Anglican clergy to rectify the "loose and prophane Principles" that had been promulgated among the public. The letter unfortunately caused a crisis in the convocation because the bishops and "lower clergy" communicated poorly about its contents. However, unlike other political troubles, such "Inconveniences" in the church cannot be cured simply by altering the ministry. Rather, "time and morality" are the only

remedies, and it looks as though those factors are beginning to effect a positive change.

*Number 22, Thursday, January 4, 1711*
Entitled, "The *Examiner* Cross-examined: Or, A full Answer to the last *Examiner,*" this paper is written "in the true Style" of responses that had appeared following earlier issues of the *Examiner.* The writer assumes the voice of a despondent Whig, embittered by Queen Anne's recent change of ministry and by the *Examiner* itself, which he calls a batch of "insipid Papers." He promises to limit the first part of his discussion to some of the ludicrous claims made in the most recent *Examiner* (number 21).

The first of the many ridiculous assertions made in that paper was that "*The Queen began her Reign with a noble Benefaction to the Church.*" It is typical for High-Church Tories to think of the "church" as composed of priests who are "*hired* to teach *the Religion of the Magistrate,*" and obvious to everyone that the author of the *Examiner* wants the kingdom to be "*Priest-ridden*" once again. Even this, however, does not sum up the paper's argument because the *Examiner*'s writer is so "inconsistent:" One never knows "whether to call him a Whig, a Tory, a Protestant, or a Papist."

Convinced that he has provided "a *full, satisfactory* Answer to the *Examiner*'s last Paper," the writer states that he will now proceed to a more significant endeavor and prove that "the late Ministry" was (despite the *Examiner*'s claims) composed of "true friends to the Church." There are several pieces of evidence to support this truth. First, the apostle Paul himself had written that heresies in the church are necessary for the truth to "be made manifest" (1 Cor. 11:19). It follows then that "the more Heresies there are, the more *manifest* will the Truth be made," and the Whigs actually promoted the light of truth by "propagat[ing]" as many heresies as they did when they were in power. Second, the Whigs who were part of the late ministry showed how much they loved the church by taking "the Care of it intirely out of the Hands of God"—a "foreign jurisdiction"—and making it "their own *Creature.*" Third, these ministers epitomized charity (the principal Christian virtue) by refusing to shut "*Dissenters*" out of the church. In fact, they were willing to open the church to anyone and everyone, even to the point of razing its walls so no one would be left out. Fourth, the former ministry—"Pillars of the Church"—worked to "ease the Bishops from that grievous Trouble of *laying on Hands*." In doing so, they permitted everyone to exercise that power. This convenience avoided "*unchurching* those" who refused to believe that Anglican bishops had exclusive rights to the practice. Fifth, since truth is even more beautiful when compared with falsehood, the former ministry arranged for books to be printed which denied truths such as the existence of God, the divinity of the second and third Persons of the Trinity, and "the Immortality of the Soul." This fixed religion in everyone's mind and fueled a deep love for the clergy "among the Youth of our Nation." And finally, to make life easier on the clergy, leaders of the late ministry made it so that "*Convocations* should meet as seldom as possible" and never actually conduct any business when they met. This created all sorts of leisure time for the clergymen.

Having outlined ways in which the Whig ministry, in general, promoted the good of the church, the writer now promises to address "several Instances of particular Persons" who epitomized this party's love of that institution. The first individual (the earl of Wharton) was attacked in an earlier *Examiner*—number 17—under the name of *Verres*. This man "felt a pious Impulse" to donate funds to the church, but wondered about the best manner in which to do so. Finally he decided to sneak into the church, mount the altar, and void his bowels on top of it. He was, of course, arrested and fined £1,000, which provided the opportunity he had desired to support the church. Another lover of the church (William Cowper, targeted as "Will Bigamy" in *Examiner* number 17) discovered a way to help clergymen earn even more money from marriage fees. His ingenious "Invention" was to marry one wife and then marry another while the first was still alive. His convincing arguments for the legality of this strategy will, the writer hopes, soon appear in print and allow others to help the clergy in such a thoughtful way.

### Number 23: Thursday, January 11, 1711

No one, regardless of their party affiliation, should have been offended by anything that was written about the army in an earlier *Examiner* paper (number 20). Some have argued that those comments were intended to highlight "certain abuses" by specific individuals associated with the army, and those suspicions are accurate. The writer insists that although he has not taken any of those objections seriously, he intends the present paper as a "Sort of Apology" for his comments in number 20. His intention in that earlier paper was not to impugn the entire army, but only "a few Persons" guilty of the abuses he described. It is important to remember that armies are as corruptible as other groups of men, and in an ideal world it would have been better just to keep silent about the abuses he saw. However, he was compelled to write about the problems he noticed because supporters of the former Whig ministry were taking every opportunity to praise the very men who were most guilty. This was an unforgivable affront to the queen herself and left the writer no choice but to tell the truth about corruption in the military.

Based upon the attacks leveled at him after his comments on the army were published, it is clear that the writer's Whig opponents operate under a double standard: "In *Them* it is humble and loyal" to offer their opinions on the queen, her Parliament and ministry. However, when others (like the author of the *Examiner*) "defend her Majesty and her Choice" to change the ministry, the Whigs call it insolence and cry foul. Nonetheless, recent events affirm that corruption in the military is not as pervasive as some have claimed, and "the Madness of a Few" should not be allowed to stain the honor of the entire army.

It is perfectly understandable that army officers were unhappy with the recent ministry change. While the old ministry supported continuing the war at all costs, the new sought to end it as quickly as possible. Peace is something no soldier—especially a successful one—really wants, and the writer does not blame the army for supporting the former Whig ministry. All that has been said about the "Valour and Experience" of the English troops is undeniably true, and it is not the army's fault that their successes on the battlefield abroad have not resulted in more noticeable benefits at home. However, members of both parties must admit that things are better in England with the new ministry and the peace that has ensued. The queen is insightful and committed to the good of her subjects, and the army has achieved "perpetual success" in Flanders. How can these improvements be explained except by attributing them to the wise decisions made by the queen, herself, and the new ministry?

It is impossible to understand fully why the former ministry did not do more to end the war. The only reasonable explanation is that its constituents knew all along that the queen saw through their schemes, that the clergy, the "Landed Men," and even the general public had turned against them, and that the only way they could maintain their power was to increase their income by perpetuating the war. Had the queen not acted quickly, these malefactors would have "ruined the Constitution." While it was only natural for the army to want to prolong the war, the politicians in the former ministry clearly had ulterior motives for doing so. The writer ends by commenting that he has just received two pamphlets called *The Management of the War*, and he plans to examine them as soon as he has a chance.

### Number 24: Thursday, January 18, 1711

It is human nature to maintain hope, even in the face of insurmountable odds. Men use hope for various purposes, one of which is to convince their enemies that they possess some hidden advantage. This has certainly been the case with the *"Ruined Party"* of the Whigs, who have nurtured all sorts of "pretended Hopes" as their power slipped away. They hoped, for example, that the queen would make no more changes to her ministry after removing the earl of SUNDERLAND, that no one would call for a "Dissolution of the Parliament," that they could ruin England's credit, and that the kingdom would suffer some catastrophe abroad. They even went so far as to hope that the widespread support for the queen's decision was simply a passing madness in the English people—one that would be cured once the populace realized how much it had been "deceived."

The writer promises to outline the causes and symptoms of this madness, and explain how it differs

from their normal habits. Citing Machiavelli, he asserts that a people left on its own will usually act in its own best interests. Even when the citizens are deceived for a time, they will eventually recognize the deception and put things right. Recent events in England are proof of this, since the English suffered from a "long Madness" maintained "by a thousand Artifices." Once the constitution was decimated, however, they came to their senses "and peaceably restored the old Constitution." In truth, the recent wholesale changes in government resulted from the people's *recovery* from an *old* madness—not (as the Whigs argue) from their having fallen prey to a new one. The "County Elections" best measure the disposition of the people, and these showed that the overwhelming majority supported the queen's decisions.

Despite all of this, members of the ousted ministry continue to insist that the new regime "cannot possibly stand." It is important to recognize, however, that the only men who make this claim are those who fear being called to account for their past malfeasance, "those who keep Offices, from which others, better Qualified, were removed," and *"Stock-jobbers,"* who constantly spread such rumors to increase their own profits. It would be better if these individuals would simply be honest about hoping—rather than fearing—that the new ministry will fail.

When the ministry change occurred, many were worried that problems would follow, but the issues that did arise turned out to be fewer and less catastrophic than expected. Fortunately, when the Whigs were dominant the Tories never acted as the ousted Whigs do now. They never allowed resentment to get in the way of promoting the public good. In contrast, the fallen Whigs have become passive and stingy: what would have happened to England if the Tories had adopted the same strategy under the "late Administration?"

### Number 25: Thursday, January 25, 1711

The writer recently heard some malcontents damn "the *Tories* to Hell" for claiming that if the ministry had not been changed, both church and monarchy would have been destroyed. Upon asking what had caused the Tories to say so, he found that the Whigs had asserted—with characteristic lunacy—

that the new ministry was bent on bringing in "*Popery, Arbitrary Power,* and the *Pretender.*" Instead of dwelling on what may have happened if the old ministry had remained, this paper will consider what would happen if the Whigs ever regained power. The "present free Parliament" would certainly be eliminated and replaced with one of a completely different character. At least a dozen votes would then be cast against the actions of the fallen Tory ministry and a bill revived that would once again sell English citizenship for a mere 12 pence.

In a hypothetical "Paper of Votes," the writer provides a broader picture of what a new Whig ministry would seek to accomplish. His conjectures are based on projects that certain individuals have actually undertaken or "projected." Among others, these include repealing the Test Act, opening civil and ecclesiastical offices to Dissenters of all types, putting someone besides the clergy in charge of educating children, forbidding priests from preaching about "Duties in Religion, especially Obedience to Princes," and giving a certain general a lifetime commission with the added convenience of making the war last as long as the general lives (see *Examiner* number 16). These and other measures would be the result of "the *Whigs* Resurrection." England would lose all hope of peace and be plunged into even more debt, bishops would lose their offices, and clergymen would be forced to depend on individuals for their support.

The writer now turns his attention to a "Gentleman" (William Wotton) who had published a "Discourse" against an earlier *Examiner* paper that dealt with "the Convocation" of bishops (number 21). This "gentleman" claims that the *Examiner's* representations are false and its "*Reflections unjust.*" After dismissing each of Wotton's claims, the writer says that he will waste no more time on the subject, since the *Examiner* was never intended to manage controversies that were insignificant in the minds of most readers.

### Number 26: Thursday, February 1, 1711

Writers who advocate lost causes enjoy a number of distinct advantages over those who support tenable ones. Among other luxuries, they can be content simply to "carp and cavil" at writers on the opposite side, they can dismiss or affirm whatever they wish

with no limitations of "Truth or Probability, and they can get away with "a Pretence" of being truthful and disinterested, "for adhering to Friends in Distress." It is not that way at all for writers (like the author of the *Examiner*) who volunteer their services to the current "flourishing Ministry," which is dear to the people and respected by the queen, because they pursue the public good rather than any devious, self-serving schemes. The current ministry does not really need the help of sympathetic writers, and readers on their own side judge them as harshly as those who oppose them. The authors who work in support of the fallen ministry are responsible for uplifting "the sinking spirits of a whole Party." In contrast, all that those who write in support of the current ministry can hope for is to enlighten the ignorant, "and those at a Distance."

Having considered these points, the writer of the *Examiner* admits that he cannot be angry with those who write bitter replies to his papers. He rarely replies to these "answers," but it is not out of anger or "Affectation"—it is simply that once he states his facts and makes his case, he leaves it up to the world to decide the point. He laments the mistake some of these competing writers have made, however, in mistakenly identifying "a most ingenious Person as Author" of the *Examiner*. Out of concern for this gentleman's ease and reputation, the writer strictly assures these "angry People" that the individual they have accused "is *not* the Author."

If the real author has gained anything from all the responses to his paper, it is the hint that he should praise the current ministry in the same way that competing writers have so zealously lauded each member of the fallen one. These "judicious hirelings" (the writers) have praised "the whole Set of discarded Statesman" for possessing the very qualities that everyone—even their greatest devotees—said they lacked while they held public office. It is as though these erstwhile ministers cast their virtues aside upon "Employment," and have now taken them up again. The writer feels that it is his obligation to pay the same homage to the current ministry, whose members are far more deserving of the lavish praises falsely applied to their predecessors. What follows is a person-by-person encomium of the current ministry, in which the writer tempers his praise by admitting that each of the current ministers possesses undeniable flaws. These supposed shortcomings, however, are all part of an effort to point out remarkable differences between the old and new ministries: for example, the new *"Lord Keeper"* is well known and eloquent, but "it must be granted" that unlike his predecessor he knows nothing of polygamy, he is not a *"Free-thinker* in Religion," and he has never supported any *"Atheistical Book."*

### Number 27: Thursday, February 8, 1711

Avarice is undoubtedly the vice that humans take to the greatest extremes. When public officials engage in it, however, it is especially costly to everyone involved. In those cases, it initiates a chain reaction in which (for example) one incident of fraud leads to a series of others and the financial losses go far beyond the initial victim. The public ends up as the biggest loser in almost every case.

According to moralists, there are two general types of avarice. One involves wanting more wealth even though one is already well-supplied; the other is characterized by an "endless Desire of Hoarding." The first type is the "more dangerous in a State, because it mingles well with Ambition." When government officials such as prime ministers or generals indulge in this type of avarice, it can gravely impact the well-being of the public, and it is vital for someone to tell them truthfully what the world thinks of them and their greed. Constantly surrounding by admirers, these leaders are often more blind than an average citizen to their own shortcomings. The writer imagines that if he had lived in Rome at the time of the First Triumvirate (60 B.C.), he might have written anonymous letters to each of its members—Julius Caesar, Pompey, and Marcus Crassus—explaining what he saw as their most grievous vice and the dangers it posed for the state. He includes a letter to Crassus intended to help that very wealthy statesman recognize the extent of his remarkable greed.

The letter begins by praising Crassus for his grace and understanding, but quickly proceeds to tell him that he is not loved by any segment of the public (including his own army). The reason is that Crassus is "deeply stained with that odious and ignoble Vice of Covetousness." The writer explains that his goal is to convince Crassus that he is guilty, and that it will be up to the Roman to find and apply his own remedy. If there is any doubt about the truth of this accusation, the writer claims, all Crassus needs to do is disguise himself and go out among the common people. If—while in disguise—he initiates conversations with them and, for that matter, his peers, he will immediately find that everyone unanimously curses and censures him for his covetousness. When his enemies reflect upon Crassus's military victories, they attribute that success to the soldiers he commands rather than to him because even they recognize how much of a distraction his avarice has become. The good news, however, is that as soon as Crassus recognizes and turns away from this vice, he "will be a truly Great Man" (but still not a god, the writer adds).

### Number 28: Thursday, February 15, 1711

In this paper, the writer responds to a letter sent to the *Examiner* six months earlier. It would have been better to have delivered the letter privately, especially since it demands an inordinate amount of work from the writer. The letter calls upon the *Examiner* to bring together *"some of those Indignities"* that the queen suffered in 1710. The writer has already compiled a number of these and planned to publish them all together in a large book or present them individually throughout future papers. He is concerned, however, that they will give the world a negative impression of England.

Despite this risk, the writer has decided to select a few *"choice Instances"* of these indignities and include them in upcoming issues of the *Examiner.* He will also draw upon an alphabetized file of all sorts of corruption and mismanagement on the part of the former ministry. It should really be no surprise that he has furnished himself so well, considering how many *"starved* Writers" he supports each week by giving them something to carp against in each of his papers. Regretfully, he has caused an epidemic of dullness and often wonders how so many competitors can pore over the *Examiner* each week, write against it, and yet make "so little Improvement."

He also wonders about the goals of these competing writers, but has decided that their primary objective must be to promote a better opinion of the fallen ministry or simply to prove him wrong. They seek to provoke him into engaging in an ongoing game of "Rejoinder and Reply," which would altogether eliminate his credibility. He had intended in this paper to examine Francis HARE's *Management of War* and *The Treaty of Peace*, and he could easily have shown the utter inaccuracy of both. He has decided, however, to take them up in a separate "discourse" rather than violate his rule of avoiding controversy in the *Examiner*.

Despite this goal, the writer finds himself in quite a dilemma, and would appreciate the letter-writer's advice on how to handle it. The problem is that while Whigs complain against the *Examiner* for being too harsh, the Tories rail against it for being too moderate. To illustrate, the writer includes "two peculiar Letters" he recently received. The first is from an angry Whig, who warns the writer that members of the fallen ministry still have many friends who will see his throat cut if he does not stop writing immediately. The Whigs' patience, he adds, "is now at an End," and having already lost their "Employments," they do not need him to turn the entire nation against their party. The second letter is from a disgruntled Tory, who claims to be dissatisfied with the *Examiner* because it obviously stops short of presenting all the author knows about the abuses and corruption of the "knaves" who made up the former ministry: "In short, turn the whole Mystery of Iniquity inside out, that every Body may have a View of it." He adds that the writer has simply been "too favourable" toward the Whigs.

Having carefully considered each of these letters and the extremes they represent, the writer has decided to proceed as he has in the past. He will continue to seek a happy medium between the two, even though he knows his paper would be more controversial—and therefore more popular—if he adopted one extreme or the other. He is also convinced that the Whigs' outcry of concern for the "late Ministry" and its reputation is a ruse designed to prevent those "Purloiners of the Publick cause" from being called forth and held accountable for their malfeasance.

### Number 29: Thursday, February 22, 1711

The writer's only goal in producing the *Examiner* has always been to do good. He never suffered personally at the hands of the former ministry; it was simply that their politics ultimately contradicted England's constitution in ways that were impossible to ignore and reflected an utter disdain for religion. They were "justly suspected" of having anything but good intentions toward the kingdom, including its government and religion. A state faces grave danger when power-hungry politicians have to exercise their hatred for the constitution and the church in order to retain their power. They become far less selective in the individuals and standards they will allow into their party, and eventually embrace "some Principles from every Party" that is at all unhappy with the "Faith and Settlement" of the status quo.

Despite the mountains of evidence provided in the *Examiner*, some Whigs still contend that their leaders never had any designs against the constitution and that they would not have destroyed it had they remained in charge. The writer apologizes for having discovered their hidden agenda, but asks why anyone would have thought it was a secret based on the former ministry's obvious attempts to do just that. It may be that the ousted ministers and their supporters are denying the charge now in order to perpetuate the question of why "*the old Ministry*" was changed. In case this is their plan, the writer decides to answer this question with one irrefutable reason. Monarchs have always been blamed for the actions of the "minions" they empower, but England has had to suffer from the "avarice and insolence" of politicians who worked without the approval of the queen. Instead of earning her favor, they "snatch[ed] their own Dues" and treated her with disrespect—creating problems and then presenting them "as Arguments to keep themselves in Power." Considering how these disloyal courtiers joined in league against her, it is remarkable that the queen ever found the courage to dismiss them.

Initially, the queen surrounded herself with statesmen who supported the "old Constitution" wholeheartedly. Eventually, however, they became greedy and fostered divisions among her subjects.

The primary reason the queen had to make such drastic changes to her ministry was the "Insolence and Avarice" of these traitorous individuals. They made a "monstrous Alliance" with radical Whigs, who "profess Principles destructive" to England's "Religion and Government, and they left her no choice but to abdicate her own power or remove them from their offices. If this is not a sufficient explanation, doubters should simply "make an Abstract" of all the corruption detailed in other issues of the *Examiner*.

The writer recently heard patrons of a coffee-house complaining about his letter to Crassus (in number 27), since it seemed to be directed toward a well-known individual who was still in office. It is difficult, he asserts, to understand why he should be censured for such a mild "reproof," since he simply intended to help that individual recognize (and cure) his avaricious behavior. No one should have ever expected him to reserve criticism for only those politicians who were no longer in power. Certain vices are often "more or less pernicious" depending on who exhibits them, and avarice is especially dangerous in a general. Crassus, himself, was the best evidence of this truth, since his greed alone caused his own downfall and that of his army.

### Number 30: Thursday, March 1, 1711

The most unified societies are those collectively engaged in some evil endeavor and those "who labour under one common Misfortune." The reason these groups are so cohesive is that their members share a common goal. They are moved by a single spirit, and their individual interests do not impinge on those of their fellows. For a long time the Whigs fit the first criterion since "they have always been engaged in an *evil Design*." Now that their leaders have been stripped of their offices, their unanimity is even greater than before.

Members of ruling parties, on the other hand, are not so united. Even when they are devoted to promoting the public good, too often there are disagreements among individuals about how that goal can be reached. Envy and impatience can come into play as the party flourishes, while certain individuals feel undervalued and disappointed by their party. "*Retrospections*" begin, dredging up "past Mis-

carriages," and the divisions that result are nurtured at every opportunity by members of the ousted party. They, of course, seek to divide and conquer the ruling faction by any means possible. Because of these tendencies, the writer says he regards it as his duty to "*warn* the Friends" and "expose the Enemies, of the Publick Weal," and to preach the virtues of unity every chance he gets.

There are two main causes of discontent among members of a ruling party. The first is an incredible urge to punish "the Corruptions of former Managers," while the second is an equally strong desire to "reward *Merit*" to everyone who had a hand in ousting the old party and bringing in the new. The writer promises to limit his present discussion to the latter. Merit, he explains, is the worth each man assigns to his own "Deservings from the Publick." There are so many false presumptions of merit, however, that the ancients might have produced an "agreeable Fiction" on the subject, complete with allegorical personifications of real merit, an unruly impostor, and others.

The writer decides to include an example of what this allegory may have looked like had the ancients written it. Entitled *A Poetical Genealogy and Description of Merit*, it indicates that Virtue and Honor had a son named Merit. There was also "a spurious child" born to Vanity and Impudence. This son was notoriously loud and obnoxious, while Merit spoke only in whispers (and "in Assemblies"). False Merit—"the Bastard Issue"—took every opportunity to stand in front of True Merit in public, and he was constantly speaking to courtiers and ministers of all kinds. False Merit's appetite, moreover, was insatiable: "the more you fed him, the more hungry and importunate he grew." People often confused him with the genuine Merit, and although he was born deformed, False Merit had "by Force of Art" gained a more desirable appearance. Only the wise were able to recognize him for the impostor he was.

Having ended his allegory, the writer assures his readers that they (and all their countrymen) are especially adept at distinguishing true merit from false, and that no monarch has ever had a ministry as skilled as the present one at making this distinction. This reflects well upon the queen, since she freely chose the members of this ministry instead of having them forced upon her. Nonetheless, an "*unruly Faction*" continues to peddle contrived scandals in the press, and if one reads the papers it looks as though the Whigs are still in charge. The queen herself has even become a favorite target of libel.

In closing, the writer explains that he recently received a letter about a Mr. Greenshields—an Episcopal clergyman in Scotland—who had been charged with "reading Divine Service, after the Manner of the Church of *England*." The *Examiner* author claims to be entirely ignorant of the matter, and calls upon the writer of the letter to pen a discourse devoted entirely to Greenshields's case. In the discourse, he should let the public know whether or not "the Episcopal Assemblies are freely allowed in *Scotland*," especially since so many of their clergymen have "fled from thence." In any case, it is remarkable that the "*Whigs* and *Fanaticks*" in England are so focused on the "Sacred Act of Toleration" when their comrades nearby are so intolerant.

### Number 31: *Thursday, March 8, 1711*

Last week someone sent the writer a passage from Plato's work along "with some Hints how to apply it" in an *Examiner* paper. The passage details a fable (by Aristophanes) on how humans originally had four arms and four legs until Jupiter—upset with the entire population—split them in halves. This was how love originated, since the cleft halves spent the rest of their lives looking for each other. Jupiter further threatened to split them once more, and the person who sent the passage claims that this has now happened: while the first separation created love, the second has created hatred by "prompting us to fly from our *other Side*, and dividing the same *Body* [politic, in this case] into two" parties.

The writer approves of the application with one adjustment. Parties, he claims, not only divide the nation, but each person within it—"leaving each but half" of their virtues and perspective. Members of a party can see only goodness in their group, only evil in the other. Party loyalties also cause each "brood of followers" to do foolish things in order to display their party loyalty: "*Whig* Ladies put on

their Patches in a different Manner from the *Tories*," and so forth.

With his "Metaphorical Genealogy" of Merit still in mind (see number 30), the writer has decided to provide a similar account of "*Faction*" in this paper. She was the youngest daughter of Liberty and at her birth, Juno (acting as midwife) "distorted" Faction at birth out of envy for Liberty. Like many parents who love their youngest and "disagreeablest" children best, Liberty doted on Faction to a fault. As Faction grew, she became such a virago that Jupiter ordered her to leave Heaven. Liberty gathered up all of her other children and moved to Earth, where the entire family was first thrown out of Greece because of Faction's evil deeds, then from Italy, and traveled all over Europe with the Goths. They eventually found themselves with nowhere to call home. Faction's "*great Employment*" was to "*breed Discord*" wherever she could (especially among families and friends), and at the same time to create "*monstrous Alliances*" between persons who had the least in common.

The writer notes that based on his understanding of faction, the name fits "those who set themselves up against the true Interest and Constitution of their Country." Members of the former ministry should keep this in mind, or at least explain why they continue to refer to the current ministry as a "faction." Listing the characteristics of a faction may help to clear up their confusion. Unlike the queen's present ministry, a faction has leaders who are usually upstarts or men of ruined fortunes. These leaders associate with "those who dislike the old Establishment," and the leaders themselves are full of new schemes in both government and religion. They have an "incurable Hatred against the old nobility," and (among other traits) their main objective is to amass "immense Riches at the Publick Expence." When one considers what a faction really is, the writer adds, it is easy to determine which party most deserves to be called one. The current ministry simply does not fit the definition. The Whigs are known for their tendency to "appeal to the People," but in actuality they do that only when they have confused and misled the people beforehand. In this case, the public should be allowed to decide which party is the true faction.

*Number 32: Thursday, March 15, 1711*
The writer explains that he has been distracted "from the general Subject" of his paper by news that Robert Harley had recently been stabbed by Antoine de GUISCARD (a "*French Papist*") on March 8. The assault took place while Guiscard was "under Examination for High Treason," being questioned by Harley, Henry Bolingbroke, and others. Although similar incidents have happened throughout history—Caesar's murder, for example, comes to mind—this occurrence is unique based on the aggravating circumstances surrounding it. Everyone knows that for centuries the French have been "too liberal of their Daggers upon the Persons of their greatest Men," but it is remarkable that a people best known for their "Vanity and Impertinence" would commit the sort of "Villainies" one would typically expect from Spaniards and Italians. Guiscard, himself, is just the type of criminal to engage in such a heinous act. He was guilty of "several Enormities in *France*," particularly evil, and his "*Ill Look*" manifests the brooding, melancholy character he possesses.

If this stabbing had happened while the former Whig ministry was still in power, they would have ascribed it immediately to the group they call the 'faction' (the Tories), claimed it smacked of "*High-Church Principles*," and indicted the entire clergy for orchestrating the entire thing. The current ministry, however, has avoided blaming the Whigs for Guiscard's efforts, even though it would be entirely "plausible" to do so. Nonetheless, it is impossible to miss how much the Whigs have in common with the "French Papists" in terms of wanting to end Harley's life. The former ministry sought to take it away through "Subornation" rather than through violence, but the goal was the same.

As far as the details of the assault go, Guiscard confessed in prison that his original target was Bolingbroke. When, however, Bolingbroke exchanged seats with Harley, Guiscard decided that rather than abort the attempt altogether it would be better to assault the man Bolingbroke most esteemed. For his part, Harley displayed remarkable poise after the stabbing. There was no change in his expression or in his speech, and he calmly asked the surgeon whether or not the wound looked to be mortal (since, if it did, he needed to attend to some business before he died). The writer claims that he is at a loss to understand why the "*High-flying Whigs*" have joined the "Friends of *France*" in seeking to destroy so great a man. In closing, the writer congratulates England on not having produced the "Savage Monster" Guiscard. He also suspects that the evil Frenchman had been scheming to assassinate the queen, herself, at the earliest opportunity.

*Number 33: Thursday, March 22, 1711*
Each apologia written by the early Church Fathers reflects its author's habits of defending truth, exposing falsehood, and accusing adversaries of nothing more than what could be proved. In recent times, however, these noble examples have not been closely followed. Ever since the Reformation, for example, the "*Papists*" have endeavored to cover up the "Absurdities" of their faith and to heap all sorts of accusations upon the reformers. It is no different in politics, since the Whigs have portrayed the Tories in distorted ways that stereotype them and promote Whig prejudices. In reality, there are no significant differences between modern-day Tories and the group known as "*Old Whigs*." The modern Whig party, however, is composed of such "a very odd Mixture of Mankind" that only the most radical individuals are consistent with its principles. This change occurred when the Whigs (in an effort to boost their numbers) began accepting "every Heterodox Professor either in Religion or Government." Once this happened, it did not take long for the party to completely lose touch with the majority of landowners, whose beliefs were more in line with traditional thinking. Throughout the party's transformation, the Whigs themselves pretended to support the church and the monarchy even as they did all they could to erode both. At the same time, they painted an exaggerated, negative picture of the Tories to prevent people from joining that party.

The charge against the Tories that has proved most useful for the Whigs involves passive obedience. Their distorted view of this principle has been widely accepted, and yet it is the most insupportable of their positions. When a Whig asks whether or not you support passive obedience, an affirmative answer will lead him to accuse you of being "a *Jacobite*, a *Friend* of *France* and the *Pretender*." Because the Whigs have presented such an inaccurate perspective on passive obedience, the public needs someone to explain its true characteristics. To do so, the writer will first present the false version espoused by the Whigs and then explain true passive obedience as the Tories understand it.

In the Whigs' view, passive obedience means believing that the king is answerable only to God. No matter what he does—even if it is against the law—the public has no right to question or resist him, since doing so "would be to resist God in the person of his Vicegerent." One day God will hold the monarch accountable, but the subjects themselves can do nothing more than submit and obey. As "a thousand Papers and Pamphlets" illustrate, this is how the Whigs have described passive obedience. They have continually accused the Tories of supporting this ridiculous version of it, and especially those members of the queen's current ministry. They have also charged the clergy with preaching in favor of this brand of passive obedience.

Passive obedience as it is "professed and practised" by the Tories is quite different from what the Whigs have claimed. The Tories believe that every government possesses "a supream, absolute, unlimited Power," but they do not believe that a monarch should be obeyed when his commands run "directly contrary" to the laws of the kingdom. The crown is as liable to lawsuits as any private citizen, and a monarch's ministers can be prosecuted and impeached "although his own Person be Sacred." If a case should arise in which a king uses his power to support the "insolence" of corrupt ministers, citizens can justifiably "assert their own Rights" without violating "the Person or lawful Power of the Prince." In contrast to the caricature the Whigs have consistently peddled, this is how the vast majority of Tories view passive obedience.

Like all the "calumnies" hurled by the Whigs, this one is easily "wiped off." The Tories' objections against the Whigs have far more substance, and are "built upon their constant Practice for many Years." The writer himself has published numerous "instances" to back these objections, but the Whigs have failed to produce even one meaningful answer in the midst of all their carping. In last week's *Examiner* (number 32), the writer handled his subject so innocuously that he assumed he would escape their "merciless pens," but finds himself accused of "two Lies, and a Blunder" in his commentary on Guiscard's stabbing of Robert Harley. As usual, his opponents have focused their attention on minor details instead of responding to the serious charges he has leveled against them.

### Number 34: Thursday, March 29, 1711

Having grown weary of his job as *Examiner*, the writer hopes the current ministry will grant him some honors and a pension. He is concerned that continuing to write the paper may one day "sowr" his temper. Some of what he has written about members of the former ministry has been called satire by "unthinking" readers, and this may be true as long as that faction is down. However, if they ever regain power, the writer says he expects to be recognized as a "*Favourite*" while those "pretended Advocates of theirs, will be Pilloried for *Libellers*." The reason is that he has never charged that "Party, or its Leaders" with anything they would not immediately acknowledge and take pride in as soon as they recovered their positions.

For example, he has accused them of having been "Insolent to the QUEEN" and "against a Peace"—traits for which they have valued themselves all along. He also charged them with having plunged the nation into debt and "engrossed much of its Money." They have now gone even farther, and used up *all* of the kingdom's money and its credit, as well. He has written that they intended to bring about "great Alterations in Religion and Government," and if they obliterate both institutions "at their next Coming," he should receive honors for having foretold what would happen. He also claimed that they once had aspirations of taking Robert Harley's life. If they were currently in power, they would certainly cut off Harley's head and thank the *Examiner* for having justified "the Sincerity of their Intentions." Based on how much he has obviously helped their party, the writer intends to put in for an esteemed position as soon as the Whigs are restored.

All of this is perpetually confirmed by those who write in response to the *Examiner*. They constantly accuse the writer of unwittingly betraying his own party and of writing with more bitterness "against those who hire" him than against the Whigs. The writer once thought that he was praising the Tories for their treatment of the queen, their devotion to the constitution and the church, and other noble attributes. Whig readers, however, regard all of this as satire because it goes against everything they believe characterizes a good ministry—it seems that the writer has been mistaken all along. From now on, then, he will write far more satire beginning with the remainder of this present paper.

Of all the advantages the kingdom has enjoyed since the great ministry change, the most notable has been the convening of the present Parliament and the "Dissolution of the last." The men currently serving in that body do so with honor and integrity, and keep the nation's best interests in mind with every decision. The House of Commons is especially noble, as evidenced by their "Bill of *Qualification*," which stipulates that only landowners may serve in future Parliaments. The writer proposes a list "in some following Papers" of all the good this Parliament has already achieved. For the moment, he will mention "two Particulars" to illustrate "the Temper of the present Parliament." The first instance occurred after Antoine de Guiscard's "inhuman" attempt to murder Harley. Parliament passed an address to the queen condemning the act, praising Harley, and blaming his "misfortunes" on his remarkable "Zeal for her Majesty's service." The second action that clearly displayed Parliament's admirable character followed the death of the eldest son of William BROMLEY (Speaker of the House of Commons). The "Assembly" adjourned for a week so that Bromley would have time to grieve. In closing, the writer asks a favor of his readers: When they read papers written against the *Examiner*, they should not rely on the "mangled Quotation[s]" of the writer's words found in those papers. Instead, they should return to the original and read the entire paragraph in which the quoted passage appeared. If readers will do that, they will find "a sufficient Answer" to every objection these hostile writers make. The writer himself has read more than 50 of these competing papers and has yet to find one that quotes him accurately.

### Number 35: Thursday, April 5, 1711

Having considered England's constitution, religion, and the demeanor of her people, the writer is contemplating whether the Whigs or the Tories will provide the "most security" for the queen and her government. If it were simply a matter of parties, it would certainly be best for the queen to avoid putting herself "at the Head of either." In this case, however, the Whigs cannot rightly be called a party because their constituency is so "heterogeneous," united only by a common goal of robbing and ruining the people. The Whigs are also characterized by their lack of "Veneration for *crowned Heads*," by their opinion that the royal prerogative needs to be more strictly limited, and their preference for "a Commonwealth before a Monarchy." They also believe that no distinctions should be made among Protestants (which they take to describe everyone except Roman Catholics), and that a national religion is unnecessary. When individuals with these opinions are in power, they never treat monarchs with appropriate respect. Even worse, their "own Want of Duty to their Sovereign" leads them to crave power and to demand unreasonable submission from their peers. In some cases, nonetheless, there are circumstances that would lead a monarch "to deliver himself over" to a party like the Whigs.

The Tories are characterized by a completely different platform. They believe in "a well-regulated Monarchy," and they view anything that compromises that form of government as dangerous and deadly to the entire nation. In terms of their views on religion, it is simplest to say that they take "just the Reverse" of the position held by the Whigs. Another trait of the Tories explains why many monarchs in the past have elected not to employ them as public officials. When Whigs gain a little power, they immediately "grow into good Humour and good Language towards the Crown." They declare unending loyalty and praise the monarch at every turn. In contrast, the Tories ("in or out of Favour") never alter their loyalties to the current prince. Their behavior remains consistent no matter what. The writer encourages his readers to consider the distinctions he has drawn and to decide for themselves which party "a wise Prince" should look to for support and safety. Answering this question will also help readers to decide whether or not the queen was "rash" in her decision to make wholesale changes in her ministry—a choice that has been praised so highly by some and condemned so heartily by others.

### Number 36: April 12, 1711

This paper is written "for the sake of Dissenters," who (from the writer's perspective) are the fastest-growing group of Whigs who still profess to be Christians. He knows that everyone will understand that by "Dissenters," the writer means Presbyterians, and he provides a brief history of their rebellion against unsympathetic monarchs. Under JAMES II, the Presbyterians joined forces with the papists—supposedly their sworn enemies—in rebelling against the Crown. After the Glorious Revolution, the Dissenters found themselves "rewarded with an Indulgence by Law," and were treated favorably. However, once they "found all was desperate with their Protector King James," they joined the newly formed Whig party which had set itself against "old Principles in Church and State."

The Presbyterians should carefully consider how different things are now than they were seven decades ago, when they first "begain their Designs against the Church and Monarchy." Back then, they were the largest part of the Whigs, and anyone who joined the party with ulterior motives was "forced to shelter under their Denomination." Now, however, the party is controlled by those who wish to level all religion or do away with it altogether. The Presbyterians would be foolish to assume that if the Whigs ever succeeded in destroying the Church of England, they would look to the Dissenters to rebuild it anew. As things currently stand, the best course for the Presbyterians would be to ally themselves with the Anglican Church.

They should also exercise some decency and distance themselves from the present-day Whigs, who are so blatantly opposed to England's Christian monarchy. While the Presbyterians fault the Church of England for having failed to divorce itself from "Popery," they have joined with "Papists and a Popish Prince to destroy her." And while they rail against the "wicked Lives" of certain Anglicans, they continue to scheme "with *Libertines* and *Atheists*" to ruin the state church. In short, the Dissenters have lost their status as leaders of the Whig party, and should immediately work toward securing a better relationship with the Crown and the state church.

There are three steps the Presbyterians should take to achieve this goal. First, they should take care not to provoke the vast majority that now stands against them. They should end their relationships with their radical allies, "disperse themselves, and lie dormant" until circumstances change. Second, although there are no laws (except God's) against occasional conformity, they should use it with the utmost care. Exercising it too frequently might lead the Crown to take some action against them. Finally, they should drop their act of being "under horrible Apprehensions" that the Tories are conniving to bring in the Pretender (James Francis Edward STUART). This pretension, learned from the Whig leaders, is based on the ridiculous notion that the Whigs are all that protect England from "*Popery* and *Arbitrary Power.*" The writer ends by asking that those who send him ideas for *Examiner* topics would think more carefully about what they suggest.

### Number 37: Thursday, April 19, 1711

The writer observes that the Whigs have recently begun to change their language. They are saying that if the new Tory ministry continues as it has, they will have nothing left to complain about. This shows that the suspicions of those who supported the ousted Whigs were completely unfounded. Nonetheless, a number of the Tories' "Adversaries" continue to complain about the same old things. They allege, for example, that the queen was unwise to change her ministry during a time of war. This charge, like all the others, is patently false. It is impossible that an act of "Rashness or Chance" could have yielded all the "Harmony and Order" the kingdom has enjoyed since the ministry was changed. It was obvious to everyone but the Whigs that the queen had to do something: With the Whigs in charge, she had lost the power to nominate anyone for office on her own. The oligarchy (which had exercised more power than it rightfully should have) took offense when she reclaimed that power and appointed individuals without consulting them. The writer insists that anyone who knows anything about politics must admit that a "Prince" who had been treated as badly as the queen has no choice but to "extricate himself as soon as possible."

The Whigs lay all the blame for their fall on the "haughty Pride, and unsatiable Covetousness" of the duchess of MARLBOROUGH, but the fact is that in changing her ministry the queen simply acted in a way that reflected the will of the people. The war was costing more than the kingdom could afford, and only the Whigs would blame her for instituting a more qualified ministry to help get England out of a conflict it could no longer sustain. In any case, both parties should judge the wisdom of any decision by its outcome, and clearly the crown's authority (which the Whigs had "scandalously Clipped and Mangled") has been effectively restored.

Another complaint the Whigs continue to make is that they are treated too harshly in publications such as the *Examiner*. It is bad enough, they claim, to have lost their political power: it is unfair and unnecessary to have their "Infirmities" displayed "in order to render them yet more odious to Mankind." This is a remarkable charge, since only in England could the Whigs get away with the all the libelous material they have published about the Tories. When the tables were turned (before the change of ministry), the Tories never stooped to the level of impertinence that characterizes the Whigs' publications. Oddly, the most vocal Whigs are out of step with the majority of their party who, "in disputing with [Tories], do generally give up several of the late Ministry; and freely own many of their Failings"—especially in terms of the massive debts they incurred, their insolence, and avarice.

### Number 38: Thursday, April 26, 1711

The writer marvels at how much the "Dexterity of Mankind in Evil" surpasses the efforts of honest individuals and the laws of the kingdom. Those whose occupations involve the constant retail of fraud (such as attorneys) are especially ingenious in their efforts to circumvent the legal system. One reason that the laws cannot rein in such individuals may be that the aggressor in any situation always has an advantage over the defender. Another possi-

ble explanation is that men are rarely "rewarded by the Publick" for doing good, while successful fraud yields immediate benefits. When laws are made to curb the practices of dishonest citizens, there are always those who devise new and ingenious ways to continue doing what the law is supposed to prevent. They manage to still "reap the Advantage" of the fraud while narrowly avoiding the shame and danger that might accompany it.

This, the writer finds, is particularly true of "that dextrous Race of Men, sprung up soon after the Revolution." There is no way the writer can enumerate all the means these "curious Men" have discovered "to enrich themselves, by defrauding the Publick, in defiance of the Law." Their continued success illustrates the great defects in the laws of the kingdom—defects that are the result of "our best Possession, Liberty." The legal system is generally too lenient in its treatment of criminals, and an examination of numerous cases shows that "it is no wonder that the Injuries done to the Publick are so seldom addressed."

Politicians (like those in the "late Ministry") often break the laws in order to protect the power they possess, and to provide for their own safety in case that power is lost. The now-fallen Whig ministers did this through "two admirable Expedients." First they procured "a general Act of Indemnity, which cuts off all Impeachments," and then they found ways to make it look as though their self-serving decisions reflected the will of the public at large. A shining example of the second tactic was the Whigs' address to the queen (about three years ago) asserting that she should not "consent to a Peace" and end the war unless it involved making "entire Restitution" to Spain. It was obvious to everyone in England and abroad that this was simply an attempt to "pin down the War upon" the Tories, to increase the Whigs' own "Power and Wealth," and to "multiply Difficulties on the QUEEN and Kingdom."

All of this makes it clear that under the kingdom's current laws, "ill-designing Men" will continue to commit blatant crimes and yet escape any punishment from the legal system. It is simply incorrect to argue, then, that men are innocent "because the Law hath not pronounced them Guilty." Satire, the writer suspects, was invented to help deal with this problem, since shame is the only likely means of stopping evildoers from doing what the laws cannot prevent. If there were any indications that Whig leaders felt any remorse for what they had done, the writer insists that he would gladly change his style and overlook "their Million of Enormities." Each day, however, they seem increasingly "fond of discovering their impotent Zeal and Malice," so he will continue in the *Examiner* to treat them as they deserve to be treated: as "Enemies to our Country and its Constitution."

### Number 39: Thursday, May 3, 1711

For years, the Whigs and Tories have attacked one another based on a number of fairly consistent "Topicks of Reproach." The Tories, for example, allege that the Whigs seek to destroy the Established Church and the monarchy. The Whigs' charges against the Tories "may be summed up" with "three formidable Worlds, *Popery, Arbitrary Power,* and the *Pretender.*" A primary difference between the two groups, however, is that the Tories actually provide proof to support their charges against the Whigs. As far as the writer can tell, the Whigs have not bothered to find any real evidence to back their accusations.

Since the Whigs perpetually allude to popery, arbitrary power, and the Pretender (James Francis Edward Stuart) in their tirades against the Tories, the writer has "been considering" how well those terms might be employed against the Whigs themselves. As for popery, the Whigs have done far more than the Tories to pave the way for it in England. The Roman Catholic Church has supposedly worked to divide the English into as many factions as possible, and the Whigs have certainly helped in that effort. Their cry has long been that "no Man, for the Sake of a few *Notions* and *Ceremonies*" ought to lose the right to hold office.

Another constant accusation the Whigs level against the Tories is that they encourage and promote arbitrary power for England's monarchs. What they really mean, the writer argues, is "*Passive-Obedience* and *Non-Resistance*"—neither of which is equal to arbitrary power. In defending passive obedience, the writer notes that his writings represent nothing more than his own opinions. He does not

claim to be the mouthpiece of any party. Since the Tories (unlike the Whigs) have no "dark Designs" to advance, they do not need any hired scribes to promote "*Heterodox Opinions.*" The Whigs and the Dissenters are "exactly of the same political Faith," and both factions have done their part to promote the arbitrary power against which the Whigs clamor.

The Whigs have also insisted that the Tories are covertly working to bring in the Pretender. They have even argued that the queen herself is part of the scheme. Each time this charge comes up, the Whigs make it in a general way without ever pointing to any specific instances as evidence. In truth, if the Pretender ever does gain power in England, he will immediately find that "the Whigs are his Men." To this day, those who owe the most "Gratitude to King James" are also "the most zealous Whigs." Lately, the Whigs have even claimed that the Pretender is not an "impostor," but an actual prince "born of the late QUEEN'S [Mary II's] Body." It is very probable, in fact, that the Pretender's greatest hope lies "in the Friendship he expects from the *Dissenters* and *Whigs.*" He chose to invade when the Whigs were dominant, and based on the "gracious Treatment they received from his supposed Father," it is easy to understand why he was counting on them. After all, the Whigs possess a "natural Faculty" of attracting and supporting pretenders ("to Wit, Honour, Nobility, [and] Politicks"), so it is no surprise that they would seek to put a *Pretender* on the throne.

### Number 40: Thursday, May 10, 1711

On a recent visit to a coffeehouse, the writer perused a paper (*The Congratulatory Speech of William Bromley . . . to the Right Honourable Robert Harley*) and found it remarkably similar to the *Examiner*. Among other "propositions," the author asserts that even Harley's enemies recognize his greatness—as evidenced by their constant "*Endeavours against his Person and Reputation.*" This statement clearly refers to something more than Guiscard's attempt to assassinate Harley, and it is probably intended to recall "the business" of William GREGG. It has given the writer great pleasure to see so many of his charges against the Whigs confirmed by certain resolutions of Parliament. The Whigs' mismanagement, for example, caused the military defeats at *"Almanza"* and *"Toulon,"* and they "grievously" defrauded the public in various ways. Lately, however, the public seems more interested in rewarding those who saved the constitution than in punishing the Whigs who flouted it. There are two individuals, in particular, who have been "singled out, as designed very soon to receive the choicest Marks of the Royal Favour."

These circumstances have led the writer to consider the late ministry's many "Heresies in Politicks." The worst of all (and the most dangerous to England's monarchy) was their "Contempt for *Birth, Family,* and *ancient Nobility.*" While it is certainly possible to exaggerate the impact of one's lineage on character, no one can seriously deny that there is no relationship between the two. Those who are born into "what we call the better Families" simply enjoy more of the opportunities and benefits that help create great leaders. Some noble families have been known to neglect the education of their sons, but this is mainly due "to that *Whiggish* Practice of reviling the *Universities*" for supposedly "instilling *Pedantry,* narrow *Principles,* and *High-Church Doctrines.*" Thankfully, he adds, the two patriots mentioned earlier exemplify what happens when merit and virtue are combined "with ancient and honourable Birth." He is sad to recall that another shining "ornament" to true nobility (the earl of ROCHESTER) has recently died. This "late *Lord President*" distinguished himself in many ways as a public servant of the utmost character.

### Number 41: Thursday, May 17, 1711

The writer insists that he is not partial, nor has he been hired to defend the present ministry against those who write against it. When he undertook the *Examiner,* he resolved to publicize "gross Neglect, Abuse or Corruption in the publick Management" whenever he saw it. He has closely scrutinized the actions of the current ministry, and the truth is that its members have simply done nothing worthy of censure.

There is one "small Occasion of Quarrelling," however, that he has discovered. That is the ministry's failure to put a stop to the "flaming Licentiousness of several Weekly Papers" that miss no

opportunity to publish "Scurrilities against" the queen's closest officials. Specifically, he has the *Medley* in mind. The writer has simply ignored all the groundless rants that paper contains against him, but finds himself especially troubled by the *Medley* dated May 7 because it contains "two Paragraphs relating to the *Speaker* of the House of Commons, and to Mr. *Harley,*" and the writer regards it as his duty to comment on these statements. The affair began when the House of Commons resolved that the Speaker should congratulate Harley officially on his "Escape and Recovery" from Guiscard, who had attempted to murder him on March 8 (see *Examiner* number 32). After the congratulatory speech was published, the author of the *Medley* argued in print that the commendation *"was ill-chosen Flattery"* since Harley had caused *"great Difficulties"* for the nation. The *Medley's* author further alleged that the speech was an exercise in hypocrisy since the Speaker *"is known to bear ill Will to Mr. Harley."*

The writer of the *Examiner* asks the Whigs themselves whether public officials in England have ever been treated with such blatant and public disrespect. Even worse, this is not some "clandestine Libel," but one that has been "openly Printed and Sold" with the printer's name clearly indicated. The laws are "very defective" in allowing this sort of defamation to go unpunished. If the current ministry will "endure such open Calumny, without calling the Author to Account," they almost deserve it. The ministry's habit of ignoring "little Things" like this will not always have "little Consequences."

When his paper was first established, the writer intended "to *examine*" some of those publications that reflected the authors' evil tendencies toward "Religion or Government." He was soon distracted by more pressing issues, such as explaining why the Whig ministry needed to be replaced in order to save the "Constitution in Church and State." If he continues to write the *Examiner,* he intends to spend more time "exposing and overturning" the arguments of those who write in favor of the Whigs, without concerning himself with the insults they hurl at him. There is clearly a need for this sort of paper on the Tory side since Abel BOYER, "a little whiffling *Frenchman*," continues to publish his Whiggish monthly called (with incredible inaccuracy) *The Political State of Great-Britain.*

### Number 42: Thursday, May 24, 1711
The writer has received a number of letters lately regarding a plan to build 50 churches in London and Westminster. A convocation of the clergy encouraged the queen to adopt the plan, and the House of Commons is in the midst of drafting a bill to make it a reality. The clergy cannot help but be pleased at the "new Scene of publick Affairs," especially since the new Parliament consistently "takes the Necessities of the Church into Consideration." The English in recent years have appeared to be a much worse people than they really are, all because the Whigs have been in charge. When factions are overthrown in any society, the citizens always find their way back to "Reason and Religion."

By the writer's calculations, each of the 50 proposed churches will cost £6,000. This is less than "the Price of a Subject's Palace," and certainly worth the cost, considering that more than 200,000 souls will be cared for. For many years now, we have known that English parishes vary wildly in size, and the discrepancies are even worse now in London. Many districts contain far more parishioners than one minister (and all the church buildings) can possibly accommodate. This has made schism a "necessary Evil," and contributed to an overall "Neglect for Religion" worse than any the author has ever heard of.

Parliament, however, is already working on a solution to this problem in the form of "a Tax laid upon every House in a Parish, for the Support of their Pastor." The writer hopes that these wise lawmakers will refrain from setting the tax at any particular amount, and instead create a tax "in Proportion to the Rent of each House, although it be but a Twentieth or even a thirtieth part" (see "LETTER FROM A MEMBER OF THE HOUSE OF COMMONS"). In line with Parliament, the queen herself has the best "Disposition" of any prince when it comes to advancing religion, but (to England's shame) the "long and ruinous War" has severely limited her efforts to pursue her designs. Were it not for the war, the queen's "Care of Religion"

would have reached the "*American* Plantations" by now. Those colonies, inhabited by countless numbers of individuals from England, will remain a "perpetual Reproach" to the English until Christianity is promoted more intensely among them. At present, however, there are more than enough subjects at home in need of the gospel, and the writer hopes the clergy will seize every opportunity to improve the "pious Dispositions of the QUEEN and Kingdom, for the Advantage of the Church."

### Number 43: Thursday, May 31, 1711
Forced by convention to use the words *Whig* and *Tory* for the past 20 years, the writer has decided to outline the changes in meaning those words have undergone. He will also explain what he takes each word to mean. These kinds of "appellations," he admits, are usually "invented by the Vulgar," who prefer to argue by calling names instead of discussing issues. The terms *Whig* and *Tory* seem to have originated late in CHARLES II's reign. They were dropped during the reign of JAMES II, and "revived at the Revolution." Since that time, they have been used "perpetually"—often to describe "very different kinds of Principles and Persons."

In December 1688 the names were used to distinguish one group from another at the Convention of Lords and Commons (those who favored granting a "Regency" to WILLIAM of Orange and those who believed he should receive the title and all the benefits reserved for the king). The distinctions between Whigs and Tories became even more complicated when the Dissenters began making distinctions between High- and Low-Church, alleging that High-Church supporters were united with the "Papists."

Despite the confusing ways in which these terms have been applied, the writer seeks to list some "principles" that served to distinguish Whigs and Tories prior to Queen Anne's accession. *Tory* was used to describe supporters of High-Church principles who opposed a "Standing Army in Time of Peace," and disagreed with the majority of bishops. The term was used to describe those of the majority opinion in the House of Commons, particularly members of the "Country-Party or Landed Interest." Whigs, on the other hand, were

Low-Church supporters who held that the royal prerogative was superior to the laws "for serving a Turn," and touted the "King's Supremacy beyond all Precedent." Casting any doubt whatsoever that "the pretended Prince" was "Suppositious," and of common lineage was (in the Whigs' view) "perfect Jacobitism." Taking grants away from royal favorites and using them to further the public good was also "the very Quintessence of *Toryism.*" The writer explains that by the time Queen Anne "came to the Crown," the Tories and Whigs had virtually exchanged their views. The Whigs, for example, had so vehemently "renounc'd" their former view of the Pretender that they seemed to be the greatest promoters of his legitimacy. It was not long after her accession that two *"great Persons"* (Marlborough and Godolphin) turned their backs on Tory principles and agreed to a "Treaty with the *Whigs,*" who offered them more attractive terms.

Since then, the term *Whig* has come to be associated with a "certain Set of *Persons,*" rather than any specific principles. In the writer's view, the term now describes anyone who had faith in the former ministry. In the *Examiner,* he uses it to denote those who were "Partisans of the late men in Power," who knew of their schemes or who united with them out of hatred for the church and constitution of England. He also uses *Whig* to describe—among others— "Unbelievers and *Dissenters*" or "Men in Office" who feared change because of the gross corruption of which they were guilty. He does not include among Whigs those who were misled out of ignorance or "seduc'd" by crafty arguments into thinking more of the former ministry than it deserved.

*Whig* and *Tory* currently have almost no relation "to those Opinions, which were at first thought to distinguish them." Originally, Whigs were those who supported the Revolution, opposed the Pretender, and regarded England's government as a limited monarchy rather than an absolute one. In contrast, Tories were those who defended "the Queen's Hereditary Right," regarded "the Persons of Princes" as sacred, and their power never to be resisted. They also abhorred schism as "the Ruin of the *Church*" (and a serious hazard to the state) and

insisted that power should never be given to those who were not "of the Establish'd Religion." In the writer's view, the clearest and most current definition of a Tory is one who—regardless of political pressures—will do whatever it takes "to save their Prince and Country, *whoever* be at the Helm."

### Number 44: Thursday, June 7, 1711
Any "true Lover of his Country" who considers the shameful conduct of the former ministry—its dishonesty, its alarmist propaganda, the brutal character assaults it launched, and the like—cannot help but be pleased at how woefully unsuccessful its members' schemes have turned out to be. None of the "misfortunes" they predicted (and pretended to fear) ever materialized once the ministry was changed. Such a wholesale alteration was a "daring" move, and one that succeeded only because of the queen's wisdom and goodness and her ministry's capabilities. It also helped that the voice of the people clearly supported her decision to enact the change.

It was certainly no surprise that the naysayers raised such a "Noise" about the change being "dangerous and unseasonable," but present circumstances clarify that their fears were entirely groundless. When any house is swept, it is sure to raise some dust. As a matter of "Justice" to the current Parliament, the writer has decided to list several of that assembly's great accomplishments "for the Service of their QUEEN and Country." They saved the nation's credit by restoring the value of "Exchequer Bills." They also provided relief to "*Nevis* and St. *Christophers*"—British colonies that had long endured merciless plundering and destruction at the hands of the French. The Commons attempted to deal with the overwhelming number of "Foreigners of all Religions" that had flooded the kingdom since the former ministry's "Act of general Naturalization." Their attempt to repeal the act, however, was defeated in the House of Lords. Both houses enacted a "*Qualification-Bill,*" which limited eligibility to serve in Parliament to those who possessed "some Estate in Land." This may be the single most important means ever devised for preserving the constitution of the kingdom. Parliament also tackled the nation's soaring debt and established a security fund against that "immense" liability—an act that will probably "prove the greatest Restoration and Establishment of the Kingdom's Credit." In addition to the administration's clear "Concern for Religion" and its determination to engage in "a Trade to the *South-Sea*," there are numerous other achievements that further illustrate its noble character. The writer admits, in fact, that he has probably forgotten some important examples of how ably "this great Assembly" has pursued the good of those who elected them.

As far as the writer is concerned, his goal in writing the *Examiner* has now become a reality: A "great majority" of the kingdom now agrees the queen acted wisely in "changing her Ministry and Parliament," and recognizes how remarkably corrupt the former ministry actually was. He learned long ago to ignore the "little barking Pens" that have hounded him ever since he undertook the paper, and their only accomplishment has been to make him ashamed to be one of their "species."

### Number 45: Thursday, June 14, 1711

Convinced that "the main body of the *Whigs*" is now soundly defeated, the writer compares himself to a general who has defeated an army and subdued a kingdom. Now that the bulk of his work is done, he finds himself "at Leisure to *examine* inferior Abuses," and he has decided to pursue those who seek to perpetuate the war even though they have nothing left to fight for. Specifically, he now targets the pro-Whig writers who for so long have clamored against him without any retribution. In a mock petition, he promises to show that these hacks were "guided" by nothing other than a desire to "gratify a private Interest." The petition is written as though it were sent from "four Score" of the Whigs' writers and addressed to the present ministry. In it, the writers complain that since the *Examiner* may now cease to be written, they and their families are in danger of starving due to a lack of material. Having nothing original to say, they had come to rely on that paper as a source from which to quote inaccurately and as an object for other "legal Abuses." In the end, they request permission to continue as usual, even though they can produce nothing other than "the *same Stuff*" presented in exactly "the *same Manner*" as before.

## COMMENTARY

Political patronage was a key element in Swift's decision to remain in London in 1710; he had come on behalf of the Irish bishops seeking financial relief from the Whig government and stayed in the city when the chief Tory ministers took notice of him and his talents. After publishing "The VIRTUES OF SID HAMET THE MAGICIAN'S ROD" in October 1710, Swift found this lampoon against the Whig Lord GODOLPHIN well received in many quarters. Swift had written the piece because he found Godolphin's cold reception impossible, but actually he saw a ready opportunity of injecting many of his personal annoyances with the current ministry. To be fair, Godolphin had been dismissed as lord treasurer in August and could do little for this Irish cleric, but Swift would not be satisfied and may have used this opportunity to bring himself to the attention of the Tories. Robert HARLEY, the new chancellor of the exchequer, suggested to Swift that he might solve the bishops' concerns and also have some literary assignment for this talented man.

Harley and Henry BOLINGBROKE, secretary of state, needed a political propagandist to take over the government's new paper, *The Examiner*, begun in August. Swift accepted this chance to elevate himself as well as help those of like mind concerning the future of England's foreign policy. In the first week of November 1710, Swift's first essay in the paper appeared as number 14 [number 13 above], and 33 weekly articles ran during the Tory Parliament's opening session until June 1711. Printed as a single 2,000-word essay on a folio half-sheet, its main purpose was to emphasize the virtues of Tory party policy and attack the Whigs, who maintained a lively opposition. As a disinterested but critical observer, the writer promoted an attitude of independence while attempting to mold public opinion toward Tory rule. The notion of Whig corruption, financial mismanagement, and promotion of war as a tool of foreign policy remained constant references in every essay. Pointing out the incompatibility of Whig policies with the natural instincts of most citizens allowed Swift to show how the party had set aside critical principles associated with the Church of England and the constitution. All his critics were conspirators and his supporters remained patriots first and party members last. If the nation sought peace and economic stability, the Tories intended on restoring both, but more important, they as landed gentry naturally represented traditional, conservative values of security and order.

The nature of reform was to invest each essay, and Swift used his command of the facts on various issues and events (supplied by ministerial resources or his own research) and a deep well of moral idealism. He wrote successfully not simply because of his literary skill but more particularly because he held the moral high ground. The extended War of the Spanish Succession and the superb victories of the English Captain-General MARLBOROUGH did not answer the Whigs' continued interest in maintaining the war and keeping the country on a war footing. Swift used both reason and moral rightness as weapons against this now unjust war.

In terms of his rhetoric, Swift rejects Addison and Steele's technique of "examining" statement after statement from the Whig opposition press, which would have added to its credibility. Instead, his style stresses his personal integrity and general disdain for what he regarded as a group of hypocrites. Calmly indifferent, he avoids close analysis of his enemies' words, reserving the power of his words to suggest the faith readers should have in the Tory effort for peace. For example, in number 16 (November 23, 1710), Swift taunts his favorite subject, Marlborough, as a symbol of British ingratitude, contrasting him with Roman gratitude for one of their successful generals. Using parallel columns, he lists each gift and expenditure for a Roman versus those for Marlborough. No reader can miss the results of this budgetary statement as British gratitude amounts to a huge sum, but Swift calls it "a trifle, in comparison of what is untold." With surgical precision, his irony reveals the corruption at the heart of the Whig ministry and how essential was his exposure of these degenerate policies that misled a well-meaning people.

His additional technique of charging Marlborough with serious faults and then denying the abusive intent was a recognized rhetorical device, and

protected Swift and his publisher from a lawsuit. He knew how dangerous attacking a famous and popular general could be, but he manages to turn his popularity against him. By hinting at his defects or suggesting the general's services to the nation may have been overstated, Swift begins his attack in number 16 by accusing him of avarice and personal faults, anticipating number 27 (February 8, 1711), known as the "Letter to Crassus," where a love of money seems inappropriate for a man of his stature. His public image suffers from this "little vice," as Swift calls it, and Marlborough's immunity fails under this charge of avarice.

The propaganda of the *Examiner* and Swift's talent gave him unparalleled access to power, especially from early 1711 when he shouldered an increasingly important role for public relations in the Oxford ministry, often treading lightly between Harley and Bolingbroke, whose power struggle became an obvious problem. Both ministers now were of a different mind concerning the tone and content of Swift's paper: Harley sought a milder, less vitriolic quality but Bolingbroke urged harsher methods. From number 25 (January 25, 1711), number 26 (February 1, 1711), the earlier mentioned number 27, and number 28 (February 15, 1711), Swift has clearly accepted St. John's views and sharpened his attacks. First, he poses the question: "What would have been the consequence if the late ministry [the Whigs] had continued," followed by "What may we reasonably expect they will do, if ever they come into power again?" The answer, delivered in a style that should frighten any independent Englishman, suggests the ruination of the constitution, ongoing war, further debts, and the eventual destruction of the current church. Then in number 26 he meditates on how the current Tory ministry has functioned, providing "meat for babes," not worthless cures to a dying man like the earlier government. Reviewing the virtuous character of the Tories in contrast to that "routed cabal of hated politicians," he names each of the chief Tory ministers as great men. After exposing the great Marlborough, he proceeds in number 28 to shift the blame from Marlborough to "the weakness of his advocates," and his main subject: "the conduct of the late ministry, the shameful mismanagement in Spain, or the wrong steps in the treaty of peace." Alluding to his being too severe against the Whigs, he pretends to having received a letter supposedly written by a Tory member of Parliament urging him to write a "few good stories" on how the Whigs have violated their duties and responsibilities to the queen and people of England. "In short, turn the whole mystery of iniquity inside out, that everybody may have a view of it."

Little did Swift know that the whole project would end in a few months and that the strained relationship between Harley and Bolingbroke would become so damaged that he could not survive as author during the turmoil. Critics suggest Swift may have been glad to let go of his post, especially when it placed him between the warring camps of the two politicians he respected most. But it may also be true that he wished to remain more independent and not suffer once again from the whims of great men, as he had experienced with Sir William TEMPLE in his first visit to Moor Park. His name and talent were known in the best circles, but he hoped for some practical, career-enhancing promotion in the church: an English bishopric or deanery. Oxford would ask Swift for his continued help, even as the ministry collapsed, but the deanship would not come until nearly two years later.

### FURTHER READING

Downie, J. A. *Jonathan Swift: Political Writer*. London: Routledge & Kegan Paul, 1984.

———. *Robert Harley and the Press: Propaganda and Public Opinion in the Age of Swift and Defoe*. Cambridge: Cambridge University Press, 1979.

Ehrenpreis, Irvin. *Swift: The Man, His Works and the Age*. 3 vols. Cambridge, Mass.: Harvard University Press, 1962–83.

Ellis, Frank H., ed. *Swift vs. Mainwaring: "The Examiner" and "The Medley."* Oxford: Clarendon Press, 1985.

# "Excellent New Ballad, An"

Poem by Swift; first published in Dublin as an anonymous broadside in 1730, written the same year. Subtitled "The True English Dean to be Hanged for a Rape," it deals with the prosecution

on June 2 of Dr. Thomas SAWBRIDGE (Dean of Ferns) for the attempted rape of Susanna Runcard. Although Sawbridge was acquitted, Swift's poem has him hanged for the crime. The speaker in Swift's poem sarcastically concludes that the Irish should "be glad" England sends them "holy" clergymen like Sawbridge. As Carole Fabricant has pointed out, Sawbridge's acquittal (despite his crime) serves as a reminder that "in eighteenth-century Ireland, persons of Swift's class and position were least likely to be among those imprisoned and hanged" ("Speaking for the Irish Nation" 349).

A ballad by definition is "a form of verse adapted for singing or recitation and primarily characterized by its presentation in simple narrative form of a dramatic or exciting episode" (Thrall, Hibbard and Holman 42). In this poem, however, Swift focuses less on the excitement surrounding Sawbridge's trial and instead cites it as a poignant example of England's lack of concern for the well-being of Irish parishioners. Near the outset, he sarcastically claims that the "brethren of England" have sent Sawbridge (a "true English Dean" who spends his days "drinking" and night "whoring") to Ireland as a "blessing" for the good of the church. Significantly, Swift counts himself among the Irish who suffer from England's neglect ("*Our* brethren [. . .] who love *us* so dear," etc.). Although he had long wished for an ecclesiastical appointment in England, Swift identified with the people of Ireland (or, at least, a segment of that population) and deeply resented what he viewed as English exploitation of the Irish in social, religious, and economic terms. He had, for example, spent a great deal of time in England in the early 1700s, arguing that Irish clergymen should enjoy the same tax benefits as their counterparts in England. Like the "Ballad," his "MODEST PROPOSAL, PROPOSAL FOR THE UNIVERSAL USE OF IRISH MANUFACTURE," and *DRAPIER'S LETTERS* help to illustrate the extent to which Swift championed Ireland's interests in the face of English oppression.

# "Excellent New Song, An"

Poem by Swift; first published in 1711, written the same year. Subtitled "Being the Intended Speech of a Famous Orator against Peace," it satirizes Daniel Finch, second earl of NOTTINGHAM. Swift's journal entry for December 5 (the day prior to the poem's appearance) provides details: "Lord Nottingham, a famous TORY and speech-maker, is gone over to the WHIG side: they toast him daily, and Lord Wharton says, It is Dismal (so they call him from his looks) will save England at last" (quoted in Rogers, *Complete Poems* 647). The poem contains what Swift wryly presents as a copy of Nottingham's speech to the Whigs. It is written in couplets and highlights his disloyalty to the Tories. See also "TOLAND'S INVITATION TO DISMAL TO DINE WITH THE CALVES' HEAD CLUB."

## "Excellent New Song on a Seditious Pamphlet, An"

Poem by Swift; first published in 1735, written 1720. It was occasioned by the uproar following publication of his "PROPOSAL FOR THE UNIVERSAL USE OF IRISH MANUFACTURE," in which he urged the Irish to forsake their devotion to imported clothing and wear goods made in Ireland. The speakers or singers of the "Song" are Irishmen who vow to ignore Swift's protests and continue buying English clothing (the refrain is, "Then we'll buy English silks for our wives and our daughters, / In spite of his Deanship and journeyman Waters"). The poem mocks Lord Chief Justice William WHITSHED (who jailed and vehemently sought to convict Swift's printer, Edward WATERS), accusing him in the prologue of "injustice" and "violence" in his treatment of the printer. When the jury did not return a guilty verdict against Waters, Whitshed angrily sent them back for further deliberation. He did so nine times (not 11, as the prologue suggests) until they returned a "special verdict" which left Waters's fate in the judge's hands. In a show of utter disdain for Whitshed's immorality and abuse of authority, Swift throughout the poem "deliberately flaunt[s] the open secret of his authorship of the *Proposal*" (Nokes, *Hypocrite Reversed* 268). Other poems by Swift against Whitshed include "VERSES ON THE UPRIGHT JUDGE" and "WHITSHED'S

MOTTO ON HIS COACH." See also "A LETTER FROM DR. SWIFT TO MR. POPE."

## "Excellent New Song upon His Grace Our Good Lord Archbishop of Dublin, An"

Poem by Swift; first published anonymously in 1724, written the same year. The subtitle names "Honest Jo, One of His Grace's Farmers in Fingal" as the author. It praises Archbishop William KING for his integrity, generosity and his opposition to William WOOD's patent for Irish coinage. See also *The DRAPIER'S LETTERS*, "DOING GOOD: A SERMON ON THE OCCASION OF WOOD'S PROJECT," "AN EPIGRAM ON WOOD'S BRASS MONEY," "ON WOOD THE IRONMONGER," "PROMETHEUS," "A SERIOUS POEM UPON WILLIAM WOOD," "A SIMILE," "TO HIS GRACE THE ARCHBISHOP OF DUBLIN," "WOOD, AN INSECT," and "WOOD'S HALFPENCE."

## "Fable of Midas, The"

Poem by Swift; first published as a broadside in 1712, probably written the same year. It compares John Churchill, First duke of MARLBOROUGH, to the mythical king Midas, portraying the duke as greedy and corrupt. See also "The CONDUCT OF THE ALLIES," "A SATIRICAL ELEGY ON THE DEATH OF A LATE FAMOUS GENERAL," and "A FABLE OF THE WIDOW AND HER CAT."

## "Fable of the Bitches, The"

Poem by Swift, subtitled "Wrote in the Year 1715, on an Attempt to Repeal the Test Act"; first published in 1762. The fable involves two dogs, Bawty and Music. Music allows the pregnant Bawty to move in with her and soon finds that she cannot be rid of her guest and the hungry new pups. Explaining the moral at the end of the poem, Swift compares Music's action to the Trojans' fatal acceptance of the Greeks' wooden horse (and, implicitly, the proposal to do away with the Test Act). A lifelong opponent of repealing the act, Swift likely wrote this poem after the General Assembly of the Church of Scotland met in May 1715. See also "LETTER FROM A MEMBER OF THE HOUSE OF COMMONS IN IRELAND" and "ON THE WORDS 'BROTHER PROTESTANTS AND FELLOW CHRISTIANS.'"

# "Fable of the Widow and Her Cat, A"

Poem by Swift; first published in 1712, written 1711. It details the fall of a haughty cat who exploits the kindness of the widow who owns him. Like "The FABLE OF MIDAS," this poem is directed against John Churchill, first duke of MARLBOROUGH. The duke—portrayed as the cat in this poem—was formally accused of embezzlement on December 21, 1711. Within days Queen ANNE—the widow—dismissed him from all his appointments. Swift's poem elicited an anonymous reply called "When the Cat's Away, the Mice May Play. A Fable. Humbly Inscribed to Dr. Swift." Swift found the response (which defended Marlborough) "Whiggish" and "good for nothing."

# "Fabula Canis et Umbrae"

Poem by Swift; first published in 1735, probably written 1727. Recalling a fable by Aesop on a similar theme, this poem depicts two attempted bribes. The first involves a thief who offers to pay a dog to open the door to his master's house, the second a "stockjobber" who is running for Parliament and tries to buy the vote of a "freeman." Both bribes are refused, and the poem ends with an allusion to aspiring London politicians who go out into the countryside determined to swindle "the silly people" out of their votes. Pat Rogers suggests that

Swift probably wrote the poem while visiting England in August 1727, when a general election was under way (*Poems* 770).

# "Faggot, The"

Poem by Swift; first published in 1735, written 1713–14. Its subject is the initial breakdown of the ministry of Robert HARLEY, first earl of Oxford. The poem begins with a fable of a "dying father" exhorting his sons to remain undivided. He illustrates the importance of remaining united by having his sons try (unsuccessfully) to break a bundle of sticks in half. He then separates the bundle and easily breaks the sticks himself, one by one. Swift applies the fable to "treasurers, controllers, stewards, / And others, . . . at court," who refuse to bind their "slender wands" together for common causes and use them instead to lash one another.

# "Family of Swift, The"

Composed in the late 1730s, Swift's autobiographical fragment holds a great deal of interest for biographers, though the dean forgets or misremembers certain facts, which over the years have led some scholars astray. Despite the flawed results, his intention had one overriding quality: a plain rendition of his life from birth to early middle age. At about 5,000 words, the essay discusses family, focusing his praise on the Reverend Thomas SWIFT, vicar of Goodrich, Herefordshire and his grandfather. Writing from memory and apparently ignoring good genealogical practice of checking facts and doing research in the existing sources, Swift got his facts wrong in certain cases. Knowing his penchant for irony and exaggeration for effect, Herbert Davis suggests that Swift did not seek to mislead his readers for devious purposes, though Denis Johnston argues in *In Search of Swift* that the fragment was designed to conceal Swift's illegitimacy. When Deane SWIFT printed the "Family," he corrected many errors and annotated the essay extensively, providing such details as "Captain Thomas Swift [a nephew] . . . having inherited the complexion and beauty of his mother, was supposed to have been the handsomest man in the Queen's army."

Swift probably was writing two famous poems about the time he was composing this sketch: "The LIFE AND GENUINE CHARACTER OF DR. SWIFT" and "VERSES ON THE DEATH OF DR. SWIFT, D.S.P.D." Both poems offered Swift the opportunity to fantasize about his own death, and to imagine how his friends and enemies might respond. He had always found death a fascinating subject, and seemed determined to write an autobiography. These pieces are the equivalent in verse, with a full spectrum of literary, political, and clerical histories of his career. In contrast to the poems, the "Family" is more detached, dry, and (at least as a commentary on the events of Swift's life) far less expansive.

References to Swift's relatives pile up quickly, with his early family squandering away an estate in Yorkshire; a wife of William Swift (a 16th-century relative) who is a "capricious, ill-natured and passionate woman" deceiving her family and disinheriting her only son; and another, Godwin Swift, who has a portrait of his wife and himself altered so her arms are joined with his; and his kindest description of his grandfather Thomas Swift, whose merits die with himself, ignored by king and church. The last half of the essay focuses more directly on Swift himself, beginning with the "very indiscreet" marriage of his parents (who lacked sufficient funds to run a household) and the early death of his father. His eventual birth, separation from his mother when his nurse "stole him on shipboard" and carried him off to England, and return nearly three years later must have produced a deep psychological reaction in him. Though the loss or separation from both parents would seem a signal event in one's life, Swift delivers these facts without any outward sign of regret or alienation. This catalogue of estrangement continues with his being sent off to Kilkenny School at the age of six, further separation from his mother who left for England, and his matriculating at 14 to the University of Dublin. Knowing how this bare list, coldly delivered, would be interpreted, Swift may have intended that such obvious references to abandonment, banishment,

and rejection would serve two purposes: He represents the condition of all Irishmen who have been rejected by their mother country, England, and dispossessed through loss and death of their origins (language and culture) and pastoral estates and now must exist in a bleak world. He might suggest also the nature of all men born into this life whose joyless childhood and later unhappy struggle of life against the evil of the fallen world prepares one for welcoming the paradise promised in the next life: This pattern exists in Protestant doctrine, and Swift effectively shows how his life matches the post-lapsarian world of the lost Eden.

The subject of Swift's attitude toward women may have its origin in his childhood—in the lonely life of a "posthumous" [fatherless] child. Certainly the references in this fragment to unpleasant and abrupt actions by his mother and his nurse (though she left Dublin for Whitehaven on practical concerns of expecting a legacy) which led to kidnapping, estrangement, and abandonment may have contributed to the debasement of a normal view of women. When discussing the women Swift men married, the bitterness increases with references to "the Shrew" and the capriciousness and ill-nature of other Swift women. His emphasis here on their unreliability and the disappointing model of his parents' marriage may have affected his response to the possibilities of his ever marrying, though in his other works, Swift reveals his fascination with women, enjoying their wit, beauty, and his own opportunities for expressing gallantry toward them. The woman to whom he was closest and wrote the most confident letters, Esther JOHNSON (Stella) was, in J. A. Downie's words, "another in a long line of surrogates." In this autobiographical fragment, Swift partially reveals why he conducted a lifelong search for emotional stability.

# "Famous Prediction of Merlin, the British Wizard, A"

This short piece published in early 1709, courting WHIG favor, is associated with the Bickerstaff Papers, where Swift's victim was John PARTRIDGE, a successful astrologer, almanac maker, and thoroughgoing charlatan who annually published his almanac *Merlinus Liberatus*. Because Partridge had successfully disputed other astrologers in the art of prophecy, Swift believed it was time to out-Partridge Partridge. He began with "PREDICTIONS FOR THE YEAR 1708," "THE ACCOMPLISHMENT OF THE FIRST OF MR. BICKERSTAFF'S PREDICTIONS," and "A VINDICATION OF ISAAC BICKERSTAFF ESQ."

## SYNOPSIS

The author, T. N. Philomath, explains that a paper was published last year supposedly written by Isaac Bickerstaff. However, the true motive behind it was to make fun of "the Art of Astrology" and its professors. The prophecy in the present paper is intended to affirm Dr. Partridge's entirely successful defense of that art in his almanac. Reportedly, the prophecy was written by "the famous *Merlin*" around a thousand years ago, but the translation is only 200 years old. Merlin's predictions are presented here in the authentic "old Orthography" with "a few explanatory Notes." At first glance, the prophecy is dark and difficult to understand, but upon closer reading it clearly applies to the current year (1709), and serves as a remarkable prediction of certain things that have come to pass and others that are highly probable. For example, it figuratively forecasts the rise of John MARLBOROUGH, the failure of the Pretender, the "happy *Union*" of all Britain, and CHARLES VI's overthrow of King PHILIP V of Spain. Whether or not Merlin was the real author, this prophecy exemplifies astrology at its finest and shows that it is certainly not "an Art to be despised" (no matter what Bickerstaff or anyone else thinks).

## COMMENTARY

The approach with "MERLIN" would parody political dogma and prophetic statement, what Irvin Ehrenpreis calls "cryptic doggerel" (*Swift* II.344). The humor Swift displays fits well with his earlier Bickerstaff pieces, and now the pretension extends back to the reign of Henry VII with sufficient verisimilitude to fool the noteworthy Samuel Johnson. Relying on a bit of prophecy provided in Sir William TEMPLE's *Memoirs*, Swift creates a preface, explanatory notes, and an antiquarian tone and

seriousness, adding a final coup de grace in having the piece printed in black letter, a kind of heavy-faced, ornamental printing typeface, sometimes called Gothic or Old English. He uses the pseudonym T. N. Philomath, a name suggestive of a person who loves learning and literature.

His final sentence offers readers, especially those who may be doubtful of its authenticity, the opportunity to verify what he has discovered: "I shall give order to have the very book sent to the printer of this paper, with directions to let anybody see it that pleases; because I believe it is pretty scarce." These kinds of assurances are familiar in the history of literature or journalism, and within the same century at least two famous publications offer to let readers check the facts and substantiate for themselves the truth behind the works: James Macpherson's *Poems of Ossian* (1765), whose purported translations of ancient Gaelic poetry had initiated a determined controversy that culminated in a desperate attempt at locating the Gaelic originals (later research substantiated an extensive oral tradition, though no exact text). The influence of the Ossianic controversy was not lost on the gifted, if pathetic, Thomas Chatterton, who fabricated the Rowley poems (1769–77), recording the medieval splendor of Bristol with spurious antique poems, and could show only his modern specimens.

# "First Ode of the Second Book of Horace Paraphrased and Addressed to Richard Steele, Esq., The"

Poem by Swift; first published January 7, 1714, written the same year. Like Swift's "IMPORTANCE OF THE GUARDIAN CONSIDERED," it was part of an ongoing pamphlet war between Swift and Richard STEELE that occurred during the administration of Robert HARLEY, first earl of Oxford. The poem is a scornful, insulting commentary on Steele's promotion of *The Crisis*, his controversial book supporting Hanoverian succession, which led to his expulsion from Parliament in and sparked Swift's "PUBLIC

SPIRIT OF THE WHIGS." Long before Steele's work was finally published on January 19, 1714, he had engaged in an extensive publicity campaign characterized by "repeated pompous advertisements and protracted delay" (Williams, *Poems* I.180). Swift's poem suggests that *The Crisis*—like its author—is entirely unworthy of such spectacle.

# "First of April, The"

Poem by Swift; first published in an undated Dublin broadside. It was probably written in April 1723, during one of Swift's visits with Robert COPE and his family at Loughall. Inscribed to "Mrs. E. C.," the poem is a tribute to the Copes, especially Robert's second wife, Elizabeth, whom Swift admired "as a model gentlewoman" (Ehrenpreis III.346). In the poem, Apollo sends the muses to the Copes' home with orders to bless the children. They soon discover, however, that Apollo has played an April Fool's joke on them, since the Cope children already have everything good under Mrs. Cope's loving management.

# *Fraud Detected: or, The Hibernian Patriot*

See FAULKNER, GEORGE.

# "From Dr. Swift to Dr. Sheridan"

Poem by Swift; first published in 1745, written in 1719. One of many verse letters Swift wrote to his friend Dr. Thomas SHERIDAN, this one is signed "STELLA" and contains three verse postscripts. Sheridan replied within hours with "A Letter from Dr. Sheridan to Dr. Swift," which sparked Swift to write "DR. SWIFT'S ANSWER TO DR. SHERIDAN." Nora Crow Jaffe compares the poem to "MARY THE COOK-MAID'S LETTER TO DR. SHERIDAN," since the humor in both depends on "conversational rhythms and absurdly elongated lines" (*The Poet Swift* 125).

# "Furniture of a Woman's Mind, The"

Poem by Swift; first published in 1735, written in 1727. It is an unflattering list of characteristics and habits suggesting that women's minds contain only trivial preoccupations. The poem ends inviting anyone who finds otherwise to send their evidence for publication to Sarah HARDING, who may have printed "Furniture" in a separate edition before its first recorded appearance in 1735. See also "The JOURNAL OF A MODERN LADY" and "MY LADY'S LAMENTATION AND COMPLAINT AGAINST THE DEAN."

# "George Nim-Dan-Dean, Esq. to Mr. Sheridan"

Poem by Swift; first published 1746, written during Swift's lengthy stay at the home of George ROCHFORT in the summer of 1721 (see "PART OF A SUMMER"). The speaker presents the poem as a collective effort by "a loving pair / Of Gaulstown lads"—Gaulstown House was the name of Rochfort's estate. Citing verses Dr. Thomas SHERIDAN had sent to the "lads," the poem makes fun of Sheridan's poetic abilities. "George Nim-Dan-Dean" refers collectively to George Rochfort, John ROCHFORT (nicknamed "Nimrod" for his love of hunting), Daniel JACKSON, and "Dean" Swift. See also "GEORGE NIM-DAN-DEAN'S INVITATION TO MR. THOMAS SHERIDAN."

# "George Nim-Dan-Dean's Invitation to Mr. Thomas Sheridan"

Poem by Swift; first published 1765, written during Swift's lengthy stay at the home of George ROCHFORT in the summer of 1721 (see "PART OF A SUMMER"). The speaker asks SHERIDAN to leave the city and come join his friends. See also "GEORGE NIM-DAN-DEAN, ESQ. TO MR. SHERIDAN."

# "Grand Question Debated, The"

Poem by Swift; first published in 1732 under the title "A Soldier and a Scholar," written in the period 1728–29 during one of Swift's visits to MARKET HILL (Pat Rogers's edition of Swift's *Poems* provides an explanation of the poem's complicated bibliographic history). Swift refers to it as "Hamilton's Bawn" in a 1732 letter to Rev. Henry JENNEY. A satire built on Sir Arthur ACHESON's uncertainty over the "grand question" of what to do with Hamilton's Bawn (a large old house he owned north of Market Hill), the poem dramatizes a lengthy dialogue among the principal figures of Acheson's household as they bicker over whether it would be best to turn the property into a malthouse or barracks. Sir Arthur argues for a malthouse based on the profit it would yield, while Lady Anne ACHESON and her maid Hannah maintain that military barracks would attract much-needed company to offset the annoying dean who (as Louise K. Barnett states) has become their "insufferable and unwelcome guest." (*Swift's Poetic Worlds* 64).

In *The Poet Swift*, Nora Crowe Jaffe calls this "the best of the Market Hill poems" (compared with "DEATH AND DAPHNE" and "ON CUTTING DOWN THE OLD THORN") and analyzes Swift's success in creating unique, recognizable voices for each of the speakers (134). She writes that, "In the eighteenth century, and until the twentieth, only novelists attempted to render conversation as realistically as Swift," and that in "The Grand Question" he displays "his skill in impersonating four completely different people"—the Achesons, Hannah, and the narrator (136).

# "Gulf of All Human Possessions, The"

See "RIDDLES."

# Gulliver's Travels (Travels into Several Remote Nations of the World)

A work of incomparable value and interest, *Gulliver's Travels* is easily the most popular of Swift's works among modern readers. Having studied the *Travels*, students of Swift will find themselves drawn to "A TALE OF A TUB," his English political writings, the writings on Ireland, the early writings on religion, and his poems. Reportedly, between 1726 and 1815 more than 100 editions of the *Travels* were published, and 330 further editions since that period, which would establish it as the best-selling prose fiction work of the 18th century. Enjoyed for its world of fantasy and adventure as well as its subversive satire, which effectively redefines humanity's view of itself to bring some clarity into our dull view of this world, the *Travels* invite us to reassess the definition of humankind. Most modern anthologies of British literature include the entire work or a careful selection of one or two of its four "parts," though in some cases the editors' preface announces that it is not satisfactory to present anything but the whole of the work and they choose not to offer a mere selection from it. The work looms over the entire period for both the scholar and student of early 18th-century British literature, and one might argue without exaggeration that one's education would sadly lack an important component if one had not read this masterpiece.

*Gulliver's Travels* has a curious publication history, beginning with the first edition published on October 28, 1726, by the printer and bookseller Benjamin Motte in London. Since he never saw an original manuscript, Motte used a "faithful" transcript, but to protect himself from arrest for libel he had a colleague, Andrew Tooke, rewrite certain sections. Swift, noting these unacceptable changes, had his friend Charles FORD complain to Motte, who corrected a few passages but in general did not restore the full text as originally conceived in later editions. Thanks to Ford and Swift's continued interest in a true copy with his personal corrections, George FAULKNER produced a new edition in 1735 in Dublin that seems on the whole a more exact rendering of Swift's manuscript. Though modern readers believe the 1735 edition is now the standard version, debate continues, and the Penguin edition (as the reference text for this volume) combines the 1726 edition with readings from the Ford copies and the 1735 Faulkner edition.

## SYNOPSIS

### Part 1: A Voyage to Lilliput

#### Chapter 1

After providing some biographical information about himself and his family, Lemuel Gulliver describes his early employments (including several sea voyages) and the shipwreck of the *Antelope,* which led to his arrival on what he eventually finds out is the island of Lilliput. Following his exhaust-

Gulliver stretches after his release from the Lilliputians' bonds. Part 1, chapter 1 *(Arthur Rackham)*

ing struggle for survival after the shipwreck, Gulliver finally swims ashore and falls asleep. He awakens to find himself tied to the ground and discovers that he has been made prisoner by a group of miniature human creatures of about six inches in height. The Lilliputians are able to communicate with Gulliver even though they do not speak his language. After feeding him, they place him (still confined) on a large carriage designed to haul trees and transport him to a large vacant temple. There they chain Gulliver's left leg to the gate and inform him that this is where he will stay.

#### Chapter 2

Gulliver outlines the landscape of Lilliput and apologetically explains the arrangement worked out to accommodate what he calls the "Necessities of Nature," by which he means his daily bowel movements. The Emperor (see Lilliput, Emperor of, under Characters) and his family come to visit Gulliver, and the Emperor himself attempts to converse with him. When this fails, he orders a number of priests and lawyers to try to talk with Gulliver, but to no avail. They leave him under heavy guard to protect him from the rabble. Several renegade Lilliputians unexpectedly shoot arrows at Gulliver, and the Emperor orders that they be bound and handed over to their giant guest. Gulliver pretends to eat them and then releases them—an act of "clemency" that earns him a great deal of clout with the Emperor and his court. The Emperor and his advisers hold meetings to decide what to do with Gulliver. They are concerned that keeping him fed will deplete the kingdom's resources but worried that if they let him starve, his rotting "carcass" might cause a plague. The Emperor ultimately orders Lilliputian-style clothes to be tailored for Gulliver and makes arrangements for him to be fed regularly and taught the language of the kingdom. He stipulates, however, that Gulliver must allow appointed officers (Clefren and Marsi Frelock) to search his pockets in case he is carrying any weapons. Gulliver consents, and they take an inventory of all the commonplace items he is carrying, except for a pair of glasses and a small telescope that are hidden inside a pocket he does not reveal to them.

Gulliver stands "like a Colossus" while the emperor reviews his troops. Part 1, chapter 3 *(Arthur Rackham)*

## Chapter 3

Gulliver's good behavior begins to earn the trust of the Lilliputian Emperor and his subjects. The Emperor even arranges for him to enjoy some "Country Shows" in which aspiring courtiers display their skill at dancing on a rope. Whenever an important office becomes vacant, a rope-dancing competition is held, and whoever jumps the highest on the rope without falling is awarded the position. The Emperor also calls upon his chief ministers from time to time to show their skill, and Gulliver watches as Flimnap (the treasurer) and Reldresal (principal secretary for private affairs) prove that they "have not lost their Faculty." Another similar

test requires courtiers to show their agility by leaping over or creeping under a stick. Gulliver delights the Emperor with a diversion of his own, using his handkerchief to create a giant stage on which he arranges mock battles between the Lilliputian troops.

There is a great fuss among the Lilliputians when they find what turns out to be Gulliver's hat lying on the shore. He further entertains the Emperor by standing "like a *Colossus*" while the soldiers of Lilliput march under him. The Emperor finally discusses Gulliver's request for liberty with his council, where it is supported by all except for Skyresh Bolgolam. That official ultimately assents, however, upon the condition that Gulliver agree to abide by a number of "articles and conditions" governing his liberty. Among other things, these articles require Gulliver to serve as Lilliput's ally in the ongoing war against Blefuscu. In that capacity, he must seek to destroy their navy, which is preparing to attack. Gulliver is set free when he formally swears to uphold these stipulations.

## Chapter 4

Gulliver visits Mildendo, the capital city of Lilliput and is entertained at the Emperor's palace, which is located in the center of the metropolis. After Gulliver returns to his house, Reldresal pays him a visit and outlines the political situation in Lilliput. He explains that his people "labour under two mighty Evils"—one violent Faction at home, and the Danger of an Invasion by a most potent Enemy from abroad. A perpetually bitter quarrel is ongoing between the rebellious Tramecksan faction (the "High-Heels") and the ruling Slamecksan ("Low-Heel") party. The foreign enemies that worry Reldresal are the High-Heels, who have fled Lilliput to find refuge on the island of Blefuscu, from which they are waging war against their homeland. Reldresal tells Gulliver that the strife between the High- and Low-Heel parties began many years ago with a rancorous disagreement over whether eggs should be broken at the larger end or the smaller end. The traditionalist Big-Endians refuse to break their eggs at the smaller end, which is required by law in Lilliput. Reldresal adds that the Lilliputians have recently received intelligence suggesting that Blefuscu is preparing to send a "numerous Fleet" to attack Lilliput, and the Emperor just wanted Gulliver to know about it. Recalling the articles to which he had sworn in order to obtain his liberty, Gulliver asks Reldresal to tell the Emperor that while he thinks it would be inappropriate for him (as a foreigner) to get involved in the war, he stands ready "to defend the Emperor and his kingdom "against all Invaders."

### Chapter 5

In response to the Emperor's thinly veiled request, Gulliver wades across to the island of Blefuscu. As he is in the process of commandeering the Blefuscudian ships, the inhabitants of that kingdom recover from their initial horror and assault him

Gulliver seizes the Blefuscudian navy. Part 1, chapter 5 *(Arthur Rackham)*

with "several thousand Arrows." He dons his spectacles to guard his eyes from the arrows, cuts the moorings from the ships and drags the 50 Men of War back to the royal port of Lilliput. The Emperor greets him joyfully and makes him a Nardac "on the spot, which is the highest Title of Honour among them." The celebration is short-lived, however, since the Emperor encourages Gulliver to go back and get the rest of the ships and ultimately wants him to destroy Blefuscu altogether so the Lilliputians can make its citizens their slaves.

Although the majority of the Emperor's ministers support Gulliver's refusal, the Emperor never forgives him. He joins in a malicious "intrigue" with a group of ministers who are hostile to Gulliver. About three weeks after Gulliver's robbery of the Blefuscudian navy, a "solemn Embassy" from Blefuscu arrives with humble offers of peace to Lilliput. They also invite Gulliver to visit their kingdom. When Gulliver asks permission to go, the Emperor's cold agreement causes Gulliver to "conceive some imperfect Idea of Courts and Ministers."

One night a fire breaks out in the Empress of Lilliput's royal apartment, caused by the "carelessness" of a maid of honor who fell asleep reading a romance. Gulliver is awakened by the commotion and ends up extinguishing the fire by urinating on the burning portion of the "magnificent Palace." Gulliver is a little concerned that he has broken the law by "mak[ing] water within the Precincts of the Palace," but the Emperor promises to seek a pardon for him. The pardon never materializes, and the Empress—"conceiving the greatest Abhorrence" at Gulliver's method for putting out the fire—vows revenge against him and swears never to set foot in her apartment again.

### Chapter 6

In this section Gulliver provides an overview of the Lilliputians, their culture, and his own "manner of living" there during his stay of nine months and 13 days. He explains that everything in that country—including animals and plants—is sized in proportion to the citizens, who are less than six inches tall. Their laws are "very peculiar," requiring (for example) that if someone accused of treason is found innocent "the Accuser is immediately put to an ignominious Death." They treat fraud and ingratitude as serious crimes punishable by death, and reward citizens who consistently abide by the laws. In choosing public officials, morality is more important to the Lilliputians than ability, and atheists are ineligible for selection. Gulliver notes that the apparent contradiction in using rope-dancing as a means of gaining and holding public office (see chapter 3) was a newfangled idea instituted by the current Emperor's grandfather, and illustrates the extent to which Lilliputian institutions have become corrupt.

The Lilliputians view marriage as a union motivated solely by sexual desire. They do not, therefore, expect children to feel any natural obligation to their parents. There are public schools for all children, and parents (except for tenant farmers and laborers) are required to provide financial support for each of their offspring. The schools vary in the education they provide, with the entire system designed to prepare children "for such a condition of Life as befits the Rank of their Parents." Students are also separated according to sex, with different preparations for each.

Gulliver describes how the Lilliputians go to great lengths in order to keep him fed and clothed. He also outlines how two informants, Clustril and Drunlo, allege that he and Lady Flimnap are having an illicit affair. Gulliver dismisses the accusation as patently false, but adds that it gives Flimnap all the excuse he needs to speak badly of him to the Emperor, with whom Gulliver quickly loses credit.

### Chapter 7

As Gulliver prepares to visit Blefuscu, he is privately visited by "a considerable Person at Court." This unnamed courtier claims that for two months, Skyresh Bolgolam, Flimnap, Limtoc, and Lalcon have all been plotting against Gulliver and have prepared articles for his impeachment, charging him with treason "and other capital Crimes." The articles (of which Gulliver's visitor provides a copy) cite him for making water within the palace precincts, failing to obey the Emperor's order to destroy Blefuscu, consorting "like a false

Traitor" with the Blefuscudian ambassadors, and intending to visit Blefuscu even though he had received "only verbal Licence" from the Emperor of Lilliput. Gulliver's informant tells him that Bolgolam, Flimnap, and others have demanded that Gulliver be put to a torturous death, but that the Emperor has "graciously" decided on the more lenient punishment of blinding Gulliver by having archers shoot "very sharp-pointed Arrows into the Balls of [his] Eyes." The Emperor assumes that Gulliver will "gratefully and humbly" submit to this reduced sentence. Upon learning of what the Emperor has in store for him, Gulliver hurriedly leaves Lilliput and makes his way to Blefuscu.

Gulliver learns of his treason charges. Part 1, chapter 7 *(Thomas Moore)*

*Chapter 8*

Three days after he arrives in Blefuscu, Gulliver notices an overturned boat floating in the waters off the shore of Blefuscu. He investigates and, upon discovering that it is a full-sized vessel, uses 20 Blefuscudian ships to bring it ashore. With help from the Emperor of Blefuscu, he begins restoring the boat in hopes that he can use it to sail home. In the meantime, the Emperor of Lilliput sends an envoy to his counterpart in Blefuscu demanding that Gulliver be "bound hand and foot" and returned to Lilliput. The Emperor of Blefuscu refuses, citing "the many good Offices [Gulliver] had done him in making the Peace" and adds that Gulliver will soon be leaving for good, anyway. About a month later (on September 24, 1701), Gulliver departs after an obsequious farewell ceremony in which he kisses the hands of each member of the royal family and receives many gifts and supplies for his voyage. Two days later he is rescued by Captain John Biddel and his crew, who are on their way back to England from Japan. Among the crew is Peter Williams, one of Gulliver's old friends. They arrive on April 13, 1702, and Gulliver is reunited with his family. After remaining with them for only two months, Gulliver settles his wife and children in a "good House at *Redriff*" and then departs once again—this time on a voyage to Surat aboard the *Adventure*.

### Part 2: A Voyage to Brobdingnag

*Chapter 1*

On June 20, 1702, Gulliver and the rest of the crew set sail on the *Adventure* with Captain John Nicholas. They reach the Cape of Good Hope and remain there until the end of March. Once they pass the Straits of Madagascar (on April 19) they encounter a storm that drives them off course. On June 16, 1703, they finally sight land, drop anchor, and send a small party (including Gulliver) ashore in search of fresh water. Gulliver ends up being left behind when the others flee while being pursued by a "huge Creature" who wades out after them into the sea. One of these giants, who look human but are 12 times larger than Gulliver, dis-

covers him hiding in a cornfield. He picks Gulliver up and (after warily examining him) tucks him away in the lapel of his coat and takes him to the Farmer, who attempts to communicate with him. The Farmer takes Gulliver home and shows him to his wife, who is shocked at first but ends up treating Gulliver kindly. During dinner, Gulliver is fed, and the Farmer's 10-year-old son frightens him by lifting him high into the air. He is awed by the sight of the Farmer's giant cat and dogs, and horrified when he sees the "monstrous Breast" (with all of its imperfections magnified by its size) of a Nurse who is breastfeeding the Farmer's youngest child. The Farmer orders his wife to take

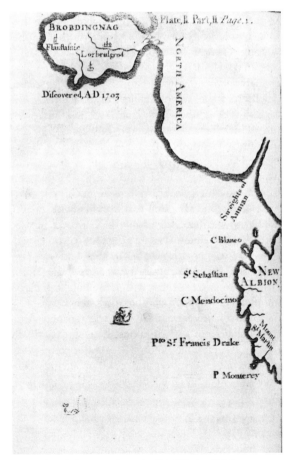

Map of Brobdingnag from Swift's *Works,* 1726
*(Courtesy of Duke University Libraries)*

care of Gulliver, and she places him carefully on their giant bed for a nap. Awakened by "natural Necessities," he encounters two giant rats that have climbed onto the bed. He draws his sword, kills one of them and wounds the other, who flees for its life. The Farmer's wife arrives and, after ensuring that Gulliver is not injured, takes him out into the garden and leaves him alone to "discharge the Necessities of nature."

### Chapter 2

The Farmer's nine-year-old daughter quickly develops a strong affection for Gulliver. She names him Grildrig and treats him as her own little doll. Gulliver calls her Glumdalclitch (which in the language of Brobdingnag means "little nurse"). Word soon gets around about the strange little creature lodged at the Farmer's house, and his neighbors begin to visit in order to have a look at him. Another Farmer who lives nearby comes to examine Gulliver, and is offended when Gulliver laughs at his comical appearance. The visiting Farmer encourages Glumdalclitch's father to put Gulliver on public display in a neighboring town and charge admission to see him. This upsets Glumdalclitch, but she is unable to discourage her father from going ahead with the plan. The Farmer transports Gulliver to an inn, where many people come and pay to see him perform various acts such as taking up a thimble filled with liquor and drinking to the audience's health. All of this wearies Gulliver, but the Farmer is pleased with the profit he makes and decides to travel with Gulliver to numerous "considerable Cities of the Kingdom." They set out for Lorbrulgrud, the capital city, on August 17, 1703, with Glumdalclitch carrying Gulliver inside a small box tied to her waist and designed to protect him during the journey. After stopping at various towns along the way, they finally reach the capital on October 26. As the Farmer prepares to put Gulliver on display, Glumdalclitch continues to teach him the language of Brobdingnag.

### Chapter 3

Gulliver's health declines because of the demanding performance schedule to which the Farmer subjects him. The Farmer, worried that Gulliver will soon die, readily accepts an invitation to appear with him before the Queen of Brobdingnag to divert her and her ladies. Upon seeing him and speaking with him briefly, the Queen offers to purchase Gulliver from the Farmer. At Gulliver's request, Glumdalclitch is allowed to remain with him as his "Nurse and Instructor." The Queen presents him to the King of Brobdingnag, who receives him coldly at first but ends up conversing with him at length. The King also has Gulliver questioned by three Scholars, who decide that Gulliver must be a freak of nature. The Queen has her craftsmen prepare a lavish little bedchamber for Gulliver. She dines with him regularly, although he reports that watching her eat was a "terrible" sight. At the King's request, Gulliver provides an account of "the Manners, Religion, Laws, Gov-

Gulliver kisses the hand of the queen of Brobdingnag. Part 2, chapter 3  *(Arthur Rackham)*

Gulliver defends himself from wasps. Part 2, chapter 3
*(Arthur Rackham)*

the geography and landscape of the kingdom and provides a detailed account of Lorbrulgrud, the capital city. He also describes the royal palace and its vicinity, where he sees a number of beggars. They are characterized by their gross deformities and diseases, which are magnified by the tremendous size of their bodies in comparison to Gulliver's. The greatest temple in the kingdom is a disappointment to Gulliver since (relatively speaking) it turns out to be much smaller than those in Europe. In contrast, the King's gigantic kitchen is "a noble Building" with an oven that is almost as wide as the cupola of St. Paul's Cathedral in London. The royal stables house about 600 horses, each of which is between 54 and 60 feet high.

### Chapter 5
Gulliver recounts several "troublesome Accidents" that plagued him during his stay in Brobdingnag. Provoked by an insult from Gulliver, the Dwarf shakes an apple tree and causes a dozen apples to pelt Gulliver, who is standing below. In another incident, Gulliver is caught in a sudden hailstorm and suffers numerous bruises from hailstones that are 18 times larger than those in Europe. In the same garden, a spaniel takes Gulliver up in its mouth and carries him to one of the gardeners. Gulliver narrowly escapes being whisked away as prey by a giant kite, and suffers several injuries by tripping over various obstacles as he walks along absentmindedly "thinking on poor *England.*" Glumdalclitch regularly takes him to visit the Maids of Honor at the court of Brobdingnag. Their treatment of Gulliver soon makes him uneasy and resentful, since they use him "without any manner of Ceremony"—stripping him and themselves naked and using him as a kind of sexual toy. Their giant bodies, which from Gulliver's perspective are riddled with all sorts of disgusting imperfections, make these strange experiences all the worse for him.

Gulliver also witnesses the public execution of a convicted murderer, whose larger-than-life beheading is remarkably gory. At the Queen's request, Gulliver displays his nautical skill by sailing a little boat in a huge trough filled with water. In the midst of sailing one day he defends himself

ernment, and Learning of *Europe.*" The King finds this information laughable, and observes that Gulliver is a great example of how "contemptible" human vanity is, since it can be mimicked by such "diminutive Insects." Gulliver finds himself at odds with the Queen's Dwarf, who is overcome with jealousy at having been replaced as her favorite. Determined to embarrass Gulliver at every turn, the Dwarf drops him into a bowl of cream and (on another occasion) jams his legs into a marrow bone. Gulliver is also pestered by giant flies and wasps in Brobdingnag, from which—by his own account—he courageously defends himself.

### Chapter 4
The King and Queen of Brobdingnag regularly take Gulliver along on tours of their realm. He describes

Gulliver's defends himself from a frog. Part 2, chapter 5 *(Arthur Rackham)*

## Chapter 6

Gulliver amuses the court by making a comb out of stubble from the King's beard. He also makes two chairs and a purse from strands of the Queen's hair, and further entertains the King and Queen by playing a giant spinet (harpsichord) with large sticks he designs for that purpose. The King frequently converses with Gulliver, and during one of these interchanges Gulliver tells the monarch that the contempt he has developed for Europe and the rest of the world is unbecoming. This leads Gulliver to deliver (over the course of several meetings with the King) a number of lengthy discourses on English government. The King asks a number of questions at each of these "audiences" and—after picking Gulliver up and petting him like a small animal—finally concludes that these conversations have

from a giant frog, but (like the episodes involving the insects in chapter 3) in Gulliver's view this is just another chance for him to show his courage. A monkey accosts Gulliver one day and climbs onto the palace roof with him in tow. To Glumdalclitch's horror, the animal treats Gulliver like one of its own offspring and tries to feed him all sorts of "filthy stuff." After Gulliver is finally rescued, the monkey is killed. Gulliver adds that he has become a source of great amusement at court, especially since Glumdalclitch takes every opportunity to tell the Queen about each of his embarrassing mishaps.

Gulliver tells the king of Brobdingnag about English government. Part 2, chapter 6  *(Thomas Morten)*

proven beyond doubt that the vast majority of Gulliver's "natives" are "the most pernicious Race of little odious Vermin that Nature ever suffered to crawl upon the Earth."

## Chapter 7

Insulted and frustrated with the King's assessment of England and its people, Gulliver convinces himself that it is only a "miserable" effect of the ruler's *"confined Education"* and lack of worldliness. As a remedy, Gulliver decides to impress the King by telling him all about gunpowder and how the English use it to subdue their enemies and assert their dominance. This strategy backfires, however, and causes the King to react with horror rather than admiration. He expresses his amazement that "so impotent and groveling an Insect" as Gulliver "could entertain such inhuman Ideas" and threatens him with death if he ever mentions gunpowder again. This leads Gulliver to give up trying to change the King's negative opinion of the English. Instead, he provides a detailed (and generally negative) description of Brobdingnagian education, laws, books and language, and military. He asserts that their learning is "very defective," their laws excessively simple, and their books few and unimpressive. The King's army, furthermore, is sizable but made up of tradesmen and farmers, rather than professional soldiers, and thus unlikely to be very powerful.

## Chapter 8

Despite the kind treatment he has received during his two-year stay in Brobdingnag, Gulliver longs to regain his freedom "among People with whom [he can] converse upon even Terms." On a trip with the King and Queen to the southern coast of the kingdom, a Page takes Gulliver (in his box) to the shore for some air. Gulliver decides to take a nap, and the Page goes off in search of bird eggs among the rocks. While Gulliver sleeps, an eagle swoops down and takes up his box by the ring fastened to the top. Eventually the bird drops the box (and Gulliver) into the sea. After nearly drowning, Gulliver is finally rescued by sailors on their way back to England under the command of Captain Thomas Wilcocks. The captain and his crew are amazed by Gulliver's story. After several stops, the vessel arrives in England on June 3, 1706—about

nine months after what Gulliver calls his "escape" from Brobdingnag. Upon his return home to Redriff, Gulliver's family decides (as Captain Wilcocks had) that Gulliver has gone mad. He soon comes to a "right Understanding" with his family and friends, but his wife nonetheless begs him not to go on any more sea voyages.

## Part 3: A Voyage to Laputa, Balnibarbi, Luggnagg, Glubbdubdrib and Japan

## Chapter 1

After Gulliver is at home for only 10 days, Captain William Robinson (an old acquaintance) offers him a position as ship's surgeon on a vessel bound for the East Indies. Gulliver agrees, and they set out on August 5, 1706. They stop in Tonquin (northern Vietnam), and while Robinson awaits his freight, Gulliver is put in charge of a sloop filled with goods to sell to the inhabitants of nearby islands. Three days after Gulliver and his men set out, they encounter a storm, and then two pirates overtake them. Persuaded by a particularly brash Dutchman who has some authority among the pirates, their Japanese captain agrees to have Gulliver set adrift in a small canoe. Gulliver makes his way to a nearby island and prepares to remain there for as long as he must. The next morning, however, he sees a giant island—which he later learns is called Laputa—floating in the sky. He waves his cap and handkerchief to attract the attention of some people who are fishing at the edge of the island, and they eventually rescue him by lowering a chain with a seat on the end and pulling him up.

## Chapter 2

Gulliver describes the strange population of Laputa. The inhabitants keep their heads tilted to one side or the other, with one eye turned inward and the other looking upward. Their clothing fits poorly and is decorated with suns, moons, stars, and various musical instruments. They are perpetually distracted—caught up in intense speculations regarding mathematics and music—and require servants called Flappers to accompany them everywhere. During conversations, each Flapper's job is to remind his master when to speak and when to listen by strik-

The flying island of Laputa  *(Thomas Morten)*

the attention of men who visit Laputa "from the Continent below," and (since their husbands are always preoccupied) married women make no attempt to hide their adulterous affairs with these visitors from Balnibarbi.

In about a month, Gulliver becomes reasonably fluent in the language and is able to answer the King's questions about the lands in which he has traveled. To Gulliver's chagrin these inquiries are limited to the state of mathematics in each kingdom, since the King has no interest in foreign laws, government, or cultures.

### Chapter 3

Curious to discover what causes the island of Laputa to fly, Gulliver gets permission from the King to go

ing his mouth or ear, respectively, with a large bladder filled with peas or pebbles and fastened to the end of a short stick. The Flappers also occasionally strike their masters on the eyes to keep them from falling down in the midst of their deep thought. Gulliver meets the King of Laputa, who arranges for Gulliver to be taught the language of Laputa. The King also sends a Tailor, who makes a suit of clothes for Gulliver in the Laputian style, which is "ill made, and quite out of shape." As the island flies toward the metropolis of Lagado, Gulliver notes that it stops above each town along the way to receive petitions (along with wine and food) from those who dwell on the land below.

The Laputians' houses are "very ill built" without any right angles, reflecting their disdain for practical geometry, "which they despise as Vulgar and Mechanic." They live in a state of constant worry, mainly concerned with "several Changes they dread in the Celestial Bodies." They are especially anxious about the possibility that the sun will eventually go out, leading to their utter destruction. The women of Laputa exist in a state that reflects their frustration at living among men who are always lost in thought. Not allowed to leave the island without a royal dispensation, they welcome

Gulliver meets the Laputian King. Part 3, chapter 2
*(Thomas Morten)*

exploring. With his "Tutor" in tow, he learns the dimensions and other characteristics of the giant floating land mass. Gulliver also finds out that the island's movement is controlled by a giant magnet that causes Laputa to rise, fall, proceed in different directions, or stop, depending on which way the "loadstone" is turned. Laputian astronomers maneuver the magnet according to the King's orders.

Gulliver notes that the King's power is limited because he cannot "prevail on a Ministry to join him." Potential associates are unwilling to unite with him because they fear losing favor with him and what he may do to their relatives living below on Balnibarbi. In cases of insurrection among the citizens beneath Laputa, the King's normal course is to make the island hover so that it deprives the rebels of sun and rain (and sometimes he has them pelted with rocks dropped from the edge of the island). In extreme cases, however, his seldom-used "last Remedy" is to have the island dropped on top of the insurrectionists—causing "a universal Destruction both of Houses and Men." Three years prior to Gulliver's arrival on the floating island, the citizens of Lindalino (a city in Balnibarbi) had rebelled against the King, demanding what Gulliver describes as a number of "Exorbitances." Through a creative use of magnetism that threatened to destroy the floating island by bringing it down on top of four giant towers, the inhabitants of Lindalino were successful in forcing the King to honor their demands. Gulliver ends the chapter by men-

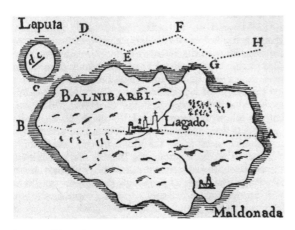

A map of Laputa

tioning that it is against the law for the King or his two sons to leave Laputa, and the same is true for the Queen until she is too old to bear children.

### Chapter 4

Dissatisfied with the amount of attention he receives from the Laputians, Gulliver asks a "great Lord at Court" to intercede on his behalf and ask the King to allow him to leave the island. The King grants this petition, and Gulliver departs for Balnibarbi. His first stop is the metropolis of Lagado, where he meets Lord Munodi, who will be his guide and host. Munodi is a friend of the courtier who helped Gulliver obtain permission to leave Laputa. He takes Gulliver on a tour of the city, and Gulliver does not hesitate to comment disparagingly on the barren, unimpressive surroundings he sees. Munodi eventually takes Gulliver to his country house, about 20 miles outside Lagado. As they travel farther away from the city and closer to Munodi's estate, Gulliver notices that the landscape becomes more and more attractive. The estate itself is magnificent: The house reflects "the best Rules of Ancient Architecture," while "the Fountains, Gardens, Walks, Avenues, and Groves were all disposed with exact Judgment and Taste." Munodi tells Gulliver that until about 40 years earlier, all of Lagado used to be as lush and neatly kept as his estate. That all changed, though, when some citizens visited Laputa. They returned to Lagado filled with new-fangled ideas and established an Academy of Projectors, which was shortly replicated in almost every town on the continent. Soon the academies succeeded in promoting new (but ineffective) strategies in agriculture and building, leaving the kingdom in its current fallow state. Munodi's estate thrives because he still follows the old ways of cultivating land and building structures. He encourages Gulliver to go see the Academy of Lagado for himself, posing as "a great Admirer of Projects."

### Chapter 5

Gulliver visits the Academy of Lagado, where he meets a variety of projectors engaged in a number of ludicrous experiments that reverse natural processes and parody the endeavors of the Royal Society. The projects are aimed at goals such as extracting sunbeams from cucumbers, turning human excrement back into its original food, transforming ice into gunpowder, and building houses from the roof down. After completing his tour of this side of the Academy, he ventures into the wing "appropriated to the Advancers of speculative Learning," where he meets the Universal Artist and other professors conducting various (and equally ridiculous) experiments in language, education, and mathematics. One is working on an invention that would allow even "the most ignorant Person" to write books on any subject. Three other professors are developing a strategy for improving the language of their country by cutting "polysyllables into one," and eliminating all words except nouns. They even consider doing away with

Projectors of the grand Academy of Lagado. Part 3, chapter 5  *(Arthur Rackham)*

words altogether, proposing instead that it would be better for individuals simply to carry around all the objects "necessary to express the particular Business they are to discourse on." The master of the Mathematical School teaches his students by having them fast and then swallow a "thin wafer" on which the "Proposition and Demonstration" are written. His theory is that as the wafer is digested, the ink (a "Cephalic Tincture") will make its way into the student's brain, depositing the proposition there, as well. Gulliver reports that unfortunately, the students most often vomit before the wafers can produce their desired effect.

### Chapter 6

The next stop on Gulliver's tour of the Academy is the School of Political Projectors. He finds these projectors to be "wholly out of their Senses," evidenced by (what he views as) the preposterous schemes they propose. One such proposal is that monarchs should choose their favorites based on wisdom and virtue. Another calls for educating ministers of state on how to consider the public good as they make decisions. Other plans seek to reward merit, ability, and eminent service. Gulliver dismisses all of these as "wild impossible Chimeras." There is, however, one "Ingenious Doctor," who stands out among these lunatics. Having devoted himself to devising remedies for the "Diseases and Corruptions" of public officials, this projector has decided that diseases of the state are best cured by the same prescriptions used for curing diseases of the body.

Based on this hypothesis (which Gulliver enthusiastically endorses), this projector argues that if physicians would administer medicines to senators just before their meetings it would greatly improve the efficiency of government. He also claims that he has discovered a way to cut down on the forgetfulness for which the "King's Favourites" are notorious. His solution: After requesting favors from these ministers, citizens should inflict physical pain upon them (kicking them in the "belly," pinching their arm "black and blue," and so forth) until the favor is granted "or absolutely refused." With great admiration, Gulliver describes the Ingenious Doctor's other schemes for improving government.

Laputa's School of Political Projectors. Part 3,
chapter 6 *(Thomas Morten)*

vices and folly or taxing "those Qualities of Body and Mind for which Men chiefly value themselves. Another professor shares with Gulliver his project for "discovering Plots and Conspiracies against the Government." The most memorable part of his plan is that "great Statesmen" should meticulously examine the excrement of "suspected Persons," paying careful attention to its color, odor, taste, consistency, and other qualities. Gulliver offers some suggestions for improving the plan.

### Chapter 7

Having decided that it is time to return home to England, Gulliver travels to the port of Maldonada in hopes of finding a ship bound for Luggnagg, an island from which he has learned he can easily sail to Japan. When he arrives at Maldonada, however, he finds that no ship will be ready for about a month. On the advice of a "Gentleman of Distinction," he decides to visit the nearby island of Glubbdubdrib while he waits. The inhabitants of this island are sorcerers, and the Governor is capable of calling spirits back from the dead. The Gentleman and one other acquaintance agree to accompany Gulliver during his visit. Upon their arrival, one of Gulliver's party goes to the Governor and gains permission for Gulliver to visit the palace. As he and the others make their way through the Chamber of Presence, Gulliver is horrified at the appearance of the guards they pass: "their Countenances," he writes, make his "flesh creep." The Governor asks Gulliver to give an account of his travels. Recognizing Gulliver's trepidation at seeing some of the royal attendants vanish, the Governor assures him that he will "receive no hurt." After Gulliver provides a brief relation of his journeys, the Governor directs his guests to dinner. They are served by a different group of ghosts, but Gulliver finds himself "less terrified" than he had been that morning. Nonetheless, he humbly declines the Governor's invitation to spend the night and (along with his companions) retires to a house in an adjoining town for the evening.

They return to the palace the following morning, and repeat the same routine for 10 days. Within a few days, Gulliver becomes so accustomed to seeing ghosts that he accepts the Gover-

Senators, he claims, should vote the exact opposite of their opinion since it would "infallibly terminate in the Good of the Public." And finally, "when Parties in a State are violent," he argues that the best solution is to take a hundred leaders of each party, slice their brains in half, and interchange the halves—"applying each to the head of his opposite Party-man." His rationale for this plan is that when the two half-brains are "left to debate the Matter between themselves" in the same head, they will eventually reach an agreement.

Gulliver next describes a heated debate he witnessed between two professors on the best ways to raise money without "grieving" the citizens. Among other strategies, they consider imposing a tax on

Dining with the governor of Glubbdubdrib. Part 3, chapter 7 *(Thomas Morten)*

nor's invitation to summon "whatever Person" he wishes from the dead and question them about anything "within the compass of the times they lived in." Based on his requests, the Governor summons Alexander the Great, Hannibal, Caesar, and Pompey. He also shows Gulliver the Senate of Rome in one Chamber, "and a modern Representative, in Counterview in another." Gulliver concludes that while the Roman senators constitute "an Assembly of Heroes and Demigods," the modern group is nothing but a "Knot of Pedlars, Pickpockets, Highwaymen and Bullies."

### Chapter 8

Gulliver decides to ask the Governor of Glubbdubdrib to summon "those Ancients, who were most renowned for Wit and Learning." His first request is to see Homer and Aristotle appear along with all of their commentators. He discovers that in the underworld, these modern commentators avoid the ancient philosophers because of the shame they feel at having so grossly misrepresented Homer's and Aristotle's work to posterity. Gulliver introduces Didymus and Eustathius to Homer, who finds that they lack the genius to be poets. He also gives Aristotle an account of Duns Scotus and Ramus as he introduces them to him, causing Aristotle to ask "whether the rest of the Tribe were as great Dunces as themselves." To further demonstrate the supremacy of Ancient learning, Gulliver asks the Governor to summon Descartes and Gassendi, who explain their principal theories to Aristotle. He responds by exploding their theories and asserting that "new Systems of Nature" are like fashions, and always "flourish but a short Period of time."

The two gentlemen who accompanied Gulliver to Glubbdubdrib tell him that they must return to Lugnagg in three days. He decides to spend his remaining time having the Governor summon "some of the modern Dead, who had made the greatest Figure for two or three hundred years." He is disappointed with the "dozen or two" kings and royal ancestors he sees and finds himself to be "chiefly disgusted with modern History." The world, he concludes, had been grossly misled by historians, who habitually ascribe qualities such as bravery, virtue, piety, and honor to those who (in reality) were only cowards and scoundrels. He also discovers that most of the famous modern dead had achieved their "Greatness and Wealth" through "Sodomy," incest, prostitution, treason, and other evils.

Gulliver is surprised to learn that those who truly served their "Princes and States" are not listed on any record, except when they are misrepresented by historians as "the vilest Rogues and Traitors." When the Governor summons these noble but forgotten moderns at Gulliver's request, most report that they died "in Poverty and Disgrace, and the rest on a Scaffold or a Gibbet." Intrigued by one among these whose "case appear[s] a little singular," Gulliver goes out of his way to talk with

Charles Mordaunt, third earl of PETERBOROUGH (a friend of Swift's who failed to receive preferment despite his bravery in the War of the Spanish Succession). Disillusioned and troubled by what he has learned, Gulliver reflects on the remarkable physical degeneration of humankind within the last century alone. For encouragement, he finally asks the Governor to call up a few "English *Yeomen*," and he is pleased to recall the simplicity, justice, valor, and patriotism that once characterized his countrymen.

### Chapter 9

Gulliver returns to Maldonada with his two companions. After a two-week wait, he begins the monthlong voyage to Luggnagg and arrives at Clumegnig (a southeastern seaport town) on April 21, 1709. Gulliver's fellow sailors reveal that he is a stranger, and upon landing he is questioned about his identity by a Custom-House Officer. Gulliver lies to the officer, saying that he hails from Holland. He represents himself this way since he intends to travel to Japan, and knows that the Dutch are the only Europeans allowed to enter that country. He recounts his shipwreck and his visit to Laputa, and tells the officer that he is on his way to Japan. The Custom-House Officer decides that he must detain Gulliver until he receives orders from court on what to do with him. Gulliver's lodgings (though guarded) are quite comfortable.

Since he receives visitors from time to time, Gulliver hires an interpreter to help him converse with them. Within a couple of weeks a dispatch from court arrives containing a warrant for Gulliver to be transported to the royal city of Traldragdubb, where he will visit the King of Luggnagg. When he arrives in the throne room, he approaches the King in the customary manner by crawling on his belly and licking the floor as he goes, until he comes within four yards of the throne, when he raises himself up on his knees and strikes his forehead on the ground several times. In an aside, Gulliver describes the King's technique of having extra dust strewn on the floor for those who have powerful enemies at court, and his "gentle indulgent manner" of putting certain nobles to death by sprinkling a poisonous brown powder on the floor for them to lick up and ingest. Since Gulliver is a

stranger, however, the King extends him the "peculiar Grace" of having the floor swept clean before his approach. After an hour's conversation (through the aid of Gulliver's interpreter, whom he brought from Clumegnig), the King arranges for Gulliver to receive lodging, board, and gold for his "common Expenses." Gulliver remains in Luggnagg for three months before deciding to return home to his wife and family.

### Chapter 10

Gulliver praises the Luggnaggians for their politeness, generosity, and kindness to strangers, but admits that they (like the inhabitants of all "*Eastern Countries*") possess their fair share of pride. One day during his three-month stay in that country, a "Person of Qualtity" asks if he has seen any of their Struldbrugs. When Gulliver says he has not, the gentleman describes this immortal race, leading Gulliver to exclaim ("as in a Rapture") how wonderful it must be to live forever. Despite his assertion in the previous chapter that it was time to return home, he declares that if the King will allow it, he will spend the rest of his life conversing with "those superior Beings the *Struldbrugs*."

He goes on to assert that if he had the "good Fortune" to have been born a Struldbrug, he would strive to become the wealthiest, most learned man in the kingdom. He would also keep careful records of important events, write impartial biographies of public figures, and describe every cultural change for posterity. He declares that he would become "a living Treasury of Knowledge and Wisdom, and certainly become the Oracle of the Nation." In his estimation, there would be no end to the good he and his fellow immortals could achieve as they lived forever.

At the end of Gulliver's oration, his interpreter and the others who have listened laugh hysterically at all he has said. The interpreter tells Gulliver that the "System of Living" he has described is entirely flawed because it is based on the false supposition that immortality also includes perpetual "Youth, Health, and Vigour, which no Man could be so foolish" as to expect. Instead of living the wonderful life Gulliver has imagined, the Struldbrugs live in absolute misery by the time they reach 80. They are hated by society and denied the death they crave as their bodies and minds continue to decay. When Gulliver finally encounters some Struldbrugs, he finds them to be the "most mortifying Sight" he "ever beheld," and he immediately loses his "keen Appetite for perpetuity of Life."

### Chapter 11

After a brief commentary on originality in travel narratives, Gulliver describes his departure from Luggnagg on May 6, 1709. The King provides him with a giant red diamond, more than 400 large pieces of gold, and a letter of recommendation to the Emperor of Japan. After a 15-day voyage, Gulliver and the others on his ship arrive at the Japanese port of Xamoschi. He presents his letter and is treated with all the pomp and circumstance usually reserved for public ministers. The Emperor receives him almost immediately, and Gulliver repeats his earlier claim (in chapter 9) that he is "a *Dutch* Merchant" who was "shipwrecked in a very remote Country" and found his way to Japan as he traveled back to Europe. He asks the Emperor to provide him with transportation to Nangasac and to excuse him from engaging in the "ceremony" of "trampling upon the Crucifix," which is normally required of all Hollanders trading in Japan. The Emperor is surprised at Gulliver's second request, and warns him that he should keep quiet about it during his upcoming voyage in order to avoid being murdered by "his Countrymen" along the way.

Gulliver arrives at Nangasac on June 9, 1709, "after a very long and troublesome journey." He soon joins a group of Dutch sailors aboard the *Amboyna*, bound for Amsterdam. He lies once again about his identity, assuring the sailors that he was born and raised in Holland and even devising fake Dutch names for his parents. The captain, Theodorus Vangrult, charges Gulliver only half the normal fare on the condition that he serve as ship's surgeon during the voyage. Following an uneventful trip, the crew arrives in Amsterdam on April 6, 1710 (this date appears as the *16th* in the 1726 edition of the *Travels*). Gulliver soon makes his way back home to Redriff five days later. Having been away for five years and six months, he finds his "wife and Family in good Health."

### Part 4: A Voyage to the Country of the Houyhnhnms

### Chapter 1

After spending five months at home "in a very happy Condition" with his wife (who is now pregnant) and children, Gulliver sets sail as captain of the *Adventure* on August 2, 1710. His orders are to "trade with the *Indians*, in the *South-Sea*, and make what Discoveries" he can. When a number of his crewmen die of distemper, most of the replacements Gulliver hires turn out to be pirates. They lead the entire crew to mutiny against him, and Gulliver finds himself confined as a prisoner in his cabin.

On May 11, 1711, James Welch comes to Gulliver and warns him that he is about to be put ashore. Welch and several others pack Gulliver and some of his belongings into a longboat, row him to an unknown beach, and leave him marooned there. Gulliver decides to move inland and surrender "to the first Savages" he meets, buying his freedom from them with bracelets and other trinkets. Expecting to be "shot with an Arrow from behind or on either side," Gulliver proceeds along a "beaten Road." After seeing a great deal of livestock, he happens upon some "very singular" and "deformed" animals—the Yahoos—which he stops to observe. He describes their appearance in detail and concludes that they are the most "disagreeable" animal he has ever seen.

When one of the Yahoos approaches him, Gulliver draws his hanger and smacks the animal on the side of the head. The yelp that follows draws a herd of other Yahoos, many of which climb a tree and defecate on Gulliver's head. This continues until a horse appears in a nearby field, which causes the Yahoos to flee in terror. The horse (a "Dapple-Grey" Houyhnhnm) examines Gulliver carefully, reacting with disdain when Gulliver attempts to stroke its neck. Soon another horse (a "brown Bay") approaches and joins the examination. Based on the civilities they show each other and the seeming conversation they conduct in neighs and whinnies, Gulliver decides that these horses must be magicians who have "metamorphosed themselves" to look like horses. He addresses them

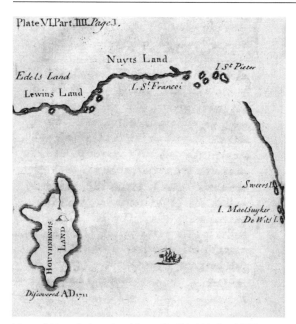

Map of Houyhnhnmland from Swift's *Works,* 1726
*(Courtesy of Duke University Libraries)*

humbly, and picks up on their frequent use of the word *Yahoo* while they converse as though they are amazed. The Bay soon departs, and the Dapple-Grey leads Gulliver away.

### Chapter 2

After a three-mile walk, Gulliver and his equine guide come to a large building. Gulliver assumes that it houses savages, and prepares to offer trinkets to secure his life. Inside, however, Gulliver finds more horses. A "very comely Mare" approaches Gulliver, gives him "a most contemptuous Look," and (in a conversation with the grey horse) repeats the word *Yahoo* several times. The Grey—whom Gulliver soon refers to as "the Master Horse"—leads Gulliver out into a courtyard and then into another building, where three Yahoos are tied up and "feeding upon Roots" and the flesh "of Asses and Dogs." The Master has a Sorrel Nag untie one of the Yahoos and bring him out into the yard. The horses stand Gulliver and the Yahoo side-by-side, and conduct a careful comparison. Gulliver is horrified when he realizes what they are doing, which is intensified when he notices that the "abominable

animal" beside him sports "a perfect Human figure." The Houyhnhnms are perplexed by Gulliver's clothing, however, which seems to distinguish him from the fur-covered Yahoo standing next to him. The Master and the Sorrel Nag offer Gulliver some of the Yahoos' rotten fare, but he refuses it. When they offer some hay and "a Fetlock full of Oats," he refuses that, as well. Gulliver indicates that he wants cow's milk, which the Houyhnhnm Master immediately provides.

An old steed (who, in Gulliver's view, appears to be "of Quality") arrives for lunch in a sledge drawn by four Yahoos. During the meal he and the Master treat Gulliver as the centerpiece of attention (as Gulliver notes, they frequently repeat the word *Yahoo* during their conversation). They are particularly befuddled at Gulliver's gloves, which he removes and puts into his pocket. The Master also gives him a brief lesson in the Houyhnhnm language, ordering him to speak "the few words" he understands. After dinner, Gulliver makes some oat cakes for himself, allaying the Master's concerns over what he will eat. As evening approaches, the Master orders that a place be made for Gulliver to sleep. His lodging is six yards from the Houyhnhnms' house, and "separated from the Stable of the *Yahoos*."

### Chapter 3

The Houyhnhnm Master and his entire household endeavor to teach Gulliver their language, which Gulliver describes as sounding something like High Dutch or German. The Master is intrigued by Gulliver's "Teachableness, Civility, and Cleanliness," but is nonetheless convinced that he must be a Yahoo. Gulliver describes his journey and the mutiny that resulted in his coming to the Houyhnhnms, but his hosts immediately dismiss his story as *"the thing which was not."* He notes that they describe it this way because (since all Houyhnhnms always speak the truth) they do not have a word in their language for lying. Gulliver learns that the word *Houyhnhnm* simply means "horse" in their language, but "in its Etymology" signifies *"the Perfection of Nature."*

Gulliver develops a widespread reputation among the Houyhnhnms as "a wonderful *Yahoo*" that can "speak like a *Houyhnhnm*." Those who come to see him, however, have trouble believing he is a Yahoo because his body "had a different Covering from others of [his] kind." The Sorrel Nag—who becomes Gulliver's companion—inadvertently catches Gulliver in a state of undress one night, and reports what he has seen to the Master. The Master is baffled, but agrees to Gulliver's request that he (and the Sorrel Nag) keep the entire incident a secret.

The Houyhnhnm Master asks Gulliver to give a further account of himself, his ship, and his origins. Gulliver assures the Master that the ship in which he sailed was indeed designed by creatures like himself, and that in his homeland (and everywhere else he has traveled) those creatures are the only

Gulliver learns the Houyhnhnm language. Part 4, chapter 3 *(Thomas Morten)*

rational beings. He adds that if he ever has the good fortune to return home and describe his experiences with the rational Houyhnhnms, his countrymen will swear that he is saying *"the Thing which was not."*

## Chapter 4

The Houyhnhnm Master has difficulty believing what he hears, especially since the concepts of lying and doubting are so unfamiliar to him. Gulliver explains that "the *Yahoos*" are the only governing "Animals" in his homeland and that the Houyhnhnms serve as beasts of burden. The Master is incredulous and indignant, asserting that even the weakest Houyhnhnm could easily "shake off" the strongest *Yahoo,* or even roll over on it and "squeeze the brute to death." Gulliver laments that it is "impossible to express" the Master's "noble Resentment" at what he hears—especially when Gulliver tells him about the common practice of castrating male horses when they are two years old.

Gulliver's Master asserts that he cannot believe any Yahoos anywhere could dominate Houyhnhnms, since the latter are far superior in terms of intellect and physical strength. He further observes that the *Yahoos* of Gulliver's kind are even more inferior to the Houyhnhnms than the *Yahoos* with which he is familiar. Among other flaws, their nails are useless, their hands (which he calls "Forefeet") are "too soft" to bear any weight, and the profile of their faces makes it difficult for them to eat.

The Master ends by asking Gulliver to provide a more detailed account of his country "and the several Actions and Events" of his life prior to his arrival in the land of the Houyhnhnms. Over the course of several days, Gulliver accommodates the request, explaining that he left home in search of riches, lost his crew at sea, and "was forced to supply them by others picked out from several Nations." The Master often interrupts, at a loss to understand why anyone would have agreed to travel with Gulliver after all of his losses. After explaining that poverty and crime forced these individuals to flee their homelands, he struggles to describe "the Desire of Power and Riches" and "the terrible Effects of Lust, Intemperance, Malice, and Envy"—all of which are completely unknown to the Master and all Houyhnhms.

The Master is amazed, but at last gains what Gulliver calls "a competent Knowledge of what Human Nature" is capable of performing.

## Chapter 5

Gulliver summarizes highlights of conversations he had with his Houyhnhnm Master over the course of two years. During these dialogues, he describes the Glorious Revolution of 1688–89 and the War of the Spanish Succession (1701–14), and he attempts to explain the many motives that drive countries to wage war against one another. In response, the Master asserts that all of this affirms "the Effects of Reason" to which Gulliver "pretends," but he adds that Nature has nonetheless left Gulliver—and other Yahoos like him—essentially harmless.

Reiterating his earlier assessment of Gulliver's physical characteristics, the Master points out that Yahoos like him cannot bite one another, nor can they defend themselves with their "short and tender" claws. Amused by his Master's ignorance, Gulliver describes the variety of weapons (including gunpowder) used in wars, explaining the massive carnage the Europeans can achieve despite their physical limitations. Appalled, the Master orders Gulliver to be silent. Gulliver's account, he says, shows beyond doubt that Yahoos who pretend to possess Reason are far more detestable than those who do not. Gulliver and his kind, the Master concludes, have (instead of reason) "some Quality fitted to increase [their] natural Vices."

The Master changes the subject and asks Gulliver to explain in more detail what he meant by all of his references to "*Law* and the Dispensers thereof," since in the Houyhnhnm's view "Nature and Reason" are "sufficient Guides" for reasonable animals, and laws should therefore be unnecessary. Gulliver provides a lengthy description of lawyers, their strategies and activities, the importance of legal precedents, and other related matters. The Master finally interrupts, saying that it sounds to him like lawyers should be called upon to instruct Yahoo society in "Wisdom and Knowledge." Gulliver, however, assures him that this would never occur since it is unanimously agreed that lawyers are "the most ignorant and stupid Generation" among all Yahoos, dedicated to destroying "Knowledge and Learning" and perverting reason at every turn.

## Chapter 6

With the Master "wholly at a Loss to understand" what could possibly drive lawyers to do all the evil they do, Gulliver attempts to explain "the use of *Money*" and the great lust for it among the Yahoos. He describes the relationship between wealth and power, the oppression of the poor by the rich, and the various luxuries available to the latter group. He also explains how those who become rich enough to devote themselves to luxury have great need of doctors to cure the ills that come from sloth and overeating. After outlining the various diseases—both real and imagined—to which the rich are vulnerable, Gulliver describes the numerous techniques doctors use in an attempt to heal their patients. These physicians, he explains, are especially adept at predicting when their patients will die, sometimes even helping to bring about that result.

Gulliver then attempts to help his Houyhnhnm Master understand the title "*Chief Minister of State,*" which he defines as a creature driven only by "a violent Desire of Wealth, Power, and Titles." One can obtain this title, he says, in one of three ways: (1) by selling the sexual favors "of a Wife, a Daughter, or a Sister," (2) by "betraying or undermining his Predecessor," or (3) by publicly attacking "the Corruptions of the Court" with a "*furious Zeal.*"

The Houyhnhnm Master concludes that Gulliver must have been born a nobleman, since he outdoes all the Yahoos among the Houyhnhnms "in Shape, Colour, and Cleanliness" (although he lacks their strength and agility). The Master explains that among the Houyhnhnms there are also different classes, evident in their different colors and shapes. The white, sorrel, and iron-gray Houyhnhnms, he points out, live in perpetual servitude to their bay, dapple-gray, and black masters. Gulliver tries to explain that he is not, in fact, a nobleman, and that members of that class in Europe (although they wield a great deal of power) are actually riddled with diseases and health problems due to their excessively luxurious lifestyles.

## Chapter 7

Gulliver explains how his perspective on himself and "Human Kind" has changed during his time among the Houyhnhnms, and he concludes that it is no longer possible for him to argue that humans possess any virtue whatsoever. He also admits that he had earlier decided never to return home, preferring instead to spend the rest of his days "among these admirable *Houyhnhnms* in the Contemplation and Practice of every Virtue." After their numerous conversations in which Gulliver is brutally honest in describing humankind, the Master calls him in one morning and explains that he believes Gulliver has repeatedly *"said the Thing which was not"* regarding himself and his countrymen. Further, he asserts that the apparent dissimilarities between Gulliver and common Yahoos are insignificant since the race Gulliver described has a great deal in common with those brutes—especially in terms of greed, drunkenness, disease, laziness, and a penchant for violence.

## Chapter 8

Appalled by the parallels his Master has drawn between humans and Yahoos, Gulliver asks permission to spend some time among the Yahoos and gather evidence against those conclusions. The Master agrees, and sends the Sorrel Nag along to be Gulliver's guard. He catches a three-year-old male Yahoo and tries to examine it, but is forced to let it go after it urinates all over him and draws the attention of other Yahoos by squalling loudly. Gulliver decides that the Yahoos are "the most unteachable of all Animals" and that they are incapable of being anything more than beasts of burden.

He describes their physical characteristics, feeding habits, and the kennels in which they sleep, along with their instinctive ability to "swim like frogs." One day, while bathing in a stream, Gulliver is assaulted by a young female Yahoo who, having seen him without his clothes, is "enflamed by Desire" for him. The Sorrel Nag ultimately saves him from the Yahoo's grasp.

Noting that he has lived among the Houyhnhnms for three years, Gulliver explains that he feels compelled to offer some account of their

"Manners and Customs." They are, he claims, "endowed by Nature with a general Disposition to all virtues" and utterly unfamiliar with evil. Their "grand Maxim is, to cultivate *Reason,* and to be wholly governed by it." The Houyhnhmns are particularly devoted to friendship and benevolence, and treat neighbors and strangers alike with the utmost respect. Among the nobility, it is standard practice to cease breeding once they produce one Houyhnhnm of each sex (unless one of the offspring dies "by some Casualty"). In selecting marriage partners, they value strength in the males and comeliness in females, and they are careful to avoid combining colors that might yield some "disagreeable Mixture in the Breed." The Houyhnhnms provide equal education to "the young ones of both Sexes," and this training is focused on *"Temperance, Industry, Exercise, and Cleanliness."* Vigorous physical exercise is an important component of their education.

The Houyhnhnms govern themselves by means of a "Representative Council of the whole Nation." The council meets once every four years ("at the *Vernal Equinox*") to discuss and immediately solve any problems that come up, but these meetings last only five or six days since there are never many issues to resolve.

## Chapter 9

Gulliver's Master attends the Houyhnhnms' Representative Council meetings during Gulliver's stay. The representatives "resumed their old Debate" on "whether the *Yahoos* should be exterminated from the face of the Earth." This, Gulliver adds, is the only thing they ever argue about. In response to a number of speeches in favor of killing all the Yahoos, Gulliver's Master asserts that castrating them when they are young (just as Gulliver's race castrates Houyhnhnms) would be a more preferable strategy for doing away with them. To replace them as beasts of burden, the Master argues, the Houyhnhnms should work toward cultivating a certain "Breed of Asses."

Gulliver explains that the Houyhnhnms do not have any system of writing, nor do they suffer from any diseases (although they do possess a number of medicinal herbs "to cure accidental Bruises and

Cuts.") They have a limited knowledge of astronomy (which they use to calculate the year), and "excel all other Mortals" in poetic ability. Gulliver also finds that they dexterously "use the hollow Part between the Pastern and the Hoof of their Forefeet" just as humans use their hands. They are thus able to milk cows, reap oats, and even make and use tools.

Except for "casualties," the Houyhnhnms die only of old age (and never of illness). They usually live to 70 or 75, and treat death with stoic acceptance. They die painlessly, Gulliver notes, in remote locations of their own choosing. The only word in the Houyhnhnm language for expressing anything evil is *Yahoo*, and they use it as an epithet to describe ills such as "the Folly of a Servant, an Omission of a Child, a Stone that cuts their Feet," and so forth. Gulliver ends by saying he could go into much greater detail describing the Houyhnhnms' character and manners (and intends to do so in another book), but must proceed to relate his "own sad Catastrophe."

### Chapter 10

Gulliver describes the room in which he lived happily among the Houyhnhnms. He also provides details on the clothing he contrived, including the shoes he made with soles fashioned from "the Skins of *Yahoos* dried in the Sun." Living on bread, honey, and water, he exclaims that he has "enjoyed perfect Health of Body and Tranquillity of Mind" during his stay. Completely free of the problems and distractions of human society, Gulliver has frequently held lengthy dialogues with his Master and other Houyhnhnms. The Master, he claims, "appeared to understand the Nature of *Yahoos* in all Countries, much better than" he did.

These conversations have had a profound effect on Gulliver's view of himself and other humans. Whenever he was bothered by thoughts of his family, friends, countrymen, or the "Human Race in general," he writes that he simply "considered them as they really were, *Yahoos* in Shape and Disposition, only a little more civilized, and qualified with the Gift of Speech, but making no other use of Reason, than to improve and multiply those Vices, whereof their Brethren in this Country had only

Gulliver says goodbye to the Houyhnhnms. Part 4, chapter 10 *(Thomas Morten)*

the share that Nature had allotted them." He also admits that he could not behold his own reflection without the utmost loathing, and began to imitate the Houyhnhnms' "Gait and Gesture," and even their speech.

Regarding himself happily and "fully settled for Life," Gulliver is surprised when his Master calls him in early one morning with some bad news. The Houyhnhnm Representative Council, he explains, has taken offense at his relationship with Gulliver and is worried that Gulliver, a Yahoo, might "seduce" hordes of other Yahoos from the mountains to come down and destroy all the Houyhnhnms' cattle. The council has decreed, therefore, that Gulliver's Master must begin to treat him like other Yahoos or command him to swim back to the place from which he came.

The Master promises to provide servants to help build a vessel to carry Gulliver away from the Houyhnhnms' country. Gulliver is so disturbed that he falls into a swoon, but eventually recovers and agrees to comply. The Master gives Gulliver two months to finish building the vessel and assigns the Sorrel Nag to help with the task. They work together to build a large canoe out of wood and Yahoo skins, and sealed with "*Yahoos'* Tallow." In a tearful seaside ceremony, Gulliver kisses his Master's hoof, bids the other Houyhnhnms farewell, and departs.

## Chapter 11

Gulliver notes that he left the land of the Houyhnhnms at nine in the morning on February 14, 1714. Based on what he recalls from his days confined to his cabin following the mutiny of his former crew, Gulliver decides to make his way eastward, intending "to reach the *South-West* Coast of New Holland" (Australia) and ultimately an island to the west of it. His plan is to find a deserted island and live out the remainder of his days there, rather than returning to "live in the Society and under the government of *Yahoos*." He arrives at the southeast point of Australia, comes ashore, and remains there for several days—deterred from venturing inland when he sees a number of "stark naked" natives. They eventually see him, and as he rows away in his canoe one of them wounds him "deeply" in the leg with an arrow. He makes his way northward, but when he sees the sail of a ship he decides to row back to the shore from which he came, choosing to trust his fate to the "Barbarians" rather than to "live with *European Yahoos*."

The ship comes close to the shore where Gulliver is hiding, and sailors in a longboat come ashore in search of fresh water. They find his canoe and eventually locate him, but are awed by his strange dress (which leads the sailors to conclude that he must not be one of the natives since they all go naked). They converse with Gulliver in Portuguese and laugh hysterically at his speech, "which resemble[s] the Neighing of a Horse." Interestingly, when they ask who he is, Gulliver tells them that he is "a poor *Yahoo*, banished from

the *Houyhnhnms*." Convinced that he is a European, the sailors kindly assure Gulliver that their captain will transport him to Lisbon, where he can easily find passage to England. He is eventually bound with cords and thrown aboard the ship, where he meets the captain, Pedro de Mendez.

De Mendez treats him with the utmost kindness, but Gulliver regards the captain and his crew as revolting Yahoos, and even attempts to jump overboard in order to escape what he describes as their awful smell. After this incident Gulliver is chained in his cabin. Gulliver reluctantly tells de Mendez about his travels and his three years among the Houyhnhnms, a story which the captain finds impossible to believe. Gulliver and the Portuguese crew arrive at Lisbon November 15, 1715. De Mendez gives him a suit of clothes and takes Gulliver in as a guest in his home. Eventually Gulliver brings himself to venture out of the house, and sails for England on November 24.

On December 5, Gulliver returns home to Redriff, where his wife and children receive him joyfully. In contrast, he can hardly bear to be around them since he regards them as nothing more than beastly Yahoos. He adds that he was especially filled with horror upon seeing his children, since it reminded him that "by copulating with one of the *Yahoo* species" he had "become a Parent of more." He even faints when his wife embraces him.

Gulliver explains that for an entire year he could not "endure" his wife or children to come anywhere near him, while he immensely enjoyed spending time in the stable conversing with two young "Stone-Horses" he had purchased almost as soon as he returned home.

## Chapter 12

Gulliver explains that he has devoted himself to truth in describing the history of his travels over a period of more than six and one-half years. It would have been easy, he asserts, to have concocted all sorts of strange tales, but he preferred to avoid doing what too many travel writers have done in the past. He adds that his goal in writing has not been fame, but rather the "PUBLIC GOOD," which (he claims) is especially well-served when each reader considers the virtues of the Houyhnhms and becomes "ashamed" of his own "Vices." Gulliver is pleased that no one can really offer any objections to his work, simply because he is "a Writer who relates only plain Facts that happened in such distant Countries." He has, he concludes, "carefully avoided every Fault with which common Writers of Travels are often too justly charged."

He admits that some have chided him for failing to provide a Secretary of State with an account of the lands he visited, since "whatever Lands are discovered by a Subject belong to the Crown." This is ludicrous, according to Gulliver, since the Lilliputians are not worth the effort, the Brobdingnagians would certainly be invincible, and he wonders how effective the English army would be against a flying island like Laputa. As for the Houyhnhms—although they are unprepared for war—Gulliver asserts that he could never advocate invading them. Besides, he says, he has developed "a few Scruples" regarding European imperialism and colonization, which have (in countries other than England) turned the sacred enterprise of spreading the gospel into an exercise in cold-blooded butchery.

Having addressed what he sees as the only possible objection that can be raised against him, Gulliver takes leave of his readers, hoping to lead a quiet life at home. He reports that he is making some progress in terms of allowing his wife to eat with him, and is generally learning to feel more at ease around the "Yahoos." He explains that it would be easier for him to tolerate them if they would "be content with those Vices and Follies only, which Nature hath entitled them to." What bothers him is that so many of these disease-ridden "Lump[s] of Deformity" allow themselves to be "smitten with *Pride*," which he simply cannot tolerate. He concludes by declaring that Yahoos "who have any Tincture" of pride should "not presume" to come within his sight.

## COMMENTARY

Though the *Travels* are often read as a novel, Swift uses the vehicle of a travel book, complete with fantastic adventures, to deliver a satiric attack on humanity. He seeks nothing less than his reader's participation in a thoroughgoing physical, intellectual, political, and moral analysis of mankind's condition. We must take his condemnation of our vices and stupidities seriously, but the comedy inherent in every page demands we laugh at these follies and ourselves. The satire functions as a censor, attempting through laughter and self-knowledge to inspire us to redesign our world. To understand how Swift designed the work and its techniques, we will study each book as a separate document while recognizing that the work stands as a whole: No adventure exists as well on its own without its associated travels. Critics who oppose this view argue that the books are episodic voyages—different in form and theme to the point of lacking cohesion. Other critics have suggested additional problems associated with the text. Among the many critical uncertainties are the role of the main character, the place of the reader, the role of the satiric structure, and the meaning of the fourth book, "A Voyage to the Country of the Houyhnhms."

### Parts 1 and 2

The voyages of parts 1 and 2 can be discussed together since the emphasis in both remains on Lemuel Gulliver himself and the theme of disproportion. With the opening details typical in travel literature, Swift establishes the "truth" of Gulliver's story by having the Letter from Richard Sympson suggest how the manuscript came into Sympson's hands, with particular reference to his editorial work in bringing the manuscript before the public. Creating Gulliver's character depends first on a series of rather dull biographical details which create the image of a rather gentle, observant, well-educated, uncomplicated Englishman who finds himself a stranger in a strange land, experiencing fantastic adventures without being capable of useful critical judgment regarding what occurred. Although a more well-rounded character than any other figure in Swift's work, Gulliver exists more in form than substance; he is more a character who is acted upon than one who acts. The changes he undergoes are a result of the experiences he has, but only in the last voyage to the land of the Houyhnhnms does he seem clearly affected, and then his drift into madness occurs quickly.

Most readers find Gulliver an unreliable narrator. His uncritical view of events and beings forces us to doubt his judgment and motivation. "Gulliver" turns out to be gullible, and a "gull": "a credulous person; one easily imposed upon; a dupe, simpleton, fool" (*Oxford English Dictionary*). Readers should not make the common mistake of identifying Gulliver with Swift, because the author is clearly using his character as the vehicle for activating and encouraging the satire. When the misanthropic Gulliver returns to the stable to live with the horses, rejecting his wife and family at the end of the fourth book, Swift portrays a good man destroyed by the corruption of a world gone mad. But to refer to Gulliver as a man implies that he has human credibility, that he is realistic. Since through his experiences Gulliver does not grow and mature emotionally and intellectually, he becomes (according to J. Paul Hunter) a " 'personation'— someone who can put on different acts and faces at various moments when a particular stance or effect is needed—but does not add up to anything coherent . . . or plausible." Yet his final withdrawal to the stables and the beings which remind him of the Houyhnhnms does seem a cogent act, in the middle of general lunacy, and one that shows his character to be less flat and more rounded.

Keeping readers uncertain of how they should view Gulliver produces the necessary interest in the satire. What are we to understand when Gulliver, who seems so careful and cautious, lurches from one accidental landing after a shipwreck in Part 1 to another unexpected landing after being abandoned by his shipmates in Part 2? When the Lilliputians capture him and conduct an inventory of all that he carries on his person, Gulliver has a full set of objects that identify him as the quintessential 18th-century traveler—a silver watch and chain, a small purse of gold coins, a handkerchief, a snuff box, a notebook, a comb, a brace of pocket pistols along with powder and ball, silver and copper coins, a razor and a knife, and a curving sword or cutlass. But could he also be a survivor of a shipwreck weighed down by

these items? The scale of implausibility begins its rise toward the impossible, and Swift continues the litany of possessions: spectacles, a magnifying glass ("a pocket perspective"), and other small inconsequential items. When Crusoe struggles ashore in Daniel Defoe's *Robinson Crusoe* (1719), he has nothing, arriving naked, as it were, to this new world, and must return to the wreck for each item that will keep him alive. Swift loads Gulliver down with all the trappings of his society, not to make him more realistic but less so.

The absurdity persists as the Man Mountain (Gulliver) shows more compassion and kindness than these physical pygmies who possess man-sized vices. When Gulliver secures the Blefuscudian fleet and ends the war, the Lilliputian triumph seems reduced as the Emperor and his ministers expect and demand total annihilation of their defeated enemies. Ludicrously, Gulliver is accused of initiating a sexual affair with the chief Lilliputian minister's six-inch wife; but instead of ignoring this foolish charge, he proceeds to offer a straightforward defense, making him seem absurd.

The emphasis on disproportion extends to Part 2, where Swift reverses the conceit. The Brobdingnagians, towering giants, now look down on the relatively minuscule Gulliver, whose perspective suffers a wrenching change from his earlier view of the Lilliputians. He had left Lilliput finally feeling only contempt for their viciousness and uncontrolled pride, but the king of Brobdingnag, among others of his people, quickly points to the ridiculousness of Gulliver's petty ambitions and expresses his horror at the "little hateful Animal['s]" moral insensitivity. When the King questions Gulliver about his homeland, he describes its constitution, class system, military activities, and history without once exercising any critical judgment. The King, having listened and observed, finds "some lines of an institution, which in its original might have been tolerable; but these half erased, and the rest wholly blurred and blotted by Corruptions." Ironically, Gulliver has heard pronounced on him the exact statement he had earlier made to the Lilliputians, and in the eyes of these giants he also seems a Lilliputian.

The King (who is genuinely shocked at Gulliver's report) suggests how his society, which was once at war with itself, its politics tearing the country apart, had reformed through wise monarchy. Less willing to accept the easy conclusion that physical smallness symbolizes moral smallness, the enlightened King responds to Gulliver's description of European hypocrisy, avarice, and hatred, and memorably declares "the bulk of your natives, to be the most pernicious race of little odious vermin that nature ever suffered to crawl upon the surface of the earth." The conversation between these two figures provides a highly suggestive allegory where Swift can pose the King as an example of what it is in man's power to become, with Gulliver representing how far man is from reaching that goal. One influential modern critic finds the essential theme of the work here, at the end of these first two voyages, where the issue becomes Swift's attack on pride. Gulliver's pettiness is revealed in the moral and physical disproportion between him and the good giants, which damages our sense of self-importance and our complacency regarding the perfection of the human form.

A further interpretation of Parts 1 and 2 (which early readers recognized) treats them as Swift's twofold discussion of political man, especially contemporary English politics where WHIG interests and personalities are flayed and TORIES celebrated for their conservatism and their opposition to innovation. Swift's fascination with history and his own participation in the internal party politics of an emerging modern society are reflected in a number of now famous scenes, such as the feuding of the High-Heel Party and Low-Heel Party in Lilliput, where the height of one's shoes and the degree of hobble in an individual's gait signify levels of political power, and the vicious war between Blefuscu (France) and Lilliput (England) that began over a religious question of which end of an egg should a believer and patriot break (the Big Endians versus the Little Endians). Satirizing the long War of the Spanish Succession (1701–13), Swift points to the symbolic difference between a Catholic nation and a Protestant one in terms of willingness to engage in destructive warfare over

such absurdities. The integration of political, diplomatic, and religious history constitutes an important element of the *Travels,* as do Swift's objections to war and colonization.

### Part 3

Gulliver's voyage to the flying island of Laputa and the metropolis of Lagado, on a nearby continent, as well as the other lands he visits in this book do not conform aesthetically to the earlier voyages. Swift's scheme depends on using episodes, often quite loosely connected, with little interest in orderly action and an often ironic, comic, or contemptuous attitude toward the subject. Since he wrote this book last, one may conjecture, as a number of critics have, that he presents here all the other ideas he had considered for this work but could not use in the other three books. Gulliver moves from one diverse group of people to another, unceasingly changing locus, and in doing so disrupts the reader's sense of direction. Having enacted a complete physical reversal from micro to macro views of being in Parts 1 and 2, Swift distorts the reader's view again in Part 3 with emphasis on the grotesque. Certainly, Gulliver's description of the Maids of Honour and their handling of him in chapter 5 of Part 2 gives special attention to the grotesqueries of the physical view, involving nearly all the senses. The third voyage adds the perversion of reason—how the intellect can suffer distortion through misuse. The culprits here are the speculative and rationalist philosophers who deny the possibility of faith and obscure humankind's understanding of its place in the world: "The minds of these people [Laputians] are so taken up with intense speculations, that they neither can speak, nor attend to the discourses of others, without being roused by some external taction [touch] upon the organs of speech and hearing."

The quality of Laputian lives has not improved with their strict reliance on reason, which resulted in the loss of their mathematical skills, particularly plain geometry, resulting in poorly constructed homes and a skewed sense of the physical dimensions of their world. Also, for all their scientific advancement, the Laputians' moral conduct has not improved; instead, their wives are unfaithful and the Laputian king uses his island to tyrannize Balnibarbi. The rather obvious parable of England's oppressive colonization of Ireland exhibits a kind of political viciousness that some critics believe anticipates the Yahoos of Part 4, who have much in common with the native Irish. Certainly this shifting perspective is introduced in Part 3 and extended with more complexity in the last voyage.

When Gulliver arrives in the metropolis of Lagado on the continent of Balnibarbi, he finds the Academy of Projectors staffed by professors who waste both money and intelligence on absurd plans. These so-called intellectuals pretend to explain the inexplicable, as did the scientists of the British Royal Society, but provide analysis on issues of no importance. Though the society did make major contributions to science, Swift focuses on its reputation for bizarre speculation, embracing the perception rather than the reality. If, as Swift argues in this satiric episode, these second-raters were involved in activities for the common good, then one might find an admirable result. Unfortunately, no one, least of all Gulliver, asks what would be the proper activity of intellectual investigation.

The most interesting episode for exposing corruption in this environment is identified with the visit to the Struldbruggs, a people who are immortal but cannot preserve their youth. They degenerate, and the physical loss symbolizes their moral decay as they fear the passage of time. Loss of memory and an unwillingness to compromise or tolerate others become the center of their being. The Struldbruggs "offer a chastening spectacle of decrepitude and a paradoxical indifference to life," and this section of the *Travels* highlights what Swift saw as "humankind's first folly"—"to ignore the essential, inescapable, limiting conditions of life" (Knowles 113). The haunting spectacle of these Immortals leads naturally to the discovery of the humanoid Yahoos of Part 4, who embody (in Martin Price's view) "in a crude animal form most of the vices (and supposed glories) of civilized man" (85).

### Part 4

Gulliver's final voyage takes him to island of the Houyhnhnms, horse-shaped creatures endowed with reason who live in a well-ordered society which follows the most rational, if not sterile, means of existence. The irony of this scene forces humans to acknowledge that their characteristics do not resemble those of the Houyhnhnms. Swift explains man as a rational animal capable of cognitive functioning, but quite different from the Houyhnhnms, whose rational nature and institutions create a utopia, one ironically alien to humans. The Yahoos, on the other hand, are obscene caricatures of human form and have no reasoning capacity but exist on a plane of pure appetite and passion. The appearance of the Yahoos reminds the reader of the existence of slaves. With these creatures Swift urges the question of what is a human being. Are we abominable animals or reasonable persons? Gulliver is so pushed by such questions that he forgets who he is and loses sight of his own humanity. The irony remains sharp, as Gulliver, who was one of the greatest propagandists for his own species, becomes a few short voyages later a hater of the shape, actions, and smell of humans.

The captain of the ship that rescues Gulliver at the end of Part 4, Don Pedro de Mendez, treats him with kindness, generosity, and what may be called Christian charity. Neither a rationalist stoic nor a deist who spouts passages on the natural benevolence of human nature, de Mendez can make no effective headway with Gulliver, who has lost his power to evaluate. Significantly, Don Pedro must have virtues of an exemplary kind, since Gulliver, after his contact with the Houyhnhnms, can tolerate him only for a short time.

Swift, who has exercised our vision, our sense of perspective throughout the work, now leaves us with an unsettling mirror image of ourselves, one that emphasizes pettiness, savagery, and innocence all contending for predominance. He gives us no recommendations for a program of social reform; we cannot rely on Gulliver, for he has retreated to the stables, resisting all claims on him as husband, father, and citizen. In Gulliver's foolish, gullible wake, we might decide that Swift seems more humanist than misanthrope, especially since he does not abandon his fellow man but asks that we rethink our humanity.

In two well-known letters to Alexander POPE in late 1725, Swift revisits his reasons for this book and emphasizes its themes. He writes that the chief end for all of his work (and he is certainly thinking especially of the *Travels*) is "to vex the world rather than divert it." He urges Pope to move beyond his translations (Homer's *Odyssey*) and cease allowing various critics to accuse him "of misemploying your genius for so long a time." Though he asks Pope to give "the world . . . one lash the more at my request," Swift denounces professions and bureaucrats as a group but insists he respects and admires individuals, no matter their chosen profession. When he says "I hate and detest that animal called man," he is objecting to human absurdity, not human nature. As the critic Paul Hunter suggests, Swift insists that if man is only capable of reason but is not necessarily a reasonable being, then human history after the Fall (the cause of "all our woe") is nothing more than a record of successive failures through which man has dragged down the divine plan.

## CHARACTERS

### Lemuel Gulliver and His Family

**Burton, Edmond** In *Gulliver's Travels* I.1, hosier in Newgate Street, London, and Lemuel Gulliver's father-in-law. Gulliver provides only a sparse number of details about Burton, including his occupation, address, and the amount of the dowry he provides when Gulliver married Mary Burton (Edmond's second daughter). The dowry—or "Portion," as Gulliver calls it—was £400, which would have been a remarkably high sum to accompany a bride from a middle-class family.

**Burton, Mary** See Gulliver, Mary Burton.

**Gulliver, Betty** Lemuel Gulliver's daughter in *Gulliver's Travels*. She is "at her Needlework" when Gulliver leaves home to sail on the *Adventure* two months after returning from Lilliput. Betty is "well married and has Children" by the time Gulliver writes the *Travels*.

**Gulliver, John** Lemuel Gulliver's eldest uncle, mentioned in *Gulliver's Travels*, Part 1. He joined Gulliver's father and some other unnamed family members in providing Gulliver with an initial sum of £40 "and a Promise of Thirty Pounds a Year" to support his study of "physic" at Leiden following his departure from London, where he had been working as an apprentice to James Bates. He also left Gulliver "an Estate in Land near *Epping*, of about Thirty Pounds a Year." Johnny Gulliver (Lemuel Gulliver's son) is named after John Gulliver.

**Gulliver, Johnny** Lemuel Gulliver's son in *Gulliver's Travels*. He is named after Gulliver's uncle John Gulliver, and Gulliver describes him as "a towardly [promising] Child." Johnny is away at grammar school when Gulliver leaves home to sail on the *Adventure* two months after returning from Lilliput.

**Gulliver, Lemuel** Narrator and adventurer in *Gulliver's Travels*. The details of his biography appear in the synopsis of Part 1 ("A Voyage to Lilliput"). Despite his humble beginnings, Gulliver becomes a successful physician and sailor, consistently driven by a penchant for travel. Marriage and a growing family do little to deter him from repeated voyages, and by the end of the *Travels* he can hardly bear to remain in the presence of his own wife and children. Gulliver prides himself on what he views as the objectivity of his writing, and regards his unbiased approach as raising his travel writing above that of other less scrupulous authors. As he declares in the final chapter of Part 4, while other adventurers "impose the grossest Falsities on the unwary reader, . . . I imposed on myself as a Maxim, never to be swerved from, that I would *strictly adhere to Truth*."

Obsessively committed (at least in his own mind) to absolute objectivity and accuracy in meticulously recording the details of each voyage, Gulliver includes numerous humiliating episodes that add up to what is on one hand a remarkably self-deprecating travelogue. On the other hand, however, the *Travels* are filled with pompous descriptions of what he clearly sees as his own heroism in action (when, for

Portrait of Lemuel Gulliver, from the frontispiece of Swift's *Works*, 1726 *(Courtesy of Duke University Libraries)*

himself is an attribute he generally ascribes to others, and his desire to remain unbiased in recording his adventures leads to remarkable credulity. Even in the midst of utter foolishness (such as that he encounters during his visit to the Academy of Projectors in Part III), Gulliver uncritically accepts and describes whatever explanations and assertions he is offered. He has an acute ability for missing or at least ignoring the obvious, and the truth tends to sneak up on him (when, for example, he finally realizes that his physique and that of the Yahoos share some disturbing similarities). He reports—but does not reflect upon—the events he experiences, and offers little commentary on their significance.

Ironically, at the end of the *Travels* Gulliver unwittingly embodies all that he claims to despise in the Yahoos. He explains that his "Reconcilement to the *Yahoo*-kind" would be far easier if "they" (as a species from which he believes he is distinct) would simply limit themselves to pursuing their natural "Vices and Follies." When, however, he "behold[s] a Lump of Deformity, and Diseases both in Body and Mind, smitten with *Pride*," it is more than he can stomach. Desperate in denying his own humanity and yearning to be a horse, Gulliver typifies the pride and willful delusion that Swift condemns in "VERSES ON THE DEATH OF DR. SWIFT": "He spared a hump or crooked nose, / Whose owners set not up for beaux. True genuine dullness moved his pity, / Unless it offered to be witty." As a poignant illustration of the vice Swift regarded as satire's rightful target, Gulliver exemplifies what he himself describes as the unforgivable Yahoo flaw—ignoring his own flaws and taking pride in virtues he does not possess.

example, he extinguishes the palace fire in Lilliput). In the end, however, this modulation between self-deprecation and prideful boasting ceases during Gulliver's visit with the Houyhnhnms in Part 4. By the conclusion of the *Travels*, he has become ridiculously hypocritical in terms of his own humanity. Having wholeheartedly adopted the Houyhnhnms' negative view of mankind (including their conclusion that humans' limited reason actually makes them worse than normal Yahoos), Gulliver convinces himself that he is somehow exempt from all that his equine hosts have criticized.

Gulliver's willingness to embrace the Houyhnhnms' perspective on humans as disadvantaged Yahoos highlights one of his more notable traits. As his name implies, Gulliver is incredibly naïve—or gullible. The unabashed honesty on which he prides

**Gulliver, Mary Burton** Lemuel Gulliver's wife. She is first mentioned in Part I, chapter 1, of *Gulliver's Travels*. The only details Gulliver initially provides about Mary is that she is the second daughter of Edmond Burton and that marrying her earned him a substantial dowry of £400. Gulliver explains that he consulted Mary before leaving his failing medical practice in London to travel as surgeon on several ships for six years. At the end of that period he intended to remain at home with

Mary indefinitely, but in 1699 Captain William Prichard made it worth his while to accept a job as ship's surgeon on the *Antelope,* which eventually sank and led to his adventures in Lilliput.

Throughout the *Travels,* Gulliver makes it clear that his "insatiable Desire for seeing foreign Countries" (as he describes it) is stronger than his desire to remain with Mary and their children. At the end of Part I, he writes that after his return from Lilliput he stayed with her for two months, gave her £1,500, moved her and the family to Redriff, and departed "with Tears on both sides." At the end of Part II, Mary begs Gulliver never to go to sea again, but he explains that his "evil Destiny so ordered that she had not Power to hinder" him from sailing. At the beginning of Part IV, he writes that following his return from Laputa he remained at home with Mary and the children for five months, and left his "poor Wife big with Child, and accepted an advantageous Offer" to sail as captain of the *Adventure.*

During his stay with the Houyhnhnms in Part IV of the *Travels,* Gulliver loses whatever desire he once had to return to Mary and his children. He happily determines that he is "fully settled for Life" far away from them, and is greatly disturbed when he finds out that he must go back to England, since he has come to think of his wife and family as revolting "*Yahoos* in Shape and Disposition." By the time Gulliver returns home, his affection for Mary has turned to palpable "Hatred, Disgust, and Contempt." He describes his wife as "one of the *Yahoo* Species" and laments the horror he feels at considering that he had "copulated" with her to produce more Yahoos. When she kisses him, he faints at the embrace of what he calls "that odious Animal." At the end of the *Travels,* he explains that even five years after his return he is scarcely able to endure her presence.

**Gulliver, Mr.** Lemuel Gulliver's father; mentioned in chapter 1 of *Gulliver's Travels* Part 1. He had five sons and maintained "a small estate in *Nottinghamshire.*" He sent Gulliver (at the age of 14) to Emmanuel College, Cambridge, but could not afford to keep him there. When Gulliver completed his time in London as an apprentice to James Bates, his father (along with his uncle John Gulliver and

other family members) provided funds for him to study "physic" at the University of Leiden.

### Part 1

**Balmuff** "Grand justiciary" of Lilliput. A *justiciary* or *justiciar* is "a judge presiding over, or belonging to, one of the king's superior courts, or exercising special judicial functions" (*Oxford English Dictionary*). Balmuff is the highest-ranking official of this type in Lilliput. In *Gulliver's Travels* I.7, he (along with Skyresh Bolgolam, Flimnap, Limtoc, and Lalcon) prepares articles of impeachment against Lemuel Gulliver "for Treason, and other capital Crimes." The goal of these proceedings is to have Gulliver put to death by setting his house on fire while he sleeps and having 20,000 Lilliputian soldiers shoot him in the face and hands with poisoned arrows. In *A Gulliver Dictionary* Paul Odell Clark translates *Balmuff* as "raven" and suggests that Swift is "coupling the Chamberlain Lalcon"—whose name recalls *falcon*—"and the justice Balmuff as two birds of prey."

**Bates, James** Fictitious London surgeon in *Gulliver's Travels,* Part 1, chapter 1. After having to leave Cambridge after three years because the expenses were "too great for a narrow Fortune," Gulliver spent four years as Bates's apprentice. Bates recommended Gulliver as ship's surgeon to the *Swallow* and helped him find patients when he settled in London. Bates's death helped precipitate the failure of Gulliver's London practice, which led to his decision to "go again to Sea."

**Biddel, John** In *Gulliver's Travels* I.8, captain of the vessel that rescues Lemuel Gulliver following his departure from Blefuscu. Gulliver describes Biddel as "a very civil Man, and an excellent Sailor" of Deptford. His crew is made up of 50 men, and the ship he captains is an English merchantman returning to England from Japan "by the *North* and *South Seas.*" Gulliver's old friend Peter Williams happens to be aboard at the time of Gulliver's rescue, and recommends him to Biddel. When Gulliver tells of his adventures in Lilliput and Blefuscu, Biddel assumes that he is "raving" and that all of Gulliver's troubles have "disturbed" his "head." Gulliver, however, shows him the tiny cattle and sheep from Lilliput and (at least in Gulliver's mind) this convinces the captain that he is telling the truth. Gulliver also gives Biddel "two Purses of two hundred *Sprugs* each" and promises to give him "a Cow and a Sheep big with young" as soon as they reach England.

**Big-Endians**   Conservative "party" in Lilliput, as well as in Blefuscu, where some exiles have fled. Reldresal mentions them as he explains Lilliputian history to Lemuel Gulliver in chapter 4 of *Gulliver's Travels*, Part I. He explains that "about six and thirty Moons past," a war broke out between Lilliput and Blefuscu when the Emperor of Lilliput's great-grandfather issued an edict forbidding his subjects from breaking their eggs ("in primitive fashion") at the larger end. The monarch made this proclamation because his son (the current emperor's grandfather) had cut his finger while he was breaking an egg in the traditional manner.

Reldresal claims that this edict created ongoing "civil Commotions" that were "constantly fomented by the Monarchs of *Blefuscu.*" When the Lilliputians finally "quelled" the rebellion, many of the Big-Endians fled to Blefuscu in exile, and relations between Lilliput and the neighboring empire have been hostile ever since. Big-Endians who remain in Lilliput are forbidden by law from holding any official "Employments."

Reldresal's discussion of the ongoing hostility between Lilliput and Blefuscu is Swift's way of satirizing the tensions between Protestant England (represented by Lilliput) and Roman Catholic France (represented by Blefuscu). The current Lilliputian emperor's grandfather who cut his finger breaking the egg the old-fashioned way represents the English king Henry VIII, who in 1534 broke with the Roman Catholic Church—the "Big-Endians"—and created the Church of England—the "Little-Endians." The central controversy over the proper way to break eggs is most likely a reference to the different views and practices of communion in each church. Irvin Ehrenpreis cites Swift's handling "of the Reformation in terms of Big-Endians and Little-Endians" as evidence that he did not espouse "a simple form of religious faith" and as an illustration of how "Swift's

frivolous treatment of several Christian doctrines violates one's idea of an orthodox priest" (*Swift* III.69). See also Lustrog.

**Blefuscu, Emperor of**   In Part 1 of *Gulliver's Travels*, ruler of Lilliput's same-sized enemies in the neighboring kingdom of Blefuscu. The hand-kissing obsequies the relatively giant Lemuel Gulliver proffers to this tiny emperor are as ironic as those he displays toward the Lilliputian ruler (see Lilliput, Emperor of). Unlike the Emperor of Lilliput, however, his Blefuscudian counterpart consistently treats Gulliver with kindness.

After Gulliver commandeers 50 men-of-war from the Blefuscudian navy and pulls them to the Lilliputian shore in a show of his loyalty to that kingdom, the Emperor of Blefuscu sends peace-seeking ambassadors to Lilliput who give Gulliver a royal invitation to visit their homeland. When Gulliver leaves Lilliput to escape the plot against him there, the Emperor refuses the Lilliputian leader's request to send him back in chains "to be punished as a Traitor." The Emperor also helps Gulliver prepare a small vessel for his departure from Blefuscu and ceremoniously gives him a number of gifts prior to his leaving.

**Bolgolam, Skyresh [or Skyris]**   "Galbet" or High Admiral and adviser to the Emperor of Lilliput in Part 1 of *Gulliver's Travels*. In *A Gulliver Dictionary*, Paul Odell Clark translates the name as "Stylish border ass" or "Style'im Border Ass." Lemuel Gulliver describes him as "very much in his Master's Confidence, and a Person well versed in Affairs, but of a morose and sour Complexion." When the Emperor approaches his council regarding Gulliver's request for liberty in chapter 3, Bolgolam is the only adviser to oppose the petition. Gulliver explains that the admiral "was pleased, without any provocation, to be my mortal enemy." The Lilliputian Royal Council grants Gulliver's liberty despite Bolgolam's opposition, but the admiral insists upon writing the conditions governing that freedom. Gulliver explains that some of the restrictions "were not so honourable as I could have wished; which proceeded wholly from the Malice of . . . the High Admiral." In chapter 7, Gulliver is told that his success in commandeering the navy of Blefuscu for the Lilliputians has increased Bolgolam's hatred of him and that the admiral and several other officials have prepared "Articles of Impeachment" against Gulliver, seeking to have him "put to the most painful and ignominious death" for treason. Although he is sometimes viewed as representing John Churchill, first duke of MARLBOROUGH, Bolgolam is most likely modeled on Daniel Finch, second earl of NOTTINGHAM.

**Clumglum**    Lilliputian treasurer Flimnap's title in *Gulliver's Travels*, Part 1. In *A Gulliver Dictionary*, Paul Odell Clark translates it as "trimmer" or "murmur." See also Nardac.

**Clustril**    Lilliputian informant in *Gulliver's Travels* I.6. Paul Odell Clark translates the name as "real truth" in *A Gulliver Dictionary*. Clustril and Drunlo allege that Flimnap's wife has developed "a Violent affection" for Lemuel Gulliver and that she has visited his lodgings privately. This accusation turns Flimnap against Gulliver, despite the latter's protests that it is entirely false. Gulliver writes that he defies Flimnap "or his two informers . . . to prove that any Person ever came to me *incognito*, except the Secretary Reldresal."

**Drunlo**    Lilliputian informant in *Gulliver's Travels* I.6, who claims that Lemuel Gulliver is having an affair with Lady Flimnap. In *A Gulliver Dictionary*, Paul Odell Clark translates the name as "trimmer" or "turn low." See Clustril.

**Flimnap**    Lord treasurer of Lilliput in Part 1 of *Gulliver's Travels*. Generally regarded as a satiric portrait of Sir Robert WALPOLE, Flimnap is renowned among the Lilliputians for his skill at rope-dancing. Lemuel Gulliver writes that the treasurer "is allowed to cut a Caper on the strait Rope, at least an inch higher than any other Lord in the whole Empire." Flimnap's ability to dance on the tightrope satirizes Walpole's political balancing act amid what Pat Rogers calls "a succession of crises and setbacks" throughout his career. In chapter 3, the near-fatal fall Flimnap suffered "a year or two" before Gulliver's

arrival in Lilliput refers to the rescue of Walpole's political career by the duchess of KENDAL.

Based on information provided by the informants Clustril and Drunlo, Flimnap becomes convinced that his wife is having an affair with Gulliver. Gulliver denies the accusation, and the notion is ridiculous since Lady Flimnap would not be likely to commit adultery with a giant. However, the fact that Flimnap never doubts the truth of this allegation shows that his wife's supposed infidelity is no surprise to him, just as Walpole had become accustomed to hearing of his own wife's numerous extramarital affairs. Flimnap's resentment leads him to join Skyresh Bolgolam and other officials in preparing Articles of Impeachment against Gulliver (in chapter 7) and seeking to have him executed "for Treason, and other capital Crimes."

Michael W. Skau has suggested an alternative to Paul Odell Clark's interpretation of Flimnap's name in *A Gulliver Dictionary* as a code word for "Prince Knave." Citing Gulliver's comment that he has seen Flimnap "do the Summerset several times together," Skau suggests that *Flimnap* is an anagram for "Flip-man" ("a man who performs flips"). Flimnap's name thus "refers specifically to the treasurer's abilities and the sound of the anagrammatic name itself suggests his acrobatic specialty."

**Flimnap, Lady**    Lilliputian wife of Flimnap in Part 1 (chapter 6) of *Gulliver's Travels*. She is said to have developed a violent affection for Lemuel Gulliver and to have visited his lodgings alone and *"incognito."* Suspicions of an affair between his wife and Gulliver lead Flimnap to join other officials in seeking to have Gulliver executed. Lady Flimnap is generally viewed as representing Robert WALPOLE's wife, Catherine (née Shorter), who had numerous extramarital affairs.

**Frelock, Clefren**    Officer in Lilliput, who (along with fellow official Marsi Frelock) searches Lemuel Gulliver's pockets in chapter 2 of *Gulliver's Travels*, Part 1. The Emperor of Lilliput orders the search since he suspects Gulliver of carrying "several Weapons, which must needs be dangerous things, if they answered the Bulk of so prodigious a Person."

In the comprehensive inventory Clefren and his fellow officer Marsi Frelock provide, they express their frustration at Gulliver's poor communication skills. They write, for example, that "he expressed himself very imperfectly" and that "we did not always trouble him with Questions, because we found it a great Difficulty to make him understand us." In *A Gulliver Dictionary,* Paul Odell Clark translates *Clefren Frelock* as "Meddler or Maltreat Traitor" or even "Murder Traitor," and he renders *Marsi Frelock* as "Malice Traitor."

**Frelock, Marsi**    See Frelock, Clefren.

**Galbet**    See Bolgolam, Skyresh.

**Golbasto Momaren Evlame Gurdilo Shefin Mully Ully Gue**    See Lilliput, Emperor of.

**High-Heels**    See Tramecksan.

**Hurgo**    Lilliputian word for "great lord" in Part 1 of *Gulliver's Travels.* In chapter 1, a Hurgo delivers a lengthy oration to Lemuel Gulliver (which he does not understand) soon after he awakens in Lillput. When Gulliver indicates with hand signals that he is hungry, the Hurgo orders that food and drink be provided to him. In *A Gulliver Dictionary,* Paul Odell Clark translates the word as "willful" or "will go."

**Lalcon**    Chamberlain of Lilliput in Part 1 of *Gulliver's Travels.* In *A Gulliver Dictionary,* Paul Odell Clark translates the name as "(Wh)arton" or "Rare Tom," suggesting a reference to Thomas, first earl of WHARTON. Clark also suggests interpreting the name as simply "falcon," which establishes a connection between Lalcon the chamberlain and Balmuff the justice (whose name means "raven") "as two birds of prey." Lalcon joins Skyresh Bolgolam, Flimnap, Limtoc and Balmuff in bringing Articles of Impeachment against Lemuel Gulliver charging him with "Treason, and other capital Crimes" and seeking to have him put to death. A chamberlain is "an officer charged with the management of the private chambers of a sovereign or nobleman" (*Oxford English Dictionary*).

**Lilliput, Emperor of**    Ruler in Part 1 of *Gulliver's Travels.* His full name is Golbasto Momaren Evlame Gurdilo Shefin Mully Ully Gue. His remarkably long name and small stature add irony to the tiny Emperor's incredible sense of power and dominance, especially in the midst of the relatively gigantic Gulliver (in whose presence he at first comically keeps his three-inch sword drawn, just in case Gulliver "should happen to break loose"). Gulliver describes Golbasto as taller by almost the breadth of a fingernail than "any of his Court, which alone is enough to strike an Awe into the Beholders."

In a satiric reference to the notoriously unattractive King GEORGE I, the 28-year-old Emperor is also depicted as having features that are "strong and masculine, with an *Austrian* Lip and arched Nose." Robert DeMaria points out in his edition of the *Travels* that the last two traits were "Hapsburg features." In his annotations, however, Isaac Asimov notes that the Emperor's appearance is "altogether different from that of George I," a fact he views as one Swift could have used to deny that he intended any resemblance between the two. Just as George I favored the Low-Church WHIGS rather than the High-Church TORY party, the Emperor of Lilliput is partial to the Slamecksan (low-heel) faction.

At only six inches in height, the shrill-voiced Emperor embodies all the worst characteristics of tyrannical rulers who have given free rein to their vanity. This is nowhere more evident than in the terms he uses to describe himself in the articles regarding Gulliver's freedom in Lilliput. Before listing all the restrictions that Gulliver (or, as the Emperor calls him, Quinbus Flestrin) must deserve, the Emperor refers to himself as the "most Mighty Emperor of Lilliput, Delight and Terror of the Universe" and "Monarch of all Monarchs." From his perspective, he is also "taller than the Sons of Men" and at his "Nod the Princes of the Earth shake their Knees." He executes subjects for the slightest offenses and relishes the control he exerts over Gulliver. Much of the humor in Part 1 of the *Travels* stems from Gulliver's ridiculous submission to such a minuscule despot. At the same time, the descriptions of Gulliver's efforts "to cultivate [the Emperor's] favourable Disposition," also make the

The Emperor of Lilliput  *(Thomas Morten)*

more serious suggestion that political figures are powerful only because of the often undeserved authority that others unthinkingly grant them. Eventually, Gulliver recognizes the Emperor as an embodiment of the "unmeasurable Ambition of Princes," and (after refusing to help the Emperor to enslave the inhabitants of Blefuscu) learns that even "the greatest Services to Princes" carry no weight "when put into the Balance with a Refusal to gratify their Passions."

Gulliver ultimately incurs the Emperor's wrath, however, when he flees Lilliput due to the plot that certain politicians there have undertaken against him. Angered by what he views as a display of gross ingratitude, the Emperor orders Gulliver to be brought back to his kingdom from Blefuscu, bound hand and foot and treated as a traitor. In an act that finally illustrates the little Emperor's utter lack of power, Gulliver simply ignores the order and sails away.

**Lilliput, Empress of**   Wife of the ruler of Lilliput in Part 1 of *Gulliver's Travels*. In chapter 5, her palace apartment is set on fire "by the carelessness of a Maid of Honour, who fell asleep while reading a Romance." Lemuel Gulliver is summoned to the scene and extinguishes the fire in three minutes by directing a profuse stream of urine upon it. In addition to violating the law against "making water" in public anywhere near the palace, Gulliver's innovative method of putting out the fire evokes the wrath of the Empress. She moves to "the most distant side of the Court," declares that she will never reenter the contaminated buildings, and vows revenge against Gulliver. The Empress's ungrateful reaction to Gulliver's act of service links her with Queen ANNE, who was unimpressed with Swift's "TALE OF A TUB" and treated his quest for preferment with indifference.

**Lilliput, Prince of**   See Slamecksan.

**Limtoc**   Lilliputian general in Part 1 of *Gulliver's Travels*. He joins Skyresh Bolgolam, Flimnap, Lalcon, and Balmuff in bringing Articles of Impeachment against Lemuel Gulliver charging him with "Treason, and other capital Crimes" and seeking to have him executed. Paul Odell Clark translates *Limtoc* as "risk it" or "risk (his) coat" in *A Gulliver Dictionary*.

**Little-Endians**   See Big-Endians.

**Low-Heels**   See Slamecksan.

**Lustrog**   Religious prophet of Lilliput and Blefuscu. Paul Odell Clark translates the name as "godliest" in *A Gulliver Dictionary*. Lustrog is mentioned in chapter 4 of *Gulliver's Travels*, Part 1, during Reldresal's discussion of the Big-Endian controversy. He explains to Lemuel Gulliver that in accusing the Lilliputians of "making a Schism in religion" the "Emperors of Blefuscu" often claim that they have broken one of Lustrog's "fundamental Doctrine[s]" from "the fifty-fourth Chapter of the *Blundercral*," which states that *all true Believers shall break their Eggs at the convenient End.*"

**Nardac**   Title of highest honor, given to Lemuel Gulliver by the Emperor of Lilliput in Part 1 of *Gulliver's Travels*. In *A Gulliver Dictionary*, Paul Odell Clark translates it as "ill-begot," and in terms of rank it is comparable to a duke. He receives the title after commandeering 50 ships from the navy of Blefuscu and bringing them to the Lilliputian shore. As Gulliver explains it, the Emperor received him at his "Landing with all possible Encomiums, and created me a *Nardac* on the spot, which is the highest title among them." Flimnap's accusations of adultery in chapter 7 caused Gulliver to worry about his reputation even though he then "had the Honour to be a *Nardac*, which the Treasurer himself is not, for all the World knows he is only a *Clumglum*, a Title inferior by one degree, as that of a Marquis is to a Duke in *England*, although I allow he preceded me in right of his Post." After Gulliver has fled to Blefuscu in chapter 8, the Lilliputian Emperor sends an Envoy to the "Monarch of Blefuscu" who warns that unless

Gulliver returns to Lilliput within two hours, the Emperor will strip him of his title and declare him a traitor.

**Nicholas, Capt. John**   A "Cornish man" and ship's captain in *Gulliver's Travels*. He commands the *Adventure*, whose crew Lemuel Gulliver sails with two months after returning home from his travels in Lilliput.

**Pannel, Abraham**   In Part 1 of *Gulliver's Travels*, commander of Lemuel Gulliver's first ship, the *Swallow*. James Bates recommends Gulliver as a candidate for ship's surgeon, and Gulliver works in that capacity under Pannell's command for three and a half years, "making a Voyage or two into the *Levant* [eastern Mediterranean], and some other parts."

**Plune, Calin Deffar**   Earlier emperor of Lilliput mentioned in chapter 7 of *Gulliver's Travels*, Part 1. During his reign he established a law requiring "that whoever shall make water within the Precincts of the Royal Palace, shall be liable to the Pains and Penalties of High-Treason." Skresh Bolgolam and the other Lilliputian officers who seek to have Lemuel Gulliver executed cite this statute in the Articles of Impeachment they bring against him. See also Lilliput, Empress of.

**Prichard, William**   Ship captain in Part 1 of *Gulliver's Travels*. He makes Lemuel Gulliver an "advantageous offer" to sail on the *Antelope*, bound for the South Sea. Gulliver joins the crew as ship's surgeon and they depart from Bristol on May 4, 1699. At first the voyage is bountiful, but a storm overtakes the *Antelope* during its passage to the East Indies. Prichard and the crew are blown off course toward Tasmania, and eventually the *Antelope* sinks (on November 5, 1699) after being driven against a rock. Some of the sailors perish in the wreck, but six crew members (including Gulliver) escape in a small boat. It eventually capsizes and—after swimming for his life—Gulliver finds himself in Lilliput.

**Quinbus Flestrin**   The name assigned to Lemuel Gulliver by Clefren and Marsi Frelock in their official inventory of his pockets in chapter 2 of *Gulliver's Travels,* Part 1. Gulliver explains that the phrase means "Great Man-Mountain" in Lilliputian, and he is addressed by this name throughout his stay in Lilliput. In *A Gulliver Dictionary,* Paul Odell Clark proposes that this title means "dressed in buffskin," referring to the buff jerkin (a jacket made of buffalo leather) that partially protects Gulliver from the onslaught of arrows in chapter 1.

**Reldresal**   In Part 1 of *Gulliver's Travels,* principal secretary of private affairs in Lilliput. In *A Gulliver Dictionary,* Paul Odell Clark translates the name as "Real dreamer." Lemuel Gulliver regards him as a friend, and claims that his skill at rope-dancing (which represents political maneuvering) is second only to that of Flimnap, the Lilliputian lord treasurer. Reldresal may correspond to Swift's friend John, second baron CARTERET of Hawnes.

In chapter 4 of Part I, Reldresal approaches Gulliver "about a Fortnight" after the latter has gained his liberty and provides an outline of Lilliputian history. Reldresal describes what he calls "the two mighty Evils" that he and his countrymen face: "a violent Faction at home, and the Danger of an Invasion by a most potent Enemy from abroad." The domestic threat he refers to stems from the rift between the Tramecksan (High-Heel) and Slamecksan (Low-Heel) parties, while the foreign danger comes from Blefuscu, which Reldresal calls "the other great Empire of the Universe." He explains that many Lilliputian exiles fled to Blefuscu as a result of the historic struggle between the Big-Endians and Little-Endians. The point of Reldresal's visit to Gulliver, however, is not the history lesson. He concludes by saying that the Emperor of Lilliput seeks Gulliver's help in preventing an impending naval strike from Blefuscu.

In chapter 7, when Skyresh Bolgolam and other Lilliputian officials seek to have Gulliver executed for treason, Reldresal respectfully argues against putting Gulliver to death and suggests putting out both his eyes instead so that "Justice might in some measure be satisfied." Bolgolam and Flimnap angrily reject Reldresal's proposal, and the Emperor

says that while killing Gulliver is not an option, simply putting out his eyes may not be a sufficient punishment. In response, Reldresal finally suggests that in addition to blinding Gulliver, perhaps the Emperor could give orders to have him starved to death—a proposal the Emperor decides to pursue.

**Slamecksan**   One of what Reldresal describes to Lemuel Gulliver as "two struggling parties" of Lilliput in Part 1 of *Gulliver's Travels.* The low heels on their shoes distinguish them from the Tramecksan (high-heel) party. The hatred between these two groups is so great "that they will neither eat or drink, nor talk with each other." Although Reldresal estimates that the Slamecksans are outnumbered by the opposing Tramecksan party, they have exclusive rights to serve in the "Administration of the [Lilliputian] Government."

The Emperor of Lilliput is the exemplary "low-heel," since the heels on his shoes "are lower at least by a *Drurr* [about one-14th of an inch] than any of his Court." His son the Prince, however, has "some Tendency towards the High-heels"—a reference to the Prince of Wales who became King GEORGE II. Swift has Reldresal paint a ridiculous picture of the Prince, who (because of his divided allegiance) wears one high heel and one low, "which gives him a Hobble in his Gait."

The Slamecksan faction—favored by the Emperor of Lilliput—represents the WHIGS, who were similarly esteemed by King GEORGE I. Their low heels signify the Whigs' character as a "Low-Church" party as opposed to the more conservative, "High-Church" TORIES (represented by the Tramecksans), who were generally more devoted to preserving the sacraments and liturgical worship. In *A Gulliver Dictionary,* Paul Odell Clark translates *Slamecksan* as "Low-set man" or "Lose-it man," and he renders *Tramecksan* as "Closet-man" or "Claim-it man."

**Sympson, Richard**   Lemuel Gulliver's cousin; fictitious first publisher and editor of *Gulliver's Travels.* In Sympson's remarks from "The Publisher to the Reader," he calls Gulliver his "antient and intimate Friend" with whom he has "some Relation" by his "Mother's side." He further indicates that Gulliver left the manuscript of the *Travels* in his hands "with the Liberty to dispose of [it] as [Sympson] should think fit." In a April 2, 1727, letter to Sympson following publication of the *Travels* with Sympson's emendations, Gulliver writes of the "great and frequent Urgency" with which his cousin had urged him "to publish a very loose and uncorrect version" of the work. He laments the inaccuracies within the edition Sympson saw into print and urges him to make corrections "if ever there should be a second Edition."

**Tramecksan**    One of what Reldresal describes to Lemuel Gulliver as "two struggling parties" of Lilliput in Part 1 of *Gulliver's Travels.* See Slamecksan.

**Williams, Peter**    An "old Comrade" of Lemuel Gulliver. In Part 1 of *Gulliver's Travels,* Williams happens to be aboard the vessel that rescues Gulliver following his escape from Blefuscu. Williams recommends Gulliver to the captain, John Biddel.

*Part 2*

**Birds**    Lemuel Gulliver has dangerous encounters with several giant birds (in addition to other animals and insects) during his stay in Brobdingnag in Part 2 of *Gulliver's Travels.* In chapter 5 he records specific episodes involving a kite (which swoops down and threatens to grab Gulliver in its talons) and a thrush (which takes a piece of cake from him). He also relates how he threw his cudgel once at a linnet. Believing he had killed it, he seized the bird by the neck and "ran with him in Triumph" to Glumdalclitch, only to have the bird regain consciousness and severely assault him. His final encounter with a giant bird comes in chapter 8, when an Eagle picks up the box in which he is kept and drops it into the sea. These encounters, like those with the Flies, the Frog, the Monkey, the Rats, and others, highlight Gulliver's ridiculous pride among the giant inhabitants of Brobdingnag and underscore the view of him throughout Part 2 of the *Travels* as a strange little Splacknuck rather than a human being.

**Brobdingnag, King of**    Ruler of the kingdom Lemuel Gulliver visits in Part 2 of *Gulliver's Travels.* Unlike the tiny Emperor of Lilliput, the King of

Brobdingnag is a giant in comparison to Gulliver. The size difference highlights important distinctions between their personalities as rulers. While he treats Gulliver coldly at times, when it comes to his subjects the Brobdingnagian monarch is far less malicious and vindictive than his Lilliputian counterpart. The King's interactions with Gulliver not only highlight Gulliver's remarkable pride, but provide a satiric perspective on England and its institutions.

Gulliver first encounters the King in Chapter 3. After purchasing Gulliver from the Farmer, the Queen of Brobdingnag brings him to her husband, who asks her "how long it was since she grew fond of a *Splacknuck*" (see Brobdingnag, Queen of). Gulliver describes the King as "a Prince of much Gravity and austere Countenance" who is "as learned a Person as any in his Dominions," having been trained "in the Study of Philosophy, and particularly Mathematics." The King initially believes Gulliver to be a "piece of Clockwork," but dismisses this possibility upon hearing him speak. He refuses to believe the story Gulliver tells of how he and Glumdalclitch arrived at court, and suspects the Farmer of having made it all up in an attempt to sell Gulliver "at a higher Price." He sends for "three great Scholars" to examine Gulliver and offer an explanation of what he might be. Later in the same chapter, Gulliver explains that the King became fond of dining with him, taking every opportunity to ask many questions about "the Manners, Religion, Laws, Government, and Learning of *Europe.*" The King, who (according to Gulliver) makes "very wise Reflections and Observations" on all that is said, concludes that "human Grandeur" is "contemptible" since it can "be mimicked by such diminutive Insects" as Gulliver.

Gulliver consistently seeks to please and impress the King. In chapter 6, after describing the horror of seeing the giant monarch's face shaved by the royal barber, Gulliver explains how he makes a comb from the stubble. When he discovers that the King "delight[s] in Music" and holds frequent concerts at court, he works diligently to play an "*English*" Tune" on a giant spinet (an early version of the harpsichord). Gulliver's effort to impress the King also extends to the many private conversations he has with "His Majesty" in the King's bedroom. In

Gulliver is presented to the king of Brobdingnag. Part 2, chapter 3 *(Thomas Morten)*

these exchanges Gulliver is seated in a little chair "within three Yards distance upon the top of the Cabinet, which brought [him] almost to a level with [the King's] face." During one of their conversations, Gulliver suggests (with great obsequies) that the King's poor opinions of "*Europe,* and the rest of the world" are all wrong and do not become one of such "qualities of Mind." The King responds by asking Gulliver for a full account of England's government, so that he can decide if it has any characteristics worth imitating in Brobdingnag.

With as much grandeur as he can muster, Gulliver has several lengthy meetings with the King in which he describes England and its various institutions (as the King takes notes and asks questions). Ultimately, however, Gulliver's praise of England

backfires, leading the Brobdingnagian monarch to conclude that England's history is just a series of "Conspiracies, Rebellions, Murders, Massacres," and other evils. The King further declares that Gulliver has provided ample evidence that the bulk of England's "Natives" are "the most pernicious Race of little odious Vermin that Nature ever suffered to crawl upon the Surface of the Earth." Gulliver heartily resents the King's assessment, and it causes a drastic change in his attitude toward "his Majesty." In chapter 7 he explains that the King's low opinions of England are simply a result of his very limited education, which has produced "a certain *Narrowness of Thinking,* from which we and the politer countries of *Europe* are entirely exempted." In a frustrated attempt "to ingratiate [himself] farther into his Majesty's Favour," Gulliver tells the King about gunpowder and how the English use it in wars. This last-ditch effort on Gulliver's part to impress the King also backfires, causing him to be "struck with Horror" and to angrily threaten Gulliver (whom he now calls an "impotent and grovelling . . . Insect") with death if he ever mentions gunpowder again.

**Brobdingnag, Queen of**   In Part 2, chapter 3, of *Gulliver's Travels,* the monarch who invites Lemuel Gulliver to come live at court and buys him from the Farmer for a thousand pieces of gold. At Gulliver's request, she also allows Glumdalclitch to remain with him as his "Nurse and Instructor." Gulliver treats the Queen with ridiculous obsequies: "I fell on my Knees, and begged the Honour of kissing her Imperial Foot; but this Gracious Princess held out her little Finger towards me . . . which I embraced with both Arms, and put the tip of it, with the utmost respect, to my Lip." She and her Maids of Honor find him entertaining and amusing, but their affection for Gulliver is very similar to that of Glumdalclitch, who regards him as a little plaything or pet: "The Queen giving great Allowance for my Defectiveness in speaking, was however surprised at so much Wit and Good Sense in so diminutive an Animal." While she is intrigued by Gulliver's wit, the Queen nonetheless enjoys making fun of her little guest for his "Fearfulness" (see Flies).

The Queen becomes so fond of Gulliver that she has him dine with her regularly. Seated at his own little table (fully provided and placed at her left elbow), Gulliver gets a close-up view of the giant woman's eating habits, which he finds to be "a nauseous sight." He explains that she "took up at one Mouthful, as much as a dozen *English* Farmers could eat at a meal" and "would craunch the Wing of a Lark, Bones and all, between her Teeth, although it were nine times as large as that of a full-grown Turkey." The Queen's fondness for Gulliver causes her "favourite Dwarf" to become jealous of him and to take every opportunity to place him in dangerous and embarrassing situations. The Dwarf's pranks—such as wedging Gulliver's legs into an empty marrow bone during dinner—amuse the Queen but (at least in Gulliver's view) also leave her "heartily vexed."

**Carpenter**   Character in Part 2 of *Gulliver's Travels.* He is a member of Captain Thomas Wilcocks's crew, who rescue Lemuel Gulliver (in chapter 8) after his departure from Brobdingnag. The crew finds Gulliver bobbing in the ocean trapped inside the box in which he was carried around in that kingdom. The Carpenter saws a four-foot hole in the box to allow Gulliver to come aboard the ship.

**Dwarf**   Antagonist of Lemuel Gulliver in Part 2 of *Gulliver's Travels*. The favor Gulliver gains with the Queen of Brobdingnag sparks remarkable hatred and jealousy from the Dwarf and leads him to place Gulliver into several embarrassing and dangerous situations (see Brobdingnag, Queen of). The Scholars who interview Gulliver soon after his arrival at court entertain the notion that Gulliver is a dwarf, but they soon reject this possibility since the Queen's dwarf is "near thirty Foot high."

In Chapter 3, Gulliver explains that nothing in Brobdingnag "angered and mortified" him "so much as the Queen's Dwarf." The Dwarf (who before Gulliver's arrival had always been the "of the lowest Stature that was ever in that Country") "becomes insolent at seeing a Creature so much beneath him." In an ironic illustration of the relationships among perspective, size, and status, Gulliver relates that the Dwarf "would always affect to swagger and look big as he passed by me in the

Gulliver quarrels with the Queen's dwarf in Brobdingnag. Part 2, chapter 3  *(Thomas Morten)*

Queen's Antechamber . . . and he seldom failed of a small Word or two upon my littleness." Gulliver himself contributes to the irony surrounding size and perspective in Brobdingnag, referring to the relatively giant Dwarf as a "malicious little Cub." Gulliver repays the Dwarf's insults by calling him "*Brother,* challenging him to wrestle," and uttering "such Repartees as are usual in the Mouths of *Court Pages.*"

Gulliver tells of two specific incidents in which the Dwarf assaults him. Both occur at meals, and each is as embarrassing to Gulliver as it is dangerous. The first happens "at Dinner," when the Dwarf ("nettled" by something Gulliver has said to him) drops Gulliver "into a large Silver Bowl of Cream," and then flees the scene. Gulliver describes the tragedy in terms that emphasize how deadly the result may have been if he "had not been a good Swimmer." Glumdalclitch ultimately saves him, since the Queen is so frightened that she lacked "the Presence of Mind" to help. As punishment for this prank, the Dwarf is "soundly whipped" and "forced to drink up the Bowl of Cream" (Gulliver had swallowed a quart of it himself). As Richard Webster has pointed out, the fact that the Dwarf is forced to drink the now-spoiled cream emphasizes the view of Gulliver throughout Part II of the *Travels* as a little unclean insect or small animal (see also Flies, Monkey, Rats, Spaniel, Splacknuck, and Wasps). The Dwarf also loses favor with the Queen, who "soon after bestowed him on a Lady of high Quality," and Gulliver never sees him again.

Gulliver also discusses an earlier "scurvy Trick" the Dwarf played on him during a meal. He explains that when no one was looking, the Dwarf "took me up in both Hands, and squeezing my Legs together, wedged them into" a hollow "Marrow-bone" on the Queen's plate. This left Gulliver's torso sticking out of the bone with his legs immobilized, making what he describes as "a ridiculous Figure." He adds, "I believe it was near a Minute before anyone knew what was become of me, for I thought it below me to cry out." This "set the Queen a Laughing," but in Gulliver's view she would have immediately dismissed the Dwarf if (as he explains) "I had not been so generous as to intercede."

**Eagle**   In Part 2, chapter 8, of *Gulliver's Travels*, an eagle takes up the box in which Lemuel Gulliver travels and carries it away from Brobdingnag. The bird is pursued by some other eagles and eventually drops the box (with Gulliver still inside) into the sea. After being rescued by Captain Wilcocks and his crew) Gulliver finally returns home to Redriff. Although Swift has Gulliver attribute his capture to the eagle's "sagacity and smell," Horace Perry Jones has pointed out that "ornithological studies reveal that an eagle locates his quarry by eyesight alone. . . . Thus Gulliver, completely hidden within his box, would have been invisible to the eye of the eagle, and the container would not have been seized."

Like Gulliver's many other encounters with animals and insects throughout Part II of the *Travels*, this one underscores the view of him as a strange little beast rather than an undersized human being: "some Eagle had got the Ring of my Box in his Beak, with an intent to let it fall on a Rock like a Tortoise in a Shell, and then pick out my Body, and devour it." See also Splacknuck, Flies, Frog, Rats, Spaniel, and Wasps.

**Farmer in Brobdingnag (1)**   In *Gulliver's Travels* II.1, he is Lemuel Gulliver's first owner in Brobdingnag. Gulliver refers to the Farmer as his "Master." Even though he initially treats Gulliver as a rational creature, the Farmer puts him on display around Brobdingnag for money. Taking advantage of the power he has by virtue of his large size, he works Gulliver (who is much smaller) strenuously as a laborer and comes close to starving him to death. When (in chapter 3) the Queen of Brobdingnag purchases Gulliver from the Farmer for a thousand pieces of gold, Gulliver ignores the Farmer's farewell and explains resentfully to the Queen that his coldness is based on the fact that he owes his "late Master" nothing, other "than his not dashing out the Brains of a poor harmless Creature found by chance in the Field" (see Brobdingnag, Queen of).

**Farmer in Brobdingnag (2)**   In *Gulliver's Travels* II.2, an elderly friend of the Farmer Lemuel Gulliver refers to as his "Master." This second Farmer lives close by, and comes to visit in order to see Gulliver for himself. Like a pet showing off for his owner's benefit, Gulliver is brought out and put onto a table where he walks around ("as I was commanded"), draws his sword, and makes "Reverence" to the "Master's Guest." He also addresses the visiting Farmer in the Brobdingnagian language. When this Farmer dons his eyeglasses, Gulliver laughs at him and causes everyone else to join in. This leads the old man "to be Angry and out of Countenance."

It is the visiting Farmer who suggests to Gulliver's Master that he could make money by putting Gulliver on public display as a kind of circus freak. Gulliver explains, "He had the Character of a great

Miser, and to my Misfortune he well deserved it by the cursed Advice he gave my Master to show me as a Sight upon Market-Day in the next Town."

**Farmer's Son in Brobdingnag**   Youngest of the Farmer's male offspring and elder brother to Glumdalclitch in Part 2 of *Gulliver's Travels.* Lemuel Gulliver describes him as "an arch Boy of ten Years old." During Gulliver's first meal with the Farmer and his family, the boy grabbed him by the legs and held him up so high that Gulliver "trembled at every Limb." The Farmer immediately "snatched [Gulliver] from him," and "gave him such a Box on the left Ear, as would have felled an *European* Troop of Horse to the Earth." In terms that highlight the view of Gulliver as a small animal (a perspective that runs throughout this section of the *Travels*), Gulliver explains how he intervened when the Farmer angrily ordered the boy to be "taken from the Table": "being afraid the Boy might owe me a spite, and well remembering how mischievous all Children among us naturally are to Sparrows, Rabbits, young Kittens, and Puppy Dogs, I fell on my Knees, and pointing to the Boy, made my Master [the Farmer] to understand, . . . that I desired his Son might be pardoned." See also Reaper and Splacknuck.

**Flies**   In Part 2 of *Gulliver's Travels*, Lemuel Gulliver is plagued by them during his stay in Brobdingnag. Gulliver reacts to them with such fear that the Queen of Brobdingnag regularly makes fun of him for his "Fearfulness" and asks "whether the People of [his] Country were as great Cowards" as he is (see Brobdingnag, Queen of). He explains that these insects, "each of them as big as a Dunstable *Lark*," perpetually bother him as he eats by buzzing around his ears, stinging his face, and sometimes landing on his food to leave "their loathsome Excrement or Spawn behind" (which is invisible to the giant Brobdingnagians but clearly visible to him). The evil Dwarf likes to catch flies and use them to torment Gulliver, but Gulliver explains that this gives him the opportunity to "cut them in pieces" in midair with his Knife, "wherein," he adds, "my Dexterity [is] much admired." Gulliver's pride in describing the valor and dexterity he

displays in killing the flies makes this episode as ironic as the one involving the Wasps in the same chapter.

**Frog**   In Part 2 of *Gulliver's Travels,* one of Lemuel Gulliver's adventures in Brobdingnag involves an encounter with a giant frog. It happens while he is entertaining the Queen of Brobdingnag by rowing a little boat in a small trough of water made especially for him (see Brobdingnag, Queen of). When a servant tasked with filling the trough empties a pail of water into it, the frog enters and climbs onto Gulliver's boat. It proceeds to hop back and forth, "daubing" Gulliver's "Face and Clothes with its odious Slime." Gulliver triumphantly declares that he told Glumdalclitch "to let [him] deal with it alone," and proceeded to smack the frog with one of his oars, "at last" forcing "it to leap out of the Boat." The grandeur with which Gulliver describes the episode makes it an ironic addition to a series of encounters he has in Brobdingnag with giant animals and insects. Like each of the other similar "battles," this one emphasizes the view of Gulliver throughout Part II of the *Travels* (even in Glumdalclitch's eyes) as a strange little animal rather than a human being. See also Splacknuck, Eagle, Flies, Monkey, Spaniel, Rats, and Wasps.

**Glumdalclitch**   In Part 2 of *Gulliver's Travels,* she is Lemuel Gulliver's keeper and friend in Brobdingnag. In the Brobdingnagian language her name means "little nurse"—an ironic title since she is 40 feet tall, and "little" only in relation to the other giant inhabitants of Brobdingnag. In *A Gulliver Dictionary,* Paul Odell Clark translates her name as "clutch doll grim(ly)." She is the nine-year-old daughter of the Farmer who nearly starves Gulliver to death while exploiting him as a laborer. Unlike her father, Glumdalclitch treats Gulliver well. She makes clothes for him; feeds, washes, and teaches him; and generally cares for him as though he is a living toy. She assigns the name *Grildrig* ("mannequin") to him and ultimately earns a place for herself at court as his babysitter. The relationship between Gulliver and Glumdalclitch is an odd one, mainly because the little nurse regards Gulliver as a living toy rather than a human being. Leo Sonderegger's novel *Glumdal-*

*clitch* (2000) is based on Part 2 of the *Travels* and outlines what happens in the little nurse's life after Gulliver leaves Brobdingnag.

**Grildrig**   In Part 2 of *Gulliver's Travels*, Lemuel Gulliver's name in Brobdingnag. It means "mannequin" in Brobdingnagian. The name is given to Gulliver by Glumdalclitch, the nine-year-old girl who serves as his nurse and friend during his stay among the giants. The name is particularly appropriate, since the little girl regards him as a living doll and treats him as a favorite toy. In *A Gulliver Dictionary*, Paul Odell Clark translates *Grildrig* as "girl-thing."

**Grultrud**   Brobdingnagian word for town crier. In Part 2 of *Gulliver's Travels*, the Farmer (in an attempt to increase his wealth) hires a Grultrud "to give notice through the town" that "a Strange Creature"—Lemuel Gulliver—is on public display at a local inn. In *A Gulliver Dictionary*, Paul Odell Clark translates *grultrud* as "dirt rul'd."

**Monkey**   In an episode involving what he describes as "the greatest Danger I ever underwent in the Kingdom," Lemuel Gulliver is assaulted by an elephant-sized monkey in Part 2 of *Gulliver's Travels*. It occurs after Glumdalclitch has locked Gulliver in her bedroom (like a pet or a toy) "while she went somewhere upon Business or a Visit." The monkey, "who belonged to one of the Clerks of the *Kitchen*," comes in through the bedroom window and pulls Gulliver out of the box in which Glumdalclitch keeps him for safety. The animal holds Gulliver "as a Nurse does a Child she is going to suckle," and eventually leaps out of the window and onto the roof with Gulliver in tow. As the monkey stuffs Gulliver's mouth full of some food it is carrying in its own mouth, a number of Brobdingnagians gather below to watch the spectacle and (to Gulliver's chagrin) cannot help laughing at his plight. One of the Queen of Brobdingnag's footmen ultimately climbs up and rescues Gulliver, who by this time is severely injured and ends up bedridden for a "fortnight" (see Brobdingnag, Queen of). The monkey is killed and "an Order made that no such Animal should be kept about the Palace."

Following his recovery, Gulliver becomes angry with the courtiers who laugh at him when he explains how mightily he would have defended himself against the monkey had he only thought to use his sword. Like his descriptions of the other encounters he has with animals and insects in this section of the *Travels*, this one emphasizes Gulliver's ridiculous pride as the smallest being in Brobdingnag. Also, the monkey's treatment of Gulliver as one of its own young underscores the Brobdingnagians' view of Gulliver as a little weasel-sized animal rather than an undersized human (see Splacknuck). See also Eagle, Flies, Frog, Rats, Spaniel, and Wasps.

**Maids of Honor**   Members of the royal household of Brobdingnag in Part 2 of *Gulliver's Travels*. The Farmer is originally ordered to take Lemuel Gulliver to the palace "for the Diversion of the Queen" and these women (see Brobdingnag, Queen of). In chapter 5, Gulliver explains that the Maids "often invited Glumdalclitch to their apartments, and desired she would bring me along with her, on purpose to have the pleasure of seeing and touching me." In one of the better-known passages of the *Travels*, he goes on to lament the giant Maids' habit of using him as a kind of sexual toy—an erotic "Grildrig"—stripping him and themselves naked and placing him "at full length in their bosoms." In terms that recall his description of watching the Nurse in the Farmer's household breastfeed a baby, Gulliver relates the disgusting experience of being exposed to the "offensive Smell" and revolting sights of the Maids' nude bodies. He explains that because the Maids are so much larger than he is, their odors and skin imperfections are painfully obvious and offensive to him. His small size gives him the ability to see the women as they really are, a perspective similar to that of the narrator in "Beautiful Young Nymph Going to Bed" in that it discourages the view of women as "nymphs."

The liberties the Maids take with Gulliver greatly disturb him, mainly because he feels that they "use" him "without any manner of Ceremony" as "a Creature" who has "no sort of Consequence." The "handsomest" of the group ("a pleasant frolicsome Girl of sixteen") would even "set [him] astride upon one of her Nipples, with many other Tricks." Gulliver is so disturbed by this experience, however, that he asks Glumdalclitch to "contrive some excuse for not seeing that young Lady any more." Since the Maids do not regard Gulliver as an actual man, they also have no qualms about urinating in front of him. Gulliver describes this as quite a revolting spectacle since they regularly discharge a "quantity of at least two Hogsheads [more than 120 gallons], in a Vessel that held above three Tuns" (compare the similar episode—on a much smaller scale—in lines 163–86 of "STREPHON AND CHLOE").

**Nurse**   In Part 2 of *Gulliver's Travels*, Lemuel Gulliver (in chapter 1) recounts a frightening episode involving a wet Nurse in Brobdingnag. It happened during his first dinner with the Farmer and his family, when the household Nurse "came in with a Child of a Year old in her arms." Seeing Gulliver caused the child to squall and—after several unsuccessful attempts to pacify him—the Nurse "was forced to apply the last Remedy by giving it suck." This turned out to be a revolting spectacle for Gulliver, who writes, "I must confess no Object ever disgusted me so much as the sight of her monstrous Breast." He proceeds to describe the sight in careful detail. In later chapters of the same section of the *Travels*, Gulliver consistently refers to Glumdalclitch as his "little nurse."

**Pirates**   Kidnappers of Lemuel Gulliver and his crew in Part 2 of *Gulliver's Travels*. In chapter 1, Captain William Robinson puts Gulliver in charge of a sloop and crew of 14 men. Their goal is to sell various goods among the islands neighboring *Tonquin* (Tonkin—northern Vietnam) while Robinson waits for his cargo to be made ready for passage. Less than three days after Gulliver and his men set out, however, they are overtaken by two pirates (one of whom is a Japanese captain) who ultimately kidnap Gulliver's crew and set him adrift in a small canoe. This leads to his rescue by the inhabitants of Laputa. See also Dutchman.

**Rats**   In Part 2 of *Gulliver's Travels*, Lemuel Gulliver is attacked by two giant rats in Brobdingnag.

The wife of the Farmer leaves Gulliver on her bed for a nap, and the rats (each of which is the size "of a large Mastiff, but infinitely more nimble and fierce") climb up the curtains and onto the bed shortly after he has awakened due to some "natural Necessities." Gulliver draws his sword, but these "horrible Animals" nonetheless have "the Boldness" to attack him. He mortally wounds one of them by "rip[ping] up his Belly," and the other ("seeing the Fate of his Comrade") escapes but "not without one good Wound on the Back." Gulliver's triumphant description of how he kills one of these formidable adversaries and vengefully draws blood from the other adds irony to the entire episode. This is one of several similar encounters between Gulliver and various animals and insects in Brobd-

Gulliver is attacked by the rats in Brobdingnag. Part 2, chapter 1 *(Thomas Morten)*

ingnag. See also Eagle, Flies, Monkey, Spaniel, and Wasps.

**Reaper in Brobdingnag**    In Part 2, chapter 1, of *Gulliver's Travels,* character who finds Lemuel Gulliver and takes him to the Farmer. As the Reaper approaches Gulliver (who is cowering "between two Ridges" in a field of corn), Gulliver screams to get his attention. The giant then picks Gulliver up, treating him with "the Caution of one who endeavors to lay hold on a small dangerous Animal." Although Gulliver fears that the Reaper will "dash [him] against the Ground" at any moment, he does not harm him.

The episode involving the Reaper is described in ways that draw unmistakable parallels between Gulliver and a helpless "little animal," in sharp contrast to the Lilliputians view of him (in Part I) as "the greatest Prodigy that ever appeared in the World." This contrasting perspective runs throughout Part II, as when Glumdalclitch complains that her parents' decision to display Gulliver publicly for money reminds her of "when they pretended to give her a Lamb, and yet, as soon as it was fat, sold it to a Butcher." See also Splacknuck.

**Scholars in Brobdingnag**    In Part 2 of *Gulliver's Travels,* the King of Brobdingnag sends for "three great Scholars" to examine Lemuel Gulliver (see Brobdingnag, King of). Although they each have some of their own unique opinions of him, they all concur that he "could not be produced according to the regular Laws of Nature," since in their view he lacks the "Capacity of preserving [his] Life, either by Swiftness, or climbing of Trees, or digging Holes in the Earth." As this assessment suggests, the scholars—like every other Brobdingnagian (including Glumdalclitch) who comes in contact with Gulliver—do not view him as an undersized human but as a strange little beast (see Splacknuck). When they examine his teeth, they conclude that he is "a carnivorous Animal" but cannot understand how he sustains himself, "unless [he] fed upon Snails and other Insects."

After agreeing that Gulliver cannot possibly be an "abortive birth" or a dwarf, the scholars finally decide that they can describe him only as a "*Relplum*

*Scalath,* which is interpreted literally, *Lusus Naturalis,*" or freak of nature. Gulliver comments that this "Determination" is "exactly agreeable to the Modern Philosophy of *Europe,*" whose proponents "have invented this wonderful Solution of all Difficulties to the unspeakable Advancement of human Knowledge." Swift's portrayal of the scholars makes fun of "modern" scientists (one segment of the group he targets in "The BATTLE OF THE BOOKS" and in Part III of the *Travels*) who habitually use this designation to describe anything that violates their particular understanding of natural law. This issue arises again in chapter 7, when Gulliver reads a "little old Treatise" written by a Brobdingnagian on "the Weakness of Human kind." The author asserts "that the very laws of Nature absolutely required we should have been made in the beginning, of a size more large and robust, not so liable to Destruction from every little Accident"—a particularly ironic statement since even the smallest inhabitant of Brobdingnag is a giant compared to Gulliver. After recognizing many similarities between this author's claims and those of European writers, Gulliver concludes that there is an unfortunately universal talent for lecturing on "Discontent" and raising "ill-grounded" quarrels with Nature.

**Slardral**    Brobdingnagian word for "Gentleman Usher" from the royal court of Brobdingnag. In chapter 3 of Part 2 of *Gulliver's Travels,* a Slardral comes to the Farmer (Lemuel Gulliver's first master in that kingdom) and orders him to bring Gulliver "immediately" to court "for the Diversion of the Queen and her Ladies." In *A Gulliver Dictionary,* Paul Odell Clark translates *slardral* as "sland'rer."

**Spaniel**    One of several animals Lemuel Gulliver perilously encounters in Brobdingnag in Part 2 of *Gulliver's Travels.* After Glumdalclitch has left Gulliver alone (at his request) in the palace garden, a "small white Spaniel belonging to one of the chief Gardeners" picks him up in its mouth. The dog carries Gulliver to its master, who (like Gulliver) is terribly frightened by the entire episode. In describing the event, Gulliver adds that "the Thing was hushed up, and never known at Court" since Glumdalclitch "was afraid of the Queen's Anger," and Gulliver is worried that his "Reputation" would be damaged if "such a Story should go about." It is ironic that Gulliver describes the spaniel as "small" since compared with him it is relatively giant. This episode, like those involving the Flies, Frog, Rats, Wasps, and other pests, underscores Gulliver's powerlessness in Brobdingnag and highlights the view of him throughout this section of the *Travels* as a Splacknuck rather than an undersized human being.

**Splacknuck**   In Part 2 of *Gulliver's Travels*, the type of animal to which the inhabitants of Brobdingnag compare Lemuel Gulliver. Gulliver explains that it becomes the talk of the neighborhood that the Farmer "had found a strange Animal in the Field about the bigness of a *Splacknuck,* but exactly shaped in every part like a human Creature; which it likewise imitated in all its Actions." This comparison adds to the suggestion throughout Part II of the *Travels* that Gulliver is more of a little animal than the great "Prodigy" the tiny inhabitants of Lilliput believed him to be. The King of Brobdingnag, for example, after hearing Gulliver's description of his homeland in chapter 7, picks Gulliver up, and "stroking [him] gently," declares that he "cannot but conclude the Bulk of your Natives, to be the most pernicious Race of little odious Vermin that Nature ever suffered to crawl upon the Surface of the Earth" (see Brobdingnag, King of). Adopting the Brobdingnagians' perspective, Gulliver eventually refers to himself consistently as an animal in this section, as when he explains to the Queen of Brobdingnag in chapter 3 that the life he led while in the Farmer's possession was hard enough to have killed "an Animal of ten times my Strength" (see Brobdingnag, Queen of). See also Reaper, Farmer's Son, Eagle, Flies, Monkey, Spaniel, Rats, and Wasps.

**Wasps**   In Part 2 of *Gulliver's Travels*, Lemuel Gulliver is attacked by "above twenty Wasps" in Brobdingnag after Glumdalclitch has left the box in which he travels on a windowsill. Attracted by a piece of "Sweet Cake" he is preparing to eat, the insects are "as large as Partridges" and terrorize Gulliver with their loud humming, which is "louder

than the Drones of many Bagpipes." The wasps threaten him with their giant stings, but he kills four of them with his sword and the others flee. Gulliver removes the stings from each of the dead wasps, keeping one for himself and giving the others to Gresham College (home of the Royal Society of London for Improving Natural Knowledge). At the end of chapter 3, he describes the episode as a feat of great bravery and strength on his part, adding irony to the reality that from a different perspective it was simply a matter of killing a few bugs. See also Flies.

**Wilcocks, Thomas**   In Part 2 of *Gulliver's Travels*, captain of the crew of sailors who rescue Lemuel Gulliver (in chapter 8) following his departure from Brobdingnag. His ship is returning to England from northern Vietnam ("*Tonquin*"). Upon their return to England, Gulliver "borrow[s]" five Shillings from Wilcocks to pay for a "Horse and Guide" to take him home to Redriff.

Wilcocks and his crew find Gulliver bobbing in the ocean trapped inside the box in which he was carried during his stay in that kingdom. Gulliver describes Wilcocks as "an honest worthy *Shropshire Man*" who treated him hospitably: "observing I was ready to faint, [he] took me into his Cabin, gave me a Cordial to comfort me, and made me *turn in* upon his own Bed." When Gulliver asks to have his box brought into the cabin because it is filled with valuable items, Wilcocks assumes that he is "raving." After hearing Gulliver explain how he "came to be set Adrift in that monstrous wooden Chest," the Captain asks whether he had committed some horrible crime and been sentenced to brave the seas "in a leaky vessel without Provisions." However, Gulliver notes that this "honest worthy Gentleman, who had some Tincture of Learning, and very good Sense" was eventually convinced of his "Candour and Veracity." Gulliver shows Wilcocks various items he obtained in Brobdingnag, and gives the Captain a giant "Footman's Tooth" as a gift of appreciation.

Gulliver and Wilcocks have several conversations about issues such as why Gulliver speaks so loudly and why he can barely contain his laughter at meals. These show that Gulliver has clearly adopted a Brobdingnagian perspective on sound and size—he had to speak very loudly to be heard among the giants, and became accustomed to seeing relatively giant portions of food served in their kingdom. He explains that while there, he "winked at [his] own Littleness as People do at their own Faults." Significantly, Gulliver also notes that it was Wilcocks who encouraged him to "oblige the World" upon his return to England by publishing an account of his travels. Gulliver's answer was that the world was "already overstocked with Books of Travels" and "nothing could now pass which was not extraordinary." See also Carpenter.

### Part 3

**Advancers of Speculative Learning**   See Projectors at the Academy of Lagado.

**Agrippa, M. Vipsanius** (b. 63 B.C.)   Deputy of the Roman emperor Augustus. Agrippa was the admiral of Augustus's fleet at the battle of Actium in 31 B.C., and was primarily responsible for the defeat of Mark Antony's forces. During Lemuel Gulliver's visit to Glubbdubdrib in Part 3 of *Gulliver's Travels*, Agrippa is called up from the dead by the Governor. His spirit tells Gulliver that the real hero at Actium was an unknown captain (see Peterborough, Charles Mordaunt). Although Agrippa was born to an obscure family, he and Octavius (who later became the emperor Augustus) had studied together as boys and were friends at the time of Julius Caesar's murder in 44 B.C. Agrippa's military prowess and administrative abilities were important factors in Augustus's success during the civil wars following Caesar's death and throughout his reign.

**Alexander the Great** (356–323 B.C.)   Macedonian conqueror whose spirit is called up from the dead in Part 3 of *Gulliver's Travels*. The son of Philip II and Olympias, Alexander became King of Macedonia after the murder of his father in 336. He put down a rebellion in his own kingdom and began a lifelong conquest of other lands including Greece, Egypt, and Persia. During Lemuel Gulliver's visit to Glubbdubdrib, the Governor uses his magical powers to summon Alexander's spirit so

that Gulliver can talk with him. Despite Gulliver's difficulties in understanding ancient Greek, he is able to find out that Alexander was "not Poisoned, but died of a Fever by excessive Drinking."

**Aristotle**   See entry under "BATTLE OF THE BOOKS, The."

**Bliffmarklub**   High Chamberlain of Luggnagg in Part 3 of *Gulliver's Travels*. *Chamberlain* refers to "an officer charged with the management of the private chambers of a sovereign or nobleman" (*Oxford English Dictionary*). After Lemuel Gulliver has ingratiated himself to the King of Luggnagg in chapter 9, the King orders this official to provide lodging, food, and gold for Gulliver and his Interpreter. In *A Gulliver Dictionary*, Paul Odell Clark translates *Bliffmarklub* as "Love vile trash" or "Ever love trash."

**Brutus, Marcus Junius** (c. 78–42 B.C.)   Ancient Roman statesman and leader of the group of conspirators who assassinated Julius Caesar on March 15, 44 B.C. During Lemuel Gulliver's visit to Glubbdubdrib in Part 3 of *Gulliver's Travels*, the Governor calls Brutus's spirit up from the dead. Gulliver is awed at what he describes as Brutus's palpable virtue, intrepidity, firmness of mind, love of his country, and other noble qualities. He is also pleasantly surprised to see that Brutus and Caesar (who has also been summoned) appear to be on good terms with one another despite the violent death Brutus and the other conspirators inflicted upon the latter. Caesar tells Gulliver that all of his great accomplishments do not equal the greatness Brutus gained by killing him.

**Caesar, Gaius Julius** (102–44 B.C.)   Ancient Roman statesman and general; character in *Gulliver's Travels*. Along with Pompey and Marcus Crassus, Caesar was the third member of the Great Triumvirate until relations between Caesar and Pompey deteriorated. During the Roman civil war, Pompey's forces were ultimately defeated by Caesar's at the Battle of Pharsalus in 48 B.C.

During Lemuel Gulliver's visit to Glubbdubdrib in Part 3 of *Gulliver's Travels*, the Governor calls Caesar's spirit up from the dead along with that of

Marcus Brutus, leader of the conspirators who assassinated him. Gulliver is primarily impressed with Brutus, but pleased to learn that he and Caesar are "in good Intelligence with each other." Gulliver also explains that by Caesar's own admission, Brutus gained far more well-deserved fame by taking his life than Caesar ever acquired through his many valiant deeds.

**Climenole**   Laputan word for Flapper in *Gulliver's Travels*, Part 3. In *A Gulliver Dictionary*, Paul Odell Clark translates it as "criminal."

**Custom-House Officer**   Character in Part 3, chapter 9, of *Gulliver's Travels* who examines Lemuel Gulliver "very strictly" upon his arrival in Luggnagg. A custom-house is "a government office situated at a place of import or export, as a seaport, at which customs are levied on goods imported or exported" (*Oxford English Dictionary*). Gulliver lies to the Officer, stating that he is from Holland. He does this because he intends to travel to Japan, which is closed to all Europeans except the Dutch.

Gulliver encounters other Customs-House Officers upon his arrival at Yedo in Japan. He is allowed to pass after showing them a letter written on his behalf by the King of Luggnagg, whose seal they immediately recognize.

**Didymus** (63 B.C.–A.D. 10)   Early Greek scholar and commentator on Homer's writings. He was nicknamed "Chalcenterus" (brass guts) based on the massive amount of work he produced. During Lemuel Gulliver's visit to Glubbdubdrib in Part 3 of *Gulliver's Travels*, the Governor calls Didymus's spirit up from the dead so that Gulliver can introduce him and Eustathius to Homer. Gulliver explains that he asked Homer to treat these commentators with more respect than they probably deserved, and Homer ultimately decided that they lacked the "Genius to enter into the Spirit of a Poet."

**Duns Scotus, John**   See entry under "Battle of the Books, The."

**Dutchman**   Particularly antagonistic member of the Pirates' crew that kidnaps Lemuel Gulliver in

Part 3, chapter 1, of *Gulliver's Travels*. Gulliver notes that he "seem[s] to be of some Authority, though he was not Commander of the ship." The Dutchman threatens Gulliver and his small crew with death by drowning and is particularly offended when Gulliver begs him (in Dutch) to move the pirates to mercy since he and his crew are Christians from a neighboring country. Vitriolic and insulting, the Dutchman not only curses Gulliver soundly but finally convinces the more merciful Japanese captain to set him adrift to die alone in a small canoe.

Part of what fuels the Dutchman's anger is Gulliver's statement that he is "sorry to find more Mercy in a Heathen [the Japanese captain], than in a Brother Christian." Swift furthers this portrayal of the Dutch as anti-Christians at the end of Part III, when Gulliver—at the court of Japan—poses as a shipwrecked Dutch merchant because (as he states in chapter 9) he knows the Dutch are "the only *Europeans* permitted to enter into that Kingdom." When he petitions to be excused from "*trampling upon the Crucifix*" (a ceremony normally required of merchants trading in Japan who were suspected of being Christians), the Emperor of Japan is surprised since no other Dutchman "ever made any scruple in this Point." Swift makes clear his view that "Dutch" and "Christian" are mutually exclusive when Gulliver adds that the Emperor even "began to doubt whether I was a real *Hollander* or no; but rather suspected I must be a Christian." The Emperor also warns Gulliver that if his "Countrymen" (the Dutch) find out that he has refused to participate in trampling the Crucifix, they will cut his throat. See also "Conduct of the Allies."

**Eliogabulus (Heliogabulus or Elagabulus)** (204–222)   Roman emperor from 218–222, notorious for his gluttony and debauchery. During Lemuel Gulliver's visit to Glubbdubdrib in Part 3 of *Gulliver's Travels*, the Governor (at Gulliver's request) calls some of Eliogabulus's cooks to prepare a dinner. They have only limited success, however, "for want of Materials." In his edition of the *Travels*, Isaac Asimov explains that Elagabulus reportedly dined "on rare, imported delicacies such as peacocks' tongues."

**English Yeomen**   Characters in Part 3, chapter 8, of *Gulliver's Travels. Yeoman* here refers to "a man holding a small landed estate" who "cultivates his own land" (*Oxford English Dictionary*). During Lemuel Gulliver's visit to Glubbdubdrib, the Governor calls a number of spirits up from the dead so that Gulliver can converse with them. The more spirits he encounters, the more disturbed Gulliver becomes at how "degenerate" the human race had become (both physically and morally) within the past hundred years. In order to offset his sadness at the devolution of his own countrymen, Gulliver asks the Governor to call up "some *English* Yeomen of the old stamp" to recall the rugged simplicity and upright character for which they were famous. Instead of bolstering Gulliver's nationalism, however, the Yeomen's appearance serves as a painful reminder of "how all these pure native Virtues" have been "prostituted for a piece of Money by their Grandchildren" who had sold their votes and learned all sorts of corruption at court. See also "BAUCIS AND PHILEMON," in which Philemon is described as "a good old honest yeoman."

**Eustathius**   (c. 1175–1194)   Archbishop of Thessalonica and early commentator on the works of Homer. During Lemuel Gulliver's visit to Glubbdubdrib in Part 3 of *Gulliver's Travels*, the Governor calls Eustathius's spirit up from the dead so that Gulliver can introduce him and Didymus to Homer. Gulliver explains that he asked Homer to treat these commentators with more respect than they probably deserved, and Homer ultimately decided that they lacked the "Genius to enter into the Spirit of a Poet." In his edition of the *Travels*, Albert Rivero notes that Eustathius's treatise on Homer's poems was mainly a series of excerpts from the work of earlier commentators.

**Flapper(s)**   In Part 3 of *Gulliver's Travels*, a special type of domestic servant in Laputa who wields a "blown Bladder [filled with peas or small pebbles] fastened like a Flail to the end of a short Stick." In chapter 2, Lemuel Gulliver notes that Laputans of quality never leave home without a Flapper, who is charged, "when two or three more Persons are in Company, gently to strike with his Bladder the Mouth of him who is to speak, and the Right Ear of him or them to whom the Speaker addresseth himself." The Laputans require this service because their minds "are so taken up with intense Speculations, that they neither can speak, nor attend to the Discourses of others, without being roused by some external Taction [touch]" on their mouths and ears. A Flapper is even expected to attend his master on walks, "and upon occasion to give him a soft Flap on his Eyes, because he is always so wrapped up in Cogitation, that he is in manifest danger of falling down" and bumping into obstructions. A Flapper taps Gulliver on the right ear during his first encounter with the King of Laputa, but Gulliver indicates that he has no need for this assistance (see Laputa, King of). This leads the King and the entire court to decide that Gulliver has very limited intellectual capabilities.

In the introductory remarks to his annotated edition of the *Travels* (1814), Sir Walter Scott writes that Swift's friends believed "that the office of a flapper was suggested by the habitual absence of mind of the great" Isaac NEWTON. Scott claims that Swift told Deane SWIFT "that Sir Isaac was the worst companion in the world, and that, if you asked him a question, he would revolve it in a circle in his brain, round, and round, and round, (here Swift described a circle on his own forehead,) before he could produce an answer" (*Critical Heritage* 290). The Flappers and their masters in this section of the *Travels* are all part of Swift's lampoon of those who (in his view) overvalued their own intellectual capabilities and neglected the need for faith and the kind of common sense displayed by Lord Munodi.

**Footman**   Character in Part 3 of *Gulliver's Travels*. Part of Lemuel Gulliver's description of Laputa in chapter 2 includes an explanation of how the great lords of the floating island are so wrapped up in speculation that they normally do not even notice when their neglected wives (forbidden to leave the island) blatantly pursue other men and even "proceed to the greatest Familiarities before his Face." He cites one specific example involving a "great Court Lady" who is married to the Prime Minister. She visited Lagado once and refused to return to Laputa, preferring instead to remain with an "old deformed Footman, who beat her every Day." Ultimately she was forcibly returned. The "Prime Minister" is likely a reference to Sir Robert WALPOLE, whose wife was notoriously unfaithful.

**Glubbdubdrib, Governor of**   Ruler of a small island located "about five Leagues off to the South-West" of Maldonada. Lemuel Gulliver visits Glubbdubdrib in Part 3, chapters 7–8 of *Gulliver's Travels* while he waits for a ship to take him to Luggnag. The Governor lives in a "noble Palace" on 3,000 acres, enclosed within a stone wall 20 feet high and containing "smaller Enclosures for Cattle, Corn, and Gardening." As a skilled sorcerer, he is able to call spirits up from the dead at will and to command their service for up to 24 hours at a time. Gulliver is initially frightened by the Governor's ability to make his servants vanish "with a turn of his Finger," and refuses to sleep in the Palace during his visit to the island. To entertain Gulliver during his 10-day visit, the Governor causes numerous famous Ancients and Moderns to appear and converse with him. Gulliver finds great satisfaction in speaking with the Ancients, but talking with the Moderns leaves him "disgusted with modern history."

**Hannibal** (247–182 B.C.)   Carthaginian general famous for his attacks on Rome, especially the one he mounted after crossing the Alps in 218 B.C. During Lemuel Gulliver's visit to the island of Glubbdubdrib in Part 3 of *Gulliver's Travels*, the Governor calls Hannibal's spirit up from the dead so Gulliver can converse with him. He tells Gulliver that there is no truth to the popular legend that he used vinegar and fire to crack a large boulder blocking the path as he crossed the Alps. In his "DISCOURSE TO PROVE THE ANTIQUITY OF THE ENGLISH TONGUE," Swift jokes that the name *Anibal* (a "sworn enemy of the Romans, [who] gained many glorious victories over them") repeats "a metaphor drawn from tennis, expressing a skilful gamester, who can take *any ball*; and is very justly applied to so renowned a commander."

**Helot of Agesilaus**   One of the spirits called up from the dead during Lemuel Gulliver's visit to

Glubbdubdrib in Part 3 of *Gulliver's Travels*. After Eliogabulus's cooks find themselves unable to prepare a meal for Gulliver and the Governor, the Helot makes them a dish of Spartan broth, which tastes so awful that Gulliver cannot eat more than a single spoonful. Agesilaus was king of Sparta from about 399 to 360 B.C. The "Helot" was one of Agesilaus's slaves—a native of the Greek city of Helos whose citizens had been enslaved by the Spartans during the Dorian conquest. The Helots (a term eventually used to describe any Spartan slave) constituted about half of the population of Sparta.

**Homer**   Greek epic poet of the eighth or ninth century B.C., author of the *Iliad* and *Odyssey*. During his visit to Glubbdubdrib in III.8 of *Gulliver's Travels*, Gulliver has Homer (and Aristotle) called up from the dead along with all their commentators. Homer is there described as taller and "comelier" than Aristotle, and as one who "walked very erect for one his age." In opposition to traditional portrayals of Homer as blind, Gulliver claims that the ancient's eyes "were the most quick and piercing" he had every seen. The commentators who appear with Homer and Aristotle are so numerous that they spill out into the outward rooms of the Governor's palace. One ghost tells Gulliver that in the underworld, these commentators always stay as far away as they can from "their Principals," because of the "Shame and Guilt" they feel at having so "horribly misrepresented the meaning of those Authors to Posterity" (Swift makes similar points about these "learned commentators" in "A TALE OF A TUB" and "ON POETRY: A RHAPSODY," as discussed below). When Gulliver introduces Didymus and Eustathius to Homer, the ancient quickly discovers that these commentators lack "the Genius to enter into the Spirit of a Poet." He responds more patiently than Aristotle, however, who (after meeting two of his own commentators) asks if they are all such "great Dunces."

As commander of the ancients' cavalry in "The BATTLE OF THE BOOKS," Homer rides a "furious" horse that he alone of all mortals is capable of keeping under control. During the battle Homer violently kills Gondibert (leaving him and his horse to be trampled "and choak'd in the Dirt"), and then impales John DENHAM with a long spear. Homer also dispatches Samuel WESLEY—"with a kick of his horse's heel"—along with Charles PERRAULT and Bernard FONTENELLE.

An important part of Swift's lampoon of the Moderns and their pedantry in *A Tale of a Tub* involves the narrator's commentary on Homer. He describes the Greek poet as "a Person not without some Abilities, and *for an Ancient,* of a tolerable Genius." Claiming to have read Homer's work "with the utmost Application usual among *Modern Wits,*" however, the narrator adds that he has "discovered many gross Errors" in the ancient poet's work. While we are told, for example, that Homer "design'd his Work for a compleat Body of all Knowledge Human, Divine, Political, and Mechanick; it is manifest, he hath wholly neglected some, and been very imperfect in the rest." Homer was utterly ignorant, the narrator explains, of England's common laws and knew absolutely nothing of the doctrine and discipline of the Anglican Church. In "On Poetry: A Rhapsody," Swift makes further fun of "learned commentators" who "view / In Homer more than Homer knew."

Swift's cousin alludes to Homer in responding to the widespread tendency among Swift's admirers to compare him with the Roman satirist Horace. In the second edition of his *Essay upon the Life, Writings and Character of Dr. Jonathan Swift* (1755) Deane SWIFT writes that, "Homer was the darling author both of Horace and Swift." He explains that, like Horace, Swift believed that "Homer had more genius than all the world put together." This admiration was undoubtedly influential in Swift's role as an early and active promoter of his friend Alexander POPE's translation of Homer's *Iliad.* The first of the five volumes of Pope's massive effort appeared in 1715 and the last in 1720. This successful translation made Pope famous as the best poet of his age, earned him a great deal of wealth, and "laid the foundation of a lifelong friendship" with Swift (Ehrenpreis, *Swift* II.609).

**Interpreter** Character in Part 3, chapter 9, of *Gulliver's Travels.* Lemuel Gulliver hires this "young man" to help him during his visit to the island called Luggnagg. Gulliver encounters another interpreter in chapter 11 at the court of Yedo in Japan. When Gulliver arrives with a letter of introduction from the King of Luggnagg, an interpreter explains the letter to the Emperor of Japan.

**Japan, Emperor of** Character in *Gulliver's Travels.* In Part 3, chapter 10, Lemuel Gulliver sails from Luggnagg to Japan, armed with a letter of recommendation from the King of Luggnagg to the Emperor, who graciously receives Gulliver. The two rulers know each other because their realms are engaged in ongoing trade. Presenting himself as a Dutch merchant (since—as he notes in chapter 9—the Dutch are the only Europeans allowed to enter that kingdom), Gulliver makes two requests of the Emperor. The first is to be safely conducted to the port of Nagasaki, and the other to be excused from participating in a ceremony that involves trampling on the crucifix (see Dutchman). The Emperor honors Gulliver's wishes on both accounts. See also "ACCOUNT OF THE COURT AND EMPIRE OF JAPAN."

**Japanese Captain** One of the Pirates who kidnap Lemuel Gulliver in chapter 1 of Part 3 of *Gulliver's Travels.* He commands the larger of the two pirate ships and (in Gulliver's view) embodies paganism mixed with virtue. Gulliver approaches him with great obsequies and is able to communicate with him in Dutch. The Captain promises Gulliver that he and his crew will not be killed and refuses to comply with the evil Dutchman's request to have Gulliver thrown into the sea. This leads Gulliver to tell the Dutchman that he is sorry to find more mercy in a heathen than in a fellow Christian, prompting the Dutchman angrily to order Gulliver to be set adrift in a canoe. The Japanese Captain, however, supplies him with provisions and forbids any of his men to search him.

**Laputa, King of** Unnamed monarch of the flying island in Part 3 of *Gulliver's Travels.* Attended by Flappers, the King of Laputa epitomizes the perpetual state of preoccupation with abstract speculations that characterizes most of the inhabitants of Laputa. When Lemuel Gulliver first meets the King in chapter 2, he notes that in front of his Majesty's throne there is a giant table "filled with Globes and Spheres, and Mathematical Instruments of all kinds." These implements reflect the King's keen interest in mathematics and music, but like his fellow Laputans he concentrates exclusively on abstractions and theories at the expense of common sense and practical applications. In his edition of the *Travels*, Greenberg notes that in this sense the King is a lampoon of GEORGE I, "who, though a patron of music and science, had no real knowledge of either."

When Gulliver arrives at court, the King of Laputa is so lost in thought regarding issues related to math and music that he initially takes no notice. After an hour, however, he assigns two servants to attend upon Gulliver and to take him to a comfortable palace apartment. Gulliver claims that this monarch "would be the most absolute Prince in the Universe" if he could convince any leaders from Balnibarbi to join him. This is unlikely ever to happen, though, since his potential ministers all own "Estates below [Laputa] on the Continent, and considering the Office of a Favourite hath a very uncertain Tenure, [they] would never consent to the enslaving [of] their country."

Like his abstract interests in music and science, the Laputan king's character as a disengaged monarch also links him with George I, whose lack of popularity among many of his English subjects was partly due to his "hands-off" approach to ruling the kingdom. Perceived as being preoccupied with Hanover and devoting himself to foreign policy, he entrusted others (especially Robert WALPOLE) with the power to handle domestic affairs. Also, just as the King of Laputa was forbidden by law from leaving the island, George I was confined to England until he gained the right to visit Hanover. The five trips he made there during his reign further exasperated many of his English subjects, who already felt alienated from their monarch.

A tenuous relationship exists between the King and his subjects who live below Laputa on the island of Balnibarbi. The King tolerates no "Rebellion or Mutiny," and provides severe punishment for any townspeople who "fall into violent Factions, or refuse to pay the usual Tribute" to the crown. His mildest means of punishing such crimes is to suspend the island of Laputa above the town containing the offending citizens. This deprives them of sun and rain, which afflicts them "with Death and Diseases" of all kinds. In more serious cases, he has the offending town also "pelted from above with great Stones," driving the inhabitants into cellars and caves while their houses are destroyed. If these measures fail to bring the offenders to submission, the King's final option is to have the island of Laputa dropped "directly upon their Heads, which makes a universal Destruction of both Houses and Men." See Lindalino.

**Luggnagg, King of**　Ruler in Part 3 of *Gulliver's Travels*. In chapter 9, Lemuel Gulliver gains an audience with the King two days after arriving in Traldragdubb, the capital city of Luggnagg, and is commanded to approach the monarch by crawling on his belly and licking the floor as he goes. Gulliver notes, however, that since he is from out of town, the Luggnuggians take great care to sweep the floor before him. Others are not so lucky: sometimes the King has the floor covered with extra dust on purpose, and those he truly dislikes find themselves forced to lick up a poisonous dust that kills them within one day. Pleased with Gulliver's obsequies, the King invites him to remain as his guest at court, ordering his Bliffmarklub to provide lodging, food, and "a large Purse of Gold" for Gulliver and his Interpreter. Gulliver ends up staying in Luggnagg for three months.

The strange court custom in which Gulliver engages during his initial encounter with the King has been traced to at least two possible sources. In his edition of the *Travels*, Isaac Asimov explains that Swift is making fun of the Chinese custom (especially when Gulliver strikes his forehead "seven times on the Ground," since *kow-tow* literally means "bump-head"). DeMaria, however, provides a biblical precedent for the King's strange requirement, citing the statement in Psalms 72:9 that those who live in the wilderness would "bow before" King Solomon "and his enemies shall lick the dust."

**Munodi, Lord**　"Person of the first rank" in Part 3 of *Gulliver's Travels*. A friend of his intercedes on

Lemuel Gulliver's behalf with the King of Laputa (see Laputa, King of) and successfully obtains permission for Gulliver to visit Balnibarbi. Gulliver stays at Munodi's house during the visit and accompanies him on a tour of the island. He arranges for a friend to escort Gulliver on a visit to the Academy of Lagado.

Munodi was once governor of Lagado, and the King of Laputa treats him "with Tenderness, as a well-meaning Man, but of a low contemptible Understanding." His common sense and commitment to the practical application of knowledge distinguish him from the inhabitants of Laputa and Balnibarbi. They regard him as a simpleton because he employs time-tested agricultural and architectural practices rather than the faddish, impractical theories that have left his neighbors' lands barren and their houses in shambles. In a society blindly devoted to speculation and the uncritical pursuit of progress for its own sake, Munodi's practical traditionalism renders him unpopular and alone. Munodi's name was probably derived from 'mundum odi' (Latin for "I hate the world"). As Isaac Asimov notes in his edition of the *Travels*, "there is considerable disagreement as to whom Lord Munodi might represent." Because of his withdrawal from public life, he has been identified with Robert HARLEY (who was impeached in 1714) and/or Henry St. John, first viscount BOLINGBROKE (dismissed in 1715). He has also been linked with Alan Brodrick, viscount MIDDLETON, who alienated other WHIGS when he opposed William WOOD's halfpence. Others have cited Munodi's traditionalism as evidence for identifying him with Sir William TEMPLE.

**Pompey (Gnaeus Pompeius Magnus)** (106–48 B.C.) Ancient Roman statesman and general. During Lemuel Gulliver's visit to Glubbdubdrib in Part 3 of *Gulliver's Travels*, the Governor calls Pompey's spirit up from the dead. He appears at the head of his troops preparing to engage the forces of Julius Caesar, a fellow member of the Great Triumvirate. Caesar ultimately defeated Pompey and brought the Roman civil war to a close at the decisive Battle of Pharsalus in 48 B.C. Pompey was assassinated in Egypt later that same year. In "CON-TESTS AND DISSENTIONS IN ATHENS AND ROME," Swift writes that Pompey and Caesar were "two Stars of such a Magnitude, that their *Conjunction* was as likely to be fatal, as their *Opposition*."

**projectors at the Academy of Lagado**  Sham scientists visited by Lemuel Gulliver in Part 3, chapters 5 and 6 of *Gulliver's Travels*. To varying degrees, the projects in this section are based on actual endeavors of the Royal Society of London and on similar episodes in the satirical writings of François Rabelais. The first group of projectors is housed in the side of the Academy opposite that of the Advancers of Speculative Learning. They are part of what Ronald Knowles calls Swift's "most concerted attack on a major branch of modernism"—his lampoon of modern experimental science and the Royal Society. Because of his practicality and traditionalism, Lord Munodi had gained a bad reputation among the projectors, so he arranges for a friend to take Gulliver to see them. Gulliver anticipates his visit with excitement, noting that Munodi introduces him to his guide "as a great Admirer of Projects, and a Person of much Curiosity and easy Belief; which indeed was not without Truth; for I had my self been a Sort of Projector in my younger Days." *Projector* here refers to "one who forms a project, who plans or designs some enterprise or undertaking" (*Oxford English Dictionary*).

Like all the others who work in the Academy, the first devotee of the new science is pursuing a ridiculous and hopeless project: He has been working for eight years to find a means for extracting sunbeams out of cucumbers. These sunbeams "were to be put into Vials hermetically Sealed, and let out to warm the Air in raw inclement Summers." Gulliver describes him as "meager" and unkempt, and before Gulliver leaves, the projector asks for some money "as an Encouragement to Ingenuity." Lord Munodi had prepared Gulliver for this to happen, explaining that those at the Academy were known for "begging from all who go see them."

The second projector Gulliver visits is the "most ancient Student of the Academy." His face and beard are "of a pale Yellow; His Hands and Clothes daubed over with Filth," and his project is to find a way of turning "human Excrement to its original Food. The third projector works to turn ice into Gun Powder, while the fourth ("a most ingenious Architect") has devised a new—and entirely impractical—way of building houses, "by beginning at the Roof and working downward." The fourth professor was born blind, and seeks to teach blind apprentices to mix colored paints for artists. They distinguish one color from another "by feeling and smelling." The fifth has "found a Device of Plowing the Ground with Hogs," and the sixth is seeking to eliminate the need for silk by replacing it with colored spiderwebs. The seventh projector Gulliver encounters is an astronomer who, by placing a sun dial on top of a weathervane, seeks to adjust "the annual and diurnal Motions of the Earth and Sun, so as to answer and coincide with all accidental Turnings by the Wind." Gulliver ends his visit to this side of the Academy by watching "a great Physician" employ a set of bellows as a new way of curing illness by blowing air into the anus. The unfortunate subject of the experiment is a dog, who "died on the Spot." See also Universal Artist.

The second group of projectors (whom Gulliver distinguishes as "Advancers of Speculative Learning") work on the other side of the Academy. The first of these professors—accompanied by 40 students working six hours a day—has invented a "Contrivance" to allow even "the most ignorant Person" to write books on various subjects such as philosophy, law, and mathematics. This "engine" works by placing random words into equally random combinations, which are recorded by scribes so that the professor can piece them together later.

In the School of Language, three professors are "in Consultation upon improving that of their own Country." Their first project (which lampoons the Royal Society's efforts to improve the English language) seeks to "shorten Discourse by cutting Polysyllables into one, and leaving out" all words except for nouns. Their other undertaking is an attempt to do away with words altogether. Having decided that "Words are only Names for *Things*," the projectors propose that rather than speaking "it would be more convenient for all Men to carry about them, such *Things* as were necessary to express the particular Business they are to discourse on." Gul-

liver notes that in addition to its convenience, this plan would also result in a "Universal Language to be understood by all civilized Nations"—a joke aimed at John WILKINS, a founder of the Royal Society who proposed a universal language in his *Essay towards a Real Character and Philosophic Language* (1668).

The Master of the Mathematical School teaches his students by having them fast and then swallow a "thin wafer" on which the "Proposition and Demonstration" are written. His theory is that as the wafer is digested, the ink (a "Cephalic Tincture") will make its way into the student's brain, depositing the proposition there as well. Gulliver comments that this project has so far been unsuccessful, mainly because each of the "perverse" lads "generally steal aside" and vomit up the wafer "before it can operate." Rivero calls this experiment a "mock Eucharist" reminiscent of "St. John's acquisition of his prophetic powers by eating the 'little book' given him by the angel in Revelation 10:10," adding that Swift may also be making fun of the Catholic doctrine of transubstantiation. This doctrine asserts that as the priest handles the bread and wine during the Eucharist, they are physically transformed into the blood and body of Christ. The opposing Protestant doctrine of consubstantiation holds that the bread and wine are only symbols of Christ's body and blood. Swift satirizes this doctrine in Section IV of "A TALE OF A TUB," in which Peter acts as though a loaf of bread is *excellent good Mutton* and presents the crust as fine wine.

In chapter 6, Gulliver notes that he "was but ill entertained" in the "School of Political Projectors," and that the professors there seemed "wholly out of their Senses." This signals an important (but temporary) shift in the satiric technique Swift employs in this section of the *Travels*. During Gulliver's visits to other parts of the academy, he depicts fruitless, unreasonable projects as very promising. Early in chapter 6, however, he describes reasonable, worthwhile endeavors as entirely ridiculous: "These unhappy People," he explains, "were proposing Schemes for persuading Monarchs to choose Favourites upon the Score of their Wisdom, Capacity and Virtue; of teaching Ministers to consult the Public Good; of rewarding Merit, great Abilities and eminent Services" and other "wild impossible Chimeras, that never entered before into the heart of Man to conceive."

When Gulliver visits a "most Ingenious Doctor" among the political projectors, however, Swift resumes having him describe the ridiculous in wholly positive terms. In an attempt to make government more efficient, this doctor proposes having physicians diagnose senators' maladies and, prior to the beginning of deliberation, have apothecaries administer whatever "Palliatives, Laxatives, Cephalagicks" or other medicines might be necessary. Awed by the prospect, Gulliver comments that this project would be of little expense to the public and "be of much Use for the dispatch of Business in those Countries where Senates have any share in the Legislative Power." The doctor's next project is reminiscent of the Flappers employed on Laputa. Based on the "general Complaint" that a monarch's favorites have short memories, he argues that those who meet with "a first Minister, after having told his business with the utmost Brevity, and in the plainest Words," should inflict some sort of physical pain on the minister in order to make sure he remembers—and should continue to assault him daily until "the Business were done or absolutely refused." Another of the doctor's projects encourages senators meeting "in the great Council of a Nation" to state their opinions and then to "Vote directly contrary"—a strategy he argues "would infallibly terminate in the Good of the Public." Finally, he proposes that when a state is divided by violent political parties, the best method for restoring order is to take 100 leaders from each party and have their heads cut into halves and "interchanged, applying each to the head of his opposite Party-man." The inevitable result, he argues, will be that the two halves of each brain will be "left to debate the Matter" and "soon come to a good Understanding."

Two other professors are engaged in "a very warm Debate" regarding the best way for a government to raise money without "grieving" the people. Their proposed remedies include taxing men for their sins and women for "their Beauty and skill in Dressing," since qualities such as constancy and chastity are so scarce that they "would not bear the Charge of Collecting." The last projector Gulliver

visits before leaving the academy has invented a scheme "for discovering Plots and Conspiracies against the Government." This involves close examination of seemingly irrelevant evidence of all sorts, including taking "a strict View" of the suspects' "Excrements"—a parody of the 1722 trial of Bishop Francis ATTERBURY as a JACOBITE, in which the evidence against him included letters retrieved from his chamber pot.

**Ramus, Petrus (Pierre de la Ramée)** (1515–1572)   French humanist philosopher and logician, well-known for his unorthodox and controversial revisions of Aristotle's theories. During Lemuel Gulliver's visit to Glubbdubdrib in Part 3 of *Gulliver's Travels*, the Governor calls Ramus's spirit up from the dead to stand alongside Duns Scotus among the multitude of commentators on Aristotle's writings. After Gulliver provides a brief account of their work, Aristotle angrily asks Ramus and Duns Scotus both if all the other commentators are "as great Dunces as themselves."

**Robinson, William**   Ship's captain with whom Lemuel Gulliver sails at the beginning of Part 3 of *Gulliver's Travels*. His vessel is the 300-ton *Hope-Well*. Gulliver describes Robinson as "a *Cornish* man" with whom he had sailed before as "Surgeon of another Ship where [Robinson] was Master, and a fourth Part Owner." On that voyage, Gulliver notes, Robinson treated him "more like a Brother than an Inferior Officer." In chapter 1 of Part 3, Robinson pays a visit to Gulliver after the latter has returned from Brobdingnag. He indicates that he is planning a voyage to the East Indies in two months and hopes Gulliver will sail with him once more as ship's surgeon. As an incentive, Robinson promises to pay Gulliver twice "the usual Pay" and (based on the respect he has for Gulliver's "Knowledge in Sea-Affairs") to share command of the ship with him. Gulliver accepts the offer, due to his fondness for Robinson as well as his "violent" thirst for seeing the world. They set sail on August 5, 1706. During the ill-fated voyage, Gulliver ends up being kidnapped by Pirates. They leave him to fend for himself in a small canoe, which leads to his visit to Laputa and Balnibarbi.

**Struldbruggs**  Race of immortals in Part 3, chapter 10, of *Gulliver's Travels*. Lemuel Gulliver encounters the Struldbruggs in Luggnagg. In *A Gulliver Dictionary*, Paul Odell Clark translates the name as "stir dull blood," "stirred blood," or "sterile blood." Upon hearing of their existence, Gulliver is "struck with inexpressible Delight" and delivers a rapturous commentary on how wonderful it must be to live forever. Along with his dissertation on what he would do if he were immortal, this heightens his sobering realization that being immortal is more of a curse than a blessing. He soon learns that the Struldbruggs are all miserable because although they never die, they continually age—losing their health, their beauty, and eventually their minds.

The Struldbruggs of Luggnagg. Part 3, chapter 10 *(Thomas Morten)*

The Struldbruggs can be born to any Luggnuggian family. Very rarely, Gulliver is told, a child is born with a small red circle on its forehead, just above the left eyebrow. This mark distinguishes the Struldbruggs from their mortal relatives, and it grows and changes color as its bearer ages. They live normally until they reach 30 years of age, at which point they sink into a deep depression based on the knowledge of what sort of life is in store for them. They are forbidden by law from marrying another of their race, based on the belief that their predicament is bad enough without having "their Misery doubled by the Load of a Wife." At 80 they are officially regarded as dead, and their heirs inherit all they have other than a "small Pittance" that is "reserved for their Support." Ten years later they lose all their teeth, hair, and sense of taste, and they begin to forget what things are called.

When Gulliver finally meets some of these miserable Struldbruggs, they beg money from him and he decides that they are "the most mortifying Sight" he has ever seen: "the Women more horrible than the Men." He is heartily embarrassed at his initial envy of their immortality, and the King of Luggnagg encourages him to take some home as a means of arming his countrymen "against the Fear of Death." As Michael DePorte notes, the Struldbruggs "are the last exotic people Gulliver meets before his voyage to Houyhnhnmland," and they provide "a particularly horrifying demonstration of the point Swift makes throughout book 3: dreams of perfectibility, whether vested in utopias of the future or golden ages of the past, are just that—dreams" ("Teaching the Third Voyage" 60).

**Tailor**  Character in Part 3 of *Gulliver's Travels*. In chapter 2, the servants appointed by the King of Laputa to attend upon Lemuel Gulliver have the Tailor make him a suit of clothes (see Laputa, King of). Gulliver notes that this Tailor performs "his Office after a different manner from those of his Trade in *Europe*." He uses a quadrant to measure Gulliver's height, "and then with a Rule and Compasses, describe[s] the Outlines" of Gulliver's "whole Body," noting each measurement carefully on paper. A quadrant is an "instrument, properly having the form of a graduated quarter-circle, used for making angular measurements," normally "for taking altitudes in astronomy and navigation" (*Oxford English Dictionary*). Six days later, the Tailor returns with a suit of clothes which Gulliver describes as "very ill made, and quite out of shape." Gulliver explains that this occurred because the Tailor happened "to mistake a Figure in the Calculation," adding that "such Accidents" among the Laputans were "very frequent and little regarded." The Tailor is part of Swift's lampoon (throughout Part III of the *Travels*) of thinkers who have devoted themselves to speculation and reason at the expense of common sense. In his 1814 annotated edition of the *Travels*, Sir Walter Scott explains that "Under the parable of the tailor,. . . Swift is supposed to have alluded to an error of Sir Isaac [NEWTON]'s printer, who, by carelessly adding a cipher to the astronomer's computation of the distance between the Sun and the Earth, had increased it to an incalculable amount" (*Critical Heritage* 289–290).

**Universal Artist, The** "Illustrious" Projector at the Academy of Lagado visited by Lemuel Gulliver in chapter 5, Part 3, of *Gulliver's Travels*. Gulliver lists him last among the projectors housed on the side of the academy devoted to experimental science. The Artist tells Gulliver that for 30 years he has "been employing his Thoughts for the Improvement of human Life." In two large rooms "full of wonderful Curiosities," he and his 50 associates work on projects as hopeless and impractical as those of the other Projectors. One venture, for example, involves "softening Marble for Pillows and Pincushions." Another is geared toward preventing "the Growth of Wool upon two young Lambs," and eventually propagating "the Breed of naked Sheep all over the Kingdom." Like the descriptions of the other projectors' experiments, this one is part of Swift's lampoon of what he viewed as the Royal Society of London's pursuit of learning divorced from practical application and common sense. As Rivero points out in his edition of the *Travels*, Swift may have based the Universal Artist on Robert BOYLE, "whose many publications featured experiments and observations on virtually all natural phenomena."

**Vangrult, Theodorus** Dutch captain of the *Amboyna* in Part 3, chapter 11, of *Gulliver's Travels*. Lemuel Gulliver sails with Vangrult and his crew from the Japanese port of Nagasaki to Amsterdam. Gulliver explains that he was prepared to pay whatever Vangrult thought fit to charge for conducting him to Holland, but when it was discovered that Gulliver was a surgeon, the Captain "was contented to take half the usual rate, on the Condition that" he act as ship's surgeon during the voyage.

**Yeomen, English** See English Yeomen.

*Part 4*

**Houyhnhnms** Ultrarational pseudo-horses that inhabit the kingdom Lemuel Gulliver visits in Part 4 of *Gulliver's Travels*. The word itself recalls the sound of a horse's whinny, and some critics read it as a corruption of "human." Gulliver explains that in the Houyhnhnm language it simply means *horse*, but "in its Etymology" it refers to "*the Perfection of Nature.*" In keeping with this explanation of the name, Gulliver describes the Houyhnhnms with increasing admiration throughout Part 4. To him, they come to exemplify perfection and innocence—a simplicity and total devotion to reason made even more distinct in Gulliver's mind by the grotesque brutishness of the Yahoos. As Gulliver explains in chapter 8, the Houyhnhnms' "grand Maxim is, to cultivate *Reason,* and to be wholly governed by it."

Even though Gulliver himself does so, it is not quite accurate to refer to the Houyhnhnms as horses, since they engage in activities of which normal equines are mentally and physically incapable. They speak and reason, hold objects between their hooves and pasterns, sit "upon their hams," and feed themselves with their forehooves: They milk cows, and "do all the Work which requires Hands, and this with [great] Dexterity." The highest-ranking Houyhnhnm is called the "Master" or "Master-Grey" throughout Part 4. He regularly converses with Gulliver and ensures that he is provided with food and shelter. An "honest and very good-natured" Sorrel Nag (a chestnut-colored horse who is the Master's valet) cares for Gulliver, helps him learn the Houyhnhnm language, and protects him

The general assembly of Houyhnhnms. Part 4, chapter 9  *(Thomas Morten)*

from the Yahoos during his stay. In chapter 6, the Master explains to Gulliver that the white, sorrel, and "iron-grey" Houyhnhnms are mentally and physically inferior to those that are bay (reddish brown), "dapple-grey" (gray with spots), or black. Houyhnhnms of the lower sort are born into servitude and never aspire to move beyond that rank throughout their lives.

The Houyhnhnms treat Gulliver well during his stay in their kingdom, although they are at first somewhat perplexed by his identity, particularly because he shares certain physical similarities with the Yahoos but is also clearly different from them. He can speak, he is "much more cleanly, and not altogether so deformed," and he is not as strong or agile as even "a common Yahoo." This uncertainty is clear in their initial decision to "lodge" Gulliver in a place about "Six Yards from the House" where the Houyhnhnms reside but still "separated from the Stable of the *Yahoos*." When (in chapters 4–7) Gulliver provides his Master with a wealth of infor-

mation on English and European cultures, this heightens the Master's suspicion that Gulliver truly belongs to the Yahoo race. However, it is not until the young female Yahoo accosts Gulliver while he is bathing (in chapter 8) that the Houyhnhnms decide once and for all that he is "a real Yahoo, in every Limb and Feature."

As his fear and hatred of the Yahoos intensify, Gulliver's admiration of the Houyhnhnms becomes so extreme that he begins to think of himself as one of them, despite their judgment that he is just a Yahoo in disguise. In chapter 11, for example, he refers to himself as the Sorrel Nag's "Fellow Servant." Adopting the Houyhnhnms' perspective on humans (except as it applies to himself), Gulliver decides that he is "fully settled for Life" in their country. He readily renounces his countrymen and even his own family, deciding that they are all "Yahoos in Shape and Disposition, only a little more civilized," able to speak, and using reason only to multiply their vices. Desperate to distinguish himself from the Yahoos, he imitates the "gait," "gesture," "voice," and "manner" of his equine Master. The Houyhnhnms eventually force Gulliver to leave their country because they suspect that, as a Yahoo endowed with the "Rudiments of Reason," he might incite the Yahoos to destroy their cattle. One of the great ironies of this part of the *Travels* is that the Houyhnhnms decide to expel Gulliver precisely because he convinces them that he is not simply a run-of-the-mill Yahoo. If he were, they could accept him, although only as a beast of burden and not in the terms he desires. Instead, his prideful campaign to show that he is more than a Yahoo worries the Houyhnhnms, and finally makes it impossible for him to remain among his beloved hosts. As Martin Price explained it years ago, "The Houyhnhnm, who is unacquainted with the possibility of rational creatures other than of his own kind, is reluctant to admit a new species as long as man can be accounted for in terms of previous experience" (99). Even after returning dejectedly to England, Gulliver continues to conduct himself in ways that, in his mind, suggest he is really more of a Houyhnhnm than a Yahoo. His neighing, trotting around, and "conversing" with horses provoke ridicule back in Redriff, while he disdains his family as "odious" Yahoos.

Early readings of Part 4 (such as Thomas SHERIDAN's in his 1784 *Life of Swift*) often presented it as Swift's "lesson to mankind" urging his audience "not to suffer the animal part" of human nature—embodied in the Yahoos—"to be predominant in them." Instead, they should "emulate the noble and generous Houyhnhnm, by cultivating the rational faculty to the utmost; which will lead them to a life of virtue and happiness" (*Critical Heritage* 237). This view, in which the Houyhnhnms are regarded as ideal, characterizes what has become known as the "hard school" of interpreting the *Travels*. In contrast, "soft school" readings present the *Travels* as a satire in which humans, Yahoos, and Houyhnhnms are targeted. Soft school readings argue that the Yahoos and the Houyhnhnms both embody extremes that are equally undesirable and unnatural for humans. As Samuel Holt Monk puts it his well-known soft school interpretation of the fourth voyage, "Swift simply isolates the two

elements that combine in the duality of man, the middle link, in order to allow Gulliver to contemplate each in its essence." The absolute lack of emotion among the Houyhnhnms of quality and the corresponding absence of reason in the Yahoos highlight Gulliver's character as existing somewhere in between. Despite his overwhelming desire to imitate the Houyhnhnms, even Gulliver refers to them as "inimitable" near the end of chapter 11. Swift quietly provides a more realistic model for Gulliver in the positive portrayal of the charitable Captain Pedro de Mendez. At the end of Part 4, the Captain's kindness and sound advice have the potential to remind Gulliver of what it means to be human: to strike a balance between the raw passion of the Yahoo and the cold rationality of the Houyhnhnm. Upon returning to his family in Redriff, however, Gulliver shows that he has lost sight of this balance as a requirement for human interaction. Along with the "Hatred, Disgust, and Contempt" he exhibits toward his family, Gulliver's sad and ridiculous attempt to find fulfillment in conversation with his horses shows that by the end of Part 4 he refuses to recognize the Houyhnhnms' limitations and his own inability to be anything other than human. As John B. Radner notes, "The self-sufficient, unfallen Houyhnhnm may be a pattern of virtue, but Houyhnhnms offer no cure for fallen men" like Gulliver (431).

**Mare** One of the Houyhnhnms in Part 4 of *Gulliver's Travels*. She is the mate of the gray Houyhnhnm who becomes Gulliver's master during his visit. Lemuel Gulliver describes her as "very comely" and notes that she is accompanied by her offspring—one colt and one foal. When Gulliver first enters his Master's house, the Mare walks over and examines him closely. Obviously disgusted with what she sees, she gives Gulliver "a most contemptuous Look" and mutters something about a "Yahoo"—a statement he does not understand at the time, although it becomes clear to him later that she and the other Houyhnhnms regard him as one of those animals.

**Mendez, Pedro de** Portuguese ship captain in *Gulliver's Travels*, Part 4, chapter 11. Lemuel Gulliver reluctantly joins de Mendez and his crew after

Gulliver is discovered by Pedro de Mendez, Part 4, chapter 11 *(Thomas Morten)*

they find him hiding on the "South-East Point of New Holland" following his forced departure from the Houyhnhnms. Gulliver describes de Mendez as "courteous and generous" and "wise," but the captain's kindness does nothing to quell Gulliver's revulsion toward other Yahoos, highlighting the depth and irony of his misanthropy. After Gulliver unsuccessfully tries to jump overboard and escape from his rescuers, de Mendez transports him safely to Lisbon. Gulliver stays at the captain's home for almost three weeks, leaving only after de Mendez convinces him that he has a moral obligation to return to his family in England. The captain is traditionally regarded as a Good Samaritan figure. Pedro's surname is probably a reference to Ferdinand Mendez Pinto (c. 1509–83), a famous Euro-

pean traveler whose accounts of his journeys were notorious for their exaggeration.

**Pocock, Captain**   Unfortunate sailor in Part 4, chapter 1, of *Gulliver's Travels*. After setting sail on the *Adventure* from Portsmouth on August 2, 1710, Lemuel Gulliver and his crew (including Robert Purefoy) meet with Pocock at Teneriffe. Pocock is "going to the Bay of *Campeche* to cut Logwood," but a storm drives his ship off course. Gulliver explains that he heard the ship had "foundered, and none escaped, but one Cabin-Boy." He adds that Pocock was an honest man, "and a good Sailor, but a little too positive in his own Opinions, which was the Cause of his Destruction, as it hath been with several others." In a statement that illustrates the extent of his overwhelming pride, Gulliver claims that if Pocock "had followed my Advice, he might have been safe at home with his Family at this time, as well as myself."

**Purefoy, Robert**   "Skilful young Man" and ship's surgeon in Part 4, chapter 1, of *Gulliver's Travels*. He sails with Lemuel Gulliver on the *Adventure*, and becomes part of the crew that ultimately mutinies against Gulliver and leaves him marooned in the country of the Houyhnhnms. Ironically, the literal meaning of Purefoy's name is "pure faith." In his edition of the *Travels*, Turner suggests that the name is also a play on "Puritan."

**Sorrel Nag**   Character in Part 4 of *Gulliver's Travels*. See Houyhnhnms.

**Welch, James**   Member of the crew that mutinies against Lemuel Gulliver during his voyage as captain of the *Adventure* in Part 4, chapter 1, of *Gulliver's Travels*. On May 9, 1711, Welch warns Gulliver (who is incarcerated in his cabin) that he is about to be set ashore as soon as they can find some land. Gulliver argues with Welch, but cannot succeed even in finding out the name of the new captain. The *Adventure* finally arrives at an unknown shore and, having no idea "what Country it was," the crew sails away after leaving Gulliver to his own devices in the country of the Houyhnhnms.

**Yahoos** Characters in Part 4 of *Gulliver's Travels*. These foul, repulsive animals live as livestock among the Houyhnhnms, who use them to perform manual labor. According to the *Oxford English Dictionary*, Swift himself coined the word *Yahoo* and it has come to mean "a person lacking cultivation or sensibility, a philistine; a lout, a hooligan." Lemuel Gulliver claims that unlike *Houyhnhnm*, (which he says means "horse" in their language and "in its etymology" refers to the "perfection of Nature") *Yahoo* is impossible to translate. Many editors and critics have offered various theories on the origin of the word—Isaac Asimov, for example, claims that Europeans in Swift's day were familiar with a "primitive tribe of Indians" called Yahoos.

Gulliver unquestionably finds the Yahoos disgusting, but the amount of time he spends describing their appearance, demeanor, and habits suggests that he is also intrigued (if not fascinated) by these strange creatures. The Houyhnhnms house a number of Yahoos in huts "for present use" but send the rest to live in designated fields where they dig holes or "kennels" in which to sleep. They feed on roots, herbs, carrion, small vermin, and (since they can swim "like frogs" from birth) fish. The Yahoos are "nimble" climbers, mainly because of their long, hooked claws. They normally move about "with prodigious Agility" on all fours, but are capable of standing on their hind legs. They do not speak, and are covered (to varying degrees) with hair. The red-haired Yahoos, Gulliver notes, are "more libidinous and mischievous than the rest, whom yet they much exceed in Strength and Activity." All the males have "Beards like Goats," and their heads and chests are covered with thick, coarse hair. The females are smaller than the males and except for the long hair on their heads, their bodies are covered with a "sort of Down." Gulliver also notices that the "dugs" (breasts) of the females hang down between their "fore-feet" and commonly reach almost to the ground. The skin of both sexes is a "brown buff Colour" and emits a repugnant odor. As evidenced by the Yahoos' immediate departure when the Houyhnhnms appear during their assault on Gulliver in chapter 1, they are afraid of their equine masters and live in complete submission to them. Gulliver concludes in chapter 8 that the Yahoos are "the most unteachable of all Animals, their Capacities never reaching higher than to draw or carry Burdens." They are characterized by a "perverse, restive Disposition" and are altogether "cunning, malicious, treacherous and revengeful."

Gulliver's first encounter with the Yahoos in chapter 1 abruptly familiarizes him with the sort of beastly behavior that characterizes their species. Even before he interacts with them, he decides that he has never in all his journeys seen so "disagreeable an Animal, nor one against which [he] naturally conceived so strong an Antipathy." When Gulliver strikes one of the Yahoos with the broad side of his hanger (in order to encourage the animal to get out of his way), a whole group of them backs him up against a tree while others climb up and defecate onto his head. In instances like this and, for example, those involving the Yahoos' ravenous consumption of rotten asses' flesh, Swift consistently emphasizes the Yahoos' grossness. These episodes intensify the horror with which Gulliver responds when the Houyhnhnms finally decide that he is simply a Yahoo who for reasons unknown has become physically unfit to live and work as the Yahoos do.

Although the Houyhnhnms do not announce their view until late, throughout Part 4 of the *Travels* all the characters except Gulliver assume that he is a Yahoo despite some obvious anomalies in his appearance and abilities. His hosts use the word *Yahoo* to describe him when they first see him, and in chapter 8 Gulliver notes that the Yahoos themselves "had some Imagination that I was of their own Species." Although they view him as one of their kind, the Yahoos consistently treat Gulliver with contempt (with the notable exception of the amorous young female who accosts him in while he is bathing). In addition to voiding their excrement on him, they "imitate [his] Actions after the manner of Monkeys, but ever with great signs of Hatred." Even the three-year-old Yahoo that Gulliver catches and tries to examine ends up urinating all over his clothes.

In the Yahoos, Swift provides a balanced and equally exaggerated contrast to the cold and emotionless rationality of the Houyhnhnms. While the pseudo-horses live according to the dictates of reason alone, the Yahoos are guided exclusively by their brute instincts. While Gulliver is attracted to the Houyhnhnms because of their dominance, they (like the Yahoos) embody an extreme—an unrealistic model for him to follow. Along with his revulsion at being identified with the Yahoos, Gulliver's ridiculous attempt to distinguish himself by imitating the Houyhnhnms illustrates his refusal to recognize his humanity: the duality of his nature as a being whose character is not limited to instinct *or* reason, exclusively. Unlike the Houyhnhnms, Gulliver's decisions are influenced by emotion and instinct. But in contrast the Yahoos, he (like all humans) is *rationis capax,* capable of reason. As Swift explained in a 1725 letter to Alexander POPE, this for him is the defining characteristic of "that animal called man." It is also what separates Gulliver from the Yahoos, who lack reason and the potential to exercise it. The Houyhnhnms and Yahoos define Gulliver as one of the latter because they know of no other category in which to place him since he is clearly not a horse. Gulliver's adoption of their dichotomous perspective, however, leads to frustration and madness as he discovers that despite his trotting and whinnying it is impossible for him to be *entirely* rational. Instead, he exists somewhere in between. He is neither pure instinct like the Yahoo nor pure reason like the Houyhnhnm, but *human.* The Yahoos' continued appearances throughout the narrative in Part 4 show that they are a constant, larger-than-life reminder of one aspect of Gulliver's identity that, to his chagrin, he cannot escape—any more than he can grow hooves, a mane, and a tail and live in bliss as a Houyhnhnm among the Yahoos he despises.

## PLACES, SHIPS, AND TERMS

*Part 1*

**Antelope**   Ship on which Lemuel Gulliver sails in Part 1 of *Gulliver's Travels.* Captain William Prichard makes "an advantageous Offer" to convince Gulliver to join the crew of the *Antelope* as ship's surgeon on a voyage to the South Sea. It departs from Bristol on May 4, 1699, only to capsize during a storm on November 5 of the same year. Following this mishap Gulliver finds himself in Lilliput.

**Belfaborac**   Royal court of the Emperor of Lilliput in Part 1 (chapters 3 and 4) of *Gulliver's Travels.* The palace there is "in the Centre of the city [Mildendo], where the two great Streets meet" and it is "enclosed by a Wall of two foot high, and twenty foot distant from the Buildings." According to Paul Odell Clark in *A Gulliver Dictionary,* the word *Belfaborac* means "ever favor at" or "evil favor at."

**Blefuscu**   Island north of Lilliput in Part 1 of *Gulliver's Travels.* In chapter 4, Lemuel Gulliver explains that the inhabitants of Lilliput regard this rival nation as "the other great Empire of the Universe." It is similar in size to Lilliput, and separated from that nation by a channel that is 800 yards wide. The inhabitants of Lilliput and Blefuscu have been engaged in an ongoing war for 36 years (see Slamecksan), and the Emperor of Lilliput convinces Gulliver to help ward off an impending attack by wading across the channel to steal ships from the Blefuscudian navy. Gulliver ultimately escapes to Blefuscu after the Emperor of Lilliput charges him with treason (among other crimes) and issues orders for his arrest, torture, and imprisonment.

The ceaseless enmity between Lilliput and Blefuscu has traditionally been read as a reflection of the ongoing hostilities between England and France, respectively. In *A Gulliver Dictionary,* Paul Odell Clark suggests that the *f* and *c* in *Blefuscu* hint that it is an anagram for France, "once the enclosing letters are dropped, and *us* turned to *an.*" See also Blefuscu, Emperor of.

**Blundercral**   Holy book of Blefuscu ("their *Alcoran*" or Koran). In chapter 4 of *Gulliver's Travels,* Part 1, Reldresal mentions it in his discussion of the Big-Endian controversy. See also Lustrog.

**Brundrecal**   Holy book containing the doctrines of Lustrog, ancient prophet of Lilliput in Part 1 of *Gulliver's Travels.* In chapter 4, Reldresal explains to Lemuel Gulliver the divide between the Big-Endians and Little-Endians sprang from a disagreement over a statement in "the fifty-fourth Chapter" regarding the end at which eggs should be broken.

**Lilliput**   Island empire near Tasmania in Part 1 of *Gulliver's Travels*. After being shipwrecked, Lemuel Gulliver awakens to find himself captured by its tiny inhabitants, who are less than six inches tall. The term *Lilliput* has been interpreted in various ways. In *A Gulliver Dictionary*, Paul Odell Clark explains that *lilli* should be read as "little," and that *put* in Swift's time "was a dialectical form of the word *pretty*." He concludes that *Lilliput* is most likely a combination of the adjectives "little" and "pretty" or, perhaps, should be understood as "pretty little." The Emperor of Lilliput seeks to enlist Gulliver's help in the ongoing conflict with the neighboring island of Blefuscu. The Lilliputians' small size underscores their pettiness, but provides an ironic contrast to their incredible brutality (as evidenced in the various gruesome punishments they consider using against Gulliver after he leaves Lilliput for Blefuscu).

**Mildendo**   Metropolis of Lilliput in Part 1 of *Gulliver's Travels*. In chapter 4, Lemuel Gulliver visits the city for the first time. The city is "an exact square" in shape, with the Emperor of Lilliput's palace in the center. The entire city is surrounded by a wall that is two-and-a-half feet high and wide enough for "a Coach and horses [to] be driven very safely round it." Each side of the wall is 500 feet in length, and fortified with "very strong Towers" every 10 feet. There is a large gate on the western side of the city. Mildendo is divided into quarters by two intersecting "principal Streets," each with lanes that are five feet wide. Other lanes and alleys in the city are between 12 and 18 inches in width. Gulliver describes the houses as "from three to five Storeys" in height and the shops and markets as "well provided." Citing Paul Odell Clark's interpretation of the name *Mildendo* in *A Gulliver Dictionary*, DeMaria notes in his edition of the *Travels* that it is "a near anagram for London in a word order that brings to mind Mile End," which in Swift's day was "a poorer place east of the City proper."

**Nottinghamshire**   Lemuel Gulliver's birthplace; East Midlands county in England. In chapter 1,

Part 1, of *Gulliver's Travels*, Gulliver notes that his father "had a small Estate" there. In his remarks "To the Reader," Richard Sympson writes that Gulliver has moved his home from Redriff to "Newark, in Nottinghamshire."

**Redriff**   In *Gulliver's Travels*, the suburb of London where Lemuel Gulliver's house is located. Now called Rotherhithe, this area "lies within a loop of the river on the north-east corner of . . . Southwark" and "faces Wapping across the river" [*The London Encyclopedia*, edited by Ben Weinreb and Christopher Hibbert (Bethesda, Md.: Adler and Adler, 1983)]. In "The Publisher to the Reader," Richard Sympson indicates that Gulliver has "quitted Redriff" for Nottinghamshire due to the "Concourse of curious People coming to him at his House."

***Swallow***   Ship in *Gulliver's Travels*, Part 1: "A Voyage to Lilliput." In chapter 1, Lemuel Gulliver joins the *Swallow*'s crew as surgeon. In his first posting after completing a surgery apprenticeship, Gulliver travels to the Levant (the shores of the eastern Mediterranean) for four years, before returning to England. Swift's use of benign names for both ships in Part 1 (the *Antelope* wrecks off Lilliput) sets an ironic tone reflecting Gulliver's naïve goodwill.

*Part 2*

***Adventure* (1)**   In Part 2 of *Gulliver's Travels*, the 300-ton merchant ship on which Lemuel Gulliver sails on "the *20th* day of *June* 1702." (It is first mentioned at the end of I.8). Bound for Surat, the *Adventure*'s captain is John Nicholas, "a *Cornish* man" of Liverpool. The crew abandons Gulliver in Brobdingnag.

**Brobdingnag (or Brobdingrag)**   Land of giants in Part 2 of *Gulliver's Travels*. Lemuel Gulliver is abandoned there in June 1703 and taken in by a Farmer (1) and his family. In *A Gulliver Dictionary*, Paul Odell Clark translates *Brobdingnag* as England.

**Flanflasnic**   City in Part 2 of *Gulliver's Travels*. It is located in Brobdingnag "within eighteen English

Miles of the Sea-Side." In *A Gulliver Dictionary*, Paul Odell Clark translates the name as "fantastic, fancy," or "far fancy." Lemuel Gulliver visits Flanflasnic (in chapter 8) as he accompanies the King and Queen of Brobdingnag on a trip "to the South Coast of the Kingdom" (see Brobdingnag, Queen of). It is the last city he visits in that kingdom.

**Lorbrulgrud**  Brobdingnagian metropolis in Part 2 of *Gulliver's Travels*. It is located in the center of the kingdom of Brobdingnag. Lemuel Gulliver explains that the name of the city means "Pride of the Universe" in the Brobdingnagian language. In *A Gulliver Dictionary*, Paul Odell Clark translates *Lorbrulgrud* as "London." Gulliver first arrives there (he notes in chapter 2) on October 26, 1703, during his series of degrading public appearances with the Farmer.

Gulliver describes the city in detail in chapter 4. He explains that it is equally divided by a river, "contains above eighty thousand Houses," and has a population of about 600,000. The city covers almost 3,000 square *English* miles," and the royal palace is located within its bounds. Lorbrulgrud also has its own militia, which conducts drills (as Gulliver explains in chapter 8) on "a great Field near the City, of twenty Miles square."

## Part 3

***Amboyna***  Vessel on which Lemuel Gulliver sails from Japan to Amsterdam in Part 3, chapter 11, of *Gulliver's Travels*. It is a "stout Ship of 450 Tuns" with Theodorus Vangrult as captain. After arriving at the port of Nagasaki on June 9, 1709, Gulliver sails on the *Amboyna* with a group of coarse Dutch sailors. During the voyage, he perpetuates his charade as a Dutch merchant (see Dutchman), inventing a name for himself and telling the sailors that he belongs to an obscure family from "the Province of *Gelderland*."

The name of this ship adds to Swift's intensely negative portrayal of the Dutch that begins in chapter 1 of Part 3. Now Ambon, Indonesia, "Amboyna" (or Amboina) was a small island in the East Indies and was notorious as the site of a gruesome massacre in 1623. Intent on discouraging the English from competing for the abundant spices and other

commodities available on the island, the Dutch tortured and killed a number of English merchants (and Japanese "conspirators") whom they believed were preparing to take over the island. In 1670 John DRYDEN had written a tragedy called *Amboyna* that focused on this incident.

**Balnibarbi**  Island in Part 3 of *Gulliver's Travels*, with Lagado as its capital city and Maldonada its primary port. Located northeast of Luggnagg and east of Japan, Balnibarbi is included within the dominions of the King of Laputa. Gulliver arrives there in chapter 4, where he meets Lord Munodi and eventually visits the Academy of Projectors. In *A Gulliver Dictionary*, Paul Odell Clark translates *Balnibarbi* as "Barbary."

**Clumegnig**  "Sea-port Town" located "at the South-East Point of Luggnagg" in Part 3 of *Gulliver's Travels*. Lemuel Gulliver arrives there on April 21, 1709 (in Chapter 9), and is held captive until a warrant is issued for him to be transported to the royal city of Traldragdubb and brought before the King of Luggnagg.

**Glubbdubdrib**  "Island of *Sorcerers or Magicians*" in Part 3 of *Gulliver's Travels*. Lemuel Gulliver reports that it is "about one third as large as the Isle of *Wight*" and located "about five Leagues off to the South-West" of Maldonada. In *A Gulliver Dictionary*, Paul Odell Clark translates the name as "Dublin." Accompanied by a "Gentleman of Distinction" and one other companion, Gulliver visits there in chapter 7 to pass the time while he waits for a ship to be prepared to transport him to Luggnagg.

***Hopewell***  The "stout Ship of Three Hundred Tons" on which Lemuel Gulliver sails with Captain William Robinson at the beginning of Part 3 of *Gulliver's Travels*.

**Lagado**  Metropolis of Balnibarbi in Part 3 of *Gulliver's Travels*. In *A Gulliver Dictionary*, Paul Odell Clark translates the name as "London" (although Lemuel Gulliver indicates that Lagado is only half as large). Gulliver arrives there in chapter 4, and after touring the city with Lord Munodi, describes it as barren, unimpressive, and filled with houses that are "strangely built" and in general disrepair. Lagado is also the site of the Academy of Projectors, which Gulliver visits beginning in chapter 5.

**Laputa**   Flying island in Part 3 of *Gulliver's Travels*. After being overtaken by pirates and left adrift in the sea, Gulliver is rescued and brought onto the island by some of its inhabitants. He explains that he was never able to learn the origins of the word *Laputa* in their language, but believes it is derived from a combination of *Lap* (which means "dancing of the Sun Beams in the Sea") and *outed* ("a Wing"). The word *Laputa* has commonly been translated as "the whore" (from the Spanish *la puta*), but Paul Odell Clark in *A Gulliver Dictionary* reads it as an anagram of "All-up-at." In chapter 3, Gulliver provides a detailed description of the island, noting (among other things) that it is "exactly circular," four-and-a-half miles in diameter, and "three Hundred Yards thick." From beneath, Laputa appears to be "one even regular Plate of Adamant." The King of Laputa travels around on the island exacting regular tributes from his subjects who live below on the island of Balnibarbi. The island's movements are controlled by rotating a giant magnet, which is suspended in the middle of the island on "a very Strong Axle of Adamant." It cannot move beyond the boundaries of Balnibarbi, "nor can it rise above the Height of Four miles" above the surface. Those who travel with the King on the floating island are constantly lost in speculation and worry over the possibility of dangerous changes in the "Celestial Bodies."

**Lindalino**   "Second city" on the island of Balnibarbi in Part 3 of *Gulliver's Travels*. In chapter 3, Lemuel Gulliver explains that three years before his arrival in Laputa, the "Lindalinians" had rebelled against the King of Laputa and attempted to destroy the flying island by bringing it down on top of "four large Towers." Unable to quell the rebellion, the king was forced to meet their demands. Traditionally, the account of the rebellion has been read as a reference to Ireland's resistance in 1724 to King GEORGE I's attempt to introduce William

WOOD's halfpence in Dublin (see *DRAPIER'S LETTERS, The*). The five paragraphs describing the rebellion were not published in any edition of the *Travels* until 1899.

**Luggnagg**   Island in Part 3 of *Gulliver's Travels*, located "about five Leagues off to the South-west" of Balnibarbi. Having learned that there are "frequent Opportunities" to travel between Luggnagg and Japan, he decides in chapter 7 to travel to Luggnagg and begin his journey back to England. In *A Gulliver Dictionary*, Paul Odell Clark argues that when the final g's in *Luggnagg* are dropped and the remaining letters read backward, the word sounds like "Anggul" and echoes "England"—highlighting the connections between England and Luggnagg that Gulliver fails to recognize.

**Maldonada**   Primary port of Balnibarbi in Part 3 of *Gulliver's Travels*. Lemuel Gulliver travels there in chapter 7 (after leaving Lagado) in hopes of sailing to Luggnagg and then to Japan. Since no ship is available when he arrives, he visits Glubbdubdrib to pass the time during the delay. In *A Gulliver Dictionary*, Paul Odell Clark calls *Maldonada* a "transparent" reference to London.

**Traldragdubh (or Trildrogdrib)**   Royal city of Luggnagg in Part 3 of *Gulliver's Travels*. Lemuel Gulliver travels there (with his Interpreter) to appear before the King of Luggnagg in chapter 9. In *A Gulliver Dictionary*, Paul Odell Clark translates *Traldragdubh* as a blending of "Lorbrulgrud" (London) and "Glubbdubdrib" (Dublin).

**Yedo (or Edo)**   Capital city of Japan. Following his encounter with the Struldbruggs and his departure from Luggnagg, Lemuel Gulliver visits Yedo and the court of the Emperor of Japan in Part 3, chapter 11, of *Gulliver's Travels*. *Yedo* was the name for the city until 1868, when it became known as Tokyo. In his edition of the *Travels*, Isaac Asimov notes that in Swift's day the Japanese emperor did not actually reside in Tokyo. The seat of that ceremonial leader was farther inland in the city of Kyoto while the "shogun, or prime minister" (who actually ruled the country) resided in Yedo.

## Part 4

**Adventure** (2)    In Part 4 of *Gulliver's Travels*, Lemuel Gulliver captains a ship called the *Adventure* ("a stout Merchantman of 350 tons") until the crew mutinies and leaves him marooned in the country of the Houyhnhnms. See also Pocock, Captain, and Purefoy, Robert.

### FURTHER READING

Asimov, Isaac. *The Annotated Gulliver's Travels*. New York: Clarkson N. Potter, 1980.

Bloom, Harold, ed. *Jonathan Swift's Gulliver's Travels*. Modern Critical Interpretations. New York: Chelsea House, 1986.

Clark, Paul Odell. *A Gulliver Dictionary*. Chapel Hill: University of North Carolina Press, 1953.

Darby, Robert. "Captivity and Captivation: Gulliver in Broddingnag," *Eighteenth-Century Life* 27, no. 3 (2003): 124–139.

Donoghue, Denis. "The Brainwashing of Lemuel Gulliver," *Southern Review* 32 (1996): 128–146.

Ehrenpreis, Irvin. "How to Write *Gulliver's Travels*," *Swift Studies* 18 (2003): 5–19.

Fox, Christopher, ed. *Gulliver's Travels (A Case Study in Contemporary Criticism)*. Boston and New York: Bedford/St. Martin's, 1995.

Gravil, Richard, ed. *Swift: Gulliver's Travels: A Casebook*. London: Macmillan, 1974.

Hunter, J. Paul. "*Gulliver's Travels* and the Novel." In *The Genres of Gulliver's Travels,* edited by Frederick N. Smith, 56–74. Newark: University of Delaware Press, 1990.

Jaffe, Lee. "*Gulliver's Travels* by Jonathan Swift." Jaffe Bros. Available online. URL: http://www.jaffebros.com/lee/gulliver/. Accessed on November 10, 2005.

Knowles, Ronald. *"Gulliver's Travels": The Politics of Satire*. New York: Twayne, 1996.

Lock, F. P. *The Politics of Gulliver's Travels*. Oxford, England: Clarendon Press, 1983.

Mezciems, Jenny. "Swift's Praise of Gulliver: Some Renaissance Background to the *Travels*." In *The Character of Swift's Satire: A Revised Focus,* edited by Claude Rawson, 245–281. Newark: University of Delaware Press, 1983.

Probyn, Clive T. *Gulliver's Travels*. Penguin Critical Studies. New York: Penguin, 1987.

Seidel, Michael. "*Gulliver's Travels* and the Contracts of Fiction." In *The Cambridge Companion to the Eighteenth-Century Novel,* edited by John Richetti, 72–89. Cambridge: Cambridge University Press, 1996.

Stillman, Peter G. " 'With a Moral View Design'd': *Gulliver's Travels* as a Utopian Text." *Qwerty* 11 (2001): 97–107.

Tippett, Brian. *Gulliver's Travels: An Introduction to the Variety of Criticism*. Basingstoke and London: Macmillan, 1989.

Wiener, Gary, ed. *Readings on Gulliver's Travels*. Literary Companion Series. San Diego, Calif.: Greenhaven Press, 2000.

# "Hardship Put upon Ladies, The"

Poem by Swift; first published 1735, written 1733. It is a mocking commentary on the lives ladies lead, suggesting that if women were in charge of making laws, men would have to do the difficult work of playing cards day and night.

# "Helter Skelter"

Poem possibly by Swift; first published in 1731, probably written in 1726/27. In his edition of Swift's poems, Pat Rogers calls it a very dubious attribution. Subtitled "The Hue and Cry after the Attornies, Going to Ride the Circuit," the poem lampoons lawyers as greedy, dishonest, and immoral. Nora Crow Jaffe (*The Poet Swift* 31–33) and Louise K. Barnett (*Swift's Poetic Worlds* 188–189) discuss the rhythm of the poem.

# Hibernian Patriot

See FAULKNER, GEORGE.

# "Hints on Good Manners"

This short essay was first printed by Deane SWIFT in 1765 in *Works* and later reprinted in George FAULKNER's edition, though the date of composition remains unknown. Its companion piece, "Treatise on Good Manners and Good Breeding," was published in 1754. Swift focuses on modesty and humility as the keys to good manners, and suggests that flattery is the worst technique for showing respect for another person. He particularly scorns the court scene as the most damaging environment for teaching or maintaining good manners. Good conversation remains a threatened species at court or, for that matter, any place where many people gather since few people listen to what another person has to say and even fewer can listen without frequent interruption.

Almost everything in this essay has been anticipated in some earlier periodical, particularly the *Tatler* or *Spectator*. Swift's views, delivered in a somewhat pedantic and patronizing manner, nonetheless provide a lightly balanced combination of learning and good humor. He criticizes those who perpetually try to be witty since they generally fail, leaving "a sort of insult on the company, and a constraint upon the speaker." The idea behind this point is that we all have the power to engage in good conversation, even though few actually do so. Because we do not, we miss a signal pleasure of life and even worse, reduce further the credibility of human nature. Excessive talking, focusing one's conversation on oneself while ignoring any balance in the discourse, attempting to show one's learning (pedantry) as if it were a flag that should be waved about, and false smiles and laughter—each of these faults adds to the ruined state of conversation.

As in much of his work, Swift here tries to redirect man's awareness to what is essential in life: "Good manners is [sic] the art of making every reasonable person in the company easy," and the enemy of achieving this result exists in an individual substituting form and artifice for good sense, decency, kindness, and generosity. Artificial ceremonies hide the true purpose of the meeting or event. Conversation takes on a kind of ritualized dance of artifice, and the most severe criticism one can make of another is that he is unskillful in conversation.

## "Hints towards an Essay on Conversation"

This essay was first printed by George FAULKNER in 1763 in the *Works*, but was probably composed

while Swift was in London working for the Robert HARLEY and Henry BOLINGBROKE ministry (1710–14). Scholars find his contribution to the *Tatler*, number 230 (dated September 28, 1710), on the style of language and speech, suggestive of what he was thinking on the subject: "conversation [should] entertain and improve" both the speaker and listener. This essay completes the group of essays containing also "A Treatise on Good Manners and Good Breeding" and "HINTS ON GOOD MANNERS," but clearly he anticipates the later "Proposal for Correcting, Improving and Ascertaining the English Tongue" (1712) with comments on how men of wit and understanding do not necessarily make good conversationalists. The problem often arises from a matter of propriety as when individuals rely too strongly on "Raillery" (appearing smart by making someone else look ridiculous). It can also be blamed on those who wait impatiently to interrupt others, and yet express "uneasiness at being interrupted" themselves. These errors do not add to our good sense.

Using parody, irony, and comedy, Swift offers practical suggestions for avoiding further errors in human relations, especially in the nature of our moral lives. When we converse, we exhibit our moral structure and attitudes, and Swift certainly makes this point in his terminology: "this degeneracy of conversation, with the pernicious consequences thereof upon our humours and dispositions, hath been owing . . . to the custom arisen . . . of excluding women from any share in our society." Here his comments on errors and abuse of language serve as metaphors for the ills of society and senselessness of a class system hidden behind the affectation of polite language—a system that excludes an entire group of reasonable people from anything except social frivolities.

## "His Grace's Answer to Jonathan"

Poem by Swift; first published as a broadside in 1724, written the same year. This was Swift's response to a 1724 verse epistle by Jonathan SMED-

LEY in which he begged Charles FitzRoy, second duke of GRAFTON, "to find him a small sinecure" to accompany "his new deanery so that he might retire with his family to a more favourable climate than that of Clogher" (Rogers, *Poems* 737). The verse letter also contained numerous insults against Swift, whom Smedley refers to as "St. *Patrick's* sawcy Dean." Written in the voice of Grafton, Swift's response makes fun of Smedley's request and ultimately predicts that his wife will turn him into a cuckold.

# "History of Poetry, The"

The Dublin printer Edward WATERS published this two-page essay in 1726 during Swift's visit to London for several months when he stayed with Alexander POPE and arranged for the publication of *GULLIVER'S TRAVELS*. With his consistent interest in the English language, especially considerations of rhetoric, dialect, vocabulary, and etymology, he maintained a lifelong passion for puns and language games. This minor piece is a bit of fun with literary history from Chaucer to Pope, exhibiting Swift's own unconstrained sense of humor and a plain style masking a remarkable inventiveness for twisting names and words into forms of verbal play.

As he had done in *Gulliver's Travels* and *The JOURNAL TO STELLA*, he turns names into a "little language" and, as Ian Higgins points out in *Swift's Politics*, "writing on the English language and English literary history in Swift's lifetime was a profoundly politicized activity." He had already taken a stand in the *Tatler*, number 230, against affectation in speech and for a plain and natural language. In Swift's TORY version of the past, much of what has occurred in corrupting the English language is due to the loss of the Stuart monarchy: The reign of Charles I produced new poets, many of whom Swift found to his liking, and CHARLES II provided "very numerous" opportunities for more poets and dramatists. But the Commonwealth and Cromwell served to advance only burlesque and the Glorious Revolution with the exile of JAMES II, and the succession of WILLIAM and Mary caused a further decline in poetry. Swift refuses the embrace of the culture of politeness that Joseph ADDISON and Richard STEELE promoted and shuns ornaments in favor of a more controlled style using concrete diction and uncomplicated syntax.

# "History of the Four Last Years of the Queen, The"

*The JOURNAL TO STELLA* suggests Swift was planning a historical analysis and defense of the policy of Queen ANNE's last ministry from about August 1712, when he was at Windsor. Soon after, he began a nine-month project, setting this "long work" aside in May 1713. Swift had been a close observer of these final months of the ministry and had watched as the relationship between Robert HARLEY and Henry BOLINGBROKE deteriorated to the point that their efforts to settle the War of the Spanish Succession reached a serious impasse. Finally, in April 1713 Bolingbroke arranged the Treaty of Utrecht, and Swift could adopt the persona of a trusted insider and impartial historian as he began his last work for the ministry. With Queen Anne's death in August 1714, Swift left for Ireland, and the *History* remained in manuscript for nearly 50 years.

## SYNOPSIS

### Preface

Swift explains that he had planned to have the "History" published sooner, but his responsibilities as dean of St. Patrick's Cathedral forced him to put those plans on hold. However, now that Queen Anne's reign has come to an end, he feels compelled to publish it to combat the rampant misrepresentations of her and her ministry. He asserts that it is an unbiased description (aside from reflecting his own opinions) and that he has not glossed over the ministry's missteps and shortcomings.

### Book 1

Swift describes this section as a public account of the most significant affairs in England during the last session of Parliament (which opened in December 1711) along with the peace negotiations "abroad" to end the War of the Spanish Succession. It highlights the schemes of what he calls the "discontented Faction" of WHIGS against the queen and her ministry. Swift focuses on the crisis initiated by the earl of NOTTINGHAM's speech in the House of Lords in which he (and the Whig majority) demanded that no plan for peace should leave Spain "and the *West-Indies*" to "any Branch of the House of *Bourbon*." Irvin Ehrenpreis remarks that "Swift took that episode as the grand peripety of the struggle for peace" (*Swift* II.600). In addition to reviewing all the reasons behind Queen Anne's decision to change her ministry, this section outlines what Swift saw as the leading qualities of the Whigs' "Principal leaders" (John SOMERS, John MARLBOROUGH, and others) and portrays Marlborough's dismissal as a landmark illustration of "the Instability of all Greatness, which is not founded upon Virtue."

### Book 2

This section outlines the queen's efforts toward peace and her sensitivity to the House of Lords' opposition to any treaty that left Spain to the Bourbons. It relates the "several Steps by which the Intercourse between the Courts of *France* and *Britain* was begun and carried on," and highlights Queen Anne's firmness in preserving the interests of her kingdom. Swift admiringly explains how she "provided for the Security and Advantage" of her subjects without compromising the goodwill of her allies. Ultimately, she skillfully obtained from France the "Preliminary Articles" that paved the way for the Treaty of Utrecht in April 1713 and the end of the war.

### Book 3

In this section, Swift outlines the affairs of Parliament from Marlborough's dismissal in December 1711 through the summer of 1712. During this time, the House of Commons reviewed "Abuses relating to the Accounts of the Army" and the terms of all treaties between Britain and the allies. The Commons also reviewed a report on the former from the Commissioners for Stating the Public Accounts, and Swift recounts all the censures that followed. Here also is the lengthy examination

Swift promised in the preface of "the State of the Nation with respect to its Debts." He covers the abuses that initiated the debts and caused them to increase, along with the "Courses" that had been taken under Queen Anne's ministry to pay the debts, prevent new ones, and restore the kingdom's credit. Swift surmises that his overview shows "in how ill a Condition the kingdom stood with relation to its Debts, by the Corruption as well as Negligence of former [Whig] Management."

This section also includes a lengthy representation (presented to the queen by the Commons) that sums up "all Debates and Resolutions of the House of Commons in that great Affair of the War." Swift notes that the supposed author was Sir Thomas HANMER. In *The* JOURNAL TO STELLA, Swift explains that the representation is "where all the wrong steps of the Allies and late Ministry about the war [are] mentioned" (letter 41). Specifically, it deals with discussions and resolutions on the "Deficiency of the Allies in furnishing their quotas," on "certain Articles in the Barrier-Treaty," and on "the State of the War." Swift comments that the representation was written "with much Energy and Spirit" and concludes that nothing could better "justify the Proceedings of the Queen and Her Ministers" over the past two years. Swift credits Lord Treasurer Bolingbroke with having led the House of Commons in conducting all of its inquiries: "by the force of an extraordinary Genius, and Application to Publick Affairs," he eloquently "laid open the Scene of Miscarriages and Corruptions through the whole Course of the War."

### Book 4

This section outlines in detail all the obstacles and advances leading up to the Treaty of Utrecht. Hindrances included "the Opposition raised by a strong Party in France, and by a virulent Faction in Britain," a conspiracy between Dutch leaders and the English Whigs "to prolong the War," and "the restless Endeavours of the Imperial Court to render the Treaty ineffectual." Despite these threats, Queen Anne and her wise, courageous ministers succeeded in having "a Peace signed in One Day by every Power concerned, except that of the Emperour" CHARLES VI.

## COMMENTARY

Serving as the trusted confidante—"a witness of almost every step they made in the course of their administration"—and a nonpartisan historian, Swift "endeavors to set future ages right in their judgment of that happy reign." He positions his history as a contribution to understanding European realpolitik where the great game of power politics requires the new party coming into office to attack their predecessors "with as much infamy as the most inveterate malice and envy could suggest, or the most stupid ignorance and credulity in their underlings could swallow." Knowing this, Swift, as a good historian, will rely on original documents, letters, instructions to ambassadors, and other notes—all written by Oxford or Bolingbroke—in describing the events, and let no critic say that prejudice, ambition, malice, or bribery served as the true impulses for this history. Apparently, Swift had accepted no payment from the ministers for his support and his pen, but clearly he hoped for a more lasting reward in the form of an English bishopric or deanery.

This valedictory essay has a curious evolution that began with Swift's tedious efforts to collect the letters and other documents necessary for his research. He found that he could not access all the indispensable documents that he knew existed. Neither minister, though much appreciative of Swift's efforts on behalf of TORY policy, would reveal his true intent in the negotiations with Prince James STUART (the Old Pretender to England's throne) who lived in exile in France. Enthusiasm for his research and a projected history was minimal, but Swift continued to forge ahead, apparently trying to refrain from thinking too often about his own ambitions, which were being ignored. Elizabeth Villiers (Lady ORKNEY and wife of George Hamilton, a Scottish peer) came to his rescue with information and advice on the actions of the major figures in this drama, drawn from her excellent contacts as the sometime mistress of WILLIAM III. With all the delay and procrastination, however, the history became irrelevant as a timely document, one that was meant to recover the reputations of the ministry in its devious efforts toward peace. In fact, the title of the piece is misleading, since the text has less to do with the last

four years than with the last 16 months and the Treaty of Utrecht. With the peace signed, friends and others worried about the dangers of publishing such an inflammatory document and urged him to set it aside permanently.

As propaganda, the "History" has few equals, but Swift confidently believed the document would be viewed as the true history of peacemaking. In a series of letters to John ARBUTHNOT in July 1714, Swift described his frame of mind as he was writing this work and watching the ministry collapse: "Shall I not be miserable to stand by and see things going every day nearer to ruin; can I do the least good to myself, my friends, or the Publick." Again he emphasizes, "I would never let people run mad without telling and warning them sufficiently." History should be practical inasmuch as the historian has a responsibility to inform his readers of facts they may not know, but manipulating those facts to promote the historian's personal agenda voids all claims of impartiality.

Book 1 of the work stands as a good example of Swift's intentions. There, he makes explicit attacks on the enemies of the ministry, arguing quite fiercely for the existence of a day of infamy, December 7, 1711, when the principal Whig figures acted prominently and in confederacy set in motion the destruction of Harley and Bolingbroke during an opening session of Parliament. Referring to a "period of rage and despair," Swift blames Baron Somers, the duke of Marlborough, the earl of GODOLPHIN, the earl of SUNDERLAND, the earl of WHARTON, the earl of NOTTINGHAM, Earl Cowper, and even the duchess of Marlborough. The struggle ensuing from their conspiracy caused the effort toward peace to slow and become confused.

Swift caps his powerful first section of the history with a diatribe against Marlborough's most able military commander, Prince EUGENE of Savoy, who had traveled to England to convince the government to continue the war in Spain. He blames the prince and Marlborough for their hatred of Harley and their promotion of mob violence and other traitorous actions. His harsh language gives his position away. Swift even addresses the critics he knows will accuse him of extreme bias in favor of the Tories: "those who think I am able to produce no better, will judge this passage to be fitter for a libel, than a history."

This work did not escape the label of historical propaganda during Swift's lifetime and was generally viewed as more of a pamphlet than a history, more subjective recreation than objective reality. When Swift finished revising the work in 1737 and sensed that the time was right for its appearance, his friends dissuaded him once again. The work lacks moderation, and partisan slander often dominates—even to the point of accusing Marlborough of wanting to usurp the crown. If the reader disagrees with Tory politics, he is not persuaded to change but instead sees his position destroyed. Publication would come in 1758, long after Swift's death, but it still remained a dangerous document to the memory of those who were his enemies.

# "History of the Second Solomon, The"

This curious autobiographical piece, which was first printed by Deane SWIFT in 1765 and reprinted in the same year by George FAULKNER, has close connections to the "CHARACTER OF DOCTOR SHERIDAN" and the "BLUNDERS, DEFICIENCIES, DISTRESSES, AND MISFORTUNES OF QUILCA." Swift and Reverend Thomas SHERIDAN maintained a long friendship during which they exchanged puns, riddles, and various domestic verses. In May 1728 Sheridan and Swift had introduced the weekly paper the INTELLIGENCER, which lasted a year, but Swift had become frustrated with his friend's lack of persistence and focus on Ireland's economic problems, as well as his interest in the Whigs and the English royal family, and he may have composed the 2,000-word essay then.

Swift positions the history as a reaction against Sheridan's criticism of his poetry, but actually he admires the man. He delivers some of his most severe comments on Sheridan and his relations (calling Sheridan's wife "detestably disagreeable" and "a most filthy slut"), but does so under the mask of "a person distinguished for poetical and writings" who invited this "second Solomon" into

his house and procured him a good preferment as chaplain to the lord lieutenant of Ireland, Lord John CARTERET. But Solomon (Sheridan) then proceeded to preach an insulting sermon against King GEORGE II, and lost his chaplaincy. Swift includes a list of foolish absurdities committed by "Solomon," from renting a ruined house for 999 years, spending more on this country estate than what he receives in rents, ridiculing his best friend's literary efforts, and inviting friends to dine and then not making an appearance.

Instead of the typical character study, which was one of Swift's favorite vehicles for analysis of an individual's moral nature, he here employs the burlesque of that form. He exaggerates and distorts Sheridan's behavior and attitude, creating a discrepancy between subject matter and style: A serious subject (his friendship for Sheridan) ends up being treated frivolously. Frustrated by Sheridan's actions at various times, Swift allows himself the liberty to indulge in a romp at his friend's expense. Impersonating the reserved and rational narrator of his "CHARACTER OF PRIMATE MARSH" or "CHARACTER OF MRS. HOWARD," he steadily parodies Sheridan, making fun of his eccentricities and inflating them into gross errors of judgment.

# "History of Vanbrug's House, The"

Poem by Swift; first published in 1710, written in 1706. Like "VANBRUG'S HOUSE," this poem makes fun of John VANBRUGH, the home he built at Whitehall, and what Swift presents as Vanbrugh's utter lack of architectural skill.

# "Holyhead Journal"

This 2,500-word essay was printed from the autograph manuscript by Herbert Davis from materials in possession of the late 19th-century Swift biographer John Forster. Herbert Davis believes this piece is a document of interest to those studying Swift's life but does not view it as a literary work and asserts that it was never intended for publication.

The journal was probably begun during the last week of September 1727 and describes a five-day period when Swift had decided to return to Ireland after visiting England for what turned out to be his last time. Desperate to return as quickly as possible and knowing Stella (Esther JOHNSON) was gravely ill, Swift and a servant made the journey from London (actually Twickenham and Alexander POPE's residence) to Holyhead on the north coast of Wales.

This port served as the chief point of embarkation and disembarkation for those traveling to Ireland across the Irish Sea. Besides the trouble of actually reaching Holyhead on the land side from Coventry and Chester by coach and horseback, arriving in Ireland often depended on the weather and wind in the Channel. His journey hindered by various mishaps, Swift began a journal (which Carole Fabricant refers to as a "prison diary") noting the places and people he saw in those days of confinement—a kind of Crusoe-like existence at the mercy of a ship's captain who was waiting for sufficient passengers to make the passage worth the trip (Fabricant, *Swift's Landscape* 43).

He describes his efforts to find suitable lodging, decent food, and clean clothes and to maintain his exercise routines. Swift calls Holyhead a kind of prison where, "frighted either by the solitude, or the meaness of lodging, eating or drinking," he worries incessantly about Stella, his dearest friend. One of the usual ironies of fame occurs when Swift recognizes that even his well-known name cannot get him a quicker passage across to Dublin, and he notes the contradiction of being treated as an emperor in London and then being used as a dog at Holyhead. His attitude suggests the symbolic value of frequent episodes in his life where he met uncertainty and disappointment. His often repeated desire to be buried at Holyhead, since any place was preferable to Ireland (even Wales), was not realized, and he remains "imprisoned" in his tomb at St. Patrick's Cathedral, Dublin.

In the end, however, the picture Swift draws in the "Holyhead Journal" has less to do with self-pity than with his penchant for self-mockery. He makes fun of himself caught among those who do not recognize him, and realizes that all men are equal in this bleak spot: Everyone must eat moldy bread and drink muddy ale. The leveling between master and servant or visitor and resident provides both a comic flavor and a firm lesson in tolerating one's fellow man and adjusting to confinements. Once again, Swift puts aside his guise of misanthropy and embraces friends and place: "Here I could live with two or three friends in a warm house, and good wine—much better than being a slave in Ireland." See also "HOLYHEAD, SEPTEMBER 25, 1727."

# "Holyhead. September 25, 1727"

Poem by Swift; first published in 1882. For the circumstances of composition, see "The POWER OF TIME." In this poem Swift laments the woeful conditions of his unplanned, frustrating delay at Holyhead on his way back to Dublin from London. Today there is a high-speed ferry named the *Jonathan Swift* that runs between Dublin and Holyhead. See also "HOLYHEAD JOURNAL," "IRELAND," "WHEN MRS. WELCH'S CHIMNEY SMOKES," and "ON LORD CARTERET'S ARMS."

# "Horace, Book I, Ode XIV"

Poem by Swift; first published in 1730, written in 1726. It is subtitled "Paraphrased and Inscribed to Ireland." Based on the Roman satirist Horace's ode to the debilitated ship of state, this poem compares Ireland to a ship that has lost its oars and is tossed about by the waves. In sharp contrast to Swift's more famous writings on Irish affairs in *The DRAPIER'S LETTERS* (published in 1724), this poem presents Ireland's situation as one that is already hopeless and will only worsen with time. Other than urging Ireland to somehow "avoid the rocks" it will encounter "on Britain's angry shore," the poem offers no solutions to the problems it addresses (mainly in terms of growing English oppression of the Irish). Swift's version of Horace's ode has the overall tone of an elegy in which the speaker laments the loss of great men and resigns himself to continuing disappointment and hopelessness.

With its mast in the midst of cracking and breaking off, the ship that is the "commonwealth" becomes even more vulnerable to coming under the "foreign yoke" of English tyranny. While Horace concludes by imploring the ship to return to more peaceful waters, Swift ultimately predicts that Ireland, as a "poor floating isle," will soon be driven "to the deep again." Once there, he forecasts, it will face many dangers in the absence of its greatest protectors—the "oars" and "mast," referring to Alan Brodrick, first viscount MIDDLETON (whose time as lord chancellor of Ireland had ended in 1725), Archbishop Robert LINDSAY (who had died in 1724), and Archbishop William KING (who, in 1726, was 76 years old and—in fulfillment of Swift's prophecy—would die three years later). See also "PART OF THE NINTH ODE OF THE FOURTH BOOK OF HORACE," "FIRST ODE OF THE SECOND BOOK OF HORACE . . . ADDRESSED TO RICHARD STEELE, ESQ.," "HORACE, LIB. 2, SAT. 6," and "HORACE, EPISTLE VII, BOOK I: IMITATED AND ADDRESSED TO THE EARL OF OXFORD."

# "Horace, Epistle VII, Book I: Imitated and Addressed to the Earl of Oxford"

Poem by Swift; first published in 1713, probably written the same year following Swift's "return to England after his installation as Dean of St. Patrick's" (Williams, *Poems* I.170). Addressed to Robert HARLEY, first earl of Oxford, the poem reminds the earl of his unfulfilled promises to give Swift a life of wealth and leisure as a dean and to reimburse him £1,000 for the expenses he incurred in moving to Dublin. David Nokes calls it "a begging letter, witty, courteous, polite, and good-natured, but for all that a serious attempt to goad or shame Oxford into fulfilling" the second promise at least (*Hypocrite Reversed* 192).

Pat Rogers and Irvin Ehrenpreis both note that the events described in the poem are mostly fictive.

It recounts Harley's first meeting with Swift (having seen the dean bargaining for "old books" near Whitehall), and indicates that the earl was so impressed with Swift's demeanor that he stopped his coach and sent his friend Erasmus LEWIS to find out who this "parson" was. In a manner similar to that of "The AUTHOR UPON HIMSELF," Swift freely praises himself throughout the poem as (among other things) a "clergyman of special note" (27), who is "addicted to no sort of vice" (32), and "owed no man a groat" (34). Harley ends up being so impressed with the dean that he invites him to dine, and although (to Harley's chagrin) Swift refuses that initial offer, he accepts a second invitation and soon becomes a regular in the earl's company.

Harley eventually promises to make Swift a dean ("to live in plenty, power and ease"), but at his post in Dublin Swift finds himself in financial hardship. He had borrowed funds to finance his move, and with the "wicked laity" constantly "contriving" to "cheat" him and other clergymen out of decent livings, all of his money is soon spent (107). Desperate for cash, he rides to "Harley's gate" to seek assistance, but the earl only jokes about the dean's gaunt appearance, filthy clothes, and (in Jaffe's terms) "supposed passion for money" (*The Poet Swift* 142). Angered, the dean asks Harley to put an end to this elaborate "jest" and simply return him to the condition in which he first discovered him. The poem (which Ehrenpreis reads as a light-hearted joke) ends up presenting Swift as an embittered victim of Harley's whims, and suggests that the dean would have been better off if he had never met the earl (*Swift* II.676). See also "PART OF THE NINTH ODE OF THE FOURTH BOOK OF HORACE," FIRST ODE OF THE SECOND BOOK OF HORACE . . . ADDRESSED TO RICHARD STEELE, ESQ.," "HORACE, LIB. 2, SAT. 6," and "HORACE, BOOK I, ODE XIV."

# "Horace, Lib. 2, Sat. 6"

Poem partly by Swift; first published in 1728, written in 1714 following "The AUTHOR UPON HIMSELF." Alexander POPE also had a hand in composing the poem. As the subtitle suggests, the poem is based on part of Horace's "Hoc erat in votis," which contains the tale of the country mouse who (after being persuaded by the city mouse to come to town) decides he prefers rural life after all. In Swift's poem, the speaker longs for a time when he can enjoy the country house and acreage he has obtained without having to make regular trips into town. He depicts himself "as the reluctant politician, the man great in spite of himself" who "would be completely content if English politicians did not demand his service" (Jaffe, *The Poet Swift* 12). See also "PART OF THE NINTH ODE OF THE FOURTH BOOK OF HORACE," "FIRST ODE OF THE SECOND BOOK OF HORACE . . . ADDRESSED TO RICHARD STEELE, ESQ.," "HORACE, EPISTLE VII, BOOK I: IMITATED AND ADDRESSED TO THE EARL OF OXFORD," and "HORACE, BOOK I, ODE XIV."

# "Hue and Cry after Dismal, A"

This short essay, published July 17, 1712, as a half-sheet broadside, has a second edition with additions and a new title, "DUNKIRK TO BE LET, OR, A TOWN READY FURNISH'D WITH A HUE AND CRY AFTER DISMAL," also printed in 1712. Swift wrote this penny paper quickly, along with a number of others, to influence particular events—in this case the opportunity for peace between France and England in the War of the Spanish Succession. Though this occasional paper has little interest today as far as historical issues are concerned, Swift's desire to produce it rapidly, before the imposition of the infamous Stamp Act (an earlier version of the one that angered the American colonists nearly 50 years later) seems noteworthy. Henry BOLINGBROKE and the TORY ministry believed in the necessity of stifling attacks on their government, which were a frequent subject for the many small newspapers, penny posts, and pamphlets of the period. Swift did not agree with such repressive measures, especially with efforts to force authors to use their true names on all publications. He did not support censorship and saw an opportunity, before its imposition, to heighten the effectiveness of the government's foreign affairs policies in negotiating

a peace on the Continent. If the war could be brought to a close, then the cautionary British occupation of Dunkirk and elimination of its port facilities—with the implicit acceptance of LOUIS XIV—made excellent sense. Those politicians like Daniel Finch, the earl of NOTTINGHAM, who opposed such projects, should be shown for what they are: obstacles and fools.

Swift's rhetorical technique in this paper displays one of his favorite approaches, the use of nicknames. Often when attacking his opponents, Swift would resort to a name that would pin his victim down without mercy, as he did with the earl of Nottingham and "his dark and dismal countenance." The Tories knew their man as Dismal, especially when he shifted allegiance to the WHIG party, and here Swift turns the statesman and his servant into chimney sweeps, who roam about Dunkirk spying for the opposition. To give special emphasis, the nickname *Dismal* is printed in heavy Gothic letters throughout the penny paper.

Once again Swift's skill at blending comedy and political invective adds a liberating quality to this prose lampoon. The picture of Nottingham, pretending to be a chimney sweeper, hiding with "a leg upon each hobb, the rest of his body being out of sight" when the English soldiers arrest him, underscores this comic scene. When the English general HILL orders this apparent "Whiggish English Traitor" washed clean of the soot, after little success the soldiers "perceived some dawning of a dark sallow brown," which gave away the identity of Dismal. Completing this portrait Swift notes that Nottingham's face has become much darker since this incident, and even with "all the beauty-washes he uses, it is thought will never be able to restore it." The exhilaration of this final flourish is derived from Swift's genuine pleasure in combining comic imaginativeness with ridicule. Surely the author hates his enemies, but why not destroy them with laughter rather than with harsh satire?

The denunciation of this Whig lord surfaces again in two poems, "TOLAND'S INVITATION TO DISMAL TO DINE WITH THE CALVES' HEAD CLUB" and "An EXCELLENT NEW SONG." During the same year as this paper appeared, a couple of GRUB STREET authors, unknown otherwise, published *A Hue and*

Cry after Dean Swift (1714) and Dr. Swift's Real Diary (1715), poor attacks on Swift's established reputation as a powerful voice for the ministry.

# "Humble Address of the Right Honourable the Lords Spiritual and Temporal in Parliament Assembled, The"

This document existed only in two drafts in the Bodleian Library, Oxford, until Herbert Davis published it in his edition of Swift's Prose Works in 1951. After a torturous period of diplomacy and debate, the English government, led by Robert HARLEY and Henry BOLINGBROKE, finally negotiated a peace with France and LOUIS XIV settling the War of the Spanish Succession. This signal event had come after Bolingbroke threatened a new war with France, and Louis, who remained at Versailles, agreed to a peace (the Treaty of Utrecht) that was signed in April 1713. With this accomplishment behind her, Queen ANNE prepared to address her Parliament, particularly the House of Lords, marking this long sought-after conclusion and setting the stage for the royal succession that would come 16 months later. Harley, who had written the speech the queen would give, provided a draft for Swift's comment and improvement. As we know from The JOURNAL TO STELLA, Swift was elated at the opportunity to participate in this historic event, and in addition Harley asked him to write the thanks of the lords, which would be given to the queen.

Though the address of thanks has been called formal and colorless, this 200-word statement does repeat the essential TORY themes: respect for royal sovereignty, hope in a future free of "so long and expensive a war," an implied thanks to her Majesty's government which secured this peace, the importance of Protestant succession, the significance of "perfect friendship" with the House of Hanover, and a final repetition of the binding constitutional requirements of religion, loyalty, and

gratitude. The references to loyalty and gratitude are actually code for opposing all traitors and political factions, as well as Swift's frequently announced devotion to impartiality. He found this characteristic particularly difficult to accomplish, since he held such passionate positions on political issues.

# "Humble Petition of Frances Harris, The"

See "MRS. HARRIS'S PETITION."

# "Humble Petition of the Footmen in and about the City of Dublin, The"

This 400-word statement on class society is dated 1732, but the first edition found was published in London in 1733, and later reprinted in Dublin by George FAULKNER in 1733. Herbert Davis refers to it as a trifle, taking the usual form of a petition for presentation to the Irish House of Commons.

More occurs in this piece than a literal request that the Commons pass a law protecting footmen and their customers from the potential damage brought about by men pretending to be footmen. Since 1704 Swift had worked on a long series of essays entitled "DIRECTIONS TO SERVANTS," and critics find "The Footman" his most brilliant of the group that he was now working on again in the 1730s. Regulating servants' behavior in the most particular manner seemed a necessity for him, but even when he appears serious about correcting a certain fault, his description of the error makes the entire situation laughable. His shrewd understanding of human behavior, especially of the differences in socioeconomic levels, renders entire portions of these essays comic.

This "Humble Petition" exhibits much of the same satiric methods (such as irony and parody) seen elsewhere in his work. As in "Directions to Servants," the truth of what he means can be discovered only through a reversal of logic, where his advice encourages precisely what should *not* be done. Instead of stating what good behavior is, his counsel pinpoints exactly what is wrong with a certain behavior by describing it as if it were correct. Alluding to how different these false footmen are from the real versions, he notes they lack "an air of impudence and dullness peculiar to the rest of their brethren: who have not arrived at that transcendent pitch of assurance," so typical of genuine footmen. When the egregious is ironically shown as most acceptable, he states "the said counterfeits . . . have been found in the very act of strutting, staring, swearing, swaggering, in a manner . . . to imitate us." Opposing the deceptive practices of these yahoos, he recommends various levels of punishment as a way of preserving the honorable profession of footman. Ironically, Swift adopts the persona of a footman, a good and true citizen, writing to his House member for relief from an outrage. Though a minor essay, it resembles every important theme and tone of his most significant statements on Ireland and the proximity of disorder in his world.

# "Humble Representation of the Clergy of the City of Dublin to His Grace William [King] Lord Archbishop"

This letter was written in 1724 and first published by Deane SWIFT in the 1765 *Works* and again by George FAULKNER in Dublin in the same year. The moment of composition seems particularly fortuitous since Swift had just finished the first chapter of GULLIVER'S TRAVELS and would soon begin his DRAPIER'S LETTERS. Apparently Swift and William KING cooperated on this piece, the archbishop sharing certain information concerning one Charles M'Carthy, a clergyman who lived in College Green, Dublin, whose house had burned. M'Carthy soon submitted a church brief, which was a type of insurance policy in which the clergy of the surrounding churches would select possible examples worthy of the parish's charity from among these briefs. Aside from the various corrupt practices surrounding such fund-raising briefs, Swift, and especially King whose diocese was most directly affected, found the procedure hateful. M'Carthy even had the temerity to go over King's head to the lord chancellor to insure that a brief would be issued, even after certain suspicions grew that M'Carthy might be implicated in an arson case.

The Irish clergy were already poorly paid, and any other imposition on the funds they might raise within their parishes seemed outrageous to Swift, who decided to address his remarks to King. Though the piece could not be published because of the ingrained relationships between church and state in the capital and Ireland as a whole, apparently King enjoyed letting particular guests read this provocative letter.

Arguing that neither the archbishop nor the clergy could oppose a brief, Swift begins a detailed analysis of the faults embedded in the entire practice of these briefs. He deconstructs the typical language used in such briefs to convince the clergy of the need for sympathy. Beyond the emotional appeal, they contain commands to the clergy that, Swift points out, have no legal basis. He also sarcastically objects to the use of the word *opportunity*: "the parsons [should use the] opportunity after the receipt of the copy of the said brief, shall, deliberately and affectionately, publish and declare . . . and stir them up to contribute freely and cheerfully towards the relief of the said sufferer." No so-called opportunity exists beyond the Sunday service, and Swift opposes, as he had throughout his life, the frequent impositions made on the charity and compassion of the common people. He argues in favor of leaving members of the clergy to direct their own parishes and permitting the people to make up their minds regarding the proper use of their charitable gifts without continual pressure from outside forces.

Swift's concerns about fund-raising remain as fresh and sensible today as when they were first written. Today government authorities, as well as various religious organizations, continually scrutinize and attempt to regulate the fund-raising practices of different groups or individuals, who often rely on a church or religious designation to conceal their sophisticated persuasions for securing gifts.

Swift denigrates the practice as poorly conceived, especially if vicars, church wardens, curates, ministers, and even bishops follow their duties and responsibilities exactly. The law remains on the side of these officials in opposing such requests, and fund-raisers, as commanded in these briefs, cannot compel these churchmen to support them. Swift's argument seems directed at King, but actually the clergy should feel the full force of his words. He condemns the clergy's weakness at one level, while defending them against any persons who would attempt to extort money from this vulnerable group. Bishops, university chancellors, judges, and other officers of the court can protect and defend themselves against such commands, but the clergy, those with "the greater hardships in this case," need relief.

As he would make clear in *The Drapier's Letters*, Swift believes a bias exists in favor of protecting the English clergy against such imposition, while the Irish clergy are left to suffer whatever outrages may suit the fund-raiser. Archbishop King could not have made this case as strongly as Dean Swift, and the two churchmen joined together in opposing what both of them regarded as one more example of tyranny.

# "Importance of the *Guardian* Considered, The"

This political essay was written during the height of Swift's activity as a writer for the TORY ministry of Robert HARLEY and Henry BOLINGBROKE, and focuses on the period immediately after the signing of the Peace of Utrecht, when Swift's job focused on defending the treaty against various accusations of betrayal asserted by the WHIGS and the Dutch. The essay was first published in London in 1713.

## SYNOPSIS

After a preface in which Swift (writing as "a Friend of Mr. St—le") asserts that Richard STEELE has opened himself up to being treated like a "Brother-Scribler," he begins the letter by addressing it to "Mr. John Snow," the bailiff of Stockbridge. He explains that he intends to provide some comments and explanation on earlier correspondence sent to Snow regarding DUNKIRK.

First, he notes, London writers often assign misleading titles to their work. For example, the title of the earlier letter was "The Importance of Dunkirk." Its subject, however, was actually "the Importance of Mr. Steele." It is vital, therefore, that those in Snow's borough (who elected Steele to represent them) have a clearer understanding of his importance. He has written "two tolerable Plays," and is often referred to as a wit. He lacks "Invention" and mastery of "a tolerable Style." His "chief Talent is Humour," and after the first bottle he makes a fair companion. A number of similar details on Steele's character and employments follow.

Steele originated a paper called the *Tatler* four to five years ago. It was published under the name "Isaac Bickerstaff" and ("by Contribution of his ingenious Friends") gained a good reputation with members of both parties. After Henry SACHEVERELL's trial, however, the nature of Steele's paper changed. Steele published two "virulent Libels" targeting Harley. Despite Steele's efforts, the Whig ministry was ousted and replaced, and he resigned as "Gazetteer."

In two years' time, Steele (and the public) got tired of the *Tatler*, and he and his friends started another paper called the *Spectator*. This, too, was eventually abandoned and Steele "hath of late appeared under the Style of *Guardian*" and more recently *Englishman*. Unlike the *Tatler*, these publications have been "very coldly received," and Steele has sought relief in "the never-failing Souce of Faction." Last August, he published a letter to "*Nestor Ironside*, Esq." and signed it, "*English Tory*." In the letter he complained about a publication recently distributed containing an address from "Sieur *Tugghe*" (the Deputy of the Magistrates of Dunkirk), imploring the queen not to "demolish" Dunkirk. Steele's comments on the address provoked "the *Examiner* and another pamphleteer" to charge him with "Insolence and Ingratitude toward the Queen." This led Steele to defend himself in the letter mentioned in the preface, and that letter is the subject of the current piece.

After a lengthy commentary that systematically points out the problems with each part of Steele's letter, Swift concludes that he has "explained . . . all the difficult Parts." He adds that the queen herself is the only one who can decide whether or not Dunkirk will be demolished: Neither Steele nor anyone else (aside from her advisers) really has anything to do with it. Steele has, however, failed to show that she would break any law by choosing to leave it "undemolished."

## COMMENTARY

Using a multidimensional approach to analyze his enemies' weaknesses, Swift depends on his skill for penetrating their argument and its rhetorical structure. One of the most noticeable techniques for damaging his opponents was the use of ad hominem argument, and in this case, it worked especially well. As relentlessly supportive of Oxford as Swift was during his assignment in the ministry, he could also react to the personal attack of an old friend who had accused him of lying in support of the Tories. As the editor and chief writer of the *Guardian* (March–October 1713), Steele wrote a punishing *Guardian* essay in August and followed up with an open letter to the bailiff of Stockbridge, entitled "The Importance of Dunkirk Consider'd." It appeared in September, and accused the government of demolishing the port and fortifications at Dunkirk, as required by treaty with France. Making the usual accusations of the Tory government's Jacobite sympathies and identifying sympathetically with Dunkirk's suffering citizens, Steele and his Whig advisers did all they could to continue damaging their opponents.

Critics point out how Swift's strategy of confronting character makes this an effective argument: Concentrate on the man and not on his politics. As we know from modern political activity, negative advertisements catch the attention of the public, and Swift knew the public was less interested in the substantive argument than in a blunt appraisal of his opponent. He turns Steele, as Richard I. Cook has stated, into an "ingrate, an ignoramus, and an arrogantly presumptuous fellow"

(34). Keeping to his anonymity, Swift avoided prosecution for libel, but more important he did not cloud the reader's view of Steele with biases arising from knowing the author's name. Steele becomes the target of Swift's wit—a fool who distorts the facts and only pretends to knowledge. Demolishing Steele's personality, literary methods, and position in society leave him a wrecked man, but more significantly the Whigs seem weak by association, empty of new ideas, and casting about for a new vision for the country.

The argument between the two men had been ongoing since 1710 when Swift had become the editor of the EXAMINER, a pro-government paper, which had criticized Steele's friends and supporters. Though Swift had given up the editorship in 1711 and now provided only hints, he did maintain a connection to the paper, one which Steele misinterpreted, believing instead that Swift was fully responsible for such offending attacks as that on the earl of NOTTINGHAM, admittedly one of Swift's favorite targets. When the *Examiner* launched a renewed attack on "Dismal" in 1713, Steele immediately determined Swift was responsible and began a strong counterattack in the *Guardian*, number 53 (May 12, 1713). A fierce exchange of letters between the two men during May suggests how far apart they had become, particularly when Steele resigned his post in the government to Lord Treasurer Robert Harley because of the provocation given in the *Examiner*. Swift answers him calmly, wondering "whether you ought not either to have asked, or written to me, or desired to have been informed by a third hand, whether I were any way concerned in writing *The Examiner*." But he does demand an apology, one which Steele never provided. After a further exchange that marked the end of their correspondence forever, Steele complains of being called "the vilest of mankind" by Swift who had supposedly said this in a letter to Joseph ADDISON. Swift rather plaintively declares his innocence, "as it is possible for a human creature to be," and "you ought to act as if you believed me, till you have demonstration to the contrary."

Clearly, neither man fully reveals the truth in this exchange, and the Dunkirk controversy, as discussed in the *Guardian*, creates a furor three months later. At about the same period, Daniel DEFOE, who was working for Harley, writes an *ad hominem* reply to Steele ("The Honour and Prerogative of the Queen's Majesty Vindicated . . . in a Letter from a Country Whig to Mr. Steele"). Defoe attacks him personally, declaring that Steele should retire to an outhouse and not seek a parliamentary seat. Finally, after being called a "prostituted pen," Swift returns quickly from Ireland at Harley's request and immediately enters the fray with "The Importance of the *Guardian* Considered."

## "In Pity to the Empty'ng Town"

Poem possibly by Swift; first published in 1875 (without the final stanza) written 1708–09. In his edition of Swift's *Poems,* Harold Williams explains that the final stanza is not printed because "corrections in another hand" have made the original illegible. While Williams notes that the original "is certainly in Swift's hand," Pat Rogers suggests that Swift may have only copied it rather than having composed the poem himself but concludes that it is "highly probable, but not quite certain," that Swift authored the lines (634).

The poem depicts May Fair (an annual festival of entertainment and sideshows which began on May 1 and lasted for 15 days) as a disappointing urban substitute for real "fields" and "air." The speaker suggests that some god invented May Fair "in pity to the emptying town," whose inhabitants were leaving by the dozen in favor of more rural surroundings. Those who flock to the festivities— among whom the speaker counts himself—reveal their "corrupted taste" by embracing false, "inverted" renditions of nature's joys rather than seeking genuine pleasures such as "frisking Lambs" and the songs of a "feathered" choir.

The exclusive modern-day Mayfair district in central London was once known as "Great Brookfield" or "Brookfield Market," but was renamed not long after the May Fair was moved there in the late 1680s. At that time, the location was still relatively remote and "the fair became a popular day out for

Londoners and a welcome chance to escape the city" with its "crowded and fetid streets." Originally, the fair was to be nothing more than a cattle market, but became notorious for debauchery and raucous celebrations. It was especially popular with the poor and with members of the upper classes looking for an opportunity to go "slumming." The Grand Jury of Westminster halted May Fair in 1708 (roughly the date of Swift's poem), claiming that "disorderly persons" used the event to lure "young persons and servants to meet to game and commit lewd and disorderly practices" ("Reviving the Mayfair May Fair").

## "In Sickness"

Poem by Swift; first published 1735. The subtitle states that it was "Written Soon After the Author's Coming to Live in Ireland, Upon the Queen's Death, October 1714." Queen ANNE died on August 1, 1714, and Swift arrived in Dublin on August 24. The poem deals primarily with Swift's depression and loneliness, lamenting his sense of having "no obliging, tender friend / To help at my approaching end" (19–20). Pat Rogers views the poem as an important precursor to "VERSES ON THE DEATH OF DR. SWIFT," while David Nokes finds it hinting at "a certain resentment" of Stella (Esther JOHNSON) as embodying his woeful condition (Rogers, *Poems* 627; Nokes, *Hypocrite Reversed* 212).

## *Intelligencer, The:* numbers 5 and 7—"An Essay on the Fates of Clergymen"

Swift began the *Intelligencer* as a weekly newspaper in May of 1728 with the help of Thomas SHERIDAN, his longtime friend. Focusing his paper on informing and diverting the small Dublin audience, Swift hoped to correct and even annoy his readers in whimsical prose which might provide him with an outlet beyond his serious pamphlets and their tone of anger, weary dismay, and biting satire. Modeled on the earlier EXAMINER and Richard STEELE's *Guardian,* this effort would display little if any of the party allegiance of those earlier papers, while reviewing topics on education, economy, literary criticism, and public satirists. Contributing only seven papers, Swift gave up in December. As he later told Alexander POPE, "if we could have got some ingenious young man to have been the manager, who should have published all that might be sent to him, it might have continued longer . . . but the printer here could not afford such a young man one farthing for his trouble . . . and so it dropped."

Swift combines two essays on ecclesiastical politics and ambition into one 2,000-word paper in which the subject of political discretion, or "prudence," provides a ready discussion of his dislike for what our age would call "political correctness." Not unexpectedly, he finds those who practice this "lower prudence" to be a species of knaves and cunning cheats who deceive those they pretend to represent and ultimately themselves. The unfortunate result for the few who try to live a more virtuous existence, refusing the practice of "servile flattery and submission with a want of all public spirit or principle," becomes a loss of hope, near poverty, and inevitable regret for a life lived badly.

The Church of Ireland and its clergy were a moribund establishment—a view many shared, including Swift. Here he finds the clergy often to be drudges who live in diminished circumstances. How the church had deteriorated over the centuries begins with Henry VIII's policy of removing property from one institution and transferring it to another, with the Crown becoming the recipient of more wealth and power. The decline of church and clergy influence proceeded from this time and resulted in not only a loss of wealth, but a weakening of the character of both the clergy and those men who considered taking orders. They became pessimists who saw themselves treated with little respect and unable to free themselves from what often became a grindingly poor existence surrounded by parishioners more hopeless than themselves. Swift's pessimism arises from this reality as well as his own personal difficulties, and the characters of Corusodes and Eugenio in this essay rec-

ognize the dilemma facing a young man who contemplates entering the church.

Corusodes represents the methodical, cautious man who flatters those more powerful than himself who are capable of offering him the preferment he unapologetically seeks. Swift adds a perverse quality to this character by introducing the clergyman's sister into the household of a rich London family where the young woman immediately becomes the willing prey of the lord of the house. Corusodes' ambition recognizes no boundaries or sacrifices, and he continues rising in the ranks of the church, always treating his lower clergy with a prideful arrogance and the rich laity with complete ignorance of their faults. Ultimately, the inevitable occurs and this most undeserving clergyman becomes a bishop, "utterly devoid of all taste, judgment, or genius."

Eugenio, who also graduates from Oxford, has an unfortunate "talent for poetry" and fluency in both Greek and Latin, skills his classmate neither possesses nor considers worthy of a rising clergyman. When in London seeking his fortune, he shows himself a modest man of generous spirit, unwilling to become a slave of "application and attendance . . . making room for vigilant dunces." Though an excellent preacher, he finds no success and retreats to the provinces where he marries badly and meditates on his disappointed life.

Swift did not object to those worldly preachers and clerical preferment, and had sought promotion himself as a younger man. He did, however, disapprove of trying to disguise self-promotion. In his view, if one was interested in rising in rank, being straightforward about one's ambition would be respected.

# *Intelligencer, The:* number 9— "An Essay on Modern Education"

See the previous entry on numbers 5 and 7 for a general description of Swift's involvement with the *Intelligencer.* "An Essay on Modern Education" was one of the eight *Intelligencer* essays by Swift and comments upon the well-known thesis that one's education does not necessarily correspond with one's social status. Having a good deal of experience with the nobility, he suggests the unlikelihood of a nobleman possessing a first-rate classical education, a fact that will contribute to his being a weak, ineffective leader. Since the nobility as a group is nearly extinct (or at least so reduced in energy and spirit), he analyzes why a new race of citizens has emerged known as "New-men." This group includes individuals such as Robert HARLEY, Henry BOLINGBROKE, Robert WALPOLE, and other figures beginning with the reign of CHARLES II. Swift skewers upper-class pretensions and infighting with mad abandon, commenting on such faults as hiring French tutors who add only absurdity, impudence, and impertinence to their young gentlemen. For all its liveliness and general references to "dunghill[s] having raised a huge mushroom [which] now spread to enrich other men's lands," the overall character of the essay is a sort of holiday exercise.

# "Ireland"

Poem by Swift; first published in 1882, written in 1727. For the circumstances of composition, see "The POWER OF TIME." Written during Swift's wearisome stay at Holyhead on his way back to Dublin from London, it is a bitter commentary on his frustrations with what he calls "this land of slaves," characterized by fruitless infighting (between WHIGS and TORIES) and preferment that ignores merit by rewarding "fools" and "knaves" (1–2).

# "Journal d'Estat de Mr. T—— devant sa Mort"

Herbert Davis does not reprint this paper, which Irvin Ehrenpreis refers to in the Swift biography concerning the last few weeks of Sir William TEMPLE's life (I.257). Swift had resided at Moor Park, Temple's home near Farnham in Surrey, England,

for nearly a decade when Temple died in late January 1699. As his secretary, Swift had not only served his patron's literary and artistic efforts but in many other household capacities, ultimately becoming the retired diplomat's literary executor. Now deprived of both a substitute father and a living, Swift writes his immediate reactions to the event in an attached register to the paper. Struggling with his emotions, Swift states the fact of Temple's death in cold terms but then adds a compliment tinged with emotional regret: "He died at one o'clock in the morning and with him all that was great and good among men."

# "Journal of a Modern Lady, The"

Poem by Swift; first published 1729, written at MARKET HILL earlier that year. Swift enclosed it with a January 13, 1723, letter to John WORRALL. As Irvin Ehrenpreis notes in his biography of Swift, "About forty opening lines make an apostrophe to Lady Anne ACHESON, who is supposed (in the poem) to have asked [Swift] for a satiric journal of a woman's day. The remaining 258 lines follow a lady of fashion from her awakening to her bedtime" (III.607). The poem portrays the "modern lady" and her friends as shallow, petty, and devoted to playing cards. John AIKIN called the poem "an outrageous satire" on the female sex but praised its "animated group of *personifications*."

# *Journal to Stella, The*

*The Journal to Stella* is a series of 65 letters Swift wrote to Esther JOHNSON (Stella) and her older companion Rebecca DINGLEY while he was working in London as a representative of the Irish church between September of 1710 and June of 1713. In the second letter of the collection—dated September 9, 1710—he declares that, "Henceforth I will write something every day to MD [My Dears], and make it a sort of journal; and when it is full, I will send it whether MD writes or no; and so that will be pretty: and I shall always be in conversation with MD, and MD with Presto" (the name he assigns to himself). Although he did not keep his promise to write every day, he did—over the course of almost three years—write to "MD" frequently, often using the unique "little language" he developed that mimics the speech patterns of young children. In letter 6 (dated October 10, 1710), he adds that he will "confine [him]self to the accidents of the day," filling his letters with "news and stuff." The journal remains one of Swift's best-known works. It continues to receive a great deal of attention from scholars, mainly as a biographical and historical document but also as an important indicator of Swift's view of himself, Stella, and women in general. The letters were not published until after Swift's death, when John Hawkesworth included them in volumes 10 (1766) and 12 (1768) of his edition of Swift's *Works*.

## SYNOPSIS

The letters in this series, Swift explains, "are a sort of journal, where matters open by degrees" and that while he does not promise to send a letter every week, he will "write every night, and when it [a folio-sized sheet of paper] is full I will send it; that will be once in ten days, and that will be often enough." He departed temporarily from this method in late April of 1712 (beginning with letter 45), explaining that he had "been extremely ill." The next several letters lack numbered journal entries, and Swift blames his ill health for having robbed him of the ease and "Humor" to continue in his "Journall Method": "I dont [sic] love to write Journals while I am in pain, and above all, not Journalls to Md." Before the end of the year, however, Swift had returned to the original format.

While each entry in the journal is unique in the particular details it provides, the majority of entries are fairly consistent in their content. As Peter J. Schakel has explained, Swift regularly lists his dining companions, details how he spent the day (including "visits, conversations, business dealings"), outlines notable news, describes any "sensational" occurrences that have caught his attention, and often includes "a personal section to the

ladies" ("Jonathan Swift"). In letter 6, for example, Swift explains that he dined with Matthew PRIOR and found out that Queen ANNE had "consented to give the First-Fruits and Twentieth Parts" (the revenues Swift had been sent to London to pursue for Irish clergymen). He describes a shocking murder-suicide involving a soldier (Capt. Charles Lavallee) who returned "from Flanders or Spain" to discover that his wife had become pregnant in his absence. In a rage, Lavallee shot her dead, fell on his sword and shot himself in the head "to make the matter sure." Swift adds that his friends are saying the "DESCRIPTION OF A CITY SHOWER" is "the best thing" he ever wrote, and he agrees. He tells "MD" to "be good girls," save their money, write to him "now and then," but urges Stella not to strain her eyes.

Other letters contain similar material—Swift's displeasure at being called away before having a chance to shave in the morning, his amazement at Henry BOLINGBROKE's voluminous drinking, how it has been "a scurvy, dull, splenetick day, for want of MD," how he and his servant Patrick intervened in a street fight between a drunk parson and "a seaman," and so forth. Beginning in early 1712, Swift provides extensive details on his poor health ("I have taken a Vomit to day; and hope I shall be bettr: I have been very giddy since I writ what is before.") From this point, the letters generally have a darker, less jovial tone than those from before. As Harold Williams explains in his introduction to the journal, this shift in the character of the letters probably resulted from the illnesses Swift suffered from March of 1712 through "the date of his departure for Ireland." He was plagued with shingles and giddiness, and his poor health was aggravated by "political anxieties and personal disappointments." The last letter in the series is dated June 6, 1713. In it, Swift chastises Stella for her laziness in mailing her last letter so late ("had you writt a Post sooner, I might have brought you some Pins") and ends with comments on how much weight William TISDALL's wife has gained and how badly Tisdall's "feet stink."

## COMMENTARY

The letters that make up this unique collection of private correspondence were written as a kind of daily diary in which Swift made entries before going to sleep at night or before rising in the morning. With the change in the ministry imminent, the Irish bishops commissioned Swift to seek the Queen's Bounty concerning the remission of a tax ("First Fruits") on the Irish clergy, providing an opportunity for Swift to approach the TORY government and its chief, Robert HARLEY, in London. The psychological and historical qualities of these letters for a reader interested in Swift are inescapable, and the particular details describing the political, social, and literary milieu of early 18th-century London, the most powerful and influential capital in Europe, provide one of the best portraits of its time.

The second half of the correspondence no longer exists, and Swift intentionally preserved these letters as a history of his public life at the heart of the government during a time of national crisis. The order and method of the diary are clear, each letter numbered corresponding to the day of the month and bundled under the title *Letter*. Some of these letters contain the entry for one day, and others are far more extensive, with smaller daily entries in some cases stretching over a two-week period. Though never intended for publication, the publication history remains complicated, even in terms of the title of the series. An early editor, Thomas SHERIDAN, called the collection *Dr. Swift's Journal to Stella* in 1784, and John Nichols referred to it in 1779 as *The Journal to Stella*, which was adopted by later editors.

The question of why Swift wrote these letters has remained a central issue since they first became known. An obvious answer is that he wished to unburden his mind and spirit because he was routinely mixing with powerful, wealthy, and intriguing men and women daily. He also had the pleasure of being courted for his considerable influence by these same individuals. As he used his skills as a pamphleteer, his power increased, at least with those who wielded power within the intricacies of party politics, extending enough that his prospects for success were highly promising. Though he wished for his own advancement, he also worked on his country's behalf, believing he might help shape its future political destiny. Even after Esther Johnson's death in 1728, Swift kept this journal

both for sentimental reasons and as a vivid picture of the final years of Queen Anne's reign. He had intended during those London years on writing and publishing a work on the last Parliament of Queen Anne and the negotiations leading to the Treaty of Utrecht. He completed the manuscript, "THE HISTORY OF THE FOUR LAST YEARS OF THE QUEEN," a month before his departure for Ireland in 1713. Because of his difficulties in securing a publisher and advice from friends and others against publishing the work, Swift had hoped Alexander POPE would help him publish it in 1727, and in 1728–29 he asks Sheridan to send him the manuscript to his country residence with Sir Arthur and Lady Anne ACHESON at MARKET HILL. Clearly Swift saw *The Journal to Stella* and the "History" as inextricably connected. The irony remains that one was too personal to publish and the other could not find a publisher because of "the ill consequences" which might arise from its appearance.

Critics have found certain pervasive themes in the *Journal*, most prominently Swift's obsession with power. Swift measures his daily success in this political game against the degree of access he has with each important figure. If an individual refuses to see him or, conversely, recognizes him fully and invites him into his office or apartments, then his access to power can shift quickly from a position of no regard and no power to one of visibility, regard, and acceptance. On first arriving in London, Swift notes that the "lord treasurer [GODOLPHIN] received me with a great deal of coldness, which has enraged me so," but later the new first minister, Harley, "charged me to come to him often: I told him I was loth to trouble him in so much business as he had . . . at his levee; which he immediately refused, and said, that was not a place for friends to come to." If an acquaintance did not abuse power, Swift would esteem that person greatly and continuously assured Stella and Rebecca Dingley of the value of recognizing such virtues.

Whether he seeks remission of taxes on the clergy or hopes to settle the disagreements between Harley and Henry Bolingbroke or argues with his servant or barely avoids the assaults of the Mohocks, a gang of young men—some of whom were aristocrats—who rampaged through London on nightly outings, Swift worries whether he has the power of doing good for those who trust him or advancing the national interest, and whether his own servants or those unknown to him will regard and respect his command or person. Power or concerns with those who possess such influence continually surface as he senses how close he now is to it, but then in the later *Journal* entries he suffers frustration at the Tory ministers' neglect or perceived disregard, wondering if "they would leave me Jonathan as they found me; and that I never knew a ministry do any thing for those whom they make companions of their pleasures."

He employed what has been called a family language or "infantile baby-talk" with his own code and system of spelling, relying on terms like Presto for himself and "MD" ("my dears") for the women. Since the letters were sent regularly between the correspondents, the language and tone in Swift's correspondence has an easy familiarity and often he speaks to Stella as if both were in the same room: "I'll rise, so d'ye hear, let me see you at night, and don't stay late out, and catch cold, sirrahs. . . . I hope to send this letter before I hear from MD, methinks there's—something great in doing so, only I can't express where it lies. . . . I'd give a guinea you had it." He often shifts from one subject to another, from one domestic scene to a vignette about a friend he noticed in the street as he walked about London. The weather, always of a concern to a walker, constantly surfaces, especially as he blames his numerous colds, fevers, "giddiness," and other physical discomforts on the heat, cold, rain, or snow. Though this journal was not intended as a public text, often the entries read as a manuscript theater—a kind of play text with dialogue and stage directions—for the audience of the two spinster ladies. London and the environs of Westminster and Windsor become a stage on which Swift interacts with numerous characters, often with such liveliness that the words on the page provide little transition from one character or scene to another. The frenetic quality of the work offers a far less subdued portrait of Swift than most readers have learned to expect from his political pamphlets and satires, despite his habit of linking the playful qualities of language with his own sense of humor.

His dinners with Harley are balanced against his doubts that Patrick, his manservant, will be able to provide him with clean shirts.

With Stella, he speaks nearly without inhibition; though certainly each letter mentions both ladies, his actual correspondent remains Esther. If she is really not his wife, as has been debated over time, then she encourages his indulging himself, a fair impression from his intimacy of language, tone, and mood toward her in his letters. Swift certainly engages his public self in the meetings and duties of those London years, but his private persona expresses the fullest intimacy and intensity with Stella. As he concludes the letter of January 4, 1711, he flirts with her as a lover might who must leave the next morning but remembers the night's pleasures: "I think I am bewitched to write so much in a morning to you, little MD . . . I'll come again tonight . . . but I can nor will stay no longer now; no, I won't, for all your wheedling[;] . . . don't smile at me, and say, Pray, pray, Presto, write a little more."

These letters are "safety-valves" for the strong, even sexual feelings of the couple toward each other, but as with any writing of Swift's, the exact nature of their content remains more complex. He manages the relationship through this correspondence, so both get pleasure but avoid the dangers (entrapment) of marriage or a full physical relationship. But this conversation, which from our perspective is a monologue, reveals his joy in linguistic gamesmanship as he tests the flexibility of the language in communicating his humor and wit, his knowledge of the political and social environment of London, and his innate sense of Irish life and its citizens. As mentioned earlier, he embraces the power of controlling the description of all these matters: the intensity, complexity, and variety of feelings created in each letter. He seeks control of the idiosyncratic in life, and though affirming the orderly, he seeks independence, too. His pleasure in word play serves as a contrast to his drawing of people; the characters he describes to Stella are fixed in place before the reader. The character's nature reveals itself according to its dominant element. And finally, his portrait of Stella remains the most dominant in the journal, with the last letter showing once again his love, his need of her, as he hurries to Chester and on to Holyhead for passage to Dublin. He "cannot ride faster," and she waits for him back in Ireland.

### FURTHER READING

Doody, Margaret Anne. "Swift among the Women." *Yearbook of English Studies* 18 (1988): 69–82.

Ehrenpreis, Irvin. *Swift: The Man, His Works and the Age.* 3 vols. Cambridge, Mass.: Harvard University Press, 1962–83.

Fox, Christopher, ed. *The Cambridge Companion to Jonathan Swift.* Cambridge and New York: Cambridge University Press, 2003.

Fróes, João. "Swift's Prayers for Stella: The Other Side of the Satirist." *Swift Studies* 18 (2003): 56–62.

Glendinning, Victoria. *Jonathan Swift: A Portrait.* New York: Henry Holt, 1998.

Gubar, Susan. "The Female Monster in Augustan Satire." *Signs: A Journal of Women in Culture and Society* 3 (1977): 380–394.

Hardy, Evelyn. *The Conjured Spirit, Swift: A Study in the Relationship of Swift, Stella, and Vanessa.* London: Hogarth Press, 1949.

Nokes, David. *Jonathan Swift: A Hypocrite Reversed.* Oxford: Oxford University Press, 1987.

Rosslyn, Felicity. "Deliberate Disenchantment: Swift and Pope on the Subject of Women." *Cambridge Quarterly* 23, no. 4 (1994): 293–302.

Swift, Jonathan. *Correspondence.* Edited by David Woolley. 4 vols. Frankfurt, Germany: Peter Lang, 1999.

———. *Journal to Stella.* Edited by Harold Williams. Reprint. Oxford, England: Clarendon Press, 1975.

## "Judas"

Poem by Swift; first published in 1735, written in 1732. It is a bitter diatribe against contemporary Irish bishops, comparing them to Judas Iscariot. Pat Rogers points out that in "The STORM," Josiah HORT is cast as "Bishop Judas," and Swift may be referring to Hort by that name in this case, as well. The poem may have been prompted by Parliament's consideration of the Bill of Residence and the Bill of Division, both of which Swift strongly opposed. The poem ends by forecasting ignomin-

ious deaths for each modern Judas. See also "ADVICE TO A PARSON," "CONSIDERATIONS UPON TWO BILLS . . . RELATING TO THE CLERGY OF IRELAND," and "ON THE IRISH BISHOPS."

## "Lady Acheson Weary of the Dean"

Poem by Swift; first published in 1730, written at MARKET HILL as early as 1728. With a great deal of self-effacement, Swift stages a lengthy complaint from Lady Anne ACHESON to her husband, Sir Arthur ACHESON, regarding Swift's extended stay with them at Market Hill (where he visited frequently between 1728 and 1730). The Lady ends her protest with a reference to the grief Swift gives her about being "skinny" and "boney," and she calls "the Dean" an "insulting tyrant."

## "Lady's Dressing Room, The"

Poem by Swift; first published in 1732, written around 1730. One of Swift's most popular (if infamous) scatological poems, it appeared in numerous editions in his lifetime and elicited many responses. For example, John Boyle, fifth earl of ORRERY, wrote in 1752 that the poem had been "universally condemned, as deficient in the point of delicacy, even to the highest degree." Sir Walter Scott thought it contained "the marks of an incipient disorder of the mind, which induced the author to dwell on degrading and disgusting subjects" (*Critical Heritage* 121, 296). Citing the work of Horace as a literary precedent, Swift defended the poem anonymously in "A Modest Defence of a Late Poem . . . Call'd The Lady's Dressing Room" (1732). In the poem, Strephon sneaks into CELIA's dressing room during her absence. There he finds abundant evidence that Celia is not quite the goddess he thought her to be. Most of the poem is an inventory of her personal effects—all of which are stained, soiled, and reeking from her sweat and other bodily sub-

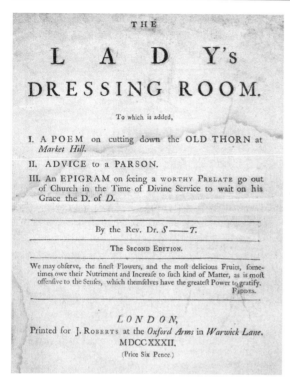

Title page of *The Lady's Dressing Room,* second edition, 1732 *(Courtesy of University of Pennsylvania Libraries)*

stances. Strephon's search culminates in the unfortunate discovery of her full, putrid commode. This taints his perception of women, in general, and he is henceforth unable to see any dame without thinking of "all her stinks." Swift separates himself as narrator at the end of the poem, pitying Strephon for failing to realize that just as "order from confusion sprung, / Such gaudy tulips [are] rais'd from dung." The "Dressing Room" has generated a great deal of psychoanalytic and gender criticism and has been read as a grotesque lampoon of the "Puffs, powders, patches, bibles, billet-doux" littering Belinda's dressing table in "The Rape of the Lock" by Swift's friend Alexander POPE. Using a technique similar to that in "A BEAUTIFUL YOUNG NYMPH GOING TO BED" and "STREPHON AND CHLOE," Swift in this poem heartily discourages idealized views (so popular in pastorals and cavalier love lyrics) of women as anything more than mortal.

# Last Farewell of Ebenezor Elliston to This Transitory World, The

See "LAST SPEECH AND DYING WORDS OF EBENEZOR ELLISTON, The."

# "Last Speech and Dying Words of Ebenezor Elliston, The"

This paper and "The LAST FAREWELL" were both printed within 24 hours of Ebenezor Elliston's execution on May 2, 1722. Herbert Davis suggests the latter was "cried about in his own hearing, as he was carried to execution," and thus printed the day before so it might be hawked. John HARDING, the Dublin printer who would print many of *The DRAPIER'S LETTERS* in 1724–25, published these two papers presumably because he could expect a quick return on his costs. "The Last Farewell" may have been written shortly after Elliston's conviction in April, since Swift was not in Dublin on the execution day, but Harding had been advertising for four days that readers could expect "The Last Speech." More than likely, after comparing both papers, Swift did not write "The Last Farewell," but having read it, found the vehicle for his prose satire.

The last speeches of criminals or social outcasts, or criminal lives, had become immensely popular among a semiliterate reading public who had found their most successful author in Daniel DEFOE. His novels *Colonel Jack, Moll Flanders,* and *Roxana* set the stage for some of the genre's most famous examples in the 1720s. He focused on England's best-known criminals, John Sheppard and Jonathan WILD, writing a *History of the Remarkable Life of Sheppard, A Narrative of all the Robberies, Escapes, etc. of John Sheppard* (both 1724), and *The Life of Wild* (1725). Earlier in this period, Defoe had gone to the Newgate cells of these London criminals and received from them manuscripts of their "authentic lives," which were published in *Applebee's Original Weekly Journal,* a TORY paper. Certainly, Defoe wrote these lives first and handed them to the criminal who would then at the scaffold in front of thousands of spectators hand over the manuscripts to his "biographer." Swift's last speech was following in a similar mode, with one unmistakable difference: This is a parody of what Defoe had made successful.

He intended to comment on contemporary Irish life, a scene of rampant poverty, widespread unemployment, and often vicious criminal activity, as seen through the eyes of one of its so-called victims, who was a product of this dysfunctional environment. Elliston rose to preeminence in Dublin with the increased activity of criminal gangs who conducted street robberies with such belligerence and apparent ease as to make walking in the streets of the capital impossible at night. The reader learns from "The Last Farewell" that Elliston, who had been raised by honest, working-class parents of modest means, apparently lived honestly until nearly the age of 30 but inexplicably joined a robber gang and over a four-month period carried out numerous robberies and assaults throughout the city. He was arrested after being pursued (according to his account) for a crime he did not commit. While attempting to escape from this false charge, he stole a horse, that he intended "to bring back again," and was captured, tried, and sentenced to death. Using the supposed facts of this autobiography, Swift employs generic satiric devices in manipulating the occasion of Elliston's execution for his real purpose of condemning England's colonial policies. He focuses here not on Irish ecclesiastical issues or WHIG outrages in England but on the welfare of the Irish people as a whole faced with the all too contemporary problem of urban crime.

"The Last Speech" begins cleverly with a denunciation of these gallows speeches in which properly convicted criminals claimed a kind of innocence and declared themselves fully repentant. Swift's persona, Elliston, speaks boldly of "pretended accounts" badly written and embarrassing to even the ignorant and illiterate (who supposedly agreed with such accounts), but then changes from this complaint to present a different face to the reader. As someone "having had an education," he is prepared to reflect "proper[ly]" on the occasion. Unlike the earlier

paper suggested, he is not penitent and does implicate women (the "common whores" with whom his comrades spend the night before their executions and "are ten times more bloody and cruel than men"). He adds that if these malefactors were allowed to escape, they would become "the wickedest rogues [he] ever knew, and so continued until they were hanged." If these words do not serve as an effective deterrent to further criminal activity, Swift continues his assault: the real culprit in encouraging crime is "the mercy of the government in ever pardoning or transporting us." The English government and the weak Irish parliament become directly responsible for refusing to take proper action; in Swift's view an enlightened country must exterminate "such vermin" or be overrun. He made this prescription clear for the Yahoos in Part IV of GULLIVER'S TRAVELS (1726), for transient beggars in "A Proposal for Giving Badges to Beggars" (1737), and by allusion to "a colony of frogs" in "CONSIDERATIONS ABOUT MAINTAINING THE POOR" (1765). This bitter rhetoric has the effect of pushing the satiric message forward, shocking the reader, Swift hopes, into recognition and action against a rising tide of chaos.

The indictment proceeds with a verisimilitude that surely convinced readers that this life was true: Elliston would not be reformed and given the chance would redouble his attacks on the public. In a final act of betrayal against the criminal fraternity he has willingly joined, he leaves the names of his gang members and other accomplices, their safe houses, and the receivers of stolen goods with "an honest man" who will turn over the list to the authorities at the first opportunity. As Swift states extending his meaning far beyond this little paper, "I here give . . . fair and public warning, and hope they will take it." Some critics suggest this paper is a variation on a theme begun in the Bickerstaff pamphlets, but with increased psychological realism and focus on the Elliston character, who centers the reader's attention on the immediate danger he poses, the specific actions he will take against the community, and the need for the government to take verifiable action when faced with rampant crime. The reading public did not miss the effect of Elliston's words. For them, it was literal truth, and

Swift's deception was successful. What more could we expect from a man who hoped "you shall see me die like a man, the death of a dog."

# "Last Speech and Dying Words of the Bank of Ireland, The"

John HARDING printed this paper in 1721, but the document does not offer sufficient evidence of Swift's authorship, though he had been involved in opposing the creation of an Irish National Bank. A group of projectors had convinced the lord lieutenant and various members of the Irish parliament that a financial institution that might regulate the money supply and the availability of credit could serve the nation well. Swift objected to any charter for such a bank, anticipating a dysfunctional funding structure between real money, "and the other half altogether imaginary." Speculation and projectors received severe criticism in "A PROPOSAL FOR THE UNIVERSAL USE OF IRISH MANUFACTURE," as well as other works probably by Swift, "CAUSES OF THE WRETCHED CONDITION OF IRELAND," "The Wonderful Wonder of Wonders," "The Wonder of All the Wonders That Ever the World Wondered At," "Subscribers to the Bank Placed According to Their Quality," "A LETTER FROM A LADY IN TOWN TO HER FRIEND IN THE COUNTRY, CONCERNING THE BANK," and "A Letter to the King at Arms." The association of this scheme with the South Sea Bubble poisoned any chance of its success, since thousands had lost money in that adventure, and Swift expected only the worst might happen in Ireland with its unstable economy. Relying on his usual efforts at satirizing the failed British colonial effort in Ireland, he examined his own sense of balance and discontent, too, knowing that the country's ills also emerged from homegrown avarice and an unwillingness to practice self-help policies.

Aside from prose responses, Swift wrote at least three poems opposing a national bank: "The BANK THROWN DOWN," "PART OF THE NINTH ODE OF THE FOURTH BOOK OF HORACE," and "The RUN UPON THE BANKERS," the latter precipitated when the South Sea Bubble panic became prominent in

late 1720 and the loss of capital doomed any suggestion of a bank scheme. Though these pieces and the pamphlets seem economic in their theme and focus, they also represent a political point of view, one that he hoped would alert the Anglo-Irish establishment whose response to English oppression had generally been weak and ineffective.

"The Last Speech" pretends to support the proposal for a national bank with the narrator impersonating the bank itself, complete with children named "Trade" and "Credit." The 500-word statement contains an opening section in which "B. B. Banker" seeks sympathy and understanding for his effort to gain a charter. The final section functions as a harsh diatribe against the Irish and their ignorance concerning modern finance. Though not without some merit in its use of personification, the piece as whole seems erratic and lacking in any real power to discredit the notion of a bank.

# "Laws for the Dean's Servants"

This set of instructions or codes for servants was first published by Deane SWIFT in 1765 but dated December 7, 1733. As a 360-word statement, it remains essentially part of a larger collection of writings on "the government of his servants"—their duties, responsibilities, fines for misconduct, and general advice delivered sarcastically. Though not a satiric project in the same vein as his "DIRECTIONS TO SERVANTS," Swift projects a similar need of avoiding the chaos and subversion perpetrated by those who would serve another. Or as Carole Fabricant has usefully described it: he "presupposes a stratified social order in which one class is responsible for cleaning up the mess made by another" (*Swift's Landscape* 41). These *"Laws"* provide another view of the balancing act Swift conducted between imagination and reality; he had the vision of Alexander POPE's *Essay on Man:* "Created half to rise, and half to fall; great Lord of all things, yet a Prey to all." Though master and servant were separated economically in this class society, both exist recognizing the bond between them while each measures the bond's tensile strength before the vision tears itself apart.

# "Left-Handed Letter to Dr. Sheridan, A"

Poem by Swift; first published in 1762, written in 1718. Along with other poems such as "MARY THE COOK-MAID'S LETTER TO DR. SHERIDAN" and "SHERIDAN, A GOOSE," it is one of a number of items in an extended series of trifles circulated among Swift, Dr. Thomas SHERIDAN, Rev. Patrick DELANY, Rev. Daniel JACKSON, and the ROCHFORT brothers. In this poem Swift chides Sheridan for failing to heed Delany's warning to bow out of what has become an ongoing paper war, and promises to continue embarrassing Sheridan as a "dunce."

# Lelop-Aw

See "ACCOUNT OF THE COURT AND EMPIRE OF JAPAN."

# "Lesbia"

Poem by Swift; first published in 1746, written in 1736. Subtitled "From Catullus," it is based on the Roman poet's *Carmina* 92. The speaker of the poem claims that his mistress's constant railing is proof of her love, since he likewise curses her hourly but loves her all the same.

# "Letter from a Lady in Town to Her Friend in the Country, Concerning the Bank, A"

As noted in the commentary on "LAST SPEECH AND DYING WORDS OF THE BANK OF IRELAND," Swift found the topic of the national bank and the subject of projectors (who suggest how Irish money properly invested might help the nation) inescapably fascinating for a series of economic pamphlets. Since

1695 when the Banks of England and Scotland were established, the issue of an Irish bank had surfaced, as it did again in 1719, but not until 1783 did a royal charter provide the structure for a bank of Ireland. Ironically, though providing a range of public and commercial banking services, the bank did not compete well against a group of private banks throughout Ireland and not until the early to mid-19th century did the National Bank, along with a group of joint-stock bank creations, actually evolve into a stable system. Published in Dublin on December 1, 1721, the "Letter from a Lady" is one several pamphlets Swift wrote regarding subscribers to the (at that point hypothetical) Bank of Ireland.

## SYNOPSIS

Writing from Dublin to her friend "in the Country," the lady explains that she has arrived in the city three days before the new national bank will open, found the representative her friend knows, and told him of her friend's plan to subscribe £2,000. He explained that she may have arrived too late (since so many others had already applied), but that he would be willing to "assign one half of his own Subscription" to her if necessary. He then made a long speech about all the advantages the bank would bring "to the Subscribers and to the Kingdom" and explained how it was completely impossible for the bank to fail. When he ran out of breath, he instructed her to bring the cash in guineas when she was summoned the next day.

Having heard nothing at the end of the following day, the lady concluded that her friend had missed out on the opportunity to subscribe. While she was waiting, however, she "accidentally" found out "that SOME of the Nobility and Gentry were violently bent against" the national bank. Among those who opposed it was "a certain LORD" to whom she happened to be related, and so she sought him out. She told him what had happened and asked his opinion. After a fit of hysterical laughter, he assured her that the bank's books were not filled with subscribers and that the bank had failed to gather even half of the capital it needed to open. When she asked how it came about that "so great a Majority could oppose" the bank, he explained that there were four main reasons. First, the bank could offer no "Sufficient Security" for the property of its subscribers. Second, there could be no guarantee that "the Presumptive Power, which must be lodged in this BANK" would not be used to destroy the "Liberties of the People." Third, it was clear that any wealth the bank acquired would undoubtedly "be apply'd to its own Preservation." And finally, since it was a *Protestant* Bank it would take the bulk of hard currency away from Protestants, leave them with worthless paper, and vulnerable to the wealthier "*Irish Papists.*" The gentleman added that he could not understand how Ireland—"a Country wholly Crampt in every Branch of its Trade, of large Extent, ill Peopled, and abounding in Commodities" it could not export— would reap any benefits at all from a national bank.

The lady writes that most of what the "certain LORD" told her was above her capacity, but fortunately he had written it all down. After hearing what he had to say, the lady immediately went back to the bank's representative and told him that her friend had changed her mind and would not subscribe to the bank. She also asked "his Lordship" about the accuracy of reports stating that "the LORD LIEUTENANT" (Charles GRAFTON) supported the bank. He responded that these reports were patently false, and that Grafton had offered no opinion on the bank, instead "leaving it to the Wisdom of the Nation" to decide whether or not it would be profitable. She also asked how the leaders of the bank could open the books and begin to collect subscriptions before the people had decided whether or not they even wanted the bank. He saw "no possible Reason for this Proceeding," and added that the bank's managers had grossly misrepresented King GEORGE I's intentions by making it appear that he ordained the bank. In reality, he had ordered only that the people of Ireland should have a national bank if they wanted one.

Several days later, a list of the bank's subscribers was published, and it was hardly a who's who— composed only of persons such as a "French *Corn-Cutter*" and a "Butcher." In fact, those who appeared on it were so embarrassed that at least one of them had gone into hiding. The lady met this individual, and learned that all attempts to recoup the money she had invested had failed.

## COMMENTARY

In 1720 Swift found "the Thing they call a Bank" worrisome, and a projection that would cause long-lasting economic damage to Ireland. As with the collapse of the South Sea Company bubble in the same year, the idea of a bank seemed an irrational plan, and this paper makes that clear in an entertaining, charming yet unmistakably pointed manner. A Dublin lady serves as Swift's persona as she narrates how a friend has sent her to invest in the bank and why after much encouragement from a ridiculous promoter she decides against buying shares in the firm. The whole fraudulent exercise is examined from the perspective of a rather innocent, if not giddy woman who finds out from a "certain Lord" that the entire enterprise is a shadow, depending on "conclusions by no means calculated for the circumstances and condition of Ireland." As a number of critics point out, it is this key theme of Ireland's uniqueness—"a crazy exception"—to which Swift often turns in opposing such schemes. What might work well in England or seem good legislation as posed by the mother country to its colony has little to do with economic realities: poor investment security, stock and security crashes throughout Europe, and untried, unproven subscribers—all of which threaten Ireland's stability.

# "Letter from a Member of the House of Commons in Ireland"

This pamphlet emerged during late 1708, when (with the urging and warrant of the Irish bishops) Swift had spent nearly two years soliciting relief from the English parliament concerning particular Crown rents on church land in Ireland, known as the first fruits and twentieth parts. While in London, Swift was encouraged to visit with Earl GODOLPHIN, the lord treasurer and leader of the WHIG ministry, and directly lay the Irish claims before him. Godolphin, who treated Swift rather coolly, was the ultimate modern politician, telling Swift that if anything were to be done concerning the first fruits, a promise of support from the Irish clergy for the removal of the Test Act in Ireland as a favor to the Dissenters must be forthcoming. Swift understood the nature of this *quid pro quo* arrangement, but any effort to maneuver the Irish Presbyterians into positions of greater influence in Ireland would be opposed by the Anglican Church of Ireland. The Sacramental Test had served Irish Anglicans well since 1704, keeping all public offices free from the competition of a member of any other sect (nonconformists), including Catholics, who might seek political power. In this letter, Swift argues against doing away with the Test—something he saw as a vital means of protection against granting political (and, by extension, ecclesiastical) power to dangerous Dissenters.

## SYNOPSIS

The letter is written in response to a missive the English M.P. (mentioned in the title) had sent earlier regarding the repeal of the Sacramental Test Act. This act limited eligibility for public office to those who received Angelican Communion. The Irish M.P. acknowledges the earlier letter, which in his view explains the "strange Representations" made of the Irish in England. He asserts that there are countless rumors circulating in English "Coffee Houses" that exaggerate the plight and power of Irish Presbyterians, and that "weekly Libellers" end every story about Ireland "with an Application against the *Sacramental Test.*"

In the next section of the letter, the Irish M.P. gives his opinion (as requested) on whether or not the act should be repealed. He proclaims—with clear sarcasm—that the Irish were surprised at England's "wonderful Kindness" to them "on this Occasion," in teaching them to see their own interests. He admits that this has raised suspicion among many Irishmen but insists that he understands it is for their own good. Far from the heart of the debate, the Irish have been "forced, by mere Conjecture, to assign two Reasons" for England's desire to repeal the act. One is that they "imagine it will be a Step towards" having it repealed in England. The other is that it will make it possible to reward "*several*" deserving "*Persons*" who, in the past, were unqualified for public office because of

the act. It would be best if the English would save conjecture and simply explain why they want to repeal the act in Ireland. After all, the Irish value England's interests far more than their own: if, for example, an Englishman's "little finger be sore," and he thinks "a Poultice" made of an Irishman's vital organs would ease the pain, all he must do is "speak the Word, and it shall be done."

Given the freedom to judge for themselves, however, the Irish see many benefits associated with keeping the Test Act and a number of "Mischiefs" that would come from repealing it. Their greatest objection is that doing away with the Act would cause "an entire Alteration of Religion" in Ireland, and it would not take long for it to happen. The majority of Dissenters are certainly in favor of doing away with it, and "many of them care not three Pence whether there be any *Church* or no." Once they gained access to public office, it would not be long before they grew into a "Majority in the House of Commons, and consequently make themselves the National Religion."

The English M.P. also asked whether the repeal would be successful in the Irish Parliament. It is not possible to predict the outcome based only on whether Whigs or Tories would win, since in this case those terms "do not properly express the different Interests" in Ireland's Parliament. Nonetheless, it would surely be difficult to get the repeal passed in the House of Commons. In the House of Lords it would be at least as challenging, and the "intire Body of" the Irish "Clergy is utterly against repealing the Test," despite their devotion to the queen.

There are several arguments commonly offered in favor of repealing the act in Ireland. One claim is that the "*Popish* Interest" is so strong among the Irish that doing away with the Test Act is the only way "to unite all *Protestants.*" The Irish M.P. dismisses this as "Misrepresentation and Mistake." He also wonders what would happen to Anglicans in Ireland if the Dissenters succeeded in having the act repealed. Would, he asks, the Dissenters "be so kind" to allow members of the Church of Ireland to hold office? Would they seek to make traditional religion illegal? The Presbyterians claim that they have been persecuted, but in reality they view persecution as everything that prevents them from persecuting others.

Some who favor repealing the Test Act find it offensive that the "Lord's Supper, should be made subservient to such mercenary Purposes, as the getting of an Employment." These individuals are usually those who attend Anglican services in the morning, and then "go with their Wives to a *Conventicle* in the Afternoon." The law should really forbid men like this from holding office simply because they take communion in an Anglican Church—they should be required to swear that they are members of the Church of Ireland. Whenever this issue comes up, however, they fall back on the argument that no man should be deprived of the right to serve queen and country "on Account of [his] Conscience."

Another "Topick of Clamour" is the requirement that military officers are also subject to the Test Act. The Dissenters point to this and cry that they are "disarmed" and "used like *Papists*." When, however, the House of Commons suggests that the government would never "hang them" for defending their country, the Dissenters tell them to go and fight their own battles. In other words, they cry out against the restriction until the opportunity to fight is actually presented.

To sum up, if the Dissenters in Ireland can be content with a law of toleration ("as hath been granted them in *England*"), both houses of the Irish Parliament would probably support it. Anything more than that, however, will be difficult to accomplish: "we make a mighty Difference here between suffering *Thistles* to grow among us, and wearing them for *Posies*." Repealing the Test Act would certainly allow the Presbyterians to "work themselves up into the National Church," and this would create "eternal Divisions" among Protestants instead of uniting them against the "Papists."

## COMMENTARY

Swift knew his political and religious beliefs were being severely tested as he lobbied for an exemption from the First Fruits tax, but his personal ambitions in church were also threatened when it came to the Sacramental Test. A few members of the Whig Junto—Charles SUNDERLAND, Thomas WHARTON, John SOMERS, Charles HALIFAX, and William Cowper—who hoped to sway the younger churchman,

urged Swift toward a position where if he would send notice to the Irish bishops of his support for doing away with the Test Act then a special piece of preferment might be arranged for him. When he refused and made his mentor, Bishop KING, understand his firmness on this point, his mission had failed, though he struggled against this fact through the middle of 1710. Reflecting on his failure back in Ireland, Swift had been writing for a few months on the value of the church's remaining moderate between the political extremes both in church and state. This subject had caused him to consider deeply the question of religious toleration earlier in the "DISCOURSE OF THE CONTESTS AND DISSENSIONS IN ATHENS AND ROME, A" (1701) and again more recently in "The SENTIMENTS OF A CHURCH OF ENGLAND MAN WITH RESPECT TO RELIGION AND GOVERNMENT" (1708), in which he assured his readers of his lack of prejudice and bigotry, suggesting that the constitution deserved more consideration and protection than the extreme pleadings of either the Whigs or the Tories. In these papers he would combine wit and humor in engaging both a healthy skepticism and good common sense in an effort to rally his Whig acquaintances toward a more acceptable political position, one which would preserve the Test Act.

Now, his tone and approach to the problem shifted into an offensive mode, where, as Herbert Davis suggests, Swift challenged the Tories. He encouraged them to take action, and warned Whigs of the power of the Established Church in Ireland against the immoderate efforts of the English government. Anarchy, disorder, and revolution would result if the Test Act was repealed, but at the same time Swift continued his anxiety over the government's involvement in the affairs of the church. The Whigs were seeking support from other constituencies in the country, particularly in England where the same effort to dissolve the Test Act was under way. In conciliating the Dissenters and demonstrating toleration beyond what was prudent, the English Parliament, in Swift's mind, was interfering in Irish affairs as an experiment, hoping to gain insight on how the repeal might proceed in England. But in conducting this experiment, Parliament would once again threaten the order of the Irish House of Commons and throw the country into the hands of wild men.

Swift's attitude toward the Dissenters developed from a long-held belief, one which emerged from the undeniable history of the English Civil War and the resulting Commonwealth, where a minority of the population, the Puritans, successfully persecuted the majority. Without full acceptance of the English constitution and agreement with the principles of the Church of England, Swift could not permit the Dissenters his usual reasonableness and tolerance. His satire punctures English hypocrisy: "I am hugely bent to believe that whenever you concern your selves in our affairs, it is certainly for our Good." If the issue actually has to do with "Liberty, Property, and Religion," then how could a law established for the protection of these interests in Ireland need elimination? When the Dissenters have taken over the country after the repeal of the Test Act, and taken all church revenues and lands and "disposed [them] among their pastors or themselves," what will the English parliament think about toleration then? Question after question is posed as Swift deconstructs the entire controversy, extending his criticism to the bishops who have a responsibility to protect the lower clergy and the welfare of the church, but instead seem on equal footing with the Whigs who abuse ecclesiastical patronage for their own personal gain. English interference, often a common theme in Swift's writings on Ireland, takes a particular noteworthy aspect when he attacks Daniel DEFOE's pamphleteering on the Test Act; "so grave, sententious, dogmatical a rogue, that there is no enduring him." Surely, Defoe's writing had produced the necessary response, and Swift recognized his opponent's skill. As Paula Backscheider notes, Defoe's major tactic was to focus on the Anglicans' primary arguments and expose what he viewed as their true message (*Daniel Defoe: His Life* [Baltimore: Johns Hopkins University Press, 1989]). Two years later, both Defoe and Swift would be working for Robert HARLEY and the TORY ministry, and the issue would once again be power rather than religion or aesthetics. The letter ends with a blunt challenge: the Irish Commons will never submit to a change in the law; the Dissenters must tolerate the majority since "we are in possession."

# "Letter from Dean Swift to Dean Smedley"

Poem possibly by Swift. Although its original printing gives no indication of place or date of publication, allusions throughout the poem suggest that it was written in response to Jonathan SMEDLEY's hostile *Satyr* on Swift (Dublin, 1725). Pat Rogers doubtfully includes it among Swift's verses.

# "Letter from Dr. Swift to Mr. Pope, A"

This letter is dated January 10, 1721, but the intriguing element is that Alexander POPE said in 1740 that he had never received such a letter but saw it for the first time as a pamphlet, never printed, but written in Ireland. David Woolley calls this letter a masquerade and asserts that Pope added the date when he printed it in Cooper's London edition of 1741. It was published again by George FAULKNER in Dublin the same year.

Swift writes in anger based on: (1) the prosecution of Edward WATERS (a Dublin printer who had published "PROPOSAL FOR THE UNIVERSAL USE OF IRISH MANUFACTURE"), (2) the false attribution of another pamphlet engineered by Edmund Curll, and (3) his own chronic illness. He reflects on his literary activity from 1714 to 1720: "what concerns the credit of a writer, the injuries that are done him, and the reparations he ought to receive." Focusing on autobiographical detail, Swift continues to describe his affiliation with and departure from the TORY party, his composition of the "HISTORY OF THE FOUR LAST YEARS OF THE QUEEN" and lost hopes for a government preferment, and his acceptance of the inevitable in Ireland although he seeks its improvement. The condition of the nation rests in the hands of a dysfunctional Irish House of Commons whose neglect is exceeded only by the malevolence of the English parliament. Less a history and more a statement of Swift's conclusions regarding Ireland's history and its political suffering (which mirrored his own disappointments), the "Letter to Mr. Pope" reasserts Tory party philosophy and criticizes WHIG tyranny. Swift's early biographer, Charles ORRERY, however, finds that "He was neither Whig nor Tory, neither Jacobite nor Republican. He was Doctor Swift." The compliment to Swift's independence and the courage of his prose seems appropriate; it is also true the dean believed an effective political writer must have well-informed opinions and scorn threats of censorship and legal manipulations. Vulnerable as a writer on Irish affairs, he felt deeply the plight of the Irish and by this time had already begun his next great satiric project, one that might free him intellectually and spiritually from what he viewed as the prison that was Ireland: GULLIVER'S TRAVELS. As Carole Fabricant reminds us, Swift felt himself an innocent man under constant assault by a corrupt system where his moral judgment counted little in his battle for survival (*Swift's Landscape* 49). Living in a virtual totalitarian nightmare, Swift, at one point a victim, at another a warrior fighting the final battle, does not delude himself concerning the seriousness of the conflict. The theme of rampant, uncontrolled power identifies the issue for him, and the trope of a prison as a parallel theme melds perfectly with the environment in which he finds himself confined. He needed the freedom of fantasy after the repressive experience of writing about Irish affairs; he now had the other worlds of Lemuel Gulliver as pathways for his escape.

# "Letter from the Pretender to a Whig Lord, A"

The letter is dated July 8, 1712, and labeled as coming from St. Germain, the French home in exile of Prince James STUART, also known as the "Pretender" or "Old Pretender." This pretended confidential letter was actually published in July 1712 and reprinted for J. Nichols in London in 1779.

Critics often comment on Swift's ventriloquism when discussing these essays, referring to his method of portraying either WHIG statesmen as the writers or, in this case, the exiled "King" James as both in a conspiracy of disloyalty to their supporters. Supposedly, James R. (Rex) was replying to suggestions from Lord W. (Thomas WHARTON) that he had entertained the Tories and sympathized with them. James offers promises of support to the Whigs and asserts his loyalty to them; he will make one a duke and another will have his debts paid. Swift's prose has the shock of accuracy, and the psychological impact on the reader is profound. With a putative letter from the Pretender who willingly suggests that if he can be permitted 12 Catholic domestics, he will not interfere with any changes the Whigs might have in mind for the Anglican Church. Turning the typical relationship of the Tories with the Jacobites upside down remains the single most significant virtue of this short letter: Now the Whigs are the culprits, and Swift has easily increased the anxiety of a public already worried about a long, costly continental war.

# "Letter of Thanks from My Lord Wharton"

This fictional letter was printed in July 1712 and reprinted for J. Nichols in London in 1779. Whether one calls Swift's approach in this piece impersonation or ventriloquism, the effect remains memorable, as he comically attacks the despised Thomas WHARTON, "the most universal villain I ever knew." This hated former lord lieutenant of Ireland praises Bishop William FLEETWOOD for affirming that any true value for the Protestant religion depends on maintaining the English constitution—which means supporting the settlement of the Glorious Revolution and Protestant succession of Mary and her husband, WILLIAM III of Orange, in 1688. The WHIGS, who chafed at their dismissal from government, saw this publication as supporting their principles. Though the House of Commons condemned it,

Richard STEELE deviously printed 14,000 copies of the paper, assuring its wide distribution even to Queen ANNE's own apartments.

Fleetwood had published *Four Sermons* in 1712 with a preface that was reprinted in the *Spectator* for May 21, 1712, and Steele added a highly complimentary paragraph as an introduction to the bishop's words. A variety of publications followed attacking Steele for publishing this supposed Whig party pamphlet, but Swift took a more inventive approach with the profane Wharton commending the bishop and the pamphlet for its effectiveness: "we have never been disappointed in any of our Whig bishops, but they have always unalterably acted up, or, to speak properly, down to their principles."

Though a minor piece, other connections add to its interest: Wharton was the same Whig whom Swift had attacked in the EXAMINER, "A SHORT CHARACTER OF HIS E[XCELLENCY] T[HOMAS] E[ARL] of W[HARTON]," "The HISTORY OF THE FOUR LAST YEARS OF THE QUEEN," and "Memoirs, Relating to That Change Which Happened in the Queen's Ministry in the Year 1710." In this last essay, he received Swift "with sufficient coldness and answered the request I made in behalf of the clergy with very poor and lame excuses." The effect of making Wharton the spokesman for the Kit-Cat Club, a quasi-literary organization founded by the Whigs in 1703, associates such men as Joseph ADDISON, William CONGREVE, Charles HALIFAX, John SOMERS, John VANBRUGH, and others, with his words. Swift disparages Wharton for his anti-Irish, antiliterary, and anti–Church of England attitudes.

# "Letter on Maculla's Project"

Swift remained hopeful regarding the restoration of Ireland and its people's ability to recover from English colonial oppression and those mistaken schemes that had damaged (and would continue to erode) their economic, political, and ecclesiastical foundation. At least one undercurrent of his confidence in Ireland depended significantly on what he saw as Irish uniqueness: It was a kingdom, not a colony, though the English never accepted this position.

In the late 1720s Swift wrote a series of pamphlets on Irish questions, often responding to specific issues or individuals who had for one reason or another provoked his anger or contempt. James MACULLA, a Dublin pewterer and coppersmith who had involved himself in various coinage schemes, became the focal point of one of these papers for his impractical, "visionary" projections concerning the Irish monetary system. Having recently in *The DRAPIER'S LETTERS* dealt with the greed of another projector, Swift was really in no mood for further amendments to current practice, but he had befriended Maculla in the past and the smith had visited the deanery and even left a copy of his book. Later, Swift visited Maculla at his home, believing him to be well-intentioned, although his project seemed ultimately flawed.

In *Jonathan Swift and Ireland*, Oliver Ferguson explains the origin of this discussion, which repeats Swift's long-held theme on the scarcity of hard currency, one he embraced earlier in the INTELLIGENCER and other essays. Maculla proposed in his "A New Scheme . . . for Increasing the Cash of this Kingdom" a plan for issuing promissory notes worth a very small amount and stamped on copper. Swift did not object as much to the idea of having currency without royal approval as to the entire responsibility falling to one man, which seemed impractical and encouraged potential fraud (Ferguson 160). The essay ultimately dismisses Maculla's suggestion in favor of the writer's own scheme: As the dean had argued for at least five years, the essential need was to establish a national mint. However, like other sensible suggestions for handling what was in effect a national emergency, this one was never implemented.

# "Letter on the Fishery"

Swift wrote to Francis Grant, a London-based Scottish merchant, on March 23, 1734, and Grant published the letter in his own pamphlet, "The British Fishery Recommended to Parliament," in

December 1749. Later, it was published as a part of *The Supplement to the Works of Dr. Swift* in 1752, and again in the *Gentleman's Magazine* in 1762 and in George FAULKNER's edition of the *Works*. The reason for Swift's letter was Grant's well-known attitude concerning the herring and fishing industry in Britain: He had argued for increased mercantile industry leading to a better economic position for all. After much consideration, the English Parliament (fearing they had already absorbed ambitious newcomers from across Europe and created a complex system of financial credit rivaled only by the Dutch Republic) did not support this proposal. Unwilling to lose this opportunity, Grant hoped he could encourage the Irish Parliament to see the benefit of this plan and believed Swift might assist him.

Swift realized "corruptions are apt to make me impatient, and give offence. . . . I was enraged at the folly of England, in suffering the Dutch to have almost the whole advantage of our fishery, just under our noses." Acknowledging the Dutch as highly capable seamen and astute businessmen, Swift regrets the English have dealt so ineffectively in countering their competitiveness. The English Parliament seems more concerned about the fish in the Grand Banks off Newfoundland than those in the North Sea off their own coast. In a particularly dramatic one-paragraph autobiographical statement, Swift describes how he has become old and sick in the service of Ireland, defending its interests against tyranny, corruption, and the ignorance of its own citizens. "I believe the people of Lapland, or the Hottentots, are not so miserable a people as we," and Swift sees no escape from the curse of oppression. The irony of introducing viable, practical ideas to a people too downtrodden to escape their own fear and ignorance ("oppressed beggars are always knaves") becomes quite sharp in his reply to Grant. Though assuring Grant that there was no hope for this proposal, Swift offers to speak with members of the Irish Parliament, while expecting nothing. The bill was later enacted, but Swift does not mention that here. Ferguson points out how Swift reviews many of his oldest grievances against both England and Ireland, while seeming less the devoted son of Ireland for which he has often been given credit (184–185).

## "Letter to a Member of Parliament in Ireland, upon the Choosing of a New Speaker There, A"

This letter was written on eight quarto pages in late 1709, though dated 1708, but not published during Swift's lifetime until Hawkesworth and FAULKNER's editions in 1765. During the same period, he had written in Ireland "A Letter Concerning the Sacramental Test," and both essays reflect his decided opposition to the WHIGS' efforts to repeal the Test Act. Within this unstable environment of shifting political allegiances, the power was shifting from the Whigs to the TORIES, and the lord lieutenant of Ireland, Thomas WHARTON, had just returned from England, after leaving Ireland to seek help from friends at Westminster, since he was under threat of impeachment. Unfortunately, his first Irish test was choosing a replacement for Speaker of the House of Commons. The current speaker, Alan Brodrick (see MIDDLETON), was a vigorous Whig who worked diligently with Wharton to repeal the Test Act, and earned Swift's particular dislike. But now as a new lord chief justice, Brodrick supported his own relative and urged Wharton to select him and ignore any other candidate, especially a proven Church of Ireland man like Swift.

A fictional letter, the essay remains unfinished and approaches the selection of a speaker without the closely reasoned manner of its companion piece. Irvin Ehrenpreis mentions that the choice for Swift was clear—the viable candidate must support the Test Act, since compromises and half measures will no longer serve (*Swift* II.374). Characteristically, the choice became important, not because of the candidate chosen but because the principle of maintaining the Test was connected to Irish independence. What might well serve Whig political interests in England would more than likely not advance Irish national interests. Swift knew Wharton was quite capable of manipulating the Irish Parliament into acting in accordance with England, and this letter implies the harsh political reality of these times: "For the bare acting upon a principle from the dictates of a good conscience, or prospect of serving the publick, will not go very far under the present dispositions of mankind." He examines the issue with his usual acuteness, finding that "the High-flying Whigs" are the great enemies of the country and "the High and Low Church" members of Parliament should join together in countering any effort to "abolish the Sacramental Test." The candidate should be nonpartisan and willingly supportive of all policies that would further Ireland's economic condition.

Even at this early point in his Irish residence, Swift had contributed more than any other Anglican cleric to the welfare of Ireland, though his worries in this case were not fully realized. Though Brodrick's protégé, John Forster, was chosen as speaker, the Parliament did not dismantle the Test Act, apparently unwilling to take such radical action. Within three months, a new government was in place at Westminster (August 1710), and the Tories and Robert HARLEY gave heart to the Irish bishops who readied Swift, once again, for his mission to request relief from the First Fruits.

# "Letter to a Very Young Lady, on Her Marriage, A"

The manuscript copy of this letter in Swift's hand, written in early February 1723, was sent to the young lady, Deborah Staunton, wife of John ROCHFORT, married three weeks earlier. Later, the letter appeared in the 1727 POPE-Swift *Miscellanies* and the 1735 edition of the *Works*. Scholars have typically commented on the irony of Swift's giving advice to a bride while struggling with the knowledge of Esther (Vanessa) VANHOMRIGH's illness and his unresolved anxiety about their feelings for each other, and his relationship with Stella (Esther JOHNSON), which apparently provided emotional stability for him. Swift, however, seems to have had no difficulty in sublimating his emotions to the task of providing straightforward advice to her, as if he were a respected uncle or trusted friend who, possessing long experience himself, can properly guide this young naïve woman.

His announced reason for writing this letter is to divert the young woman "from falling into many errors, fopperies, and follies to which [her] sex is subject." Though harsh and unfair in this and other generalities, he offers his friendship, alerting her to his respect for her new husband and his long friendship with her mother and father. His advice stresses the need for education and the cultivation of common sense. If a woman remembers that love has as much to do with friendship and esteem, then her marriage may prevail against the many tests it faces. Swift proceeds with a list of recommendations for the virtuous life: Remain a modest, reserved person; show affection for your husband without public displays or excessive bouts of regret when he is away; dress modestly without spending excessively on clothing; keep to a personal hygiene regimen, since "the capacities of a lady are sometimes apt to fall short in cultivating cleanliness and finery together"; select your female friends carefully, as you may contract some form of vice or foolishness; associate with sensible male acquaintances; avoid close friendships with a favorite maid; and preserve at all times the friendship and respect of your husband. Swift's ironic pose though critical of women seems more intent on teasing the young Deborah into recognizing the complexities of married life, where men and women often act unreasonably and their conduct toward one another becomes petty and unfeeling. Urging both sexes to depend as much on their intellects as their hearts in creating a healthy relationship and marriage seems thoroughly sensible advice.

Most critics of this letter hold rather different views on its meaning; the early moderns like Ricardo Quintana find Swift "belligerently anti-romantic," where his realistic view of marriage seems a further example of his remaining forever "anesthetized to so much that is valid in normal emotional experience" (*Mind and Art of Jonathan Swift* 355–56). Irvin Ehrenpreis at first concludes that the dean's essay suggests "that virtue itself has no gender," and one might celebrate his elevating men and women "to the status of intellectual creatures" (III.397). Unable, however, to set aside the harshness of Swift's comments on women and marriage in general, this more recent biographer decides the piece would better serve a spinster intent on educating herself about male society than a young woman who has married a well-educated, cultured gentleman (III.401).

Even though his emphasis on female faults is aggravating, the positive connections arising from his advice—"he will have regard for your judgment and opinion" and "I am ignorant of any one quality that is amiable in a man, which is not equally so in a woman"—add somewhat to the credibility of his statements on the conduct of marriage. By implication, one would have to be married an extended period in order to experience all the various points Swift raises, which suggests he writes not only for the new bride but a woman who has had a long-standing marriage. The fact that a woman might manage a relationship with a reasonable man over a longer period of time suggests Swift's basic belief in the status of current marriages and for that matter in the existence of reasonable women.

# "Letter to a Young Gentleman, Lately Entered into Holy Orders, A"

This letter was first printed in Dublin in 1720 with the title "A Letter from a Lay-Patron to a Gentleman Designing for Holy Orders." Later that year, it was published in London with the title by which it is now known. Whereas the earlier title suggests that the recipient is only contemplating becoming a clergyman, the latter name indicates that he has already made his decision. In his edition of Swift's prose, Herbert Davis notes that the letter was probably never intended for any specific recipient but was instead designed to "answer the general need of the young clergy" for advice on how to succeed (9.xxii–xxiv). Swift signed it anonymously as "Your Friend and Affectionate Servant"—posing as a member of the laity rather than offering his advice as dean of St. Patrick's.

## SYNOPSIS

Swift begins by saying that even though the "young gentleman" has ignored his advice and proceeded

in becoming a priest (despite mankind's current attitude toward the church), he will provide a few thoughts "upon this new Condition of Life." It would have been far better to have attended the university for several more years, since rushing into the ministry leaves little time for improving one's mind and adequately furnishing one's library. The young man should have studied the English language more extensively. Neglecting it "is one of the most general Defects among the Scholars of this Kingdom, who seem to have not the least Conception of a Stile." It simply means putting "proper words in proper places," but a full explanation would require more space than this letter allows.

The letter provides advice on the proper goals of preaching. Swift writes that striving to move the "Passions" is very popular among "Preachers and Hearers of the *Fanatick* or *Enthusiastick* Strain" nowadays, but this practice is not at all helpful in "directing Christian Men in the Conduct of their Lives." The best course is to use this strategy sparingly and cautiously, if at all. If you have compelling arguments, present "them in as moving a Manner as the Nature of the Subject will properly admit," but never let "the pathetick Part swallow up the rational." There are "two principal Branches of Preaching": explaining to people what their duty is, and then convincing them that what you have said is true. The "Topicks" in each case come from "*Scripture* and *Reason*," respectively. Skilled preachers can help even the most ignorant person understand both.

Swift also offers advice on sermon delivery: Preachers, he insists, should not read their sermons. It is far better to write the sermon out in large print with ample margins, go over it several times "on *Sunday* morning," and deliver it in a way that makes the hearers believe it was memorized. Most clergymen write so small that they end up stammering and stuttering in front of their congregations, "at a Loss in reading [their] own Compositions." It is best to avoid striving for wit in your sermons. For one thing, Swift writes, it is very likely that you do not possess any. For another, too many clergymen have made themselves to look "ridiculous by attempting" to display it. It is best to use quotations sparingly, and to avoid filling sermons with many obscure philosophical terms.

The letter also includes instructions on how to prepare for preaching. Swift advises the gentleman to read what the heathen philosophers actually wrote before presuming to "disparage" them in his sermons. While it is true that their "System of Morality" is far inferior to that of the Scriptures, the worst than can be said of them is that "they were ignorant of certain Facts which happened long after their Death." Swift advises him to "make their Works a considerable part of [his] Study," along with "the principal Orators and Historians, and perhaps a few of the Poets." Doing so will go a long way to enhancing his intellect, imagination, and judgment.

The letter also stresses the importance of the young gentleman's occupation. Currently, Swift asserts, the English people are more morally corrupt than anyone else in the world. This is the result of many factors, but mainly "the perpetual bandying of *Factions* among us for Thirty Years past." Several centuries prior to the Reformation, learning was "more equally divided between the *English* Clergy and Laity" than it is today. With today's corrupt education system, it is difficult to find even one "Young Person of Quality with the least Tincture of Knowledge," while the clergy are more educated and yet more "scurvily treated" than ever before.

## COMMENTARY

The essay offers advice to young clergymen on one of their most important duties—writing and delivering sermons to their parishioners. Herbert Davis and David Nokes both believe Swift had two goals in mind: practical suggestions on becoming an effective clergyman and his ever-present interest in the use of the English language. Appropriate style, symmetry, and simplicity are all characteristics of an effective writer and speaker, especially one whose profession demands understanding often from the poor and illiterate. Employing the persona of a well-educated and cultured layman—"person of quality," Swift could write to his fellow clergymen, as well as their influential bishops, without giving offense or presuming bias. Acknowledging his surprise that anyone might enter a profession lacking completely in material reward, he argues

for increased formal education as the first method of achieving success in the church. If a young man persists in this field, practicing one's craft in rural areas and with a friend and critic present seems the best approach.

Irvin Ehrenpreis tracks the origins of Swift's views of effective preaching back to Restoration churchmen (who opposed the Puritans) or to the Latitudinarians (who believed in free thought and more liberal church practices) (*Swift* III.83). Avoiding witty turns of phrase or elegant vocabulary while showing energy and enthusiasm for the views presented form the best preaching method. Swift, however, never departs from his main theme—more study of the English language. His problem with contemporary clergy centers on their inadequate education, including the quality of their preparation or curriculum. The current of anti-intellectualism which runs through this essay seems in contradiction with his encouraging better education, but he subtly argues for a clergyman who grasps the power of language to sway people's beliefs and who refrains from using obscure language or depending on other linguistic abuses. Instead, the effective clergyman relies on straightforward, plain language and a tenacity of purpose. What most readers find most curious about this essay is its complete lack of irony. Since Swift's use of ironic reasoning, reference to classical learning, and sense of humor and wit have emerged as typical characteristics in his writing, one expects to find his persona using these implements here. To find him criticizing the dependence on these tools by a clergyman strikes one as surprising—so much so that, as David Nokes argues, Swift must have felt thoroughly unsuitable as an Anglican preacher (*Hypocrite Reversed* 279). Another point of view is possible here: He may have felt unworthy of the important task of directing men and women in the conduct of their lives, yet he took his own advice quite seriously by all reports, in telling people what their duty was and then attempting "to convince them that it is so." Reading classical writers would improve the quality of the young clergyman's sentences and make him less tedious, while reliance on common sense would guide his parishioners far better than explaining the mysteries of faith. A constant effort toward balancing his duty with the needs of his audience suggests how Swift managed his own religious profession in Ireland and avoided "English linguistic imperialism."

# "Letter to the Archbishop of Dublin, Concerning the Weavers, A"

Though this essay was not printed until after Swift's death, the dean wrote it in the early months of 1729 while in Dublin, before leaving the city for his usual summer retreat. His theme focuses on the damage done to Ireland's most famous trade, weaving, the economic injury created through the English absentee landlords, the foolishness of the Anglo-Irish and Irish who imported foreign cloth and other articles into Ireland, and the ruination of an already weak agricultural environment. Though little can be done at this point to rectify what have been decades of misuse and ignorance, Swift, whose spirit of reformation never seems diminished, suggests his readers purchase and wear their national cloth (wool or linen), support their own economy by purchasing goods made in Ireland, and review agricultural practices. His call seems as fresh and recognizable today, nearly 300 years later, when various economists and social critics remind Americans, who have the benefit of goods imported in a thriving global economy, to buy products made in America as an act of patriotism and good economic practice.

A distinct difference exists, however. Ireland was in national crisis—"emigration to America, grain shortages, the lack of silver money"—and the leading members of the government and the church were using their names and talents to assist those suffering from famine and poverty. Though Archbishop William KING was ill and would die shortly, the Lord Lieutenant, John CARTERET, raised money in support of those starving, and Swift did his best, writing four well-conceived essays which he intended to publish as a way of motivating the public and the government to action. None of the essays was published during this time because, according to Irvin Ehrenpreis, "they were either too offensive or not finished enough" (*Swift* III.610). What might be closer to the truth is also hinted at, since Swift felt himself a failure, unable to correct problems he had long before recognized but was powerless to alter or improve. His frustration maintains a particularly sharp edge when he refers to the people in the Dublin streets as "those animals which come in my way with two legs and human faces, clad, and erect, be of the same species . . . like them in England . . . but differing in their notion, natures and intellectuals more than any two kinds of brutes in a forest."

His efforts toward building the weavers' sense of economic self-sufficiency remained active throughout the period of the late 1720s and 1730s. Ireland's domestic industry, including its agricultural economy, were in a deplorable state, and if the Irish could be made to understand the virtue of refusing the importation of finished cloth, then possibly a correction could occur in the balance of trade. Groups of weavers and members of the archbishop's immediate staff urged Swift to do what he could in support of woolen manufacturers. A related essay, "Observations Occasioned by Reading a Paper, Entitled 'The Case of the Woollen Manufacturers, Etc.'" (1733), addresses the corporation of weavers once again, and his approach remains the same as the earlier piece. The weavers should petition Parliament for relief, and in the "Letter to the Archbishop" he urges the members of the House to "wear no cloaths but such as are made of Irish growth or of Irish manufacture, nor will they permit their wives or children to wear any other." As always in these Irish tracts, the economic or political subject at hand must be balanced against the moral lesson where examples of pride, vanity, and dishonesty receive regular attention in their damage to the human spirit. Women also receive a troubling degree of Swift's anger, and some argue, prejudice, as he punishes what he refers to as their vanity and luxury, while he condemns the rules of modern education that have led them to despise their own country's products. Warming to his attack, he suggests each husband is "nourishing a poisonous, devouring serpent in his bosom with all the mischief but none of its wisdom."

His satire focuses on men's cultural traditions which have shaped women's response to these issues, and although the language remains harsh, he avoids the typical forms of antifeminist satire.

## "Letter to the King at Arms from a Reputed Esquire, One of the Subscribers to the Bank, A"

This letter forms part of a miscellaneous collection of essays, printed in Dublin by Thomas Hume, concerning the proposal to establish an Irish national bank. Though not signed by Swift, it has always been considered his work and certainly captures his well-known ridicule of this proposal. Dated November 18, 1721, the essay assumes the tone of one of the bank's subscribers who complains that a suggestion has been made that diminishes him. Skewering his pretensions at wealth and position, Swift reveals this "subscriber" for the fool that he is, and does so while implying the bank will make fools of anyone who considers it a legitimate operation. He believed that the Irish Parliament would once again revert to English pressure and approve the bank, but in this he was quite mistaken. The collapse of the South Sea Bubble in 1720 in England actually encouraged the proposal of a national bank with the hope it would improve credit and moderate price fluctuations in the economy. But once again, threats of corruption and irregular stock trading damaged its chances for passage.

Establishing a national bank had begun with the granting of a royal charter on July 27, 1721, and Lord Lieutenant Charles GRAFTON officially presented the document for parliamentary approval on September 12, 1721, at Dublin. These formal efforts were preceded by a vigorous pamphlet campaign opposing the bank, which Swift had opened in May 1720 with "A PROPOSAL FOR THE UNIVERSAL USE OF IRISH MANUFACTURE." When he wrote to Archbishop KING on September 28, 1721, Swift was afraid King would face the supporters of the bank alone, but a sufficient number of M.P.'s were

of like mind and voted the whole proposal down. Ireland would wait another 10 years before reviving such plans again.

## "Letter to the Reverend Dr. Sheridan, A"

Poem by Swift; first published 1735, written 1718. Along with other poems such as "MARY THE COOK-MAID'S LETTER TO DR. SHERIDAN" and "SHERIDAN, A GOOSE," it is one of a number of items in an extended series of trifles circulated among Swift, Dr. Thomas SHERIDAN, Rev. Patrick DELANY, Rev. Daniel JACKSON, and the ROCHFORT brothers. Each couplet in this poem rhymes on three syllables, and Swift concludes by inviting Sheridan to "return" verses of equal difficulty.

## "Letter to the Right Worshipful the Mayor, Aldermen Sheriffs, and Common Council of the City of Cork, A"

The correspondence of certain writers has always held much fascination for readers, and Swift's letters have long been considered the best examples of the genre. David Woolley reports that from 1690 to 1740, more than 230 of Swift's contemporaries decided on preserving the dean's letters, and he kept many of theirs, though not with the assidity of his friend Alexander POPE, who collected and published their joint correspondence. Swift had from the first believed in the value of preserving the letters of eminent figures in England and Ireland, and their correspondence contains the heart of many of his political and religious views. Certain other letters, such as the "Letter to the Mayor of Cork," have none of the laboriousness of those from his political friends, and his familiar letters to Stella (Esther JOHNSON) will always remain examples of his highly charged emotional and intellectual capacity, while offering us a glimpse of his intimate life.

George FAULKNER published this letter in the *Works* (1762) as a miscellaneous piece connected with Swift's public life in Ireland and his continuing preoccupation with his country's economic condition. Though dated August 15, 1737, the origins of this piece begin earlier with a note from his friend John Boyle, fifth earl of ORRERY, dated March 15, 1737, in which the nobleman informs Swift that he is "the idol of the Court of Alderman: they have sent you your freedom; the most learned of them having read a dreadful account in *Littleton's Dictionary* of Pandora's gold box." As a mark of their approbation, the Cork city council had decided to honor Swift for his frequent defense of Ireland's national interests. Typically, the honoree would receive a gift and a proclamation in the form of a certificate making him the equivalent of its chief citizen for the day. Instead, in a haphazard and embarrassing manner, a silver box, not gold, was delivered to Swift without any of the usual formalities, and the box had no inscription nor was it engraved properly.

The dean writes to the mayor explaining his generally poor health, but his undiminished capacity for recognizing when an event or ceremony has been poorly managed: "A private man, and a perfect stranger, without power or grandeur, may justly expect to find the motives assigned in the instrument of his freedom, on what account is he distinguished." Maintaining a polite but severe tone, Swift continues with a description of the box with "not so much as my name upon it, or any one syllable to show it was a present from your city." Though the letter is remarkable for its combination of resigned disappointment and bristling language, it does not quite match one of the most famous letters in literary history: the January 20, 1775, note written by Samuel Johnson to James Macpherson, the poet of Ossian. Johnson had detected, he felt, fraudulent behavior and materials in Macpherson, the man and his work, and was willing to challenge him in what became a quite public quarrel. Swift simply wants to be shown proper respect; if an organization intends to celebrate one of their native sons for services performed, then they should do it well and properly. Even after the mayor of Cork wrote him a letter of apology and had the box engraved and the proclamation written out, Swift never seemed very impressed with the gift, leaving it in his will to a friend for storing his worst tobacco.

# "Letter to the Writer of the Occasional Paper, A"

Published by Deane SWIFT in 1765, Swift's essay had been started in London in 1727 during his last visit there from April to September but left unfinished. In a sense this piece had been commissioned by Henry BOLINGBROKE, who had begun an opposition paper, *The Craftsman*, the year before with the help of a coalition of "patriots" who concentrated on attacking the Robert WALPOLE ministry. Many of the most able literary figures of the period wrote against Walpole, and Swift's willingness to immerse himself in politics again suggests how disturbed he was with the unsympathetic and unresponsive serving minister. His satire of Walpole in GULLIVER'S TRAVELS had already angered the minister, but the prince and princess of Wales had told Swift in private meetings that they enjoyed the work.

Swift wrote to the writer of the Occasional Paper, a smaller, more concise version of *The Craftsman*, urging the necessity of effective, cogent writing. Effective pamphlet writers, meaning those who agree with the antiministerial coterie, do not resort to the weapons used by the worst of the GRUB STREET newsmongers who depend on "scurrility, slander, and Billingsgate," and in doing so prove themselves no better than the government officials they supposedly defend. Deciding to attack an official's family is another tactic to which an ethical writer does not resort: "allowing this heap of slander to be truth, and applied to the proper person; what is to be the consequence?"

When Swift learned that GEORGE I had died on June 15, 1727, it seemed for a moment that his dreams (at least his ideological issues) might be realized, both his public and private ones. The opposition party and their writers would be returned to power and its immediate supporters "made easy." From his contacts at court, he believed the new king would discard Walpole, but this was not to be, as GEORGE II felt he needed this man, whom he began to respect, and rather soon found he liked and trusted. Swift, as one critic bluntly states, had been backing the wrong horse. Now, he would neither associate himself with a government which could modestly relieve Ireland's pains nor one that might rescue him from his own personal purgatory.

# "Libel on the Reverend Dr. Delany and His Excellency John, Lord Carteret, A"

Poem by Swift; first published 1730, written the same year. This was Swift's second response (after "AN EPISTLE UPON AN EPISTLE") to Rev. Patrick DELANY's "Epistle to Lord Carteret." Swift's argument in this poem is that "servility to politicians wins incomparably more patronage than talent does" (Ehrenpreis III.648). He complains that by seeking even more preferment from Carteret, Delany risks disappointing his patron and losing more than he can gain. As a broad satire against what Joshua ALLEN described as "the King, the Queen, and the government," this poem had scandalous results. Two newsboys were arrested for crying the poem in the streets, and Allen himself attempted to have Swift prosecuted for writing it (see "ON THE IRISH CLUB" and "TRAULUS").

# "Life and Genuine Character of Dr. Swift, The"

Poem by Swift; first published 1733. In his biography of Swift, Irvin Ehrenpreis argues that Swift wrote the poem between 1731 and 1733 as a less inflammatory version of "VERSES ON THE DEATH OF DR. SWIFT" (III.708–09). Like the earlier "Verses," "The Life and Genuine Character" is a mock-auto-biography based on Maxim XCIX from the first edition of François La Rouchefoucauld's *Reflexions ou Sentences et Maximes Morales* (1665). Swift translates the maxim differently in each poem. In this case, he renders it as " 'Whenever fortune sends / Disasters, to our dearest friends, / Although, we outwardly may grieve, / We oft, are laughing in our sleeve' " (7–10). Despite Swift's repeated disavowals of the poem, many of his friends recognized it immediately as his own. Laetitia PILKINGTON, for example, "told Swift to his face" that the poem "was an unsuccessful attempt at disguised self-parody" (Rogers, *Poems* 844). The verses were published with a prefatory letter ostensibly written by "L. M."— "Little Matthew" PILKINGTON—through whom Swift had arranged for the poem to be published. In the letter dated April 1, 1733 (April Fool's Day, not coincidentally), L. M. claims to have received the verses by accident and explains that they are the result of "the Dean" having told some friends "he could guess the discourse of the world concerning his character after his death."

The poem is staged as a debate between two persons, one who speaks well of Swift and a critic who points out (as Ehrenpreis notes in his biography) "the main faults charged against Swift since his death," portraying him as a spiteful, faithless misanthrope who "would have truckled to the men in power if he had received better preferments" (III.711). The advocate makes the stronger argument and has the last word, arguing that Swift's writings were intended to "please" and "reform mankind" (197). This poem is usually discussed in relation to "Verses on the Death of Dr. Swift" as what Louise K. Barnett calls one of Swift's two "greatest poems of fictive self-portraiture" concerned with reputation and how death affects it (76). In what Barnett describes as "the familiar ritual of Swiftian exorcism," Swift presents "The Life" as "a disarming apologia within the fictive world of his poem" as a way of imposing "aesthetic order" on the troublesome prospect of being vilified after his death (81).

# "Lines from 'Cadenus and Vanessa'"

A set of two poems by Swift; first published 1814, written 1720. Swift included the first poem in a letter written in July of that year to Esther VANHOMRIGH. The second was part of a separate letter sent to her in August. Swift introduces the first poem ("Nymph, would you learn the only art") as having been sent by a "Friend." These verses assert that only a fool would reject a nymph as virtuous and sensible as Vanessa. In the second poem, the speaker rejects "dainties" in favor of "peace" and "the highest mount in Wales." See "CADENUS AND VANESSA."

# "Louisa to Strephon"

See "RIDDLES."

# "Love Song in the Modern Taste, A"

Poem by Swift; first published 1733 as "A Song, by Dr. Swift" in the *Gentleman's Magazine*; probably written the same year. The poem is a series of well-known poetic clichés brought together in a satire of contemporary love songs. Nora Crow Jaffe finds that it "recalls passages from [Alexander] POPE where he uses and parodies the pastoral at the same time" (*The Poet Swift* 53).

# "Mad Mullinix and Timothy"

Poem by Swift; first published 1728, written the same year. One of several satires Swift wrote against Richard TIGHE. Along with "TIM AND THE FABLES," it first appeared in the *INTELLIGENCER* number 8. The poem dramatizes a conversation between Tighe ("Timothy") and a beggar named

Molyneux ("Mullinix"), "a half-crazed beggar who went round Dublin spouting TORY sentiments" (Rogers, *Poems* 776). See also "TOM MULLINEX AND DICK."

# "Mary the Cook-Maid's Letter to Dr. Sheridan"

Poem by Swift; first published 1732, written 1718. Along with other poems such as "TO THOMAS SHERIDAN" and "SHERIDAN, A GOOSE," it is one of a number of items in an extended series of trifles circulated among Swift, Dr. Thomas SHERIDAN, Rev. Patrick DELANY, Rev. Daniel JACKSON, and the ROCHFORT brothers. Like his earlier "MRS. HARRIS'S PETITION," this poem is written in the voice of a woman Swift knew. "Mary" is based on Swift's cook, who was, according to Delany "of a large size, and very robust constitution" (quoted in Rogers, *Poems* 680). Nora Crow Jaffe notes that in this poem "Swift portrays Mary as a pious old woman scandalized by Sheridan's insults to her master"—a technique that enables Swift to "chastise Sheridan indirectly for his real abuses of raillery" (*The Poet Swift* 125–126).

# "Mechanical Operation of the Spirit"

See "DISCOURSE CONCERNING THE MECHANICAL OPERATION OF THE SPIRIT IN A LETTER TO A FRIEND: A FRAGMENT, A."

# "Meditation upon a Broomstick, A"

Subtitled "According to the Style and Manner of the Honourable Robert Boyle's *Meditations*," this essay was printed in 1710 by Edmund Curll. The circumstances surrounding its composition are particularly interesting, since Swift wrote it as a hoax in the hopes of fooling Lady Elizabeth BERKELEY, the wife of Charles, the earl of BERKELEY (though David Woolley believes the real person concerned is Lady Betty GERMAIN, their daughter, and ultimately a friend of Swift's for more than 30 years). While visiting their castle in Gloucestershire (England) in August of 1704, Swift supposedly wrote this parody as a way of correcting Lady Betty's fascination with the natural philosopher and Fellow of the Royal Society, Robert BOYLE—whose writings, particularly *Occasional Reflections upon Several Subjects* (1665)—Swift found silly. Various writers report Swift patiently reading this spoof to the countess of Berkeley as if it were a true Boyle "Meditation."

"Surely mortal man is a broomstick" remains an often quoted line from the essay since it captures both Swift's sense of irony and his predilection to direct whimsy at an innocent friend. It also diminishes the Puritan Boyle, one of the "Moderns," and all the writers this chemist praised. He anticipates a later discussion in Part 2 of GULLIVER'S TRAVELS where the King of Brobdingnag finds the proud Gulliver so "groveling an insect" for suggesting the use of gunpowder, and then Gulliver bemoans the fact that these beings (unlike English intellectuals) cannot be taught to think in abstractions and understand transcendental thought.

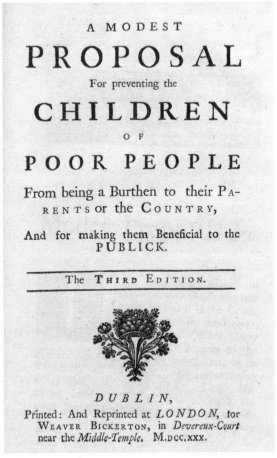

Title page of "A Modest Proposal," third edition, 1730
*(Courtesy of University of Pennsylvania Libraries)*

## "Modest Proposal, A"

Written in September 1729 and first published in Dublin the same year, "A Modest Proposal" has become the most famous short satire in English literature. Although GULLIVER'S TRAVELS remains Swift's best-known extended satiric work, this essay combines sustained irony and parody to devastating effect in less than 2,000 words. As a political document, it has no parallel, combining Swift's concerns for Ireland's recurrent famines, extensive poverty, and corrupt economy, and his frustration with the English landlords and their remarkable neglect of their tenants.

### SYNOPSIS

Overrun with beggars, the streets of Dublin present an awful scene. Many of the vagrants are mothers with multiple children who spend their lives doing nothing besides seeking sustenance for their offspring. To compound the problem, most of the children grow up to be thieves or traitors, and some even sell themselves into slavery. Undoubtedly, he who could devise a plan to turn these children into contributing members of society would deserve the highest honors.

The scope of this writer's plan, however, is not limited to helping impoverished children. It would also yield great benefits for their parents. A child "*just dropt from its Dam*" can be nursed for a full year at a cost of no more than "two Shillings" (which its mother can easily obtain through begging). Once such children reached their first birthdays, the author's plan would enable them to help thousands instead of becoming even more of a burden to their starving parents. Enacting the plan will also cut down on "*voluntary Abortions*" and help to prevent women from "*murdering their Bastard Children.*"

Based on the author's computations, there are about 120,000 poor children born each year for the Irish to deal with (once you subtract those who die for various reasons). He has learned from "a very knowing *American*" acquaintance in London that at one year old, a "well-nursed" healthy child is "a most delicious, nourishing, and wholesome Food"— no matter how it is cooked. Based on this information, his proposal is that (1) Ireland should "reserve" 20,000 of the poor children born each year for breeding, and (2) it should sell the remaining 100,000 to "*Persons of Quality and Fortune*" throughout the kingdom to be prepared and eaten at the family table. These children will make excellent fare for entertaining and can (when properly salted) even be served as leftovers "in *Winter.*"

This dish will quickly become a delicacy, "very *proper for Landlords*; who, as they have already devoured most of the Parents, seem to have the best Title to the Children." Since Roman Catholics eat so much fish during Lent, and fish is known to be a "*prolifick Dyet*," the market will be flooded with "*Popish*" infants nine months after. This suggests yet another benefit of the author's program, which will cut down on the number of "*Papists*" in Ireland. The costs of this proposal are minimal. No gentleman will refuse to pay the "two Shillings *per Annum*" needed to yield "*the Carcase of a good fat Child,*" and those who are "more thrifty" can even use the children's hides to make ladies' gloves and boots for the gentlemen.

A friend suggested to the author that he might refine his plan by adding that the lack of venison in Dublin could "be well supplied by the Bodies of young Lads and Maidens" between the ages of 12 and 14. The problem with this idea is that his American acquaintance has told him that by that age, children's flesh is "generally tough and lean"

and not very tasty. Nonetheless, plump young girls might be an exception, and using them for this purpose would certainly cut down on the number of them in Dublin who (despite their poverty) spend their days in playhouses wearing "foreign Fineries."

Some may object that the author's plan would do nothing to reduce the number of elderly beggars in Dublin. This group, however, is already dying so quickly that there is really no need to add any provisions for dealing with them. As for the "younger Labourers," they cannot find work and are starving to death almost as rapidly as their elders.

There are several distinct advantages to the author's proposal: First, "it would greatly lessen the *Number of Papists.*" This will be especially helpful since they are currently "the principal Breeders of the Nation" and its "most dangerous Enemies." Second, the plan would give impoverished tenants "something valuable of their own." Third, it would increase "the Nation's Stock" by £50,000 per year (besides adding a new dish to delight the palates of the kingdom's gentlemen). Fourth, the "constant Breeders" will earn eight shillings a year by selling their offspring and be freed from the burden of raising them beyond a year. Fifth, the proposal will cause a remarkable increase in business for the taverns. Sixth, it will "be a great Inducement to Marriage," make mothers more loving toward their children (because of the profits they can bring), and cause men to treat their wives more fondly during pregnancy. With fears of miscarriage—and the loss of future earnings—in mind, men would certainly refrain from beating and kicking their wives. There are numerous other advantages of the proposal but too many to "enumerate" in detail.

The only reasonable objection that might be raised against the proposal is that it would greatly reduce the number of people in the kingdom. This, in fact, is precisely what it is designed to do. The author has heard of other ideas for dealing with overpopulation and widespread poverty: taxing absentees and imports, putting aside petty quarrels, and such, but he wants to hear nothing more about them until there is some "Glimpse of Hope" that these plans might actually be put into practice. There is no danger that the Irish will "disoblige" England by implementing his proposal. The children's flesh is too tender for export, since its consistency could not stand being preserved for long periods with salt. (In an aside, the author admits that he "*could name a Country, which would be glad to eat up*" the "*whole Nation*" of Ireland—even without salt.)

As for nay-saying politicians who might be tempted to oppose his plan, the author invites them to ask the parents of current beggars whether or not they think "having been sold for food at a Year old" would have been preferable to the miserable lives their children now lead. To those who suspect him of having private profits in mind, the author asserts that the public good has been his only motive: His nine-year-old is too old to earn him anything, and his wife is too old to bear any more children.

## COMMENTARY

What strikes readers from Swift's time to now is the shocking proposal of the nameless projector who unites, in one personality, a cold rationality and a systematically inhuman response to the crisis. His failure to grasp the horror of his solutions suggests the distortion of the culture and the success of prevailing political and economic logic taken to its extreme. By explaining his scheme using arithmetic formulas and an annoying scientific detachment, the projector adopts a tone of superiority and snobbery, which aids in convincing his readers of the wisdom of the argument. Swift crafts this character effectively so the projector seems to compete with all other schemers for the prize for reasonableness and the eternal gratitude of his fellow citizens.

To cannibalize the children of the poor as a commercial venture would obviously by impossible for any culture that considers itself civilized, yet this "modest proposal" does encourage the reader to at least admit the logical extreme leading from England's conduct toward Ireland. The Modest Proposer's outrageous plan unfolds without apology or regret, implying that the efficiency and feasibility of the ideas must surely outweigh other considerations. The difference between the proposer and Swift remains quite distinct, as Swift implicitly urges the reader toward a more compassionate answer to this problem.

The persona of the speaker will remind readers of those social engineers or actuaries who calculate risks, life expectancies, and premiums based on endless lists of statistics and computations. The projector's cool use of figures and bestial imagery (casually referring, for example, to a "child dropped from its dam" and proposing that wives become breeders in some national program, as if we were visiting a national collective farm) becomes an unforgettable emblem of English indifference to Irish humanity and suffering. However, this analysis does not precisely answer the situation as presented: The speaker, whom we have already come to distrust and regard as crazy, is an Irishman, not an Englishman. Swift has little toleration for those Irish who submit to this pattern of brutalization and blindly follow the mad projector's scheme.

This occasional essay, parodying the well-recognized "projects" of many contemporary writers, reveals a straightforward design with clear grouping of paragraphs offering the proposal in a reasonable voice, which heightens the effect of the absolutely mad plan. The first half of the essay (or paragraphs 1–16) presents the scheme as a way of alleviating famine, reducing or eliminating abortion, and putting good scientific methods into practice. Arguing that little money can be made from selling "a boy or girl, before twelve years old" into slavery, Swift shows the merchants willingly engaging in whatever commodity may turn a profit. A later example accuses Americans of using cannibalism as an acceptable food source, which certainly suggests the degree to which Swift blamed the Irish for emigrating to America and depopulating Ireland. The last half of the proposal (which has two sections, containing paragraphs 17–28 and 29–33) continues to puncture dishonesty and complacency by appealing to readers' patriotism and love of his fellow citizens.

The proposer's success in turning the most shameful plan into a reasonable defense has much to do with the success of the essay, as the proposer answers the major objection of cruelty to his fellow man. Professing a complete sense of humanity, he envisions a method for ridding the society of the aged and the sick. Returning to his calculations, he poses the distinct advantages of his scheme, enumerating each while adding a sentence or two of clarification: "Fourthly, the constant breeders, besides the gain of eight shillings sterling per annum, by the sale of their children, will be rid of the charge of maintaining them after the first year." Having studied numerous pamphlet proposals and parliamentary debates over the years for the improvement of the Irish, Swift finally grew tired of their impracticality and general self-destructiveness, and created his own hellish projection—one meant to shock the reader by the force of his rhetoric.

The final five paragraphs heighten his tone of despair as he discounts all objections to his proposal—"let no man talk to me of other expedients." The debater's technique of denouncing all other arguments that might refute his own has the effect of sweeping aside what are the implied humane and compassionate solutions while embracing the inhuman expedients. Rising to his final peroration, the proposer announces his qualifications for making such projections and reiterates his most convincing arguments, while suggesting his annoyance that any reader might accuse him of seeking personal financial gain in realizing this proposal. A final sentence undercutting his character delivers the last stroke of irony in this cannibalistic world: "I have no children by which I can propose to get a single penny."

Whether one decides Swift wrote the essay because he was angry or in a fit of despair over Ireland's economic condition, the fact remains he blames both the English and Irish for the people's misery. Critics suggest the tone and essential theme recall the Old Testament prophet Jeremiah, who rebuked a corrupt people, but Swift complicates this voice with impersonations of a projector, a scientist, and a moralist. As with all of his strongly ironic essays, there is a clear difference between the voices of the proposer and the author, so the projector's political and economic views secure the most commanding presence while nearly muting the author's call for moral understanding. In addition to the "Proposal," numerous other writings reflect Swift's concern with what he saw as England's oppression of the Irish. Some examples are "A SHORT VIEW OF THE STATE OF IRELAND" (often read as a preface to "A Modest Proposal"), "The STORY OF AN INJURED LADY," *The DRAPIER'S LETTERS,* and the episodes involving Laputa in Part 3 of *Gulliver's Travels.*

## FURTHER READING

Fox, Christopher, ed. *The Cambridge Companion to Jonathan Swift.* Cambridge and New York: Cambridge University Press, 2003.

Fox, Christopher, and Brenda Tooley, eds. *Walking Naboth's Vineyard: New Studies of Swift.* South Bend, Ind.: University of Notre Dame Press, 1995.

Flynn, Carol Houlihan. *The Body in Swift and Defoe.* Cambridge: Cambridge University Press, 1990.

Real, Hermann J. "Birth Weight in *A Modest Proposal,*" *Scriblerian* 35, no. 1–2 (2002–03): 106.

Richardson, John. "Swift, A Modest Proposal and Slavery," *Essays in Criticism* 51 (2001): 404–423.

Ross, Ian Campbell. " 'More To Avoid the Expence than the Shame': Infanticide in the Modest Proposer's Ireland," *Swift Studies* 1 (1986): 75–76.

Wittkowsky, George. "Swift's *Modest Proposal:* The Biography of an Early Georgian Pamphlet," *Journal of the History of Ideas* 4 (1943): 75–104.

# "Mr. Collins's Discourse of Free-Thinking, Put into Plain English, by Way of Abstract, for the Use of the Poor"

Swift published this essay in the last years of Anthony COLLINS's life, after the well-known deist and WHIG had published a *Discourse of Freethinking* (1713), a work Swift found unconvincing and a direct attack on Church of Ireland doctrine. The abstract delivers a severe reprimand against Collin's historical accuracy, an attack that had begun earlier with the EXAMINER, number 17 (November 30, 1710).

## SYNOPSIS

In a short preface, the "friend of the author" explains that the Whigs, having failed to regain their power, need to set down and publish their system of divinity. This would help to offset the oppressive TORY publications that strive to keep the public in awe by touting a supreme being in heaven and a monarch here on earth. There is no need for the Whigs to worry about retaliation from the Tories, since any ministry that allows so much to be said against itself and its "sovereign" will never act against those who speak out against its religion. The Tories have resigned themselves to the view that God is "able enough" of taking revenge against those who injure him. Having come across the following letter, the "friend of the author" decided that it was exactly the sort of declaration the Whigs needed to affirm and publish (at least in the form of an abstract). Infusing "these Doctrines" into the public, he knew, would contribute to the "continuance of the War, and the Restoration of the late Ministry." Publishing an abstract of Collins's discourse would also make it "impossible" for the "Jacobite, High-flying, Priest-ridden" Tory faction to "misrepresent" the Whigs.

The letter begins with a statement that it contains an "Apology for *Free Thinking*," written at the recipient's request. Everybody knows that priests are nothing but "crackt-brained Enthusiasts" and that the Bible (which supposedly outlines their religion) is "the most difficult Book in the World" to understand. As such, those who believe the Bible should "do so by force of his own *Free Thinking*, without any Guide or Instructor." In fact, a man cannot think at all if not freely. Even "the wickedest Thoughts" are harmless, "provided they be free." Freethinking is the best way to banish the devil (since to think freely of the devil is not to believe in him at all), and while priests insist that we should believe the Bible, freethinking says just the opposite "in many Particulars." It is all well and good for England to send Christian missionaries abroad, but it would really be better if heathen missionaries were also allowed to come and seek to convert the English. Encouraging such freethinking would certainly prolong the war, restore the late ministry and put an end to faction.

Another project that would be exceptionally helpful would be to allow freethinkers to disturb "our Priests." While the traditionalists are "prating in their Pulpit[s]," the freethinkers should have the liberty to come right in (even to St. Paul's) and seek to convert as many in the congregation as would listen. After all, Christ commanded us to be freethinkers when He said to search the Scriptures "and take heed what and whom we hear; by which

he plainly warns us, not to believe our Bishops and Clergy" who are clearly "mortal Enemies to Christ, and ought not to be believ'd."

With so many different religions and scriptures out there to choose from, it is impossible to know which one is right without freethinking. The priests themselves disagree about all the various copies and readings of the Bible, and even about what it means. They argue about the nature of the Trinity, the resurrection of the dead, and the "Eternity of Hell-Torments." Since there is "no end of disputing among Priests," there should really "be no such Thing in the World as Priests, Teachers, or Guides, for instructing ignorant People in Religion." Instead, "every Man ought to *think freely* for himself." At present, however, the best course is to allow freethinkers to receive or reject—at their discretion—anything on which the priests disagree. For example, if priests debate the Trinity, freethinkers should have the freedom to "reject one, two, or the whole three *Persons*." Besides all of this, the many mutually contradictory Christian doctrines make it impossible *not* to be a freethinker and conclude "that Christianity is all a Cheat." Freethinkers must try to force everyone else to think exactly as they do, and this means that free speaking and free writing are inseparable from freethinking. No man can rightly call himself a freethinker if he fails to differ from "the received Doctrines of Religion." Anytime someone "falls in, though by perfect Chance, with what is generally believed, he is in that Point a confined and limited Thinker."

The priests who promote these doctrines habitually label anyone with more wit than they as an atheist. The various books they write against atheism and heresies, however, do more to promote freethinking than to discourage it. In other words, their conduct at every turn leaves the public with no choice but to think freely and reject Christianity altogether. Even the best-known priests (such as St. Jerome, Eusebius, "and several others") all engaged in "arrant Forgery and Corruption," since when they "translated the Works" of freethinkers they called heretics, they failed to include all of their own "Heresies or *Free-thinkings*."

There are a number of possible objections to this apology for freethinking, including the notion that most people are no more capable of thinking than they are of flying. In truth, however, if someone incapable of thinking freely "freely thinks that he cannot think freely," he should certainly not "*think freely,* unless he *thinks* fit." Another objection is that widespread freethinking will result in "endless Divisions in Opinion" and cause utter chaos. This disorder would certainly be no worse than that created by the priests, and "difference of Opinion, especially in Matters of great Moment, breeds no Confusion at all." Others may object that freethinkers "will *think* themselves into *Atheism.*" Even so, certain divines have argued that atheism is no worse than "Superstition and Enthusiasm." Some argue that people should rely upon priests just as they do upon lawyers and physicians "because it is their Faculty." This makes sense in that men who are not lawyers are not allowed to plead their own cases, but anyone can "be his own Quack if he pleases," and any place that lacks lawyers, doctors, and priests would certainly be a *"Paradise."*

Others may object that public officials need to promote "false Speculations" to keep the populace under control. The truth is "that Zeal for imposing Speculations, whether true or false . . . has done more hurt than it is possible for Religion to do good." It has saddled the public with the giant financial burden of maintaining priests, and it has shown that imposing faith upon people consistently reduces their morality. This clearly shows that a perfectly "moral Man must be a perfect Atheist." Finally, "it is objected that *Free-thinkers*" epitomize mankind's infamy and wickedness. The freethinkers, however, level the same charge at "Priests and other Believers." In reality, those of "all Sects are equally good and bad; for no Religion whatsoever contributes in the least to mend Mens Lives." Freethinkers actually have more understanding than religious individuals, and they are "the most virtuous Persons in the World." There are numerous examples throughout history to prove that this is true: Socrates, Plato, Epicurus, Plutarch, Varro ("the most Learned among the *Romans*"), Cato, Cicero, and Seneca were all freethinkers, and all men of remarkable virtue. Even biblical figures such as Solomon and the Old Testament prophets (including Isaiah, Ezekiel, Amos, and Jeremiah)

were really freethinkers, and if Solomon were alive today all that would prevent the priests from calling him an atheist would be "his Building of Churches." Other historical examples of virtuous freethinkers include Josephus, Origen, Minutius Felix, and Synesius. England has also had its share of respected freethinkers: Sir Francis Bacon affirmed that "whatever has the least Relation to Religion, is particularly liable to Suspicion." Thomas Hobbes was also devoted to freethinking ("except in his *High-Church* Politicks"). The head of all English freethinkers, however, is Archbishop John Tillotson, whose "virtue is indisputable" mainly because he has been called an atheist and has been accused of causing "several others to turn Atheists" and "ridicule the Priesthood and Religion."

The letter ends with the author affirming that he has done what the recipient asked, and granting permission to publish the letter. In a short epilogue, the "friend" (who turned the letter into an abstract and arranged for its publication) assures readers that he has done his best to provide a faithful abstract of Collins's original letter. He also reminds readers that *"the Author"* has never specifically declared himself an atheist—he has only stated *"that Atheism is the most perfect degree of Free-thinking; and leaves the Reader to form the Conclusion."*

## COMMENTARY

Swift criticized Gilbert BURNET and Collins in this paper as bad writers and historians, but some scholars believe he did not take their positions seriously, suggesting the whole matter is portrayed as ludicrous. Actually, Swift employs a method that takes Collins and deistic logic as a palpable threat to the order and effectiveness of the church, and his ironic language reduces Collins's arguments to nonsense. Characterizing Collins and his likeminded supporters as absurd has the beneficial effect of diluting the dignity and seriousness of their arguments. Swift understood the necessity of appearing to judge these ideas with an opposite point of view, and in effect his method connects with the psyche of his reader. If the reader believes the arguments as Swift has restated them, then the entire Collins argument may collapse of its own accord. "Crafty designing men, that they might keep the world in awe, have, in their several forms of government, placed a supream [sic] power on earth to keep human kind in fear of being hanged . . . but the mystery is now revealed."

When Collins argues for a new interpretation of the Bible, one which permits us to decide privately what may be meant by particular biblical passages, he posits that deliverance from the burdens of sin is clearly available to mankind now. Anglican priests who may become influenced by deistic thinking will decide that the more complicated the testament the greater the need for free inquiry. Swift manages to make deists support the telling of lies as a pathway to the truth. If we focus not on a search for the logic in the dean's argument against the deists, but instead on the fallacies he reveals in their philosophy, then the essence of what he intends becomes clear: Treating deists as thinkers locked into their own absurdities seems an effective technique in Swift's hands.

Swift's attack on the deists has as much to do with his religious convictions as his political views, coinciding with the rising power of the Whigs, whom the retired Tory journalist had recently been confronting in London. Connecting the distortion and falsification of the deists with the Whigs seems a profitable line of attack. Deflecting any suggestion of a political agenda, Swift proceeds directly to similar themes that are easily found in his political essays. Complete freedom of speech, abuses of the Established Church, falsifying biblical Scripture, encouraging party dissension, and breeding chaos and heresy—these characteristics remain at the center of his political debates and reflect the destructiveness of the deist philosophy. The "Abstract" reveals inventiveness and his basic distrust of human nature, which alludes to his rejection of the Whig Junto.

# "Mr. Jason Hassard, a Woollen Draper in Dublin"

Poem by Swift; first published in 1746, written about 1720. Alluding to the Jason of ancient Greek myth—who recovered the golden fleece from a dragon—the poem suggests that this modern Jason has his own (unidentified) "watchful dragon" to tame. Like "An Excellent New Song on a Seditious Pamphlet," this poem may have been written in response to the uproar caused by the publication of Swift's "Proposal for the Universal Use of Irish Manufacture."

# "Mrs. Harris's Petition"

Poem by Swift; first published in unauthorized editions 1709–11, written in 1701 during his stay at Berkeley Castle. Having lost her entire savings (which she carried around with her at all times and was in the habit of counting frequently), Mrs. Harris recounts her futile efforts to recover her funds and asks the lord justices of Ireland for help. John Irwin Fischer has pointed out that "in both her loss and her subsequent frustration she embodies a paradox: not only are wordly goods transitory in themselves, but they perversely prove most ephemeral to those who value them most highly" (On Swift's Poetry 61).

David Nokes calls this famous poem the first of Swift's "many evocations of the muddled animation of below-stairs life" (Hypocrite Reversed 62). It is written in doggerel couplets, mimicking the voice and vocabulary of Frances Harris, waiting-maid to Lady Betty Germain. As Nora Crow Jaffe has pointed out, Swift had both an affinity and a talent for creating unique "voices" in his poems for various speakers—especially those of the lower class (see "The Grand Question Debated" for more information on Jaffe's discussion). In his 1758 Life of Swift, W. H. Dilworth cites this poem as an example of "low humour," but adds that it nonetheless "abounds with entertaining raillery, and strong characterizing strokes." Nineteenth-century physician and critic John Aikin insists that the poem is distinguished by its "loose measure," and is "scarcely to be called verse" (Critical Heritage 159, 268). The "loose measure" of Harris's speech throughout the poem gives it a frantic, digressive tone as she recounts all that occurred before the after she lost her purse and begs for help from the lords justices. Having given up hope of ever finding her lost fortune, she ends the "Petition" by requesting that the officials allow her to "have a share in next Sunday's collection."

## "My Lady's Lamentation and Complaint against the Dean"

Poem by Swift; first published in 1765, written in 1728. Probably the earliest of the poems Swift wrote during his three long visits to MARKET HILL, it is written in the voice of Lady Anne ACHESON. She complains about the treatment she receives as Swift's pupil, enduring insults on everything from her reading to her lanky build.

## "New-Year's-Gift for Bec, A"

Poem by Swift; first published in 1765, written in 1724 for Rebecca DINGLEY ("Bec"). Swift had spent Christmas with Dingley and Esther JOHNSON at Dr. Thomas SHERIDAN's house at QUILCA. The poem jokingly details all the cares Janus has sent to Dingley as a New Year's gift.

## "Occasioned by Sir William Temple's Late Illness and Recovery"

Poem by Swift; first published in 1789, written in 1693 during Swift's stay at MOOR PARK. As David Nokes has noted in his biography of Swift, "the poem is less about Temple's illness than Swift's dejection" at not having found preferment (26). In the first half of the ode, the muse chides the poet for neglecting to celebrate Temple's recovery from a serious illness. In the second half, the speaker accuses the muse of being "the cause of all [his] woes" since she has inspired him to seek fame—an

undertaking he now recognizes as "madness" (82, 147). Irvin Ehrenpreis calls the poem "an odd sort of dialogue" and links it with Abraham COWLEY's "The Complaint" and one of Temple's essays, *Of Poetry* (I.139). In *Swift's Poetic Worlds*, Louise K. Barnett cites the poem as evidence that Swift had become confident enough to "repudiate" the muse "as a delusion of the wayward feminine part of his nature" (55–56).

## "Ode to Dr. William Sancroft"

Poem by Swift; first published 1789, written about 1692 after William SANCROFT had been removed as "Late Lord Archbishop of Canterbury" (as the subtitle reads). The poem is incomplete. In a May 3, 1692, letter to his cousin Thomas SWIFT, Swift wrote that he "had an ode in hand these five months inscribed to . . . Dr Sancroft, a gentleman I admire at a degree more than I can express" (*Corr.* I.8). The poem praises "holy Sancroft" as a shining image of truth on earth. Irvin Ehrenpreis calls it "a large Pindaric ode" and the opening lines "Miltonic" (I.129–30). See also "ODE TO THE ATHENIAN SOCIETY," "ODE TO THE HONOURABLE SIR WILLIAM TEMPLE," and "ODE TO THE KING."

## "Ode to the Athenian Society"

Poem by Swift; first published in 1692 in the supplement to the *Athenian Gazette* (later *Athenian Mercury*), written 1691/92. It was Swift's first publication, and provides an unflattering response to Abraham COWLEY's ode "To the Royal Society." In *Swift as Nemesis*, Frank Boyle notes that it is "a poem praising the authors of the *Athenian Gazette* as if they were learned men comparable to the members of the Royal Society of London, but working toward different, even contrary ends." Boyle also contends that the "confused reputation this poem has had with critics" results from a failure to consider its implications as an answer to Cowley's poem, attacking the Modern attempt "to decontextualize knowledge—to make truth independent of history, tradition, and poetry" (83). See also "ODE TO DR. WILLIAM SANCROFT," "ODE TO THE HONOURABLE SIR WILLIAM TEMPLE," and "ODE TO THE KING." See also DRYDEN, John.

# "Ode to the Honourable Sir William Temple"

Poem by Swift; first published in 1745, written in 1692/93 (not in 1689, as the first printing suggests). David Nokes calls it Swift's "third and least successful ode" following the "ODE TO THE ATHENIAN SOCIETY" and "ODE TO THE KING" (*Hypocrite Reversed* 23). Like the other odes, it reflects the profound influence of Abraham COWLEY. Swift presents William TEMPLE as having brought lost virtue back "in one single breast" to a fallen land. More effective than "antique relics of the dead" and "the gleanings of philosophy," Temple's living example promises to set his contemporaries back on the path to virtue. "Learned, good, and great," Temple simultaneously typifies the virtues of Virgil, Epicurus, and Caesar as he works tirelessly to promote peace. After depicting Temple as one who exposes the deceitful tactics of guileful politicians, Swift briefly takes to task those at court who have stifled Temple's political progress. Their treachery is embodied in a single "serpent" that "still lurks in palaces and courts." Irvin Ehrenpreis finds this treatment of the villain unique in comparison to those in the other odes: "Swift seems so powerfully dazzled by his master's virtues that he merely glances at the enemy," focusing instead on his own "comparative unworthiness" (I.119). After asking whether or not he can believe that Temple was cast from the "same mould" as himself, Swift spends the rest of the poem contemplating his own lot as one who is roped "to the muse's galley." Ehrenpreis and Nokes both find hints of possible irony in the poem, but disagree on its significance. While Ehrenpreis

sees "some ironic squints at the [earlier] ode to the king" (*Swift* I.119), Nokes suggests that the exaggerated "hero-worship" of the ode to Temple renders its own "hyperbole" slightly ironic (*Hypocrite Reversed* 23).

# "Ode to the King"

Poem by Swift; first published in Samuel Fairbrother's *Miscellanies* (1735), written 1690–91. It is Swift's earliest extant poem and the first of his early odes imitating Pindar and Abraham COWLEY. Concerned throughout with distinguishing "goodness" from "greatness," the poem celebrates King WILLIAM III by contrasting him with JAMES II ("Bajazet") and LOUIS XIV ("that restless Tyrant") and by praising his victorious leadership during the Battle of the Boyne. It suggests that Williams's victory was good for Ireland ("glad Iërne"), despite opposition from the "giddy British" and "murmuring Scots."

# "Of Mean and Great Figures Made by Several Persons"

The "Figures" was first published in 1765 (first in London by Deane SWIFT and then in Dublin by George FAULKNER). In his edition of Swift's prose, Davis lists it among things Swift "jotted down for his own amusement" (5.x).

## SYNOPSIS

This short prose piece is divided into two sections. The first lists "those who have made great figures in some particular Action or Circumstance in their Lives." Of the 22 individuals listed, most are historical (such as Socrates, Alexander the Great, and Virgil) but several were Swift's contemporaries (including, for example, the earl of STRAFFORD and Robert HARLEY). Along with each name, Swift briefly describes the situation in which he believes that individual earned a good name for himself. For

Socrates, it was his conduct during "the whole last Day of his Life." For King CHARLES I ("the Martyr"), it was his handling of his trial and execution. The second, less flattering, section features 28 persons "who have made a mean contemptible Figure in some Action or Circumstance of their Life." This slightly longer list includes more English officials than the first, such as Oliver Cromwell (who "refused the Kingship out of Fear") and "King John" (who "gave up his Kingdom to the Pope").

### COMMENTARY

At various points in his career, Swift wrote pieces solely for his own amusement, though his social, political, religious, and personal views were essentially embedded in these prose works, too. Herbert Davis finds "a romantic fascination for the dramatic moment in the lives of heroes and villains" in this piece. As with certain other literary fascinations conceived by highly inventive and curious authors, this composition has no clearly defined thesis to lead the reader to a moment of clarity or insight. Instead, Swift has collected a group of entries, ones that remind the reader of a proposal for a biographical encyclopedia, and the operative concern is what makes these figures "great" and in what circumstance or action did their greatness become obvious. Yet he decides to follow this listing with one centered on a group of individuals whose actions display contemptible behavior, in which many of the same historical and literary figures show themselves undeserving of his respect.

The greatness of Cicero—exiled when his political enemy took power but then recalled by the people—symbolizes the qualities Swift held in esteem: powerful oratory, the vision of a statesman, and the intelligence and capacity as a successful man of letters. Near the end of the list, he strikes the note his readers would have expected: Swift praises Robert Harley, the earl of Oxford not only for physical and spiritual courage while under the assault of the assassin GUISCARD, but for his intellectual and moral strength while under impeachment, imprisonment, and trial for acts done, in Swift's mind, for the national interest. The list of despicable figures offers the weak and defeated Mark Antony, whose passion for a woman ends in his own destruction,

and then leaps nearly 1,800 years to criticize Cromwell, JAMES II, WILLIAM III, the duke of MARLBOROUGH, and CHARLES II. He suggests Queen ANNE, who refused him a bishop's post, was practiced at humiliating her own ambassadors. And he includes a curious anecdote concerning Charles I, whom Swift admired for doing his duty to the last, who gives a gift to his wife, Henrietta Maria, which injures her—all this to point out the king's gallantry. Swift's satire punctures such false displays of chivalry and pride, especially as the kingdom crumbles under dissension and strife.

# "On a Printer's Being Sent to Newgate"

Poem by Swift; first published in 1746, written in 1736. Its subject is George FAULKNER's imprisonment at Newgate for printing Swift's revision of Archbishop Josiah HORT's satiric "New Proposal for the Better Regulation and Improvement of Quadrille." The work contained a passage (probably by Swift rather than Hort) that Richard BETTESWORTH found personally offensive. Soon after the "Proposal" was printed, Bettesworth raised the matter in the Irish Parliament and initiated Faulkner's arrest. Faulkner was released after apologizing, but Edward WATERS was subsequently imprisoned for reprinting the work. Swift's poem is a bitter commentary on the affair, attributing it to the condition of living "in slavery to slaves." See also "ON NOISY TOM" and "A CHARACTER, PANEGYRIC, AND DESCRIPTION OF THE LEGION CLUB."

# "On a Very Old Glass"

Poem by Swift; first published 1746, written between 1728 and 1730 during one of Swift's visits with Sir Arthur and Lady Anne ACHESON at MARKET HILL. It records Swift's response to an epigram (concerning mortality) written on an old glass belonging to Sir Arthur.

# "On Brotherly Love"

This sermon was preached on December 1, 1717, at St. Patrick's Cathedral, and composed on November 29. Swift arranged for printing the piece in March 1754 by George Faulkner in Dublin and R. and J. Dodsley in London with an agreement between the two publishers. It was later reprinted in Glasgow as part of *The Sermons of the Reverend Dr. Jonathan Swift* in 1763 and 1776.

## SYNOPSIS

The preacher's thesis seems straightforward, arguing that peace and mutual love have been instruments of more good than all the statesmen and politicians in the world. Though papists have caused much trouble in former times, the Dissenters remain the main cause of all the hatred and animosity in the land. Too many people follow the voices of the Dissenters as sheep and their unthinking herd mentality harms others. The Established Church clergy do not provide a rock of support for the people because they do not insist on the duty due the church, and parishioners drift away toward more powerful voices. With the additional interference of politics among the common people, one finds flattery and artifice developing among them. Posing as an oppressed minority, the Dissenters plead for toleration but if shown such charity, refuse toleration to others. The response to such behavior seems obvious: Dissenters should not be tolerated. At the midpoint of the sermon, the preacher begins deconstructing the word moderation and determines that moderate behavior will only increase the power of the Dissenters, which will be used in further increasing the divisions among Protestants. Finally, the political implications of the use of language as manipulated by the Dissenters become in the preacher's passionate diatribe a serious warning call to his parish. Semantic confusion becomes another weapon the destroyers of the church and those politicians who embrace factionalism will employ in dismantling the society.

## COMMENTARY

Those who have analyzed this sermon quickly note its seeming innocence (especially the title), but admit its partisan content as a political document.

After reviewing the complicated structure of Christian charity, the preacher suggests that equal application of the idea to all men throughout society remains unacceptable. His bitter attack on the Dissenters and how such a term as *moderation* has been misused seem his intended targets. His traditional themes on the status of the Established Church, schism, toleration, and dissent remain paramount. Those who really intend to weaken the Anglican Church (and the state) as well deserve little charity or brotherly love, particularly since the church is established by law, and holds exclusive right, as he views it, and should not tolerate schismatics. As Swift says, "A man truly moderate is steady in the doctrine and discipline of the Church, but with a due Christian charity to all . . . as long as it is not abused, but never trusted with power." The moderate Tory who supports the Church of England, the lower clergy, and royal prerogative will preserve the nation. See its companion piece "On False Witness."

# "On Burning a Dull Poem"

Poem by Swift; first published in 1735, written in 1729. It describes the speaker's negative response to a poem so bad it could only have come from a brainless "ass's head."

# "On Censure"

Poem by Swift; first published in 1735, written in 1727. It contemplates the problem of jealous detractors and how best to deal with the lies they spread about those they envy. The narrator concludes that the best option is simply to let such individuals talk, since their words cannot alter the person being slandered.

# "On Cutting Down the Old Thorn at Market Hill"

Poem by Swift; first published in 1732, written in 1728. Centered on the imminent destruction of a diseased but "spacious thorn before the gate" of the ACHESON estate at MARKET HILL, it brings together techniques from a variety of literary genres in an effort to assign epic proportions to the tree's demise.

# "On Dan Jackson's Picture"

Poem by Swift; first published in 1745, written around 1718. One in a series of poems by Swift, Rev. Patrick DELANY, Dr. Thomas SHERIDAN, and George ROCHFORT making fun of Rev. Dan JACKSON's large nose. This poem was occasioned by a portrait silhouette of Jackson made by Lady Betty Rochfort. See also "TO MR. DELANEY," "DAN JACKSON'S REPLY," "ANOTHER REPLY BY THE DEAN," and "SHERIDAN'S SUBMISSION."

# "On Dreams"

Poem by Swift; first published in 1728, written about 1724. Subtitled "An Imitation of Petronius," it is based on one of T. Petronius Arbiter's poems in the *Satyricon*. It suggests that dreams are not useful as omens and do not merit serious interpretation. Rather, they are "mere productions of the brain" and result from the guilt immoral persons feel based on the acts that characterize their lives. Among others, tyrants, murderers, lawyers, and hangmen all provide examples of those who are plagued with nightmares that recall their evil deeds. In *Swift the Poet*, Nora Crow Jaffe discusses this poem as an example of Swift's ability to "exploit prosody in familiar ways, along with the best of his contemporaries." She points out that the first two lines of each stanza "describe the dreams of men [such as the lawyer] whose crimes the world exonerates, even exalts," while lines 3–4 "equate these men with those . . . the world reviles." Or, as Louise K. Barnett explains it, the only difference between the immoral individuals described in each couplet is that one has a "criminal, the other a respectable label" (*Swift's Poetic Worlds* 123).

With its repeated equation of high and low crimes, the poem can be read as Swift's indictment of English society for having established a category (debunked in each stanza of the poem) of socially acceptable crimes. As such, it has less to do with dreams and their functions than with Swift's frustration at the high levels of systematic corruption society had come to allow. One poignant example of that is what Swift viewed as the Robert WALPOLE ministry's unjust arrest and banishment of Francis ATTERBURY in 1722—all based on their determination to "find a plot" (19). It also suggests that unlike the instinct-driven Yahoos in Part 4 of *GULLIVER'S TRAVELS*, humans (such as the lawyer, the murderer, and others cited in the poem) cannot claim ignorance when it comes to the immorality of their actions. Even when they consciously rationalize or ignore the wrongs they regularly commit, their dreams remind them of the truth and affirm their culpability.

# "On Dr. Rundle"

Poem by Swift; first published in 1762, written 1735–36. It outlines Swift's displeasure at Thomas RUNDLE (an "Arian") having been appointed bishop of Derry in February 1735. Swift concludes that Rundle is really just as qualified as most other Irish bishops, and would be even if he were "heathen, Turk or Jew" (9). See also "An EPIGRAM."

# "On False Witness"

Herbert Davis links this sermon with two others, "ON BROTHERLY LOVE" and "UPON THE MARTYRDOM OF KING CHARLES I," since each one concerns a political topic arising out of the contentious nature of late 17th- and early 18th-century relationships between church and state. Based on "topical allusions and the nature of the contents," Louis Landa dates the composition of "On False Witness" sometime during the reign of King GEORGE I (*Prose Works* 9.133), 1714 to 1727. The sermon was first published in 1762 in Dublin by George FAULKNER.

## SYNOPSIS

Based on Exodus 20:16 (which forbids bearing "false Witness against thy Neighbour"), the sermon begins with the assertion that government officials must seek to prevent mischief in countries undergoing significant change. Even though no one likes an informer, it is vital—especially in the midst of such changes—for subjects to share information if it will help protect the monarch and the public good. Problems arise, however, when "parties are violently enflamed" as they are now and men begin to accuse their brethren falsely for the sake of personal gains.

The sermon is divided into three parts. The first explains "several Ways" a person can rightly "be called a False Witness" against his neighbor. The second sets down rules of conduct for protecting oneself "against the Malice and Cunning of false Accusers," and the third shows how it is each subject's duty "to bear faithful Witness" when "lawfully called" to do so by the authorities.

There are several situations in which a man deserves to be called a false witness. The first is when he accuses his neighbor of something "without the least Ground of Truth." Likewise, when someone mixes "Falshood and Truth together, or concealeth some Circumstances, which, if they were told, would destroy the Falshoods he uttereth." He is also a false witness if he accuses his neighbor of having said something evil, when in fact that neighbor was simply repeating something he had heard from someone else. The worst kind of false witness is the one who does "the Office of the Devil, by tempting" others "in Order to betray them." Another type is the one who "beareth Witness against his Neighbour" based solely on malice or on a desire for revenge, "from an old Grudge, or Hatred to his Person." Those who "make a Trade of being Informers in Hope of Favour and Reward" are false witnesses, along with those who bring their neighbor "into Trouble and Punishment" over matters that are of no consequence to the public. There is one last type of false witness, and that is the one who accuses his neighbor "out of Fear of Punishment" for something he himself has done.

When it comes to protecting oneself against false witnesses, innocence is the best defense. However, innocence is often inadequate "in jealous and suspicious times," which call for other measures. There are a number of rules that even the most ignorant can follow to defend himself against a false witness. First, "have nothing at all to do" with "Politicks, or the Government of the World." Second, be consistently ready to display your "Loyalty to the King that reigns over you." Third, "avoid Intemperance": It is difficult enough to control the tongue when a man is sober, and almost impossible when he is drunk. Fourth, avoid conversing with those who are prone to discuss "publick Persons and Affairs," particularly when your opinions are different from theirs.

With all of this in mind, it is undoubtedly the duty of every subject to bear faithful witness when he is lawfully called to do so "by those in Authority or by the sincere Advice" of his own Conscience." To be a faithful witness, a man must "not undertake it from the least Prospect of any private Advantage to himself." A "good Subject" must bear witness against his neighbor "for any Action or Words, the telling of which would be of Advantage to the Publick, and the Concealment dangerous, or of ill Example." Conspiracies that threaten the peace, speech that suggests a rebellious attitude toward the monarch, and other similar acts should clearly be reported to the authorities. Understanding what makes a faithful witness comes in part from knowing what characterizes a false one is. There are, however, several specific traits of a faithful witness: He is truthful, he has no personal malice against the accused, he refrains from aggravating the circumstances against the accused (and from concealing anything "in his Favour"), and his only motive is "the Safety and Service of his Prince and Country."

Swift admits that he considered adding some advice to those who are engaged in the sin of bearing false witness, but decided against it. He is confident that no one among his "Hearers" belongs to "that destructive Tribe." False witnesses rarely "frequent these holy Places," unless they think they can "pick up any Materials" to help them "misrepresent or pervert the Words of the Preacher."

## COMMENTARY

Swift returned to Ireland in August 1714 as dean of St. Patrick's Cathedral, a promotion that marked his rise to prominence in the Church of Ireland, though it was a level and place of advancement he had not sought after his service to the TORY party. With the Robert HARLEY ministry dismissed and the WHIGS seeking revenge, Swift had very little choice now but to accept an Irish deanship when he had sought a bishop's post or a deanery in England. Knowing he had three months from his installation to take the oaths of allegiance to the new king, GEORGE I, Swift took up his self-imposed exile in Ireland, vowing to remain solely concerned with his parish and not involve himself in Irish politics.

During this period of bitterness and self-pity, Swift took up his duties and began preaching to his congregation with this sermon an early result. His attack on Whigs consumes the whole of this preaching pamphlet, where the business of a false witness actually refers to political informers. These informers were busy tracking down disaffected Tories and supposed Jacobites on the slightest evidence. Swift knew his mail had been opened on the pretense that he posed a danger to the present government. So his decision to concentrate on this hated race of informers seems an early effort to assist the Irish in spotting another form of insidious English oppression.

Davis suggests, however, that the piece rises above personal issues, and condemns faction and political cronyism as seen in the extreme Whig policies of this period in Ireland. The Irish had become a nation of informers, thanks to the folly and baseness of the Whigs, and their agents in Ireland. Swift selects the worst type of informer, one who tempts his countryman in order to betray them. His reference to the impeachment activities of the Whigs, who were sweeping across Ireland searching for those who might convert on a moment's notice as they balanced between parties is directly connected to the fears he outlines in the sermon. His analysis carefully delineates seven kinds of informer, and supports the description of each type with details from his own experience. Swift, who had been warned by his friends to hide his papers, began doing so on a limited basis.

Beyond condemning the Whigs for seeking revenge in such a low manner, Swift pointedly divides the sermon into two parts: The first marks those who have practiced betrayal of their fellow man for profit, and

the second serves as useful advice to his friends and others of similar political interest on how to survive this dangerous climate. Knowing that George I's edict had expressly forbidden any meddling in affairs of state, especially for churchmen, Swift's tone and language express regret, bitterness, anger, and pain at the political and economic condition of Ireland. However, he does advise his parishioners "to have nothing at all to do with that is commonly called politics." Though this sermon may have been a dangerous choice of topic, Swift had already begun preparing himself for other pro-Irish publications.

## "On His Own Deafness"

Poem by Swift; first published in 1734, probably written the same year. The poem first appeared in English only and was then published (also in 1734) together with the four-line Latin version. It may have been occasioned by the particularly severe attack of giddiness and deafness Swift suffered in mid-September of 1734.

## "On Lord Carteret's Arms"

Poem by Swift; first published in 1735, written in 1727. It is the last of Swift's Holyhead poems, and predicts that John, second baron CARTERET, will prove to be as unhelpful to Ireland as previous lord lieutenants from England. For circumstances surrounding its composition, see "The POWER OF TIME." See also "An EPIGRAM ON WOOD'S BRASS MONEY," "A LIBEL ON THE REVEREND DOCTOR DELANY AND HIS EXCELLENCY JOHN, LORD CARTERET," and "Vindication of His Excellency the Lord Carteret."

## "On Mr. Pulteney Being Put Out of the Council"

Poem by Swift; first published in 1735, written in 1731. While the title suggests that its subject is Sir

William PULTENEY's dismissal from the Privy Council on July 1, 1731, the poem is really more of an attack on Sir Robert WALPOLE.

## "On Mrs. Biddy Floyd"

Poem by Swift; first published in 1709, probably written the same year. It praises "the famous Mrs. Floyd of Chester," whom Swift regarded as "the handsomest woman" he had ever seen" (JOURNAL TO STELLA II.282). She was one of Lady Betty GERMAIN's friends.

## "On Noisy Tom"

Poem by Swift; first published in 1762, written in 1736. An attack upon Sir Thomas PRENDERGAST, the poem is a sequel to "ON A PRINTER'S BEING SENT TO NEWGATE" and a precursor to "A CHARACTER . . . OF THE LEGION CLUB," in which Swift calls Prendergast "a rampant ass" (63). Prendergast's hostility toward printer George FAULKNER during his imprisonment incurred Swift's anger and provided the immediate occasion for the poem.

## "On Paddy's Character of 'The Intelligencer' "

Poem possibly by Swift; first published as an anonymous broadside late in 1728 or 1729. Thomas SHERIDAN, rather than Swift, may have been the author. The poem is a reply to Rev. Patrick DELANY ("Paddy"), who—unaware of Swift's involvement in the publication—had attacked the INTELLIGENCER on more than one occasion.

## "On Poetry: A Rhapsody"

Poem by Swift; first published in 1733, probably written the same year. It was one of several controversial poems Swift sent to London with Mary BARBER in August 1733 to be delivered to Matthew PILKINGTON so he could arrange for them to be printed. The poem is an important and extensive statement of Swift's views concerning poets and poetry, explaining how each should and should not function. The subtitle was originally spelled "A Rapsody," and reflects the poem's character as a satire, punning on "rapp" (a counterfeit coin) and "rap" (a blow to the head). The poem has three sections. In lines 1–70, after outlining the prevalence of false poets the speaker laments the ways poets, in general, are mistreated by the ungrateful public. This opening section also refers to the work that had occasioned the poem: Edward YOUNG's Love of Fame: The Universal Passion. Lines 71–420 make up the body of the poem, recording the advice of a veteran poet to a "young beginner." And finally, in lines 421–448 the "old experienced sinner" shows his pupil how to engage in the profitable political flattery in which lesser poets tend to engage.

"On Poetry" has received a relatively large amount of critical attention, of which only a few examples are mentioned here. In The Poet Swift, Nora Crow Jaffe cites the poem as having been misinterpreted in ways that have led readers to steer clear of Swift's poetry. She suggests that the contempt Swift shows in this poem (for bad poets and for critics) has been misunderstood as a disdain for poetry itself. She argues that "the common view fails to distinguish between Swift's attitude toward the poet and his attitude toward poetry," as well as "between his attitude toward poetry and his feelings about bad verse, especially when decked out in hackneyed heroic ornaments" (44). John Irwin Fischer cites this poem as significantly distinct from the rest of Swift's verse, since instead of asserting his ability to draw good out of evil (in imitation of God's providence), it "demonstrates" divine sovereignty by "illustrating the catastrophic consequences" of "choosing one's own will in preference to God's" (On Swift's Poetry 178). Louise K. Barnett gives it even more distinction as "one of Swift's greatest satiric poems," and "a definitive statement on . . . the connection between political corruption and a pervasive misuse of language" (Swift's Poetic

*Worlds* 140). In his biography of Swift, Irvin Ehrenpreis prizes the poem (albeit unfinished) for its "unforgettable descriptions" of King GEORGE II, the royal family, and Sir Robert WALPOLE (III.775–76). Pat Rogers provides particularly extensive notes on this poem, explaining its complex publication history, allusions, and analogues (including an important source in *Tatler* 229 for Swift's depiction of GRUB STREET writers).

## "On Psyche"

Poem by Swift; first published in 1762, written 1730–31. The first publication included a note identifying Mrs. SICAN as the subject. The poem is a good-natured satire on "Psyche" as a late-rising, talkative, and witty woman.

## "On Reading Dr. Young's Satires"

Poem by Swift; first published with "TO A LADY" in 1733, written in 1726. The title refers to Edward YOUNG's *Love of Fame: The Universal Passion, in Seven Characteristical Studies* (published between 1725 and 1728). Young's sixth satire was dedicated to Lady Elizabeth GERMAIN. Swift jestingly suggests that depending upon how one reads Young's work, England is either the most blessed or most cursed land in the world. See also "ON POETRY: A RHAPSODY" for an additional reference to Young's satires.

## "On Seeing Verses Written upon Windows in Inns"

Poem by Swift; first published in 1735, probably written in 1726. It contains four epigrams. The first three comment on the bad poetry lovers tend to write, while the fourth jokes that the clergy are a lot like their churches—weather-beaten on the outside and "empty . . . within."

## "On Stephen Duck, the Thresher, and Favourite Poet"

Poem by Swift; first published in 1735, written in 1730. Subtitled "A Quibbling Epigram," it makes fun of DUCK's poetry, the favor his poems gained him with Queen CAROLINE, and his candidacy for poet laureate (eventually awarded to Colley CIBBER) following the death of Laurence EUSDEN on September 27, 1730.

## "On the Archbishop of Cashel and Bettesworth"

Poem by Swift; first published in 1765, written in 1734. Like "ON THE WORDS 'BROTHER PROTESTANTS AND FELLOW CHRISTIANS,' " it bitterly insults Richard BETTESWORTH. The impetus for the poem seems to have been his attacks in the Irish Parliament upon Theophilus BOLTON, archbishop of Cashel, whom Swift respected.

## "On the Burning of Whitehall in 1698"

Poem by Swift; first published in 1814, probably written shortly after the Whitehall fire in 1698. Most editors do not accept the poem as Swift's, but Pat Rogers cites an article by George Mayhew to support including it in his edition. The poem refers to the January 1698 fire that destroyed most of Whitehall—the palace built by Cardinal Wolsey and seized by Henry VIII as in 1530. Swift traces the history of Whitehall as a place of royal corruption and depravity, concluding that the fire (like that which burned Sodom) was divine retribution for all that had occurred there.

# "On the Collar of Mrs. Dingley's Lap-Dog"

Poem by Swift; first published in 1762, written in 1726. Its subject is Rebecca DINGLEY's devotion to Tiger, her spoiled dog. Swift makes fun of Dingley's attachment to Tiger in "BEC'S BIRTHDAY."

# "On the Day of Judgment"

Poem by Swift; first published about 1762 (but see Pat Rogers's notes in his edition of Swift's *Poems* for its complex bibliographic history), probably written in 1731. This well-known and often analyzed poem describes the speaker's vision of God's ultimate judgment on humanity, with the world trembling as it awaits the sentence. In this all-inclusive satire Jove spares no one—condemning the entire human race for its hypocrisy. The poem illustrates Swift's aversion to pride (particularly that of those who deny their own fallenness), sectarianism, and ignorance that he found pervasive in humanity. He suggests that even those clergymen who preached the truth knew nothing more of "Jove's designs" than their congregations. Jove describes the human race—or at least a majority of its members—as a group of "blockheads" who have wasted their lives in "mad business" and now find themselves worthy of damnation.

Both Louise K. Barnett and Nora Crow Jaffe have commented on the poem's broad scope but disagree on whether or not Jove condemns everyone. Barnett finds the poem's "indictments" to be "sweeping," suggesting that "almost everyone belongs in hell" (196). For Jaffe, however, the condemnation is even more comprehensive: "First, [Swift] makes sure the reader sees that every single human being is involved in the satiric damnation. Second, he includes himself in that damnation and so destroys the reader's only hope for protection" (*The Poet Swift* 26). Like the question of whether or not Jove spares anyone in his condemnation, another important issue in this poem is the relationship Swift understood between humankind's blindness

and "nature, reason, and learning." While the race's ignorance of its fate (and terrifying vulnerability while waiting to find it out) are certainly distinctive characteristics, Swift may be suggesting that the widespread misuse of reason and learning has aggravated humans' "natural" moral blindness rather than reduced it.

# "On the Death of Mrs. Johnson"

This character essay portrays Stella's (Esther JOHNSON's) essential qualities of goodness and compassion, particularly the enjoyment Swift took in their friendship. As "the truest, most virtuous and valuable friend," Stella, who died on January 28, 1728, had moved to Ireland from Moor Park, where Swift as secretary to Sir William TEMPLE had first met and begun tutoring the eight-year-old girl in "what books she should read, and perpetually instructing her in the principles of honour and virtue." In Dublin, where Stella lived with Rebecca DINGLEY (Sir William's spinster cousin), they met regularly with Swift, and the relationship between the young woman and the older man grew to one based on love, trust, and respect. Though debate has often been raised on whether Stella and Swift married, which seems unlikely, the birthday poems, the personal JOURNAL TO STELLA, and this final commemorative biographical essay reveal deep affection and an admiration that the dean never gave lightly.

Published in 1765 in Deane SWIFT's *Works* and reprinted in the same year by George FAULKNER in Dublin, the essay's power derives partially from its sincerity of tone and sense of being a private expression of Swift's feelings within hours of learning of her death. His discipline of mind and spirit and long habit of taking refuge in composing at moments of greatest despair and concern serve him well here. The clear need he exhibits in wanting to retreat from even attending her burial in St. Patrick's Cathedral two days later—"that I may not see the light in the church"—suggests the degree that her death affected his emotional well-being.

Though the despair was present, he had long ago trained himself to keep emotion at bay when faced with a writing assignment. The intellectual exercise of listing her strengths, facing her weaknesses unabashedly, and alluding to their close personal relationship in a piece he knew one day would be published reveal Swift's character as an artist and human being. "On the Death" achieves an effective tension in describing a private matter in a public voice, though Davis believes "the character of Stella was written for his own satisfaction." Though one does not disagree that he is seeking relief, he in no way apologizes or retreats from his affection for this woman and the value she had in his life.

### FURTHER READING

Ehrenpreis, Irvin. *Swift: The Man, His Works and the Age.* 3 vols. Cambridge, Mass.: Harvard University Press, 1962–83.

Fox, Christopher, ed. *The Cambridge Companion to Jonathan Swift.* Cambridge and New York: Cambridge University Press, 2003.

Nokes, David. *Jonathan Swift: A Hypocrite Reversed.* Oxford: Oxford University Press, 1987.

Rosslyn, Felicity. "Deliberate Disenchantment: Swift and Pope on the Subject of Women," *Cambridge Quarterly* 23, no. 4 (1994): 293–302.

Swift, Jonathan. *Journal to Stella.* Edited by Harold Williams. Reprint. Oxford, England: Clarendon Press, 1975.

Vieth, David M. "A Symposium on Women in Swift's Poems: Vanessa, Stella, Lady Acheson, and Celia," *PLL* 19, no. 2 (1978): 115–151.

# "On the Five Ladies at Sot's Hole, with the Doctor at Their Head"

Poem by Swift; first published in 1735, written in 1728. It is subtitled "The Ladies Treated the Doctor Sent as from an Officer in the Army." It is written in imitation of various satires on Pat Walsh—the Dublin officer referred to in the subtitle and nick-named "the little Beau." This poem satirizes Rev. Thomas SHERIDAN. Referring to him as "little Tom," the speaker expresses surprise that five fine ladies would waste their time with "a dull Divine" like Sheridan. Sheridan responded with "The Five Ladies Answer to the Beau with the Wig and Wings at His Head" (included in Harold Williams's edition of Swift's poems), which led Swift to write "The BEAU'S REPLY TO THE FIVE LADIES' ANSWER." George FAULKNER noted that Sot's Hole was "A famous ale-house in Dublin for beefsteaks," and Harold Williams adds that it "was built in a recess between Essex Bridge and the Custom House."

# "On the Irish Bishops"

Poem by Swift; first published in 1732, written the same year. Like "ADVICE TO A PARSON," "JUDAS," and "CONSIDERATIONS UPON TWO BILLS . . . RELATING TO THE CLERGY OF IRELAND," it was prompted by Parliament's consideration in late 1731 and early 1732 of the Bill of Residence and Bill of Division, both of which Swift strongly opposed. The poem bitterly portrays contemporary Irish bishops—with few exceptions—as prideful, greedy, and guilty of exploiting the clergymen over whom they preside. Swift points to the mitre as an emblem of his argument, claiming that just as it is split at the top but whole at the bottom, the bishops seek to divide the church, but the clergy work to unite it. The poem ends praising the House of Commons for "biting the biters," referring to its defeat of both bills on February 26, 1732.

# "On the Irish Club"

Poem by Swift; first published 1765, written 1730. The club mentioned in the title is the Irish House of Lords. The poem was Swift's response to the uproar against his "LIBEL ON THE REVEREND DR. DELANY," evident in the arrest of two newsboys for "crying" the poem in the streets. Swift insults the lords and "bishops" for their greed and hypocrisy, and suggests that instead of being outraged they should mend their ways and actually perform the duties entrusted to them.

## "On the Little House by the Churchyard of Castleknock"

Poem by Swift; first published in 1746, written about 1714 after Swift's return to Ireland. The "little house" was the building Swift's friend Archdeacon Thomas WALLS used as his vestry while officiating at Castleknock church, northwest of Dublin.

## "On the Trinity"

Sermon by Swift, first published in 1744. It is based on I John 5:7. The date on which it was first preached is unknown, but in the sermon Swift explains that he has chosen to speak on this topic because it is the "Day being set apart to acknowledge our Belief in the Eternal TRINITY" during the "Season appointed . . . to celebrate the Mysteries of the Trinity, and the Descent of the Holy Ghost." This statement suggests that the sermon was preached on Trinity Sunday, one week after Easter. After lamenting how much the doctrine of the Trinity has suffered, Swift explains that many men wish there were no truth in Christianity at all, and that when they find one aspect of religion that seems counter to their "corrupted Reason," they conclude that the entire Gospel "must sink."

The word *Trinity* does not appear in the Scriptures, but was "invented in the earlier Times" to express a biblical doctrine with a "single Word." The doctrine of the Trinity is scriptural, and can be summed up in a few words: "the Father, the Son, and the Holy Ghost, are each of them God, and yet . . . there is but one God." The Athanasian Creed had been developed earlier to oppose the heresy of the Arrians, who denied that Christ was God. That heresy had been revived 100 years earlier, and has "continued ever since."

Unfortunately, the manner in which many "learned Men" have attempted to defend the Trinity has been ill conceived. They strive to explain it in rational terms, and this will never work. The simple facts are that God commands us to believe "that there is a Union and there is a Distinction" within the Godhead, even though we will all remain ignorant about the nature of those things until Judgment Day. Christianity "abounds in Mysteries," and it is sufficient for most believers to understand that there are certain things God has not chosen to reveal. Those who "declare against" mysteries (such as the Trinity) are actually renouncing "the whole Tenor of the New Testament."

The best way to distinguish a legitimate mystery in religion from a false one is first to ask whether or not it is found in the Scriptures. It is also vital to discover whether or not it "turns to the Advantage of those who preach it." The Roman Catholics, for example, have devised a number of unscriptural mysteries in order to gain "temporal Wealth and Grandeur." Among others, these include "*Transubstantiation, Worshipping of Images, Indulgences for Sins, Purgatory,* and *Masses* for the *Dead.*" It may appear strange that God requires His followers to believe in mysteries, but not when one considers the importance of faith "both in the Old and New Testament." Faith enables Christians to believe things (such as the Trinity) that are *above*—not *contrary to*—their reason.

The bottom line is that "we must either believe what God directly commandeth us in Holy Scripture" or reject the Scriptures altogether. There are several inferences to be drawn from this discussion. First, people should place less emphasis on their own reason when it comes to religious matters: "*Reason* itself is true and just, but the Reason of every particular man is weak and wavering." Second, when tempted to abjure mysteries of the faith, people should search their hearts and make sure they are not motivated by some "favourite Sin." Third, people should realize that "raising Difficulties" regarding religious mysteries will not have any desirable results and will only weaken their faith. Fourth, those "strong Unbelievers" who demand that everything in religion must fully "square" with their reason should think about all the completely unreasonable things they believe, such as the idea "that the World was made by Chance." Finally, those who continue to write "pestilent Books" arguing that it is impossible for God to be both three and one have missed the point. The Scriptures nowhere say that He is three and one, but only that "there is some kind of Unity and Distinction in the Divine Nature, which Mankind cannot possibly comprehend." These authors should realize that the scriptural doctrine is thus "short and plain, and itself uncapable of any Controversy." Those well-meaning divines who attempt to answer these books should also keep that in mind, and stop "answering Fools in their Folly" by trying to "explain a Mystery which God intended to keep secret from us."

## "On the Words 'Brother Protestants and Fellow Christians'"

Poem by Swift; first published in 1734, written in 1733. The impetus was Richard BETTESWORTH's reference (during a speech in favor of repealing the Test Act) to himself and Swift's friend Henry SINGLETON as "brother serjeants." Swift compares this association to a popular fable by Aesop portraying a lump of horse dung floating beside an apple and saying, "See, brother, how we apples swim." The poem reflects Swift's extreme dislike of Bettesworth and his opposition to the Irish Presbyterians' attempt to have the Test Act repealed in 1733. See also "The YAHOO'S OVERTHROW."

## "On Wisdom's Defeat in a Learned Debate"

Poem possibly by Swift; first published in 1725, written the same year. One of several poems Swift wrote against William WOOD and his patent for Irish coinage. This one resulted from a protracted debate in the Irish House of Lords over how to word Parliament's official response to King GEORGE I

following the withdrawal of Wood's patent. See also *The DRAPIER'S LETTERS*, "DOING GOOD: A SERMON ON THE OCCASION OF WOOD'S PROJECT," "An EPIGRAM ON WOOD'S BRASS MONEY," "An EXCELLENT NEW SONG UPON HIS GRACE OUR GOOD LORD ARCHBISHOP OF DUBLIN," "ON WOOD THE IRONMONGER," "PROMETHEUS," "A SERIOUS POEM UPON WILLIAM WOOD," "A SIMILE," "WOOD, AN INSECT," and "Wood's Halfpence."

## "On Wood the Ironmonger"

Poem by Swift; first published in 1735, written in 1725. One of several statements by Swift against William WOOD, it compares Wood to Salmoneus, a Greek king who wanted to be a god. He had his subjects call him Zeus, and while driving a brass chariot he flung torches in the air to imitate thunderbolts. Zeus eventually killed him. Swift suggests that once the Drapier (see *The DRAPIER'S LETTERS*) exposed Wood as a fraud, the Irish recognized Wood's halfpence as worthless just as Salmoneus's subjects—after his death—realized his "thunderbolts" were fake. See also *DRAPIER'S LETTERS*, "DOING GOOD: A SERMON ON THE OCCASION OF WOOD'S PROJECT," "An EPIGRAM ON WOOD'S BRASS MONEY," "An EXCELLENT NEW SONG UPON HIS GRACE OUR GOOD LORD ARCHBISHOP OF DUBLIN," "PROMETHEUS," "A SERIOUS POEM UPON WILLIAM WOOD," "A SIMILE," and "WOOD, AN INSECT."

## "Panegyric on the Dean, A"

Poem by Swift; first published in 1735, written in 1730. A mock-encomium to Swift written in the person of Lady Anne ACHESON, it "salutes" him in a variety of capacities such as "Dean, butler, usher, jester, tutor," etc. Swift is self-effacing throughout much of the poem, wryly celebrating qualities he was notorious for lacking. This poem is traditionally classed among the scatological or "excremental" poems because of its long digression "deal[ing] in startling detail with Swift's construction of two outdoor privies" at MARKET HILL (Ehrenpreis, *Swift* III.670).

## "Panegyric on the Reverend Dean Swift, A"

Poem possibly by Swift; first published in 1730, written the same year. According to the subtitle, it was written to answer Swift's "LIBEL ON THE REVEREND DR. DELANY AND HIS EXCELLENCY JOHN, LORD CARTERET," but the long "Panegyric" scorns Swift and DELANY both. Pat Rogers calls it an "exceedingly dubious item" for inclusion among Swift's poems (810). Following George FAULKNER and further evidence from D. F. Foxon, Irvin Ehrenpreis attributes it to Scotch-Irish author James Arbuckle (*Swift* III.653). Rogers suggests that this attribution is probably correct.

## " 'Paper Book Is Sent by Boyle, A' "

Poem by Swift; first published 1733, written 1732. It refers to gifts Swift received on his 65th birthday—November 30, 1732—from John Boyle (see ORRERY) and Patrick DELANY. Both had written commendatory verses to accompany their gifts for the occasion. Swift writes that when he dies he wants the gilt book from Boyle and the silver writing stand from Delany placed beside his tomb and the poems they wrote for him engraved on his tombstone. He predicts that these will gain him more praise than any of his own writings and will cause the "vandals of the present age" to "burst with envy, spite, and rage."

## "Parson's Case, The"

Poem possibly by Swift; first published 1734. It initially appeared in Dublin and London newspapers and then in the December *Gentleman's Magazine*

along with "VERSES SPOKEN EXTEMPORE BY DEAN SWIFT ON HIS CURATE'S COMPLAINT OF HARD DUTY." Pat Rogers treats the poem as a doubtful attribution. It is addressed to a curate named Marcus who wishes to die and be remembered "in strain heroic." The speaker suggests that should Marcus be promoted and become a dean, he might revoke his pious wish to die humbly.

## "Part of a Summer, The"

Poem by Swift; first published in 1721–22, probably written 1721. Based on Swift's long stay at the house of George ROCHFORT during the summer of 1721, it describes the daily activities of those who lived there. In addition to Rochfort, that included his wife, Lady Betty; his brother John ROCHFORT; and his friends Daniel JACKSON and Swift. In "Swift and the Poetry of Allusion," Aubrey Williams reads the poem as a "seriocomic inversion" of Epicurean verses on country living, the second part (lines 61ff.) "shattering" the "atmosphere of bucolic tranquility and conviviality established in the first half" (quoted in Rogers, *Poems* 714). Citing an October 6, 1721, letter from Swift to Jackson, Williams argues that Swift may have worn out his welcome with the Rochforts (*Corr.* 2.407–08). See also "GEORGE NIM-DAN-DEAN, ESQ. TO MR. SHERIDAN" and "GEORGE NIM-DAN-DEAN'S INVITATION TO MR. THOMAS SHERIDAN."

## "Part of the Ninth Ode of the Fourth Book of Horace"

Poem by Swift; first published in 1730, written 1720–21. As the subtitle indicates, it was originally "Addressed to Doctor William KING, Late Lord Archbishop of London." The original ode by Horace suggests that failing to sing the virtues of those who deserve it is laziness on the part of writers. In his imitation, Swift applies this principle in praising King, whom he respected in part because of their shared opposition to the proposal in 1720 for establishing a national Bank of Ireland. Like

Swift, Archbishop King was forthright in expressing his opinion of the bank, which he claimed would "only put it in the power of a few to cheat the whole kingdom, and bring in a villainous trade of stock jobbing and paper credit to the ruin of the unwary" (quoted in Ehrenpreis, *Swift* III.161). See also "LAST SPEECH AND DYING WORDS OF THE BANK OF IRELAND" and "TO HIS GRACE THE ARCHBISHOP OF DUBLIN."

## "Pastoral Dialogue, A"

Poem by Swift; first published in 1732, written in 1729. Dramatizing a conversation between two Irish peasants weeding Sir Arthur ACHESON's courtyard, it is a coarse lampoon of pastoral conventions. In his biography of Swift, Irvin Ehrenpreis suggests that this poem "looks like a parody of [Alexander] POPE's *Spring*" (III.626). Other mock-pastorals by Swift include "DESCRIPTION OF THE MORNING," "DESCRIPTION OF A CITY SHOWER," and "A PASTORAL DIALOGUE."

## "Pastoral Dialogue between Richmond Lodge and Marble Hill, A"

Poem by Swift; first published in 1735, written (as the subtitle indicates) in June 1727 shortly after the death of King GEORGE I. Richmond Lodge was the country house of the prince of Wales (soon to become King GEORGE II), and Marble Hill was that of Henrietta HOWARD. The poem dramatizes a conversation between the houses in which they sadly predict the neglect and loneliness they will suffer once the prince becomes king.

## "Peace and Dunkirk"

Poem by Swift; first published 1712 as an undated broadside. It celebrates the French surrender of DUNKIRK to Major-General John HILL on July 8 of that year. See also "A HUE AND CRY AFTER DISMAL" and "The HISTORY OF THE FOUR LAST YEARS OF THE QUEEN."

## "Pethox the Great"

Poem by Swift; first printed in *Miscellanies* (1727), written about 1723. "Pethox" is an anagram for "the pox" (syphilis), and the poem is a mock encomium—complete with classical allusions—to the disease. Swift's friend Patrick DELANY wrote in his *Observations upon Lord Orrery's Remarks* (1754) that "Swift hath made his *Pethox* the Great, a piece truly historical and learned; with as many fine strokes of satire as any in Hogarth's. I wish, the subject had been less disagreeable, and the colouring in some places, less strong."

## Philomath, T. N.

See "FAMOUS PREDICTION OF MERLIN."

## "Phyllis"

Poem by Swift; first published 1728, written 1719. Like "The PROGRESS OF BEAUTY," it is primarily concerned with deterioration rather than progress. Phyllis, who by all appearances is a pious prude, inexplicably leaves her new husband the day after their wedding. The abandoned groom sends his butler, John, to find Phyllis and bring her back "alive or dead." After running away together, John and Phyllis eventually become destitute, regret the day they met, and end up a "rogue and whore" running an inn just outside London.

Nora Crow Jaffe compares this poem to "The PROGRESS OF MARRIAGE" as a work in which Swift is "uncommonly hard on people who make matrimonial mistakes" (*The Poet Swift* 132). However, Phyllis's *seeming* modesty and virtue at the beginning of the poem may provide a more accurate explanation of the downfall Swift has her suffer at the end of the poem. Swift highlights discrepancies between appearance and reality throughout the poem. The first two lines, for example, indicate that Phyllis is "desponding" and "endued / With every talent of a prude"—not that she actually is one. The speaker further insists that she would "rather take you to bed, / Than let you see her dress her head," suggesting that her modesty is misapplied at best (7–8). We also find out that even in church she bites her lips "to make them red" and "heave[s] her bosom"—supposedly "unaware"—so that "neighboring beaux" can "see it bare" (17–18). Her "bashful way," in other words, turns out to be a sham. Swift's aversion to women who engage in any sort of false-seeming (and to the men who fall for it) is clear in other poems such as "The PROGRESS OF BEAUTY," "STREPHON AND CHLOE," "CASSINUS AND PETER," "The LADY'S DRESSING ROOM," and "A BEAUTIFUL YOUNG NYMPH GOING TO BED." Whether or not Swift is suggesting that Phyllis's false modesty is typical of most women, in the context of this poem that hypocrisy (rather than her "matrimonial mistake") is the central concern. It is the character flaw that leads to her punishment as the wife of an impoverished innkeeper. The unnamed first husband and John are both punished, too, but their crime was in regarding Phyllis as anything more than a well-mannered "whore."

# "Place of the Damned, The"

Poem by Swift; first published as a broadside 1731, written the same year. The speaker claims that everyone "pretend[ing] to religion and grace" agrees that hell exists but has differing views on where it is located. He sets out to define hell "by logical rules," and describes it as any place where the damned "do chiefly abound." After a lengthy list of whom that includes—everyone from "damned" poets and critics to politicians and parsons—the poem ends satirically with a sigh of relief that hell must be far away at Paris or Rome (rather than here "at home").

One of the poem's most distinctive features is the repeated use of the word *damned*—it occurs 17 times within the 18 lines of the poem. The speaker uses the adjective to describe a variety of persons, from poets (which, of course, would include himself) and critics to senators, liars, "ignorant prelates," priests, spies, and friends. On the whole, the poem suggests that the application of the term *damned* has become so ubiquitous that it no longer has much meaning. Swift may be affirming his prediction of universal condemnation in "ON THE DAY OF JUDGMENT," or, as Louise K. Barnett has argued, he may be suggesting that meaningful distinctions no longer exist among the nouns *damned* describes: "To couple *Friends* with *Spies, Informers,* and *Liars* is to strip it of positive connotations and provoke a reassessment of the word itself. This proximity suggests that the ordinary meaning of *friends* can be a hypocritical cloak for the same kinds of evil plainly indicated by the other terms, while the blanket condemnation of lawyers, judges, lords, and squires implies that every positive or neutral label potentially masks corruption." In Barnett's view, Swift in this poem moves beyond the use of language for satiric purposes, and engages in a "satiric questioning of language itself" to point out "a serious breakdown of the labeling process" (125). He subjects other positive labels to a similar process of erosion in other poems such as "The LADY'S DRESSING ROOM," "A BEAUTIFUL YOUNG NYMPH GOING TO BED," and "STREPHON AND CHLOE." In these verses, terms like *lady, goddess,* and *nymph* are shown to be woefully misapplied when used in an attempt to elevate women beyond mortality and the "necessities of nature" ("Strephon and Chloe" 25).

# "Poems from the 'Holyhead Journal'"

See "HOLYHEAD JOURNAL," "The POWER OF TIME," "HOLYHEAD. SEPTEMBER 25, 1727," "IRELAND," "WHEN MRS. WELCH'S CHIMNEY SMOKES," and "ON LORD CARTERET'S ARMS."

# "Poetical Epistle to Dr. Sheridan, A"

Poem possibly by Swift; first published 1814, written 1724. In his edition of Swift's poems, Pat Rogers calls it a dubious item. The poem calls upon Dr. Thomas SHERIDAN to mend his ways and offers Swift as an example of how to do so.

# Polite Conversation

See COMPLETE COLLECTION OF GENTEEL AND INGENIOUS CONVERSATION, A.

# "Portrait from the Life, A"

Poem by Swift; first published in 1765, written between 1718 and 1738 (which Pat Rogers calls "the approximate duration of the friendship of Swift and Sheridan"). Filled with insulting comparisons, it presents a very negative "portrait" of Elizabeth SHERIDAN, the wife of Dr. Thomas SHERIDAN.

# "Power of Time, The"

Poem by Swift; first published in 1735, written in 1727. It is one of several poems written at Holyhead (a port and the largest town on the island of Anglesey in north Wales) during Swift's September journey from London back to Dublin. Bad weather delayed him there for several days. In this poem, a "Welsh divine" asks why he should complain that his cassock is wearing out when nothing else withstands "the mortal force of Time's destructive hand." See also "HOLYHEAD JOURNAL," "HOLYHEAD. SEPTEMBER 25, 1727," "IRELAND," "WHEN MRS. WELCH'S CHIMNEY SMOKES," and "ON LORD CARTERET'S ARMS."

# "Predictions for the Year 1708"

Associated with "The ACCOMPLISHMENT OF THE FIRST OF MR. BICKERSTAFF'S PREDICTIONS" and "A

VINDICATION OF ISAAC BICKERSTAFF ESQ.," this initial installment begins the dean's extended satire against astrologers and almanac makers. Swift's irony, however, actually delves more deeply into criticizing the results of their popular publications: their exorbitant profits, the establishment's approval through a royal charter, and the self-important tone that often convinced the unsuspecting of their supposed truth.

Throughout the latter part of CHARLES II's reign, John PARTRIDGE flourished with a mix of mysticism, superstition, and political and religious bigotry, persuading both the gullible and those who should have known better that he was possessed of rare wisdom and insight. With the accession of WILLIAM III, the climate had changed and the almanac maker's Low-Church, anti-Tory perspective became unendurable to the TORY wits, especially Swift, who showed the power of his words in this highly charged environment.

In his parody of Partridge's annual almanac, *Merlinus Liberatus*, Swift used the pseudonym Isaac Bickerstaff—a persona that was later adopted by Richard STEELE in the *Tatler*. Swift made even further predictions than Partridge had and in a laughable scene, foretold Partridge's death. When the "fateful day" arrived, the Company of Stationers, in a moment of real-life irony, struck Partridge's name from the rolls of living writers, and he lost his right to publish the almanac. Partridge's arrogance brought about this burlesque, since Swift found the astrologer's criticism of the Church of England's clergy to be unacceptable propaganda. Swift here plays a role we recognize well today—the establishment intellectual who will not tolerate the constant dumbing down of the culture by publishers bent solely on embracing profits. Though Swift's attitude toward authority remains contradictory, he had no compunction in discrediting those who make greater fools of their fellow human beings.

# "Probatur Aliter"

Poem by Swift; first published in 1746. It may have been composed around the same time as "A RID-

DLING LETTER," which also poses a number of riddles with answers that all begin with "ass."

## "Problem, The"

Poem by Swift; first published in *Works* (1746), written around 1699. A manuscript version of the poem is subtitled, "That [Henry] Sidney, earl of ROMNEY stinks, when he is in love." Swift had unsuccessfully asked Romney to recommend him for preferment in 1699. The "problem" satirized in the poem is the chronic flatulence the earl suffers whenever he feels "love's fire."

## "Progress of Beauty, The"

Poem by Swift; first published in 1728, written in 1719. Like "PHYLLIS" it is primarily concerned with deterioration rather than progress. In an extended comparison of (the "beauty") CELIA to the waxing and waning moon, it details with mock admiration the skill "earthly females" use to hide their physical imperfections. It suggests, however, that even these remarkable skills cannot hide the continual "rotting" of the bodies women strive to beautify. In his biography of Swift, David Nokes lists this work among several of Swift's poems that "develop the contrast between the idealistic notion of women as angels in petticoats and the cynical rejection of them as beasts in skirts." Like the later "LADY'S DRESSING ROOM," this poem goes into great detail about the various makeup items "Celia" uses (albeit unskillfully) to mask her actual appearance. According to Nokes, Swift in this sense was working in a familiar vein. He cites Alexander POPE's *Rape of the Lock* to show that Swift and other "satirists of the Restoration and Augustan period were fascinated by cosmetics which turned women's faces into testing-grounds for the conflicts between art and nature, truth and falsehood" (253).

Louise K. Barnett also recognizes this poem's relationship with the "Dressing Room," but she argues that although both poems tell the same story, "Progress" is more successful because of the "distance" it maintains from the central figure. In Barnett's view, Swift's technique in "Progress" "keeps Celia satirically remote," while in the "Dressing Room" he "approaches his subject at close range" and "expose[s] his conflicting attitudes" about nature and art (*Swift's Poetic Worlds* 174). Nora Crow Jaffe reads "Progress" as more of a "relatively light piece of literary criticism" in which Swift offers a "negative critique" of "certain conventions of Renaissance and Restoration poetry." She does not draw a specific parallel between "Progress" and Shakespeare's Sonnet 130 ("My mistress' eyes are nothing like the sun"), but her reading suggests that Swift (like Shakespeare) mocks poetic conventions in order to show how useless they are when it comes to describing reality. Even the techniques are similar, in that in both poems, "wherever the reader might expect a romantic compliment, he finds a dramatic insult instead" (103, 105). As suggested above, "Progress" is often discussed alongside others categorized as "excremental" or "scatological" verses, such as "A BEAUTIFUL YOUNG NYMPH GOING TO BED," "CASSINUS AND PETER," and "STREPHON AND CHLOE."

## "Progress of Love, The"

See "PHYLLIS."

## "Progress of Marriage, The"

Poem by Swift; first published in 1765, written 1721–22. It satirizes the marriage of Benjamin PRATT to the much younger Lady Philippa Hamilton, daughter of James Hamilton, sixth earl of ABERCORN.

## "Progress of Poetry, The"

Poem by Swift; first published in 1728, written in 1719 or 1720. It begins with a fable of a goose who, after having to give up a lavish and sedentary lifestyle, learns she can fly. The narrator applies the fable to the poet, who produces nothing of worth as long as he is wealthy and gluttonous. His "exalted spirit" comes through in his work only after poverty and want have removed the "incumbrances" of fancy foods and extravagant clothing. See also "To STELLA, WHO COLLECTED AND INSCRIBED HIS POEMS" and "ADVICE TO THE GRUB STREET VERSE-WRITERS."

## "Prometheus"

Poem by Swift; first published anonymously as a broadside in 1724, written the same year. George FAULKNER published it in *Fraud Detected: or, The Hibernian Patriot* (1725), which also contained the first collected edition of *The DRAPIER'S LETTERS*. Like a number of other poems, this one denounces William WOOD and his patent for Irish coinage. In an original expansion of several classical myths Swift compares Wood to Prometheus, who stole the gold chain connecting Earth to Jove's throne and then melted it to make coins. In order to hide the theft, Prometheus replaced the gold chain with a brass one. The poem contends that Wood committed a similar crime by ensuring that nothing but brass would pass between the Irish and King GEORGE I. It further suggests that just as Prometheus received a gruesome punishment for his misdeed, Wood should be hanged (and his body left to the crows) for his. See also "DOING GOOD: A SERMON ON THE OCCASION OF WOOD'S PROJECT," "An EPIGRAM ON WOOD'S BRASS MONEY," "An EXCELLENT NEW SONG UPON HIS GRACE OUR GOOD LORD ARCHBISHOP OF DUBLIN," "ON WOOD THE IRONMONGER," "A SERIOUS POEM UPON WILLIAM WOOD," "A SIMILE," and "WOOD, AN INSECT."

## "Proposal for the Universal Use of Irish Manufacture, A"

As Swift's earliest pamphlet on Ireland, the "Proposal" acknowledges the rights of the Irish against the English, and rejects in particular the economic and political oppression practiced by the British Parliament. The timing of its composition and publication during the 60th-birthday celebration of the Hanoverian king GEORGE I (along with the continued rise of the WHIG party) made the essay in the eyes of the Dublin establishment an especially hated document. Though its thesis seems directed toward enlightening the Anglo-Irish consciousness and correcting "the blunders of his deluded countrymen," the essay attacks the wearing of clothes produced from English cloth and sold by English traders. The argument suggests instead that the Irish would prosper from wearing clothes produced by their own countrymen. The quite modern notion of reducing foreign imports and relying on domestic goods as a remedy for stabilizing the economy seems eminently sensible, except for the English imperialist notion that Ireland had no authority to declare a boycott of English trade goods.

As a reaction to this publication, the Irish authorities charged the pamphlet's author (unknown to them) and the printer, Edward WATERS, with sedition and proceeded to arrest Waters. Provoked beyond any typical response that would be urged by English heavy-handedness, Lord Chief Justice William WHITSHED—a strong Whig—urged a Dublin grand jury and hounded a trial jury into prosecuting and imprisoning Waters in June of 1720. Swift was outraged at the actual reason for Whitshed's actions. Many knew his pursuit of Waters had little to do with the pamphlet's call for peaceful resistance against the government's trade policies and more to do with the justice's overt bias toward Whig party politics. Swift decided to bring his considerable influence to bear in hopes of saving Waters before sentencing. He launched a letter-writing campaign that included missives to Sir Thomas HANMER (most recently Speaker of the British House of Commons) and Constantine PHIPPS (lord chancellor of Ireland), and a report of the entire incident to his friend Alexander POPE.

The correspondence with each of these men has one embedded question: Why does a free man in England seem to lose his autonomy by simply crossing the Irish Sea? It was a query he had often posed in his earlier writings, but in this case it was asked with particular frustration: He wrote to Pope (January 10, 1721), "I rather chuse to appeal to you than to my Lord Chief Justice, under the situation I am in. . . . [He] had so quick an understanding, that he resolved if possible to outdo his orders. The Grand Juries of the county and city [were given] the said pamphlet with all aggravating epithets, for which they had thanks sent them from England[;] . . . the printer was seized, and forced to give great bail." After summarizing the trial, the unwillingness of the jury to come to judgment, and the justice's prejudicial comments at the bar, Swift tells Pope that "the cause [the trial of Waters] being so very odious and impopular, the trial of the verdict was deferr'd from one term to another, till upon the Duke of GRAFTON's arrival, . . . was pleased to grant a noli prosequi [unwilling to prosecute]." A short letter to Hanmer reviews the entire situation as a miscarriage of justice and asks the former Speaker if he would "prevail on the Duke of Grafton to write to the Chief Justice to let the matter drop, which I believe his Grace would easily do . . . and I believe him ready to do a thing of good nature and well as justice."

In his biography of Swift, Irvin Ehrenpreis draws some particularly important connections for the origin of the essay, remarking how Irish nationalism combined with economic necessity in reaction against the 1699 English Woollen Act and the dangerous importation of foreign goods into Ireland (III.123ff.). The concern for English imperialist notions seems equally weighted against Swift's despair for the Irish, who seem to be their own worst enemies: "it is wonderful to observe the bias among our people in favour of things, persons, and wares of all kinds that come from England." But the issue of the Irish landlords a frequent theme in the Irish essays, surfaces, citing their guilt in "unmeasurable screwing and racking their tenants all over the kingdom [having] reduced the miserable people to a worse condition than the peasants in France." He makes a famous call for rebellion: "burn everything from England except their people and their coals." But the broader point of the essay comes in Swift's full declaration of the necessity for freedom and self-determination. His appeal for a government that leads with the consent of the governed is the central thesis, and Swift once again anticipates the future: The Irish must face their colonial predicament or accept their enslavement.

## FURTHER READING

Fabricant, Carole. "Swift the Irishman." In *The Cambridge Companion to Jonathan Swift*, edited by Christopher Fox, 48–72. Cambridge: Cambridge University Press, 2003.

Fauske, Christopher J. *Jonathan Swift and the Church of Ireland, 1710–1724*. Dublin and Portland, Ore.: Irish Academic Press, 2002.

Ferguson, Oliver. *Jonathan Swift and Ireland*. Urbana: University of Illinois Press, 1962.

Kelly, James. "Jonathan Swift and the Irish Economy of the 1720s," *Eighteenth-Century Ireland/Iris an dá Chultúr* 6 (1991): 7–36.

Landa, Louis A. *Swift and the Church of Ireland*. 2d ed. Oxford, England: Clarendon Press, 1965.

Mahoney, Robert. "Protestant Dependence and Consumption in Swift's Irish Writings." In *Political Ideas in Eighteenth-Century Ireland*, edited by S. J. Connoly, 83–104. Dublin: Four Courts Press, 2000.

Real, Hermann J. *Securing Swift: Selected Essays*. Irish Research Series 1. Dublin, Oxford, England, and Bethesda, Md.: Maunsel, 2001.

# "Quibbling Elegy on the Worshipful Judge Boat, A"

Poem by Swift; first published in 1735, written about 1721. It satirizes Judge Godfrey Boate, punning on his last name and portraying him as a blockhead. To explain Swift's dislike of the judge, Harold Williams cites Boate's participation in the 1720 trial of Edward WATERS, who had printed Swift's "PROPOSAL FOR THE UNIVERSAL USE OF IRISH MANUFACTURE." According to F. Elrington Ball, however, the hostility may have arisen from a demand in Boate's will involving Swift's friend Knightley CHETWODE (whose wife was Boate's niece).

# "Quiet Life and a Good Name, A"

Poem by Swift; first published in 1735, written in 1719. It is subtitled "To a Friend, Who Married a

Shrew." Pat Rogers discounts the suggestion that Swift based the poem on Thomas SHERIDAN's less than blissful marriage, pointing instead to the familiar maxim, "Anything for a quiet life" (which Swift includes in his COMPLETE COLLECTION OF GENTEEL AND INGENIOUS CONVERSATION). The poem details the plight of Dick, whose wife, Nell, abuses him incessantly. When Dick's neighbor Will tries to intercede, Nell responds by giving him a sound beating. Will tries to convince Dick to stand up against Nell's scolding, but Dick argues that he endures her scorn to preserve his quiet life and good name. Despite his efforts, Dick ironically becomes the object of ridicule around the parish as he continues to suffer Nell's abuse at home. The narrator ends the poem accusing Dick of "false patience and mistaken pride" and lamenting the number of husbands who are just as foolish as he is.

# "Receipt to Restore Stella's Youth, A"

Poem by Swift; first published in 1735, written in 1725. Stella—Esther JOHNSON—visited Swift during his stay at Quilca from April through September of 1725 (see "TO QUILCA" for details). The "receipt" Swift prescribes to improve Stella's declining health is beef and wine along with mirth, exercise, and air during her stay at Quilca. See also "VERSES FROM QUILCA" and "BLUNDERS, DEFICIENCIES, DISTRESSES, AND MISFORTUNES OF QUILCA."

# "Revolution at Market Hill, The"

Poem by Swift; first published in 1735, written in 1730 at MARKET HILL. It describes the plight of Swift and Henry LESLIE ("a Spaniard"), who find themselves living at Market Hill "on conditions cruel." Leslie had moved there upon retiring from the Spanish army, and Swift's last visit there took place in 1730. Swift considered building at nearby Drumlack (also known as Drapier's Hill), but abandoned his plans. Constrained to be the "slaves" of

"the triumphant knight" (Sir Arthur ACHESON) who "reigns" at Market Hill, Swift and Leslie decide to revolt against Sir Arthur and Lady Anne ACHESON and take control of their estate. The poem ends with Swift deciding they have no real need for Lady Acheson's maid Hannah, so they should simply hang her "As all your politicians wise / Dispatch the rogues by whom they rise." See also "DEAN'S REASONS FOR NOT BUILDING AT DRAPIER'S HILL, The."

# "Riddles"

A group of nine poems by Swift; first published as a group in 1735, written in the 1720s. George FAULKNER's headnote to the riddles suggests that Swift wrote them as part of an ongoing diversion among friends, but thought little of them. Only two have titles: Riddle 7 is named "The Gulf of All Human Possessions" and Riddle 8, "Louisa to Strephon." Riddle 1 ("In youth exalted high in air") was originally published as a broadside (Dublin, 1726).

# "Riddling Letter, A"

Poem by Swift; first published in 1746, written about 1731. George FAULKNER printed this verse letter as addressed to Dr. Thomas SHERIDAN, but John HAWKESWORTH published it as intended for Dr. Richard HELSHAM. This letter is "riddling" because each couplet poses two different riddles, both of which have the same answer. Faulkner printed it along with "TO DR. HELSHAM," "TO DR. SHERIDAN," and "CAN YOU MATCH WITH ME," suggesting that it may have been part of the word game in which Swift and Helsham engaged (via these poems) during November 1731.

# "Robin and Harry"

Poem by Swift; first published in 1765, written in 1729. It contrasts the characters and habits of two brothers, Robert and Henry LESLIE. Swift visited Henry during his stays with Sir Arthur and Lady Anne ACHESON at MARKET HILL. Robert was married to the niece of one of Swift's friends, Peter LUDLOW. Robin is profligate and talkative, while Harry pinches pennies and says little. Harry marries and becomes a farmer, but Robin, "all his youth a sloven," is "doomed to be a beau for life." The poem ends suggesting that Robin's extravagant dress is an attempt to compensate for unnamed "defects," possibly including sexual impotence.

# "Run upon the Bankers, The"

Poem by Swift; first published in 1735, written in 1720. Based on concerns similar to those reflected in "UPON THE SOUTH SEA PROJECT," this satire details the troubles following the failure of the SOUTH SEA COMPANY in 1720. It portrays English bankers as largely dishonest and indicates Swift's general lack of sympathy for those who lost money in the South Sea affair. Debt, the poem suggests, is crucial to maintaining bankers' wealth, and they would be "ruined" if those who had borrowed money suddenly paid it all back. At the end of the poem, the speaker predicts that "Few bankers will to heaven be mounters" and will instead end up in hell in spite of all the "gold and bills" they have accumulated. Pat Rogers calls the poem "wholly characteristic" of Swift, "blending wit, mythology, biblical allusion, and parody of commercial language" (*Poems* 703n.).

# "Satire on an Inconstant Lover, A"

Short poem by Swift included in an April 9, 1737, letter to Dr. Thomas SHERIDAN. It is one of many contributions to the word games in which Swift and Sheridan regularly engaged. See also, for example, "ANGLO-LATIN VERSES."

# "Satirical Elegy on the Death of a Late Famous General, A"

Poem by Swift; first published in 1764, written in 1722. The "Famous General" insultingly memorialized is John Churchill, first duke of MARLBOROUGH (whom Swift had satirized earlier in "The FABLE OF MIDAS"). Swift penned this very unflattering elegy as numerous poems were being published praising Marlborough for his successes. Louise K. Barnett notes that Swift inverts the conventions of the genre as he "draws a general picture of unworthiness by constantly questioning" Marlborough's "ability to live up to the honors conferred upon him" (*Swift's Poetic Worlds* 127–128). As he does in a number of other verses, including "ON DREAMS" and "PLACE OF THE DAMNED," Swift in this poem capitalizes on what he views as an important discrepancy between language and reality. At the beginning of the poem, for example, Swift adopts the terms used in laudatory elegies to describe Marlborough ("His Grace," "Mighty Warrior"). By the final stanza, however, he has depicted the general as a typical "bubble"—"empty," and temporarily "raised by breath of kings" only to end up dead with nothing but past (and now meaningless) "honours" as he awaits "the last loud trump" of divine judgment. The poem ends with the assertion that Marlborough's accolades were undeserved and that now, "From all his ill-got honours flung" he is "Turned to that dirt from whence he sprung" (31–32).

# "Scriblerian Verses"

Group of poems, partly by Swift, circulated at meetings of the SCRIBLERUS CLUB not long before its dissolution. All written in 1714, these verses were addressed to Edward HARLEY, second earl of Oxford, inviting him to join the club. Two of the poems were first published in 1766, but the others first appeared in Harold Williams's 1958 edition of Swift's poems under the title "Jeux D'Esprit of the Scriblerus Club."

# "Sentiments of a Church of England Man with Respect to Religion and Government, The"

Pamphlet by Swift written in 1708, and published three years later. Swift composed it during his negotiations regarding the First Fruits, after GODOLPHIN told him that if anything were to be done concerning the tax, a promise of support from the Irish clergy for the removal of the Sacramental Test Act in Ireland as a favor to the Dissenters must be forthcoming (see the Commentary under "LETTER FROM A MEMBER OF THE HOUSE OF COMMONS IN IRELAND," above).

In this work, Swift argues that the most extreme views of both WHIGS and TORIES are unacceptable to reasonable persons. After asserting that he is "no *Bigot* in Religion" or in government, Swift explains that he will "describe the Sentiments of a *Church-of*-England *Man*" in order to do away with the prejudices that have come to characterize both parties. He begins with religion, arguing that anyone who claims to be a member of the Church of England "ought to believe in a God, and his Providence, together with revealed Religion, and the Divinity of Christ." He should also value the "Scheme established . . . of Ecclesiastical Government" as the best way to maintain order in the kingdom. While he is open to discussing "useful Alterations" in "Rites, Ceremonies, and Forms of Prayer" (and agreeable to adopting those the clergy or legislature approve), he can understand why many clergymen are opposed to any such changes. And although he has nothing against tolerating different forms of worship, he is thoroughly opposed to allowing "those who are tolerated, to advance their own Models upon the Ruin of what is already established."

He believes that the state should grant official powers only to those who support and "preserve the Constitution in all its Parts"—including its provision that government officials must subscribe to the Sacramental Test. Many who oppose the Constitution supposedly because it hinders them from public service are actually more interested in furthering their own interests and those of their party.

The Church of England man cannot understand how so many individuals—who claim to have a passion for the church—can treat the clergy with such hatred and abuse. He is likewise troubled by the general tendency of the age "in delighting to fling Scandals upon the Clergy in general." In his view, clergymen do not deserve charges of "*Ambition, or Love of Power*," any more than other men do. In fact, the clergy have been robbed of "all sorts" of power over the past two centuries, and even of their possessions in too many cases.

Swift argues against the notion that individuals should be free to publish whatever books they will against the central doctrines of Christianity. These authors—despite their claims—do nothing more than "undermine the Foundations of Piety and Virtue." While he does not believe that every schism in the church is as "damnable" as some pretend, he nonetheless opposes making schisms "no Crime at all." In his view, "any great Separation" from established worship presents a serious threat to the "publick Peace." He opposes those who are called "Dissenters" for the same reason. In matters of religion, it would be best for both parties to strive for moderation. Currently, one side "very justly disowns it," while the other "as unjustly pretends" to be governed by it.

Moving on to an explanation of his sentiments in government, Swift laments the presence of so much hatred in religion—especially since all parties "agree in all Fundamentals, and only differ" in a few "Ceremonies" or "speculative points." The case is the same, however, when it comes to "contending Parties of State." For the most part, the Whigs and Tories agree about important political matters ("Loyalty to the *Queen*," "Abjuration of the *Pretender*," and so forth). Their differences have received more attention because these parties have carried their mutual hatred to such extremes, and aggravated it by mixing religion and politics.

The Church of England man does not hold one form of government in any higher regard than any other, nor does he believe any particular form to be especially capable of complementing the church. At the same time, he does not take a "one-size-fits-all" approach to government, since some countries are better suited to certain forms than others. In terms of England's monarchy, he thinks it best that it remain hereditary rather than become elected. Hereditary succession is more convenient, and monarchs in that system are still limited in that they reign only by the consent of the people. There are some who argue that a king (and his offspring) own the monarchy just as any private man owns property and are therefore not subject to the consent of the people. This argument is foolish, since the effects of what a man does with his private property are minimal when compared with the results of a monarch's decisions and his responsibility to promote the public good. A nation's freedom depends upon "an absolute *unlimited legislative* Power, wherein the whole Body of the People are *fairly* represented; and in an *executive* duly *limited*."

In conclusion, Swift insists that a Church of England man may approve of one party's principles and decisions more than another's, but he will never "advance an Opinion merely because it is *That* of the Party he most approves." Likewise, those who are truly interested in preserving the "Constitution entire in Church and State" will take care to avoid the extremes of both parties. While he hopes that his pamphlet will be well-received, he knows that if it is rejected by both parties it will be "an ample Justification" of his efforts.

## "Serious Poem upon William Wood, A"

Poem by Swift; first published (anonymously) in 1724, written the same year. The subtitle refers to William WOOD as a "Brazier, Tinker, Hardware-Man, Coiner, Counterfeiter, Founder and Esquire." The poem was not published under Swift's name until 1762. Invoking a variety of insulting puns on William Wood's surname, it emphasizes his greed and dishonesty and ends with a wish for his death by hanging. See also *The DRAPIER'S LETTERS*, "DOING GOOD: A SERMON ON THE OCCASION OF WOOD'S PROJECT," "An EPIGRAM ON WOOD'S BRASS MONEY," "An EXCELLENT NEW SONG UPON HIS GRACE OUR GOOD LORD ARCHBISHOP OF DUBLIN,"

"ON WOOD THE IRONMONGER," "PROMETHEUS," "A SIMILE," and "WOOD, AN INSECT."

## "Sermon upon the Excellency of Christianity, in Opposition to Heathen Philosophy, A"

This sermon was first published in London in 1765, and then again in Dublin the same year. Its date of composition is unknown. Louis Landa describes this sermon as one that offers important insight into what [Swift] thought a proper Christian scheme of morality" (*Prose Works* 9.111).

### SYNOPSIS

Around the time of Christ's birth, "all kinds of learning flourished to a very great degree." For centuries, men have praised "the wisdom and virtue of the Gentile sages" along with that of ancient philosophers. Divine Providence allowed this to happen for "several very wise ends"—mainly to illustrate the superiority of revealed Christian wisdom in comparison to worldly alternatives. Numerous thinkers have exalted ancient and Gentile wisdom at the expense of the gospel, and have even suggested that "all Revelation is false" or "that it hath depraved the nature of man, and left him worse than it found him." Such a "high opinion of Heathen wisdom" is a relatively new phenomenon, unsupported by "primitive times" and contrary to Christ's low esteem of it (exemplified in "treatment of the Pharisees and Sadducees"). The goal of this sermon is to show that some persons' "preference of Heathen wisdom and virtue, before that of the Christian, is every way unjust, and grounded upon ignorance or mistake."

Christian wisdom is superior to "unrevealed philosophy" in various important ways. First, there is a universal defect in the latter because its proponents could never agree on what constitutes the greatest good, "or wherein to place the happiness of mankind." Second, heathen philosophy lacked any consistent "suitable reward" to encourage "progress in virtue." While almost all of its proponents referenced rewards and punishments in the afterlife, this was more of "an entertainment to poets" or a way of frightening children "than a settled principle, by which men pretended to govern their actions." Third, even the most famous heathen philosophers "were never able to give any satisfaction, to others and themselves, in their notions of Deity." Fourth, even those who believed in a "Divine Power" and "Providence" never had any intention "of entirely relying and depending upon either." Instead, they trusted only in themselves.

More evidence of the superiority of revealed wisdom lies in how "defective" the most famous heathen philosophers were in their "lessons of morality." Thales, Solon, Plato, Aristotle, Diogenes, Zeno, and Epicurus all fell short in explaining morals to their followers—some suggesting that "wisdom and morals were useless," others suggesting that happiness lies in worldly pleasures such as health and riches. All of these absurdities show that these philosophers' "defects in morals were purely the flagging and fainting of the mind, for want of a support by revelation from God."

Having focused mainly on the shortcomings of heathen philosophy, Swift proceeds to explain "the perfection of Christian wisdom from above." He quotes I Cor. 3:15–17 to show that the purity of mind and spirit associated with divine wisdom "is peculiar to the gospel." Those filled with this wisdom have pure minds and enjoy "a daily vision of God," which keeps them "unspotted from the world" and enables them to live holy lives "far beyond the examples of the most celebrated philosophers." Another advantage of revealed wisdom is that "it is *peaceable, gentle, and easy to be entreated.*" It promotes kindness without "pride or vanity," empowering men to live in peace. It is also "*without partiality*" to any nation or people (unlike other "philosophical schemes"). Finally, it is "*without hypocrisy*": The gospel forbids "publish[ing] to the world those virtues we have not," and even disallows flaunting those we have.

Unlike Christian virtue, that of "the Grecian sages" was the result of "personal merit, and not influenced by the doctrine of any particular sect." The ancients celebrated "fortitude and temperance" above all else, and regarded Socrates and

Cato as having personified both. None of these men's virtues, however, "were at all owing to any lessons or doctrines of a sect." Instead, they were simply outpourings of each man's "good natural disposition." In contrast, "examples of fortitude and patience" abounded among early Christians, and "were altogether the product of their principles and doctrines." Some may object that Christianity has failed to produce many modern exemplars of these virtues, but that is only because "pretended Christians" far outnumber "true believers." Christianity has also been compromised and "blended up with Gentile philosophy." Ultimately, however, the most compelling reason for the failure of Christianity to "produce the same effects which it did at first" is the abundance of division and dispute among modern Christians.

## COMMENTARY

Swift's role as pastor of a congregation, moral guardian of parishioners who attended St. Patrick's Cathedral, gave him immense satisfaction not only because it was his duty but also because he found his literary, political, and religious interests joined in the writing of his sermons. Every five weeks he was expected to preach, and he prepared carefully, concerned with the effect his words might have on his listeners. Balancing such characteristics as intonation, diction, and intelligibility, he strove for simplicity and clarity, though never agreeing to publish the sermons in the editions he supervised.

Of the 11 surviving sermons known to be Swift's work, "The Excellency of Christianity" serves as what one early biographer called a "preaching pamphlet." Though not focused on political issues, Swift gives the listener a statement of his ethical views— "a proper Christian scheme of morality." His purpose here is to avoid focusing on revelation and instead stress right conduct, an approach he believed would reach more of his audience than deep discussions of the mysteries of the Trinity. This sermon particularly stresses the value of the Christian system of forgiveness and understanding versus the philosophical articles of various Greek and Roman writers, especially how Christian ethics has equal importance when compared to their classical doctrines. Swift seeks to diminish the effect of deistic thought, which gave more attention to the ancient philosophers who achieved wisdom without knowing Christianity. The deist saw no need of divine revelation, but Swift, who was a practical and plain preacher, has no sympathy for setting aside Christian principles and can see only danger in placing religion in a subordinate role. If he can prove that the ancients' beliefs were defective in comparison to Christian doctrine, then his sermon will show the validity of Christian doctrine and its continued universality. By directing his analysis to the nature of mankind, Swift argues that only Christianity offers a viable answer in the debate between vice and virtue. Human nature, being altogether selfish, seeks immediate pleasure, but in this traditional discussion Swift focuses on eternal welfare.

This pattern of ethical thought concerning the future of one's soul versus the argument that virtue is in itself its own reward points clearly to Swift's opposition to Stoic and Epicurean thought. Basically his sermon argues for a true reading of human psychology, which would reveal man's compassionate nature. Though the date of composition for this sermon is unknown, Swift's theme on the doctrine of future rewards surfaces in a number of his prose works throughout his lifetime. Possibly the most memorable illustration of this design appears in GULLIVER'S TRAVELS, where the Houyhnhnms of Part 4 face their world with an icy, stoical calm and practice eugenics, or in the aphoristic "Thoughts on Various Subjects," where his criticism of the Stoic philosophy focuses on its basic folly.

# "Sermon upon the Martyrdom of King Charles I, A"

Often treated as a party piece in which Swift attacks his usual opponents (WHIGS and Dissenters), this sermon was preached on January 30, 1726—the day established after the restoration of CHARLES II for commemorating the tragic "humiliation" of the death of his father, Charles I. It was first published in London in 1765 and then again in Dublin the same year.

## SYNOPSIS

Many have complained against the church for "keeping this holy day of humiliation" (January 30) memorializing "that excellent King and blessed Martyr Charles I." Those who rail against it, however, either lack religion altogether or draw "their principles, and perhaps their birth, from the abettors of those who contrived the murder of that Prince." They object to observing the day of humiliation on several grounds. They claim that it perpetuates discord "among our country-men" and "disunite[s] Protestants." They cite a law that was made at Charles II's restoration, giving a general pardon and forbidding "all reproaches upon that occasion." Finally, they argue that it is insensitive to maintain the memory of Charles I's execution "for all generations." Assuming that most of the congregation is "ignorant in many particulars concerning that horrid murder, and the rebellion preceding it," Swift proposes to review the highlights of the story, explain the consequences "this bloody deed had upon these kingdoms," and outline the "good uses" to which this "solemn day of humiliation may be applied."

During Charles I's reign, kings had much greater powers than they do now. Many kings before him had tested the limits of those prerogatives, but as the royal lands were increasingly bestowed upon favorites, power ("which always follows property") was silently transferred to the people. Under Queen Mary I, many Protestants had fled to Geneva—"a commonwealth governed without a king." A number of them returned under the more tolerant Elizabeth I, and having become accustomed to the religion and government "of the place they had left," sought to establish both in England. These Protestants proved "extremely troublesome to the church and state." Styling themselves "Puritans," they worked to eliminate "all the errors of Popery" that remained in the Anglican Church and (not satisfied with that) proceeded to discard "many laudable and edifying institutions of the Primitive Church." Soon, they even began to question "kingly government" in favor of the commonwealth they had enjoyed in Geneva.

By the middle of Charles I's reign, the Puritans constituted "a considerable faction in the kingdom, and in the Lower House of parliament." They promulgated "false and bitter libels against the bishops and clergy," and the House of Commons became "insolent and uneasy to the King"—even refusing to supply him with the funds necessary to support his family. The "wicked" Puritan "faction" joined with a like-minded group from Scotland and forced the king to have his chief minister (Thomas Wentworth) executed for no justifiable cause. They also compelled him to "pass another law" that made it impossible for him to dissolve Parliament without its members' consent.

When a rebellion began in Ireland, Parliament left the king on his own. They even turned his army against him, instigating a rebellion in England that lasted "for four or five years" and culminated in his execution. To pave the way for this heinous murder, the evil Puritans had manipulated the soldiers in an effort to "exclude from the House" all members of Parliament suspected of having "the least inclination towards and agreement with the King." All of this shows that Charles "was, in all respects, a real martyr for true religion and the liberty of his people."

The Puritans' treason yielded a number of woeful consequences. The Irish rebellion was the result of the "rebellious spirit" they displayed and encouraged in the House of Commons. Once they had gained the power they sought, their own Parliament was never able to reach a consensus on "any one method of settling a form either of religion or civil government." Instead, they "changed every day from schism to schism, from heresy to heresy, and from one faction to another. The confusion that currently exists in Britain over "several ways of serving God" is a long-standing monument to their indecision. Their murderous rebellion against the king also initiated the "rise and progress of Atheism among us" and corrupted the "old virtue and loyalty, and generous spirit of the English nation." It forced Charles I's children to flee for their lives to foreign lands, and caused "vast numbers of God's houses" in England to be obliterated or defaced. In the time since Charles I's murder, it has become clear that that act caused "all the public evils we have hitherto suffered, or may suffer in the future" at the hands of ignoble princes or "the wickedness of the people."

There are many "good uses" to which "this solemn day of humiliation may be applied." First, it reminds monarchs to take special care in selecting "advisers in matters of law." Second, it reminds the people of their need to suppress "unruly spirits" who promote "new doctrines and discipline in the church, or new forms of government in the state." Third, it points out the need for contemporary Dissenters to publicly "renounce" the "principles upon which their predecessors acted" in rebelling against their king. Fourth, it reminds professed Anglicans who "presume in discourse to justify" what happened to the king of how dissonant that opinion is "to the doctrine of Christ and his apostles, as well as to the articles of our church." Fifth, it warns the people not to believe "those deluding spirits who, under pretence of a purer and more reformed religion, would lead them from their duty to God and the laws." Finally (as to the objection that observing the day perpetuates animosity among Protestants) it is vital for those who love the church to stand firmly against anyone who today supports the principles behind the Puritans' rebellion.

Swift qualifies all that he has said by assuring his audience that he is not arguing in favor of "absolute unlimited power in any one man." Rather, he is advocating a middle way between two extremes relating to obedience. One regards the king as equal with God and above the law, while the other subjects the king to the whims of every passing faction. The Scriptures clearly come out against authorities that fail to punish evil and to reward goodness, and the recent "Revolution under [WILLIAM] of Orange" is a clear example of justified rebellion. Being "good and loyal subjects" requires finding the middle ground between these extremes by choosing "*to obey God and the King, and meddle not with those who are given to change.*"

## COMMENTARY

Only a few of Swift's sermons survive and, as Davis makes clear, those are conservative and often predictable in their prescriptive method for counsel, wisdom, and dependence on common sense and plain reason. This sermon does more than simply outline the ideas of a conventional clergyman. It provides Swift's views on the pillars of 18th-century society: monarchy, government, and party.

Ordered for the Anglican Church, such commemorative sermons often seemed overly emotional and dramatic, but the occasion demanded high-energy orations, intended to elicit audience response. The Dissenters found the celebrations objectionable and had petitioned for their removal, a point which lent increased drama to Swift's essay since he disliked Dissenters intensely. His argument focuses on justifying the role of Anglicanism in protecting the health of the state, and how these various other religious sects contribute to weakening the nation. His conclusion reminds readers of the justified fears he had in the potential destruction of the Constitution, the dangers of instability, and the rise of absolutism. Appropriately, his views here seem in conjunction with those of other political theorists, most particularly John Locke, whose second *Treatise on Government* (1690) provided the classic statement of the principles of civil liberty underlying the Revolution of 1688. Locke and Swift both promote principles that justified the actions taken against Charles I and James II, since these kings had acted so arbitrarily as to violate the laws of their kingdom.

## "Sheridan, A Goose"

Poem by Swift; first published in 1808, written in 1718. Along with other poems such as "To Thomas Sheridan" and "Mary the Cook-Maid's Letter to Dr. Sheridan," it is one of a number of items in an extended series of trifles circulated among Swift, Dr. Thomas Sheridan, Rev. Patrick Delany, Rev. Daniel Jackson, and the Rochfort brothers.

## "Sheridan's Submission"

Poem by Swift; first published in 1735, written about 1718. Subtitled "Written by the Dean," it is one in a series of comical poems by George Rochfort, Dr. Thomas Sheridan, and Swift, making fun of Daniel Jackson's large nose. They also

wrote joking "answers" in the voice of Jackson himself. In this obsequious "Submission" addressed to Jackson, Swift (speaking as Sheridan) wryly declares that Jackson has routed his detractors. He blames Delany and the others for having compelled him to join in the lampoon, and laments the pain he feels as a result of it.

## "Short Character of His Ex[cellency] T[homas] E[arl] of W[harton] L[ord] L[ieutenant] of I[reland], A"

The essay on Thomas Wharton, whom Swift had come to know in June 1709 after returning from England to Ireland, cultivating a supposedly friendly relationship with this new chief official and representative of English parliamentary power, reveals the dean's appreciation of the lord lieutenant's intelligence and cunning. Wharton clearly has the ability and the strength to exercise his power over the Irish House of Commons, especially since all too many of the Anglo-Irish are more than willing to accede to English imperialism.

The sharp tone and unremitting suspicion that colors the essay have their origin in Swift's reaction against the immense power of the Whigs during this period. He had been for a while nursing a growing dissatisfaction with the Whigs, even disillusionment with their policies. Robert Harley's offer to join with the Tories was timely and spoke to Swift's character, which craved notice and attention, but more significant, the Tories fit his political principles. Wharton's power and position as one of leading members of the Whig Junto added considerable weight in Swift's decision to learn all he could about this new lord lieutenant of Ireland but always to keep his own counsel, since Wharton was clearly a dangerous enemy.

The close observation of Wharton would cease in August 1710, when Swift accompanied him on a return trip to England, but the Tories were now in power and the dean would seek remission of the

First Fruits and Twentieth Parts from Harley. But Wharton would continue playing a significant role in trying to undermine the Tory ministry, and Swift would attack him in the EXAMINER, number 17 (November 30, 1710), portraying him as Verres, a Roman governor of Sicily, of whom Cicero had written contemptuously. At the same time Swift had begun the "Short Character," "a study of a man whose easy insolence and complete unconsciousness of ordinary standards of behavior" surely fascinated the intelligent observer. "In his commerce with mankind his general rule is, to endeavor to impose on their understanding, for which he hath one receipt, a composition of lies and oaths. . . . [H]e is generally the worst companion in the world; his thoughts being wholly taken up between vice and politics." Whether this attack was ordered and carried out to satisfy the demands of party politics or not, Swift exhibits sincere pleasure in the vigor of his effort—he has deep contempt for Wharton.

Later, in "A PROPOSAL FOR THE UNIVERSAL USE OF IRISH MANUFACTURE," he returned to this theme of lying: "his lordship owned it was true, but swore the words were put into his mouth by direct orders of the court. [He] look[ed] down upon this kingdom, as if it had been one of the colonies of outcasts in America." Swift could often think of no finer insult or demeaning comment than of associating an English aristocrat with American immigrants: a pack of traitors, transported felons, and Dissenters. He had first built this image into exaggerated form in "The CHARACTER" with a description indicting Wharton as the arch liar: "he is without the sense of shame or glory, as some men are without the sense of smelling; and, therefore, a good name to him is no more than a precious ointment would be to these." The cunning actions of this aristocrat as he diminishes and degrades those for whom he has responsibility, whether clergy, single or married women, judges, or any person having less power than himself, create an unforgettable portrait.

When a recent critic, David Nokes, finds Wharton reduced "to a sub-human species, a kind of proto-Yahoo," the reader can appreciate, even from this one example, why the harsh satire of Part 4 of

GULLIVER'S TRAVELS seemed necessary (*Hypocrite Reversed* 127). Apparently, Wharton suffered from a complete insensitivity to the feelings of others, and his hard character made him impervious to subtler forms of criticism. Of course, as the leading Tory pamphleteer charged with presenting the best evidence to the country concerning its new ministry, Swift must punish Vice and praise Virtue. His choice for the character of Vice was perfect, and his attack on the individual accomplished without resorting to judicious balance. He must, in fact, make him into a kind of animal, "a serpent, a wolf, a crocodile or a fox," whose viciousness seems a natural quality of its being. The writer of satire has only to identify the animal, and its repellant nature will speak for itself, its indifference to moral argument and public opinion being its natural characteristics. Swift detaches himself from personal involvement and simply reveals the facts as a forensic examiner would, finding how easily Wharton has fooled the world.

# "Short View of the State of Ireland, A"

One of Swift's many pamphlets on Irish affairs; first published anonymously in Dublin on March 19, 1728, by Sarah HARDING. It was subsequently reprinted in *Mist's Weekly Journal* and the INTELLIGENCER (number 15). Asserting that his desire is not to complain but only to "relate facts," Swift lists 14 conditions necessary for any country to thrive and become "rich," and then explains how Ireland has unnecessarily fallen short on each one. The conditions include factors such as having soil that is fruitful enough "to produce the Necessaries and Conveniences of Life," having the privilege of free trade "in all foreign Countries," and "disposing" all important offices "only to the Natives, or at least with very few Exceptions."

Swift follows this catalogue with a compelling explanation of how the English government (with some complicity on the part of the Irish) has made

Though brief, the "Short View of Ireland" is one of Swift's most important commentaries on what he viewed as England's oppression of the Irish. It is commonly read as an introduction to the "MODEST PROPOSAL," but is also closely related to a number of other works in which Swift outlines the many ways in which the Irish were being programmatically exploited for England's gain. Examples include The DRAPIER'S LETTERS, "The STORY OF THE INJURED LADY," Part 3 of GULLIVER'S TRAVELS, "An ANSWER TO A PAPER, CALLED 'A MEMORIAL OF THE POOR INHABITANTS, TRADESMEN, AND LABOURERS OF THE KINGDOM OF IRELAND,'" and the "ANSWER TO THE CRAFTSMAN." While Irish oppression was certainly the primary impetus for Swift's pamphlet, the immediate stimulus (as Patrick Kelly has pointed out) was likely Sir John BROWNE's Seasonable Remarks on Trade. Swift regarded Browne's tract as "a clumsy attempt to convince Englishmen that conditions in Ireland were by no means as bad as generally represented" (Kelly 138). The "Short View" made clear that the poor conditions in Ireland had not been exaggerated, and enumerated many of the issues that had led Swift to take up Ireland's cause and, through his writings, gain heroic status as the "Hibernian Patriot."

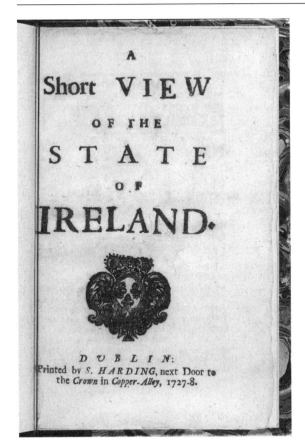

Title page of "A Short View of the State of Ireland," 1728 *(Courtesy of University of Pennsylvania Libraries)*

it virtually impossible for Ireland to enjoy any of these conditions, mainly by forcing her citizens to "obey some Laws [they] never consented to." The Irish, however, deserve some of the blame for their country's state since, for example, citizens of "both sexes, but especially the Women, despise and abhor to wear any of their own Manufactures, even those which are better made than in other Countries" (see "PROPOSAL FOR THE UNIVERSAL USE OF IRISH MANUFACTURE"). While the English enjoy each and every one of the 14 conditions needed for a kingdom to prosper, they are able to do so only because of their exploitation of the Irish. This must one day come to an end, however, because *"when the Hen is starved to Death, there will be no more Golden Eggs."*

# "Simile, A"

Poem by Swift; first published in 1735, written in 1725. This is one of several poems by Swift against William WOOD and his patent for Irish coinage. It targets Sir Robert WALPOLE and the duchess of KENDAL for attempting to conceal the harm of Wood's halfpence behind an official patent, and credits the Drapier with exposing the truth. See also The DRAPIER'S LETTERS, "DOING GOOD: A SERMON ON THE OCCASION OF WOOD'S PROJECT," "An EPIGRAM ON WOOD'S BRASS MONEY," "An EXCELLENT NEW SONG UPON HIS GRACE OUR GOOD LORD ARCHBISHOP OF DUBLIN," "ON WOOD THE IRONMONGER," "PROMETHEUS," "A SERIOUS POEM UPON WILLIAM WOOD," and "WOOD, AN INSECT."

# "Some Advice Humbly Offered to the Members of the October Club in a Letter from a Person of Honour"

See "ADVICE HUMBLY OFFER'D TO THE MEMBERS OF THE OCTOBER CLUB."

# "Some Considerations in the Choice of a Recorder"

This election broadside was printed without the usual information concerning place or printer in February 1733, in the middle of a Dublin election. George FAULKNER reprinted it in 1746 in *Works*, and again in 1751, and in London in *Miscellanies* in 1746.

## SYNOPSIS

The writer explains that since he is a stranger to all the candidates he is wholly impartial and can offer his opinions freely. Aldermen's sons usually would qualify for jobs in city government, but not in this case where being the recorder requires "good abilities in his calling, an unspotted character, and able practitioner," and nearly seven other sterling qualities. Every dealer and shopkeeper in the city needs an effective recorder of parliamentary actions who will protect his best interests. The last paragraph mirrors a prayer, where the writer asks God to direct the Dublin citizenry in their choice of this recorder because we will live with our selection for many years.

## COMMENTARY

When the Recorder of the City of Dublin died in January 1733, the authorities planned an election and several candidates came forward for the seat. Faulkner printed some verses in the *Dublin Journal* in favor of Eaton STANNARD and at the same time this Swift essay appeared. Swift does not affirm Stannard as his choice but he makes clear that the opposing candidates' backgrounds will not do for this important post and its significance with the Dublin merchants and shopkeepers. Subsequently Stannard won the election and Swift appointed him as one of the executors of his will. This interest in purely secular issues had a positive effect in this case, as well as influenced a parliamentary election which Swift wrote about in "ADVICE TO THE FREEMEN OF DUBLIN."

# "Spider and the Bee"

Fable in "The BATTLE OF THE BOOKS." See also BACON, Francis.

# "Stella at Woodpark"

Poem by Swift; first published in 1735, written in 1723. Swift wrote it as a means of reconciliation with Stella (Esther JOHNSON). Outraged after Esther VANHOMRIGH sent her a letter bluntly asking whether or not she and Swift were married, Stella had (according to Thomas SHERIDAN, Jr.) "retired in great resentment" to Charles FORD's "country seat" at Woodpark, where she was lavishly entertained as mistress of the house. Written after her return to Dublin on October 3, the poem makes fun of Stella's attempt to maintain the luxurious lifestyle she enjoyed at Woodpark even after her return to far more modest lodgings.

# "Stella's Birthday (1719)"

Poem by Swift; first published in 1728, written in 1719. Although the first line of the poem suggests that it celebrates Stella's (Esther JOHNSON's) 34th birthday, she actually turned 38 on March 13 of that year. This was the first of seven birthday poems Swift wrote for her (see below for specific titles). As a group, these tributes provide what Ricardo Quintana has called a "key to the enigmatic relations between Swift and Stella" (*Mind and Art of Jonathan Swift* 278). The birthday poem for 1719 provides clear evidence that these verses were not complimentary in any traditional sense: Swift tells Stella not to be discouraged just because her "size and years are doubled" and indicates that he wishes her plumpness and faded beauty could be separated from her wit, which the years have not diminished.

Herbert Davis, Irvin Ehrenpreis, Nora Crow Jaffe, and others have pointed out that Swift was working to distinguish his own "expressions of tenderness" from those of Petrarch in the *Canzoniere* and Sir Philip Sidney in *Astrophel and Stella* (Ehrenpreis, *Swift* III.102). David Nokes, however, suggests that while Swift's "unromantic comments" are certainly anti-Petrarchan, they simultaneously illustrate his "tendency to reduce Stella's self-esteem by de-sexualizing her." In this poem, especially, she is portrayed as having "passed from girlhood to tubby middle-age without being allowed a sexual prime" (*Hypocrite Reversed* 249). Jaffe, on the other hand, reads the birthday poem insults as Swift proving that "he can write a better compliment than his [Petrarchan] predecessors because he takes actuality into account and still manages to indicate that Stella is twice as beautiful and twice as wise as any other woman" (*The Poet Swift* 89). See also "STELLA'S BIRTHDAY (1721)," "STELLA'S BIRTHDAY (1723): A GREAT BOTTLE OF WINE, LONG BURIED, BEING THAT DAY DUG UP," "STELLA'S BIRTHDAY (1725)," "STELLA'S BIRTHDAY (1727)," "TO STELLA ON HER BIRTHDAY," and "TO STELLA, WRITTEN ON THE DAY OF HER BIRTH."

## "Stella's Birthday (1721)"

Poem by Swift; first published in 1728, written in 1721. Stella (Esther JOHNSON) wrote highly complimentary verses for Swift on his birthday the same year. Like the other birthday poems Swift wrote for Johnson (see titles below), this one tempers bluntness with praise. Swift mentions her "angel's face, a little cracked" and the "fainting rays" of her eyes as he marvels at her enduring virtue. The entire poem is built around a comparison of Stella to an inn

called the "Angel," where travelers initially stop because of the attractive sign hanging out front and end up recommending the inn to their friends based on how much they like what lies inside. Swift predicts that, like the inn whose business thrives even after its sign has faded, Stella (unlike other women) will remain attractive to those who know her even after her "locks must all be grey." See also "STELLA'S BIRTHDAY (1719)," "STELLA'S BIRTHDAY (1723): A GREAT BOTTLE OF WINE, LONG BURIED, BEING THAT DAY DUG UP," "STELLA'S BIRTHDAY (1725)," "STELLA'S BIRTHDAY (1727)," "TO STELLA ON HER BIRTHDAY," and "TO STELLA, WRITTEN ON THE DAY OF HER BIRTH."

## "Stella's Birthday (1723): A Great Bottle of Wine, Long Buried, Being That Day Dug Up"

Poem by Swift; first published in 1728, written in 1723. It was one of seven birthday poems Swift wrote for Stella (Esther JOHNSON). Irvin Ehrenpreis calls it a "charmless poem based on a grotesque image" (*Swift* III.416). The poem explains how Swift attempted to praise Stella in one of his annual birthday tributes, but had no success until he appealed to Apollo, who directed him to dig up an old bottle of wine and drink it for poetic inspiration. See also "STELLA'S BIRTHDAY (1719)," "STELLA'S BIRTHDAY (1721)," "STELLA'S BIRTHDAY" (1725), "STELLA'S BIRTHDAY (1727)," "TO STELLA ON HER BIRTHDAY," and "TO STELLA, WRITTEN ON THE DAY OF HER BIRTH."

## "Stella's Birthday (1725)"

Poem by Swift; first published in 1728, written in 1725. It is one of seven birthday poems Swift wrote for Stella (Esther JOHNSON). Like the others (listed below), this tribute tempers its praise of Stella with unflattering references to the ravages of time:

"Adieu bright wit, and radiant eyes; / You must be grave, and I be wise." It is also significantly concerned with Swift's own aging: "That half your locks are turned to grey; / I'll ne'er believe a word they say, / 'Tis true, but let it not be known, / My eyes are somewhat dimmish grown." In his biography of Swift, Irvin Ehrenpreis calls this poem "a song composed by an elderly Apollo for a middle-aged Venus" (III.425). See also "STELLA'S BIRTHDAY (1719)," "STELLA'S BIRTHDAY (1721)," "STELLA'S BIRTHDAY (1723): A GREAT BOTTLE OF WINE, LONG BURIED, BEING THAT DAY DUG UP," "STELLA'S BIRTHDAY (1727)," "TO STELLA ON HER BIRTHDAY," and "TO STELLA, WRITTEN ON THE DAY OF HER BIRTH."

# "Stella's Birthday (1727)"

Poem by Swift; first published in 1728, written 1726–27. By the time Swift composed these verses Stella (Esther JOHNSON) was suffering from the illness that would prove to be her last, and the poem suggests that Swift himself was feeling very old. In his edition of Swift's *Poems*, Pat Rogers calls this widely discussed poem "the last and most deeply felt" of the seven birthday poems Swift wrote for Stella. Nora Crow Jaffe views it as the best of that group and "the most difficult to analyze" (*The Poet Swift* 11). John Irwin Fischer agrees and writes in *On Swift's Poetry* that this is "the most moving" of the birthday poems to Stella. He argues that in it Swift is more earnest than before in utilizing the "motifs" that characterize the entire group: "recognition of age, the uses of frailty, and mythic statement" (145). According to Jaffe, in this poem Swift works out "a perspective from which he and Stella can look at the prospect of her death" and, "having made his emotions manageable, he has felt free to declare his love, the raison d'être of the poem" (*The Poet Swift* 10). He also, in her view, provides an unprecedented display of "his capacity for tenderness, honesty, and . . . strength of mind" ("Jonathan Swift" 14). Louise K. Barnett reads the poem more critically, presenting it as a failed attempt to overcome vulnerability. She explains that in other

poems (such as "The PROGRESS OF BEAUTY"), Swift can treat death "as the merited punishment of flagrant sinfulness." In this poem to Stella, however, he is "forced to confront the issue of physical decline and death . . . as the inescapable end of an admirable life" (*Swift's Poetic Worlds* 104). See also "STELLA'S BIRTHDAY (1719)," "STELLA'S BIRTHDAY (1721)," "STELLA'S BIRTHDAY (1723): A GREAT BOTTLE OF WINE, LONG BURIED, BEING THAT DAY DUG UP," "STELLA'S BIRTHDAY (1725)," "TO STELLA ON HER BIRTHDAY," and "TO STELLA, WRITTEN ON THE DAY OF HER BIRTH."

# "Storm, The"

Poem by Swift; first published in 1749, written in 1722. Swift wrote it as an indignant response to Josiah HORT being made bishop of Ferns. Subtitled "Minerva's Petition," it presents Hort unfavorably through a conversation among the gods about whether or not to destroy him. Explaining the occasion of the poem, F. Elrington Ball cites a December 12, 1722, newspaper account of a violent storm that drove the "king's yacht" into Scotland. Among others, Hort, George BERKELEY, and "an Irish Dean" are listed among the passengers. When Archbishop William KING questioned Swift about the poem following a complaint from Hort, Swift denied having written it and blamed Edmund Curll for its existence.

# "Story of the Injured Lady, The"

Cast as a letter from a jilted lady to one of her male friends, this is a commentary on Anglo-Irish relations that emphasizes England's abuse and exploitation of Ireland. It was not published until 1746 (one year after Swift's death), and George FAULKNER included it in volume 8 of his edition of Swift's *Works*, which was published the same year. Herbert Davis suggests that Swift may have written it as early as 1707 and taken it up once more early in 1720 following the passage of an "Act for the better securing the Dependence of the Kingdom of Ireland upon the Crown of Great Britain." As Davis notes, the "Injured Lady" provides a useful "introduction" to the political tracts Swift wrote in the early 1720s (such as his "PROPOSAL FOR THE UNIVERSAL USE OF IRISH MANUFACTURE") and summarizes what he saw as the most blatant forms of England's oppression of the Irish (*Prose Works* IX.x).

Personifying Ireland, the "Lady" who is the author of the letter describes how she has been rejected by her lover (England) in favor of a coarse and unattractive rival (Scotland), characterized by "her natural Sluttishness." As his inexplicable devotion to this unworthy rival has increased, the Lady's ex-lover has treated her with mounting unkindness. She was once beautiful but has grown "pale and thin with Grief and ill Usage"—herself and her household suffering because of her initial naïveté. Among other things, he has ordered that she and her entire household send all their "Goods to his Market just in their Naturals; the Milk immediately from the Cow without making it into Cheese or Butter; the Corn in the Ear;" and "the Wool as it cometh from the Sheeps Back." His explanation for this is that she and her people are filthy, and he and his household want nothing that has been tainted by their touch. His real motive, however, is to provide work for his "own Folks." In short, he has engaged freely in any form of oppression against her that promised even the smallest benefit to him and his people.

When the ex-lover and his new mistress had a quarrel in the midst of planning their wedding, the Lady dutifully promised to stand by him "against her and all the World." The rival immediately became "more tractable," and the wedding proceeded as planned. The Lady's only reward for her faithfulness was to be made a "Sempstress" to the man's "Grooms and Footment"—a position she is "forced to accept or starve." Having given up hope of ever recovering the man from her rival, all the Lady desires at this point is "to be free from the Persecutions of this unreasonable Man." He will soon deplete her resources completely unless something changes, and he has begun to impose policies on her and her household without bothering to consult them. She concludes the letter by asking for her friend's advice on how best to "protect" her freedom and resources from this "unkind, inconstant Man."

In a companion piece, "The Answer to the Injured Lady," Swift adopts the persona of the Lady's respondent and outlines what he believes Ireland's policies should be in terms of her relations with England. He urges her to convene a meeting of her tenants and have them agree to four "Resolutions": (1) that they "have no Dependence upon the said Gentleman," other than what is stipulated in an "old Agreement" that requires them "to have the same Steward" (referring to the king); (2) that they will no longer yield all their goods "to the Market of his Town" unless they wish to do so, and they will not be forbidden from selling them elsewhere; (3) that the servants whose wages are paid by the Lady will "live at Home," or lose their positions; and (4) that the ex-lover cannot break any leases the Lady grants to tenants. He ends by assuring the Lady that some of her ex-lover's own tenants oppose his "severe Usage" of her and anticipate an opportunity to rectify her situation (suggesting that many English citizens recognize and oppose their country's sins against the Irish).

# "Strephon and Chloe"

Poem by Swift; first published 1734 in a pamphlet with "The LADY'S DRESSING ROOM" and "CASSINUS AND PETER," probably written 1731. It is one of Swift's excremental or scatalogical poems. Like "Dressing Room," it dramatizes the effects of STREPHON's realization that his "goddess" (in this case it is CHLOE rather than CELIA) is "as *mortal* as himself at least." More than half of the poem describes Strephon's heightened anticipation of consummating his marriage to Chloe and his worry that she will never "permit a brutish man to touch her." Everything changes, however, when he discovers "heavenly Chloe's" bodily functions. Unlike his response in "Dressing Room," however, Strephon's reaction in this case is not revulsion but liberation: The newlyweds "soon from all constraints are freed" and "can see each other *do their need*." Swift cites the couple's neglect of "fair Decency" to encourage founding "passion" on "sense and wit" rather than unrealistic "fine ideas."

# "Swift's Account of His Mother's Death"

This paragraph appears as an entry in Swift's Account Book of Personal Expenses for 1710–11. It was written on the May 1710 page, when Swift was serving in the Laracor parish.

## SYNOPSIS

On Wednesday, May 10, 1710, Swift received a letter from his sister, Mrs. Jane FENTON, dated May 9, that included a letter from Mrs. Worrall at Leicester to Mrs. Fenton providing a report on the death of Swift's mother, Mrs. Abigail SWIFT, who had died on Monday, April 24, 1710. She had been ill for more than four months and especially weak over the most recent six weeks. "I have now lost my barrier between me and death." Swift compliments the peace and resignation of his mother to her death, and her truth, piety, and charity—all values which would have readied her for Heaven.

## COMMENTARY

Swift's good friend, Joseph ADDISON, had arrived in Ireland as secretary to Thomas WHARTON, lord lieutenant of Ireland, a few days before Swift learned of his mother's death. When he received the news, Swift was shocked, even though he was aware of how sick she had been during the past year. His early years remained difficult ones in their relationship, but since becoming an adult Swift had shown increased devotion and support of his mother who lived in southern England. His account contains a sincere, pious, and utterly unaffected valediction for her. Yet, clearly his last sentence concerning grief and loss focuses on a major Swiftian theme: keeping the darkness and chaos of life separate from the terror of death. Relatives and close friends made the world a more palatable environment, and with the loss of one of them Swift felt once again

doubts of the existence of heaven and the uncertainty of whether there was a world to come.

# "Swift to Sheridan"

Poem by Swift; first published 1808, written about 1719. Along with other poems such as "MARY THE COOK-MAID'S LETTER TO DR. SHERIDAN" and "SHERIDAN, A GOOSE," it is one of a number of items in an extended series of trifles circulated among Swift, Dr. Thomas SHERIDAN, Rev. Patrick DELANY, Rev. Daniel JACKSON, and the ROCHFORT brothers. This poem is Swift's answer to a "crambo" poem by SHERIDAN in which the end of each line rhymes with *Dean.*

# "Tale of a Tub, A"

This prose satire is Swift's first major work and one of the truly memorable achievements of the 18th century. Biographer David Nokes writes that it is impossible to assign its composition to any "particular period in Swift's life," but internal allusions suggest that much of it may have been written (like "The BATTLE OF THE BOOKS") in 1696–97, during Swift's employment with Sir William TEMPLE at Moor Park (*Hypocrite Reversed* 43). The remarkable and immediate popularity of the "Tale" is evident based on its publication history: It was first printed in London in 1704, and appeared in two additional editions that same year. A fourth edition came out in 1705, and an enlarged fifth edition five years later. John Hawkesworth was the first to include the "Tale" in an edition of Swift's collected *Works* in 1755.

## SYNOPSIS

### Apology, Preface, and Section 1

Written (as the subtitle indicates) "for the Universal Improvement of Mankind," the tale begins with an "Apology" dated June 3, 1709, that offers a brief history of the text and explains the nature and objects

Since the apology is mainly "intended for the Satisfaction of future Readers," the writer admits that it is probably unnecessary to "take any notice" of all the ephemeral responses that have been written to the tale. Nonetheless, he discusses several at great length. He concludes the apology by asserting that a combination of wit and humor "render" any work "always acceptable to the World." Readers who possess neither wit nor humor, however, allow their "Pride, Pedantry, and Ill-Manners" to prevent them from appreciating such works. The tale contains little for which a young author may not be forgiven. The "Tale" was intended for "Men of Wit and Taste," and those who fit that description have responded to it positively. Finally, it appears that the bookseller asked some gentlemen to write "explanatory Notes" for the tale. The author has never seen these notes, and therefore makes no guarantees as to their accuracy. Once they are printed, he expects to "find twenty Meanings" assigned to the tale "which never enter'd into his Imagination." More prolegomena follow, including a postscript, a letter from the bookseller to John SOMERS, comments from "The Bookseller to the Reader," and an "Epistle Dedicatory" to Prince Posterity.

There is also a preface that explains the circumstances surrounding the tale. The "grandees" of both church and state were concerned that the remarkably great wits "of the present Age" would (during peacetime) begin to "pick holes" in both institutions. They decided that something had to be done to prevent this, and devised an extensive long-term project to that effect. In the meantime, they needed a more immediate solution that would suffice until the "main Design" could be carried out. They decided to adopt the strategy of sailors who, when they encounter a whale at sea, throw an empty tub in his path to divert him from destroying their ship. That is where the "Tale" comes in: It is designed to divert the *Leviathans* and prevent them "from tossing and sporting with the *Commonwealth*." While the wits argue about what the "Tale" means, "a large Academy" can be built, and when it is completed these "unquiet Spirits" can be "disposed" into its "several Schools" and rendered harmless. After a long aside on what characterizes an admirable preface, the author ends this section and

Frontispiece of "A Tale of a Tub" *(London, 1710)*

of its satire. It further asserts that the author cannot understand why the clergy have responded so negatively to the "Tale," and insists that it is unfair that anyone should try to name the author. Lawyers, physicians, or any other group would have appreciated being frankly apprised of their abuses; when it comes to corruption in religion, however, it is clearly a different story. Many have accused the author of having had "ill intentions" in what have been misrepresented as parodies of other writers' work. This was not his intension in the least. There is also a "thread" of irony running through the entire work, but while "Men of Taste" have noticed and appreciated it, others have offered "weak and insignificant" objections.

introduces the tale in section 1 by lamenting the struggles modern writers face in seeking readers who can appreciate their works.

### Section 2

"Once upon a Time" male triplets were born, and even the midwife who delivered them was unsure about which was the eldest. Their father died when the children were young, and he left each of them a new (but plain) coat as an inheritance. On his deathbed, he commanded his sons to wear their

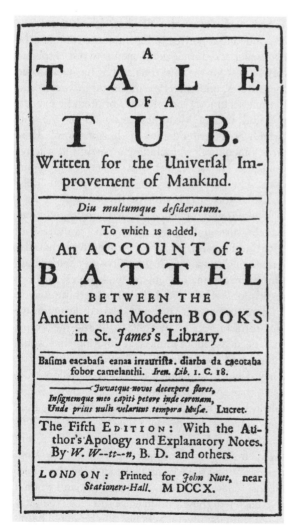

Title page of "A Tale of a Tub" and "The Battle of the Books" *(London, 1710)*

coats clean "and brush them often," adding that in his will he left more specific instructions on how to wear and care for the coats. The will also contained penalties for failing to follow the instructions. With his dying breath, he ordered his sons to "live together in one House like Brethren" so that they could thrive.

For seven years, all went well for the brothers. They traveled through "several Countries, encountered a reasonable quantity of Gyants and slew certain Dragons." Soon, however, they went to town and fell in love with some very fashionable ladies there: the Duchess D'Argent, Madame de Grands Titres, and the Countess D'Orgueil. Although the brothers found themselves alienated at first, they soon learned to fit in with the townspeople and were eventually recognized as "the most accomplish'd Persons in the Town." The ladies, however, were still not impressed.

Part of the problem was that a "Sect" had arisen among those "of good Fashion." They worshiped an idol whom they credited with having invented "the *Yard* and the *Needle*," and their principal belief was that the universe was actually a gigantic suit of clothes, "which *invests* every Thing." They further held that man himself was nothing other than a microcosmic "Suit of Cloaths with all its Trimmings:" Religion is his cloak, honesty his shoes, and so forth. Suits of clothes, in fact, "are Rational Creatures, or Men." Those who supported this "System of Religion" differed in some of their particulars, but it was clear to all of them that "outward Dress must needs be the Soul," and that the "Faculties of the Mind" should be understood primarily as ornaments of dress. For example, "*embroidery*" to them "was *Sheer wit; Gold Fringe* was *agreeable Conversation*," and "a huge long *Periwig* was *Humor*."

This strange belief system left the brothers in a dilemma. While their father's will forbade them from adding or subtracting even one thread from their well-made but very plain coats, the fashion-conscious ladies they loved could never abide anything but the most sharply dressed men. Soon everyone who was anyone in town began wearing "*Shoulder-knots*," and the brothers were mercilessly chastised for having none on their coats. One of the brothers—known for his learning—devised a newfangled way of reading the will that allowed for adding shoulder-knots to his and his brothers' coats, and the three of them quickly regained their status as fashionable gentlemen.

Shoulder-knots eventually gave way to gold lace as the ultimate fashion statement, and gold lace to flame-colored satin. That soon became less fashionable than silver fringe, and silver fringe lost out to embroidery "with *Indian Figures*" on it. At every turn, however, the learned brother always came through with a new way of reading his father's will to get around its prohibitions of adding anything to the brothers' coats. Ultimately, the brothers unanimously decided simply to lock the will away in a box. That way, they would never actually have to read the will anymore but could appeal to it as an authority whenever it was convenient. The learned brother became known as the best scholar in the land, and was hired as a children's tutor in the house of "a *certain Lord*." When the lord died, the scholarly brother used his skills to devise a *"Deed of Conveyance"* that left the lord's house to him and his brothers. They immediately turned the lord's children out into the street and lived in the house together.

### Section 3: A Digression Concerning Critics
Despite his best efforts to follow the example set by the "illustrious *Moderns*," the author realizes that he has forgotten to pay homage to his *"good Lords the Criticks."* To atone for this oversight, he will in this section provide a "short Account" of them and "the *Art*." Over the years, the term *critic* has been used to describe several different types of men. Originally, it was used to describe those who "invented or drew up Rules" by which they and others could recognize worthy "productions" and learn to appreciate the *"Sublime* and the *Admirable."* It could also describe a person who worked to restore ancient learning. These definitions of *critic*, however, are now obsolete since both types have been completely "extinct" for some time now.

The third and "Noblest Sort"—the true critic— is a hero descended "from a Celestial Stem" and an ancestry of noble figures such as Momus, BENTLEY, and RYMER. Despite the great benefits these critics have brought to the "Commonwealth of Learning,"

naysayers continue to claim that these critics are a "greater Nuisance to Mankind" than any of the abuses they subdue. Like the heroes of old, these critics travel the "World of Writings" pursuing "Monstrous Faults" and exposing them to the world. All of this yields the definition of a true critic: "a *Discoverer and Collector of Writers Faults."* Often, they deal so intensely with other writers' errors that their own works become abstracts of all that they criticize. Many detractors falsely allege that criticism, as it is currently practiced, is "wholly *Modern*" and has no ancient precedent. The author himself once held to this mistaken belief, but (through the assistance of "our Noble *Moderns*") he now recognizes that the ancients were exceptionally indebted to the much wiser moderns. Ancient writers dealt very obliquely with critics and criticism, afraid to make any "open Attacks" against such an awe-inspiring "Party." True criticism is vital to the "Commonwealth of Learning," and requires remarkable sacrifice: To become a critic, a man must be willing to give up "all the good Qualities of his Mind."

To conclude, the author offers "three Maxims" to help readers recognize "a *True Modern Critic*" when he sees one. Criticism is "truest and best" when it is the very first thing that comes to a critic's mind. True critics also have an instinctive talent for "swarming about the noblest Writers." Finally, a true critic approaches a book like a dog at a feast, "whose Thoughts and Stomach are wholly set upon what the Guests *fling away.*" Having provided this "address" to his patrons, the *"True Modern Critics,"* the author hopes they will treat him with generosity and tenderness.

### Section 4
Once the learned brother had inherited his house, his demeanor began to change. He told his brothers that he was their elder, and that their father had designated him as sole heir. He insisted that they no longer call him "brother," but "Mr. Peter," "Father Peter," and sometimes even "Lord Peter." He also began to fancy himself a *"Projector and Virtuoso,"* and devised a number of remarkable projects and inventions. He purchased a newly discovered continent directly from the men who discovered it, and then

he sold the land over and over again to other people. He also developed a cure for worms, and a "*Whispering-Office*" to aid those who found themselves "bursting with too much *Wind*." He founded an insurance company, originated puppet shows, and even developed a recipe for a "Universal *Pickle*." While other pickles were only good for preserving dead flesh, Peter's pickle (although it looked and tasted like any other) was capable of pickling live persons and animals.

The invention Peter treasured most was "a certain Set of Bulls" unlike any other in the kingdom at that time. These animals were descendants of the bulls who had guarded the golden fleece, although some argued that some degeneracy had occurred. Unlike their ancestors, Peter's bulls had leaden feet instead of brass, but they retained their predecessors' ability to roar and breathe fire. The bulls were unique in that they had "*Fishes Tails*" and were able to fly with ease. Peter routinely sent them out on various errands, and the bulls were so fond of gold that if they met anyone on their journeys they would roar, spit, belch "and *Piss*, and *Fart*, and *Snivel* out *Fire*" until the stranger "flung them a bit of *Gold*."

Peter also began issuing pardons to condemned men who were willing to pay for them. Although he wrote in very strong language that the man possessing the pardon was to be set free, those who trusted in these dicta "lost their Lives and Money too." He had many other inventions and undertakings besides these, but they are too numerous to describe. In the meantime, Peter had become incredibly rich. He had also gone mad (his brain overstrained with devising all of his inventions). He began calling himself "*God Almighty,* and sometimes *Monarch of the Universe*." He required a salute from anyone he met on the street, and eventually kicked his wife (and those of his brothers) out of the house. In their place, he had the first three "Strolers" found on the street picked up and brought to live with him and his brothers. He nailed the cellar door shut, refusing to allow his brothers "a Drop of *Drink*" with their meals. Having heard an alderman praise beef as "*the King of Meat*," he came home and insisted to his brothers that a loaf of bread was the "quintessence" of all meats, made up of beef, mutton, veal,

Illustration of Peter expelling Martin and Jack in "A Tale of a Tub" *(London, 1710)*

venison, partridge, plum pudding, and custard. He promised his brothers a glass of wine, presented them with a dry crust, and encouraged them to drink of it heartily. When the brothers—or anyone else—offered to contradict anything he said, he reacted so violently that "all the Neighbourhood" decided that "he was no better than a Knave."

Fed up with Peter's antics, his brothers decided to move out of the house. They asked for a copy of their father's will, but had to obtain it secretly after Peter denied their request. In rereading the will, they discovered that their father had designated the three of them "equal Heirs," and that Peter's claim as sole heir was groundless. They angrily broke down the door to the cellar and drank their fill, discarded their "concubines," and sent for their wives. Peter returned, saw what they had done, and "with a File of Dragoons at his Heels" banished them both from his house forever.

### Section 5: A Digression in the Modern Kind

Those whom the world honors as "*Modern Authors*" are successful only because their work has been "so highly serviceable to the general Good of Mankind." The author insists that this is what motivates his present "Adventurous Attempt." He has fully "dissected the Carcass of *Human Nature*," and has now undertaken to give a full anatomy of it. The public good, he claims, "is performed by two Ways, *Instruction* and *Diversion*." Nowadays, mankind reaps far more benefits from the latter. Nonetheless, as he completes his current "Divine Treatise" he will skillfully combine both by kneading together "a *Layer* of *Utile* and a *Layer* of *Dulce* at every turn.

In considering how greatly the moderns have outshone the "weak glimmering Lights" of the ancients, the author has found that many "Town-wits" now argue over whether or not the ancients ever truly existed. Dr. Bentley's work provides "wonderful Satisfaction" on this point, but the author bewails the fact that no modern has written "a universal System in a small portable Volume" containing everything that should be "Known, or Believed, or Imagined, or Practised in Life." An ancient philosopher once developed a recipe for such a work, and that is what the author will use as he seeks to meet the great need for such a convenient book.

Using this recipe, the author has found that the works of "a certain Author called *Homer*" are filled with all sorts of "gross Errors." While he assured readers that his work contained a complete collection of all human knowledge, it is obvious that he left out a great deal of it. Among his more notorious faults (for example) was "his gross Ignorance in the *Common Laws*" of England. It is also clear that he knew absolutely nothing about the Anglican Church—a fault for which he and all the ancients have been "justly censured" by Mr. WOTTON in his *Ancient and Modern Learning*. These and other

unforgivable defects in Homer's work have motivated the author to take up his pen. As he proceeds, he will highlight "the Beauties and Excellencies" of his writing. This is a strategy he learned from the greatest modern writers, who always point out what is sublime and admirable about their work just in case readers fail to see "one Grain of either."

The author proclaims himself to be the "*Last Writer*" and the "*freshest*" and most modern of all the Moderns. This gives him "Despotick Power over all authors" who preceded him, and he asserts that power by declaring his disapproval of "that pernicious Custom, of making the Preface a Bill of Fare to the Book." Prefaces are too important for that: John DRYDEN once said, in fact, that readers would never have suspected him to be as great a poet as he was if he had not told them so in so many prefaces. Sadly, "lazy" modern readers too often skip the preface of a work altogether or (especially among critics and wits) read nothing beyond it. The author has devised a strategy to discourage both evils by interspersing his preface throughout "the Body of the Work." Having explained his "own Excellencies and other Mens Defaults," he now returns to his subject.

### Section 6

In a state of exile, Peter's two brothers take up lodging together and resolve never again to depart from the guidelines of their father's will. They also decide to make whatever alterations are needed to bring their coats back in line with their father's commands. In rereading the will, they recognize how grossly they have transgressed its "every Point." Their coats had become agglomerations of years and years of passing fashions. They had never bothered to remove old "trimmings" as they added new ones, and "there was hardly a Thread of the Original Coat to be seen." The brothers chose names for themselves—one Martin, the other Jack—and set to work removing all the lace, ribbons, fringe, and other ornaments from their coats.

The process went quickly at first, with Martin tearing off multiple trimmings at a time. He soon decided, however, that he needed to proceed more carefully in order to avoid damaging the fabric of the coat itself. Instead of tearing the ornaments off, he meticulously used a needle and thread to undo the stitches that held them onto his coat. When he came upon an ornament that was impossible to remove without tearing the coat, he left it alone. Likewise, he did not disturb trimming that covered up some flaw in the coat's fabric.

Jack, on the other hand, continued to rip the trimmings from his coat with renewed violence. He called this intensity *zeal,* and based it on the anger he felt toward Peter. Although he removed ornaments far more quickly than Martin, Jack tore large portions of his coat in the process. Martin begged him to be more cautious, and this threw Jack into a rage. He soon left Martin for new lodgings, and the report around town was that Jack had lost his mind. He eventually founded the sect known as the Aeolists.

### Section 7: A Digression in Praise of Digressions

The author notes that he has sometimes heard of an *Iliad* in a nutshell, but he has far more frequently seen a nutshell in an *Iliad.* For the latter, the "Commonwealth of Learning" should thank the "great *Modern* Improvement of *Digressions.*" While a number of "ill-bred People" complain about long digressions in modern books, it is clear to everyone else that the "Society of writers" would be greatly reduced if authors had to confine their works to "nothing beyond what is to the Purpose."

Things have changed since the times of the Ancients. Back then, there were numerous untapped sources of knowledge and many original subjects about which to write. These days, that is not the case. In response to the lack of fresh subjects, Modern writers have found "a shorter, and more Prudent Method, to become Scholars and Wits, without the fatigue of *Reading* or of *Thinking.*" The Moderns use books in one of two ways: they either memorize their titles and tell everyone how well they know them or (and this is the more noble use) they gain "a thorough Insight into the *Index,* by which the whole Book is governed and turned, like *Fishes* by the *Tail.*"

Digressions are vital these days for two reasons. First, since the means of becoming "Wise, Learned, and Sublime" is now regular and well established,

the number of writers has greatly increased, and it is impossible for authors to avoid interfering with one another. Second, there is no longer enough "new Matter left in Nature" to fill a volume on a single subject. This problem is well illustrated by "the noblest Branch of *Modern* Wit or Invention," the "highly celebrated Talent" of "deducing Similitudes, Allusions, and Applications . . . from the Pudenda of either Sex, together with *their proper Uses.*" So many writers have engaged in this noble endeavor that soon there will be no room for new material. Based upon this example, it is clear that Modern wits have no alternative but to produce "large Indexes, and little Compendiums" based on writings that already exist. This allows for an increasing number of writers to create volumes of material to remain untouched on booksellers' shelves. How else can the Moderns avoid ending up "in an unglorious and undistinguisht Oblivion?" The author ends by assuring readers that the "Necessity of this Digression will easily excuse its length," and that despite his care in placing it in precisely this location in his book, readers may feel free to move it to any "Corner" they please.

### Section 8

The Aeolists (the sect originated by Jack) regarded wind as the "Original Cause of all Things." Spirit, Animus, and similar terms are simply different words for wind, and even life itself is commonly referred to as "the *Breath* of our Nostrils." Aeolist doctrine comprised 32 points, and the author promises to explain a few of the more important components. First, man is the "highest Perfection of all created Things" since wind "abounds" in him more than in any other creature. Second, each man is born with a unique "Portion or Grain" of wind which is to be perfected and then "freely communicated" to the rest of mankind. Based on this doctrine, the Aeolists believed that belching was "the noblest act of a Rational Creature." Their priests had developed a unique means of helping one another increase their wind: Standing in a circle, each priest places a set of bellows into his neighbor's "breech" and then proceeded to blow him up "to the Shape and Size of a *Tun.*" Thus prepared, the priests then departed to release their wind "into their Disciples Chaps." The "chief Sages" among the Aeolists were known by their contorted faces (distorted mouth, bloated cheeks)—the result of frequent and repeated belching.

The Aeolists worshiped the four winds, and regarded the *"Almighty-North"* as principal. Their mysteries and rites are based in part on one of Aeolus's own inventions: a barrel used for "carrying and preserving *Winds.*" There was one of these barrels in each of their temples, and on holy days, "a secret funnel" was run from the priest's "Posteriors to the Bottom of the Barrel." Newly inspired in this manner, the priest could then "disembogue" tempests upon his congregation. This ceremony (along with their maintenance of *"Female* Priests") has led many to conclude that the Aeolists are actually a very ancient sect. As for their devils, the Aeolists have only two: the chameleon ("sworn foe to Inspiration, who in Scorn, devoured large Influences" from the Aeolists' god "without refunding the smallest blast by Eructation") and the windmill (*"Moulinavent"*) who "with four strong Arms" waged constant war with their "divinities."

Whether the Aeolists' system of belief was devised by Jack or (as some argue) "rather copied from the original at *Delphos,*" the author cannot "absolutely determine." His goal in this section has simply been to clear up the many misconceptions that exist surrounding the Aeolists due to years of "extream" misrepresentation. Removing prejudice, ignorance, and malice is a noble undertaking, and one that he can "boldly undertake" with no regard for himself.

### Section 9: A Digression Concerning the Original, the Use and Improvement of Madness in a Commonwealth

The fact that Jack had lost his mind by the time he founded the Aeolists does nothing to detract from the reputation of that "famous Sect." Perusing history, in fact, reveals that some of the greatest acts have been performed by men whose reason has undergone "great Revolutions." Invention in the human mind is fruitful only when the understanding is "troubled and overspread by Vapours, ascending from the lower Faculties." Among many examples of this, there was once a "Great Prince" who gathered a powerful army, amassed "Infinite Treasures"

and an impressive fleet without explaining anything to his ministers or favorites. Everyone wondered what he was up to—some even thought he was planning to institute a "Universal Monarchy." In the end, however, a *State-Surgeon* cured him of his illness by (with a single blow) breaking "the bag"—the Prince's body—and allowing the vapor to escape. This remedy was almost entirely successful, except that the Prince died as it was being administered. It turned out that the cause of this disturbance had been "an absent *Female,*" who caught the Prince's attention but was then "removed into an Enemy's Country." With the Prince's desire thus frustrated, "the collected part of the semen, raised up and inflamed," burned up, turned into choler, and "ascended to the brain," causing him to commit the strange actions that confused all of his ministers.

Another example of how strangely vapors affect the human brain was that of "a mightly King" who "amused himself" for more than 30 years by subduing armies, sacking towns, frightening children, and the like. Philosophers were baffled by his actions. Eventually, however, the monarch ceased his strange behavior when the vapors that had seized his brain moved down into his lower regions and became a tumor: "The same Spirits, which in their superior Progress would conquer a Kingdom, descending upon the *Anus,* conclude in a *Fistula.*"

An examination of those who have introduced "new Schemes in Philosophy" shows that almost all of them—Ancients and Moderns alike—were mistakenly regarded by everyone as "Crazed or out of their Wits." Their words and actions set them outside the "vulgar Dictates of unrefined Reason" and illustrate how similar they were to "their present undoubted Successors in the *Academy of Modern Bedlam.*" Among many others, examples of these misunderstood individuals include Epicurus, Diogenes, Paracelsus, and Descartes. In today's "undistinguishing Age," these great innovators would be tied up, separated from their followers, and mistreated as madmen. In their natural state, men are simply incapable of hatching truly revolutionary ideas. There is no way to explain true genius apart from the phenomenon of vapors, which move from the "lower Faculties to over-shadow the

Brain" and cause "Conceptions" that (based on the limits of "our Mother-Tongue") are labeled as madness or frenzy. How, one might wonder, did men such as these ever manage to attract followers? The answer lies in the "peculiar *String* in the Harmony of Human Understanding, which in several individuals is exactly of the same Tuning." These innovators and their followers shared the same pitch, even though to everyone else they sounded out of tune.

It is truly a shame that a man regarded as a philosopher "in one Company" is treated like a fool in another. This was exactly what happened to the author's "most ingenious Friend" William Wotton, when he promoted "a new religion." Had he applied his "happy Talents" to dreams and visions instead of "vain Philosophy," the world would have treated him more kindly. Likewise, when one considers the origins of Enthusiasm, "from whence, in all Ages, have eternally proceeded such fatning Streams," it becomes clear that it had its beginnings in what the "World calls *Madness*."

All of this shows that by *madness*, the Moderns mean nothing but "a Disturbance or Transposition of the Brain" brought on by vapors ascending to it from the "lower Faculties." Madness, then, has generated every significant revolution that has occurred in "*Empire*, in *Philosophy*, and in *Religion*." It is impossible for a man with his brain "in its natural Position and State of Serenity" to do anything great and out of the ordinary. When, however, a "Man's Fancy gets astride on his *Reason*" and kicks common sense out the door, he is capable of achieving far more than common persons can. This is mainly because he is then able to maintain a constant state of self-delusion. The truth is that happiness is nothing other than "a perpetual Possession of being well Deceived," and the ultimate question is whether imagined things are at least as real as those that are remembered. The author affirms that this must be the case, especially since "Credulity is a more peaceful Possession of the Mind, than Curiosity." Credulity is content with the surface of things, while curiosity vainly yields worthless "Informations and Discoveries" from what is beneath that surface.

Several examples will clearly show how far superior the outsides of things are to their internal parts. For one, the author recently "saw a Woman *flay'd*," and as her skin was peeled away he was astounded at "how much it altered her Person for the worse." Just yesterday, he had the "Carcass of a *Beau*" stripped of its clothing, and everyone around was shocked at all the faults that were found beneath those garments. Proceeding to lay open several of the deceased fellow's organs, the author concluded that "in every Operation," the further we go the more defects we unfortunately discover. Therefore, the "Philosopher or Projector" who can find a way to cover up Nature's imperfections (and render his followers happily deceived) is far more praiseworthy than the one who works to expose those flaws.

As far as madness goes, it is always the result of "a Redundancy of Vapour," and the best way to handle it is to find some "Employment" for the redundancy. The author has devised a "noble Undertaking" in this regard: A bill should be enacted that allows the government to search for officials among the inhabitants of Bedlam (London's mental hospital). There they could find "admirable" candidates for numerous offices, both "*Civil* and *Military*." This would be a remarkable means of rescuing scores of men who have simply "misapplied" their talents, and redirecting these abilities toward improving the public good. The author himself is a convincing example of how well this plan would work: His "Imaginations" have a tendency "to run away with his *Reason*," enabling him to recognize and articulate the type of "momentous Truths" contained in this work.

## Section 10

In recent years, authors and readers have enjoyed an especially civil relationship. Hardly any work is published that does contain a sprawling preface thanking the world for receiving it so well. Based on this marvelous tradition, the author begins by expressing his gratitude "to all Inhabitants whatsoever, either in Court, or Church, or Camp, or City, or Divine Country; for their generous and universal Acceptance of this Divine Treatise."

There is also a remarkably good relationship between booksellers and authors (who these days are "the only satisfied Parties in *England*"). Ask any author how his work has been received, and he will swear that it has done well in spite of the fact that he wrote it in bits and pieces whenever he had a few minutes to spare. The booksellers will likewise insist that he has only a few of that writer's books left (which he can sell at a discount since a new edition is just about to arrive). What would have become of all these masterpieces had it not been for all the random "Accidents and Occasions" that enabled the authors to write them?

There is a "paultry *Scribbler*" in Britain who writes "pernicious" second parts to others' works under the original authors' names. The author of the "Tale" is concerned that as soon as he is finished, this impostor will immediately do the same to him. With this in mind, he appeals to Dr. Bentley, asking that should this specious second part appear, Bentley would take it home "till the *true Beast*" comes looking for it.

Meanwhile, the author publicly declares that he plans to "circumscribe within this discourse" everything that he has written about for so many years. If readers will carefully consider all that he has discussed, it will certainly cause "a wonderful Revolution" in their "Notions and Opinions." There are three types of readers—the superficial, the ignorant, and the learned. How readers react to the author's "miraculous Treatise" will depend on which category they belong in. Superficial readers will laugh, ignorant readers will simply stare, and learned readers will "find sufficient Matter" to speculate upon for the rest of their lives. In fact, a worthwhile experiment would be for "every Prince in *Christendom*" to take seven of the "deepest Scholars" in his realm, lock them up with a copy of the treatise for seven years, and command them individually to write seven commentaries on "this comprehensive Discourse." In the end, the experiment would reveal that no matter how different their "Conjectures" end up being, the text would support each one.

The author sincerely hopes someone will undertake this experiment, since he strongly desires to enjoy fame *before* he dies (rather than after, as most authors must). To give commentators a head start, he addresses "a few *Innuendo's* that may be of great Assistance." One hint, for example, is that he has "couched a very profound Mystery in the Number

of O's" in the treatise "multiply'd by *Seven*, and divided by *Nine*."

### Section 11

Having ranged so broadly throughout this work, the author now begins to "close in" with his "Subject." Unless he is distracted along the way, he will proceed at an "even Pace" to his destination. Jack had created a "fair Copy of his Father's *Will*" on a giant piece of parchment, and decided that although his Father's directions appeared to be plain and simple, they were actually dark and mysterious. Jack was also remarkably clever in making the parchment serve any purpose he wished: It served as a nightcap, an umbrella, a bandage, and a host of other uses. He engaged in a number of other odd behaviors. Among other things, he "made it a Part of his Religion" never to say grace at meals; he kept a perpetual fire in his belly by eating burning candles; he walked with his eyes shut and (whenever he ran into something) said it had been divinely ordained. He introduced a new deity, assumed the posture of prayer to play unspeakable pranks on people, and regularly asked passersby to strike him (only to return home "comforted" and explaining how much he had suffered for the public good).

The fact that Jack and his brother Peter looked so much alike caused serious problems. Despite their best efforts to avoid ever being in the same vicinity, it was their "perpetual Fortune to meet," and Jack was constantly being arrested for Peter's exploits. This had understandably "terrible Effects" on Jack's "Head and Heart." Adding to these troubles was the poor condition of the coat Jack's father had given him. After years of abuse, Jack continued to rub the coat against a rough wall for two hours every day in an effort to remove even the slightest traces of "*Lace and Embroidery*." As a result, barely anything of the original coat remained. Following a large section of missing manuscript, the author explains that "no Revolutions" in history "have been so great, or so frequent, as those of human *Ears*." After commenting on the unfortunate "falling state of Ears," he promises to deliver a "*general History of Ears*" in a later volume. Having held his readers firmly by the "handle" of their curiosity, he reluctantly resolves to free them from his grasp.

*The Conclusion*

Especially when it comes to "the *Labors* of the Brain," going too long is as harmful as going too short. Every book has its season, and these days any work that "misses its Tide" is cast aside like stale mackerel. The wise booksellers who purchased the "Tale" knew that it would fare well in what is otherwise such a dry season (even though they were skeptical at first). To help it sell, they agreed that if anyone asked privately about the author, the bookseller would name whichever "Wit" happened to be most in vogue at the time.

Currently the author is "trying an experiment very frequent among Modern Authors; which is, to *write upon Nothing.*" All it requires is that a writer, having written everything he has to say on the subject at hand, allow his pen to continue—driven by what some have called "The Ghost of Wit." In the course of a long book, authors and readers become great friends and are reluctant to part. They are like close friends who, at the end of a visit, take longer in saying good-bye than they did in the "whole Conversation before." Likewise, the end of a treatise is somewhat similar to the end of a life (which has been compared to the end of a feast, when diners are reluctant to leave the table and prefer to doze off for a while). Unlike other writers, the author of the "Tale" insists that he will be pleased if his treatise puts people to sleep, since he believes one office of "Wits" is to contribute "to the *Repose* of Mankind."

He asks a favor of the reader, which is to allow for unevenness in the treatise based on the "Author's Spleen, and short Fits or Intervals of Dullness." It would certainly be unfair to demand that every page of the treatise be equally informative and entertaining. He has attempted throughout the treatise to make Invention his master, with Method and Reason as his lackeys. The reason was that the author often found himself tempted to be witty when he had nothing wise, sound, or relevant to say. As a "Servant of the *Modern* way," however, he knew better than to put down his pen in these situations. After gathering more than 700 "*Flowers, and shining Hints* of the best *Modern* Authors" in his commonplace book, he discovered that only rarely could he force any of these gems into a conversation. In print,

however, these same "flowers" have been received with great esteem. At this point, however, he has decided to "pause awhile" until conditions make it absolutely necessary "to resume" his "Pen."

## COMMENTARY

"A Tale of a Tub" purports to tell the story of three brothers: Peter (who represents Roman Catholicism), Martin (who suggests an inspirational connection to Luther), and Jack (who symbolizes Protestant dissent associated with Calvin). Using the parable form, Swift implies that he has written a history of the development of Christianity in Europe, expanding his tale with references to God and his will among mankind and embellishing the piece with digressions on various topics. The work's structure would have been familiar to readers, who expected a diversity of material, often on moral subjects but laced heavily with comedy and figures or scenes of ridicule.

Swift's satiric method and irony attacked the corruptions in religion and learning which he had begun to note while serving as Sir William TEMPLE's secretary at Moor Park in 1696, though critics believe the work also served as his chief imaginative effort while serving in the unhappy assignment as prebendary of Kilroot, near Belfast, in 1695. When first published in 1704, along with "The BATTLE OF THE BOOKS" and "The MECHANICAL OPERATION OF THE SPIRIT," "A Tale" became very popular, permitting his conservative viewpoint on religious issues to counter the theological extremism that had held the public's attention. Later, Swift added an "Apology," because too many of his readers misunderstood his true intention of praising the established state religion and instead believed he meant to embrace religious fanaticism. His depiction of the traditional power of Catholic institutional policy and procedure, as displayed in Peter's character, was countered by a searing description of individual preference from Jack, who seemed no more than a wild anarchist, bent only on asserting egocentric beliefs. Many readers lost sight of the moderate voice of Martin, whose portrayal of Anglican thought and principle attempted a celebration of "the Church of England as the most perfect of all others in discipline and doctrine."

The apparently complex satire, with its five sections of parable and six digressions, actually pleads simply for eliminating the falsity and hypocrisy of Christianity's trappings. Yet Swift's effort parodies bad modern prose, too, and his attack begins early with the 10-page apology, a three-page dedication to John SOMERS (the beau ideal of a patron), an "Epistle Dedicatory to Prince POSTERITY" (four pages) that serves as a parody of a hack author; and a preface "extend[ed] . . . into a size now in vogue, which by rule ought to be large in proportion as the subsequent volume is small" (seven pages). Within the preface, Swift suggests the possible meaning of his title: a foolish story or story meant to divert the reader from the truth of his situation, as sailors toss out a tub to divert a whale from striking the ship. The implication of fanaticism lies heavily on the essay, and Swift intends on suggesting the link between heretical antiquity and modern zealots who have brought a disreputable character upon the Established Church.

Assuming the role of a Christian moralist, Swift uses allegory, intending on creating dual interest, one in the events, characters, and setting presented, and the other in the ideas they are intended to convey to the reader. He seeks nothing less than the reader's acknowledgment of the many corrupt practices in the name of religion and learning that have grown out of a combination of political rebellion and intellectual presumption. The quality of individualistic religion seen clearly during his experience with Ulster Presbyterianism while at Kilroot surely made him determined to reflect on how far such beliefs had grown from his own Anglican thought and practices. The debate on learning intends to put the reader further off balance, suggesting how distant the past has become for modern man, who desperately needs a model of morality, one which can be found in the classical period. The reader has no present authority, since all that can be found in political and cultural life are tyranny and revolution. Whether he was making reference to actual figures and events as examples of taste and morality or simply exhibiting an abiding respect for an earlier time, he focuses the debate on what was a well-known framework in the early 18th century, the controversy between the Ancients and the Moderns. (See also "BATTLE OF THE BOOKS, The.")

As Judith Mueller has cogently shown, the debate was the 18th-century version of our culture wars, where both groups were advancing opposing concepts of knowledge. Reading the Ancients' history, not only the re-creation of the historical record but their sensibility toward the events of their time, offered a way of living one's life according to a high moral standard. The Moderns embraced the new science and were highly progressive, breaking ranks with the moralists and recognizing experience as the true end of learning. Though Swift's position relative to this controversy may seem ambiguous, he has little problem attacking various sacred cows. If we can trust what he says in the "Apology," then his dislike for speaking in tongues, laying on of hands, and other miraculous affectations becomes quite obvious. Any deviation or dissent from the Anglican state religion would promote revolution and societal collapse.

The notion that "Tale of a Tub" is a mock-book helps explain Swift's intention with the work, since critics have noted his growing concern with the rapidly expanding print culture. The prevalence of pamphlets, cheap newspapers, and periodicals seemed a subversive development to Swift, and one can argue that in "Tale of a Tub" he seeks to alert readers to imminent danger. David Nokes mentions this work as a "bibliomaniac's fantasy, a virtuoso display of book-learning" with its apology, postscript, dedication, epistle dedication, preface, and introduction (*Hypocrite Reversed* 44). The concoction Swift devises serves as an example in his satire of how bad books distribute bad ideas and weaken the culture. "A Tale" could have become a victim of its own irony, and the satiric damage he produced could have backfired; but its density and allusiveness preserve it from the fate of the works Swift was criticizing in his text.

What may seem counterintuitive in the text—some parts seem an excellent example of bad writing—is in fact a clever, effective effort at demonstrating satirically why the padding, overwriting, arcane references, allegories, digressions, and numerous other examples of so-called wisdom create bad learning. Swift's cock-and-bull story functions as a mask for a serious critique of contemporary cultural values and icons. The famous remark in the "Digression concerning the Original, the Use, and Improvement of Madness in a Commonwealth" (section 9 of the "Tale") embraces this point: "And he whose fortunes and dispositions have placed him in a convenient station . . . can . . . content his ideas with the films and images that fly off upon his senses from the superficies of things; such a man, truly wise, creams off Nature, leaving the sour and the dregs for philosophy and reason to lap up. This is the sublime and refined point of felicity, called the possession of being well deceived; the serene peaceful state, of being a fool among knaves" (110). Though Swift certainly intends that we not trust his narrator, who is busy making various claims for wisdom, he ridicules those who find easy answers to the complex problems in their daily lives, who refuse to accept responsibility for the decisions they make and instead create scapegoats to be blamed for decisions gone wrong, and who, in condemning the faults of a few, destroy the characters of everyone around them. Dark visions of human nature, as Judith C. Mueller comments, are wedded to a healthy mistrust of interpretation, meaning the material world offers little real substance and denies spiritual reality, which after all, to Swift, seems the key to surviving this existence. Though even such authorities as the Established Church, the work of the ancient writers, the established class system, and other examples of traditional strength within the society remain important fixtures, Swift is frustratingly ambiguous on whether or not moral improvement can take place.

## CHARACTERS

**Aeolists** "Learned" sect of fictitious zealots in section 8 of "A Tale of a Tub." Founded by Jack, they are Swift's lampoon of radical Dissenters, who in his view epitomize irrational fanaticism and in their rejection of right reason and authority present an even greater threat to religion than the Roman Catholics, their "brethren" (as he calls them in "Reasons Humbly Offered to the Parliament of Ireland"). The faith of the Aeolists is founded on their belief in direct inspiration from God, and Swift highlights the literal meaning of *inspire*—"to breathe or blow upon or into" (*Oxford English Dictionary*)—in order to satirize that belief. The narrator of the "Tale" explains that the Aeolists believe that the "original cause of all things" was wind and that "the same breath which had kindled and blew *up* the flame of nature, should one day blow it *out*." Based on this doctrine, the Aeolists view "belching" (through a variety of orifices) as "the noblest act of a rational creature." Their priests often prepare for service by standing in a circle "with every man a pair of bellows applied to his neighbor's breech [buttocks]." After they inflate one another with as much air as possible, the priests then disperse to break wind "for the public good" in the faces of their "disciples." The sect is appropriately named after Aeolus, god of the winds in classical mythology, which emphasizes Swift's view of the Dissenters as being full of hot air.

**Argent, Duchess d'** Character in section 2 of "Tale of a Tub." Along with Madame de Grands Titres and Countess d'Orgueil, she is one of the three town ladies of "chief Reputation" with whom the brothers fall in love. She represents the love of wealth. Her name is the French word for "money."

**Grands Titres, Madame de** Character in section 2 of "Tale of a Tub." Along with Duchess d'Argent and Countess d'Orgueil, she is one of the three town ladies of "chief Reputation" with whom the brothers fall in love. Her name (*Grand Titres*) means "great titles" or "great honors" in French, and she stands for worldly honor.

**Jack** Along with Martin and Peter, one of the three brothers in "Tale of a Tub." His name echoes that of John Calvin, and he represents Protestant Dissenters (including Calvinists and Puritans). In the preface to his 1721 French translation of the "Tale," Juste van Effen remarked that for Swift, Jack embodies "all the different kinds of fanatics, whom he regards as having arisen from the reformed religion as it was established in England under the name of Presbyterianism" (*Critical Heritage* 56). In section 9 of the "Tale" (the "Digression Concerning Madness"), Jack is credited with having founded the Aeolists.

In the descriptions of Jack's exploits, Swift generally makes fun of what he took to be the characteristic excesses and extremism of dissenting groups. For example, after the brothers have violated their deceased father's command not to add any ornaments to the coats he left to them (each coat representing religion), Jack and Martin decide to remove all the alterations with which they have embellished their coats. In an episode suggesting that Calvinists were overzealously devoted to iconoclasm and simplicity in religion, Jack removes the decorations from his coat with such zest that he tears his coat to pieces in the process. This episode aligns Jack with the "wild reformers" in Swift's "ODE TO DR. WILLIAM SANCROFT," who "tear Religion's lovely face; / Strip her of every ornament and grace, / In striving to wash off the imaginary paint." Similarly, Jack's habit of walking down the street with his eyes closed caricatures the Calvinist doctrine of predestination: "[I]f he happened to bounce his Head against a Post," Swift writes, Jack would announce to laughing onlookers that, "*he submitted with entire Resignation*" since "*It was ordained some few Days before the Creation, that my Nose and this very Post should have a Rencounter.*"

Despite Jack's efforts, he has great difficulty distancing himself from his roots. The narrator of the "Tale" explains that "it was among the great Misfortunes of *Jack,* to bear a huge Personal Resemblance with his Brother *Peter*" (who represents the Roman Catholic Church). The fact that "Their Humours and Dispositions were not only the same, but there was a close Analogy in their Shape, their Size, and their Mien" causes Jack constantly to be mistaken for Peter, and vice versa. The estranged brothers often meet accidentally, despite their efforts to avoid ever crossing paths. A footnote explains that this reflects the ironic similarities between "*Papists*" and "*Fanaticks,*" who—although "*they appear the most Averse to each other*"—"*bear a near Resemblance in many things, as has been observed by Learned Men.*" An additional footnote attributed to William WOTTON complains that this similarity "*is ludicrously described for several Pages.*"

In the end, Jack receives more attention than either of his brothers from the narrator of the "Tale." In the process, the Dissenters he represents become the primary targets of Swift's scorn. The comic descriptions of Jack's ultimately destructive vehemence in purifying his coat and of his failed efforts to separate himself from Peter highlight Swift's serious antipathy toward religious fanaticism and radical Dissenters as posing an even greater threat to religion than the Roman Catholics. Jack does to his coat precisely what Swift feared the Dissenters would do to religion: As he claims in his "Preface to the Bishop of Sarum's Introduction," "the Presbyterians, and their Clans of other *Fanaticks* of *Free-thinkers* and *Atheists,* that dangle after them, are as well inclined to pull down the present Establishment of Monarchy and Religion, as any Sett of Papists in Christendom; and therefore . . . our Danger . . . is infinitely greater from our Protestant Enemies; because they are much more able to ruin us, and full as willing" (*Prose Works* IV.78).

**Martin**   Along with Jack and Peter, one of the three brothers in "Tale of a Tub." His name echoes that of Martin Luther, and he represents the Church of England, in which Swift was a priest.

Martin has long been regarded as the hero of the "Tale." In the preface to his 1721 French translation of the "Tale," for example, Juste van Effen remarked that Swift favored Martin "at the expense of Jack, whose ill-considered zeal is everywhere mocked" (*Critical Heritage* 56). Martin is first to begin restoring his coat to the condition in which he received it from his father, and (unlike Jack) he exercises restraint in removing the ornamentation in order to avoid damaging the fabric: "For the rest, where he observed the Embroidery to be worked so close, as not to be got away without damaging the Cloth, or where it served to hide or strengthen any Flaw in the Body of the Coat, contracted by the perpetual tampering of Workmen upon it; he concluded the wisest Course was to let it remain, resolving in no Case whatsoever, that the Substance of the Stuff should suffer Injury; which he thought the best Method for serving the true Intent of his Father's *Will*" (*Prose Works* I.85). Between Peter (who leaves all the ornamentation on his coat and adds even more) and Jack (who removes the ornamentation with such violence that he destroys his coat in the process), Martin represents a more moderate middle way. His careful "reformation" of the coat recalls the equally moderate Protestant Reformation, which recovered religion from its corruption at the hands of Roman Catholics but—unlike the Calvinists and radical Dissenters—did so without stripping it so bare that it became unrecognizable.

Despite Martin's identification with Swift's church and the via media between Roman Catholicism and radical Protestantism, critics have become increasingly skeptical of readings of the "Tale" that present Martin as a fairly transparent embodiment of moderation, reason, Anglicanism, and even Swift himself. For example, Irvin Ehrenpreis spoke for many readers when he pointed to the portrayal of Martin as compelling evidence that Swift sounds "weak or dull" whenever he "simply, positively recommends what he takes to be a middle-of-the-road course" (III.564). More recently, however, critics such as Richard Nash and Frank Boyle have proposed that Martin—like his brothers Peter and Jack—is a target of satire in the "Tale" rather than a standout personification of Swift's "positive positions." Nash argues that Swift satirizes the type of moderation that characterizes Martin, since it is what finally drives Jack mad. Boyle explains that Swift links Martin with the "Tale's chief pedant," Richard BENTLEY, in order to highlight disdainfully all that Bentley and others like him had done to "inflame" the Roman Catholics and Calvinists (Boyle 160–161). From this perspective, Martin is far from being the hero of the "Tale." Instead, he illustrates a type of doctrine and devotion that are at least as misguided as those embodied in Peter and Jack.

**Momus**    In Greek mythology, the god of ridicule and fault-finding. As punishment for constantly ridiculing other deities (including Jupiter, Aphrodite, and others), he was expelled from Olympus. In the "Digression Concerning Critics" the author of "A Tale of a Tub" cites Momus as the original ancestor of all "true critics"—those who limit their task to discovering and collecting other writers' faults. For Swift, Momus—along with the goddess Criticism—embodied the abortive pedantry to which criticism had been reduced. In "The BATTLE OF THE BOOKS," Momus is

patron of the moderns. He makes an "Excellent Speech in their Favor" which is answered by Pallas (the ancients' "Protectress") and calls upon the goddess Criticism to aid the moderns in the battle.

**Orgueil, Countess d'**    In section 2 of "TALE OF A TUB," one of the three town ladies wooed by the brothers. *Orgueil* is French for "pride," which is the trait she represents. See also Argent and Grand Titres.

**Paracelsus (Phillippus Aureolus Theophrastus Bombastus ab Hohenheim, 1493–1541)**    Swiss physician and alchemist, noted for his study of the role of chemistry in human medicine. He was the author of *Der grossen Wundartzney* (*The Great Surgery Book*), published in 1536. Swift regarded Paracelsus as a quack. In the "Digression Concerning Madness" in "Tale of a Tub," he is listed among the "great Introducers of new Schemes in Philosophy" who were regarded by everyone but their followers as "Persons Crazed, or out of their Wits." Swift adds in a footnote that Paracelsus, "*who was so famous for Chemistry, tried an Experiment upon human Excrement, to make a Perfume of it.*" In "The BATTLE OF THE BOOKS" he fights for the Moderns, hurling a javelin at Galen and leading a squadron of "*Stink-Pot-Flingers*" into the battle.

**Peter**    Along with Jack and Martin, one of the three brothers in "Tale of a Tub." The eldest, he represents the Roman Catholic Church and demands that he be addressed as Mister Peter, Father Peter, and (ultimately) Lord Peter.

As Frank Boyle has explained in *Swift as Nemesis*, in Swift's portrayal of Peter he "is seen dealing . . . with the fact of the Roman Church's pervasive corruption" (112). This is most evident as Peter leads his brothers in glossing over the prohibition in their father's will against adding ornaments to the coats he bequeathed to each of the sons. His overwhelming devotion to pedantry and tradition, along with his skill and creativity in distorting the dictates of the will, illustrate what Swift saw as the Roman Catholic Church's habit of willfully misinterpreting and adding to Scripture in self-serving ways. In a footnote he attributes to

William WOTTON, Swift writes that, "*The first part of the* Tale *[of a Tub] is the History of* Peter; *thereby* Popery *is exposed, every Body knows the* Papists *have made great Additions to Christianity, that indeed is the great Exception which the* Church of England *makes against them, accordingly* Peter *begins his Pranks, with adding a* Shoulder-knot *to his Coat.*" In describing Peter's character in section 4 of the "Tale," the narrator sums up Swift's attitude toward Roman Catholicism and its leaders: After explaining that Peter suffers from periodic fits of madness, the narrator laments, "it is certain, that Lord Peter, even in his lucid Intervals, was very lewdly given in his common Conversation, extream willful and positive, and would at any time rather argue to the Death, than allow himself to be once in an Error. Besides, he had an abominable Faculty of telling huge palpable Lies upon all Occasions; and swearing, not only to the Truth, but cursing the whole Company to Hell, if they pretended to make the least Scruple of believing him."

After Peter evicts them from his house, Jack and Martin initiate a "Protestant Reformation" of their own. Having found their father's will (which Peter had kept hidden from them) and read it for themselves, the ousted brothers come to their senses and decide to rid their coats of the ornamentation they now recognize as a clear violation of their father's dying wishes.

**Posterity, Prince**   The noble lord to whom the author of "Tale of a Tub" dedicates his text. Time is his governor, and the author begs the Prince not to believe Time's claim that the age is "almost wholly illiterate." As evidence, he cites the works of DRYDEN, Tate, D'Urfey, BENTLEY, WOTTON, and others.

### FURTHER READING

Clark, John R. *Form and Frenzy in Swift's "Tale of a Tub."* Ithaca, N.Y.: Cornell University Press, 1970.

Connery, Brian. "The Persona as Pretender and the Reader as Constitutional Subject in Swift's *Tale.*" In *Cutting Edges: Postmodern Critical Essays*, edited by James A. Gill, 159–180. Knoxville: University of Tennessee Press, 1995.

Devine, Michael G. "Disputing the 'Original' in Swift's *Tale of a Tub*," *Swift Studies* 18 (2003): 26–33.

Ehrenpreis, Irvin. *Swift: The Man, His Works and the Age.* 3 vols. Cambridge, Mass.: Harvard University Press, 1962–83.

Nokes, David. *Jonathan Swift: A Hypocrite Reversed.* Oxford: Oxford University Press, 1987.

Paulson, Ronald. *Theme and Structure in Swift's "Tale of a Tub."* New Haven, Conn.: Yale University Press, 1960.

# "Thoughts on Various Subjects"

Series of more than 40 sayings by Swift, first published in 1711. The sayings are all fairly short, and (as the title suggests) cover numerous different topics. Religion, politics, relationships, and human nature in general are all favorites, and many of the saying take up more than one of these issues at once. For example, "NO Preacher is listened to but Time; which gives us the same Train and Turn of Thought, that elder People have tried in vain to put into our Heads before." The "Thoughts" have come to be known by other titles, such as "Various Thoughts, Moral and Diverting" and (in the Oxford Authors edition of Swift's work) "Aphorisms and Maxims."

In his edition of Swift's prose, Herbert Davis suggests that Swift probably wrote most of the "Thoughts" after his return to Ireland in June of 1704, when he was spending considerable time in Dublin engaging in "great punning contests" at the castle. Davis notes that the work is dated October 1, 1706, and adds that this was probably "the time when Swift first brought together a group of [his] aphorisms for publication" (1.xxxiv–xxxv). Several editors have suggested that Swift modeled his "Thoughts" on François de LA ROCHEFOUCAULD's *Reflexions ou Sentences et Maximes Morales* (1665)—a work he admired and which also influenced some of his better-known writings, including "VERSES ON THE DEATH OF DR. SWIFT" and "The LIFE AND GENUINE CHARACTER OF DR. SWIFT." As Irvin Ehrenpreis notes, however, although Swift was almost certainly "guided by French example[s]," there are not very many specific parallels between his "Thoughts" and those works (*Swift* II.193).

## "Three Epigrams"

Group of poems by Swift, transcribed as a group by Esther JOHNSON. Poem 1 was first published in 1728, written in 1712. Poem 2 was first published in 1910 (with no indication of its date of composition). Poem 3 was first published in 1735, written in 1723. The poems all deal mockingly with unhappy marriages.

## "Tim and the Fables"

Poem by Swift; first published in the INTELLIGENCER 8 (July 1728); written the same year. It is a sequel to "MAD MULLINIX AND TIMOTHY," and is likewise directed against Richard TIGHE ("Tim").

## "To a Friend Who Had Been Much Abused in Many Inveterate Libels"

Poem by Swift; first published in 1754, written in 1730. Swift wrote this poem along with "TO DR. DELANY, ON THE LIBELS WRIT AGAINST HIM," for Rev. Patrick DELANY in the wake of a number of negative responses (including two by Swift himself) to Delany's "Epistle to Lord Carteret." Swift suggests that Delany is the object of the libels because he is virtuous, and encourages him not to be "frighted out of honour's road" (9). Delany responded with "The Pheasant and the Lark," a fable thanking Swift but also invoking his ridicule in the "ANSWER TO DR. DELANY'S FABLE OF THE PHEASANT AND THE LARK." See also "EPISTLE UPON AN EPISTLE" and "LIBEL ON THE REVEREND DR. DELANY."

## "To a Lady"

Poem by Swift; first published 1733 with "ON READING DR. YOUNG'S SATIRES," begun during a visit to MARKET HILL in 1728–30 and completed 1732–33.

This verse epistle is addressed to Lady Anne ACHESON, "Who Desired the Author to Write Some Verses Upon Her in the Heroic Style" (according to the subtitle). Instead of praising the lady, however, the poem dramatizes a conversation between her and "the Dean" in which he chides her for ignoring "good sense" as she lives the life of "an humble, prudent wife." As Swift discusses his general tendency to "encounter vice with mirth" rather than "anger," he sharply criticizes Sir Robert WALPOLE, who almost had Swift arrested after the poem's publication.

## "To Betty the Grisette"

Poem by Swift; first published in 1735, written in 1730. According to the *Oxford English Dictionary*, a *grisette* is "a French girl or young woman of the working class, esp. one employed as a shop assistant or a seamstress." Pat Rogers defines it in the context of Swift's poem, however, as "a girl who is common and rather loose, but not actually a prostitute" (*Poems* 826n). The poem is a mock encomium of Betty's supposed beauty and wit, ultimately suggesting that she possesses neither.

## "To Charles Ford, Esq. on His Birthday"

Poem by Swift; first published in 1935, written 1722–23. Pat Rogers accepts this date of composition even though the poem (in line 12) suggests it was intended for Charles FORD's 42nd birthday, which was January 31, 1724. It is a lighthearted tribute expressing Swift's and Stella's (Esther JOHNSON) affection for Ford and their hope that he will remain in Dublin.

## "To Dean Swift"

Poem; first published in 1765, written in 1729. While Swift is undoubtedly the author, the poem's subtitle is "By Sir Arthur Acheson." ACHESON calls himself Swift's landlord and expresses happiness at having Swift "grace my villa with his strains." He is thankful that the British "court and courtiers have no taste," since MARKET HILL might "never else have known the Dean."

## "To Dr. Delany, on the Libels Writ against Him"

Poem by Swift; first published in 1730, written the same year. Like "TO A FRIEND WHO HAD BEEN MUCH ABUSED IN MANY INVETERATE LIBELS," this poem was written by Swift in the wake of what Pat Rogers calls "a flurry of rejoinders" (including two by Swift himself) to Delany's "Epistle to Lord Carteret" (813). As he does in "To a Friend," Swift attempts consolation by suggesting that Delany's gifts are what cause others to attack him. Irvin Ehrenpreis compares the restrained, complimentary tone of this imagined dialogue with Delany to that of Swift's verses addressed to Stella (Esther JOHNSON) (*Swift* III.662). See also "EPISTLE UPON AN EPISTLE" and "LIBEL ON THE REVEREND DR. DELANY."

## "To Dr. Helsham"

Poem by Swift; first published in 1746 with "TO DR. SHERIDAN" and "A RIDDLING LETTER," written 1731. It is a playful verse letter to Dr. Richard HELSHAM, who was Swift's physician at the time. Like "To Dr. Sheridan," this poem is primarily an exercise in wordplay, in which every line ends in "sick." See also "CAN YOU MATCH WITH ME."

## "To Dr. Sheridan"

Poem by Swift; first published in 1746 with "TO DR. HELSHAM" and "A RIDDLING LETTER," written in 1731. Like Swift's much longer poem to Dr.

Richard HELSHAM, this verse letter to Dr. Thomas SHERIDAN is primarily an exercise in wordplay, in which each line ends in "sick." See also "CAN YOU MATCH WITH ME."

## "To His Grace the Archbishop of Dublin"

Poem by Swift; first published anonymously as a broadside in 1724, written the same year. Swift had earlier praised Archbishop William KING for opposing a national bank of Ireland (see "PART OF THE NINTH ODE OF THE FOURTH BOOK OF HORACE"), and in this poem Swift salutes him for having refused to sign Lord CARTERET's proclamation against the Drapier. See also "An EXCELLENT NEW SONG UPON HIS GRACE OUR GOOD LORD ARCHBISHOP OF DUBLIN."

## "To Janus"

Poem by Swift subtitled "On New Year's Day"; first published in 1735, written in 1729 at MARKET HILL. It records a conversation between Lady Anne ACHESON and "the Dean," who prays that the two-faced god Janus will give the Lady "half [his] face behind" since she disregards the past. Lady Anne and Swift disagree over whether it is better to focus on the future or on history, the Lady concluding that she will "have none but forward eyes."

## "Toland's Invitation to Dismal to Dine with the Calves' Head Club"

Poem by Swift; first published in 1712, written the same year. Modeled loosely on Epistle 5, Liber I of Horace, this is a satire on Daniel Finch, second earl of NOTTINGHAM—nicknamed "Dismal." Written in the voice of WHIG writer John TOLAND, it invites

Nottingham to join the Whigs in celebrating the anniversary of King Charles I's execution (the Calves' Head Club met annually to do so). The poem is concerned throughout with how much those who attend the dinner will change as they drink more and more wine. Louise K. Barnett notes that Swift has "altered" the "substance" of the original Horatian epistle, so it does little to "illuminate Swift's version" (187). See also "EXCELLENT NEW SONG, AN."

# "To Lord Harley, since Earl of Oxford, on His Marriage"

Poem by Swift; first published in 1765, written in 1713 for the marriage (on August 31) of Edward HARLEY and Lady Henrietta Cavendish Holles. Swift praises Harley for his wit and character, comparing him to Phoebus. His bride is described as having been "born to retrieve her sex's fame." Swift portrays her as Aurora descending to find a superior mortal to be her mate.

# "Tom Mullinex and Dick"

Poem by Swift; first published in 1745, written about 1728. Like "MAD MULLINIX AND TIMOTHY" and "TIM AND THE FABLES," it satirizes Richard TIGHE ("Dick"). In the first poem, Swift dramatizes a conversation between Tighe and Tom Molyneux ("Mullinix"). In this one, he compares the two in order to insult Tighe.

# "To Mr. Congreve"

Poem by Swift; first published in 1789, written in 1693 soon after the appearance of William CONGREVE's second play, *The Double-Dealer*, in October of that year. The poem is an awkward panegyric, praising Congreve as one who will reform the stage and advising him to "Beat not the dirty paths where vul-

gar feet have trod." It is, however, focused primarily upon Swift's own frustrations (with bad poets, poseurs, and critics, especially) and his comfort at William TEMPLE's home, Moor Park, where he was visiting when he composed the poem. As Swift indicated in a December 6, 1693, letter to his cousin Thomas, he hoped this poem would eventually accompany one of Congreve's plays as prefatory verses commending the author. There is, however, nothing to suggest that Congreve ever saw the poem.

# "To Mr. Delany"

Poem by Swift; first published 1765, included with a letter to Rev. Patrick DELANY, dated November 10, 1718. Concerned with what Swift calls "simple topics told in rhyme," it was written as an indirect response to a poem by Thomas SHERIDAN detailing the death and funeral of Swift's muse. Swift thought Sheridan had gone too far, and after providing a lengthy commentary on "humour, raillery and wit," he challenges Delany to "mend" or "defend" their mutual friend.

# "To Mr. Gay"

Poem by Swift; first published in 1735, included (in part) with a letter to John GAY, dated March 13, 1731. Based on a false rumor that Gay had been appointed steward to Charles Douglas, third duke of QUEENSBURY, it is primarily an attack on Sir Robert WALPOLE. Swift depicts him as a false steward who abuses his power as lord treasurer—"a brazen minister of state" who lacks the virtues associated with poets and embodied in Gay.

# "To Mr. Harley's Surgeon"

Poem by Swift; first published as part of *The JOURNAL TO STELLA* in 1766, written 1711. It was addressed to the physician treating Robert HARLEY, first earl of

Oxford, after Antoine de GUISCARD stabbed him in March 1711. Swift warns the surgeon that the safety of Europe lies in his hands. According to Pat Rogers, the attending surgeon was most likely Paul Buissière, "a Huguenot emigré who achieved some prominence in London" (642n.).

## "To Mr. Sheridan, upon His Verses Written in Circles"

Poem by Swift; first published in 1765, written in 1721. After Dr. Thomas SHERIDAN (or Rev. Patrick DELANY, in Sheridan's name) composed a reply to "GEORGE NIM-DAN-DEAN'S INVITATION TO MR. THOMAS SHERIDAN," Swift responded with this poem making fun of Sheridan's verses, which he had written in concentric circles. George ROCHFORT also penned a response to Sheridan's circular poem.

## "To Mrs. Houghton of Bormount"

Poem possibly by Swift; first published in 1762, date of composition uncertain. It is a gently goading but laudatory poem to a woman who dotes on her husband. Pat Rogers calls it a doubtful attribution.

## "To Quilca"

Poem by Swift; first published in 1735, written in 1725 during a visit to Quilca—Thomas SHERIDAN'S house in County Cavan. Swift was there from late April through September completing GULLIVER'S TRAVELS. The poem describes the house as a damp, dreary place where the goddess Want reigns with her chief officers Sloth, Dirt, and Theft. Swift wrote several other poems during his visit to Quilca, including "VERSES FROM QUILCA" and "A RECEIPT TO RESTORE STELLA'S YOUTH." See also

"BLUNDERS, DEFICIENCIES, DISTRESSES, AND MISFORTUNES OF QUILCA."

## "To Stella on Her Birthday"

Poem by Swift; first published in 1766, written 1721–22 for Esther JOHNSON's 40th (or 41st) birthday. It was one of several "annual tributes" he wrote for her. This poem is as concerned with Swift's own aging as it is with Stella's worthiness: "You, every year the debt enlarge, / I grow less equal to the charge," he writes. The verses end suggesting that unless Patrick DELANY picks up with similar poems after Swift's death, this "debt" will remain forever unpaid. See also "TO STELLA, WRITTEN ON THE DAY OF HER BIRTH" and the "STELLA'S BIRTHDAY" poems for 1719, 1721, 1723, 1725, and 1727.

## "To Stella, Visiting Me in My Sickness"

Poem by Swift; first published in 1728, written 1720, following Esther JOHNSON's (Stella's) care for Swift during an illness early that year. In his biography of Swift, David Nokes points out that the opening of this poem echoes that of "CADENUS AND VANESSA" and that in both poems Pallas argues that "male wisdom and female beauty" in one person would cause more confusion than admiration (250). Like Vanessa (Esther VANHOMRIGH) in the longer poem, Stella is praised for possessing virtues that were generally regarded as masculine.

## "To Stella, Who Collected and Transcribed His Poems"

Poem by Swift; first published in 1728, written about 1720. In it, Swift suggests that Stella (Esther JOHNSON) deserves all the credit for his poetry if it is praised by future generations. Nora Crowe Jaffe has pointed out that Shakespeare made "the same claim for his friend in Sonnets 78 and 84, and [Sir Philip] Sidney gives the praise to his Stella in Sonnets 74 and 90" of *Astrophel and Stella*. She explains, however, that while Shakespeare and Sidney claim that their subjects' "immortal beauty" will immortalize their poems, Swift focuses on Stella's virtue as what will make his poetry endure (*The Poet Swift* 88). Describing it as an "authorized version" of Swift's relationship with Stella, David Nokes compares this poem to "CADENUS AND VANESSA," in which Swift made a similar attempt to "set the record straight" about his association with Esther VANHOMRIGH (*Hypocrite Reversed* 251).

Early in the poem Swift compares himself to the famous English architect Inigo Jones (1573–1651), who received all the praise for the buildings he designed while the "workmen" were never honored. He hopes that Stella (who, like the workmen, has done the mundane but important work of transcribing and collecting his poems) will receive the praise if his "pile of scattered rhymes" stands the test of time and attracts favorable attention from future generations. He praises her as a true friend, but also lauds poets and their work, asserting that "Truth shines the brighter, clad in verse." Swift does not end the poem, however, without goading Stella for her tendency to react passionately to any hint of criticism. He concludes by saying that if she angrily burns the poem (rather than transcribing it) because of the comments it contains on her behavior, she will only have proven Swift's accusations.

## "To Stella, Written on the Day of Her Birth"

Poem by Swift; first published in 1765, written in 1724. Like the other birthday poems Swift wrote for Esther JOHNSON, it is as much concerned with the author as anything else. The subtitle reads, "Written on the Day of Her Birth, But Not on the Subject, When I Was Sick in Bed." By the time he composed these verses, Swift had reached the point he had

imagined in "TO STELLA ON HER BIRTHDAY": He had become too old and "tormented with incessant pains" to continue writing such poems for Stella. The poem is a tribute to her profound virtue, but mainly in terms of how patiently she "tends" Swift "like a humble slave" during his lengthy illness. See also "TO STELLA ON HER BIRTHDAY" and the "STELLA'S BIRTHDAY" poems for 1719, 1721, 1723, 1725, and 1727.

## "To the Earl of Oxford, Late Lord Treasurer"

Poem by Swift; first published 1730. The laudatory poem is subtitled "Sent to Him When He Was in the Tower, before His Trial" and "Out of Horace." It was written sometime between July 1715—when Robert HARLEY, first earl of Oxford, was imprisoned—and July 1717, when he was freed. It is based upon Horace's second ode of the third book with "the opening twelve lines ignored" (Rogers, *Poems* 675). Swift had written what Harold Williams calls "a noble and dignified letter" to Harley in the Tower on July 19, 1715: "You suffer for a good Cause, for having preserved Your Country, and for having been the great Instrument under God, of His present Majesty's peac[e]able Accession to the Throne" (Williams, *Poems* I.209; *Corr.* II.182–83).

## "To the Earl of Peterborough"

Poem by Swift; first published 1735, written about 1726. Its subject is Charles Mordaunt, third earl of PETERBOROUGH, whom Swift greatly admired. The poem depicts "Mordanto" as a man of poise who never stays in the same place for very long. The earl's friend Alexander POPE had mentioned this characteristic to Swift in a letter of September 3, 1726: "Lord Peterborough can go to any climate, but never stay in any" (*Corr.* III.161). The poem ends suggesting that Peterborough's heroism is rivaled only by that of "his namesake" CHARLES XII, king of Sweden.

## "To Thomas Sheridan"

Poem by Swift; first published in 1808, written in 1718. Along with other poems such as "MARY THE COOK-MAID'S LETTER TO DR. SHERIDAN" and "SHERIDAN, A GOOSE," it is one of a number of items in an extended series of trifles circulated among Swift, Dr. Thomas SHERIDAN, Rev. Patrick DELANY, Rev. Daniel JACKSON, and the ROCHFORT brothers.

## "Town Eclogue, A"

Poem by Swift; first published in the *Tatler* 301 (March 13, 1711), written the same year. Like "DESCRIPTION OF A MORNING," "DESCRIPTION OF A CITY SHOWER," and especially "A PASTORAL DIALOGUE," it is a mock-eclogue. The conversation in this poem between the "rustic" Corydon and Phyllis (his pregnant mistress) parodies pastoral conventions by emphasizing the ridiculous incompatibility of polished language and the realities of urban life.

## "Traulus"

Poem by Swift; first published in two parts in 1730 and 1732, written in 1730. It is an attack upon Joshua, second viscount ALLEN. The title comes from the Greek word "for 'lisping' or 'mispronouncing,' because Allen habitually stuttered" (Ehrenpreis, *Swift* III.656). Allen had incurred Swift's wrath by speaking out against the Corporation of Dublin's proposal to honor Swift with a gold box. The first part of the poem is cast as a dialogue between "Tom" and "Robin." Tom is based on Tom Molyneux—see "MAD MULLINIX AND TIMOTHY" and "TOM MULLINEX AND DICK"—and "Robin" on Robert LESLIE, who had defended Allen following his outburst against honoring Swift with the box. The second part is a bitter

diatribe against Allen, ultimately suggesting that he possesses more female vices than male and that his parentage may be traced back to hell itself. See also "A VINDICATION OF LORD CARTERET."

## "Twelve Articles"

Poem by Swift; first published with "DAPHNE" in 1765, written between 1728 and 1730 at MARKET HILL. The point of this poem is essentially the same: Swift repudiates Lady Anne ACHESON as his pupil based on her unreceptive behavior. He concludes that this is the only way they can "continue special friends."

## "Upon Four Dismal Stories in the Doctor's Letter"

Poem by Swift; first published in 1929. It was included with an October 15, 1726 letter Swift sent to Alexander POPE and John GAY. Soon after Swift's return to Dublin in August of 1726, he received a letter dated September 20 from Dr. John ARBUTHNOT. It described various illnesses, injuries, and other calamities that had recently befallen several of Swift's friends (William CONGREVE, Alexander Pope, Henrietta HOWARD, and Robert ARBUTHNOT). After mentioning these misfortunes in the poem, Swift reports that although he suffers minor inconveniences (such bad claret), he "gets home at night with health and whole bones" (8).

## "Upon the Horrid Plot Discovered by Harlequin the Bishop of Rochester's French Dog"

Poem by Swift; first published in 1735, written in 1722. Subtitled "In a Dialogue Between a Whig and a Tory," it derides the proceedings against Bishop Francis ATTERBURY, bishop of Rochester, who supported the plot to usurp the Hanoverian King GEORGE I and restore the Stuarts to power. The poem begins with the speaker (a TORY) asking a WHIG how the "wicked plot" was discovered. When the latter responds that "a dog" acted as an informant, the Tory assumes that the Whig is speaking figuratively since that term is often used to describe a "villain, who his friend betrays." In the comical discussion that follows, the Whig continues to use *dog* literally while the Tory metaphorically speaks to Walpole and other villains (including Whig bishops) as "dogs." Their mutual penchant for misunderstanding suggests that Whigs and Tories speak different languages, and are barely capable of holding intelligent conversations with anyone other than fellow party-men.

In his biography of Swift, Irvin Ehrenpreis points out that while Swift ridiculed the prosecution witnesses, he never argued that Atterbury was innocent of the charges (III.140). Part of the government's case against Atterbury and other conspirators was based on the fact that they all knew details about a small dog named Harlequin (a gift sent to Atterbury's wife from France), which had been mentioned throughout the incriminating correspondence. In what Pat Rogers calls "the only other direct echo of the Atterbury affair," Swift makes fun of the government's code-breaking strategies in Part 3, chapter 6 of GULLIVER'S TRAVELS (721n.).

# "Upon the South Sea Project"

Poem by Swift entitled "The Bubble" or "The South Sea" in some early editions; first published in 1721, written in 1720. Filled with classical and biblical allusions, it is a bitter satire against the corrupt leaders of the SOUTH SEA COMPANY, who in 1720 agreed to absorb Britain's national debt. They hoped to profit from selling shares of the debt and using the revenue to exercise their exclusive trade rights with Spanish America. By September 1720, however, the value of the shares had dropped and the scheme had cost many investors in England

and Ireland their fortunes. Swift calls for divine vengeance against the company's promoters for misleading the public and ruining the nation's credit. See also "The RUN UPON THE BANKERS."

# "Vanbrug's House"

Poem by Swift; first published 1711, written between 1703 and 1708–09. It is subtitled "Built from the Ruins of Whitehall That Was Burnt." Swift makes fun of John VANBRUGH, who built an extravagant home at Whitehall after it was heavily damaged by fire in 1698. After explaining that poets of old could build great edifices with their verses alone, Swift casts Vanbrugh among the far inferior modern poets and suggests that he lacks architectural skill. He goes on to compare the house Vanbrugh builds from Whitehall's ruins to the corrupt verses modern rhymers produce in perverse imitation of the ancients. See also "The HISTORY OF VANBRUG'S HOUSE" and "ON THE BURNING OF WHITEHALL IN 1698."

# "Verses from Quilca"

The title Pat Rogers assigns in his edition of the *Poems* to three poems by Swift; first published in 1746. All three describe life in the country. They were included in a 1725 letter from Swift to Thomas SHERIDAN. For the circumstances surrounding the composition of these verses see "TO QUILCA." See also "The BLUNDERS, DEFICIENCIES, DISTRESSES, AND MISFORTUNES OF QUILCA."

# "Verses Left in a Window of Dublin Castle"

Poem by Swift; first published in 1779, written about 1725 during Swift's first known visit to Dublin Castle. The Lord mentioned in the first line is John, second baron CARTERET, who allegedly penned a jesting reply to Swift's couplet (Rogers, *Poems* 746n.).

# "Verses Made for the Women Who Cry Apples, etc."

Poem by Swift; first published in 1746, written while Swift was living in Dublin but Pat Rogers calls it undatable beyond that. The poem is divided into six sections, each spoken by a woman preaching the virtues of the specific food she has for sale. Joseph Horrell notes that the poem reflects Swift's fascination with street cries, especially evident in *The* JOURNAL TO STELLA (Horrell, *Poems* II.772).

# "Verses Occasioned by the Sudden Drying Up of St. Patrick's Well near Trinity College, Dublin"

Poem by Swift; first published in 1762, written in 1729. Pat Rogers notes that although it is seldom discussed, "this is one of the most explicit statements of Swift's view of Irish politics" (791). The poem is unique among Swift's verses, mainly because of the lengthy scholarly notes that accompany it: Joseph Horrell writes that "It is not characteristic of Swift to show his erudition" (II.782).

# "Verses on I Know Not What"

Poem by Swift; first published in 1765, probably written in 1732. Pat Rogers calls the poem now unintelligible and its subject unidentifiable. He also suggests that the title may not have been Swift's, although it was found on the reverse side of a paper containing Swift's autograph version of the poem (860–861).

# "Verses on the Death of Dr. Swift, D.S.P.D."

Poem by Swift; first published in 1739, written in 1731. Swift added explanatory notes in 1732.

"D.S.P.D." stands for "Dean of St. Patrick's, Dublin." Swift made an important reference to the poem in a December 1, 1731, letter to John GAY: "I have been several months writing near five hundred lines on a pleasant subject, only to tell what my friends will say on me after I am dead" (*Corr.* III.506). He apparently did not intend for the "Verses" to be published until after his death, but the manuscript was widely read among his friends. Based on its popularity, Swift wrote and published a shorter, less inflammatory autobiographical poem, "The LIFE AND GENUINE CHARACTER OF DR. SWIFT." Both poems are based on maxim xcix from the first edition of François de LA ROCHEFOUCAULD's *Reflexions ou Sentences et Maximes Morales* (1665). Swift translates the maxim differently in each poem. In the "Verses," he renders it as, "In all distresses of our friends / We first consult our private ends, / While nature kindly bent to ease us, / Points out some circumstance to please us" (7–10).

The first printing of the "Verses" was controversial. Several years after completing the poem, Swift gave it to Dr. William KING, "with whom Swift seems to have become acquainted toward the end of 1734, when King was in Ireland on the business of a lawsuit" (Williams, *Poems* 2.551). With Alexander POPE's approval, King issued a heavily edited first edition in London during 1739 without Swift's permission. Greatly angered by the drastic changes his friends had made to the poem prior to publication, Swift himself saw to the printing of the restored "Verses" in Dublin that same year. King and Pope thought they were doing Swift a favor in their emendations, since they removed what they regarded as the most embarrassingly vain sections, along with lines that contained what Nora Crow Jaffe calls "dangerous political references" (*The Poet Swift* 14).

The poem contains three sections. In the poem (lines 1–72), Swift offers a commentary on La Rochefoucauld's maxim—first in general and then in personal terms in lines 39–72. In the following section (lines 73–298), he imagines the time just before "by the course of nature" he dies. As his friends predict his impending fall and lament his reduced faculties, they take comfort in "hug[ging] themselves" and saying, " 'It is not so bad with us.' "

When the "fatal day" finally arrives, the news of his death spreads rapidly until "every paper" contains at least one paragraph "To curse the Dean, or bless the Drapier." Lines 179–204 make fun of those who are pleased or indifferent at his death—including Lady Suffolk (Henrietta HOWARD), Queen CAROLINE, Francis Charteris, Sir Robert WALPOLE, and the bookseller Edmund Curll. In contrast, lines 205–242 imagine how those he loves (Pope, Gay, John ARBUTHNOT, Henry BOLINGBROKE, and tender-hearted "female friends") will grieve the loss. In lines 245–298, he imagines that only one year after his death there will be "No further mention of the Dean; / Who now, alas, no more is missed." The final section of the poem (lines 299–488) eavesdrops on a "club assembled at the Rose" as they converse about Swift. In the midst of this discussion, "one quite indifferent in the cause" finally speaks up to "draw" Swift's character "impartial[ly]." What follows is the controversial panegyric in which the supposedly impartial speaker presents an extremely flattering picture of Swift as a pillar of the kingdom.

As Swift's most famous poem, "Verses" has received a great deal of critical attention. Pat Rogers (*Complete Poems*) and Nora Crow Jaffe (*The Poet Swift*) both provide helpful overviews of critical responses, only a few of which can be mentioned here. A central question has long been how seriously to take all the praise lavished upon Swift in the final section of the poem: Louise K. Barnett suggests that readers have generally found the poem to be "ingenuously vain" or characterized by a "contrived" vanity that makes the work "exemplary" (*Swift's Poetic Worlds* 3). John Irwin Fischer devotes an entire chapter to the "Verses" in *On Swift's Poetry*, where he suggests that the greatest single challenge of the poem is "to discover the relationship between the panegyric with which Swift's poem ends and that maxim of La Rochefoucauld which . . . occasioned the entire poem" (152). Irvin Ehrenpreis reads the poem as Swift's fusion of "the motifs of friendship, death, and lack of recognition, which had risen constantly in his poems and letters" (III.708). In relating the "Verses" to "Life and Genuine Character," Ehrenpreis further suggests that "Verses" is superior: "more important but

more puzzling" (III.710). In his biography of Swift, David Nokes cites its central difficulty as identifying the "precise tone" of the poem, based on the many ambiguities that characterize it (358). For Barnett, reading the poem to discover how "Swift conceived the variety of his character" is to miss the point. She argues that in this and other poems of "fictive self-portraiture," we find Swift presenting the features and flaws of an ambiguous "self"—one who is less vulnerable to death, distortions, and weaknesses because he exists in a "poetic world" that can "order and contain" each of those "destructive phenomena" (90).

# "Verses on the Revival of the Order of the Bath"

Poem possibly by Swift; first published in 1814, written about 1726. Pat Rogers calls this a doubtful item. It makes fun of King GEORGE I's decision—heavily influenced by Robert WALPOLE—to reinstate this order of chivalry. Originated by King Henry IV in 1399, the Order of the Bath had become inactive at the beginning of King CHARLES II's reign.

# "Verses on the Upright Judge"

Poem by Swift; first published in 1735, written in 1724. Like "WHITSHED'S MOTTO ON HIS COACH," this poem is directed against William WHITSHED, who (as the subtitle suggests) had "Condemned the Drapier's printer," John HARDING. See also "An EXCELLENT NEW SONG ON A SEDITIOUS PAMPHLET."

# "Verses Said to Be Written on the Union"

Poem by Swift; first published in 1746, written in 1707. It reflects Swift's opposition to the Act of

Union (enacted May 1, 1707), which united the Parliaments of England and Scotland and established Sophia, princess of Hanover, and her heirs as rulers of the United Kingdom. Swift supported a union between England and Ireland, and saw the Anglo-Scottish alliance as faithless and unlawful. See also "STORY OF THE INJURED LADY."

# "Verses Spoken Extempore by Dean Swift on His Curate's Complaint of Hard Duty"

Poem possibly by Swift; first published (along with "The PARSON'S CASE") in the December 1734 *Gentleman's Magazine*. Pat Rogers calls it a doubtful attribution. The poem is a sarcastic treatment of the supposedly remarkable and difficult work of Robert Hewit, a curate in a parish neighboring Swift's.

# "Verses to Vanessa"

See "LINES FROM CADENUS AND VANESSA."

# "Verses Wrote in a Lady's Ivory Table-Book"

Poem by Swift; first printed in *Miscellanies* (1711), written in 1699 or earlier. The first of Swift's mature occasional poems, it is narrated by the table-book in which the "verses" are written. Reflecting the blotted, cluttered pages of the table-book, the poem juxtaposes the lady's jottings and her suitors' obsequies to suggest—in an ironic comment on the poem itself—that the book is full of nothing.

# "Vindication of Isaac Bickerstaff, Esq., A"

Written in the person of "Isaac Bickerstaff," this short prose piece is that fictional character's response (as the subtitle indicates) to "What is objected to him by Mr. Patrige [John PARTRIDGE], in his Almanack for the present Year 1709." It was first published in London in 1709 as part of Swift's ongoing satiric campaign against Partridge that had begun with "PREDICTIONS FOR THE YEAR 1708."

## SYNOPSIS

Bickerstaff begins by complaining of the rough treatment he has received from Partridge, and expressing his amazement that a gentleman would stoop to such a level—especially against a fellow gentleman. His main concern, he argues, is not for himself but for "the *Republick of Letters*," which Partridge has "endeavoured to wound" through his attack on Bickerstaff. This attack was particularly unwarranted, especially in light of all the praise Bickerstaff has received from many "parts of Europe" (except for Portugal, where his book was burned).

Bickerstaff asserts that he has found only two objections to his earlier predictions—one of which can be ignored since it came from a French papist, and the other based on his prediction that Partridge would die on March 29, 1708. This second objection is the subject of the present vindication, and the one that led Partridge to attack him violently in print. Partridge had the audacity, in fact, to "roundly" claim that "he *is not only now alive, but was likewise alive upon that very 29th of* March, *when* [Bickerstaff] *had foretold he should die.*" In response, Bickerstaff sets out to show that Partridge is, in fact, "not alive." First, numerous readers of Partridge's libels against Bickerstaff have proclaimed that "*no Man alive ever writ such damned Stuff as this.*" Second, Partridge claims to foretell the future "and recover Stolen goods" through his visions—both of which would require him to communicate with "the Devil" and "evil Spirits," something no man could do until after he had died. Third, Partridge asserts that he is alive now, and was alive at the time Bickerstaff predicted he would die, unwittingly revealing his belief "that a Man may be alive now, who was not alive" one year ago—and therein "lies the Sophistry of his Argument." Finally, Bickerstaff asks why he would have been so "indiscreet" as to start his predictions "with the only Falshood [that of Partridge's death] that ever was pretended to be in them."

Bickerstaff insists that he would not have bothered to defend himself against Partridge's preposterous complaints had some other prognosticators used his name without permission in their own predictions. Having "clearly proved, by *invincible Demonstration*," that Partridge truly did die at the time he predicted (and not earlier, as some have claimed), Bickerstaff ends his vindication.

## COMMENTARY

When John Partridge attacked Isaac Bickerstaff in early 1709, treating the fictional figure as an authentic opponent in his almanac, Swift found vindication for his efforts. Denying Partridge's assertion that he (Bickerstaff) was alive, Swift responded with "A Vindication," explaining slowly and carefully why Partridge had thoroughly misunderstood Bickerstaff and detracted from the learned discussion which the two astrologers might have had if Partridge could find it in himself to act without "scurrility and passion." Though Londoners understood at this point the joke which had begun with "PREDICTIONS FOR THE YEAR 1708," the foolishness seems, if possible, to have reached a new level of absurdity. Swift's imaginative impulses realized their full power here; and when Richard STEELE intended on advancing to the next stage of the hoax in naming the good-humored Bickerstaff the narrator of his periodical the *Tatler* (April 12, 1709), Swift readily agreed.

The attack on Partridge was extended, which suited Swift's original intention. The satiric attack would diminish further the anticlerical WHIG influence of Partridge's annual almanac, *Merlinus Liberatus*. Answering the foolishness of astrology and the politics of a tradesman who has rejected established authority spurred Swift into a number of other pamphlets he was writing at this time against dissent and Dissenters whom he blamed for causing the chaos of the English Civil War. Partridge and

his ilk deserved immediate response, but Bickerstaff's voice and words needed to be lively and funny and engaging and boisterous, so he might rouse a reading public whose critical sense about discerning the good from the rubbish usually needed freshening.

Swift's "Bickerstaff papers" survive today due to their intellectual heft and epitomize the way politics was discussed in the early decades of the century. He sets a tone in these that one can find again and again in his essays, longer satiric works, and correspondence—aggressive, violently witty, full of friction, sharply humorous, but containing a steely moral basis. The good will of Bickerstaff, as Herbert Davis calls it, exists also in such full measure that Steele can import it into his own periodical, and readers immediately focus on the moral and political clarity embodied in his character. Both Steele and Swift enjoyed the sense of ridicule that emanated from both Bickerstaff and Partridge—the former took an outrageous position and caused laughter, but the result fractured Partridge, whose blindness and arrogance allowed Swift to flay him alive.

# "Virtues of Sid Hamet the Magician's Rod, The"

Poem by Swift; first published in 1710, written the same year. It is an angry attack upon Sidney, first earl of GODOLPHIN, based on the resentment Swift felt for him. This was mainly due to disagreement over the First Fruits (a tax from which Swift sought to have Irish clergymen exempted) and the cold treatment Swift received during a visit to Godolphin in September of 1710.

# "When I Come to Be Old"

Set of resolutions by Swift, written in 1699. Even at the relatively early age of 32, after a series of uncertain career decisions that had not led to a clear view of whether old age would find him a success or not, Swift had decided on writing down a series of resolutions. He had during the past 10 years been in the service of Sir William TEMPLE three separate times, and come to realize that the older man represented the single most important influence on him at this stage of his life. We know Temple would acknowledge the value of listing virtues, either those one possessed or those one sought to achieve after a struggle. Certainly, Swift would likely find the process of writing a list a useful exercise, not unlike some people who jot down New Year's resolutions.

Critics debate whether this "dramatic doodle" has autobiographical value, and even if the young man reverses the typical process and decides how the old man will find himself at an advanced age, it remains a curiosity among the far more significant work of his early period. When Temple died in January 1699, Swift faced a watershed moment in his life. He would stay on at MOOR PARK and finish editing and arranging publication of his employer's work, but then he hoped for a prebend in England, some certainty where he might gain tenure and position in the world. Possibly before launching himself with BERKELEY back to Ireland in August, he wrote these in a sort of coda: The themes seem familiar—avoid the young, especially women and children; avoid boring others with one's talk or self-importance; avoid troublesome servants and friends who flatter; and cultivate friends who will tell you when you have become obnoxious. Though these seem naïve and the product of a few moments' thought, the truth, or as much of it as Swift could see at this time, does intrude. He was headed back to Ireland for a minor, short-term post, unwilling to marry Varina (Jane WARING), and determined to set his mind and soul on being deprived and forgotten. He would be proven wrong in some of his conclusions, but others, those resolutions having to do with human relationships, would remain infinitely complicated, being worked out while burdened with self-mockery and self-pity.

## "When Mrs. Welch's Chimney Smokes"

Poem by Swift; written in his "HOLYHEAD JOURNAL" September 27, 1727, regarding uncomfortable conditions in the inn where he stayed on his way back to Dublin from England. See also "HOLYHEAD. SEPTEMBER 25, 1727," "IRELAND," "The POWER OF TIME," and "ON LORD CARTERET'S ARMS."

## "Whitshed's Motto on His Coach"

Poem by Swift; first published in 1735, written in 1724. Directed against William WHITSHED, it offers an insulting interpretation of his family motto, *"Libertas et natale Solum"* ("Liberty and our native land"). The immediate occasion for the poem was Whitshed's attempt as lord chief justice to have printer John HARDING prosecuted for having published the fourth of Swift's DRAPIER'S LETTERS. In letter 6: "To Lord Chancellor MIDDLETON," Swift recalls the episode: "I observed, and I shall never forget upon what Occasion, the Device upon [Whitshed's] Coach to be *Libertas & natale Solum;* at the very Point of Time when he was sitting in his Court, and perjuring himself to betray both." Swift's other poems against Whitshed include "VERSES ON THE UPRIGHT JUDGE" and "An EXCELLENT NEW SONG ON A SEDITIOUS PAMPHLET."

## "Windsor Prophecy, The"

Poem by Swift; first published in 1711. According to David Nokes, it was written on December 23 of that year and printed on Christmas Eve (*Hypocrite Reversed* 141). The poem is a vicious attack upon Elizabeth Percy Seymour, duchess of SOMERSET, written in an attempt to gain greater favor from Queen ANNE for Swift's friend Abigail Masham (née HILL). Although Swift wrote to Esther JOHNSON that he liked the poem "mightily" (JOURNAL TO STELLA 2.144), he later recognized it as having incensed the queen and prevented him from gaining the preferment he wanted.

## "Wood, an Insect"

Poem by Swift; first published in 1735, written in 1725. It is one of numerous poems in which Swift attacks William WOOD and expresses his opposition to Wood's patent for Irish coinage. In this poem Wood is compared to "three little vermin" and sentenced to die by scalding in a vat of the copper he melts to make coins. See also *The DRAPIER'S LETTERS*, "DOING GOOD: A SERMON ON THE OCCASION OF WOOD'S PROJECT," "AN EPIGRAM ON WOOD'S BRASS MONEY," "AN EXCELLENT NEW SONG UPON HIS GRACE OUR GOOD LORD ARCHBISHOP OF DUBLIN," "ON WOOD THE IRONMONGER," "PROMETHEUS," "A SERIOUS POEM UPON WILLIAM WOOD," and "A SIMILE."

## "Yahoo's Overthrow, The"

Poem by Swift; first published in 1765, written in 1734. It is a sequel to "ON THE WORDS 'BROTHER PROTESTANTS AND FELLOW CHRISTIANS.'" In response to the insults against him in that poem, Richard BETTESWORTH threatened violent revenge on Swift and engaged in a heated exchange with him at Rev. John WORRALL's home. In this poem (and others including "AN EPIGRAM INSCRIBED TO THE HONOURABLE SERJEANT KITE"), Swift makes fun of Bettesworth's threats.

# Part III

## Related Entries

**Abercorn, James Hamilton, sixth earl of** (1656–1734) A friend of Swift who served as privy councillor to the sovereigns ANNE, GEORGE I, and GEORGE II. He was an early supporter of a proposed Bank of Ireland ("the Child's intended Governour") that Swift opposed in his bank pamphlets. He joined Swift in rejecting William WOOD's coinage patent (1720–25).

**Acheson, Lady Anne (née Savage)** (d. 1737) Wife of Sir Arthur and heiress of Swift's friend Philip SAVAGE, chancellor of the exchequer of Ireland. She was a slender, sickly (from tuberculosis), intelligent woman who enjoyed Swift's company at their rural MARKET HILL family estate for more than 18 months. Swift appreciated her charity and candor, especially during his lengthy illnesses while visiting them. The Achesons, who married in 1715, had seven children and separated about 1732. Swift, who prospered there away from Dublin, assumed the role of language and literature teacher to the good-natured pupil, her ladyship. He wrote the so-called Market Hill group of poems during his long visits. See also "TO A LADY," "DAPHNE," "The JOURNAL OF A MODERN LADY," "LADY ACHESON WEARY OF THE DEAN," "ON CUTTING DOWN THE OLD THORN AT MARKET HILL," "An ANSWER TO THE BALLYSPELLIN BALLAD," "MY LADY'S LAMENTATION AND COMPLAINT AGAINST THE DEAN," "DEATH AND DAPHNE," and "A PANEGYRIC ON THE DEAN."

**Acheson, Sir Arthur, fifth bart** (1688–1749) Irish member of Parliament and sheriff of County Armagh whose estate, MARKET HILL, was an agreeable place where the citybound Swift embraced the rural life. Between 1728 and 1730 the Achesons invited Swift for three long visits, during which he wrote poetry, dabbled in farming and landscape gardening, and educated Sir Arthur's wife, Lady Anne. As Swift's ideal of the cultivated gentleman and man of taste, Acheson could balance his pride in Ireland with the demands of the Robert WALPOLE ministry. See also "The REVOLUTION AT MARKET-HILL," "The DEAN'S REASONS FOR NOT BUILDING AT DRAPIER'S HILL," "The GRAND QUESTION DEBATED," and "TO DEAN SWIFT."

**Addison, Joseph** (1672–1719) Writer and politician who joined Richard STEELE in writing and editing the *Tatler* (1709–11) and the *Spectator* (1711–12); WHIG M.P., 1708; undersecretary of state; secretary to Thomas WHARTON, the lord lieutenant of Ireland (1709–10); among later government posts served as secretary of state (1717–18). His poem "The Campaign" (1705), celebrating MARLBOROUGH's victory at Blenheim, earned him a ministerial post. His tragedy *Cato* (1713) held the stage throughout the century. Addison first met Swift in 1705 and became a close friend despite shifting political differences, inviting him to his circle of Whig wits—Steele, William CONGREVE, Ambrose PHILIPS, and other Kit-Cat Club members. Addison and Swift complemented each other intellectually, maintaining their respect for the dignity of each other's body of work. Yet, Swift says, "Mr. Addison and I are different as black

Joseph Addison, by Michael Dahl, c. 1719 *(Library of Congress)*

and white . . . but I love him still as well as ever" (*The* JOURNAL TO STELLA, 127).

**Aikin, John** (1747–1822)   A physician, literary critic, and editor whose *Select Works of the British Poets* (1820) and *General Biography* (10 vols.) made him well known to his 19th-century readers. Aikin worries about his readers' delicate tastes, advising them to pick their way "very nicely" through Swift's poetry and leave much of it "unvisited." Yet he finds Swift a "most perfect rhymer," his diction natural and easy, and his meaning expressed with perfect precision.

**Aislabie, John** (1670–1742)   Member of Parliament from 1695 to 1702 and 1705 to 1721; treasurer of the navy, member of the privy council for the WHIG ministry, and chancellor of the exchequer in 1718. Consumed with amassing wealth, he supported the SOUTH SEA COMPANY as a way to pay off the national debt. When the company's share values tumbled in 1720, the Commons found him guilty of "infamous corruption." Swift, who did not know Aislabie, called the directors of the company "knaves cheating fools." See also "UPON THE SOUTH SEA PROJECT" and "The RUN UPON THE BANKERS."

**Albemarle, Arnold Joost van Keppel, first earl of** (1670–1718)   A Dutch courtier and favorite of King WILLIAM III of England, who became a trusted general commanding Dutch cavalry squadrons in the duke of MARLBOROUGH's army in the Netherlands campaigns of the Spanish Succession War (1701–14). Swift's intention in "The CONDUCT OF THE ALLIES" and "Remarks on the Barrier Treaty" was to discredit the WHIG ministry and its general, Marlborough. He furthers this effort with "The HISTORY OF THE FOUR LAST YEARS OF THE QUEEN," where his comments on "the Earl of Albemarle's disgrace at Denain . . . the blame of which was equally shared between Prince EUGENE [Marlborough's co-captain and commander of the imperial forces] and the Earl" might weaken Marlborough's reputation (146–147).

**Allen, Joshua, second viscount** (1685–1742)   Politician, wealthy Dublin merchant, and city alderman whose family had long associations with the political life of Ireland. As a result of Swift's successful effort to defeat William WOOD's patent for minting coins (see *The* DRAPIER'S LETTERS), the council had bestowed on him the freedom of the city (1725). Swift, however, sought the additional distinction of a gold box, one that less deserving churchmen had recently received. Allen, who along with his wife had been on friendly terms with Swift, attacked the council's proclamation in the most insulting manner. Swift, believing him mad and unwilling to forgive his malice, renounced Allen in a series of prose and verse pieces. See also "ADVERTISEMENT BY DR. SWIFT, IN HIS DEFENSE AGAINST JOSHUA, LORD ALLEN" and "TRAULUS."

**Anglesey, Arthur Annesley, fifth earl of** (1676–1737)   Member of Parliament, 1702–10; Joint vice treasurer and treasurer of war in Ireland, 1710–16; and lord justice, 1714. As an acquaintance and frequent dinner companion of Swift in London when both were admitted to Robert HARLEY's inner cabinet, Annesley's TORY beliefs and family interests in Ireland gave him credibility in the ministry. Swift lobbied him on behalf of various Irish friends seeking preferment and of the Irish woolen industry, which wanted protection against threatened export duties. Annesley's great hope for an appointment as lord lieutenant of Ireland remained unfulfilled.

**Anne, (queen of Great Britain and Ireland)** (1665–1714)  The last of the Stuart monarchs. She was the second daughter of JAMES II (then duke of York) and his first wife, Anne Hyde, who died in 1671. Though her father became a Catholic in 1672, Anne was raised in the Anglican Church. She married GEORGE, prince of Denmark, 1683, bearing him 17 children. Only William, duke of Gloucester, survived infancy, though he died in 1700. As a princess and later queen, she was influenced by her close friends and confidantes, Sarah Churchill, duchess of MARLBOROUGH, and later Sarah's cousin Mrs. Abigail MASHAM (née Hill), who attempted to sway her politically. She succeeded to the throne on the death of WILLIAM III, her sister's husband, in 1702. Anne, Swift felt, never fully appreciated his wit or his capacity for political and religious satire, finding "A TALE OF A TUB" especially disturbing. His ambition for an English bishopric, a preferment requiring royal support, remained unfulfilled, and he returned to Ireland with the lesser post of a cathedral dean.

In GULLIVER'S TRAVELS, the "Letter from Captain Gulliver to his Cousin Sympson" indicates that Anne is greatly admired by Lemuel Gulliver. He alludes to her "most pious and glorious memory" and writes that (despite his aversion to Yahoos) he "did reverence and esteem her more than any of the human species."

**Arbuthnot, Dr. John** (1667–1735)  Physician, writer, member of the SCRIBLERUS CLUB along with John GAY, Robert HARLEY, Thomas PARNELL, Alexander POPE, and Swift. A Scot educated at Aberdeen University and Oxford, Arbuthnot took his M.D. at St. Andrews (1696), becoming Queen

ANNE's personal physician and a favorite courtier. The friendship of Arbuthnot and Swift remained important to both men for 25 years. Arbuthnot introduced Swift to the princess of Wales, later Queen CAROLINE, in April 1726. Swift embraced Arbuthnot's intellect, generosity, honesty, and worldliness. Arbuthnot wrote scientific studies and political and literary satires, including *The History of John Bull* (1712) and various pieces in the Pope and Swift *Miscellanies* (1727–32), and was the chief contributor to *The Memoirs of Martinus Scriblerus* (1741).

**Arbuthnot, Robert** (c. 1669–1741)  Younger brother of John and banker at Rouen and Paris who, after having fought at Killiecrankie for JAMES II in 1689, decided to leave Scotland and seek a career. He married a rich English widow in Suffolk (1726) and was one of the PRETENDER's most useful agents in financing the Jacobite uprising in 1715. Swift (who met Robert through his brother) respected and trusted him, recommending in 1735 that the son of a Dublin friend, Mrs. E. SICAN, visit Arbuthnot in Paris. Earlier, Swift had intended to stay with Arbuthnot on a long-planned trip to France (1727), but various issues, including his poor health and the death of King GEORGE I, prevented his departure.

**Argyll, Archibald Campbell, first duke of** (d. 1703)  Scottish nobleman and government official, father of John Campbell, second duke of ARGYLL. He was an early and active supporter of William of Orange, later WILLIAM III. He recovered his Scottish estates when JAMES II was deposed. Swift recognized similar traits in the father, Archibald, as in the son, John: In outward appearance they were good-natured, civil gentlemen but their actions encompassed anything that would promote their own interests.

**Argyll, John Campbell, second duke of** (1678–1743)  Eldest son of Archibald Campbell, first duke of ARGYLL; soldier and politician. He was a distinguished general officer in MARLBOROUGH's army whose ambition led him to challenge his commander. His political timing was perfect, as the new

TORY government commended his actions and installed him as a knight of the Garter (1710). With Marlborough's influence declining, Argyll was promoted commander-in-chief of the English army in Spain, as well as ambassador extraordinary. Later, he commanded the Hanoverian forces opposing the Jacobite Rising of 1715 and was created duke of Greenwich in 1719. Swift considered himself a friend of Argyll, noting the duke's habit of "distinguishing people of merit." When Argyll, however, reconciled himself to Marlborough and changed parties, Swift (who also hated Presbyterianism and believed the Act of Union between Scotland and England unfairly ignored Ireland) responded to this and other Whig attacks on Robert HARLEY's ministry in *The Public Spirit of the Whigs* (1714). In criticizing the Hanoverian succession, Swift condemned certain "Scotch peers . . . [who] have since gathered more money than ever any Scotchman . . . could form an idea of" (*Prose Works* VIII.50–51).

## Arran, Charles Butler, first earl of (1671–1758)

Second son of Thomas, earl of Ossory, who was the eldest son of the first duke of Ormonde, created earl of Arran in the Irish peerage in 1693 and Baron Butler in the English peerage. He was often referred to as the Jacobite brother of James Butler, the second duke of ORMONDE, who was beloved by Swift. A regular companion of Swift in London when both were members of "The Club," a group of 22 noblemen and commoners founded by Henry BOLINGBROKE about 1710. Swift wrote "The end of our club [better known as The Society] is to advance conversation and friendship, and to reward deserving persons with our interest and recommendation" (*The JOURNAL TO STELLA* 294).

## Asgill, John (1659–1738)

Lawyer, deist, and M.P. in both Irish and English Houses of Commons (1703, 1705–07) who had a successful Dublin legal practice but wrote an eccentric pamphlet to prove death was not required for Christians (1699), which was ordered burned (1703; again 1707). Asgill's writings, as well as those of Matthew Tindall, John TOLAND, and William Coward, represented for Swift an attack on Christian orthodoxy.

Swift links them together, calling their work "trumpery," in his most effective essay on religion and mortality, "An ARGUMENT AGAINST ABOLISHING CHRISTIANITY" (1708–11), and earlier in "Remarks upon a Book Intitled the Rights of the Christian Church Asserted."

## Ashburnham, John, first earl of (1687–1737)

Third baron Ashburnham (1710) and first earl in 1730, wealthy son-in-law of James Butler, second duke of ORMONDE, whose younger daughter, Lady Mary Butler (1710), he married. He was an acquaintance of Swift, to whom (according to some editors) the dean addressed a "LETTER FROM THE PRETENDER TO A WHIG LORD." Ashburnham had begun his political career as a WHIG but gave his friends and father-in-law reason to doubt his loyalty, showing instead TORY interests. Swift had little use for the man, calling him "a Puppy, and I shall never think it worth my while to be troubled with him" (*The JOURNAL TO STELLA* 595), saving his admiration instead for the earl's wife, Lady Mary.

## Ashburnham, Lady Mary (née Butler) (c. 1690–1713)

Wife of John Ashburnham, first earl; younger daughter of James Butler, second duke of ORMONDE. Lady Mary was a particular favorite of Swift, who enjoyed the company of the Butler sisters, including Lady Elizabeth, while in London in 1710–11. They were social acquaintances of the VANHOMRIGHs. Lady Mary's beauty and manner attracted Swift, who paid her the ultimate compliment of finding her very much like Stella (Esther JOHNSON) and the best-looking woman in court circles. Her death from complications of pregnancy in January 1713 caused Swift profound disillusionment and sadness.

## Ashe, Dillon (c. 1666–1718)

One of three brothers, including Thomas ASHE and St. George ASHE; a contemporary of Swift whom he met when both were students at Trinity College, Dublin. Ashe had a successful career as a clergyman in the Church of Ireland (due in part to his brother St. George's influence), becoming vicar of Finglas; promoted to archdeacon of Clogher in 1704 and chancellor of Armagh, 1706. Swift later enjoyed his company in London but found his inveterate punning, excessive drinking of wine, and love of the theater tiresome. "Just such a puppy as ever; and it is so uncouth, after so long an intermission" (*The Journal to Stella*, 303–04). But Swift's complaints masked his loneliness for Stella (Esther Johnson), and seeing "Dilly," whom Stella knew and liked, brought out his desire to return to Dublin, leaving London to the ambition of others. See *Dill* reference in "A Dialogue in the Castilian Language."

**Ashe, St. George** (c. 1658–1718)   Irish bishop who successively advanced from Cloyne (1695) to Clogher (1697), and finally Derry (1716–17). First a student at Trinity College, Dublin, Ashe became a fellow in 1679, professor of mathematics in 1685, and provost in 1692. A published writer of sermons and pamphlets, fellow of the Royal Society, and secretary to the Irish Philosophical Society, he and his two brothers, Thomas Ashe and Dillon Ashe, were friends of Swift. St. George Ashe, who had been Swift's tutor at Trinity, became particularly close to the dean despite his Whig tendencies. Stella (Esther Johnson) respected the bishop, and a false story circulated that he had performed a marriage ceremony joining Swift and Mrs. Johnson. Swift depended on Ashe for business advice but mainly accepted his friendship and hospitality. See reference to *Bp. Cl.* (Bishop of Clogher) in "A Dialogue in the Castilian Language."

**Ashe, Thomas** (c. 1656–1719)   Elder than the other Ashe brothers, St. George and Dillon, he was a convivial squire, known as "captain," with an estate of £1,000 a year in County Meath, Ireland; his home Ballygall, near Dublin, served as a frequent vacation residence for Swift. He appears as Tom A. in "A Dialogue in the Castilian Language" and in "The Dying speech of Tom Ashe," a fictional account of Ashe's death written as an extended joke on the man's constant punning, a habit Swift often practiced.

**Atterbury, Francis, bishop of Rochester** (1662–1732)   Churchman and a powerful voice of ecclesiastical authority. He became the leading figure of High Church politics in England during a 20-year period from 1693 when he enjoyed a base within London as the minister of the ancient hospitals of Bridewell and Bethlehem. In 1704 he was appointed dean of Carlisle and later dean of Christ Church, Oxford, in 1711. He and Swift had been neighbors in Chelsea, where Atterbury owned a country house, and Swift had lately taken an apartment nearby. They often dined together, and Swift respected the dean and liked his wife, Katherine. Atterbury became a member of the Scriblerus Club, and bishop of Rochester and dean of Westminster, in 1713. Swift mentions Atterbury in "A Proposal for Correcting, Improving and Ascertaining the English Tongue," "Mr. Collins's Discourse on Free Thinking," and "A Preface to the B——p of S——r——m's Introduction," and refers to him as the character of Prolocutor in the *Examiner* (December 28, 1710). With the influence of Atterbury's *Dr. Bentley's Dissertation . . . Examined* (1698), Swift responds and extends his support of Temple in "The Battle of the Books" (1704). When Atterbury is arrested for an alleged Jacobite plot, imprisoned in the Tower in 1722, tried, and banished to France, Swift believes him innocent, satirizing the trial in *Gulliver's Travels*, Part 3, and accusing the Walpole ministry of predetermining his guilt. See also "Upon the Horrid Plot Discovered by Harlequin the Bishop of Rochester's French Dog."

**Bacon, Francis** (1561–1626) English philosopher. His work runs counter to Scholastic and Aristotelian thinking, promoting an inductive method of reasoning based upon empirical observation, hypotheses, and verification by experiment. In "THE BATTLE OF THE BOOKS," Aristotle shoots an arrow at Bacon but misses, killing DESCARTES instead.

Born in London and educated at Cambridge, Bacon attended Gray's Inn and had all the educational preparation for a career in law. He served in Parliament for many years and wrote a number of papers on public affairs. He also held several influential posts, including solicitor-general, attorney-general, lord keeper, and lord chancellor. In 1621 Bacon was charged with bribery and lost the privilege of any further service in Parliament. Following a brief period of confinement in the Tower of London he wrote the works for which he has become famous, including the *Essays* (1597), *The Advancement of Learning* (1605), the *Novum Organum* (1620), and the *New Atlantis* (1626).

Swift counted Bacon among men of "eminent Parts and Abilities, as well as Virtues" who found success but were ultimately disgraced" (*Prose Works* XII.39). In another reference to Bacon's conviction for bribery, Swift lists him among "those who have made a mean contemptible Figure in some Action or Circumstance of their Life" (*Prose Works* V.85). He also describes Bacon as a "great Free Thinker," who was suspicious of "all the facts whereon most of the Superstitions (that is to say, what the Priests call the Religions) are grounded" and who preferred atheism to superstition (*Prose Works* IV.47).

Bacon's use of spiders, ants, and bees in the *Novum Organum* to portray different philosophical schools was an important source for the altercation between the spider and the bee near the beginning of "Battle of the Books."

**Baldwin, Henry** (fl. 1705–1710) London printer and bookseller who published Swift's "A FAMOUS PREDICTION OF MERLIN, THE BRITISH WIZARD" on February 21, 1709. To give an appearance of a 16th-century translation, Swift had Baldwin print this half-sheet of doggerel in black letter font.

**Baldwin, Richard** (c. 1672–1758) Provost of Trinity College, Dublin, 1717. An arch-WHIG who annoyed Swift by reducing his friends' chances for success at the college, Baldwin's actions were barely legal as he set aside popular choices for receiving fellowships and turned instead to his own party's candidates (1727). Swift calls him a "wealthy ninney" in "ON DR. RUNDLE" and insults him by implication in "SWIFT TO SHERIDAN."

**Barber, John** (1675–1741) Printer, elected alderman of the City of London for life in 1722, and lord mayor of the city (1732–33). He had extensive contacts in the government, including Henry St. John, Viscount BOLINGBROKE. Swift helped arrange printing rights for *The London Gazette*, the government paper, for Benjamin Tooke and Barber. Proving reliable, if not completely trustworthy, Barber also printed "Some Free Thoughts upon the Present State of Affairs," "The Public Spirit of the

Whigs" (for which he was arrested for libel), the EXAMINER, "THE CONDUCT OF THE ALLIES," "ADVICE HUMBLY OFFER'D TO THE MEMBERS OF THE OCTOBER CLUB," and "THE WINDSOR PROPHECY." Due to the controversial nature of many of these satiric pieces, Swift kept his authorship secret even from his own publisher. Friends and correspondents for years, Swift employed Barber's mistress Mrs. MANLEY for a short time in writing pamphlets.

**Barber, Jonathan** (died c. 1733) Woollen-draper (clothier) in Capel Street, Dublin. Husband of Mary BARBER, one of the Deanery circle of women with literary aspirations or interests with whom Swift could act as patron. Swift refers indirectly to Barber in "Observations on the Case of the Woollen Manufactures," finding the clothiers responsible for being "defective both in quality and quantity of their goods." Later, Swift notes in his correspondence the dishonesty of Barber, who overcharges an important customer for a suit of clothes.

**Barber, Mary** (c. 1690–1757) Poet, member of the Deanery circle of Dublin women with literary aspirations in whose company Swift took much pleasure; wife of Jonathan, a woollen-draper, and mother of four children—two of whom had distinguished careers in medicine and the fine arts. Mary published her first poem in 1725, and A Tale in 1728 celebrating John GAY's Fables. Swift enjoyed her literate conversation and made suggestions for improvement, and she edited her work to satisfy him. Swift calls her "our chief poetess" and a woman "with a great deal of good sense." He assisted in moving her entire family to Bath and in securing a list of subscriptions for her Poems on Several Occasions (1734), to which he added a prefatory letter of introduction. See also "APOLLO'S EDICT."

**Barrett, John** (1753–1821) Vice-provost of Trinity College, Dublin, and author of the Swift biography, An Essay on the Earlier Part of the Life of Swift (London, 1808). He maintains Swift was responsible for a controversial oration, Tripos of Terrae Filius, read by John Jones (c. 1664–1715) at Trinity College in July 1688. Though this appears a misattribution, Barrett was suggesting Swift's early skills as a satirist.

**Barton, Catherine** (1679–1740) Niece of Sir Isaac NEWTON whom Swift met during his visit to England in 1708–09. A beautiful woman with excellent connections in society who was the reputed mistress of Charles Montagu, earl of HALIFAX. The Newton household was in close proximity to Swift's London apartments, and an easy walk for him to visit, dine, and talk with her. Though an ardent WHIG, Mrs. Barton won him over with her charm and intelligence. She married John Conduitt in 1717, though she was already a rich woman thanks to Halifax's legacy.

**Bass, Thomas** (fl. 1725–1730) Co-owner of a theater company in Leicester, England, with John and Thomas SWIFT, who were the dean's relatives from Leicestershire and Hertfordshire. When traveling through Holyhead in Wales (disembarkation point from Dublin) to London and on the return trip, Swift would either walk or ride in his kinsmen's wagons.

**Bathurst, Allen, first earl of** (1684–1775) TORY member of Parliament for Cirencester (1705–11); created baron (1712) and earl (1772); and one of the century's greatest arborealists. Swift and Bathurst were members of the literary club founded by Henry BOLINGBROKE, known as "The Society," consisting of Tory statesmen and writers—the party's elite. Friends and correspondents for years, Swift with Alexander POPE visited Bathurst at his Cirencester estates. Pope's dedication of his "Epistle to Bathurst" (1733) suggests the high value both writers placed on Bathurst: "the sense to value riches, with the Art / T'enjoy them, and the virtue to impart" (ll.219–20). See also BOYER, ABEL.

**Bathurst, Charles** (1709–1786) London bookseller and printer on Fleet St. (1737–86); succeeded Benjamin Motte. One of the nominal printers of the votes of the House of Commons. Printed Swift's COMPLETE COLLECTION OF GENTEEL AND INGENIOUS CONVERSATION (1738) and "VERSES ON THE DEATH OF DR. SWIFT, D.S.P.D." in 1739, now known as the Bathurst edition. It reflects Alexander POPE's editorial skills, or "improvements" of the poem. Its popularity produced two editions, but this version, considerably changed from Swift's original intentions, angered the Dean. See "William King to Martha Whiteway, March 6, 1739" in the *Correspondence*.

**Beattie, James** (1735–1803)    Poet, essayist, and professor of moral philosophy and logic at Marischal College, Aberdeen, Scotland. "The Minstrel" (1771–74), his long and excellent poem in Spenserian stanzas, made his reputation, but his *Essays* offer more compelling insights. He believed English as a literary language "was brought to perfection in the days of Addison and Swift" as he decried its present loss of elegance, simplicity, veracity, and ease.

**Beaumont, Joseph** (d. 1734)    A linen-draper and merchant of a general goods in Trim, County Meath, Ireland. Swift corresponded with him frequently and often commended him to Stella (see Esther JOHNSON), who, with Rebecca DINGLEY, used to visit Trim for country outings. Laracor, the adjoining parish to Trim, served as Swift's first appointment as rector. Beaumont had developed a method for improving the weaving of linen cloth and won an Irish government award, and Swift supported Beaumont's claim through his extensive government contacts. As one of Swift's closest friends in Ireland who visited him in London, he also proved useful to the dean as his financial and administrative agent. A handsome man who suffered from numerous bouts of mental instability, Beaumont committed suicide. As he indicates in a March 26, 1722, letter to Daniel JACKSON, Swift had requested the authorities commit him to Bedlam (*Corr*. II.425). See also the poem, "ON THE LITTLE HOUSE BY THE CHURCHYARD OF CASTLEKNOCK."

**Bedell, Bishop William** (1571–1642)    An Englishman who became bishop of Kilmore and Ardagh and in 1627 was appointed as provost of Trinity College, Dublin, where he recommended that Irish divinity students should cultivate their native language so as to work more effectively with their parishioners. He supervised the translation of the Old Testament into Gaelic with the help of Rev. Thomas SHERIDAN's ancestors. Swift and Sheridan were excellent friends until near the latter's death, but Swift did not directly take much interest in the Irish language, though Swift approved of Bedell's injunction.

**Beer, E.**    London bookseller and printer of *Mr. Partridge's Answer to Esquire Bickerstaff's Predictions for the Year 1708*, suggesting that Bickerstaff's "PREDICTIONS" were understood as false and "the work of a 'Jacobite Shuffler.'" Swift did not write *Mr. Partridge's Answer*, though one of his friends may have and, in doing so, spawned Swift's "VINDICATION OF ISAAC BICKERSTAFF" (1709).

**Behn, Aphra**    See "Characters" under "The BATTLE OF THE BOOKS."

**Bentley, Richard** (1662–1742)    Classical scholar, critic, and theologian. He became keeper of the Royal Library in 1694 and master of Trinity College, Cambridge, in 1699 and was one of the ablest intellects of his generation. Later, he became Regius professor of divinity at Cambridge (1717). His self-promotion, patronizing manner, and peremptory self-assurance annoyed Swift, who portrayed him as an enemy of good taste—the pedantic critic in "The BATTLE OF THE BOOKS." Bentley had earlier earned Swift's wrath when he had disagreed with one of Sir William TEMPLE's essays. As the antihero of "A TALE OF A TUB," Bentley becomes the perfect portrait of vice in mankind. Alexander POPE included Bentley in *The Dunciad*.

**Berkeley, Charles, second earl of** (1649–1710)    Lord justice of Ireland who had held various commissions and ambassadorships, including envoy extraordinary at The Hague, 1689–94. As Swift's patron, he often entertained the dean at his many homes: Berkeley Castle (Gloucester), Berkeley House (Clerkenwell), Cranford (Middlesex), and Durdance (Surrey). Swift had served as Berkeley's private secretary and chaplain on the earl's first voyage to Ireland and arrival in Dublin (1699), but

Swift soon after became vicar at Laracor, near Chapelizod, the Berkeley mansion on the outskirts of Dublin. He dedicated his "Project for the Advancement of Religion and the Reformation of Manners" (1708) to Elizabeth, countess of BERKELEY, Charles's wife. Swift expected Berkeley would arrange for his appointment to the deanery of Derry; though this did not occur, he remained friendly with the Berkeleys, especially their daughter Lady Elizabeth (later GERMAIN) Berkeley. Swift's poem "The DISCOVERY" reveals how Arthur BUSHE outmaneuvered him to become Berkeley's secretary in Ireland. Though Swift had described him as "intolerably easy and indolent and somewhat covetous," he agreed to write the inscription for the earl's monument in Latin at Lady Berkeley's request.

**Berkeley, Elizabeth, (née Noel), countess of** (1655–1719) Wife of Charles, second earl of BERKELEY, and daughter of Baptist Noel, third viscount Campden. Swift played a teasing joke on Lady Berkeley, who was devoted to Robert BOYLE's *Meditations*, when he inserted his own "MEDITATION ON A BROOMSTICK" in a reading that tricked her into believing it was Boyle's piece (1704). His visit to Berkeley Castle when he wrote this meditation is traced through his poem, "A BALLAD ON THE GAME OF TRAFFIC," written at the same time. Later, he dedicated "Project for the Advancement of Religion and the Reformation of Manners" to her. She convinced Swift to provide a Latin epitaph for her husband's monument—he did it willingly in remembrance of the Berkeley family's many kindnesses.

**Berkeley, George, bishop of Cloyne** (1685–1753) Irish-born churchman who became well known for his philosophical writings: *A New Theory of Vision* (1709) and *A Treatise Concerning Human Knowledge* (1710). His *Dialogues between Hylas and Philonus* (1713), though not producing converts, did mark him, as Swift says, "a very ingenious man and great philosopher." The dean took the lead in introducing Berkeley to his ministerial friends and writers while both were in London. Swift secured Berkeley's appointment as chaplain and secretary to Charles Mordaunt, earl of PETERBOROUGH, while

envoy to Sicily. Later, he became dean of Dromore (1721) and dean of Derry (1724): see Swift's poem, "The STORM." When Esther VANHOMRIGH (Vanessa) died in 1723, she named Berkeley one of her executors, leaving him a healthy sum but nothing to Swift. Throughout their long, but not close, friendship, Swift often recommended him with great esteem, as in his September 4, 1724, letter to Lord CARTERET: "either use such Persuasions as will keep one of the first Men in this Kingdom for Virtue and Learning, quiet at home, or assist him . . . to compass his Romantick design [founding a college in Bermuda], which however is very noble" (*Corr.* III.32). Though his project failed, he moved to America and upon his return to England was appointed bishop of Cloyne (1734).

**Berkeley, George Monck** (1763–1793) A minor playwright, poet, and early biographer of Swift; grandson of George BERKELEY, bishop of Cloyne, and son of Rev. George Berkeley, the bishop's favorite. His family connections gave him particular insight and fascinating anecdotes concerning Swift's life. He draws on these for his *Literary Relics* (London, 1789), which contains the chapters "Inquiry into the Life of Dean Swift" and "Correspondence of Swift."

**Bernard, Charles** (1650–1710) Renowned surgeon who became Queen ANNE's chief surgeon (sergeant-surgeon) in 1702. Swift mentions him in *The JOURNAL TO STELLA* by reputation, though he indicates he has never met Bernard. After Bernard's death, Swift admires his large, valuable library and during the auction buys only a few books, though he desires many more.

**Bernier, François** (1620–1688) French author, physician, and traveler who the astrologer and almanac-maker John PARTRIDGE had predicted would die on a particular day. Swift's "Bickerstaff Papers" begin with "PREDICTIONS FOR THE YEAR 1708," in which he announces the approaching death of Partridge as an elaborate satiric joke discrediting his occupation and teachings. Swift mentions Bernier's *Suite des Memoirs* in a "DISCOURSE CONCERNING THE MECHANICAL OPERATION OF THE

Spirit." As an avid reader of travelers' tales and voyages of discovery, Swift certainly read and may have owned Bernier's *Grand Mogol* and *Voyages*.

**Bettesworth, Richard** (1688–1741)    Irish lawyer, sergeant-at-law, and M.P. for Philipstown and Middleton, Ireland. Swift satirized Bettesworth for his political views, especially those weakening the established Church. In the lampoon, "On the Words 'Brother Protestants and Fellow Christians,'" Swift criticizes Presbyterians but takes a vigorous jab at "that Booby Bettesworth" and rhymes his name with "sweat's worth." Within days Bettesworth protests the poem and threatens to cut Swift's ears off. Avoiding harm, Swift responds in a series of poems making fun of his threats: "The Yahoo's Overthrow," "An Epigram, Inscribed to the Honourable Sergeant Kite," and "On the Archbishop of Cashel and Bettesworth." Two prose pieces related to this quarrel, "The Observations Occasioned by Reading a Paper, Entitled, the Case of the Woollen Manufacturers of Dublin" and "Some Reasons against the Bill for Settling the Tyth of Hemp, Flax, &c. by a Modus," suggest Swift's continued efforts in pointing out injustices, even when threatened by his critics.

**Bindon, David** (unknown–1760)    M.P. for Ennis, Ireland. He produced an early pamphlet leading the fight against the English manufacturer William Wood: *Some Reasons Shewing the Necessity of the People of Ireland Are Under, for Continuing to Refuse Mr. Wood's Coinage* (1724). Along with Swift's *Drapier's Letters*, this piece was written as journalistic prose, encouraging the opposition of the Irish to a new copper coinage foisted on them by the Crown in granting a patent to Wood.

**Bindon, Francis** (c. 1690–1765)    Irish painter, architect, and Irish M.P. whose reputation brought him numerous commissions. Agreeing to a request from Lord William Howth, Swift sat for his portrait in 1735. Bindon painted three more pictures of Swift, the last in 1740 when the dean's health began failing. This full-length portrait hangs in the Deanery House, St. Patrick's.

**Blachford, Rev. John** (fl. 1730–1735)    Prebendary of Wicklow, Ireland, an intelligent, scholarly man who had served in Swift's chapter for more than 12 years. Swift wrote him two letters, the first dated April 16, 1731, the other December 12, 1734. Both are excellent examples of Swift's humor, or mock rudeness: He playfully criticizes Blachford's gift of a barrel of Wicklow ale (*Corr.* III.452–453) and affectionately invites himself to Blachford's home (*Corr.* IV.275–276).

**Blackmore, Sir Richard** (c. 1650–1729)    Physician, Whig political writer, and prolific poet who attended Oxford but took his M.D. at Padua. William III made him physician-in-ordinary, knighting him in 1697; he continued as royal physician to Queen Anne. Blackmore's infamous works—especially the epic *Prince Arthur* (1695) and his *Satyr against Wit* (1700)—caused him to become the object of Swift's satire and that of Alexander Pope. Swift mentions Blackmore in Section X of "A Tale of a Tub," and he appears in "The Battle of the Books" as "a famous *Modern* (but one of the *Mercenaries*)." He hurls a javelin at Lucan during the battle, but it falls short. When Lucan throws a lance at Blackmore in response, Aesculapius prevents it from hitting him. The two end up presenting gifts to each other, Blackmore offering a pair of spurs and Lucan giving him a bridle. In 1716 Blackmore published *Essays upon Several Subjects*, including "Essay upon Wit," in which he wrote that "Tale of a Tub" was the work of an "impious buffoon" and that if it had been published "in a pagan or popish nation," the "author would have received the punishment he deserved." He also attacked Swift as an "insolent derider of the worship of his country." Swift condemned Blackmore as an enemy of good taste, with both detestable principles and prosody. In book 2 of *The Dunciad*, Pope gives him the "honor" of standing out among all the "braying ass[es]" because he "sings so loudly" and for so long. See also "On Poetry: A Rhapsody."

**Blayney, Cadwallader, seventh lord** (1693–1733)    A young Irish peer known to Swift, who had introduced him to Joseph Addison, secretary to Thomas

WHARTON, the lord lieutenant of Ireland. Though Blayney may have distrusted Swift for abandoning the WHIGS, as he saw it, and embracing the TORIES, he had no cause for threatening the dean's life. In early 1715, after coming upon Swift on horseback, he forced him off the highway and then drew a pistol on the unsuspecting dean. Though Swift was unharmed, he immediately wrote "The Dean of St. Patrick's Petition to the House of Lords against the Lord Blaney" complaining about the brutal nature of his fellow citizens.

**Blount, Martha** (1690–1763)   Patty Blount was the younger of two unmarried sisters from an ancient, impoverished Catholic family living at Mapledurham Manor, the former neighbors of Alexander POPE in Berkshire, England. She was the poet's closest female friend, and he addressed his poem "An Epistle to a Lady" to her. Swift had met her at Twickenham, Pope's villa, and treated her with special kindness. Their correspondence was brief, but he mentions her often in letters to Pope and strongly defends her character as "an honest girl" to his friends (*Corr.* IV.79). See also his poem "A PASTORAL DIALOGUE BETWEEN RICHMOND LODGE AND MARBLE HILL."

**Blount, Teresa** (1688–unknown)   Vivacious elder sister of Martha BLOUNT, whose Catholic family had long made their home at Mapledurham manor in Berkshire, England. She was well known to Alexander POPE, and he may have considered marrying her about 1709. Teresa may also have suggested certain characteristics in his portrayal of Belinda in *The Rape of the Lock.* Swift certainly knew her and defended her character, though she often took advantage of her sister's friendship with Pope (as Swift indicated in a July 8, 1733, letter to him) (*Corr.* IV.172).

**Bolingbroke, Henry St. John, first viscount** (1678–1751)   Statesman and writer who was a TORY M.P., 1701; secretary of war in GODOLPHIN's ministry, 1704–08; secretary of state, 1710–14, when he drew up the settlement known as the Treaty or Peace of Utrecht (1713), ending the War of the Spanish Succession; created Viscount Bol-

ingbroke 1712. Swift meets him and pronounces him "the greatest young man I ever knew" in November 1710, after agreeing to become editor of the EXAMINER, the government's new paper. Robert HARLEY (at that time earl of Oxford and lord treasurer) and Bolingbroke needed "an impartial observer" who appeared convinced of the superiority of Tory party policy. St. John invited Swift to join his literary club, The Society (or Brothers) in 1711, consisting of Tory elite statesmen and writers. Both his "New Journey to Paris" and "The CONDUCT OF THE ALLIES" appeared in 1711, prompted by Bolingbroke's concern to salvage the Tories' image and on the latter to convince the public that England's interests and Tory policy were identical.

Other pamphlets of this period reflect the party's focus: "A LETTER FROM THE PRETENDER TO A WHIG LORD," "A LETTER OF THANKS FROM MY LORD WHARTON," "A HUE AND CRY AFTER DISMAL," and "The Public Spirit of the Whigs." Swift was also working diligently on "The HISTORY OF THE FOUR LAST YEARS OF THE QUEEN" during this period. Once Harley and Bolingbroke had encouraged the effort, but now the political occasion had passed, and Bolingbroke advised him not to publish it. When a rift developed between the two ministers, Swift wrote "Some Free Thoughts upon the Present State of Affairs" mourning opportunities lost. GEORGE I dismissed Bolingbroke from office, and after a threat of impeachment, he fled to France in 1715 to become the PRETENDER's secretary of state. With the disastrous defeat of Jacobite forces, he requested a pardon. It was granted by Walpole in 1723, but Bolingbroke was not allowed to serve in the House of Lords. Swift remained his friend, visited him in England, and encouraged Bolingbroke's literary and philosophical interests. In launching *The Craftsman,* Bolingbroke attacks the Walpole ministry and enlists Swift's help in writing *A Letter to the Writer of an Occasional Paper* (1727) attacking corruption. The Bolingbroke-Swift correspondence contains 35 letters, and Swift mentions him in the poems "HORACE, LIB. 2, SAT. 6," "A LIBEL ON THE REVEREND DR. DELANY AND HIS EXCELLENCY JOHN, LORD CARTERET," and "VERSES ON THE DEATH OF DR. SWIFT, D.S.P.D."

**Bolton, Charles Paulet, second duke of**  (1661–1722)  Lord lieutenant of Ireland (1717–19), who had been the seventh marquis of Winchester and lord justice of Ireland. He had joined William of Orange (WILLIAM III) in Holland (1688) and held minor offices during the reign of William and Mary. His presence at court was unimpressive—Swift refers to him as a fool, "a great booby." This view is shared by other commentators, one of whom calls him a lewd, lying, rock-solid WHIG. His efforts on behalf of the Irish economy weakened it further. Bolton had been part of an inquiry into the traitorous activities of a clerk in Robert HARLEY's office during an earlier Whig administration. The Whig peers raised the public's anger with their efforts at implicating Harley in the plot, though no proof existed involving him. Swift enters the fray with "Some Remarks upon a Pamphlet, Entitled A Letter to the Seven Lords" (1711). His poems mentioning Bolton include "ON LORD CARTERET'S ARMS," "TOLAND'S INVITATION TO DISMAL TO DINE WITH THE CALVES' HEAD CLUB," and indirectly "The Problem."

**Bolton, Dr. John, dean of Derry**  (c. 1656–1724)  Ordained in Ireland, 1677; vicar of Ratoath and Laracor; and prebendary of St. Patrick's, 1690–91. He served as the official chaplain for public and state functions to the earl of BERKELEY, the lord justice of Ireland. Bolton apparently held a better position than Swift, who was Berkeley's domestic chaplain. When Bishop William KING nominated three state chaplains for the opening of dean of Derry, Swift's name was missing. Bolton accepted the deanship, vacating his other livings (Asher, vicarage of Rathbeggan, and the vicarage of Laracor), which were given to Swift. These preferments provided him with an increased yearly income, but Swift never forgave Bolton and unjustifiably asserted that he (or Berkeley) had been bribed into depriving Swift of Derry. See also "The DISCOVERY" and "MRS. HARRIS'S PETITION."

**Bolton, Theophilus, archbishop of Cashel**  (unknown–1744)  Churchman graduated from Trinity College, Dublin, 1701; received D.D., 1716;

installed as chancellor of St. Patrick's, May 1722; raised to bishop of Clonfert, September 1722; promoted to a higher-paying bishopric of Elphin, 1724, and was sworn into the Privy Council. He gained the archbishopric of Cashel, 1729. Swift's relations with Bolton went poorly, as the latter was an excellent canon lawyer and often opposed Swift in cathedral chapter business. Much later, when Bolton rose to high rank in the Irish church, he opposed a proclamation for the arrest of the Drapier and wrote a letter of recommendation for SHERIDAN. Swift and he developed a mutual respect and friendship, as both had the best interests of the church and Ireland at heart. See "The STORM," "ON THE IRISH BISHOPS," "ON THE ARCHBISHOP OF CASHEL AND BETTESWORTH," and "ADVICE TO A PARSON."

**Bothmar, Johann Caspar, count von**  (1656–1732)  GEORGE I's envoy to the Court of St. James, who worked effectively to ensure his superior's right of succession. Published *The Elector of Hanover's Memorial to the Queen of Great Britain* (1711) against the articles for peace (the Barrier treaty) and provided ideas and material to Richard STEELE, who had agreed at the WHIGS' urging to make their case clear to the nation. Steele's *The Crisis* had the elector's direct support and found an audience that reacted favorably to its call for liberty—code for Whig principles. Swift replied to his good, but now estranged friend, Steele, with *The Public Spirit of the Whigs.* See also "The FIRST ODE OF THE SECOND BOOK OF HORACE . . . TO RICHARD STEELE." Swift mentions Bothmar in "The HISTORY OF THE FOUR LAST YEARS OF THE QUEEN," and refers indirectly to his work in "Some Free Thoughts upon the Present State of Affairs" and "An ENQUIRY INTO THE BEHAVIOR OF THE QUEEN'S LAST MINISTRY."

**Boulter, Hugh, archbishop of Armagh**  (1672–1742)  Educated at Christ Church, Oxford; received M.A., 1693, and D.D., 1708; served as chaplain to GEORGE I at Hanover; bishop of Bristol and dean of Christ Church, Oxford, 1719; archbishop of Armagh, 1724. As the primate of Ireland and frequently lord justice of Ireland, Boulter was WALPOLE's main source of information, influence, and power in Ireland, after the lord lieutenant. Swift treated Boulter as the ministry's chief agent in Ireland and his enemy whom he endeavored to discredit at all times. In *The DRAPIER'S LETTERS,* Swift opposed William WOOD's patent for copper coinage and the royal prerogative that sponsored this oppressive scheme. Boulter warned the ministry of the Irish refusal and the need to rescind the patent and grant Wood a pension. For a later clash between Swift and Boulter, see Swift's version in "AYE AND NO (A TALE FROM DUBLIN)." Other works referring to Boulter include "An EPIGRAM," "ON DR. RUNDLE," "ADVICE TO A PARSON," "A Ballad," and the fourth of *The Drapier's Letters* (letter 4: "To the Whole People of Ireland").

**Bowls, Sir John (Sir John Bolles)** (1690–1702) M.P. for Lincoln and leading TORY. Swift mentions him in "A Digression Concerning the Original, the Use and Improvement of Madness in a Commonwealth," in section 9 of "A TALE OF A TUB." Bowls, who is reputed to have gone mad, becomes in the satire a part of the madness causing self-deception, "an extravagant addiction to one's own opinions."

**Boyer, Abel** (1667–1729) Huguenot (French Protestant) refugee best known for his famous French-English dictionary (1702) and a monthly publication called *The Political State of Great Britain,* which ran from 1711 to 1729. After coming to England in 1689, he served as a tutor to Allen BATHURST and to Queen ANNE's son William, duke of Gloucester. Boyer's *Political State* recorded parliamentary debates and provided a WHIG-biased commentary on current affairs. Boyer attacks Swift in at least one pamphlet, after which Swift calls him "a French dog" in the Oct. 16, 1711, *JOURNAL TO STELLA* entry. Swift further reviles Boyer as "a little whiffling Frenchman" in no. 41 of the *EXAMINER,* adding that Boyer should probably stay out of politics and stick to teaching French. Boyer summarizes and comments critically on *GULLIVER'S TRAVELS* in several issues of *The Political State* that appeared between November 1726 and January 1727. He describes the *Travels* as "a satirical romance" in which the author uses various "Fictions" to reveal "the Faults and Mismanagements of Ministers of State; and Lashes the Corruptions and Vices of the Age in Different Professions, Civil and Military; but spares the *Ecclesiastical.*" He suspected that Swift was the author. Alexander POPE lampoons Boyer in book 2 of *The Dunciad,* describing him as "a voluminous compiler of Annals, Political Collections, &c." (412n.).

**Boyle, Michael, archbishop of Armagh** (1610–1702) Head of the Church of Ireland (1678) as primate who oversaw the diocese of Armagh. In 1695, Swift entered the Kilroot parish as priest, and Boyle was an eminent, if not infirm, figure in the church. Boyle had been bishop of Cork, Cloyne, and Ross (1660) as well as dean of Cloyne (1640), serving later as lord chancellor of Ireland (1665). In his *Marginalia,* Swift disagrees with BURNET's point that Boyle's political lobbying held his religious convictions hostage. Swift admires Boyle's strength of character in the 1733 pamphlet "Reason Humbly Offered to the Parliament of Ireland, for Repealing the Sacramental Test."

**Boyle, Robert** (1627–1691) Natural philosopher and chemist born in Ireland, educated at Eton and Oxford. Working with Robert Hooke, he made an efficient vacuum pump with which he was able to establish a variety of scientific principles. He freed experimental science from much alchemical superstition, becoming a founding fellow of the Royal Society. Swift ridiculed Boyle's measuring the elasticity of air in "A TALE OF A TUB," and comments in the *Marginalia* on his being "a very silly writer." The famous anecdote of Swift playing an elaborate joke on Lady BERKELEY, who admired Boyle's *Meditations,* helps explain the origin of a "MEDITATION ON A BROOMSTICK," a parody of the chemist's devotional work.

**Brandreth, Rev. John, dean of Armagh** English clergyman, educated at Trinity College, Cambridge, served as tutor to the duke of DORSET's son and chaplain in the household, on Dorset's arrival in Ireland (1731). Alexander POPE recommended Brandreth to Swift, though the dean complains that Irish, not English, clergymen should hold preferments in Ireland. Another friend, Lady Elizabeth GERMAIN, writes to Swift on June 5, 1731, that Brandreth is "as worthy honest sensible a man as any I know" (*Corr.* III.470). In a June 30, 1732, letter, Swift gives him stern advice concerning Ireland and its troubles—"all these evils are effects of English tyranny" (*Corr.* IV.34).

**Brent, Anne (Anne Ridgeway)**    Daughter of Mrs. BRENT, Swift's housekeeper for 40 years. Anne succeeded her mother and married Anthony Ridgeway, "an idle spendthrift" who managed poorly as a cabinetmaker. He tried compelling his wife to sell an annuity left her by Lord Newtown, and Swift intervened, protecting the annuity for the remainder of Anne's life. Swift in his will further left her rental profits, a small amount of cash, rings, and silver plate. See also "DIRECTIONS TO SERVANTS."

**Brent, Mrs.**    (unknown–1735)    Swift's housekeeper at the Deanery House who served him for 40 years, beginning with his first post as prebend of Kilroot in 1694. He calls her his "Walpole above thirty years, whenever I lived in this kingdom." Reportedly intelligent and trustworthy, Mrs. Brent had cared for Swift's mother when she visited him in Ireland, and became an essential member of his household staff. She married a Dublin printer, John Brent, and paid his guild dues in 1713—the year she may have been widowed. Numerous references to her exist in *The* JOURNAL TO STELLA and the *Correspondence*. See also "STELLA'S BIRTHDAY: A GREAT BOTTLE OF WINE" and "DINGLEY AND BRENT."

**Bristol, John Hervey, first earl of the second creation**    (1665–1751)    Educated at Clare College, Cambridge (1684); LL.D. (1705); M.P. (1694–1703); close friend of the duke of MARLBOROUGH; created baron (1703). Staunch WHIG and supporter of GEORGE I; created earl of Bristol (1714). His son, Lord John Hervey, was Alexander POPE's sworn enemy. Swift refers to Bristol in "A Modest Defence of Punning" as one of three noblemen who deserve contempt for their foolishness and corruption.

**Brodrick, Alan [Middleton], viscount**    See MIDDLETON, Alan Brodrick, viscount.

**Bromley, William**    (1664–1732)    M.P. for the University of Oxford beginning in 1702 and secretary of state. Considered an important High Churchman, he was elected Speaker of the House of Commons (1710–14). Swift refers to the Speaker in a number of his prose works: "The HISTORY OF THE FOUR LAST YEARS OF THE QUEEN," "The Public Spirit of the Whigs," and the EXAMINER. Bromley was a loyal supporter of Robert HARLEY and a good friend of BOLINGBROKE. Swift seems unconvinced of Bromley's faithfulness, though he compliments him as "worthy" and "so good a servant of the publick" in commenting on the death of Bromley's son (see EXAMINER no. 34).

**Brown, Thomas**    (1663–1704)    A minor satirist and translator whose satirical pamphlets against John DRYDEN were a success. His work as a political journalist and essayist in *The London Mercury* (1692) and *Gentlemen's Journal* (1692–94) brought him notoriety. Brown's anti-Partridge burlesque, *Infallible Astrologer* (1700), caught Swift's eye and influenced his creation of the "Bickerstaff Papers" (1708–09), as well as creating an audience for Swift's final elimination of the charlatan John PARTRIDGE. Brown's works may have also served as a source for GULLIVER'S TRAVELS. Yet, Swift's final satiric review on Brown may be found in A COMPLETE COLLECTION OF GENTEEL AND INGENIOUS CONVERSATION in which Simon Wagstaff, a Swift pseudonym, claims to have read all of Brown's works, finding him "the greatest genius of his age."

**Browne, Sir John, baronet of the Neale**    (d. 1762) Member of a Catholic family with a large estate in Mayo, Ireland. Browne became involved in William WOOD's coinage controversy after escaping to England under a charge of malicious conspiracy brought by the Irish House of Commons. Swift attacks him in *The* DRAPIER'S LETTERS (Letter 3—"Some Observations upon . . . The Report of the Committee") for testifying before the Privy Council in London and acting as a traitor to the Irish cause. Later, Swift, though critical, changed his view of him after studying Browne's pamphlets on Irish trade. See also "An ANSWER TO A PAPER, CALLED 'A MEMORIAL OF THE POOR INHABITANTS, TRADESMEN, AND

LABOURERS OF THE KINGDOM OF IRELAND,' " and "A SHORT VIEW OF THE STATE OF IRELAND."

**Browne, Peter** (1662–1735)   Provost of Trinity College, Dublin (1699), bishop of Cork and Ross (1710). Browne was a well-regarded clergyman and author who became Esther JOHNSON's friend. Swift, who had known him since they were Trinity College classmates, did not fully respect him nor did he read his works, though allowing that scholars reported him "excellent in his way." References to Browne appear in "A Short Character of his Excellency Thomas Earl of Wharton, ON THE DEATH OF MRS. JOHNSON," and the *Correspondence*.

**Buchanan, George** (1506–1582)   Scottish humanist and historian. He was imprisoned for satirizing the Franciscans but escaped and became a professor at Bordeaux, where Montaigne was one of his students. Upon his eventual return to Scotland he embraced Protestantism and became a fierce enemy of Queen Mary I. He also served as a tutor to Prince James (who became King James VI of Scotland and James I of England) from 1570–78. In "The BATTLE OF THE BOOKS," Buchanan appears as a commander of the moderns' "heavy-armed" infantry.

**Buckingham, George Villiers, second duke of** (1628–1687)   An aristocratic wit and writer who possessed great wealth, a magnificent art collection, and a close friendship with CHARLES II. Swift alludes to Villiers's burlesque, *The Rehearsal* (1671), in *A Letter to the Seven Lords*, *The Public Spirit of the Whigs*, and *The Presbyterians' Plea of Merit*, as well as several poems. Villiers's other smaller prose pieces have been cited as possible sources for "A TALE OF A TUB."

**Buckingham, John Sheffield, first duke of** (1648–1721)   Aristocrat, soldier, courtier to CHARLES II and JAMES II, TORY politician much respected by WILLIAM III and ANNE, and Swift. Buckingham was appointed lord justice of Great Britain in 1710, and was a patron of John DRYDEN and friend of Alexander POPE, who edited Sheffield's papers and poems (1723). Swift mentions that the WHIGS hate him in The EXAMINER,

number 25, and praises his character in number 26. Swift associates Sheffield, if only mildly, with the Jacobite cause in "An ENQUIRY INTO THE BEHAVIOR OF THE QUEEN'S LAST MINISTRY." The JOURNAL reveals Swift's dislike of Sheffield, and the feeling became mutual.

**Burlington, Richard Boyle, third earl of** (1695–1753)   Aristocrat and leading cultural arbiter of taste. Burlington was also an architect in all but the professional sense, who launched the English Palladian movement. He was a hereditary lord treasurer of Ireland (1715) and a close friend of Alexander POPE. Swift mentions him in several letters, and wrote to Burlington (on May 22, 1729) about repairing his family's monuments in St. Patrick's Cathedral (*Corr.* III.335). Earlier, in the fourth of *The DRAPIER'S LETTERS* (*To the Whole People of Ireland*), Swift had referred to Burlington's Irish sinecures, along with other absentee landlords, "as keen against the interest of Ireland, as if they had never been indebted to her for a single groat."

**Burnet, Gilbert, bishop of Salisbury (Sarum)** (1643–1715)   Historian, theologian, and WHIG political writer who become a royal chaplain (1673). During his self-imposed exile on the Continent, Burnet became a useful adviser to WILLIAM III. In 1689 as bishop of Salisbury, he found High Church TORIES detested him for his arrogance and materialism. Swift attacked him numerous times (in, for example, the "Preface to the Bishop of Sarum's Introduction" and "Short Remarks on Bishop Burnet's History"). Though complaining of Burnet's "permanent bias," Swift also finds him a generous, good-natured man who often convinces his readers of his arguments. His *History of the Reformation* and *History of His Own Time* (1724–34) remain invaluable records on the order of high-class gossip. Swift's poetry serves as a satiric vehicle against Burnet: "A DIALOGUE BETWEEN AN EMINENT LAWYER AND DR. SWIFT, DEAN OF ST. PATRICK," "The First Ode of the Second Book of Horace Paraphrased and Addressed to Richard Steele, Esq.," and "The STORM."

**Burton, Samuel** (d. 1733)   Irish M.P. for Sligo (1713–14), later alderman and M.P. for Dublin.

Swift knew and disliked his father, Benjamin Burton (a Dublin banker, lord mayor of Dublin, and M.P.) for his WHIG sympathies. Samuel appears at Swift's London house and plays cards with the dean, but earns only the comment "a pox on him" (JOURNAL TO STELLA 201). There is a passing reference to Burton in "ADVICE TO THE FREEMEN OF THE CITY OF DUBLIN."

**Bushe, Arthur** (b. 1691)   Secretary to Charles, second earl of BERKELEY, who had been appointed a lord justice at Dublin. Swift, who had served as Berkeley's chaplain and secretary on the voyage from England, lost his position on arriving in Ireland. He never forgave Bushe for this disappointing loss of preferment, blaming him for the further loss of the deanery of Derry, when, according to the angry Swift, Berkeley's "secretary having received a bribe the deanery was disposed of to another." Proof now exists showing Bushe did not receive a bribe. See also "The DISCOVERY."

**Butler, Lady Betty (Lady Elizabeth Butler)** (d. 1750)   Eldest daughter of James Butler, second duke of ORMONDE. She lived in Richmond with her sister, Mary (d. 1713), who later married Lord ASH-BURNHAM. Betty, who never married, maintained a fond friendship with Swift, calling him a "most provoking unkle." Often Betty, the VANHOMRIGHs, and Swift would dine together since the Vanhomrighs lived close by during Swift's London years. Frequently, Lady Betty GERMAIN and Betty Butler would dine with Swift, who said "the beauty of one, the good breeding and nature of t'other, and the wit of neither, would have made a fine woman" (*The JOURNAL TO STELLA* 202).

**Butler, Humphry, second viscount Lanesborough** (1700–68)   Son of Brinsley Butler, first viscount Lanesborough; both men, along with Humphry's brother, Robert, and uncle Theophilus were familiar Dublin friends of Swift. In his *Correspondence*, Swift describes Butler as "the courteousest man, and nothing is so fine in the quality, as to be courteous" and "a gentleman universally loved."

**Butler, Robert** (b. 1704)   Son of Brinsley Butler, first viscount of Lanesborough, and younger brother of Humphry BUTLER—all familiar friends of Swift. Robert succeeded his brother as captain of the Battle-Axe Guards, in December, 1726. See also Swift's poem, "To DR. HELSHAM."

**Butler, Samuel** (1612–80)   A satirist whose reputation was based on *Hudribas* (1662), a burlesque of the Puritans and their times. Skeptical in philosophy and conservative in politics, Butler appealed to Swift, who attacked Puritan enthusiasm in "A TALE OF A TUB." The earlier poet's form and meter influenced Swift in "BAUCIS AND PHILEMON" and other verse, so much so that one critic calls Butler Swift's poetic father.

**Buys, Willem** (1661–1749)   Dutch statesman, envoy to the Court of St. James, and plenipotentiary at Utrecht who came to England (1711) as a result of the peace terms with France negotiated by Matthew PRIOR, settling finally the War of the Spanish Succession with the Treaty of Utrecht in April, 1713. Swift was not impressed with his abilities, and says as much in "The HISTORY OF THE FOUR LAST YEARS OF THE QUEEN" and *The JOURNAL TO STELLA*.

# C

**Cadogan, William Cadogan, first earl of** (c. 1671–1726)   Distinguished army officer and lieutenant general in MARLBOROUGH's forces serving at Blenheim and Ramillies; created baron (1716), earl (1718). Swift, who knew his mother in London in 1710 (see JOURNAL TO STELLA 121), mentions Cadogan in the EXAMINER (No. 20, December 21, 1710) concerning an incident where civil authority must exert control over military power. See also "ON NOISY TOM."

**Caesar, Mrs. Mary**   Wife of Charles Caesar, M.P. for Hertford and treasurer of the navy (1711). Mrs. Caesar became a good friend of Alexander POPE and kept a journal concerning the poet and his friends writing to and receiving letters from Swift. In a November 4, 1732, letter to Caesar, Swift refers to her and Mrs. Mary BARBER as "two . . . ladyes of my long acquaintance . . . [who] are still so kind to remember me, . . . since constancy is I think at least as seldom found in friendship as in love" (*Corr.* IV.80–81).

**Callières, François de** (1645–1717)   French diplomat and author whose *Histoire Poetique de la Guerre . . . entre les Anciens et les Modernes* (1688) served as a source for Swift's "BATTLE OF THE BOOKS." Swift denied that he was inspired by Callières's much richer and wittier parody of Homer.

**Camden, William** (1551–1623)   English antiquary and historian. His most famous work was *Bri-*

*tannia,* which originally appeared (in Latin) in 1586 but went through six editions and was translated into English in 1610. In "The BATTLE OF THE BOOKS," "Cambden" is one of the commanders of the moderns' "heavy-armed" infantry. Swift also mentions Camden in "DISCOURSE TO PROVE THE ANTIQUITY OF THE ENGLISH TONGUE," promising that he will use etymological evidence as he asserts the antiquity of the English language—thus treating his readers more kindly than "superficial pretenders" such as Camden have done in the past (*Prose Works* IV.231).

**Capel of Tewkesbury, Henry Capel, baron** (1638–1696)   Lord justice of Ireland (1693), governed Ireland along with two others. Capel appointed Swift to the prebend of Kilroot, County Antrim, in the cathedral of Connor in 1695. Capel became chief governor of Ireland as lord deputy in the same year. The recommendation for Swift may have come from Sir William TEMPLE, who had served with Capel in the Privy Council of Charles II. Mentioned in Swift's *Autobiography* and *Marginalia.*

**Carey, Walter** (1685–1757)   M.P. for Dartmouth, chief secretary to duke of DORSET as lord lieutenant of Ireland (1730–37). Swift mentions Carey as a witness to his assurance to the duke that he would not further criticize the English government for the condition of Ireland. Carey knew Alexander POPE's circle well, though Swift condemns him as Briareus, a recipient of bribes, in "A Character of the Legion Club."

**Caroline of Anspach, queen of England**
(1683–1737)   Wife of GEORGE II since 1705, having arrived in England as the princess of Wales in 1714 and becoming queen in 1727. She invited Swift, through John ARBUTHNOT, to visit her during one of his trips to England in 1726. This visit, and a few subsequent, were successful but she ultimately fails the test of enduring friendship in not providing gifts or the preferment she had suggested would be his or in fulfilling her promise to "use all her credit" in Ireland's behalf. He chides her for these faults in "VERSES ON THE DEATH OF DR. SWIFT." Other satires focused on the royal family, and on her directly: "DIRECTIONS FOR A BIRTHDAY SONG" and "ON POETRY: A RHAPSODY." Alexander POPE may have modeled the Queen of Dulness in *The Dunciad* on Caroline.

**Carr, Charles, bishop of Killaloe** (1671–1739)
Churchman. He was a graduate of Trinity College, Dublin; rector of Castlehaven, County Cork; chaplain to the Irish House of Commons; and then bishop of Killaloe in 1716. Swift admired him for admitting the bishops' power might be employed in bettering the condition of Irish clergy and their parishioners. Swift had entered the controversy with "CONSIDERATIONS UPON TWO BILLS," a pamphlet attacking the church bills of 1732. His poem "ON THE IRISH BISHOPS" praises Carr for voting against these bills. Ironically, Swift had earlier tried blocking Carr's nomination as bishop. Carr is also mentioned in "TO MR. DELANY."

**Carstares, William** (1649–1715)   Scottish statesman and divine who served as chaplain to William of Orange (WILLIAM III). Swift mentions him in *Marginalia* as "a true character but not strong enough." He was appointed principal of Edinburgh University (1703) and opposed a bill of Occasional Conformity (1711).

**Carteret, John, second baron, and Lady Frances**
(1690–1763)   Statesman and three times lord lieutenant of Ireland (1724–30). He served in various government posts as a WHIG and joined the Robert WALPOLE ministry until finally breaking away in 1742 to form his own short-lived govern-

ment. In 1744 he succeeded to the title of earl of Granville and Viscount Carteret. Swift respected him as a man of learning and wit whom he had known since his London days (1710). With William WOOD's coinage as the chief issue of his Irish administration, Carteret made a show of prosecuting the drapier as Swift's *DRAPIER'S LETTERS* emerged, though he knew the author's true identity. Carteret had found preferments for Swift's friends too, and Swift ironically praises him in his "VINDICATION OF LORD CARTERET." Critics believe Carteret was the model for Reldresal and perhaps the king of Brobdingnag in *GULLIVER'S TRAVELS*. See also "A LIBEL ON THE REVEREND DR. DELANEY AND HIS EXCELLENCY JOHN, LORD CARTERET," "An EPISTLE UPON AN EPISTLE," "An EPIGRAM ON WOOD'S BRASS MONEY," "WHITSHED'S MOTTO ON HIS COACH," and "ON LORD CARTERET'S ARMS."

**Castle-Durrow, William Flower, baron** (d. 1746)
Irish landowner and grandson of Sir John Temple, brother of Sir William TEMPLE, whom Swift had served as secretary. Flower was created baron in 1733 and began a sporadic correspondence with Swift in 1729, attempting to visit him at the Deanery in 1736, but Swift's butler turned him away. Both men had known each other, though not continuously, since Flower was a youth.

**Celia**   Stock name in Swift's poems for a woman whose outward purity, supposed immortality, and transcendence of base human necessities are all revealed as a sham. See "The PROGRESS OF BEAUTY," "The LADY'S DRESSING ROOM," and "ANSWER TO A SCANDALOUS POEM." See also CHLOE.

**Chandos, James Brydges, first duke of** (1673–1744)   M.P. and paymaster general of the forces during Queen ANNE's reign, making his fortune; succeeded as Baron Chandos, earl of Carnarvon (1714), and duke of Chandos (1719). Alexander POPE denies Brydges is Timon in the *Epistle to Burlington*, and asserts that his home, Cannons, is not Timon's villa. Swift knew Brydges when both worked in the TORY government, but became estranged as Brydges grew more magnificent and arrogant, ignoring in later years a civil request from Swift. See "The DEAN AND THE DUKE."

**Charles II, king of Great Britain** (1630–1685) Charles fled to France after his father's defeat in 1646, and remained in exile until proclaimed king of England in 1660. His reign contained a series of dramatic events—the Great Plague, the Fire of London, the Dutch wars, the Popish Plot, and the intrigues surrounding legitimate succession. Swift felt Charles had increased the suffering of the Irish people through bad monetary policy, especially supplying copper coinage and failing to redeem it with gold and silver. Also, Charles's court embraced intrigue in its actions, and Swift respected plain dealing. Sir William TEMPLE, Swift's patron, who had served as Charles's chief diplomat to France and Louis XIV, found his king's reversals and irresolution intolerable. Swift accepts this view: see also "VERSES ON THE DEATH OF DR. SWIFT," The CONDUCT OF THE ALLIES," "The HISTORY OF THE LAST FOUR YEARS OF THE QUEEN," "Thoughts on Various Subjects," The DRAPIER'S LETTERS, and "A TALE OF A TUB."

**Charles VI, emperor, archduke of Austria** (1685–1740) Holy Roman Emperor (1711–40) and king of Hungary as Charles III. After an unsuccessful effort to ascend to the Spanish throne, precipitating the War of the Spanish Succession, he retired to Austria, having lost much of his land in wars. Swift, who mentions him frequently in his prose and correspondence, believed the war necessary for controlling the ambitions of France but felt "the Emperor could find twenty reasons and excuses . . . for not furnishing his quota [of soldiers and funds]." See also "The HISTORY OF THE LAST FOUR YEARS OF THE QUEEN."

**Charles XII, king of Sweden** (1682–1718) King of Sweden (1697–1718) and a military hero who won victories against Denmark, Russia, and Poland, but ultimately his endless wars exhausted Sweden's resources. Swift admired him as a hero of lost causes who died young, and intended to dedicate "An ABSTRACT OF THE HISTORY OF ENGLAND" to him. Swift refers to him in "PART OF A SUMMER" and "TO THE EARL OF PETERBOROUGH."

**Chesterfield, Philip Dormer Stanhope, fourth earl of** (1694–1773) Statesman, journalist, letter writer, and a leading figure in the opposition to Walpole. Swift met Chesterfield in 1726 on a visit to England in the company of Alexander POPE, John ARBUTHNOT, and other comrades. Chesterfield maintained close relations with the prince of Wales and his mistress, Mrs. HOWARD, who served as a rallying point for antiministerial opposition. Swift hoped to exert some beneficial influence on behalf of Ireland from whoever had power. Later, Swift solicited Chesterfield's help in finding "some little employment" for a "near relation's" husband, and received a cordial reply. In 1746 George FAULKNER reprinted Swift's *Works* in eight volumes with a dedication to Chesterfield, then lord lieutenant of Ireland.

**Chetwode, Knightley** (1679–1752) Irish landed gentleman who began an awkward friendship with Swift in 1714 that lasted for 18 years. Chetwode's and Swift's families had similar origins in Ireland, though Chetwode secured his fortune through marriage. Swift found his letters (the correspondence includes nearly 70 letters) and company engaging, but Chetwode's obnoxious need for attention, fame, and self-promotion finally alienated the dean. In a last letter (dated April 28, 1731) that was written but never sent to Chetwode—whom Swift called "Ventoso"—Swift told him, "At this season in your life, I should be glad you would . . . have done with all dreams of being important in the world" (*Corr.* V.250).

**Chloe** Stock name in Swift's poems for a woman whose purity and reputation as a chaste "nymph" are exposed as hoaxes. See "STREPHON AND CHLOE," "TO STELLA, WHO COLLECTED AND TRANSCRIBED HIS POEMS," and "RIDDLES" ("Louisa to Strephon"). See also CELIA.

**Cholmondeley, Hugh, first earl of** (c. 1662–1725) WHIG courtier who became Baron Cholmondeley in 1682; treasurer of the Queen's Household (1708–13, 1714–15); created earl in 1706. Swift expressed his dislike of Cholmondeley in *The JOURNAL TO STELLA* and his *Correspondence*: "Ld Chomley came in; but I would not talk to him tho he made many advances. I hate the Scoundrel" (*Journal* 633). Swift objected to Cholmondeley's treatment of Edward HARLEY, especially after "the Court Whig" retained his office in the TORY government.

**Cibber, Colley** (1671–1757)    Playwright and actor-manager who as an ardent WHIG was made poet laureate in 1730. His success in the theater and some vapid birthday odes (as well as a personal quarrel with Alexander POPE) led to general ridicule and his selection by Pope as King Dunce in *The Dunciad.* In an April 20, 1731, letter to Pope, Swift comments that "ill taste" can result in political reward and "if the Court had interceded . . . for a fitter man, it might have prevailed" (*Corr.* III.459). See also "VERSES ON THE DEATH OF DR. SWIFT, D.S.P.D.," "ON POETRY: A RHAPSODY," "TO DEAN SWIFT," and *COMPLETE COLLECTION OF GENTEEL AND INGENIOUS CONVERSATION.*

**Clancy, Michael** (fl. 1737)    Irish playwright. He was educated both in France and Ireland but did not take a degree at Trinity College, Dublin. His comedy, *The Sharper* (1737), and two tragedies brought him small renown. Swift read the play when it was left on his desk intentionally, and upon learning about the author, wrote and sent him a Christmas gift since the play "conveyed a good moral."

**Clarendon, Edward Hyde, first earl** (1609–1674) Statesman and historian. Educated at Oxford and the Middle Temple, he became chancellor of the Exchequer (1643) after a long tenure in politics, where his respect for constitutional monarchy and the church were well established. At the Restoration, he became lord chancellor and prime minister (1660–67), until he was dismissed from office and exiled to France. Clarendon's *History of the Rebellion* (1702–04) is the first important history of contemporary English affairs. Swift considered him "a great genius in several ways" and read Clarendon's *History,* frequently providing extensive marginalia on the text. Swift believed Clarendon possessed all the requisite strengths of a historian. See also "HISTORY OF THE FOUR LAST YEARS OF THE QUEEN" for Clarendon's influence, and "A DIALOGUE BETWEEN

AN EMINENT LAWYER AND DR. SWIFT, DEAN OF ST. PATRICK'S."

**Clarke, Samuel** (1675–1729)    Rector of St. James, Westminster, London; deistic philosopher; author of *Scripture Doctrine of the Trinity* (1712). He was a close friend of the princess of Wales, later Queen CAROLINE, who had a bust of Clarke commissioned for her grotto at Richmond. Swift satirizes the pretence and dullness of the royal family in "DIRECTIONS FOR A BIRTHDAY SONG," in which Clarke serves as an exponent of anti-intellectual and antifundamental church doctrine. See also "ON THE TRINITY" for a response to Clarke's ideas.

**Cobbe, Charles, archbishop of Dublin** (1687– 1765)    Archbishop of Dublin (1743) and bishop of Dromore (1727) and Kildare (1731). Educated at Trinity College, Dublin, in 1717 he went to Ireland as chaplain to Charles, duke of BOLTON, lord lieutenant. In this capacity, he met Swift and soon became one of his younger clerical friends. While dean of Christ Church, Dublin, he was given a copy of "The FAMILY OF SWIFT" (c. 1738), later published by Dean Swift in 1765. Recently, the "lost" Cobbe copy of the fragment surfaced and Victoria Glendinning read it in preparing *Jonathan Swift: A Portrait.*

**Coghill, Marmaduke** (c. 1670–1739)    Irish M.P. for Dublin University and judge of the Prerogative Court (an ecclesiastical body) in Ireland. Coghill, as a fellow privy councillor and friend of Archbishop William KING, refused to sign prosecution orders (1724) on John HARDING, who printed various DRAPIER'S LETTERS during the copper coinage controversy. As Swift's early friend, Coghill dined with him in London (1712), suggesting he would intervene in helping Swift gain the deanery of St. Patrick's Cathedral.

**Collier, Jeremy** (1650–1726)    Ecclesiastical writer, cleric, and bishop of the Nonjuring sect, who were violently opposed to the Revolution. He was imprisoned, outlawed, and exiled but returned in 1697. His *Short View of the Immorality and Profaneness of the English Stage* (1698) became famous and was answered by William CONGREVE and John VANBRUGH. Swift, who supported Collier's views on public morality, did not agree with his antitheatrical campaign, particularly when such attacks condemned John GAY's *The Beggar's Opera*. A well-behaved clergyman, Swift asserted, might learn much from the moral effect of the play.

**Collins, Anthony** (1676–1729)   Freethinker and deistic writer of philosophical works and literary theory. He was educated at King's College, Cambridge, and Middle Temple, and later appointed justice of the peace and deputy lieutenant of the county. Swift objected to and satirized his *Discourse of Freethinking* (1713) and *Discourse Concerning Ridicule and Irony* (1729). The opportunity to associate freethinkers and the WHIGS could not be ignored, and Swift treated deism as a serious threat.

**Compton, Spencer, first earl of Wilmington** (c. 1673–1743)   WHIG politician and Speaker of the House of Commons, who became the nominal chief minister at the death of GEORGE I (1727) for a short period, until he yielded his place to Robert WALPOLE. Swift considered him weak and unconcerned about the fate of his supporters. Swift's satiric portrait of Wilmington appears in "An ACCOUNT OF THE COURT AND EMPIRE OF JAPAN" as Nomptoc, master of finances, "who secretly hated Lelop-Aw [WALPOLE]." See also "ON READING DR. YOUNG'S SATIRES" and "TO MR. GAY."

**Congreve, William** (1670–1729)   Dramatist whose family moved to Ireland in 1674; educated at Kilkenny School and Trinity College, Dublin, as a contemporary of Swift. He began studying law but soon focused his attentions on the theater, producing *The Old Bachelor* (1693) and concluding with *The Way of the World* (1700). He held minor government posts during WHIG and TORY ministries. He remained on friendly terms with Alexander POPE and Swift, and Pope dedicated his translation of the *Iliad* to him. Swift admired Congreve, though he felt resentment at the younger man's success. See "TO MR. CONGREVE," "A PANEGYRIC ON THE REVEREND DEAN SWIFT," "UPON FOUR DISMAL STORIES IN THE DOCTOR'S LETTER," and "A LIBEL ON THE REVEREND DR. DELANEY AND HIS EXCELLENCY JOHN, LORD CARTERET."

**Conolly, William** (1660–1729)   Wealthy Irish WHIG, Speaker of the Irish House of Commons, and lord justice of Ireland. Swift disparages Conolly in *The DRAPIER'S LETTERS* for supporting William WOOD's coinage and serving as a ready dupe of English influence (see Letters 1 and 7). Conolly signed both the *Proclamation against the Drapier* for his arrest, and the *Address of the Privy Council of Ireland* requesting the removal of Wood's patent so as to quiet "the fears of your people." See also "The ANSWER TO 'PAULUS.'"

**Cope, Robert** (c. 1679–1753)   TORY Irish M.P. and gentleman who during Swift's frequent rambles in the country provided welcome hospitality at his home, Loughgall, in northern Ireland. In a letter of thanks to the Copes, Swift offers his "greatest compliment . . . that I never found anything wrong in your house." Swift admired, and even envied their close family bond, even though Cope had once politically annoyed him. See "The FIRST OF APRIL," dedicated to Cope's second wife, Elizabeth.

**Corbet, Rev. Francis** (1688–1775)   Churchman, treasurer and later dean of St. Patrick's. Swift mentions Corbet (to whom he had rented a vineyard) in his will. Earlier, Corbet had been one of Esther JOHNSON's executors, and his colleagues and Swift considered him one of "the most distinguished [clergymen] for their learning and piety." See "TO CHARLES FORD, ESQ. ON HIS BIRTHDAY."

**Cowley, Abraham** (1618–1667)   Poet whose metaphysical style, so named by Samuel Johnson, can be found in his extravagant conceits. Swift greatly admired his odes and imitated the earlier poet's metrical technique, employing certain details in his own ode "To the King." As a young man, Swift told his cousin Tom, "when I write what pleases me I am Cowley to myself and can read it a hundred times over." Cowley leads the Moderns in "The BATTLE OF THE BOOKS" and suffers a glorious death at the hands of Pindar.

**Craggs, James Jr.** (1686–1721)   M.P., secretary of war (1717), and secretary of state (1718) in the

WALPOLE government. He was a friend and colleague of the duke of MARLBOROUGH and an important WHIG politician. See the INTELLIGENCER, number 9. Swift did not know him except by reputation, but he was a friend of Alexander POPE, who memorialized him in the last 10 lines of his "To Mr. Addison," despite Craggs's connection to the South Sea fiasco. His father, James Craggs, Sr. (1657–1721), was deeply implicated in the South Sea scandal, which Swift denounced, finding all parties guilty of fraud. See "The BANK THROWN DOWN," "The FAGGOT," and "UPON THE SOUTH SEA PROJECT."

**Crassus, Marcus Licinius** (c. 115–53 B.C.) Roman political figure and a successful general who amassed a vast personal fortune. With Julius Caesar and Pompey he formed the first triumvirate. Swift found MARLBOROUGH the modern-day Crassus, "covetous as hell, and ambitious as the prince of it." The "Letter to Crassus" in the EXAMINER (number 27) includes this pseudonym for Marlborough, whose appetite for power and wealth knew no bounds.

**Creech, Thomas**   See "The BATTLE OF THE BOOKS."

**Creichton, Captain John** (b. 1648) Irish-born soldier who served in Scotland in the armies of CHARLES II, JAMES II, and WILLIAM III. Swift meets the retired soldier at Arthur ACHESON's MARKET HILL home and, becoming fascinated with his history, he offers to edit Creichton's life's story for publication in hopes of providing him with an annuity. Creichton's *Memoirs* (1731) show Swift's considerable help in this collaboration.

**Cross, William**   Churchman; dean of Leighlin (1723), Ferns (1719), and Lismore (1720); lost the opportunity for bishop of Cork (1735). Swift mentions Cross in "ON DR. RUNDLE" and "TO DR. HELSHAM." He writes part of a September 17, 1735, letter to Thomas SHERIDAN in Latin "for fear the letter should fall into Dean Crosse's hands " (*Corr.* IV.393).

**Crow, Charles, bishop of Cloyne** (d. 1726) Churchman, bishop beginning in 1702 and member of the Irish House of Lords. Swift respected his efforts in explaining the burden the First Fruits and Twentieth Parts taxes placed on the Church of Ireland. Crow, who traveled to London with Swift, brought a petition to Queen ANNE for relief of these dues, but ultimately Swift's negotiations led to their abolition. See the pun on Crow's name in "A DIALOGUE IN THE CASTILIAN LANGUAGE."

**Cumberland, William Augustus, duke of** (1721–1765)   Third son of GEORGE II and CAROLINE of Anspach. He served as an army officer and was promoted to major general (1742) and then to captain-general of British forces at home and in the field (1745). Severely defeated by French forces, Cumberland did suppress the 1745 Jacobite rebellion and was nicknamed the "Butcher" for his harshness toward the Scots. Swift mentions him in the INTELLIGENCER, number 3, as the recipient of his good friend John GAY's dedication of *The Fables* (1727): "for which he [Gay] was promised a reward." See also "DIRECTIONS FOR A BIRTHDAY SONG" and "A LIBEL ON THE REVEREND DR. DELANY AND HIS EXCELLENCY JOHN, LORD CARTERET."

**Cutts, John, first baron** (1661–1707)   Distinguished general officer who fought with WILLIAM III at the Battle of the Boyne in 1690 and was created Baron Cutts of Gowran. He later joined MARLBOROUGH at Blenheim. As an Irish peer, he became lord justice of Ireland when ORMONDE returned to England. His efforts against the Irish church and his well-publicized pursuit of money and women evoked Swift's bitter attack. See "THE DESCRIPTION OF A SALAMANDER" and his character description in the *Marginalia* as "the vainest old fool alive."

# D

**Damer, Joseph (Joseph Demar)** (1630–1720) Irish merchant. Born in England, he fought on the English Parliament's side during the Civil War. Upon the Restoration of CHARLES II, he moved to France and, after selling some of his land in England, established his moneylending business in Dublin. His offices were in the London Tavern on Fishamble Street. By the time Swift wrote his "ELEGY ON THE MUCH LAMENTED DEATH OF MR. DEMAR, THE FAMOUS RICH USURER," Damer had become widely infamous for his greed. It is unclear whether or not Swift ever met him.

**Dampier, William** (1652–1715) Explorer and buccaneer who circumnavigated the world twice and purportedly rescued Alexander Selkirk, the inspiration for DEFOE's *Robinson Crusoe*, from the island on which he was marooned. Swift, who read many travel accounts, owned the third edition of Dampier's *A New Voyage around the World* (1697). Swift has Lemuel Gulliver in "A Letter to Cousin Sympson" state how he advised Dampier to "hire some young gentlemen of either University to put [his account] in order."

**Dartmouth, William Legge, earl of** (1672–1750) TORY statesman and a devout Anglican who became the second secretary of state (1710) after Henry BOLINGBROKE. Swift, who knew him well and dined with him in London often as a member of Robert HARLEY's Saturday Club, wrote in the EXAMINER (number 26) of Dartmouth's good sense, good nature, strict virtue, and admirable intellect.

Swift often mentions him in *The JOURNAL TO STELLA* and *Correspondence*.

**Davenant, Sir William** (1606–68) Poet and dramatist, attended Lincoln College, Oxford; poet laureate (1637); royalist supporter, imprisoned in the Tower; writer of operas (*The Siege of Rhodes*) and manager of the Dorset Garden Theater, London, and the Duke's Company of players. Swift mentions him in "The BATTLE OF THE BOOKS," criticizing Davenant's heroic poem, *Gondibert*: "Homer overthrew . . . [the] man to the ground, there to be trampled and choak'd in the dirt." Also, Swift and Davenant were related, since the latter's daughter married Swift's uncle, so Davenant's grandson seemed like a brother to Swift during his early years.

**Defoe, Daniel** (1660–1731) Businessman, Dissenter, government agent, pamphlet writer, and novelist. Defoe's enormously popular poem, *The True Born Englishman* (1701) satirized the xenophobia of his day. After a bankruptcy, Defoe was patronized and rehabilitated by Robert HARLEY, beginning a 10-year period as a TORY pamphleteer and journalist. *The Review* emerged during this period and later *Robinson Crusoe* (1719). In a "LETTER FROM A MEMBER OF THE HOUSE OF COMMONS IN IRELAND," Swift refers to Defoe as a "grave . . . dogmatical rogue" whose name he's forgotten. Defoe represented all that in Swift's mind threatened the social order. Though Swift never met him, he recognized Defoe's energy and grasp of English affairs, but he did not admit any agreement with him. See EXAMINER, number 15.

**Delamar, Richard** An Irish acquaintance of Swift who delivered the dean's letters to his English friends, John and Robert ARBUTHNOT, in 1732.

**Delany, Rev. Patrick** (c. 1685–1768) Churchman who became Swift's close friend in the summer of 1718 as a junior fellow of Trinity College, Dublin; later chancellor of Christ Church Cathedral, Dublin, 1728; chancellor of St. Patrick's Cathedral, 1730; dean of Down, 1744. He joined Swift in several literary efforts and eventually wrote an early biography, *Observations upon Lord Orrery's Remarks on the Life and Writings of Dr. Jonathan Swift* (London, 1754), in which he defended Swift against ORRERY's unflattering portrayal. See also "TO MR. DELANY," "ON DAN JACKSON'S PICTURE," "APOLLO TO THE DEAN," "APOLLO'S EDICT," " 'A PAPER BOOK IS SENT BY BOYLE,' " "TO STELLA ON HER BIRTHDAY" (1721), "A LEFT-HANDED LETTER TO DR. SHERIDAN," "SHERIDAN'S SUBMISSION," "DR. SWIFT'S ANSWER TO DR. SHERIDAN," "GEORGE NIM-DAN-DEAN'S INVITATION TO MR. THOMAS SHERIDAN," and "STELLA'S BIRTHDAY" (1725).

**Denham, Sir John** (1615–1669)   Poet. In "The BATTLE OF THE BOOKS," he is described as "a stout *Modern*, who from his Father's side, derived his lineage from Apollo, but his mother was of Mortal Race." A footnote (which Swift attributes to William WOTTON) explains that this mixed parentage highlights the unfortunate fact that Denham's works *are very Unequal, extremely Good, and very Indifferent.* After Homer kills Denham with a long spear during the battle, Apollo takes "the Celestial Part" of him and makes it into a star while the "Terrestrial" portion remains "wallowing upon the Ground." Born in Dublin and educated at Oxford, Denham fought for the Royalists during the English civil wars. Following the Restoration, he battled periodic insanity—reportedly due to his second wife's affair with a courtier. He translated six books of Virgil's *Aeneid* and published a drama in blank verse called *The Sophy* (1642). He became famous, however, for *Cooper's Hill* (1642)—a topographical poem in closed couplets combining a description of the landscape around Windsor Castle with meditative reflections based upon the scenery.

**Dennis, John** (1657–1734)   Dramatist and professional critic who often disagreed with Alexander POPE, though he did share with the poet a love of literature and the principles of good writing. But since popular literature was the height of bad taste, as Dennis believed, he attacked Pope's works and the poet, as well as the *Tatler,* the *Spectator,* and *Cato.* In COMPLETE COLLECTION OF GENTEEL AND INGENIOUS CONVERSATION, Swift mentions Dennis in his parody of serious works and writers on the subject of manners. See also "ON POETRY: A RHAPSODY," "The FIRST ODE OF THE SECOND BOOK OF HORACE . . . TO RICHARD STEELE, ESQ.," and "A TALE OF A TUB."

**Desaulnais, Henry (Henry Disney, Henry Desney)** (1675–1731)   French Huguenot who was a colonel in the British army, a TORY member of The Society, and a friend of John ARBUTHNOT, Alexander POPE, and Henry BOLINGBROKE. He was known to his friends as "Duke Disney." Swift mentions Desaulnais reporting on the British occupation of DUNKIRK during the War of the Spanish Succession in "The HISTORY OF THE FOUR LAST YEARS OF THE QUEEN." He is also referenced in Swift's *Correspondence* and THE JOURNAL TO STELLA.

**Descartes, René** (1596–1650)   French philosopher, mathematician, and physicist best known for his opposition to Scholasticism and its emphasis on the value of knowledge based on authority and tradition. His principal work, *Le Discours de la Méthode* (1637), contains the well-known phrase that sums up the basis of Cartesian philosophy: *"Cogito ergo sum"* ("I think therefore I am"). Swift's satiric allusions to Descartes generally make fun of his theory of vortices, which was built on the idea that since no two objects can occupy the same space, motion occurs only when small particles collide and move simultaneously in a circular pattern. For example, in the "Digression Concerning Madness" the narrator of "A TALE OF A TUB" counts Descartes among philosophers who were mistakenly regarded as insane by everyone but their followers, adding that he "reckoned to see before he died, the Sentiments of all Philosophers, like so many lesser stars in his *Romantick* System, rapt and drawn within his own *Vortex.*"

René Descartes  *(Library of Congress)*

In "The BATTLE OF THE BOOKS," Descartes commands the moderns' archers until Aristotle inadvertently kills him during the battle with an arrow intended for Francis BACON. When the arrow enters his right eye, the pain whirls Descartes around "till Death, like a star of superior Influence, drew him into his own *Vortex.*" During Lemuel Gulliver's visit to Glubbdubdrib in Part 3 of GULLIVER'S TRAVELS, the Governor calls Descartes' spirit up from the dead. At Gulliver's request, Descartes explains his "system" to Aristotle, who has also been summoned. Aristotle apologizes for his own "Mistakes in Natural Philosophy," but then finds Descartes' theory of vortices to be equally ridiculous.

**DeWitt, Johan** (1625–1672)  Dutch statesman and grand pensionary of Holland. A colleague of Sir William TEMPLE, who convinced him that the English must join the Dutch in opposing LOUIS XIV. Swift edited Temple's letters and mentions DeWitt's correspondence with Temple, noting the pensionary's excellent reputation and suggesting CHARLES II had him murdered. See "A TALE OF A TUB" and *Marginalia.*

**Dingley, Rebecca** (c. 1665–1743)  Friend and lifelong older companion of Esther JOHNSON (Stella); daughter of a cousin of Sir William TEMPLE. Swift advised the two women to settle in Ireland, where their annuity from Temple's estate (and Dingley's small annuity from her father) would provide better security. Dingley remained an essential part of Swift's personal life. See references to her in *The JOURNAL TO STELLA,* "ON THE DEATH OF MRS. JOHNSON," "A NEW-YEAR'S-GIFT FOR BEC," "DINGLEY AND BRENT," "BEC'S BIRTHDAY," and "ON THE COLLAR OF MRS. DINGLEY'S LAP-DOG."

**Dodington, George Bubb** (1691–1762)  WHIG M.P. who held the Irish sinecure of clerk of the Pells during WALPOLE's administration. Swift disliked this English acquaintance, who was known as Walpole's jackal, as no friend of the Irish. "He is too much a half-wit to love a whole-wit, and too much half-honest, to esteem any entire merit." Swift also mentions him in "A CHARACTER OF MRS. HOWARD" and *The DRAPIER'S LETTERS* (Letter 4: "A Letter to the Whole People of Ireland").

**Dodsley, Robert** (1703–1764)  Publisher, editor, poet, and dramatist; friend and disciple of Alexander POPE. In addition to printing the work of William Collins (1721–59), Thomas Gray (1716–71), and Samuel JOHNSON, Dodsley published three of Swift's sermons in 1744: "On Mutual Subjection," "On the Testimony of Conscience," "ON THE TRINITY," and a fourth in 1745, "The Difficulty of Knowing One's Self." Though he probably never met Swift, Dodsley published his unfinished "DIRECTIONS TO SERVANTS" posthumously in February 1746. Swift mentions Dodsley in his *Correspondence,* commending Pope for helping Dodsley set up as a bookseller.

**Dolben, Sir Gilbert** (1658–1722)  Justice of the Common Pleas of Ireland; wealthy M.P. at Westminster, 1685–1713. Swift stayed with the Dolbens at their home in Northhamptonshire. Dolben was a personal friend of John DRYDEN; his scholarly tastes appealed to Swift.

**Donnellan, Anne**  One of a number of Dublin gentlewomen who made Swift's acquaintance. Swift depended on the extended Irish "female society" of Mary BARBER, Mary PENDARVES, Frances Kelly, and Miss Donnellan for improving his daily routine. Anne was an accomplished musician and the sister of Rev. Christopher Donnellan, whom Swift had assisted in gaining his first church appointment.

**Dorset, Lionel Sackville, first duke of** (1688–1765)   Lord lieutenant of Ireland (1730–37); Whig peer created duke in 1720 who had been sent to Hanover to welcome GEORGE I on his inauguration as the new king in 1714. Swift, and Dorset exchanged a number of letters with Swift, assuring the chief governor that he would refrain from embarrassing England by writing about the conditions in Ireland: Since its "condition [is] absolutely desperate, I would not prescribe a dose to the dead." See "ADVICE TO THE FREEMEN OF DUBLIN," "The ANSWER TO THE CRAFTSMAN," and "EPIGRAM."

**Downes, Henry** (d. 1735)   English clergyman with successive appointments as bishop of Killala, of Elphin, of Meath, and of Derry; member of the Privy Council who represented the English bloc on the Episcopal bench. Swift made special efforts to cooperate with the bishop of Meath, even offering Downes the use of his house at Laracor until his own could be built.

**Downton, Thomas** (fl. 1670)   One of Sir William TEMPLE's chief secretaries who began his service during his first embassy at The Hague (1668–70). Downton maintained a manuscript of Temple's letters, known as the *Downton Transcript of Temple's Letters*, under the ambassador's direction. He left Temple's service shortly after their return to England. Swift relied on the Downton transcript in preparing Temple's letters for publication in 1699.

**Drogheda, Henry Hamilton Moore, third earl of** (c. 1650–1714)   Lord justice of Ireland (1701) and member of a powerful Irish family that had taken control of certain church lands and tithes. Swift's third parish, Rathbeggan, was given to him by Drogheda with the agreement it would be returned on Swift's achieving episcopal success. When Swift became dean of St. Patrick's, the earl

asked him to give up Rathbeggan, and Swift refused. See also "MRS. HARRIS'S PETITION."

**Drummond, John** (1676–1742)   Scotsman who served as a TORY agent, specifically Robert HARLEY's financial deputy, at The Hague until 1714, when he returned to London. He was under the protection of Lady Abigail Masham (née HILL), in whose company Swift had met him during a visit to England.

**Dryden, John** (1631–1700)   English poet, dramatist, and literary critic; distant cousin to Swift (see Part I). In *Lives of the Poets* (1779–81), Samuel JOHNSON writes that after reading Swift's "ODE TO THE ATHENIAN SOCIETY" when it appeared in the *Athenian Mercury* in 1692, Dryden remarked, " 'Cousin Swift, you will never be a poet;' and . . . this denunciation was the motive of Swift's perpetual malevolence to Dryden." Swift lists Dryden among the Moderns in "The BATTLE OF THE BOOKS," and lampoons his penchant for translating (or paraphrasing) the works of earlier authors. Dryden wears ill-fitting rusty armor, and when he exchanges armor with Virgil, the ancient Roman's golden armaments "became the Modern yet worse than his Own" (I.158). Dryden had translated Virgil's *Aeneid* (1697) in its entirety, and his *Miscellanies* (1693–94) and *Fables Ancient and Modern* (1700) included partial translations of Virgil's *Georgics*, Ovid's *Metamorphoses*, Homer's *Iliad*, and Boccaccio's *Decameron*, along with paraphrases of Chaucer's *Canterbury Tales*.

Dryden sided with Oliver Cromwell and the Puritans against King Charles I, but celebrated the Restoration of King CHARLES II in 1660. He was named poet laureate in 1668, but lost his title 20 years later, having refused to renounce his Catholicism following the crowning of Protestant king WILLIAM III. Dryden wrote a number of popular plays, such as *The Indian Emperor* (1665), *The Conquest of Granada* (1670), and *All for Love* (1677), numerous poems, including well-known verse satires such as *MacFlecknoe* (1678/79) and *Absalom and Achitophel* (1681), along with *Religio Laici* and *The Hind and the Panther*—both poems on religious issues. His best-known critical works are *An Essay of Dramatic Poesy* (1668) and his *Preface to Fables Ancient*

John Dryden  *(Courtesy of New York Public Library)*

*and Modern* (1700). See also "Amboyna," "DESCRIPTION OF A CITY SHOWER," and "A TALE OF A TUB" (Section 5: "Digression in the Modern Kind").

**Duck, Stephen** (1705–56)  The "thresher poet"—a natural, self-taught genius who was a Wiltshire agricultural laborer until his verses aroused the interest of members of the Court, especially Queen CAROLINE, to whom he had written complimentary lines. She gave him a house at Richmond Park, and John GAY wrote to Swift that he "is the favorite Poet of the Court." Swift displayed contempt for the so-called child of nature, and Alexander POPE responded in disgust that Duck or CIBBER would be given preference for the now vacated post of poet laureate. See "ON STEPHEN DUCK, THE THRESHER, AND FAVOURITE POET," "VERSES ON THE DEATH OF DR. SWIFT, D.S.P.D.," and "ON POETRY: A RHAPSODY."

**Dunkin, Rev. William** (c. 1709–1765)  Poet and young protégé of Swift who received an increased annuity at Trinity College, Dublin, at the dean's request. Ordained 1735 and became master of Portora Royal School, Ireland (1746). Eagerly writing on his behalf, Swift recommended him as "a gentleman of great learning and wit, true religion, and excellent morals" in hopes of adding a church living for him. He failed, and later Dunkin witnessed Swift's will and its codicil.

**Dunkirk**  Seaport town in northern France. It was an important factor in European conflicts—especially during the 16th and 17th centuries, but also during the War of the Spanish Succession. The Treaty of Utrecht required the French to destroy fortifications there in 1713. See also "PEACE AND DUNKIRK," "A HUE AND CRY AFTER DISMAL, and "A HISTORY OF THE FOUR LAST YEARS OF THE QUEEN."

**Dupplin, George Hay, viscount** (1689–1758)  Eldest son of the seventh earl of Kinnoull, was an M.P. for Fowey (1710–11). He married the second daughter of the Lord treasurer Robert HARLEY, and succeeded to the earldom in 1719.

While in London, Swift met Dupplin in Harley's company; they were members of The Society together. Dupplin brought Swift's "ADVICE HUMBLY OFFER'D TO THE MEMBERS OF THE OCTOBER CLUB" to the notice of Harley, who praised it while all acted as if the author was unknown to them. Swift refers to Dupplin in *The* JOURNAL TO STELLA and the *Correspondence*.

**D'Urfey, Thomas (Tomas Durfey)** (1653–1723)  Popular dramatist and poet whose plays were well constructed, though not original in thought. His flair for ballads and songs made him a highly efficient and prolific entertainer, and a ready source for the Scriblerian satire of Swift and Alexander POPE, especially ridiculed in "A TALE OF A TUB." See also "FIRST ODE . . . Addressed to RICHARD STEELE."

**Echlin, Rev. John, vicar-general of Tuam** (d. 1763)   Irish clergyman whom Swift consulted on the music and cathedral choir for St. Patrick's and who had written the musical setting for the dean's "A Cantata." Swift recommended him, among four other clergymen of his acquaintance, to Lord Carteret as one of "the most distinguished for [his] learning and piety." He became vicar-general of Tuam Cathedral in 1734.

**Edwin, Sir Humphrey [lord mayor of London]** (1642–1707)   Swift satirizes Edwin in "A Tale of a Tub" and "The Mechanical Operation of the Spirit" for his excesses and blindnesses. Edwin was a Presbyterian, and Swift, in describing the relevant characteristics of Nonconformity, uses the lord mayor as a coarse caricature of the supposed vices of Dissenters.

**Eglinton, Alexander Montgomery, eighth earl of** (c. 1636–1701)   An acquaintance of Swift who had married a granddaughter of Sir Robert Swift, in the dean's family. Montgomery appears very early in Swift's autobiographical essay, "The Family of Swift."

**Ellis, Welbore, bishop of Kildare** (c. 1651–1734) English clergyman who served as chaplain to the duke of Ormonde, the new lord lieutenant, on his arrival in Dublin and was promoted quickly to bishop of Kildare and concurrently dean of Christ Church, Dublin (1705). This posting caused both Swift and Archbishop King much difficulty, since

Ellis often led the opposition against both men in the law courts of England and Ireland. He later became bishop of Meath (1732). Ellis made sure Swift received no official recognition or thanks for his part in relieving the Irish clergy of the First Fruits (Queen Anne's Bounty, fees paid to the Crown by clergy). See also *The Drapier's Letters* (letter 3: Some Observations upon . . . the Report of the Committee) on William Wood's patent where, after Swift has succeeded in organizing a boycott against the copper coinage, the Irish bishops finally petition the English government requesting the patent's cancellation.

**Essex, Algernon Capel, second earl of** (c. 1670–1710)   Whig aristocrat, constable of the Tower, and acquaintance of Lord Halifax, whose relationship with Swift was complex. Essex, whom Swift apparently never met, did have reason to dislike him since he believed Swift had been partially responsible for insulting the name of his dead father and embarrassing his mother, Elizabeth Capel, countess of Essex (Temple's *Memoirs, Part III*). In the *Marginalia*, Swift notes Essex "cut his own throat," reversing John Macky's claim in *Characters of the Court of Britain* (1733) that he was murdered in the Tower.

**Essex, Elizabeth Percy Capel, countess of** (d. 1717)   Wife of Arthur Capel, first earl of Essex who, after her husband's death, continued her close friendship with Martha Temple Giffard. Swift published Temple's *Memoirs, Part III*, knowing that certain passages would severely criticize Capel's diplomatic practices while serving with Temple. Lady Giffard, who worried about accusations that she would profit from the publication of her brother's memoirs and in turn hurt her friendship with the countess of Essex, placed an ad in a London newspaper stating Swift had acted without authority and that his version of the memoirs was a false copy. His reply was devastating, silencing her.

**Eugene, prince of Savoy** (1663–1736)    French prince and general in the service of the Holy Roman Empire. He had achieved success in Austrian service against the Turks (1683–97), and in the War of the Spanish Succession (1701–14) with the duke of MARLBOROUGH he secured important victories over the French. Swift never met Eugene when the prince visited England but held firm opinions on his warlike attitudes, cruelty, WHIG behavior, hatred of Robert HARLEY, and perpetual conniving. See "HISTORY OF THE FOUR LAST YEARS OF THE QUEEN" and "The Public Spirit of the Whigs."

**Eusden, Laurence** (1688–1730)    Clergyman and poet who became poet laureate in 1718, much to the annoyance and incredulity of his peers, who found him totally without talent. In *The Dunciad*, Alexander POPE compares the alcoholic Eusden to the figure of a fat naked drunkard, usually found in art or classical poetry. Swift satirized him in "DIRECTIONS FOR A BIRTHDAY SONG" and earlier had asked Charles FORD, "Who is that same Eusden they have made laureate? Is he a Poet?"

**Evans, John, bishop of Meath** (d. 1724)    Successively bishop of Bangor (1702–16) and of Meath; a Welshman who had voted in the House of Lords as a staunch WHIG, and earlier had spent two decades in India in various East-Indian Company chaplaincies. Swift and Evans disliked each other from the first, and Evans's refusal to treat the diocesan clergy with kindness angered the dean who quickly defended his colleagues against this censure. His reports to the archbishop of Canterbury denouncing Swift and Irish interests continued until his death.

# F

**Farquhar, George** (1678–1707) Irish dramatist. The son of a clergyman, he spent a year at Trinity College, Dublin. Arriving in London in 1697, he began writing comedies and proved a fertile writer until his early death. His best-known works, *The Recruiting Officer* (1706) and *The Beaux' Stratagem* (1707), may have been on Swift's mind when he wrote against the "corruptions of the Theatre" in "Project for the Advancement of Religion and the Reformation of Manners."

**Faulkner, George** (1699–1775) Dublin printer and bookseller, whom Swift referred to as "the Prince of Dublin Printers." He published the first edition of Swift's collected *Works* in Dublin in 1735. Faulkner worked as an apprentice to Thomas Hume, and later as a journeyman in London with the well-known printer William Bowyer (1699–1777). Faulkner started a printing business in Dublin as a joint venture with James Hoey in 1724, and began printing the *Dublin Journal* soon thereafter. Faulkner opened his own shop in Dublin in 1730, and in the same year published Swift's "Vindication of Lord Carteret."

In 1725 Faulkner produced the first collected edition of Swift's DRAPIER'S LETTERS under the title *Fraud Detected: or, The Hibernian Patriot.* In his biography of Swift, Irvin Ehrenpreis writes that between 1727 and 1730, the *Dublin Journal* included regular reports of Swift's "activities," but that during that time Faulkner "enjoyed no close relation with Swift" (III.780). In 1732 Faulkner was fined and incarcerated for having printed in the

*Journal* a controversial "Queries" by Swift regarding the Irish House of Lords (see "CONSIDERATIONS UPON TWO BILLS"). He was imprisoned once again in 1736 after publishing a controversial pamphlet by Josiah HORT. Following a lengthy process of gathering manuscripts of Swift's work from various places in England and Ireland (and with Swift ultimately denying that he had anything to do with the process), Faulkner in 1735 issued the first edition of Swift's collected *Works*. The incredibly popular publication was issued by subscription and included a revised version of GULLIVER'S TRAVELS. By 1669 the edition had grown to 20 volumes. Ehrenpreis writes that the greatest significance of Faulkner's edition was that it saved a number of Swift's works from oblivion (*Swift* III.787). For Carole Fabricant, however, the true significance of Faulkner's Dublin edition is that it "presented Swift's works as part of a consciously and thoroughly Irish production," rendering Swift "inseparable from Dublin life and letters" ("Swift the Irishman" 69). Faulkner's correspondence is available in Robert E. Ward's *Prince of Dublin Printers: The Letters of George Faulkner* (Lexington: University Press of Kentucky, 1972).

**Fenton, Jane (née Swift)** (1666–1736) Elder sister of Jonathan Swift; married Joseph Fenton in 1699 at the age of 23. Joseph Fenton was a tanner or currier ("one whose trade is the dressing and colouring of leather after it is tanned" [OED]). Jane was one year old at the time of Swift's birth. When her mother Abigail SWIFT left to visit a relative in Leicester after the death of Jonathan SWIFT,

Sr., in 1667, she took Jane with her and left the infant Jonathan with a nurse. Neither Swift nor his mother thought highly of Jane's choice of a husband (he refers to Fenton as a dunce in *The JOURNAL TO STELLA*), but Jane and her brother remained intermittently in contact with each other until her death. In his biography of Swift, Irvin Ehrenpreis explains that Jane looked to her younger brother "for advice and assistance," and that Swift wrote letters to her and (at least after her husband's death) provided a "regular allowance" (II.18).

**Fielding, Henry** (1707–1754)  Novelist who first had success as a dramatist; his *Pasquin* (1736) with its satire of current poets, pantomimes, and Italian opera was an outstanding success. Mary PENDARVES wrote to Swift of the latest excitement in London and mentions this Fielding work as having "almost as long a run as the Beggars Opera, but in my opinion not with equal merit, though it has humor." Swift did not meet Fielding, but Alexander POPE knew his farces and dramatic pieces and met him in 1741. See "ON POETRY: A RHAPSODY."

**Finch, Anne (née Kingsmill), countess of Winchilsea** (1661–1720)  Poet and daughter of Sir William Kingsmill and wife of Heneage Finch, later fourth earl of Winchilsea and the brother of the earl of NOTTINGHAM. In 1682 she became a maid of honour to Mary of Modena, the wife of James STUART, duke of York, and went to live at St. James's Palace. After James succeeded his brother CHARLES II as king, the Finches became prominent members of the Court; however, soon after James was exiled the new monarchs, WILLIAM III and Mary, demanded an oath of allegiance, which the Finches refused to swear. In 1690 Finch's husband was arrested as a Jacobite but ultimately not convicted. They retired to Eastwell Park in Kent, where Anne wrote poetry. Her work circulated in manuscript (though it is also found in collections and in her first volume, *Miscellany Poems, Written by a Lady* (1713). Swift (who knew her work well) mentions in *The JOURNAL TO STELLA* in 1711 how "he hear[s] no more of Mrs. Finch," likely a comment on the political atmosphere of London. Yet, he writes a poem to her, often published in collections, "APOLLO OUTWITTED: To the Honourable Mrs. Finch (Since Countess of Winchilsea), under the Name of Ardelia," urging her to publish her poems. He had played cards with her in London, found her charming, and would have welcomed the opportunity of reading her more than 230 poems.

**Fleetwood, William** (1656–1723)  Bishop of St. Asaph and an ambitious WHIG who had been bishop of Ely. Fleetwood had written a book, *Chronicon Preciosum* (1707), which Swift had in his library, on the relative cost of commodities and the danger of inflation to a clergyman's living. Later, Fleetwood reprinted four of his sermons and wrote a preface celebrating the Glorious Revolution and praising MARLBOROUGH. The Whigs gave it much publicity, and the TORIES urged Swift to respond; his essay, "LETTER OF THANKS FROM MY LORD WHARTON," severely ridiculed Fleetwood and his hypocritical stance. This attack appeared shortly before the EXAMINER, number 34, in which Swift includes an earlier Fleetwood preface in hopes of rescuing it from "oblivion."

**Fontenelle, Bernard le Bovier de** (1657–1757)  French author and scientist. In "The BATTLE OF THE BOOKS," he is the Moderns' primary supporter in France. After unhorsing Charles PERRAULT, Homer hurls him at Fontenelle, "with the same blow dashing out both their brains." Fontenelle's best-known work was a series of dialogues called *Entretiens sur la pluralité des mondes* (1686; published in 1688 as *Conversations on the Plurality of Worlds*). Influential in promoting the Copernican view of the solar system and based on René DESCARTES' theory of vortices, this work proposed the existence of numerous worlds and living beings. Fontenelle argued that many of these worlds are incredibly small and exist all around us as well as in outer space.

**Ford, Charles** (1682–1741)  Younger friend of Swift; born in Dublin, a devoted correspondent for 30 years who was an absentee landlord with an estate named Woodpark in County Meath; educated at Trinity College, Dublin. Ford's worldliness and classical learning, as well as his sympathetic critical voice, qualified him as one of Swift's most important confidants. Their friendship began in 1708 in London, where Ford enjoyed its fashionable world and knew Swift's English friends as well as Esther VANHOMRIGH (Vanessa) and Esther JOHNSON (Stella). Ford's visits to Ireland became frequent, deepening the father-son relationship, and Swift arranged for his appointment as gazetteer in 1712. As a literary agent, Ford worked diligently in providing Swift's corrections of the first edition of GULLIVER'S TRAVELS to Benjamin Motte, the London bookseller and printer. See "TO CHARLES FORD, ESQ. ON HIS BIRTHDAY," "STELLA'S BIRTHDAY (1723)," "STELLA AT WOODPARK," "A PORTRAIT FROM THE LIFE," and nearly 70 letters in the *Correspondence*.

**Forster, John** (1667–1720)   Recorder of Dublin, lord chief justice of the Common Pleas of Ireland, solicitor general, and Speaker of the Irish House of Commons from May 1710, replacing Alan Brodrick MIDDLETON. Swift's *EXAMINER* had focused on the chief enemy of the Irish Church, Lord Thomas WHARTON, the lord lieutenant of Ireland (1708–10) and directed the pamphlet "A SHORT CHARACTER OF HIS EXCELLENCY THOMAS EARL OF WHARTON" against this arrogant politician. Wharton had in 1710 replaced one uncooperative solicitor general with Forster, and Swift makes clear in "A Continuation of a Short Character of Thomas, Earl of Wharton" that the lord lieutenant had no authority to do so. See also "A LETTER TO A MEMBER OF PARLIAMENT IN IRELAND."

**Fountaine, Sir Andrew** (1676–1753)   A sophisticated Englishman from Norfolk with extensive interests in collecting coins, books, drawings, and paintings, who held two Oxford University degrees; well traveled on the Continent, knighted in 1699; and the protégé of Thomas, earl of PEMBROKE, the lord lieutenant of Ireland (1707). Pembroke promoted Fountaine as a court officer of the Black Rod, or usher, between the lord lieutenant and the Irish Parliament. Swift and Fountaine enjoyed each other's company, both in Ireland and England, where they both met frequently, often with the older man's friends. Though a WHIG, Fountaine's politics were not an obstacle in their relationship. See "DIALOGUE IN THE CASTILIAN LANGUAGE," "A Modest Defence of Punning," and "Tritical Essay upon the Faculties of the Mind."

**Frederick Louis, prince of Wales** (1707–51)   Father of George III and the alienated eldest son of GEORGE II. He led the opposition to his father's government, resulting in Robert WALPOLE's resignation, but died before he could ascend the throne. Swift uses the conceit of the education of the young prince in 1714 to comment on the fate of the Robert HARLEY and BOLINGBROKE ministry, and the illness of Queen ANNE. See also "Some Free Thoughts upon the Present State of Affairs," "An ENQUIRY INTO THE BEHAVIOUR OF THE QUEEN'S LAST MINISTRY, "DIRECTIONS FOR A BIRTHDAY SONG," and "ON POETRY: A RHAPSODY."

**French, Humphrey** (d. 1736)   Lord mayor of Dublin (1732–33). French took early steps in opposing WOOD's patent on coinage as damaging to tax-and-revenue collection in Ireland. As unofficial agent of the Irish commissioners of the Revenue in 1722, French drew his information from Archbishop KING. Swift called him a hero and a lover of liberty, praising his efforts against dishonest traders in the city. He supported French's unsuccessful bid for election to the Irish House. See "ADVICE TO THE FREEMEN OF THE CITY OF DUBLIN."

**Furnese, Sir Henry, baronet** (1658–1712)   A well-connected WHIG who used his considerable talents for business to advance himself in London, while also an M.P. Swift and other TORIES found his self-interest and underhanded methods intolerable, satirizing him as a "brewer," a veritable "Furnese" [furnace] of mischief. See *EXAMINER*, number 40, and "A DIALOGUE BETWEEN CAPTAIN TOM AND SIR HENRY DUTTON COLT."

# G

**Gadbury, John** (1627–1704) Astrologer and almanac maker who was a predecessor to John PARTRIDGE. Gadbury's brand of scientific quackery annoyed Swift nearly as much as Partridge since both voiced anticlerical abuse. See "The PROGRESS OF BEAUTY," "A VINDICATION OF ISAAC BICKERSTAFF ESQ.," and "PREDICTIONS FOR THE YEAR 1708."

**Gallas, Johann Wenzel, count de** (1669–1719) Austrian ambassador in London during the period when BOLINGBROKE and the TORIES were attempting to settle the War of the Spanish Succession. The English government hoped to arrive at a peace even if the Dutch or Austrians were displeased with its articles. Gallas released the confidential documents to the press and to his master, the elector of Hanover, the rising GEORGE I. Swift reports in "The HISTORY OF THE FOUR LAST YEARS OF THE QUEEN" that Gallas acted "a very dishonorable part" and his expulsion from court was well deserved.

**Galway, Henry de Massue de Ruvigny, first earl of** (1648–1720) French Huguenot and lieutenant general in the English army; later lord justice in Ireland (1697–1715) who, with Charles GRAFTON, governed Ireland for nearly 18 months (1715–17). In his *Characters of the Court of Britain* (1733), John MACKY commented on Galway's modesty, vigilance, and sincerity: "a man of honor and honesty." Swift believed exactly the opposite, disliked his WHIG opinions, calling Galway (in his *Marginalia* to Macky's work) "a damnable hypocrite, of no religion," and refused to accept his positive traits. See "MRS. HARRIS'S PETITION" and "The CONDUCT OF THE ALLIES."

**Garth, Sir Samuel** (1661–1719) Physician, poet, and early friend of Alexander POPE. Swift knew him in London and admired his mock-epic *The Dispensary.* Irvin Ehrenpreis suggests Swift's "A DESCRIPTION OF A CITY SHOWER" owes much to Garth's poem, as does Pope's *The Rape of the Lock* (*Swift* II.385 n.1). As a WHIG and a member of the Kit-Cat Club, Garth had friends both in the government and literary circles. His good nature and generous spirit appealed as much to Swift as did his wit.

**Gay, John** (1685–1732) Poet and dramatist Alexander POPE met Gay in London in 1711, and "his wit and vivacity" appealed to all who knew him; though good-natured, he was excessively improvident yet was possessed of expensive tastes. Swift met him with other charter members of the SCRIBLERUS CLUB (formed in 1714), and they quickly became firm friends. Their correspondence is extensive (more than 30 letters), and Swift helped in the creation of Gay's *The Beggar's Opera* (1728). Using his paper, the INTELLIGENCER, number 3, Swift defended Gay against religious and political critics who would diminish the success of the *Opera.* Also, Gay's continual struggle with debt disturbed Swift, who worked unsuccessfully to secure him preferment. See also "TO MR. GAY," "SCRIBLERIAN VERSES," "HORACE, LIB. 2, SAT. 6," "TO CHARLES FORD, ESQ. ON HIS BIRTHDAY," "A

John Gay *(Library of Congress)*

PASTORAL DIALOGUE BETWEEN RICHMOND LODGE AND MARBLE HILL," "VERSES ON THE DEATH OF DR. Swift, D.S.P.D.," "ON POETRY: A RHAPSODY," and "TIM AND THE FABLES."

**George, prince of Denmark** (1653–1708)   Husband of Queen ANNE; lord high admiral, 1702. Swift comments on the prince's influence with the queen in "Memoirs Relating to That Change Which Happened in the Year 1710," describing his aversion to the WHIGS and efforts at having prominent ministers removed from office. The prince's unexpected death changed the political atmosphere for a time, affecting Swift's hopes for the Irish Church and his own early preferment.

**George I, king of Great Britain** (1660–1727)   Elector of Hanover (1698–1727); king of Great Britain and Ireland (1714–27). George was the great-grandson of James I of England and a Protestant, who succeeded Queen ANNE under the provisions of the Act of Settlement (1701). He favored the WHIGS over the TORIES, and suspected the lat-

ter of promoting Jacobean sympathies. In "A LETTER FROM DR. SWIFT TO MR. POPE," Swift comments that he does not know him, "nor ever had once the curiosity to enquire. . . ." Yet in GULLIVER'S TRAVELS he models the Emperor of Lilliput and King of Laputa on George I, suggesting that each character's despotic behavior and irresponsible attitude toward his people mirror George's conduct. See also "DIRECTIONS FOR A BIRTHDAY SONG."

**George II, king of Great Britain** (1683–1760)   Eldest son of George I, married CAROLINE of Anspach, became king of Great Britain and Ireland (1727–60); elector of Hanover (1698–1727). Influenced by Sir Robert WALPOLE, he supported the WHIGS. His efforts resulted in Britain's entry into the War of the Austrian Succession (1740–49) and became the last British monarch to lead his troops into battle. His suppression of the last Jacobite Rebellion, at the hands of his brother, the duke of CUMBERLAND, was remembered as especially harsh. In "An ACCOUNT OF THE COURT AND EMPIRE OF JAPAN," Swift attacks the corruption rampant in the Walpole government, assuring the monarch that "without bribery . . . the wheels of government will not turn."

**Geree, Rev. John** (1672–1761)   Rector of Letcombe Bassett, Berkshire, where Swift spent part of the summer of 1714. Apparently Geree's father, Rev. John Geree, and William TEMPLE traded favors since Temple used his influence to help the senior Geree's brother while the younger Geree could provide a local church sinecure for Thomas SWIFT, Jonathan's cousin and Temple's secretary. Geree's friendship and comfortable home afforded Swift the opportunity of writing 73 letters in a period of 78 days.

**Germain, Lady Elizabeth (Berkeley)** (1680–1769)   Daughter of Charles, earl of BERKELEY, and longtime friend of Swift, who first met her in Ireland when her father was installed as lord lieutenant. Lady Betty remains the only one of the Berkeleys whom Swift could tolerate after the old earl's death. Her intelligence and lively wit appealed to him, and she invited him to her husband's (Sir

John Germain) home, Drayton, and maintained the friendship as a widow. Though a "zealous" WHIG, Lady Betty and the now TORY Swift enjoyed each other's banter; see "A BALLAD ON THE GAME OF TRAFFIC," "A BALLAD TO THE TUNE OF CUTPURSE," and "MRS. HARRIS'S PETITION."

**Gerrard, Samuel**  A respected Irish legal friend who was introduced to Swift through a mutual Dublin friend; later Swift introduced him to Alexander POPE. A short series of letters between Gerrard and Swift in 1734 discusses the purchase of lands not far from Laracor, Swift's vicarage. Later, Gerrard assisted Pope in producing a new volume of letters between the poet and Swift and ultimately brought a copy of the new book to Swift in Dublin.

**Gibson, Edmund, bishop of London**  (1669–1748) Churchman who became bishop of London (1723) and author of the monumental *Codex Juris Ecclesiae Anglicanae* (1713). Swift disagreed with the effort to repeal the Test Act as a gesture to Dissenters, and Gibson was one of the six bishops who voted against the bill and in favor of the Established Church. Swift's pamphlets "Queries Relating to the Sacramental Test" and "The ADVANTAGES PROPOSED BY REPEALING THE SACRAMENTAL TEST" were influential in the bill's defeat. Gibson printed the first essay in *The Dispute Adjusted* (1733).

**Giffard, Lady Martha (née Temple)**  (1638–1722) Sister of Sir William TEMPLE and widow of Sir Thomas Giffard, who died 13 days after their marriage (1662). As Temple's companion and close confidante, she wrote her memoir of him in 1690, but objected to Swift's having published the third part of Temple's *Memoirs* from "an unfaithful copy." Swift, who had earlier sympathetically alluded to her widowhood in "OCCASIONED BY SIR WILLIAM TEMPLE'S LATE ILLNESS AND RECOVERY" and also helped with her literary translations, finally broke with Lady Giffard over efforts to discredit him.

**Gildon, Charles**  (1665–1724)  Dramatist, critic, and miscellaneous writer who had a long-running battle with Alexander POPE, who places him in *The*

*Dunciad.* Swift satirizes his deist views in "MR. COLLINS'S DISCOURSE OF FREE-THINKING" and earlier in "Remarks upon . . . the Rights of the Christian Church Asserted" as one of the "enemies of Christianity." He attacks Gildon's criticism in COMPLETE COLLECTION OF GENTEEL AND INGENIOUS CONVERSATION, celebrating his and his contemporaries' dullness and lack of taste.

**Godolphin, Sidney, first earl of** (1645–1712) Statesman who held office under CHARLES II and WILLIAM III; later lord treasurer in 1702 under ANNE and party manager of the WHIGS, leading member of the long-standing Whig Junto. Godolphin responded coolly to Swift's petition for assistance in repealing the First Fruits, and Swift never forgot the slight. Swift mentions him frequently in his prose, the EXAMINER and "The Public Spirit of the Whigs," among numerous other pieces. In "The VIRTUES OF SID HAMET THE MAGICIAN'S ROD," Swift accuses the earl of hypocrisy and corruption while in office.

**Grafton, Charles Fitzroy, second duke of** (1683–1757)  Statesman who was the grandson of CHARLES II and member of the Kit-Cat Clubs, he became lord lieutenant of Ireland (1720–24). Swift's "A PROPOSAL FOR THE UNIVERSAL USE OF IRISH MANUFACTURE" caused an uproar in the government, but Grafton decided against prosecuting the printer, the writer remaining unnamed. Later, Grafton's office supported an Irish bank and WOOD's coinage—Swift's crusade against these proposals in *The DRAPIER'S LETTERS* and other pamphlets and poems defeated both efforts, leading to Grafton's recall to England.

**Graham, Colonel James** (1649–1730)  Soldier, Jacobite, M.P. under Queen ANNE and GEORGE I, and brother of Sir Richard Graham, Viscount Preston. In COMPLETE COLLECTION OF GENTEEL AND INGENIOUS CONVERSATION, Swift (as Simon Wagstaff) calls Graham his "old friend and companion" who "invent[ed] a set of words and phrases." See also *The JOURNAL TO STELLA.*

**Grant, Francis**  London merchant who apparently wrote to Swift in early 1734 requesting his help in encouraging the Irish to initiate herring and cod fishing as a method for improving their economy. Swift found Grant's request most appealing and after discussing it with his friends in the Irish Parliament, a bill was enacted. His reply to Grant (in a March 23, 1734, letter) remains a superb summary of Swift's concerns for the Irish condition (*Corr.* IV.228–31).

**Granville, George, Baron Lansdowne** (1667–1735)   Minor poet, dramatist, and statesman. He was secretary of war in the HARLEY government and one of 12 aristocrats elevated to the peerage in 1711 for the TORY Peace. Confined to the Tower on suspicion of Jacobite sympathies, after his release he took a self-imposed exile abroad. Granville was an early patron of Alexander POPE, who dedicated "Windsor-Forest" to him. Swift and Granville were both members of The Society, a literary club that included Henry BOLINGBROKE, Swift, Dr. John ARBUTHNOT, and others.

**Grattan, Charles** (c. 1688–1746)   Seventh son of Rev. Patrick Grattan, Fellow of Trinity College, Dublin, and a prebendary of St. Patrick's Cathedral. Swift's attempt to help him maintain his fellowship failed in 1713. Later, Charles Grattan became headmaster of Portora Royal School, Enniskillen. In 1742 he was named as one of Swift's guardians appointed to manage his affairs. See "An EPISTLE UPON AN EPISTLE."

**Grattan, Dr. James** (1673–1747)   Third son of Rev. Patrick Grattan and a prominent Dublin physician. Swift knew and respected him, and even left him a bequest in his will. He called the Grattan brothers "men of open hearts and free spirits."

**Grattan, Rev. John** (d. 1754)   Fifth son of Patrick Grattan and rector of a parish near his ancestral home, Belcamp, who became Swift's close friend in the 1720s and member of the cathedral chapter. Grattan assisted the dean in publishing the final DRAPIER'S LETTER. Later, Grattan agreed to become the executor of Swift's will. See "STELLA'S BIRTHDAY (1723)" and "TO CHARLES FORD, ESQ. ON HIS BIRTHDAY."

**Grattan, Rev. Robert** (c. 1678–c. 1741)   Fourth son of Patrick Grattan, prebendary of Howth, and a member of the cathedral chapter. Swift helped "Robin" secure a more valuable living in Dublin in 1723. He served as an executor of Swift's will. See "A PANEGYRIC ON THE REVEREND DEAN SWIFT" and "A PORTRAIT FROM THE LIFE."

**Gregg, William** (d. 1708)   Clerk in Robert HARLEY's office when Harley was secretary of state. Gregg, whose treasonous behavior led to his trial and execution for crimes against the state while England was at war with France, provided Harley's opponents the opportunity of implicating the secretary in this affair. The WHIG peers who conducted the investigation acted with prejudice, and were roundly condemned in a series of pamphlets. Later, Swift wrote "Some Remarks upon a Letter to the Seven Lords" defending Harley, praising the writer of the *EXAMINER*, and justifying the new ministry. The dean compares Gregg's actions with the GUISCARD affair.

**Grierson, Constantia** (c. 1706–1732)   Wife of the Dublin printer George Grierson and poet, who had grown up poor but had achieved a love of learning and literary taste. Irvin Ehrenpreis suggests she is responsible for the literary ambitions of her friend, Mary BARBER, one of Swift's protégés, and encouraged the Dublin bluestocking Laetitia PILKINGTON. Swift viewed Mrs. Grierson as "a very good Latin and Greek scholar" (*Swift* III.636–37).

**Grigsby, John**   An accountant of the SOUTH SEA COMPANY with whom Swift corresponded in 1713–15. Swift owned £1,000 of stock in this company, held on behalf of three friends, and the dividend came due and was paid to his agent, John BARBER. The "South Sea Bubble" burst in 1720, but apparently Swift had earlier withdrawn his investment. See also "UPON THE SOUTH SEA PROJECT."

**Grimston, William Luckyn, first viscount** (c. 1683–1756)   WHIG M.P. and author of *The Lawyer's Fortune: or, Love in a Hollow Tree* (1705), a comedy. Swift's Colonel Atwit, a foolish character in COMPLETE COLLECTION OF GENTEEL AND INGE-

NIOUS CONVERSATION, recommends this play. See also "A PROPOSAL FOR THE UNIVERSAL USE OF IRISH MANUFACTURE," in which Grimston serves as an ironic example of "a writer of superior class" in Ireland only because he happens to be English.

**Grub Street**  Street in London near Moorfields; renamed Milton Street in 1830. In his *Dictionary*, Samuel JOHNSON characterized it as being "much inhabited by writers of small histories, dictionaries and temporary poems." Beginning in the 17th century, the term was used as an adjective to describe needy, second-rate writers and their work. Swift consistently uses "Grub-street" when discussing ephemeral, often anonymous writings devoted to controversial rumors and current events. He remarks in "ADVICE TO THE GRUB STREET VERSE WRITERS" that these poets are "dead as soon as born," but he makes similar comments about prose writers elsewhere. For example, in a June 29, 1710, letter to Benjamin Tooke, he writes that the "Apology" attached to "A TALE OF A TUB" "is so perfect a Grub-street-piece, it will be forgotten in a week" (*Corr*. I.165). Swift often described himself as a Grub Street author. In a March 22, 1708/09, letter to Robert HUNTER, for example, he writes that he is "of late" a "small Contributor" to the "*Republica Grubstreetaria*," and in "PROMETHEUS" he invokes the "Pow'rs of Grub-street" to help him complete the poem (*Corr*. I.132–33).

Writing anonymously in "A Tale of a Tub," Swift drily lists his treatise among Grub Street writings despite the "ridicule" works and authors in that category have suffered as being "unworthy of their established Post in the Commonwealth of Wit and Learning." The origin of the term *Grub Street* is unclear, but it may derive from the surname *Grubbe*, the word *grub* (which Johnson defined as "a . . . worm that eats holes in bodies"), or *grube* (ditch). Pat Rogers's *Grub Street* (London: Methuen, 1972) is a comprehensive study of the 18th-century subculture associated with this area.

**Guernsey, Heneage Finch, baron, first earl of Aylesford** (c. 1650–1719)  Brother of the second earl of Nottingham, Daniel Finch, a distinguished WHIG statesman. King's counsel (1672) and solici-

tor-general (1679) during the reign of CHARLES II and dismissed by JAMES II in 1686, during a period of constitutional remodeling and alienation of the Church of England. In May 1688 the bishop of Canterbury, William SANCROFT, and six other prominent bishops were arrested on a charge of seditious libel for failing to support the king's Declaration of Indulgence and publishing a petition suggesting the order was illegal. Guernsey served as their chief counsel and secured their freedom. He was created baron on ANNE's order in 1703, and earl of Aylesford in 1714. Swift mentions Guernsey in "The HISTORY OF THE FOUR LAST YEARS OF THE QUEEN," his marginalia to Gilbert Burnet's *History of His Own Times, 1724–34*, and his poem "TOLAND'S INVITATION TO DISMAL TO DINE WITH THE CALVES' HEAD CLUB."

**Guiscard, Antoine de** (1658–1711)  A French spy, arrested in England on March 8, 1711. During his appearance before the Privy Council on the same day, he stabbed Robert HARLEY, first earl of Oxford, with a penknife. The earl eventually recovered, but the event profoundly affected Swift. In a March 8, 1710/11, letter to Archbishop KING, he wrote that the attack had caused him a "violent pain of mind . . . greater than ever I felt in my life" (*Corr*. 1.215). Harley gave Swift the penknife, which became one of his most treasured possessions. See also "TO MR. HARLEY'S SURGEON" and *EXAMINER*, number 32.

**Gyllenborg, Karl Gyllenborg, count de** (1679–1746)  Swedish ambassador in London (1710–17), arrested for complicity in the plot to supply Swedish troops for the planned Jacobite uprising. While in London, Gyllenborg and Swift had developed a mutual respect for each other's talents. Earlier, Swift had begun writing an "ABSTRACT OF THE HISTORY OF ENGLAND" with the intention of dedicating the work to the Swedish king, CHARLES XII. The king had invited Swift to visit him in Sweden in 1710—a trip Swift regretted not making. After the king's death in battle, Swift transferred the dedication to Gyllenborg, now long since returned to his country.

# H

**Hale, Sir Bernard** (1677–1729) Lord chief baron of the exchequer of Ireland and member of the Privy Council who on the order of Lord Lieutenant CARTERET joined with other executives in issuing a *Proclamation against the Drapier* for seditious libel (1724). Swift's DRAPIER'S LETTERS (Letter 4: "A Letter to the Whole People of Ireland") had placed the government's position on WOOD's patent in serious jeopardy. Though Swift and Carteret were friends, Swift felt he had no choice but to challenge the government's authority.

**Halifax, Charles Montague, first earl of** (1661–1715) Statesman, lord of the treasury (1692), chancellor of the exchequer (1694), member of the WHIG Junto, Baron Halifax (1700) and earl of Halifax (1715). His rise to power began during WILLIAM III's reign but was halted during ANNE's, and he returned to office during GEORGE I's ascension. Swift's first political pamphlet, "A DISCOURSE OF THE CONTESTS AND DISSENSIONS BETWEEN THE NOBLES AND THE COMMONS IN ATHENS AND ROME," effectively defends Halifax and other Whig ministers from a threatened impeachment. Though a generous patron of literary artists, Halifax later lost favor with Swift; see "A LIBEL ON THE REVEREND DR. DELANY AND HIS EXCELLENCY JOHN, LORD CARTERET" and "TOLAND'S INVITATION TO DISMAL TO DINE WITH THE CALVES' HEAD CLUB."

**Hamilton, James Douglas, fourth duke of** (1658–1712), and **Elizabeth (née Gerard), duchess of** (d. 1744) Scottish peer in the House of Lords whose support of SACHEVERELL against the WHIGS brought him political reward. Swift finds him "a worthy good natured person, very generous, but of middle understanding," adding "I loved him very well, and I think he loved me better." Hamilton died as a result of wounds received in a duel, and Swift wrote articles for the *Post Boy* and the *Evening Post* (both London newspapers) suggesting that his death was the result of a Whig conspiracy. He revisited this idea in "HISTORY OF THE FOUR LAST YEARS OF THE QUEEN." The duchess was a young, appealing second wife of Hamilton, and Swift enjoyed her "abundance of wit and spirit," especially when she returned his friendship. Swift consoled her immediately after Hamilton's death. See further references to her in *The JOURNAL TO STELLA*.

**Hampden, Richard** (c. 1675–1728) Politician with strong family ties to the WHIG party, who gained only minor government posts, such as treasurer of the navy (1720). His involvement in the South Sea Bubble speculations caused a public outcry, when it was learned he had invested and lost public money. See SOUTH SEA COMPANY and "UPON THE SOUTH SEA PROJECT."

**Hanmer, Sir Thomas, fourth baronet** (1677–1746) Politician; TORY M.P. (1708–27); and Speaker of the House of Commons (1713–14). Swift relied on his long acquaintance with Hanmer in asking him for help in setting free the printer of the dean's political pamphlet, "A PROPOSAL FOR THE UNIVERSAL USE OF IRISH MANUFACTURE"

(1720). Earlier, Swift collaborated with Hanmer on "The Humble Representation of the House of Commons" for the queen, and later published this in "The HISTORY OF THE FOUR LAST YEARS OF THE QUEEN." See also "SCRIBLERIAN VERSES."

**Harcourt, Simon, first viscount** (1661–1727) Lawyer and TORY M.P. (1690) whose courtroom skills led to his directing the impeachment of John SOMERS (1701) and his selection as attorney general (1707–08). Harcourt led the defense of Henry SACHEVERELL (1711) and served as lord keeper, member of the Privy Council. He was appointed lord chancellor in 1713. Swift and Harcourt respected each other: Harcourt wrote "Dr. Swift is not only all our favorite, but our governor." On first meeting Harcourt, Swift's impression was not favorable—"sir chancellor Coxcomb." Created Baron Harcourt in 1711, he offered to secure preferment for Swift but was refused, and Swift instead requested a living for his friend, John GEREE. Often mentioned in Swift's prose, Harcourt (a friend and patron of Alexander POPE) also appears in "The FAGGOT."

**Harding, John** (d. 1725) Irish printer. Harding was arrested and imprisoned (along with his wife, Sarah) in 1724 for sedition in publishing Letter 4 of Swift's *DRAPIER'S LETTERS* and refusing to identify their author. In his biography of Swift, Irvin Ehrenpreis notes that Harding "was no stranger to brushes with authority": In 1719 he reportedly hid "from arrest for issuing a Jacobite document," in 1721 he was jailed for printing one of Lord Lieutenant CARTERET's speeches without permission, and he had already "published several pieces by Swift" (III.277).

**Harding, Sarah** Irish printer and wife of Dublin printer John HARDING. She was arrested and imprisoned along with her husband in 1724 for having published the fourth of Swift's *DRAPIER'S LETTERS*. After her husband's death in 1725, she printed Swift's "ON WISDOM'S DEFEAT IN A LEARNED DEBATE" and (as a result) was called before a committee of Irish lords and arraigned.

**Hare, Francis** (1671–1740) Bishop of Chichester and chaplain to the duke of MARLBOROUGH. Hare wrote a number of pamphlets defending Marlborough against the criticisms leveled in "The CONDUCT OF THE ALLIES" and the EXAMINER. Swift, though hardly feeling the sting of these retorts, did reply in "Some Reasons to Prove . . . in a Letter to a Whig-Lord" and under Mrs. MANLEY's name, "A Learned Comment on Dr. Hare's Sermon." See also EXAMINER, number 28.

**Harley, Edward, second earl of Oxford** (1689–1741) Son of Robert HARLEY; collector of books, coins, and medals. A patron and friend of Alexander POPE, Matthew PRIOR, and Swift, Harley inherited his father's outstanding collection of manuscripts as well as his passion for book collecting. Swift and Harley maintained an active correspondence, and the dean celebrates Harley's marriage in "TO LORD HARLEY, SINCE EARL OF OXFORD, ON HIS MARRIAGE."

Harley's home, Wimpole (in Cambridgeshire), became known for its vast library, which reflected a love of books inherited from his father, Robert, who collected manuscripts. Oxford did not manage his finances well, especially his estate, though every branch of learning and its experts, especially artists' and scholars' works, were promoted and acquired to the fullest. He maintained a close association with the Scriblerus circle.

Nearly bankrupt, Harley sold Wimpole before his death, and the books soon went to the newly founded British Museum for the eminently fair price of £10,000. Oxford had been a founding member of the Brothers Club from 1711, and referred to Swift as Brother. His wife, Henrietta (Harriot) Cavendish Holles, was the only daughter of John Holles, the duke of Newcastle who had been lord privy seal since 1705. When the young Harleys after their marriage in 1713 took up residence at Newcastle House in London, Swift was supposed to have helped in the apportionment of the large inheritance after the unexpected death of Henrietta's father, and later noted in his marginalia that the duke cheated his daughter. Swift wrote the poem celebrating their marriage that Irvin Ehrenpreis calls "a eulogy of bride and groom, congratulating them on a range of moral and intellectual virtues" (*Swift* II.673). Swift hoped in praising the son that the father would appreciate his loyalty and accordingly act as a patron. No matter what might result, Swift called Lord Harley "a person of the world for whom I have the greatest love and esteem." Pope held a similar opinion and makes this point clear in "The Epistle to Bathurst." The Dublin printer George FAULKNER thanked Harley in his preface to his edition of Swift's *Works* (1763), writing that Harley had been most hospitable to him and had given "many valuable and curious presents." Swift intended to leave two valuable gifts that had once belonged to Queen ANNE to Harley in his will, but he outlived the earl. Earlier, when Swift had hoped finally to publish his "HISTORY OF THE FOUR LAST YEARS OF THE QUEEN," Harley and another friend, Erasmus LEWIS, made a strong argument against publishing until the work could be vetted. Though Swift protested, insisting he had only the best intentions regarding the young lord's father, the work was not published until years after the dean's death. In 1737 Swift told Pope that he never corresponded with the Harleys any longer since "we have nothing to say to each other."

**Harley, Robert, first earl of Oxford** (1661–1724) Statesman and consummate politician, who eventually became chancellor of the exchequer and then lord treasurer (1710–14). He was born in London and became a lawyer and a WHIG M.P. in 1689. In 1701 he was elected Speaker of the Commons, and in 1704 became secretary of state. Shortly after, he became sympathetic to TORY principles, and from 1708 when he was forced to resign as secretary, worked to undermine the power of the Whigs. In 1710 with the dismissal of Sidney GODOLPHIN, Harley formed the Tory ministry, whose principal aim was to end the War of the Spanish Succession. First, as chancellor of the exchequer (head of government before the title *prime minister* came into vogue) and in 1711 earl of Oxford and lord high treasurer, Harley employed Daniel DEFOE (in the *Monthly Review*) and Swift (in the *EXAMINER*) in an effort to hold sway over a contentious Parliament and a weak monarch whose opinions were often shaped by the powerful figures in her immediate circle.

Swift met Harley on October 4, 1710 (see *THE JOURNAL TO STELLA*), and for the next four years Swift wrote pamphlets for the ministry and tried valiantly to maintain an effective working relationship between Harley and BOLINGBROKE. Harley's shrewdness in selecting Swift was aided by the cleric's work in securing relief from the First Fruits and Twentieth Parts (taxes levied against clergymen in Ireland). Needing an effective editor and political manager for the *Examiner*, Harley noted Swift's talent, his ambition, and his excitement at being led into the secret counsels of English government. With the failed assassination attempt on Harley, critics mark this event as the beginning of the end of the ministry. Bolingbroke, a young and superbly talented politician, became more jealous, suspicious, and estranged from Harley. Swift worked to mend the rift to no effect and finally retreated into the English countryside to await the inevitable dissolution of the ministry. Soon after the signing of the Treaty of Utrecht (1713), the

Robert Harley, earl of Oxford; engraving by J. van Huchtenburg, based on a portrait by Sir Godfrey Kneller

principal act of his administration, Harley, now earl of Oxford, was dismissed in August 1714, subsequently impeached by vengeful Whig managers, and imprisoned in the Tower of London on a charge of high treason for two years during the Hanoverian succession. Released from prison, he retired to his estate at Brampton Castle in Herefordshire, since the Whigs could not proceed with the indictment and acquitted him of all charges.

As a member of the Scriblerus Club and friend of Pope, Arbuthnot, Gay, Parnell, and especially Swift, Harley would join them occasionally. Pope in 1721 published his "Epistle to the Right Honourable, Robert, Earl of Oxford, and Earl Mortimer," celebrating those golden years when a statesman loved and valued poets. Pope included Swift and Parnell in his praise, as well as recalling Harley's faults, errors which brought down the ministry before its time. Swift refers to Harley in numerous prose works, including (among others) "The Conduct of the Allies," "Advice Humbly Offer'd to the Members of the October Club," "The History of the Four Last Years of the Queen," "An Enquiry into the Behaviour of the Queen's Last Ministry," and the "Importance of the Guardian Considered." Swift's *Correspondence* contains numerous letters between Swift and Harley and traces their complex relationship. Poems by Swift that contain references to Harley and his ministry include "A Description of a City Shower," "The First Ode of the Second Book of Horace Paraphrased and Addressed to Richard Steele, Esq.," "Scriblerian Verses," "The Faggot," "Verses on the Death of Dr. Swift, D.S.P.D.," "The Windsor Prophecy," "A Panegyric on the Reverend Dean Swift," "Atlas," "Horace, Lib. 2, Sat. 6," "To Mr. Harley's Surgeon," "Horace, Epistle VII, Book I: Imitated and Addressed to the Earl of Oxford," "The Author upon Himself," "To the Earl of Oxford, Late Lord Treasurer," and "To Lord Harley, Since Earl of Oxford, on His Marriage."

**Harley, Thomas** (d. 1738) Cousin of Robert Harley; M.P. and secretary to the treasury. The ministry sent Harley to The Hague and Utrecht to consult with the plenipotentiaries on peace negotiations. Later, sent to Hanover, Harley provided the future king all assurances "for settling the succession in him and his family." Swift and he were good friends, and his diplomatic efforts are mentioned in "An Enquiry into the Behaviour of the Queen's Last Ministry" and the "The History of the Four Last Years of the Queen." Harley also appears in the *Tatler* (number 230) as Tom, a figure who "begins to gi'mself airs, because he's going with the Plenipo's."

**Harris, Frances** A servant to Lady Betty Berkeley. Harris inspired Swift in 1701 to write a poem in doggerel couplets entitled "Mrs. Harris's Petition." The story of a woman who has lost her savings and her potential husband at the same time and requests the assistance of the lord justices had significance for Swift, as he considered his own now forgotten matrimonial offer to Varina (Jane Waring) and his new interest in Esther Johnson (Stella).

**Harrison, Rev. Theophilus** (d. 1714) First husband of Mrs. Martha Whiteway, née Swift, and the dean's cousin. Harrison's mother had been the last wife of Swift's eldest uncle, Godwin Swift. The widowed Martha and her two children of this marriage were substitutes for the family he never had.

**Harrison, Theophilus, Jr.** (c. 1713–1736) Martha Whiteway's eldest son who died unexpectedly of typhus. Swift was especially kind to the grieving mother, whose son had become the dean's friend and companion. He arranged for an obituary to be published in the *Dublin Journal.*

**Harrison, William** (1685–1713) Poet, friend, and protégé of Swift who helped Richard Steele to continue the *Tatler* through one volume (52 numbers) in 1711 (although Swift actually sponsored it after giving it up himself). He had some success in the diplomatic corps, thanks to Swift's efforts, but this soon faded and he seemed left without any viable options. Earlier, Swift was intent on making Harrison's fortune, but no interference from Joseph Addison, Henry Bolingbroke, and Thomas Tickell could improve his status.

**Hartstonge, John** (1654–1717) Bishop of Ossory (1693) and Derry (1714). Swift's London commission to negotiate the return the First Fruits to the Irish clergy should have had the support of two powerful bishops of the Irish church who were in England at the same time. Instead, Swift found that both Hartstonge and Thomas LINDSAY had left town. Later, Swift complained in "Memoirs, Relating to That Change Which Happened in the Year 1710" that though he succeeded in his efforts he neither received a stipend, like Hartstonge, nor thanks. In *The JOURNAL TO STELLA*, he agrees with her that Hartstonge "is the silliest, best-natured wretch breathing, of as little consequence as an egg shell."

**Hawkshaw, Dr. John** (d. 1744)   An Irishman who graduated from Trinity College, Dublin, as well as took two law degrees, and often handled various business affairs for Esther JOHNSON and Swift. Mentioned frequently in *The JOURNAL TO STELLA*, Hawkshaw was responsible for insuring Swift's funds were properly dispensed while the dean was in London.

**Helsham, Dr. Richard** (c. 1683–1738)   Swift's physician, companion, and executor of his will. Helsham was senior Fellow of Trinity College, Dublin, where he was also professor of medicine and moral philosophy (1714–27). He and Swift shared a love of books, especially collecting fine editions. Thomas SHERIDAN and Patrick DELANY introduced Helsham to Swift, though the dean "had never shown deep respect for Helsham," referring to him as "Dr. Arrogance" (Ehrenpreis, *Swift* III.620). See "TO THOMAS SHERIDAN," "TO DR. HELSHAM," and "A LETTER FROM DEAN SWIFT TO DEAN SMEDLEY."

**Henley, Anthony** (c. 1666–1711)   Affluent WHIG writer, wit, and M.P. On friendly terms with Swift, Henley had known the MOOR PARK circle and had excellent contacts in political and literary circles in London. He contributed to the *Tatler* and the *Medley*, and helped William HARRISON with his continuation of the *Tatler*. Swift enjoyed his company but finally found him provoking and refused to have further dinners with him. See *JOURNAL TO STELLA*.

**Henley, John** (1692–1756)   Eccentric clergyman and propagandist, known as "Orator Henley." Walpole employed him to write a newspaper called *The Hyp-Doctor* (1730–41). Henley attacked Alexander POPE from his Oratory Chapel and in the paper, and criticized Swift along with anyone else the government did not like. Pope lampoons him in *The Dunciad*, and Swift condemns him in "VERSES ON THE DEATH OF DR. SWIFT, D.S.P.D."

**Hervey, Rev. John, baronet of Ickworth** (1696–1743)   WHIG intimate of the royal family, especially Queen CAROLINE. As an M.P. under Robert Walpole, he became vice chamberlain in 1729 and lord privy seal in 1737. His friendship with Lady Mary Wortley MONTAGU further encouraged an ongoing literary skirmish with Alexander POPE. Swift satirizes Hervey in *A Modest Defence of Punning* and *COMPLETE COLLECTION OF GENTEEL AND INGENIOUS CONVERSATION*.

**Higgins, Rev. Francis** (1669–1728)   Archdeacon of Cashel and provocative preacher; also a classmate of Swift's at Trinity College, Dublin. He eventually became prebendary of Christ Church, Dublin. Often in trouble with the authorities due to his violent speeches, he was arrested and charged with sedition or serving as "a common disturber of her Majesty's peace." Swift, who questioned his sincerity and decided the noise was about gaining preferment, frequently mentions him in *The JOURNAL TO STELLA*.

**Hill, Abigail**   See MASHAM, ABIGAIL.

**Hill, Alice** (1685–1762)   Unmarried younger sister of Abigail, Baroness Masham (née Hill), and General John Hill. She served the royal family for many years, first in Princess Anne's son's household and then as woman of the bedchamber to Queen ANNE (1707–14). Mrs. Hill and Swift frequently dined, rode, and played cards together during his London years. Swift teases Stella (Esther JOHNSON) that he has romantic interests in Mrs. Hill. See also *The JOURNAL TO STELLA*.

**Hill, Major General John** (d. 1735)   Soldier, M.P., privy councillor, member of The Society, and brother of Alice HILL and Abigail, Baroness MASHAM (née Hill). A family connection to the MARLBOROUGHs ensured his rise at court and in the army. Urged on by Henry BOLINGBROKE, who had split with Robert HARLEY, General Hill took command of an expedition against the French at Quebec, resulting in failure (1711), but he was soon named commander of British forces at DUNKIRK and governor there. Swift celebrated his friend's accomplishments in "A HUE AND CRY AFTER DISMAL," "PEACE AND DUNKIRK," and "The CONDUCT OF THE ALLIES."

**Hoadly, Benjamin, bishop of Bangor** (1676–1761)   Churchman whose famous Erastian sermon in 1717 set off a violent eruption of WHIG party spirit, known as the Bangorian controversy. Swift found Hoadly, even in 1710, "a great deal of ill company." Hoadly's attacks on the Tory churchmen, Francis ATTERBURY and Henry SACHEVERELL, made him a Whig hero, with bishoprics in Bangor, Hereford, Salisbury, and Winchester. See "A LEFT-HANDED LETTER TO DR. SHERIDAN" and "The Public Spirit of the Whigs."

**Hoadly, John, archbishop of Dublin** (1678–1746) Churchman who became successively bishop of Leighlin and Ferns, archbishop of Dublin (1730), and archbishop of Armagh and primate of Ireland; younger brother of Benjamin HOADLY. Swift initially had strong reservations against Hoadly: "our gardens join, but I never see him except on business." Eventually, however, the two managed to maintain an amicable professional relationship, although Hoadly's charge reflected the English interest.

**Hobbes, Thomas** (1588–1679)   Influential philosopher and political scientist. In Swift's "BATTLE OF THE BOOKS," he commands the Moderns' archers. Hobbes's best-known work is *Leviathan* (1651), his study of human nature and the dynamics governing the relationship between the individual and society. In opposition to Aristotle's view of humans as social beings who voluntarily act upon a sense of obligation to their community, Hobbes argues that humans are ultimately selfish and driven to a state of constant conflict by two primary impulses: fear and the desire for power. As Swift puts it in "ON POETRY: A RHAPSODY," "Hobbes clearly proves that every creature / Lives in a state of war by nature" (335–336). Hobbes had argued that in order to escape the conflict naturally caused by these impulses, individuals voluntarily give up some of their freedoms and submit themselves to certain "Laws of Nature." These laws are that (1) all members of a society should seek peace, (2) individuals should exercise only those freedoms that they would also extend to others, and (3) all people should honor the covenants they make. Hobbes proposes that enforcing these laws requires external sovereignty, sustainable only when individuals agree to "confer all their power and strength upon one man, or upon an assembly of men." In his view, an individual ruler with absolute power (rather than a governing body) is necessary to maintain order in any human society by protecting its members from one another and from themselves.

Thomas Hobbes *(Courtesy of New York Public Library)*

A number of years ago, one critic summed up Swift's reaction to Hobbes this way: Swift "was a basically philanthropic man convinced against his will that Hobbes's *Leviathan* is truer to human nature than the Sermon on the Mount. As a result, he often intellectually accepted what he instinctively and emotionally disliked" (quoted in Ehrenpreis I.244). There are a number of generally unfavorable allusions to Hobbes and his ideas throughout Swift's works, only several of which can be outlined here. In "SENTIMENTS OF A CHURCH OF ENGLAND MAN," Swift endorses Aristotle's view that the abuse of government occurs whenever power is seized by "any one Person, or Body of Men, who do not represent the Whole," adding that "arbitrary Power" is always harmful, "despite all that Hobbes . . . and others have said to its Advantage." Many scholars have discussed the ways *Leviathan* figures satirically in "A TALE OF A TUB." In the preface, for example, the Hack presents his "Tale" as a diversion—as a Swiss reviewer put it in 1721—to amuse "the Hobbeists, to give them something to do which distracts them from attacking civil society" (Williams, *Critical Heritage* 59). Critics have more recently described how imagery and parodies throughout the "Tale" wryly echo Hobbes's materialism, and particularly his view of ideals as worthless superstitions.

Swift also makes fun of Hobbes's mechanistic philosophy in "DISCOURSE CONCERNING THE MECHANICAL OPERATION OF THE SPIRIT" by describing the human brain as a "Crowd of little Animals but with Teeth and Claws extremely sharp," who "cling together . . . like the Picture of *Hobbes's Leviathan*." Irvin Ehrenpreis explains that "the whole web of the *Mechanical Operation* seems involved with Hobbes's materialistic doctrines concerning 'Christian politics,' spirit and inspiration, and prophets" (I.243). In "The Public Spirit of the Whigs," Swift refutes Hobbes's claim that "the Youth of *England* was corrupted in their political Principles, by reading the Histories of *Rome* and *Greece,* which having been writ under Republicks, taught the Readers to have ill notions of Monarchy." As a staunch supporter of the ancients, Swift not surprisingly concludes that "In this Assertion there was something specious." Finally, in "Remarks upon a Book, Intitled, The Rights of the Christian Church," Swift lists Hobbes among the "Enemies of Christianity."

**Hogarth, William** (1697–1764) Painter and engraver. Apprenticed as a silversmith but achieved independence by making engravings of his satiric paintings, one of which complemented Alexander POPE's and Swift's poetry. Though Hogarth and Swift probably never met, the dean mentions him in "A CHARACTER, PANEGYRIC, AND DESCRIPTION OF THE LEGION CLUB."

**Holdernesse, Lady Frederica Schomberg, countess of** (d. 1751) Granddaughter of Fredrick Herman, created duke of Schomberg in 1689, who served William of Orange (WILLIAM III) as commander in chief in Ireland during the Ulster campaign and died at the Battle of the Boyne. Swift asked the countess to erect a monument in St. Patrick's Cathedral, where he was buried. She refused by ignoring Swift's letters, and finally he had a black marble slab ordered, on which he placed an inscription proclaiming the virtues of strangers over one's relations. See also *The JOURNAL TO STELLA.*

**Holt, Sir John** (1642–1710) Lord chief justice of Ireland. In letter 6 of *The DRAPIER'S LETTERS,* Swift mentions Holt's penchant for interpreting words by relying on their most favorable definition, particularly when the words affected the progress of criminal cases.

**Hopkins, Edward** (c. 1675–1736) WHIG M.P., chief secretary to the duke of GRAFTON (1721–24), commissioner of revenue (1716–22), master of the revels (1722), and privy councillor. Swift refers to him in *The DRAPIER'S LETTERS* (Letter 4) as an example of an Englishman who has achieved preferment and an income solely from his contact with powerful men. Swift implicates him in the WOOD's coinage controversy since he ignored Archbishop KING's warnings and the dean's requests for help on another matter. He also accuses him of considerable acts of "credit and extortion" at the Smock Alley playhouse, Dublin. See also "BILLET TO THE COMPANY OF PLAYERS."

**Hort, Josiah, archbishop of Tuam** (c. 1674–1751)  English churchman who became successively bishop of Ferns, of Kilmore and Ardagh, and archbishop of Tuam (1742–51). Swift had disliked him immediately—"that rascal . . . a wretch"—and found him to be the perfect example of the nonresident clergyman who becomes one of the most self-seeking of the Irish bishops. Irvin Ehrenpreis argues that Swift bitterly attacks Hort in "The STORM" and "ADVICE TO A PARSON" (*Swift* III.171–72, 720). See also "JUDAS."

**Howard, Henrietta (née Hobart), countess of Suffolk** (1681–1767)  Wife of Charles, ninth earl of Howard, (1706); mistress of GEORGE II; bedchamber woman to Princess CAROLINE; became countess (1731). After retiring from Court, she married again and lived at Marble Hill close to Alexander POPE and often saw the other Scriblerians. She was a friend and frequent correspondent of Swift, who first met her in 1726 and decided she was characterized by "justice, generosity and truth." However, when she offered to find Swift preferment and not only failed at Court with him but also with other friends, he became angry and found "her good for nothing but to be a rank courtier." See "CHARACTER OF MRS. HOWARD," "A PASTORAL DIALOGUE BETWEEN RICHMOND LODGE AND MARBLE HILL," and "VERSES ON THE DEATH OF DR. SWIFT, D.S.P.D."

**Howard, Robert, bishop of Elphin** (1683–1740)  Churchman who became successively prebendary of Maynooth, St. Patrick's; vicar of St. Anne's, Dublin; chancellor of St. Patrick's; bishop of Killala; and bishop of Elphin (1729). Swift had a highly favorable opinion of Howard, but the latter's ambition and WHIG tendencies ultimately alienated the dean. Howard had gained the friendship of Archbishop KING, and Swift found it necessary to acknowledge Howard's growing political reliability, at least with the government. See "ON THE IRISH BISHOPS" and "ADVICE TO A PARSON."

**Howe, John Grubham (Jack How)** (1657–1722)  TORY politician whom Swift refers to in "A TALE OF A TUB" and as the model for Clodius in "DISCOURSE OF THE CONTESTS AND DISSENSIONS IN ATHENS AND ROME." His stridency first caused the WHIGS to eject him, and then the Tories who accepted him had to acknowledge Swift's criticism that Howe was acting like a "new Whig." Swift briefly makes fun of Howe in "A BALLAD ON THE GAME OF TRAFFIC."

**Howth, [Lady] Lucy St. Lawrence (née Gorges)** (b. 1711)  Wife of Lord William HOWTH and daughter of Lieutenant General Richard Gorges of Kilbrew, Ireland. Swift was a welcome visitor to Howth Castle, and in partial thanks for their hospitality he attempted to use his political and religious contacts in helping members of their family. She is mentioned in Swift's *Correspondence*.

**Howth, [Lord] William St. Lawrence** (1688–1748)  The descendant of a long line who had held Howth Castle near Dublin, he married Lucy Gorges in 1728. As his *Correspondence* indicates, Swift found the couple most entertaining, often dining with them, adopting them as a regular part of his Dublin community. Lord Howth engaged the painter Francis BINDON to paint Swift's portrait in 1735.

**Hunter, Robert** (d. 1734)  Scholarly friend of Richard STEELE and Joseph ADDISON who had distinguished himself at Blenheim and secured a promotion to lieutenant colonel of dragoons and later lieutenant governor of Virginia. During the voyage to the colonies, his ship was attacked by French privateers and Hunter was imprisoned in France (1707). Later, he was exchanged and received the governorship of New York and New Jersey in late 1709. He became governor of Jamaica in 1729. Hunter and Swift met as early as 1707, and exchanged a number of letters later. Hunter is mentioned in "The FIRST ODE OF THE SECOND BOOK OF HORACE . . . TO RICHARD STEELE, ESQ."

# J

**Jackson, Rev. Daniel** (b. 1686?) Clergyman, brother of Rev. John Jackson, to whom Swift gave an edition of Lucretius and who was named in Swift's will as the recipient of his "Horses and Mares" and "Horse Furniture." Daniel Jackson was a cousin to the GRATTANs, a friend of the ROCHFORTs, and a third-generation vicar at Santry (near Dublin). Swift and his friends regularly treated "Dan's long nose" as an object of humor ("GEORGE NIM-DAN-DEAN . . . TO MR. SHERIDAN"). See also "TO MR. DELANY," "SHERIDAN, A GOOSE," and "ON DAN JACKSON'S PICTURE."

**Jacobite(s)** See STUART, JAMES FRANCIS EDWARD.

**James II, king of England** (1633–1701) Second son of CHARLES I who became prominent as duke of York, winning a naval victory against the Dutch (1672). As King, he alienated his subjects with his ardent Catholicism and was compelled to flee (1689) and live in exile the rest of his life. Swift wrote "ODE TO THE KING," celebrating WILLIAM III's achievement at the Boyne and calling James his "enemy," noting "his scrap of life is but a heap of miseries." Later, in "SENTIMENTS OF A CHURCH OF ENGLAND MAN," he dismisses the dogmas of absolutism and divine right. See also STUART, JAMES.

**Jenney, Rev. Henry** (c. 1655–1742) Archbishop of Dromore (1690) and rector of Mullabrack, whom Swift had known since his year at Kilroot (1695). Part of a circle of Swift's Irish friends including Robert COPE, Jenney was a wealthy cler-

gyman in his mid-70s when he agreed to travel with Swift to visit the ACHESON family at MARKET HILL. Swift addresses him as "Dear friend, Dr. Jenney" in "MY LADY'S LAMENTATION AND COMPLAINT AGAINST THE DEAN," and as a dinner companion in "The GRAND QUESTION DEBATED."

**Jervas, Charles** (c. 1675–1739) An Irish-born portrait painter who lived in London, Paris, and Rome and studied with Kneller. He became friends with POPE, ADDISON, and STEELE. Jervas served as painting instructor and host to Pope during 1713 when the poet lived with him in London. In the *Tatler*, Steele had claimed Jervas "as the last great painter Italy has sent us." He became the king's painter to both GEORGE I and GEORGE II. His earliest portrait of Swift dates from 1709–10, but Swift seems to have avoided him later, either because of his WHIG politics or the demand on his time for more sittings. A number of copies of this portrait exist, as well as a purported Jervas portrait of Esther (Stella) JOHNSON. See "The GRAND QUESTION DEBATED."

**Johnson, Bridget (later Mose)** (d. 1743) House-keeper to Sir William TEMPLE at Moor Park and mother of Esther JOHNSON (Stella). Bridget was considered a higher-ranking employee of the Temple household and received an increased legacy in his will. She continued working for Lady GIFFARD, and when Swift broke off with Giffard, he still enjoyed excellent contacts with Stella's mother, whom he had first met in 1689. As a widow, Bridget finally married Ralph MOSE (Temple's steward) in 1711 and seems to have taken a motherly interest in Swift.

**Johnson, Esther ("Stella")** (1681–1728)   Swift's closest lifelong friend, and an intimate source of literary inspiration. She was the daughter of parents who were in the household service of Sir William TEMPLE at Moor Park, Surrey. In 1701, Swift advised Stella and her guardian, Rebecca DINGLEY, to settle in Ireland to ensure their small legacy from the now dead Temple. Though he loved her, Swift insisted on the intellectual and imaginative loneliness of living in that country. His disappointment at not receiving English preferment became a constant source of depression for him, though he was hardly paralyzed and made new literary, clerical, and government friends in Ireland, and initiated other friendships during his various trips to England.

Evidence of his invincible attachment to Esther Johnson comes in *The JOURNAL TO STELLA*, the collection of letters addressed to her and Rebecca that Swift wrote between September 1710 and June 1713. Swift secured a commission from the bishops of Ireland to travel to London and persuade the government and the queen to extend to the Irish clergy the same benefits their brothers in the English church enjoyed. Not only do his allusions to contemporary political and historical events, pamphlet literature, and the numerous contemporary figures add to the importance of this document, but also the insights into his personal and psychological character are revealed here, as well as the intimacy and humanity few people understood or would acknowledge.

When Stella was 38 years old, Swift began writing poems in celebration of her birthday, and as with all his work these poems reveal deeper intentions. He intended to criticize the elaborate birthday odes written for the Court (puncturing the false gallantry of the earlier poems of Waller, Cowley, and Butler), and to condemn the lust of Rochester's naturalistic verse. See "STELLA'S BIRTHDAY (1719)," "STELLA'S BIRTHDAY (1721)," "STELLA'S BIRTHDAY (1723): A GREAT BOTTLE OF WINE, LONG BURIED, BEING THAT DAY DUG UP," "STELLA'S BIRTHDAY (1725)," "STELLA'S BIRTHDAY (1727),"

Esther Johnson (Stella)   *(From The Journal to Stella, 1897)*

"TO STELLA ON HER BIRTHDAY," and "TO STELLA, WRITTEN ON THE DAY OF HER BIRTH." He also composed "STELLA AT WOODPARK," "TO STELLA, VISITING ME IN MY SICKNESS," "A RECEIPT TO RESTORE STELLA'S YOUTH," and "TO STELLA, WHO COLLECTED AND TRANSCRIBED HIS POEMS."

On the subject of a marriage between Stella and Swift, many critics now believe that the two were married in Dublin in 1716, though the couple lived separately and the marriage was kept secret. This lively, intelligent woman, whose social skills were evident in Dublin, was often sick and weak. Her long illness and death caused Swift much suffering. His analysis and celebration of her character in "ON THE DEATH OF MRS. JOHNSON" exhibits deep feeling, sincerity, and love.

**Johnson, Samuel** (1709–1784)   Preeminent English literary figure of the late 18th century. His works include a remarkable *Dictionary*, a travel book, an edition of Shakespeare, two series of essays, moral/philosophical fiction, and a striking collection of short biographies.

Born the son of a bookseller in Lichfield, England, Johnson attended Oxford but left (for financial reasons) without a degree. He began teaching, and soon settled in London. Working as a journalist, Johnson started his famous *Dictionary* in 1747 and published it in 1755. On the strength of his writing for the *Rambler*, a periodical, and his prose tale, *Rasselas* (1759), Johnson secured a royal pension and became a central voice for letters and aesthetic issues, particularly in the Literary Club (known later simply as "The Club"), which he helped found in 1764. During this early period (in 1738), Alexander POPE—who had not met the talented Johnson but had read his work—urged John, Lord Gower, to write to a Dublin friend who might solicit Swift's aid in securing an M.A. degree for the young Johnson. Nothing resulted from this effort, and Swift may never have seen the letter.

Johnson first mentions Swift in an early letter to his friend Hester Thrale, in which he tells her that their relationship reminds him of Swift's and Stella's in *The* JOURNAL TO STELLA. He refers to the "CONDUCT OF THE ALLIES," *The* DRAPIER'S LETTERS, GULLIVER'S TRAVELS, "A Proposal for Correcting . . . the English Tongue," "SENTIMENTS OF A CHURCH OF ENGLAND MAN," and "A TALE OF A TUB" in his letters, conversation, and published work. Certainly Johnson had read Swift's work thoroughly, relying on John Hawkesworth's 1755 edition, prefaced by his "Life of Swift"—an essay that Johnson depended upon when preparing his short biography of Swift for the *Lives of the English Poets* (1779–81). Though he admired the breadth of Swift's work and accepted the older man as a genius, Johnson nurtured a thoroughgoing antipathy for him, arising from what he believed was Swift's lack of self-esteem and confidence. He said that Swift "was not a man to be either loved or envied [and] he seems to have wasted life in discontent."

Like Swift, Johnson possessed the fully developed talents of an accomplished satirist, and both men had determined that the great evils in humanity were rampant egotism and vanity. Yet, as Jackson Bate has pointed out, Johnson harbored a "hatred and fear" of satire, "which is what led him to be so antagonistic and unfair to Swift" (493). Johnson's hostility so severely colored his "Life of Swift" that even James Boswell (Johnson's most famous biographer) could not ignore the unfairness of his analysis and the "unaccountable prejudice against Swift" that it reflected (Williams, *Critical Heritage* 204). Today, many critics see past Johnson's overt bias to his perceptive comments on Swift's complicated stance toward religion and hypocrisy, political independence and service, and morality versus pleasure.

**Jones, Elizabeth (Betty)**    The daughter of Rev. John Jones, vicar of Wanlip, Leicestershire, and a cousin of Swift's mother, Abigail SWIFT. Swift met her during 1689 in Leicester while visiting his mother, just before leaving to join William TEMPLE's household. He soon became involved with Betty, and his "prudent" mother encouraged him to end his visit.

# K

**Kelly, Rev. George** (b. 1688) An Irishman who graduated from Trinity College, Dublin, who refused to take the oaths of allegiance to William III and would not accept the legitimacy of the Revolution of 1688. He joined the JACOBITE cause as a secretary and courier between Bishop ATTERBURY and the Old Pretender, JAMES II. He was finally arrested in 1722 in London, along with his brother, and sentenced to the Tower indefinitely. He later escaped to Paris, joined the group supporting Prince Charles, participated in the 1745 Jacobite revolt, and avoided capture. Swift grudgingly respected him. See "UPON THE HORRID PLOT DISCOVERED BY HARLEQUIN THE BISHOP OF ROCHESTER'S FRENCH DOG."

**Kendal, Ermengarde Melusina, née countess von der Schulenburg, duchess of** (1667–1743) Influential mistress of GEORGE I who became involved with William WOOD (after receiving a hefty bribe) in providing him a patent to manufacture copper coins for Ireland. Both SUNDERLAND and WALPOLE hoped for King George's support, and in helping the duchess secure a patent they thought to advance themselves. Swift added this outrage to a list of other greedy acts on the part of the English government and launched *The DRAPIER'S LETTERS*. In Part 1 of *GULLIVER'S TRAVELS*, Kendal becomes "one of the King's Cushions" breaking the fall of Flimnap, who represents Walpole. See also "A Wicked Treasonable Lie," "WOOD, AN INSECT," "A Simile on Our Want of Silver," "A SERIOUS POEM UPON WILLIAM WOOD," and "PROMETHEUS."

**Kendall, Rev. John** (1684–1717) Vicar of Thornton, Leicestershire, who married Swift's first cousin, Jane Ericke. The Thornton cure was part of Swift's maternal grandfather Rev. James Errick's parish. Swift also refers to Kendall as his cousin, and "a good [WHIG] himself." In the first surviving letter of the Swift correspondence, he explains to Kendall some of his attitudes toward women and marriage.

**Kendrick, Roger** Verger (in charge of the interior of a church) of St. Patrick's Cathedral, master of the charity school, and amanuensis for Swift. He served as a witness to a codicil to Swift's will. His manuscript copy, written in his own hand, of "The HISTORY OF THE FOUR LAST YEARS OF THE QUEEN," marked and corrected by Swift, served as the source for George FAULKNER's Dublin edition of this work (1758).

**Kennett, White, bishop of Peterborough** (1660–1728) WHIG clergyman and anti-Jacobite who wrote a well-known polemical tract criticizing Bishop ATTERBURY's views on convocation in the Anglican Church. Kennett believed in the philosophy of "the wisdom of looking backwards" as a historian and scholar. He despised Swift and wrote a malicious, often reprinted "Picture of Swift" while the dean was in attendance at Windsor Castle in 1713. Swift "was the principal man of talk and business, and acted as a master of requests. . . . [H]e turned to the fire and took out his gold watch . . . and complained it was very late. A gentleman said 'he was too fast'. 'How can I help it', says the doctor, 'if the courtiers give me a watch that won't go right?' " (*Corr.* V.228–29).

**Kent, Henry de Grey, first duke of**  (1671–1740) A WHIG who held various offices in the GODOL-PHIN ministry but was dismissed as Lord Chamberlain when Queen ANNE was persuaded to change governments. He was created duke of Kent in 1710, and on the queen's death he was named lord justice of England. Swift mentions in his *Marginalia* to MACKY's *Characters of the Court of Britain* (1733) that "he seems a good natured man but of very little consequence" (*Prose Works* V.259). Glendinning reports on Kent's curious nickname, explaining that he was "known as the Bug because he stank" (93).

**Kerry, Lady Anne Fitzmaurice (née Petty)**  (d. 1737)  Daughter of Sir William Petty and sister of Lord Shelburne. In 1693 she married Thomas Fitzmaurice, who became baron of Kerry and Lixnaw in 1697 and was created earl of Kerry on January 17, 1723. Her father was a highly intelligent and respected Oxford professor of anatomy and later physician-general to the Parliamentary army in Ireland and founder of the Dublin Philosophical Society. Irvin Ehrenpreis calls him one of the most extraordinary Englishmen of the 17th century (*Swift* I.81). Swift believed Anne had inherited much of her father's ability, and found her company entertaining and stimulating. His desire for Lady Kerry to meet Esther JOHNSON and Rebecca DINGLEY suggests the quality of their relationship: "we have struck up a mighty friendship; and she has much better sense than any other lady of your country. We are almost in love with one another: but she is "most egregiously ugly; but perfectly well bred" (*The* JOURNAL TO STELLA, May 4, 1711). With her, her family, and servants, Swift traveled about London. He suffered from the same dizzy spells as she, and they relied on similar kinds of medicine—a commonality that added to their connection. Kerry would later ask Swift (in a letter dated September 20, 1715) to commend her younger son to Westminster School (*Corr.* II.187–88), as he had earlier done for her eldest son

on his entrance into Christ Church, Oxford, where he matriculated on March, 1713.

**King, Rev. James**  (c. 1699–1759)  Vicar of St. Bride's, Dublin, and prebendary of Tipper in St. Patrick's Cathedral, Dublin (1731–59); Fellow of Trinity College, Dublin (1720–35). Along with a number of other clergymen and Dubliners, King became a friend and companion of Swift's during his last decade. In "TO CHARLES FORD, ESQ. ON HIS BIRTHDAY," the dean mentions "Jim," who cannot be equaled in Dublin or London for his friendship (though Pat Rogers suggests the reference is to James STOPFORD, Harold Williams disagrees).

In his will, Swift left King (an executor) his "large gilded medal of King Charles I and on the reverse a Crown of Martyrdom, with other devices," and in the codicil to his will an annuity or yearly rent charge of 20 pounds sterling, per annum. King also agrees to serve as witness to the document, which creates the position of subdean, naming John Wynne precentor of the cathedral, when Swift declares his "infirmities of age and ill-health" have prevented him from maintaining "the good order and government of my Cathedral Church . . . in person" (*Exhortation to the Chapter of St. Patrick's, Dublin*).

**King, Peter, first baron**  (1669–1734)  Lawyer and politician who was born into the merchant class, yet was called to the bar in 1698. He was elected to Parliament in 1701, becoming a trustworthy WHIG, then appointed recorder of London and knighted in 1708. He joined with LECHMERE in helping to manage the prosecution of SACHEVERELL in 1710. Later, as chief justice of the Common Pleas, he appears in Swift's "Public Spirit of the Whigs" as one of the Whigs condemned for arrogance, false logic, and in general depriving Englishmen of their liberty (1714). Created Baron King of Ockham in 1725, and later in the same year, he became lord chancellor. As chancellor, King, who was Sir Robert WALPOLE's close friend, served as his adviser on questions of constitutional law. When Swift and his friendly enemy, William KING, archbishop of Dublin, agreed the latter should seek the posts of lord justice and the primacy in 1723,

Archbishop King was putting the Irish case before Lord Justice King. William King was not offered the post, though Justice King apparently supported his friend's application. Swift, who disliked the chancellor, apparently never met him, though he is mentioned in "The FAGGOT."

**King, William** (1685–1763) Principal of St. Mary Hall, Oxford. King devoted himself to scholarship and the JACOBITE cause, and the latter compulsion led some critics to believe he was the spokesman for English Jacobitism during the period of the uprisings in 1715 and 1745. Swift did not approve of the cause. Many of his friends and acquaintances were sympathizers, but for the most part he left them to what he viewed as their own madness. King's interest in satire, dislike of the present government, and admiration for Swift led to a correspondence and later meeting in 1734. A protracted Dublin lawsuit in which King had offered to help his uncle, Sir Thomas Smyth, whose finances were threatened, led to a number of visits to Ireland beginning in the late 1720s. During this period, King wrote an early draft of his verse satire, "The Toast, An Epic Poem" (1732), attacking his family's enemies, while avoiding a charge of libel by appending his accusations in Latin as notes to the text. Swift's encouragement caused King to expand the work to four volumes inscribed to the dean (1736).

Apparently, Swift suggested King might cooperate in arranging the publication of "The HISTORY OF THE FOUR LAST YEARS OF THE QUEEN," and with this agreement Lord ORRERY delivered the manuscript to King in England. The less than enthusiastic response to the news of its publication, especially from Robert HARLEY, convinced King that Swift should make extensive revisions, otherwise all those involved would face legal difficulties. Swift withdrew the manuscript, but later entrusted the manuscript of the ironic poem on his own death, "VERSES ON THE DEATH OF DR. SWIFT, D.S.P.D." to King for publication in England. On the advice of POPE and ORRERY, King made complicated revisions so as to represent Swift more appreciatively to both current readers and posterity. Swift did not appreciate these "improvements" in the London version, and another edition of the complete poem

was printed in Dublin in 1739. King, who felt justifiably nervous at his role in revising the poem, could only express his "love and honor" for Swift and an ongoing fear that his superiors may suspect his involvement in treasonable behavior.

**King, William, archbishop of Dublin** (1650–1729) Churchman and theologian who was educated at Trinity College and ordained a priest in 1674. Promotions came quickly for King, from the provost position at Tuam cathedral to the chancellorship of St. Patrick's Cathedral in 1679. His work in preventing the spread of Roman Catholicism came to the attention of his superiors, who respected his energy and intelligence and especially his pamphlets arguing various Church of Ireland issues. Elected as dean of St. Patrick's in 1689, King took his Doctor of Divinity degree in the same year. The government had him arrested for his support of William of Orange (WILLIAM III) and other anti-Jacobite efforts, but William's victory at the Boyne ended his sufferings. After a number of well-publicized sermons congratulating William, King was promoted to bishop of Derry in 1691 and archbishop of Dublin in 1703, succeeding Narcissus MARSH.

During the period after 1700, Swift (then prebendary of St. Patrick's) was closely associated with King as both men drew upon their common concern for Ireland, though their relationship always remained in delicate balance. "The STORY OF THE INJURED LADY" describes the unhappy condition of Ireland, especially after the Union of England and Scotland—this allegory is a result of their association. King sent Swift to London as his agent to solicit remission of the First Fruits and Twentieth Parts, and Swift's success drew them closer. Though English politics and WHIG principles remained King's constant focus, and alienated Swift at various points, King suffered for his support of Irish interests, losing the senior archbishopric of Armagh in 1723. Louis Landa explains that the "era of better feeling between Archbishop King and Swift set in after the controversy over WOOD's coinage in 1724" (*Swift and the Church of Ireland* 92). Reaction against further English government policy infringing on the opportunities of Irish-born clergy united both men in the archbishop's last years. See also

"Letter to the Archbishop of Dublin, Concerning the Weavers," *The Drapier's Letters*, "History of the Four Last Years of the Queen," "Proposal for the Universal Use of Irish Manufacture," "Letter from a Member of the House of Commons in Ireland," "Part of the Ninth Ode of the Fourth Book of Horace," "Epilogue to a Play for the Benefit of the Weavers in Ireland," "To His Grace the Archbishop of Dublin," and "On Wisdom's Defeat in a Learned Debate."

**Kingsmill, Anne**    See Finch, Anne.

# L

**Lambert, Ralph, bishop of Meath** (c. 1666–1732)   Contemporary of Swift's at Trinity College, and later in London. Thomas WHARTON, a capable (if corrupt) WHIG, became lord lieutenant of Ireland (1708) and quickly chose Lambert as his chaplain, a post Bishop KING had urged Swift to seek. Rev. Lambert was expected to join in Wharton's mission of repealing the Test Act in Ireland; his sermon in favor of closer unity with the Nonconformists against Catholics annoyed Swift and proved another example of England's effort to weaken the Church of Ireland. Swift felt strongly that occasional conformity was a great danger to the Established Church. Writing his "LETTER FROM A MEMBER OF THE HOUSE OF COMMONS IN IRELAND," Swift attacked Lambert's arguments pointing out the differences between Irish political alignments and those in England. Lambert's opposition to "inferior" Irish clergy in the bitter convocation disputes of 1709 also upset Swift. Soon after Wharton nominated Lambert to fill the vacancy of the deanery of Down (1710), King had written again to Swift "if you could either get into it, or get a good man with a comfortable benefice removed to it, it might make present provision for you." Lambert's rapid promotion followed, with the bishoprics of Dromore (1717) and Meath (1727).

**Land, Henry** (d. 1757)   Sexton of St. Patrick's Cathedral, Dublin. Land lived in a house leased by Swift in Deanery-Lane alias Mitre-Alley. In his will, Swift leaves this lease and others to Martha WHITEWAY. After Swift's death, Land married the widowed Mrs. RIDGEWAY, and kept his office in the cathedral until his death.

**Lanesborough, Humphry Butler, second viscount**   See BUTLER, HUMPHRY.

**La Rochefoucauld, François, duc de** (1613–1680)   French classical writer and moralist. His *Maxims* (1665) reflect the wave of pessimism at that time and his belief that self-interest is at the root of all human behavior. Swift admired these aphorisms and brought together his own in "Thoughts on Various Subjects" with additions in the *Miscellanies* (1727) and the *Works* (1735). They cover a wide range of subjects with wit and elegance, and none of the distraction of irony. In the poem "VERSES ON THE DEATH OF DR. SWIFT, D.S.P.D." he states "as Roche Foucault his Maxims drew/From Nature, I believe'em true." See also "The LIFE AND GENUINE CHARACTER OF DR. SWIFT," which reflects this view: La Rochefoucauld "is my favorite because I found my whole character in him." "A TALE OF A TUB" also draws on La Rochefoucauld's interest in such themes as time, posterity, and the innocence of the present age. Though Swift found him and other French moralists instructive, one finally sees very few parallels to Swift's ideas.

**Lechmere, Nicholas, first baron** (1675–1732)   WHIG lawyer and statesman, member of the bar (1698), M.P. from 1708; queen's counsel, attorney general (1718–20); created baron (1721). Sarah, duchess of MARLBOROUGH, called him "the worst man that ever I knew in my life." He and James STANHOPE, Peter KING, and Thomas Parker were the leading managers for the prosecution of Rev. SACHEVERELL (1710). Swift respected his intelligence but detested his politics, and in "A FABLE OF THE WIDOW AND HER CAT," Lechmere becomes a champion of the freethinkers and deists. His skill as an orator provoked many Tories into an intense dislike of him, though Swift calls him simply worthless in "The FAGGOT." References in the prose show Lechmere as a well-known figure, but Swift's satiric tone diminishes his significance—see EXAMINER, number 25 (January 25, 1710).

**Lee, James (James Leigh)**    Irish landholder in Westmeath with residence at Walterstown, near Dundalk, and brother of Rev. Thomas Leigh, a minor canon of St. Patrick's, Dublin, both frequently mentioned in *The JOURNAL TO STELLA*. James was an absentee landlord who preferred living in London and maintained a friendly relationship with Stella (see Esther JOHNSON). Swift liked James, or Jemmy, as he was known, dining and playing cards with him and Leigh's frequent companion, Enoch Stearne, cousin of the dean and later clerk to the Irish House of Lords, when all three were in London (1711). In "A DIALOGUE IN THE CASTILIAN LANGUAGE," Swift humorously refers to Jemmy in this conversation piece as "Gemelli," an honest man that both speakers know.

**Leslie, Charles** (1650–1722)    Clergyman and journalist. Leslie was educated at Trinity College, Dublin, becoming an Anglican minister who later refused to swear allegiance to WILLIAM and Mary in 1689, his refusal marking him as a JACOBITE. His loyalty to JAMES II remained firm, and he soon began writing and publishing a series of pamphlets attacking the government and the court for numerous crimes and acts of corruption. His attacks on WHIG divines such as Gilbert BURNET and Tillotson became famous, as well as his treatises against the Quakers, Dissenters, and Jews, and mixed marriages between Catholics and Protestants, but Swift found Leslie's political views

impossible ("[He] is most unhappily misled in his politics but . . . I distinguish between the principles and the person."). Leslie had criticized Swift's "DISCOURSE OF THE CONTESTS AND DISSENSIONS IN ATHENS AND ROME" (1701), and once again Swift became convinced of his old acquaintance's lack of balance and moderation. Swift's censure surfaces in "SENTIMENTS OF A CHURCH-OF-ENGLAND MAN" and even in "A TALE OF A TUB," in which Leslie's pamphlets become "the vilest things in nature." Later, in the "Preface to the Bishop of Sarum's Introduction," Swift indicted Burnet for encouraging attacks on the TORY clergy, inspired in part by Leslie's words.

**Leslie, Henry**    Younger son of Charles LESLIE, the Irish JACOBITE, who had served in the Spanish army as a lieutenant colonel until losing his commission when a regulation against employing Protestants became law. He resided at MARKET HILL with his Spanish wife as both were friends of the ACHESONs. He and his brother Robert LESLIE became friends of Swift during his extended visit to the area. Swift wrote "ROBIN AND HARRY," one of the Market Hill group of poems during the middle of his second visit to the Achesons, on August 4, 1729. Harry is portrayed as a farmer of above average means, a loving husband, and a generous man who shows compassion for the less fortunate of his neighbors, while his brother exhibits many of the opposite characteristics.

**Leslie, Robert** (born c. 1680)    Eldest son of Charles LESLIE, who lived at Glaslough House, County Monaghan, Ireland (close to Armagh and MARKET HILL) and brother of Henry LESLIE. Robert, or Robin, had married a niece of Swift's friend Peter LUDLOW. Swift wrote "ROBIN AND HARRY" as a jest at the two brothers—complimenting one and insulting the other, hoping to elicit some reaction. Robin talks constantly—"from noon to night." In "TRAULUS, Part I," Swift relies on a dialogue between two characters, Robin and Tom. Robin is the sane man who patiently deals with the lunatic Tom. Leslie had once acted as an intermediary, offering an apology when Joshua ALLEN, as privy councillor, had publicly insulted Swift.

**L'Estrange, Sir Roger** (1616–1704) TORY journalist and pamphleteer. As an avid supporter of Charles I, he was arrested on a mission against the parliamentarians and sentenced to death but managed to escape from Newgate Prison. From the Continent and later in England, he wrote a series of pamphlets attacking various Puritan points of view, though Oliver Cromwell, whom he met, found no reason to prosecute him further. His efforts to support the restoration of the monarchy continued, as well as attacks on the liberty of the press, Dissenters, and the WHIGS in his own two newspapers, the *News* and the *INTELLIGENCER*. After the Revolution, he lost all favor at Court and supported himself mainly by a series of translations, including *The Fables of Aesop and other Eminent Mythologists* (1692).

Swift shows the influence of L'Estrange in "The BATTLE OF THE BOOKS," particularly in the fable of the spider and the bee, where his use of language and dialogue parallels the earlier writer's discussion of Aesop. The spider's love of dirt and other associated images makes him in this prose satire the analogue of the modern, and Swift condemns L'Estrange as one of the chief Moderns, the leader of "infinite swarms of calones [unbound pamphlets], a disorderly rout." Earlier, in "A TALE OF A TUB," L'Estrange becomes associated with "a pernicious kind of writing" and may be "a certain paultry scribbler." In his marginalia, Swift calls him "a superficial meddling coxcomb," since he represents everything Swift disliked in a writer who invented advertising and other money-making devices. See also "ON THE WORDS 'BROTHER PROTESTANTS AND FELLOW CHRISTIANS.' "

**Levinge, Sir Richard** (1656–1724) Attorney general for Ireland, later Speaker of the House of Commons, and then lord chief justice of the Common Pleas (1720–24). Levinge was born in England, where he became a lawyer in 1678 and an M.P. for Chester (1690–1702). As solicitor-general for Ireland, he began a distinguished career there. Swift knew him personally, dining with him in London in 1710, and working with him to develop impeachment materials against Earl WHARTON, who, as lord lieutenant of Ireland, had dismissed Levinge as solicitor-general, among other "barbarous injustices." Wharton represented a dangerous opponent to Swift, and a WHIG whose every action violated Swift's political principles. He denounced Wharton in the *EXAMINER*, number 17 (November 30, 1710), and again discredited him in "A SHORT CHARACTER OF HIS EX[CELLENCY] T[HOMAS] E[ARL] OF W[HARTON]." Levinge cannot be removed, Swift says in "A Continuation" (possibly by Levinge) of Wharton's "Short Character," "without the Queen's letter, it being outside [Wharton's] commission." In "The PROBLEM," Swift refers to Levinge's wife, Mary Corbyn, using a familiar name for the couple—"Levens." See also *The JOURNAL TO STELLA* for further insight into Levinge's role in these pamphlets.

**Lewis, Erasmus** (1670–1754) Welsh bureaucrat who served in diplomatic and other government posts and became the personal agent for Robert HARLEY. As undersecretary to the second secretary of state, Lord DARTMOUTH, Lewis introduced Swift to the first secretary, Henry BOLINGBROKE. His skill for arranging various meetings between influential people would make him invaluable to the Harley ministry. Swift had met Lewis through a mutual friend in London in September 1710 when the latter had promised to introduce Swift to Harley. The first planned meeting fell through, and in the meantime Swift primed Lewis with a story about how the former ministry had ignored him "for not being Whig enough." With this story, Swift hoped Harley would see the similarity in how both had been treated and invite him to a private meeting. Harley, either at Lewis's urging or because he had intended on speaking with Swift for his own purposes, met the clergyman with the greatest cordiality and immediately invited him to return to discuss fully his mission concerning the First Fruits.

Lewis, who transmits Robert Harley's views, continually surfaces during Swift's London years as the clergyman publishes a series of pamphlets in support of the ministry. Later, Swift came to the rescue of his friend Lewis when the agent was accused of treasonable activity with JACOBITES. The dean's skill in explaining the truth as a "public service" in the *EXAMINER* helped destroy this scandalous gossip and save Lewis's reputation. Yet Swift enjoys provoking him too, saying "this Lewis is an arrant shaver, and very much in Harley's favour" in "HORACE, EPISTLE VII, BOOK I: IMITATED AND ADDRESSED TO THE EARL OF OXFORD." He refers to Lewis again in "HORACE, LIB. 2, SAT. 6." To the end, Lewis served the Harley family in trying to convince Swift to make extensive changes to "The HISTORY OF THE FOUR LAST YEARS OF THE QUEEN" to ensure the dean "do[es] justice to truth." Swift found the letter annoying though his reply is polite, and ignored its request, but the "History" was not published until 1758. Swift's *Correspondence* contains more than 20 letters between the two men.

**Lightburne, Rev. Stafford** (b.1662)   Clergyman and Swift's curate (1722–33). Lightburne belonged to a family with an estate in County Meath, graduated from Trinity College, Dublin (1684), and married Hannah Swift, daughter of Swift's older cousin Willoughby, a merchant working in London who had contributed support to Jonathan. Lightburne could not obtain his wife's fortune, which was in litigation, and the couple needed financial help. Swift's curacy at Laracor was available; but when Lightburne applied the first time, Swift turned down this "foolish" man. In 1722 Swift decided the clergyman would have the post, including a house at Trim and the paid assignment as schoolmaster of Trim. From that period until his death, Swift would periodically come to his aid, recommending Lightburne to Lord Lieutenant Grafton for a position. Later, he petitioned members of the House of Lords in London for justice on this lower clergy's behalf (the appeal was successful in 1725). The dean finally secured a rectory in Churchtown, County Westmeath, for the struggling Lightburne, whom he had come to respect.

**Lincoln, Henry Clinton, seventh earl of** (1684–1728)   Courtier and knight of the garter. He was a lord of the bedchamber to GEORGE, Prince of Denmark, and the consort of Queen ANNE. As an ardent WHIG, he held several minor offices under GEORGE I: joint paymaster general to the forces (1715–20) and cofferer (treasurer) of the household (1725–28), and constable of the Tower. His own income was modest, and these posts were a financial necessity. As a member of the Kit-Cat

Club, which flourished between 1696 and 1720 as a distinguished dining society of Whig writers and politicians, Clinton had his portrait painted for Godfrey Kneller's series of Kit-Cat portraits done between 1702 and 1717. Swift mentions Clinton in a comic poem, "TOLAND'S INVITATION TO DISMAL TO DINE WITH THE CALVES' HEAD CLUB," as part of a gang of deists and republicans in this probably mythical club whose members gather in celebrating the anniversary of the death of Charles I.

**Lindsay, Robert** (d. 1743)   Justice of the Common Pleas of Ireland. Lindsay graduated from Trinity College, Dublin, and was called to the Irish bar in 1709. He was appointed legal counsel (or seneschal) to the proctor and Chapter of St. Patrick's Cathedral in 1722, possibly at Swift's endorsement. Swift respected his legal abilities and liked him as a friend: "an intimate . . . of mine upon the score of virtue, learning and superior knowledge in his own profession." With "The ANSWER TO 'PAULUS,' " Swift criticizes lawyers as "common drudges" who are "always for saving their own bacon," yet he begs Lindsay to practice discretion and seek virtue. His criticism of politicians and members of Parliament remains harsh; he suggested to Lindsay, who had been elected to the Irish Parliament in 1729, that "scrambling to get a place: must lose the honour you have gained." "A DIALOGUE BETWEEN AN EMINENT LAWYER AND DR. SWIFT, DEAN OF ST. PATRICK'S" positions a careful lawyer and a vigorous satirist as examining each other's values. In the final analysis, the lawyer recognizes the long-lasting influence of the satirist, who may help humankind but in the end will damage his own chances for personal success. Lindsay may have also served as legal adviser to Swift during the writing of the sixth of *The DRAPIER'S LETTERS* ("A Letter to the Lord Chancellor Middleton"), an essay Swift waited 11 years to publish. In 1740 Swift made his last will, asking 10 different men to serve as executors; Lindsay was one of four lawyers in this group.

**Lindsay, Thomas, archbishop of Armagh** (d. 1724)   Irish churchman. Lindsay, a Scot, was born in England and came to Ireland in 1693 as chaplain to Henry Lord CAPEL, a neighbor of the TEMPLE family at Sheen, who provided Swift with his first post at Kilroot in January 1695. Lindsay became dean of St. Patrick's Cathedral in 1694, bishop of Killaloe (1695), and bishop of Raphoe (1713) and ascended as primate of all Ireland and archbishop of Armagh in 1714, with the death of Narcissus MARSH.

Swift, who had earlier found Lindsay's beliefs troublesome, became especially annoyed after arriving on his 1710 mission to recover the First Fruits in London, where he expected two Irish bishops would be waiting to advise and assist him in his petition to the government. Neither John HARTSTONGE nor Lindsay was disposed toward helping Archbishop KING or his agent, Swift, and both had left the city. Swift's *Correspondence* and *The* JOURNAL TO STELLA provide ample evidence of his annoyance with them, and his uncertainty in this predicament. King soon authorized him to take the full management of the commission, and Swift had interviews with Sidney GODOLPHIN and Robert HARLEY. Ironically, Swift found himself later supporting the undistinguished Lindsay's preferment as primate over his respected colleague, Bishop King, because he feared that the post would not go to an Irish Tory. Lindsay's reputation as a devoted servant of government policies gave him a stronger argument for this promotion than the independent and sometimes Whiggish King. Swift also felt his own advancement was more likely with Lindsay's promotion than with King's, yet most critics argue political over personal considerations in understanding the dean's actions. "HORACE, BOOK I, ODE XIV" alludes to Lindsay's death, as well as the loss or decline of Viscount MIDDLETON and King, and the effect these events will have on an already vulnerable Ireland. Swift mentions Lindsay in several prose pieces, including "LETTER FROM A MEMBER OF THE HOUSE OF COMMONS IN IRELAND," "Memoirs Relating to That Change Which Happened in the Queen's Ministry in the Year 1710," and "Some Arguments against Enlarging the Power of the Bishops."

**Lloyd, William, bishop of Killala** (d. 1716) Welshman who graduated from Trinity College, Dublin, and became a Fellow in 1684. His rise in the church occurred quickly with promotions to precentor of Killala and dean of Achonry. In 1691 he was established as bishop of Killala. The bishop was a friend of both Swift and Esther JOHNSON (Stella), and supported Swift in his commission to solicit a remission of First Fruits (1710). "ON THE DEATH OF MRS. JOHNSON" provides a poignant note concerning Stella's friends and acquaintances, of whom Lloyd is mentioned as one "who . . . respected her highly, upon her good sense, good manners, and conversation."

**Long, Anne** (d. 1711)  Friend of Swift and a celebrated beauty of London society, an elected member of the Kit-Cat Club, who voluntarily exiled herself to escape her creditors. Swift notes in his yearly account book for 1711–12 a particularly revealing comment about his affection for Mrs. Long on hearing of her death. Though he was "never more afflicted at any death," he also intends on placing a death notice in the London newspaper, the *Post-Boy*, to shame her brother, Sir James Long (1682–1729), a TORY M.P., into spending the money to have her body brought to London from King's Lynn, Norfolk (her place of exile). But in a December 26, 1711, letter, Swift explained to Anne's minister in Lynn (Thomas Pyle) that he should "bury her in some part of your church . . . where a plain marble stone may be fixed, as a poor monument for one who deserved so well" (*Corr.* I.279–80).

Mrs. Long was a friend and distant relative of the VANHOMRIGH family, and Swift had first met her at their house about 1708. After long expecting a £2,000 legacy from an "odious grandmother," Anne had accumulated so many debts that to escape collectors she felt forced to hide out using the assumed name "Smyth." Swift used a number of ruses in writing to her, and they carried on a lively correspondence. At one point he wrote a letter to a third party in which he enclosed a letter to Vanessa (Esther Vanhomrigh) that included a final letter to Mrs. Long. His enjoyment was doubled in permitting Vanessa to eavesdrop on his praise of her to Anne. Swift's comments in *THE* JOURNAL TO STELLA and "A Decree for Concluding the Treaty between Dr. Swift and Mrs. Long" reveal the degree to which Swift appreciated amiability and good sense in his often difficult professional and personal life.

**Louis XIV, king of France (1643–1715)** (1638–1715)   Known as the "Sun King" and celebrated as an absolute monarch, he ruled from 1643 to 1715. In 1661, after a long minority in which Cardinal Jules Mazarin dealt with state matters, Louis was determined to overcome any weaknesses in French central authority. He warred in the Netherlands in 1667 and 1672; and during 1683–84 he was laying new claims in the Netherlands, Alsace, and Genoa. The War of the League of Augsburg (1688–97) created German enmity and little gain. His enemies—England, the Netherlands, the Holy Roman Empire—in the War of the Spanish Succession (1701–14) forced him to separate the crowns of France and Spain for his future heirs.

Swift adopted his patron William TEMPLE's point of view regarding Louis XIV that national policy springs from the character of the ruler who enunciates it. Temple, who had negotiated a peace between England and Holland and forged the Triple Alliance (of Sweden, England, and Holland), had long recognized and opposed Louis's territorial imperative. In the early "ODE TO THE KING" Swift praises WILLIAM III and the Glorious Revolution and denounces JAMES II and Louis XIV. The French king remains, for all his supposed greatness, a bad and tyrannical ruler. Swift rises to his theme, considering Louis first as a false meteor, then a "fearful star," finding it will all end "in vapour, stink, and scum." This allusion appears in "The Digression Concerning Madness" section of "A TALE OF A TUB" where Louis's brain relocates itself to the human anus, forming a tumor or fistula there. Aside from this excremental imagery, Swift describes the French king as a small bully, a little boy stubbornly determined to have his way in the world. This condition leads to the madness of military conquest, and later Swift continues the attack in "The VIRTUES OF SID HAMET THE MAGICIAN'S ROD" and "A DISCOURSE OF THE CONTESTS AND DISSENSIONS." The latter portrays Louis XIV as "a vulture." Other references to the king appear in "The HISTORY OF THE FOUR LAST YEARS OF THE QUEEN," "The Public Spirit of the Whigs," and "The IMPORTANCE OF THE GUARDIAN CONSIDERED."

**Louis XV, king of France** (1710–1774)   He became king at the age of five, succeeding his great-grandfather, LOUIS XIV. During his minority, he was educated by Cardinal Fleury, and after his adviser's death in 1743, Louis took personal charge of the country, with disastrous results. Finding court life boring and government bureaucratic operations even more so, he entertained himself with various court intrigues. His support of the Seven Years' War (1756–63) caused France to lose much of its colonial influence and weakened its economy. In general, his reign was marked by disasters—financial, military, and political.

Swift opposed Louis's plan of sending French officers to raise recruits in Ireland for service in the French army in Europe. In a clever piece of irony, Swift builds on his friend BOLINGBROKE's argument in the TORY periodical *The Craftsman* against this unacceptable plan. In *An* "ANSWER TO *THE CRAFTSMAN*," the author argues for this policy in the character of a loyal WHIG who defends the current English government position while opposing the Tory view. The notion of sending 60,000 Irishmen to fight and die in the service of the French or Spanish might serve English trade interests while reducing the number of rebellious subjects in the kingdom. Swift's approach, in this example and throughout the pamphlet, reminds his readers of his "MODEST PROPOSAL," and the irony remains as sharp and effective.

**Lucas, Charles, M.D.** (1713–71)   Irish apothecary, physician, patriot, pamphleteer, and editor of Andrew Millar's edition of Swift's "The HISTORY OF THE FOUR LAST YEARS OF THE QUEEN." In 1758, when preparing the "History," Lucas felt the necessity for injecting an advertisement in the beginning of the text that remarked on the passions and political party prejudice of the author. His caution did not prevent his being harassed by the authorities for earlier conduct. In his publications, Lucas challenging the legitimacy of the government and the corruption rampant in the Irish Parliament. He was arrested as a common libeler and faced imprisonment in 1749 but fled the country. He practiced medicine in London, returning to Dublin in 1761, and he continued his campaign against the oligarchic control of city politics by the lord mayor and aldermen. Soon after, he won a Dublin seat in Parliament and became a leading figure in the emerging patriot opposition.

In his *Life of Swift*, Samuel Johnson mentions Lucas as the editor of the "History," and apparently held the editor's work in high esteem. Boswell records Johnson's description of Lucas "as a man well known to the world for his daring defiance of power, when he thought it exerted on the side of wrong. . . . Let the man thus driven into exile, for having been the friend of his country, be received in every other place as confessor of liberty." Though no record exists of Swift's having met Lucas, the two men clearly shared a similar political philosophy, especially when Ireland was the topic.

**Lucy, Lady Catherine** (d. 1740) Daughter of the poet Charles Cotton and wife of Sir Berkeley Lucy, baronet, of Facombe and Netley, in Hampshire. Her mother-in-law was the second daughter of George, first earl of Berkeley, and Swift probably first met the Lucys through his friendship with the Berkeleys. His skill at cultivating social connections as well as entertaining himself at cards (one of his favorite pastimes) led to meeting various people in London or court society. Lady Lucy and Swift dined together periodically and played ombre (1710–11), as seen in *The JOURNAL TO STELLA*, but soon the relationship became difficult: at one dinner her guests pounced upon a couple of his recently published poems without knowing the author was Swift, and at another meal Lucy's sister,

"the most insupportable of all women," attacked the most recent issue of the EXAMINER. These "plaguy Whigs," as Swift called the sisters and their guests, apparently did not suspect their dinner partner was the author. He soon dropped his friendship with the argumentative Lady Lucy once his political allegiance changed, but kept in contact with the Berkeleys.

**Ludlow, Peter** (d. 1750) Irish M.P. for Dunlear, County Louth, and during the Hanoverian period, for County Meath, and friend of Swift. By his marriage into the Preston family, he became owner and resident of Ardsallagh House, overlooking the River Boyne, between Trim and Navan. Swift often visited Ludlow in his country rambles, and their friendship remained firm for more than 30 years.

The family relationships by birth and marriage between the Prestons and a number of families and persons close to Swift seem remarkable today, but in the relatively small Protestant Irish and Anglo-Irish communities of this period, not necessarily unusual. An earlier Preston had married the mother of Charles FORD (Swift's good friend), and she was related, as a Hammond, to Swift's patron, Sir William TEMPLE. She also had a family connection as a cousin to Elizabeth Dingley, mother of Rebecca DINGLEY. When Rebecca and Stella (Esther JOHNSON) arrived in Ireland, Mrs. Letitia Hammond-Preston-Ford introduced them and the Dean to the Fords and the Ludlows. Apparently, Ludlow also knew Knightley CHETWODE, who cultivated a friendship with Swift.

# M

**Maccartney, George (George Maccartney)** (c. 1660–1730)   British army general. He rose to command a brigade in Spain but was badly defeated along with the allied army at Almanza in 1707, later his commander, MARLBOROUGH, at the Battle of Malplaquet, 1709, in the Netherlands, praised Maccartney's superb leadership in achieving this costly victory and promoted him to lieutenant general. During a period of bitter political argument between the TORIES and WHIGS in 1712, Maccartney allied himself with Lord Charles MOHUN, a notorious rake and tool of Whig interests. Mohun quarreled with the duke of HAMILTON, a Tory, on a personal issue, and the two carried out an illegal duel in which Mohun was killed and the duke mortally wounded. The duke's second accused Maccartney of taking advantage of the situation to kill the duke, and a murder warrant was issued for his arrest. This evidence was not confirmed by servants who were looking on, but the whole issue aroused heated public debate and partisanship.

The Tories regarded Hamilton's death as another in a long series of Whig plots to weaken their ministry. Swift, in his marginalia to John MACKY's *Characters of the Court of Britain* (1733), states categorically that the "worthy, good natured" Hamilton was murdered "by that Villain McCartny an Irish Scot ambitious, covetous, cunning Scot has no principle but his own interest and greatness. A true Scot in his whole conduct now very homely and makes a sorry appearance." In one of his contributions to the *Post Boy* (November 15–18, 1712), Swift wrote "it was found that Gen. Maccartney, Esq. was aiding and assisting the Lord Mohun to commit the murder on the said Duke; and the said Maccartney is fled for the same; . . . that the wound whereof the said Duke died, was given him by the said Maccartney." In "The HISTORY OF THE FOUR LAST YEARS OF THE QUEEN," Swift accuses Maccartney of stabbing the duke, "who died after a few minutes in the field and the murderer made his escape." After escaping to Holland, Maccartney, who did not return until the accession of GEORGE I, was tried for murder, and found guilty of being an accessory to murder. Once the sentence of having his hand burnt was carried out, he was immediately restored to his former rank and given an active assignment. Swift mentions him in "The FIRST ODE OF THE SECOND BOOK OF HORACE PARAPHRASED AND ADDRESSED TO RICHARD STEELE, ESQ." In a February 19, 1732, letter to the Rev. John WINDER (a friend from his early Kilroot days), Swift offered assistance in a matter of preferment; ironically, Winder's daughter, Elizabeth, was married to Maccartney (*Corr.* IV.3–4).

**Macky, John** (d. 1726)   Author, government agent, and spy. In his *Memoirs of the Secret Services of John Macky, Esq.* (1733), he recalls his acquaintance or observation of English and Scottish nobility and officers of the various military services. At the request of Princess Sophia, the electress of Hanover, Macky, who attended her at Court in 1703, provided impressions he had formed during the period before WILLIAM III's death, when as a government agent he made it his business to investigate and thoroughly learn the character of any person connected with the ministry or Court. Swift, who found his work fascinating, provided extensive marginalia (later transcribed) in his copy of Macky's work. His comments can savage an individual such as MARLBOROUGH, whom he finds "detestably covetous," or the earl of Sandwich, "as much a puppy as ever I saw very ugly and a fop." His knowledge of these figures is firsthand, from the period 1710–14 when he worked for the Harley ministry and spent time in Court circles, and often allows for a physical description as well as a character impression.

**Maculla, James**  Dublin pewterer and coppersmith, also pamphleteer. Maculla wrote an early and influential pamphlet attacking William WOOD's patent for coining Irish halfpence. His *Ireland's Consternation in the Loosing [sic] of Two Hundred Thousand Pounds of their Gold and Silver for Brass Money* denounces the entire idea as poorly conceived and injurious to the Irish economy. This effort gave Swift the last bit of encouragement as he prepared to launch his DRAPIER'S LETTERS in 1724, resulting in the eventual defeat of Wood's patent. Later, in 1729, Maculla, ever ready in proposing revenue-producing schemes, wrote a pamphlet offering to sell promissory notes worth a halfpence and a penny, in the form of copper discs. Swift was properly indignant, yet he restrained himself, met Maculla, and heard him out. Deciding on a measured response to Maculla, Swift wrote the essay "LETTER ON MACULLA'S PROJECT" focusing on the profits Maculla would gain from this, and proposing his own scheme. The public response to both schemes was lukewarm and dismissive, but Swift's idea for a public mint made good sense.

**Mainwaring, Arthur** (1668–1712)  Auditor of the Imprests (a government loan-granting agency), commissioner of the Customs, WHIG politician, satirist, and a journalist. Mainwaring (or Maynwaring), who came from a well considered and wealthy family, now much reduced—held Jacobite sympathies. He was a leading Kit-Cat member, a friend of ADDISON and STEELE, and a controller of Whig publicity. In an attempt to counter the effectiveness

of the EXAMINER, Addison brought out the *Whig-Examiner*, and followed with *The Medley* (1710–11), edited by John Oldmixon and Mainwaring, who had become an M.P. and the duchess of MARLBOROUGH's unpaid secretary and political adviser. Steele dedicated the first volume of the *Tatler* to Mainwaring in gratitude for having recommended him as gazetteer (see Swift's "The IMPORTANCE OF THE GUARDIAN CONSIDERED"), a preferment HARLEY had available. A proposal with less overt political references yet certainly showing the enmity between the two parties was Swift's project for reforming and purifying the English language, "A Proposal for Correcting, Improving and Ascertaining the English Tongue" (1712). Mainwaring answered this essay with his own, *The British Academy* (1712), in which he dismisses Swift's plan for an academy "to fix the language for ever." Less biting and more urbane than Oldmixon in his *Reflections on Dr. Swift's Letter to the Earl of Oxford*, both Mainwaring and Swift agree that the use and condition of a nation's language serve as an indication of its taste. Soon Mainwaring died, leaving the Whigs with a shortage of effective writers capable of responding to the opposition press.

**Manley, Isaac** (d. 1735)  Postmaster-general in Ireland. Manley became general in Dublin in August, 1703, after a successful term as Comptroller of the Inland Post at the General Post Office, Lombard Street, London. As a WHIG, he constantly worried about whether he could retain his job in a TORY administration, but his job security improved with the arrival of the Hanoverians. The Tories had accused Manley of tampering with the mail and opening Swift's letters, but apparently the dean ignored this accusation and advised Manley on how he should counter these attacks. Esther JOHNSON (Stella), urged Swift to do whatever he could to protect their friends, and he promised to do so. In a February 2, 1713, letter to Thomas WALLS, Swift refers to Manley as "the most violent Partyman in Ireland" in support of Whig issues (*Corr.* II.11), and says he would not have been surprised to learn of Manley's involvement in reporting on confiscated letters between the dean and his correspondents the following year. But Swift and Stella played cards with Manley and his wife in Dublin, and the dean, while involved in his ministerial work, had visited Frances Manley, their daughter, in London in 1712. Frances married the Rev. Samuel Holt, who became a prebendary of St. Patrick's Cathedral, Dublin, from 1723 to 1763. Manley is also referenced in *The JOURNAL TO STELLA*.

**Manley, Mary de la Riviere** (1663–1724) Writer and daughter of Sir Roger Manley, a soldier in the forces of Charles I. Mary Manley married her cousin, John Manley, brother of Isaac MANLEY, under the false pretenses that his wife was deceased. Whether she knew the true circumstances of this union or not, she does move on to a series of affairs with various men, some of whom keep her as a mistress. John BARBER, the alderman and lord mayor of London, maintained her for a period of time, but she continuously supported herself through her writing. Her apparently scandalous romans à clef, *The History of Queen Zarah and Zarazians* (1705), an attack on the MARLBOROUGH WHIGS, or her more infamous *The New Atlantis* (1709), in which she and her printers were arrested for libel, became best sellers. Her melodramatic picture of ANNE's court brings "their jasmine-scented seraglio to life." As a minimally successful dramatist with tragedies and a ballad opera to her credit, Manley's prose brought her the most credit, revealing the liveliness of a skilled journalist, but her connection to Swift, whom she probably met at the end of 1710, provided the clearest sense of her facility as a writer.

Mrs. Manley took over writing the *EXAMINER* from Swift on June 14, 1711, with number 45, though he wrote the first part of that number. He may have provided hints and information to her for subsequent numbers. He did provide suggestions for "A Learned Comment upon Dr. Hare's Excellent Sermon," which she wrote but which editors include among his productions as prompted and partly written by him. Early in 1714, Mrs. Manley wrote, with Swift's help, "A Modest Enquiry into . . . a Report of Her Majesty's Death," exploring the real grievances of the Whigs toward Queen ANNE. When Swift alludes to her in *The JOURNAL TO STELLA* or the *Correspondence*, he mentions her

kindly: "our friend was ill in the country . . . but she is in no danger" and "she has . . . a great deal of good sense and invention." His "CORINNA" satirizes the main character's birth and morals in a humorous but often stinging critique. Some critics argue the character is Manley, but others are convinced that the figure is likely a composite of Manley, Eliza Haywood, Elizabeth Thomas, and Martha Fowke.

**Mansell, Thomas** (c. 1668–1723) Privy councillor, TORY M.P., and comptroller of the royal household (1704–08, 1711–12), succeeded his father as sixth baronet in 1706, and created Baron Mansell of Margam in 1712 when the queen formed a group of 12 new peers necessary to ensure a majority in the House of Lords. Swift mentions him as a favorite of Queen ANNE in "An ENQUIRY INTO THE BEHAVIOUR OF THE QUEEN'S LAST MINISTRY." Mansell had earlier resigned his post as comptroller and joined Robert HARLEY, but left the government during the ministerial crisis of 1708. Swift knew him well and sometimes trusted his perception of events, though the dean complains about the poor quality of the food when he dines with "this man [who] has ten thousand pounds a year in land and is lord of the treasury." His opinion of Mansell comes through in the marginalia for MACKY's *Characters of the Court of Britain:* "of good nature but a very moderate capacity." *The JOURNAL TO STELLA* and *Correspondence* contain numerous references to Mansell.

**Margaret** Esther JOHNSON's (Stella's) maid in Dublin. The first known reference to Margaret can be found in the account books for 1709–12; she would have served both Rebecca DINGLEY and Stella and traveled with them on their holidays. Swift speaks of her in *The JOURNAL TO STELLA*, often recalling or projecting humorous incidents involving the ladies and Margaret. As a corollary to these references, Swift extends his satiric comment on maids in his "DIRECTIONS TO SERVANTS," especially chapter 9: "Directions to the Waiting Maid" (1745).

**Market Hill (Markethill), County Armagh** Later called Gosford Castle, the seat of Sir Arthur and Lady Anne ACHESON in County Armagh, Ireland.

Swift made three long visits there, the first from June or July 1728 to February 1729, the second from June 1729 to October of the same year, and the third from June to September 1730. During these extended stays he spent a great deal of time with Lady Anne as her tutor. He enjoyed being outdoors at Market Hill, and often helped with the farming and landscaping. He even supervised the construction of two outhouses there (see "A PANE-GYRIC ON THE DEAN"). Although in 1729 he purchased land north of Market Hill at Drumlack (also called Drapier's Hill) on which to build a home, he eventually abandoned those plans. Swift produced a "mass of occasional and more than occasionally scatological verse" at Market Hill, "mostly written in the assumed voice of Lady Anne" (Glendinning 157). Among the poems Swift wrote during visits to Market Hill are "DAPHNE," "DEATH AND DAPHNE," "JOURNAL OF A MODERN LADY," "LADY ACHESON WEARY OF THE DEAN," "A REVOLUTION AT MARKET HILL," "TO DEAN SWIFT," "TO JANUS," "TO A LADY," and "TWELVE ARTICLES."

## Marlborough, John Churchill, first duke of

(1650–1722)  Soldier and statesman. Churchill was born in Ashe, Devon, England, and was commissioned in the Guards (1667), receiving further promotions, including those after his 1678 marriage to Sarah Jennings, an attendant of Princess Anne. On JAMES II's accession (1685), he was elevated to a barony and given the rank of general. After assisting in the defeat of Monmouth's Rebellion, Marlborough, now lieutenant general and commander of the King's forces, deserted to William of Orange (WILLIAM III), fighting on the Protestant side in campaigns in Ireland and Flanders (1688). Under Queen ANNE he was appointed supreme commander of the British forces in the War of the Spanish Succession and captain-general of the Allied armies against LOUIS XIV. His military and organizational skills resulted in a number of superb victories against the French, and Anne granted him great wealth and noble rank. His decision to side with Sidney GODOLPHIN in politics and the collapse of the WHIG ministry, along with the public's exhaustion with war caused his own influence to wane. His wife's fall from royal favor, combined

with the growing power of the TORIES who pressed for his downfall, led to his dismissal on charges of embezzling large sums of government money (1711). He went into exile on the continent (1713), and returned to England only after GEORGE I's accession (1714).

During the period 1710–12, Swift had a leading role in attacking Marlborough's character: in "The HISTORY OF THE FOUR LAST YEARS OF THE QUEEN" (published much later but intended for immediate release) he wrote, "I am persuaded, his chief motive was the pay and perquisites by continuing the war . . . that liberality which nature hath denied him with respect to money, he makes up by a great profusion of promises." Greed and ambition seemed the predominant passions, both of which Swift focused on in "The CONDUCT OF THE ALLIES," adding a list of lying allegations of corruption.

Marlborough prolonged the war on the Continent to increase his profits in hopes of further destroying the queen's credibility with her subjects and making himself king. Critics do argue that Swift's accusations were part of a larger effort to bring down the Whig party, and not the result of any particular animosity between the two men. The business of placing Robert HARLEY and BOL-INGBROKE in power remained the essential concern, and after Marlborough's fall Swift wrote little against him.

However, in the EXAMINER papers of November 23, 1710 (number 16), and February 8, 1711 (number 27), Swift ruthlessly attacked the duke and Thomas WHARTON, ex–lord lieutenant of Ireland, now on the Whig front bench. Using a common rhetorical technique of the polemicist, Swift refers to Marlborough with a nickname. In this instance, he is "Crassus"—with all its attendant allegorical and historical analogies. The references to the Roman general who (in Swift's words) was "deeply stained with that odious and ignoble Vice of Covetousness" and whose victories translated into immense financial gain insinuates further Marlborough's true interest. Virtue is set aside and vice becomes the main motivation for the general's every action.

"The FABLE OF MIDAS" addresses the same theme of uncontrolled avarice and alleged corruption, though Irvin Ehrenpreis calls it "a stingless, charmless" poem without much ingenuity (*Swift* II.533). Later, after Marlborough's death, Swift apparently still felt the general approached the perfect example of a classical tyrant, as seen in "A Satirical Elegy on the Death of a Late Famous General," brought down to the equal of other men. See The Journal to Stella for Swift's incisive explanations to the ladies of his efforts.

**Marlborough, Sarah Jennings, duchess of** (1660–1744)   Wife of John Churchill, first duke of Marlborough (1678), keeper of the privy purse, groom of the stole, and mistress of the robes, and Queen Anne's closest confidante. Brought up in the court of Charles II, Sarah became the intimate friend of his niece, the princess Anne, so that by 1702, with Anne's accession to the throne, Sarah had risen to a position of power beyond expectation. They called one another "Mrs. Morley" and "Mrs. Freeman" as a code and a kind of private game. She and her husband, and Sidney Godolphin joined with the queen in successfully governing England during the War of the Spanish Succession, reducing the power of France. A shift of political power began in 1710 as the queen turned away from her Whig advisers and relied more on Harley and his Tory followers. Sarah's partisan Whiggism annoyed the queen, and their long friendship suffered irreparable damage. Ultimately, she resigned her posts and ironically found her replacement would be one of the Queen's waiting women, Abigail Masham, whom she had introduced to the monarch.

Sarah remained kind to Swift while he supported Whig causes, but his allegiance to Harley produced some of her most venomous statements: "the Revered Mr. Swift . . . quickly offered [himself] to sale . . . ready to prostitute all [he] had in the service of well rewarded scandal. . . . [L]ong ago [he] turned all religion into a *Tale of a Tub* and sold it for a jest." She had a great affection for Gulliver's Travels, but her imperious and quarrelsome nature was more than Swift could bear. "The History of the Four Last Years of the Queen" describes her character as "sordid Avarice, disdainful Pride, and ungovernable Rage." "An Excellent New Song" takes a jab at the Marlboroughs and

their supposed love of money and position. Sarah's memoirs, *Account of the Conduct of the Dowager Duchess of Marlborough from her First Coming to Court to Year 1710*, dealt severely with Swift. His *Correspondence* and The Journal to Stella reflect his attitude toward this lady.

**Marsh, Narcissus, archbishop of Dublin** (1638–1713)   Churchman. Marsh was educated at Exeter College, Oxford, and distinguished himself as a studious scholar. The first Duke of Ormonde, the father of Swift's friend, appointed Marsh as provost of Trinity College, Dublin, in 1679. His lifelong interest in books and manuscripts resulted in an early gift of Oriental manuscripts to the Bodleian and the founding of the Marsh Library in Dublin. He was created bishop of Ferns and Leighlin in 1683, but he fled Ireland during the three-year-long Williamite War, also known as the revolution of 1688, which was both an episode in a major European conflict and an Irish civil war. After William III's accession, Marsh became archbishop of Cashel in 1691, and was promoted to archbishop of Dublin (1694), and of Armagh (1703).

Marsh was provost of Trinity during Swift's residence at the college and one of the founding members of the old Dublin Philosophical Society (1683) along with Swift's tutor, St. George Ashe and Bishop William King. After leaving Moor Park for the second time in 1694, Swift returned to Dublin to become ordained, but Marsh (by then archbishop) required logically a letter of reference from William Temple. Swift wrote his famous "penitential" letter to Temple requesting a testimonial of his "good life and behaviour." Soon Swift was ordained as a deacon and then a priest and appointed to the prebend of Kilroot (1695). Denying him the dean of Derry, Marsh made him prebend of Dunlavin (1700), giving Swift a living, although a meager one. Apparently, Swift retained hard feelings toward Marsh for insisting on this certificate and for his difficulties with Archbishop King, as we see in his "A Character of Primate Marsh" (1710). The essay, a paragraph in length, severely criticizes the churchman, suggesting his reputation for scholarship remains unproven, his compassion disappoints, and no one will be sorry or glad at his passing. Swift could only hope, as he told

Esther JOHNSON (Stella), that in the event of Marsh's death, King would be chosen primate.

## Masham, Abigail, baroness (née Hill) (d. 1734)

Lady-in-waiting and confidante to Queen ANNE and a distant cousin of Sarah, duchess of MARLBOROUGH, who secured a position for her as bedchamber woman to the queen in 1704. She was treated with such confidence, given access to state matters, that Mrs. Masham soon began advising the queen. Abigail was also a cousin of Robert HARLEY's, with whom she maintained a close correspondence and, through her influence with Anne, had suggested the strengths in Harley's character and the TORY party.

Critics call Abigail a quiet, self-denying sort of person who enjoyed and played the music of Purcell and actively read newspapers and books, suggested by Harley, to Anne. Though not as intellectual or beautiful as Sarah, she had an instinct for understanding her sovereign's character and anticipating her needs, whether political news or court rumors. For a variety of reasons both personal and political, Sarah began losing her sway over Anne, and Abigail gradually supplanted the duchess in the queen's favor.

In 1707 Abigail secretly married Samuel MASHAM, a groom in the bedchamber to Prince GEORGE of Denmark, and from that point on the duchess realized the growing link between Anne and Abigail, which infuriated her. The various conspiracies she hatched for removing Abigail failed, and with the dismissal of Sarah in 1711 from her offices Abigail was given full powers. She remained at court through the queen's last illness, attending her with the special attention she had always displayed toward Anne.

Swift found Abigail "a person of a plain sound understanding, of great truth and sincerity, without the least mixture of falsehood or disguise; of an honest boldness and courage, superior to her sex; firm and disinterested in her friendship, and full of love, duty, and veneration for the Queen her mistress" ("An ENQUIRY INTO THE BEHAVIOUR OF THE QUEEN'S LAST MINISTRY"). Their friendship lasted to the end of her life. In a May 12, 1735, letter to Alexander POPE, Swift refers to her as "my dear friend my Lady Masham, my constant friend in all changes of times" (*Corr.* IV.334). Abigail had advised him against printing "The WINDSOR PROPHECY" because of its nasty attack on the queen's friend, the duchess of SOMERSET, even though Swift recommends to Anne that she keep close to Mrs. Masham. Other references to her appear in "Memoirs, Relating to That Change Which Happened in the Queen's Ministry in the Year 1710," the EXAMINER, and *The JOURNAL TO STELLA*.

## Masham, Samuel, baron (c. 1679–1758)

Courtier in the retinue of Prince GEORGE of Denmark and husband of Abigail Hill MASHAM. He was the son of Sir Francis Masham, baronet, and had been a page to the queen when she was princess of Denmark, as well as page, equerry, and groom of the bedchamber to the prince. The duchess of MARLBOROUGH claimed she had secured these posts for him. Masham, who was distantly related to ANNE, secretly married Abigail in a private ceremony at Kensington Palace, attended by the queen, in 1707. In the spring of 1710 he was created brigadier general in the army and also won a general election, in the fall, as a member of Parliament. Anne elevated him to a peerage in January 1712, as one of the 12 new peers created to ensure a TORY majority in the House of Lords.

As Baron Masham of Oates in the county of Essex, he and his wife owned a home at Langley Marsh in Buckinghamshire, where Swift was often invited but did not visit. Swift found their London homes in Kensington and at St. James's congenial retreats where he would play with the Mashams' children or dine and play cards with the parents. Masham was an early member of The Society, the club founded by BOLINGBROKE to consolidate his influence on the Tories, where his "brothers" were Swift and his brother-in-law, John HILL, among others. Swift had hoped to heal the breach between HARLEY and Bolingbroke during a 1712 dinner at the Mashams' apartments in Windsor Palace, where the dean had arranged the meeting for this purpose; the effort failed to achieve any results. Swift mentions Masham frequently in *The JOURNAL TO STELLA* and the *Correspondence*, as well as in

"An ENQUIRY INTO THE BEHAVIOUR OF THE QUEEN'S LAST MINISTRY."

**Mather, Charles**   A well-known London toy maker and dealer whose shop was in the Fleet Street district, near Chancery Lane and the Temple Bar. Swift mentions him in "The VIRTUES OF SID HAMET THE MAGICIAN'S ROD." The object of his attack in this poem is Lord GODOLPHIN, associating the great man with various images meant to diminish his importance and insult him. Mather is mentioned in the *Tatler* as Charles Bubbleboy (meaning toy) in numbers 27, 113, 142 and by his own name in the *Spectator* in numbers 328, 503, and 570.

**Matilda (Maude), empress of Germany**   (1102–1167)   Wife of Henry V of Germany (1114), daughter of Henry I of England, and mother of Henry II. On Emperor Henry V's death in 1125, Henry summoned the empress Matilda back to England and made his barons do homage to her as his heir. In 1128 Matilda married Geoffrey Plantagenet, heir to the county of Anjou, and in 1133 she bore him her first son, the future king Henry II. When Henry I died at Lyons-la-Forêt in eastern Normandy, his favorite nephew, Stephen of Blois, disregarding Matilda's right of succession, seized the English throne. Although he established himself as king, Stephen could not thereafter control his barons. Matilda's subsequent invasion of England unleashed a bitter civil war that ended with the Treaty of Wallingford (1153), when Stephen conceded the succession to Matilda's son, Henry, but not before besieging her at Oxford (1142) and forcing her to leave England. The struggle ended with King Stephen's death and Henry II's unopposed accession in 1154.

By 1697 Swift has many references to Maude in the "ABSTRACT OF THE HISTORY OF ENGLAND," a work projected as a continuation of William TEMPLE's history. In summarizing the struggle between Stephen and Maude, Swift draws parallels with WILLIAM III (as Irvin Ehrenpreis finds), to "the succession problem, the contractual element in the royal election, the new king's preoccupation with wars, and his difficulties with the pretender (the Empress Maude)" (*Swift* II.64–65).

**Maximilian II, Emilia Emanuel, elector of Bavaria**   (1662–1726)   Elector of Bavaria beginning in 1679 and an able soldier whose ambition drove him into a series of wars through which he hoped to expand his kingdom. His connection as an ally to the Hapsburg family became severely strained and later was damaged so much that it nearly cost him his holdings. As the son of the elector Ferdinand Maria, he joined the Austrian army in 1683 in the war against the Ottoman Turks, achieving renown at the capture of Belgrade (1688). As a Hapsburg ally, he was appointed governor of the Spanish Netherlands during the War of the Grand Alliance against Louis XIV of France. With his marriage and the subsequent birth of a son, Maximilian had hopes of rising in the Hapsburg succession. All these dreams failed with deaths in his family and his inability to retain his lands. During the War of the Spanish Succession, he joined the French against the English and Prussia in the hope that his dynasty, the Wittelsbachs, could supplant the Hapsburgs on the imperial throne. After the Bavarians and his allies the French were soundly defeated at Blenheim (1704), he lost his principality, and the failure at Ramilles (1706) cost him the governorship. Under the Treaty of Utrecht (1713), he could return to Bavaria as ruler in 1715. Nearly 10 years later, Maximilian's leadership increased the significance of his dynasty's power in German affairs, and his son ultimately became emperor of the Holy Roman Empire in 1742.

Swift comments on the man and his character frequently in "The HISTORY OF THE FOUR LAST YEARS OF THE QUEEN," describing how both LOUIS XIV and ANNE were concerned that Maximilian would be restored to his electorate and given one or two other small kingdoms "to efface the stain of his degradation." In *The Public Spirit of the Whigs*, Swift's references to Maximilian have less to do with his historical role than with providing a means for allusions to Richard STEELE and the WHIGS, and their "mishandling" of foreign affairs. He denounces the Whigs' politics using an ad hominem argument, and the linkage between their behavior and the elector's half-friendships and hungry ambitions discredits both.

**Maxwell, Henry** (d. 1730) M.P. for Donegal, Ireland. Maxwell was one of the most active propagandists in favor of founding a National Bank of Ireland. His pamphlets, *Reasons Offered for Erecting a Bank in Ireland* (1721) and *Mr. Maxwell's Second Letter to Mr. Rowley . . . Objections against the Bank Are Answered* (1721), caused much discussion and moved the issue forward in the Irish House. Swift found the proposal outrageous: Ireland was in a miserable economic state, due in part to the Jacobite rebellion of 1715 and the bursting of the South Sea Company bubble. In a recent and very contentious pamphlet war over Irish affairs, Swift had argued for protection for the Irish weavers, who were destitute because native manufactures were denied a market. Now, once again his services would be required, though BOLINGBROKE told the dean to remain silent. After two years of projecting a bank, various local and English advocates (Arthur ABERCORN, Viscount Boyne, and Sir Ralph Gore) announced in a 1720 proposal a plan to erect an institution "to save our moneys (sic) in the kingdom."

These backers had requested a charter from the king (which was approved in July 1721), and now at the end of the year, a series of carefully planned pamphlets arguing the good sense of founding such a bank began appearing. Swift feared a few rich backers would have the power to cheat the whole kingdom, and bring in all the corruptions associated with WHIG speculation and English and Irish monied interests. To oppose Maxwell and others who supported this scheme, Swift wrote a number of pamphlets, some of which can only be attributed to him with uncertainty: "The Wonderful Wonder of Wonders," "The Wonder of All the Wonders," "A LETTER FROM A LADY IN TOWN TO HER FRIEND IN THE COUNTRY, CONCERNING THE BANK," "The Subscribers to the Bank," and "A LETTER TO THE KING AT ARMS." The Irish Parliament voted the proposal down in December of 1721, and Swift once again, along with a number of others concerned with Irish interests, felt vindicated. Swift would allude to this controversy in at least three other works, "PART OF THE NINTH ODE OF THE FOURTH BOOK OF HORACE," "The BANK THROWN DOWN," and in the imagery of the mill in Part 3 of GULLIVER'S TRAVELS.

**McAulay, Alexander (Alexander M'Aullay, Alexander Macaulay)** (fl. 1735–1766) A distinguished barrister, legal scholar, and judge of the Consistorial Court of Dublin (an ecclesiastical court); M.P. for Thomastown (1761–66); recipient of an honorary doctorate from Trinity College, Dublin (1746); and unsuccessful candidate as M.P. for the University of Dublin in 1739. Swift and McAulay had known each other since 1736, and the dean had read McAulay's pamphlet, *Property Inviolable,* arguing in favor of the clergy's right to their property, especially tithes. Clergymen had both a temporal and spiritual role in the community, and as such should expect the same protection of their property as any other citizen. Using statutes, precedents, and a variety of legal authorities, McAulay made a solid, reasoned case. In 1737, Swift recommends to his printer George FAULKNER another McAulay tract, *Some Thoughts on the Tillage of Ireland* (1738), with a private note praising the writer as "a very worthy person of much ancient learning . . . a most loyal subject to King George . . . and a gentleman of as many virtues, as I have any where met . . . [who] cannot be blind or unconcerned at the mistaken conduct of his country in a point of the highest importance to it's [sic] welfare." The dean did write a prefatory commendation, "Letter to the Printer," which was appended to the published version of the pamphlet.

Swift, still had hopes of publishing "The HISTORY OF THE FOUR LAST YEARS OF THE QUEEN," and consulted McAulay on the legal issues surrounding this controversial manuscript. When the dean wrote his last will in May 1740, he asked McAulay to act as one of his executors and bequeathed him the gift of the gold box in which Swift had received the freedom of Dublin. Earlier, Swift had contacted his most powerful friends both in Ireland and England in support of McAulay's candidacy for Parliament representing Trinity College. Though McAulay ultimately lost in a recount, the dean's influence had made an important difference.

**McGee, Alexander** (d. 1722) Swift's personal servant, whom he called Saunders, from January 1718 until his death in March 1722. At the age of 29, McGee became ill and died in the deanery.

Swift wrote, "he was the first good one I ever had, and I am sure will be the last. I know few greater losses in life." He is buried inside the cathedral (at the southern end of the west wall in the south transept) and commemorated with a stone slab which the dean had engraved with McGee's name, position in the household, and the statement, "His grateful master caused this monument to be erected in memory of his discretion, fidelity and diligence in that humble station." Apparently, Swift originally intended to have said "grateful friend and master" but was convinced not to in the end. McGee had made Swift the sole executor of his will, and bequeathed to him various personal items including his pipes and nets "as the last mark of duty and affection from a faithful servant." Swift presided at McGee's funeral service and became quite emotional at the loss of his friend. In "Mary the Cook-Maid's Letter to Dr. Sheridan," McGee (as Saunders) plays a small part in this humorous and witty portrait of life below stairs in the deanery. He is also mentioned in "Stella's Birthday (1723)" and a number of Swift's letters.

## Medlycott, Thomas (Thomas Medlicott) (1662–1738)

Politician born in Binfield, Berkshire, and raised in Dublin, who began his career in Ireland as secretary and estate manager to the second duke of Ormonde, a Hanoverian Tory M.P. for Westminster from 1708–15, who in 1714 became commissioner of customs for Ireland, as well as an Irish M.P. Swift first mentions him in The Journal to Stella as a High Church London Tory who won a hotly contested reelection in October 1710 when the public desired peace and wanted to rid themselves of the Whigs, the so-called war party. To celebrate the occasion, Swift, who knew him personally, wrote a ballad (now lost) full of puns that was apparently entitled "An Excellent New Ballad, Being the Second Part of the Glorious Warrior."

The collapse of the South Sea Bubble in August 1720 nearly ruined Ireland's economy, and domestic trade slowed so much that tradesmen, especially those in the weaving industry, were unemployed. Swift, who became the Drapier, joined with Archbishop William King in various money-raising schemes to assist these weavers. One benefit performance of Hamlet given in their support on April 1, 1721, had Thomas Sheridan writing the prologue and Swift the epilogue ("An Epilogue to a Play for the Benefit of the Weavers in Ireland"), a 46-line poem urging improved efforts to stimulate trade. Medlycott, though he knew the overall effect of the poem on the local economy would be negligible, still praised it to his English superiors; it was reprinted numerous times in London newspapers. Later, Swift would write others describing how Medlycott had "overruled the tedious forms of the custom-house" to bring certain items to the deanery that had been ordered from England.

## Ménager, Nicolas le Baillif, count of St. Jean Ménager (1658–1714)

French merchant and peace envoy who was a knight of the Order of St. Michael and an important member of the Council of Trade to Louis XIV. His cleverness and adroit skill in negotiating a peace treaty with the English required the best skills available in the Tory ministry, and Bolingbroke was the most effective in countering the various ploys of this French agent. Bolingbroke also employed Matthew Prior to debate terms in Paris with another French representative, and Prior returned to London with Ménager, who had special knowledge of commercial affairs. These activities would result in the Treaty of Utrecht (1713), concluding the War of the Spanish Succession.

Swift's direct involvement occurred when Prior and the French diplomats were arrested on suspicion of being spies on entering London. The entire affair became a great embarrassment to the ministry, and Swift suggested writing a fictional narrative of the event so as to discredit the whole story and reduce the negative impact on Robert Harley and Bolingbroke. The pamphlet, "A New Journey to Paris," accomplished its goal—even Prior and Ménager were captivated by the report. On September 29, 1711, after having signed preliminary articles of peace on behalf of Louis XIV, Ménager and his colleague had a secret audience with Queen Anne. Swift had dinner with a small group of senior ministry figures and the Frenchmen, including Ménager, involved in the preliminaries at

Windsor, and begins considering the framework for his argument in "THE CONDUCT OF THE ALLIES," published in November 1711. "The HISTORY OF THE FOUR LAST YEARS OF THE QUEEN" contains numerous references to Ménager.

**Middleton, Alan Brodrick, viscount** (1656–1728) Lawyer and politician who held various important posts in the Irish government, became Speaker of the House of Commons (1703), and lord chancellor (1714); created a baron (1715) and Viscount Middleton (1717). Swift disliked his WHIG attitudes, especially his opposition to the Test Act. When the controversy over Wood's coinage emerged, Brodrick opposed the patent but ultimately signed a proclamation against the drapier. Swift wrote the sixth of The DRAPIER'S LETTERS ("A Letter to the Lord Chancellor Middleton") to rebut the proclamation and to clarify the resistance to the patent, especially Middleton's defiance. Both intimidation and incrimination, Irvin Ehrenpreis believes, worked to stiffen Middleton's decision to resist English pressure (*Swift* III.274). See also "A PROPOSAL FOR THE UNIVERSAL USE OF IRISH MANUFACTURES" for Middleton's decision to prosecute the printer, and Swift's poem "WHITSHED'S MOTTO ON HIS COACH."

**Milton, John** (1608–1674) English poet and political writer. Milton was born in London, studied at Cambridge University, and undertook a six-year program of self-directed reading in ancient and modern theology, philosophy, history, science, politics, and literature. During this period, he began writing occasional poems in Latin and several English poems in the pastoral mode: lyrics, the masque *Comus* (1634), and the pastoral elegy *Lycidas* (1683). His support of the Civil War and the revolution made him the polemical champion and official apologist for the Commonwealth in a series of publications against episcopacy, on divorce, in defense of the liberty of the press, and in support of the regicides. Blind from 1752, he devoted himself wholly to poetry, achieving an outstanding reputation with the great epic *Paradise Lost* (published in 10 books in 1667 and then in a second edition of 12 books in 1674).

Although Swift ranks Milton among the Moderns in "A TALE OF A TUB," he seems generally to have admired Milton's writing—a reminder that Swift did not categorically reject *all* modern works as worthless in favor of ancient ones. He did, however, find Milton's controversial *Doctrine and Discipline of Divorce* to be problematic because of the conditions surrounding its creation. In *Remarks upon a Book, Intituled, The Rights of the Christian Church, &c.*, Swift points to this work as a notable example of how knowing the author's personal circumstances is often useful in judging (and especially in refuting) the value of a book: "when *Milton* writ his Book of Divorces, it was presently rejected as an occasional Treatise; because every Body knew, he had a Shrew for his Wife. Neither can there be any Reason imagined, why he might not, after he was blind, have writ another upon the Danger and Inconvenience of Eyes." Swift makes a similar point later in the same work, where he writes, "*Milton* wrote for Divorces, because he had an ill Wife." Swift believed in the education of women and their intellectual powers, disagreeing with Milton's view "that woman was created for man, and not man for woman." Swift's rejection of this work was also based on what he saw as Milton's personal stake in making an argument for divorce—a bias that (in Swift's view) compromised whatever logic that argument may contain.

At various points in the prose and in a few poems, Swift alludes to *Paradise Lost* (two copies were in his library), finding appropriate references to how mankind remains susceptible to the power of evil, particularly the abuse of power. He apparently marked one volume with notes for the use of Stella (Esther JOHNSON) and Mrs. DINGLEY. In "The LADY'S DRESSING ROOM," Swift relies on Milton for various classical tags and references which he then parodies to suit his own thesis. "The ODE TO THE HONOURABLE SIR WILLIAM TEMPLE" contains a strong Miltonic element with critics suggesting that Temple plays the part of Christ, the second Adam, restoring the empire of Virtue. In an August 1732 letter to an Irish friend, Charles WOGAN, Swift announces his willingness to read the young man's poems, in the pose of an admirer of Milton and a critic; however, Harold Williams believes

Swift's knowledge of Milton is in doubt, the allusions few, and the evidence little. In a discussion of Swift's portrayal of the Houyhnhnms in Part 4 of GULLIVER'S TRAVELS as a "mode of proving . . . great truths," Samuel Taylor Coleridge encourages comparing it with the Paradise scenes in *Paradise Lost*. After asking the reader to weigh "the moral effect on his heart and his virtuous aspirations of Milton's Adam" against "Swift's horses," he concludes that genius manifests itself differently in different men and that "Swift's may be good, tho' very inferior to Milton's; they do not stand in each other's way" (William *Critical Heritage* 333–334). A particularly interesting parallel is Swift's portrayal of the goddess Criticism in "The BATTLE OF THE BOOKS." This character shares important similarities with Milton's depiction of Sin in the second book of *Paradise Lost*.

## Mohun, Charles, fourth baron (1677–1712)

A boisterous rake and duelist whose WHIG sympathies were as well known as his pleasure in confronting anyone who might challenge his politics and attitudes. He joined the Kit-Cat Club in 1702 when a colonel of an infantry regiment and later became a lieutenant general and the least admirable member of the club. Mohun, who had killed three other men in duels and been charged with murder in each case, quarreled with James Douglas, the fourth duke of Hamilton, whose Jacobite leanings provided the obvious reasons for the November 1712 duel. But the real enmity between the two began as a family lawsuit, though Swift in the *Post Boy* (November 18–20, 1712) believes the lawsuit had gone on for years without any "personal quarrel of consequence." The duke's second was Colonel John Hamilton of the Scots Foot Guards; Lord Mohun chose General George MACCARTNEY. The actual duel became a vicious combat, with each of the primaries, using swords, being wounded three or four times. Mohun apparently died on the spot in Hyde Park, but not before mortally wounding the duke in a last, desperate lunge.

This final wound has been the subject of much controversy, as Swift and others for political purposes have used the false story that the Whig Maccartney attacked the wounded Duke and stabbed

him. The deaths of these two men affected many lives: Maccartney, under threat of arrest, escaped to France; Colonel Hamilton was arrested and tried for murder, though finally released; the young duchess of Hamilton, Swift's friend, became an inconsolable widow; Lady Elizabeth Mohun, mourning her own condition, wrote the duchess of MARLBOROUGH about Joseph ADDISON's new tragedy, *Cato;* and the duke of Shrewsbury was declared ambassador extraordinary to the court of France in Hamilton's place and departed a month after the duel.

Swift saw Mohun as a Whig tool manipulated to serve party interest, and his comments in "The HISTORY OF THE FOUR LAST YEARS OF THE QUEEN" substantiate this view. In the marginalia to MACKY's *Characters of the Court of Britain* (1733), Swift adds "Mohun was little better than a conceited talker in company." "The FIRST ODE OF THE SECOND BOOK OF HORACE PARAPHRASED AND ADDRESSED TO RICHARD STEELE, ESQ." alludes to Mohun as a "pious patron's ghost."

## Molesworth, Robert, first viscount (1656–1725)

WHIG writer and politician who began as a member of WILLIAM III's Privy Council for Ireland; envoy extraordinary to Denmark (1692); author of *An Account of Denmark* (1694), which severely criticized that government as tyrannical; Irish M.P. (1695–99 and 1703–05); English M.P. (1705–08); created Baron Molesworth of Philipstown and Viscount Molesworth of Swords (1719) in reward for his support of the Hanoverian succession. As a member of the Royal Society, Molesworth was considered an ingenious and extraordinary man by his peers, among them John Locke and John TOLAND. During the 1720s Molesworth became the patron for a group of New Light Presbyterians, mainly writers and intellectuals, who numbered among this circle such figures as James Arbuckle, editor of the *Dublin Weekly Journal;* John Smith, Irish publisher of leading works in the commonwealth tradition; and Francis Hutcheson, a moral philosopher.

Swift had much respect for Molesworth, and dedicated the fifth of The DRAPIER'S LETTERS (dated December 14, 1724) to him. He knew Molesworth was a Whig with liberal views but admired his defense of Ireland's rights. The entire paper projects a tone of assurance and confidence that his readers will respond, as he has done, to the idea of liberty as a blessing. Satirically remarking on his having read too much of Locke, MOLYNEUX, and Molesworth, the Drapier complains that "a certain Dean" had warned him against the goodwill of a people who are governed by laws made with their own consent. Support for Molesworth was not universal, and Swift may have influenced HARLEY in 1714 to remove this politician from his place on the Privy Council for his siding with Dissenters against High Church interests. Richard STEELE had defended Molesworth in his paper *The Englishman* (January 19, 1714), but Swift attacks both men in "The Public Spirit of the Whigs" for this damaging point of view. However, though they disagreed respectfully at other times, both men found their outrage at William WOOD's patent for issuing coins a common cause.

**Moll, Herman** (d. 1732)   Dutch mapmaker and geographer who began work in London in the late 1690s. Swift was familiar with his 1719 *New and Correct Map of the Whole World*. In Part 4, chapter 11, of GULLIVER'S TRAVELS, Lemuel Gulliver alludes to Moll as his "worthy Friend." Gulliver explains that after the mutiny of his crew on the *Adventure* (detailed in chapter 1), he discovered that New Holland—Australia—is actually three degrees west of where it normally appears on most maps and charts. He claims that he shared this information with Moll, who ignored it and chose "to follow other Authors."

**Molyneux, William** (1656–1698)   Philosopher, scientist, and political writer. He was born and raised in Dublin of an English family who had arrived in Ireland in the late 16th century. Educated at Trinity College, Dublin, and the Middle Temple, he was joint surveyor-general and chief engineer, supervising civil and military construction projects during the period 1684–88. His long interest in optics, astronomy, and applied mathematics led to a number of essays and other publications, as well as his helping to found the Dublin Philosophical Society (which first met formally in 1683), on the model of the Royal Society. He resumed his work as chief engineer after 1691 and became commissioner of army accounts and M.P. for Trinity College, Dublin (1692–98). As a correspondent of Locke, the astronomer Edmund Halley, and other well-known figures, Molyneux not only increased his knowledge of the new sciences (he translated Descartes's *Meditations* in 1680) but also took particular interest in investigating the effect that recent legislation of the English Parliament was having on the Irish linen and woolen industries. His concern produced his best-known work, *The Case of Ireland's Being Bound by Acts of Parliament in England* (1698).

In *The DRAPIER'S LETTERS*, letter 4: "To the Whole People of Ireland," Swift repeats Molyneux's arguments "that the people of Ireland have equal rights with the people of England under the same King but . . . Ireland is in no sense a depending kingdom." Swift relies on Molyneux—"the famous English Gentleman born here"—in stating that Ireland has always opposed England's effort to bind that country and ignore the inherent liberty of its people. Later, in letter 5: "To Viscount Molesworth," Swift refers to Locke and Molyneux as dangerous authors who refer to liberty as a blessing that only unlawful force can take away. Earlier, in "The STORY OF THE INJURED LADY," Swift had shown the influence of Molyneux, arguing the universal law of nature required being governed only by laws to which the Irish had given their consent. As the first statesman to claim legislative independence for Ireland, Molyneux began a protest that would last for more than a hundred years.

**Montagu, John, second duke of** (1690–1749)   Courtier. His connections at an early age at Court provided him with a number of ceremonial offices and opportunities for enriching himself. GEORGE I appointed him governor general of the Caribbean islands of St. Lucia and St. Vincent's (1722), and Montagu outfitted ships and recruited colonists and their families to settle the islands. After a series of disasters the colonial enterprise failed, and Montagu, who had sent a lieutenant governor in his place, lost an immense sum of money. He spent the remaining 25 years of his life serving in various impressive-sounding offices, but typically his duties were nonexistent. As an active WHIG, Montagu joined the Kit-Cat Club and supported its informal political forum where the objectives of limited monarchy, a strong Parliament, resistance to French aggression, and the succession of the House of Hanover were paramount. One writer has said, "the duke appears to have been a man of some talent, but with much of the buffoon about him." He married Mary Churchill, youngest daughter of the duke of MARLBOROUGH and celebrated for her beauty (1705), though Montagu, then 15 years of age, was described as sickly and immature.

Swift mentions Montagu's wife in "To CHARLES FORD, ESQ. ON HIS BIRTHDAY," and certainly he knew of the duke, whom he may have met when he and Alexander POPE apparently joined the Lodge of Freemasons in 1730. The duke was the Grand Master of the London Grand Lodge and may have amalgamated it with one of the loosely organized individual lodges at the time.

**Montagu, Lady Mary Wortley** (1689–1762) Daughter of the first duke of Kingston-upon-Hull and wife of Edward Wortley Montagu, M.P. (1678–1761), an eminent WHIG and grandson of the first earl of Sandwich, whom she married in 1712 after eloping with him against her father's will. Montagu proved himself a rather dull, self-contained man and indifferent to his wife's many talents. Considered vivacious, ambitious, aggressive, self-educated beyond other women, and beautiful, Lady Mary could be viciously witty both in person and in the mock pastorals she wrote. Her renown at Court as the confidante of the Princess of Wales (later Queen CAROLINE) and as a notable figure in the beau monde evoked in Alexander POPE's *Rape of the Lock* aided her husband's political ambitions. Traveling to Constantinople with her husband, who was appointed ambassador to Turkey (1716–18), she embraced the language and culture, as her embassy letters so effectively display. Returning to England with information on smallpox inoculation, she diligently worked to popularize the practice there.

At Court she grew close to Lord HERVEY and anonymously engaged in playwriting and publishing

a political paper supporting Robert WALPOLE. Her husband made little progress in politics and then focused wholly on business and becoming immensely wealthy, while their marriage grew stale. By 1728 her friendship with Pope turned to mutual hate, and they lashed each other in various satiric pieces. Finally in the 1730s she separated from her husband and followed a young Italian lover to the Continent, intending to live with him. This did not happen, but she remained abroad. She maintained an active correspondence for the next two decades with the literary world in England, only to return for a final flourish and death in 1762.

She wrote a poem, "Epistle to Mr. Pope," in 1730 with a group of lines insinuating a sexual liaison between Swift and Vanessa (see Esther VAN-HOMRIGH) and alluding to the dean's "CADENUS AND VANESSA." In 1726 on a visit to England, Swift, who was staying with Pope at Twickenham, met Lady Mary, who lived nearby and held a salon for wits, poets, and painters. They disliked each other immediately, and later she suggests in commenting on "The LADY'S DRESSING ROOM" that Swift had written the poem as revenge against a woman with whom he had been impotent. In an April 5, 1733, letter to his friend Charles FORD, Swift wrote that he thought "her Devil enough" (*Corr.* IV.138), and Pope told Swift in a missive of April 20 that "they [Lady Mary and Hervey] are certainly the Top wits of the Court" (*Corr.* IV.147). Ironically, Swift's relationship with Edward Wortley Montagu seems more balanced from the time they first met in 1710 in London, having dined together with Joseph ADDISON.

**Moore, Arthur** (c. 1666–1730) Lord commissioner of Trade and Plantations, M.P. for Grimsby, and comptroller of army accounts. Moore was born in Ireland of poor origins, but through talent and energy he learned finance and trade. Swift mentions him in "A New Journey to Paris" (1711) as the person who assisted Matthew PRIOR, the diplomat, in his efforts to negotiate the Peace of Utrecht. Moore accompanied Prior as he secretly left Windsor with instructions for the French Court, traveling to Kent and on to Dover where a boat, prepared by Moore, waited offshore for a signal to pick Prior up and carry him to Calais. He was a known agent for BOLINGBROKE, who developed the commercial terms for the treaties with the French, and Robert HARLEY's allies often attacked him for supposed corrupt practices in hopes of diminishing the secretary. Harley saw an opportunity to investigate Moore and damage Bolingbroke in June 1714 with the result that Moore was found guilty of illicit trade and diverting money into various secret accounts. Also, he was declared incapable of further employment and lost his director's position with the SOUTH SEA COMPANY. These battles between the secretary and lord treasurer disappointed Swift who regretted the infighting and demise of the ministry.

Moore's son, James Smythe Moore (1702–34) was an author and man about town who wrote the play *The Rival Modes* (1727) and quarreled with POPE, who added him to *The Dunciad,* his community of dunces. See also *The JOURNAL TO STELLA* and Swift's *Correspondence* for further insight into Arthur Moore.

**Moore, Betty**    The youngest daughter of Henry Moore, third earl of Drogheda, married in 1704 to George ROCHFORT, son of Robert Rochfort, chief baron of the exchequer in Ireland. In a whimsical yet tender letter to Esther JOHNSON (Stella) in *The JOURNAL TO STELLA* (March 25, 1711), Swift imagines Stella waking up and looking out her window as various Dublin ladies, including this friend, come past from church. Baron Rochfort had given George the family seat at Gaulstown when he was married, and Swift spent many holidays in the intimacy of their wealthy family. The dean was friends with both the father and Lady Betty's parents, and the hospitality at Gaulstown was the most lavish, especially in its liberality: He might exercise whenever he wished, keep his own hours, and read all the good books in the Rochfort library.

Early editors have often understood Swift's "A LETTER TO A YOUNG LADY," written on the occasion of the marriage of one of Rochfort's sons, as advice meant for Lady Betty, instead of John's wife, Deborah Staunton. But John Rochfort was the dean's favorite, and the very young lady mentioned in this essay surely was Deborah. Lady Betty did

participate in a humorous game involving Swift, Thomas SHERIDAN, Patrick DELANY, Daniel JACKSON, and her husband resulting in a series of verses poking fun at Jackson's nose and various replies: see "TO MR. DELANY," "ON DAN JACKSON'S PICTURE," "DAN JACKSON'S REPLY," "ANOTHER REPLY BY THE DEAN," and "SHERIDAN'S SUBMISSION." And as a result of a June 1721 visit lasting months, Swift wrote "The PART OF A SUMMER," in which all these same friends are together at Gaulstown for a house party, and Lady Betty shows herself briefly as both affectionate and controlling toward her husband. See also "TO THOMAS SHERIDAN," "TO MR. SHERIDAN, UPON HIS VERSES WRITTEN IN CIRCLES," and "ON DAN JACKSON'S PICTURE."

**Moor Park**    See TEMPLE, Sir WILLIAM.

**Morgan, Marcus Antonius** (b. 1703) M.P. of Athy, County Kildare, Ireland, and chairman of the Irish Commons committee considering the petition of graziers for relief from the pasturage tithes on grazing lands (1736). The Church of Ireland worried that with tithe adjustments of any kind, the clergy would suffer further financial hardship. The universal hatred, as Swift saw it, toward the church resulted in his writing a very effective poem, "A CHARACTER, PANEGYRIC, AND DESCRIPTION OF THE LEGION CLUB," and following with the pamphlet "CONCERNING THAT UNIVERSAL HATRED WHICH PREVAILS AGAINST THE CLERGY." During an earlier piece of related legislation, Swift had written "Some Reasons against the Bill for Settling the Tyth of Hemp, Flax, &c. By a Modus" (1734). In this piece, he was successful in having the proposed legislation dropped, but the tithe on pasturage opposition was better organized, and Swift adopted his harshest diatribe and tone in hoping to stop passage of the bill. Morgan, who had been on friendly terms with Swift, was chastised in the poem as a traitor to his school and a gorgon who has turned his classmate to stone. Both he and Swift had graduated from Trinity College, Dublin. Morgan is assigned in the poem to this legion of unclean spirits, sitting in their handsome new parliament building as a club of inmates in a veritable madhouse. Swift mentions Morgan, with his "heathenish Christian name," and his wife frequently and with affection in his *Correspondence* during the last months of 1735.

**Mose, Ralph**    Second husband of Esther JOHN-SON's (Stella's) mother, Bridget JOHNSON. Mose was William TEMPLE's steward at Moor Park, and Mrs. Johnson had been a widow and housekeeper at the time when Mose's first wife was still alive. Mose and Swift shared some of the same duties in the household during the 1690s as higher-ranking employees. During absences of the Temple family, Swift and Mose were responsible for the proper running of Moor Park. When Temple died in 1699, Mose received a good settlement from the estate, testimony of the value he retained in the Temple family. Mose married Bridget Johnson in 1711, long after Stella had grown up. According to a recent biographer, Mrs. Johnson had married Mose beneath her cultivation and status because he had blackmailed her, threatening to reveal certain secrets concerning the origins of Stella's birth.

**Mountjoy, William Stewart, second viscount** (d. 1728)    He succeeded to his title in 1692 on the death of his father, who was killed at the Battle of Steinkirk, where the British army was nearly cut to pieces and William of Orange (WILLIAM III) embarrassed by French forces. Mountjoy served in the army, becoming a general officer and finally lieutenant general in 1709. As a reward for his services, Mountjoy held the post of master general of ordnance from 1714 to 1728.

Swift and Mountjoy had become friends when the latter took his seat in the Irish House of Lords and later became a member of the Privy Council; and on receiving his commission for the remission of first-fruits and traveling in 1710, Swift joined a group of bishops and Irish M.P.s from Dublin to London. Mountjoy paid Swift's expenses from Chester to London, and the favor was much appreciated. The men dined and played cards with each other during his London stay (1710–13), often accompanied by other Irish and English friends or recent acquaintances. Mountjoy's brother, Richard Stewart, became a regular at their table. Later, in 1724, during the WOOD coinage scandal and the subsequent publication of *The DRAPIER'S LETTERS,* Swift took distinct pleasure

in Mountjoy's signing the *Address of the Privy Council of Ireland,* in which the members requested the removal of William Wood and the base coin he was to produce. See *The JOURNAL TO STELLA* for frequent references to Stewart as Mountjoy.

**Mountrath, Charles Coote, fourth earl of** (1680–1715)    Son and heir to the third earl of Mountrath, whom he succeeded in 1709; the family were WHIGS. Swift dined with him and MOUNTJOY in London during 1710, playing cards until late in the evening and feeling "like a fool." Later, he accepts a dinner invitation at Mountrath's apartments but finds the wine poor and leaves early. Swift was familiar with the current earl's grandfather, Sir Charles Coote (d. 1661), an able military and political figure in Ireland whose support of CHARLES II had resulted in his being rewarded with the lands and the title of earl of Mountrath. Assuming the dean does not know the man, the duchess of Queensberry describes the current earl in a November 10, 1733, letter to Swift: "a modest well bred spleenatick good natturd man, . . . he has a very great regard for you. . . . [W]e were all highly pleasd with him he seems to have a better way of thinking than is common and not to want for sense or good humour" (*Corr.* IV.205–06). A month later, Coote writes a complimentary letter to Swift thanking him for the indulgence of using his name among various acquaintants and promising to give him at the first opportunity Queensberry's gift of a walking stick.

**Musgrave, Sir Christopher** (1631–1704)    Statesman, aristocrat, and long-serving English M.P. Musgrave was an Oxford graduate and student at Gray's Inn who underwent imprisonment in the Tower for his support of the Crown. He served in Parliament for 43 years and remained a staunch supporter of royal prerogative, opposing the Exclusion Bill and refusing JAMES II's order to vote for a repeal of the test and penal laws. Swift mentions Musgrave in "A TALE OF A TUB" in "Section 9: A Digression Concerning Madness" as one of the leading TORY M.P.s who, according to Swift's suggestion, should search Bedlam Hospital for potential civil servants. Alexander POPE satirizes Musgrave's reputed corrupt dealings with WILLIAM III in his *Epistle to Bathurst* (1733).

# N

**Newton, Sir Isaac** (1642–1727)   Physical scientist and mathematician. He discovered the laws of gravitation and published his account of them in *Principia* (1687). He also invented the reflecting telescope, which enabled him to discover the composition of white light and the nature of colors. He published these theories in *Opticks* (1704). Alexander POPE admired him greatly, keeping a bust of Newton in his house and writing his epitaph for Westminster Abbey.

Swift first mentions Newton in "A TALE OF A TUB," alluding to a point he is making about humor and wit and an association with mathematics. For Swift truth is revealed through intuition or revelation, but not through scientific investigation. Later, in "A DISCOURSE TO PROVE THE ANTIQUITY OF THE ENGLISH TONGUE," Swift makes an ironical reference to Richard BENTLEY making learning expire just as Newton did with mathematics. With this barb, the dean shows himself still angry with Newton's support of the William WOOD copper coinage scheme. As warden and then master of the mint, Newton took his duties seriously during the great recoinage and assayed the copper in Wood's coins, and much to Swift's horror, found the copper "to be of same goodness, and value . . . [as] is coined in the King's Mint for England." The second DRAPIER'S LETTER condemns the Newton assay as a poor example of the scientific method and implies sarcastically that Newton is in the employ of Wood. In *COMPLETE COLLECTION OF GENTEEL AND INGENIOUS CONVERSATION*, Swift calls him an instrument maker and a workman in the mint, who made

"Sun-dyals better than others of his trade, and was thought to be a conjurer, because he knew how to draw lines and circles upon a slate, which no body could understand." Yet Swift found warm and spirited company in the companionship of Newton's niece, Catherine BARTON, who cared for her uncle's home and his daily household requirements in the area of Leicester Fields and the Haymarket near the dean's apartments. At some point during the 1720s Swift had met Newton and discussed the problems inherent in determining longitude, a popular topic among projectors during this period. *GULLIVER'S TRAVELS* explores the issues of travel in its parody of that genre, and Gulliver carries with him a pocket telescope and spectacles: Both offer opportunities for references to optics, as well as magnification and reduction. The major assault on Newton comes in Part 3, where mathematicians receive a thorough criticism of their values and practices.

**Northey, Sir Edward** (1652–1723)   Lawyer and politician, educated at Oxford and the Middle Temple. He served as attorney general of England (1701–07 and 1710–18), appointed by the lord keeper of the Great Seal, Sir Simon Harcourt (1661–1727), who later became lord chancellor (1713). He tended to move between the WHIG and TORY parties, becoming an M.P. in 1710, and often voted favorably on Tory issues but survived into the Hanoverian regime, voting appropriately so as to retain his office. He had a significant role in a number of state trials, as well as various cases requiring his opinion, one concerning Joseph ADDISON and his appointment to a diplomatic post. Knighted in 1702, Northey had ambitions to possess the Great Seal. Swift, in "The FAGGOT," calls him "that Rascal Northey . . . [who] is prepared to leap o'er sticks" to supplant Harcourt. He led an undistinguished career but made good use of his political connections in retaining various political appointments. Swift met him in London in 1710.

## Nottingham, Daniel Finch, second earl of

(1647–1730) Statesman, High TORY, High Churchman, and trusted leader of the country clergy. He was ultimately appointed senior secretary of state (1702–04); he served earlier as first lord of the admiralty (1681–84), then as secretary of war (1688), and in other government posts during Queen ANNE's reign. Educated at Oxford and the Inner Temple, he was first elected to Parliament in 1679 and soon became a privy councillor who found himself at odds with JAMES II's policies, particularly regarding Jacobites. Both parties respected him, and the clergy saw him as a champion of their concerns, yet he refused to join the revolution against the Stuarts.

Swift nicknamed him "Dismal" for his dark complexion (or, as Pat Rogers suggests, for his gloomy aspect and sober attire), and listed him as one of the principal WHIG party figures in "The HISTORY OF THE FOUR LAST YEARS OF THE QUEEN," describing his holding principles opposite to party belief, yet his ability to retain government appointments was legendary. Though admiring him for this balancing act, Swift could not abide Nottingham's cynical ambition of gaining Whig support for his bill against Occasional Conformity by supporting that party's decision in opposing the Peace of Utrecht. Nottingham's will-

ingness to sacrifice strict truth for expediency, not to indulge in gross distortion or dishonesty but merely to place his concerns in the best possible light, became a frequent practice, at least as Swift viewed his character. Even earlier than the writing of the "History," Swift had published "An EXCELLENT NEW SONG" condemning Nottingham's desertion of the Tory party. During this period, "TOLAND'S INVITATION TO DISMAL TO DINE WITH THE CALVES' HEAD CLUB" portrays a meeting of a republican society called the Calves' Head Club, held on the date of Charles I's execution, where Nottingham is the most sought-after guest of this Whig gathering. "Suspend a while your vain ambitious hopes, leave hunting after bribes," advises Swift's narrator, and join us to "talk what fools call treason all the night." Swift follows up this piece with a broadside containing a prose satire on Nottingham, entitled "A HUE AND CRY AFTER DISMAL," where Dismal and his servant, horribly costumed as chimney sweeps, are discovered in Dunkirk on a spying mission for the Whigs. Two poems in 1712, "PEACE AND DUNKIRK" and "Dunkirk to Be Let," refer to Dismal, and the latter poem Swift inserted into the "Hue and Cry" pamphlet as if the French, when arresting Nottingham, found it in his pocket. Later, "The AUTHOR UPON HIMSELF" reflects on the personal attack made against him by Nottingham on the floor of the House of Lords. Finally, this enemy receives Swift's coup de grâce in GULLIVER'S TRAVELS, becoming the reprehensible character of Part 1, Skyresh Bolgolam, the high admiral of Lilliput and counselor of the emperor. Bolgolam, as a great noble and high functionary with a solemn demeanor, seemed the perfect mirror to Nottingham. See also The JOURNAL TO STELLA, "A PANEGYRIC ON THE REVEREND DEAN SWIFT," "The WINDSOR PROPHECY," and "SCRIBLERIAN VERSES."

**O'Carolan Turlough (Turlough Carolan)** (1670–1738) Irish Gaelic musician. Born in County Meath and blinded by smallpox as a young boy, O'Carolan was trained as a harper, his instrument the ancient symbol of Irish music. He played for the remnants of the Gaelic aristocracy and was welcomed at the houses of the Catholic gentry but also had such Anglo-Irish patrons as Swift and his friend Patrick DELANY. In the first collection of Irish secular music, he had 20 tunes published (1724), marking him as the chief musician of Gaelic Ireland. He avoided political and religious controversy in his lyrics and attracted a diverse audience.

Swift did not take much interest in Irish/Gaelic culture, though he insisted on mixing with the poor Catholic Irish at Quilca House, County Cavan—the home of Thomas SHERIDAN and his wife. His tastes, however, were far too tolerant and his enjoyment of people and conversation too vast to exclude an interest in this ancient culture—its language, music, and history, though he did write in "An ANSWER TO SEVERAL LETTERS SENT ME FROM UNKNOWN HANDS" that "it would be a noble achievement to abolish the Irish language," hoping to improve the economic conditions of Ireland if all the Irish spoke English. "The DESCRIPTION OF AN IRISH FEAST" suggests Swift knew and admired O'Carolan, who set the words of this poem to music. Since O'Carolan knew Delany, the harpist visited Dublin and the deanery, entertaining all with his music. Interest in Irish crept into "MY LADY'S LAMENTATION AND COMPLAINT AGAINST THE DEAN" and GULLIVER'S TRAVELS, where certain linguistic similarities between foreign vocabularies and Irish can be found.

**Ogleby, John (John Ogilby)** (1600–76) Scottish cartographer, printer, and translator of Virgil, Homer, and the *Fables* of Aesop. He is referred to in "The BATTLE OF THE BOOKS" as the spiritual father of Thomas Creech. Ogleby is also targeted as an object of satire in John DRYDEN's *MacFlecknoe* and Alexander POPE's *Dunciad*.

**Oldham, John** (1653–83) Satirist, writer of Pindarics. John DRYDEN wrote a well-known elegy in his honor after Oldham died of smallpox. In that poem ("To the Memory of Mr. Oldham"), Dryden calls Oldham "the Marcellus of our Tongue" and writes that he and his "young Friend" were "Cast in the same Poetic mold" in that they both abhorred "Knaves and Fools." Among Restoration poets, Oldham helped popularize the "imitation" as a genre, producing his own imitations of Boileau, Horace, and Juvenal. In his *Satire against Virtue* (a Pindaric ode published in 1679) and *Satires upon the Jesuits* (1681), he targeted general problems rather than specific individuals. In "THE BATTLE OF THE BOOKS," he is slain by Pindar during the battle.

**Orford, Edward Russell, first earl of** (1653–1727) WHIG statesman and naval officer who became first lord of the Admiralty and M.P. from 1689. His famous career in the navy led to a position in the Whig government during the final years of the reign of WILLIAM III. Orford had been an early and active agent for the prince of Orange, and later when he became king. After 1695 he did not return to sea and soon after, he became a peer and sat in the House of Lords. As the TORIES became more powerful during the early months of 1700, they argued that William's partition treaties for the division of the Spanish empire had been negotiated without the consent of Parliament but on the advice of four lords (the Whig Junto): Hans Willem PORTLAND, Charles HALIFAX, John SOMERS, and Edward Russell, first earl of Orford. The House of Commons began impeachment proceedings against these Whig ministers, and Swift immediately went into action in their defense.

"A DISCOURSE OF THE CONTESTS AND DISSENSIONS IN ATHENS AND ROME" (1701) served as a powerful statement on the balance of power and the dangers of political parties. Swift uses parallel history as a mask to discuss contemporary politics, referring to Orford as a modern day Themistocles, the Athenian naval hero and political leader. See also "TOLAND'S INVITATION TO DISMAL TO DINE WITH THE CALVES' HEAD CLUB."

**Orkney, Elizabeth Villiers, countess of** (1657–1733)  Mistress of WILLIAM III for six years and wife of George Hamilton, sixth earl of Orkney. Elizabeth was the first cousin of Barbara Villiers, the well-known mistress of CHARLES II, and her family was closely associated with the royals, which brought the young woman into William's presence. As a reward for her devotion, William presented her with the immense property in Ireland once belonging to JAMES II, nearly 100,000 acres, worth more than £26,000. Though these grants were rescinded later, she gained value from this munificence for more than 10 years, even after William had removed her from his side.

Swift became friends with Lady Orkney in 1712. She invited him to her home at Cliveden, giving him presents and portraits of her. In The JOURNAL TO STELLA he wrote that "she is the wisest woman I ever saw," and appreciated her efforts in trying to raise his spirits as the TORY ministry began its collapse. Some writers suggest Orkney helped Swift in the writing of "The HISTORY OF THE FOUR LAST YEARS OF THE QUEEN." Her knowledge of the court circle and her perspective on political issues made her advice worth having, especially for HARLEY, who frequently consulted her. In his will, Swift returns two of her gifts to him, especially her portrait to her husband. Other commentators mention her physical plainness and a disfiguring, "hideous" squint. Her chief virtue was her willingness to serve as Swift's confidante during this difficult period, and in 1712 Swift wrote a comment on her character and added it to Lady Orkney's Character of Oxford. Aside from the virtues mentioned, Swift complains that her formal education remained unsatisfactory for a person of her obvious intellectual talents and damaged her prose.

**Orkney, George Hamilton, first earl of** (1666–1737)  A career army officer who served in the field for nearly 30 years and was remembered by Swift in 1733 as "an honest good Natured Gentleman." He married his cousin Elizabeth Villiers, countess of ORKNEY, in November 1695 and was created earl of Orkney, a Scottish peer, in January 1696. Earlier in 1695, Hamilton was promoted to brigadier general after his excellent leadership during the siege and conquest of Namur. Promoted twice again, Lieutenant General Hamilton commanded a brigade of what is now the Royal Scots and other troops, creating confusion and the collapse of the French command in the village of Blenheim in 1704. He fought with great distinction in the most important battles of the War of the Spanish Succession, and on his return to England sat in Parliament, became a Privy Council member, and received various military appointments as a reward for his fine service. He was also named governor of Virginia in 1714, governing by proxy, and field marshal of all his majesty's forces in 1736. Swift mentions him frequently in later sections of The JOURNAL TO STELLA as a dinner companion and member with Lady Orkney in numerous card games.

**Ormonde, James Butler, second duke of** (1665–1745)  Soldier, courtier, Irish aristocrat, early and constant supporter of WILLIAM III, and Jacobite; lord lieutenant of Ireland (1703–05, 1710–11, 1713); commander-in-chief and captain general of the allied army on the Continent, after MARLBOROUGH was relieved of command (1712). BOLINGBROKE insisted that Ormonde avoid engaging in any siege or battle while the peace negotiations were ongoing, and this order would later form the main article in this minister's impeachment for high treason. In July 1715 he fled to France to avoid imprisonment, losing all his estates and forfeiting his honors. At various points during the next 25 years he was involved in assisting or consulting with those Jacobites planning "risings." Opinions regarding Ormonde's character remain evenly divided, with Winston Churchill calling him a "weak, base creature," and others, like Swift, considering him one of most glittering and noble men of his age. His family, education, intelligence, charm, and courage set him apart from normal mortals in Swift's eyes. If Ormonde made mistakes, and he made many in his long life, Swift felt he was not to blame: "he is governed by fools . . . and has much more sense than his advisers."

Swift celebrates him as the favorite hero of the Jacobite and TORY party, a true son of Dublin in "TO CHARLES FORD, ESQ. ON HIS BIRTHDAY." In 1713, with the direct help and assistance of Ormonde, Swift secured the preferment of an appointment. After arranging to move John STEARNE out of the deanery of St. Patrick's to the bishopric of Dromore, Ormonde and Robert HARLEY created the place for Swift. As the breakup of the Tory ministry proceeded, Swift wrote to Ormonde, who was a fellow member of the Brothers' Club, seeking his support to reconcile the ministers. Ironically, the queen had already asked the duke to serve in a similar role. "The FAGGOT" alludes to this story in its image of arrows that individually are easily broken but, bound together, resist breakage. Swift, after hearing of Ormonde's conviction, began writing "An ENQUIRY INTO THE BEHAVIOUR OF THE QUEEN'S LAST MINISTRY," believing "it looks like a dream to those who will consider the nobleness of his birth . . . and sweetness of nature." "The HISTORY OF THE FOUR LAST YEARS OF THE QUEEN" stresses Ormonde's respect for the orders of Bolingbroke and Harley to suspend operations against the French while peace negotiations proceeded. The JOURNAL TO STELLA and Swift's Correspondence

contain extensive references to Ormonde's work as lord lieutenant of Ireland, chancellor of the University of Dublin, in the Tory ministry, and as a leading Jacobite.

**Ormonde, Mary (née Somerset) Butler, duchess of** (d. 1733)   Wife of James Butler, second duke of Ormonde, second daughter of Henry, first duke of Beaufort (d. 1700). She became Butler's second wife in August 1685, and the couple enjoyed a friendly relationship with Swift. She frequently referred to herself as Swift's sister, and to her only surviving daughter, Lady Betty Butler, as his niece. In a letter to Swift (dated May 3, 1715) Ormonde refers to his wife as "Corinnikin," a term of endearment. After Ormonde fled to France in 1715, she never saw him again. In writing to Swift in October 1715, she begins realizing the enormity of his departure and the couple's loss of all his properties. Their correspondence remained limited after the duke's impeachment; a government bounty on his head for thousands had government authorities investigating all mail to the duchess and often never delivering it to her. Both used Charles FORD as a courier for their few letters, as he traveled between Ireland and England regularly. The duchess's final letter to Swift, December 9, 1723, suggests her resignation about the future of her marriage: "I have no sort of correspondence with the person you have not seen, and wonder at nothing they do, or do not do." See Swift's JOURNAL TO STELLA and Correspondence for further references to this friend.

**Orrery, Charles Boyle, fourth earl of** (1676–1731)   Statesman and general; educated at Christ Church, Oxford. Orrery joined a group of university wits who were objecting to Richard BENTLEY's defense of modern learning. Like Swift, Orrery was a staunch advocate of the ancients in the Ancients versus Moderns controversy. Orrery was the editor of the so-called Epistles of Phalaris published in 1695. In response to Sir William TEMPLE's lavish praise of Phalaris in his essay on Ancient and Modern Learning (1690), William WOTTON and Bentley successfully argued that Phalaris could not have been the author of the Epistles. Dr. Bentley's Disserta-

*tion . . . Examin'd* (1698) was published as a response to both Wotton and Bentley. Orrery allowed this refutation to be printed listing him as the author, although Francis ATTERBURY had written it.

Swift mentions Orrery in the Apology attached to "A TALE OF A TUB," and he also appears in "The BATTLE OF THE BOOKS." The episode there recalls the Phalaris controversy and the assault Orrery waged in print against Wotton and Bentley: After Wotton hurls a lance at Temple during the battle, Apollo orders Orrery (as Boyle) to seek revenge. Wearing armor *"given him by all the gods,"* Boyle eventually impales Wotton and Bentley simultaneously with a single lance—just as he had using a single publication (the *Dissertation . . . Examin'd*) to attack their arguments regarding the *Epistles of Phalaris.* Swift's return to Moor Park in 1696 and the influence of Temple may have caused him to enter the controversy and write "A Tale of a Tub" and the "Battle of the Books." Orrery was chosen to prepare an edition of Phalaris, but to no effect, though his colleagues at Christ Church were pleased. Later, he became an M.P. in the Irish House of Commons and joined the army, fighting at Malplaquet and becoming a general officer in 1709. He knew Swift in England and Ireland as a member "The Society," a TORY club, and spoke freely about the character weaknesses of his heir, John Boyle, earl of ORRERY. In 1721, Orrery was implicated in a Jacobite conspiracy and thrown into the Tower for six months.

**Orrery, John Boyle, fifth earl of** (1707–1762) Aristocrat, author, and friend and biographer of Swift. Educated at Christ Church, Oxford; his father, Charles Boyle, apparently did not respect his son's intellectual abilities and left his library to the university because (in his view) his son had no use for books. This report does not seem an accurate portrayal of John Boyle, who became the respected friend of Swift and Alexander POPE.

Swift first met Orrery in mid-August 1732, and the young man displayed all his powers of charm and obsequiousness—which worked on the dean, who was feeling physically unwell and emotionally unsettled. Swift had been invited to England and offered a lesser post in a church near BOLING-BROKE's home, Dawley, but had turned it down, deciding his duty was in Ireland. He responded to Orrery's gift of verses with excessive praise: "go on to be the great example, restorer, and Patron of Virtue." Orrery became Swift's trusted agent, someone with impeccable credentials in both kingdoms, who could carry important manuscripts to Principal William KING of Oxford, especially COMPLETE COLLECTION OF GENTEEL AND INGENIOUS CONVERSATION, "The HISTORY OF THE FOUR LAST YEARS OF THE QUEEN," and letters for Pope. Orrery's role in convincing Swift to release Pope's original letters and return them to the author shows the young earl reveling in the company of both of these famous artists. In his will, the dean left Orrery a small amount of silver plate and a painting of the countess of ORKNEY, Orrery's mother-in-law. Lord Orrery published his *Remarks on the Life and Writings of Dr. Jonathan Swift* in 1752, the earliest biography, though earlier Laetitia PILKINGTON published reminiscences in her *Memoirs* (1748–54). Although Orrery's work improved the level of reliability in reporting the facts of Swift's life, Thomas SHERIDAN, Patrick DELANY, John Hawkesworth, and Deane SWIFT all found elements in Orrery's biography that could not be defended. Swift's *Correspondence* contains nearly 40 letters between the two men. See also "A PAPER BOOK IS SENT BY BOYLE."

**Oxford, Edward Harley, second earl of** (1689–1741)　See HARLEY, EDWARD.

**Oxford, Robert Harley, first earl of** (1661–1724) See HARLEY, ROBERT.

# P

**Palmerston, Henry Temple, first viscount** (c. 1673–1757) Eldest son of Sir John Temple, speaker of the Irish House of Commons, and nephew of Sir William TEMPLE. As a child, he was named to the sinecure of chief remembrancer of the court of exchequer of Ireland for life at an income of £1,200. In *The DRAPIER'S LETTERS* (Letter 4—"To the Whole People of Ireland"), Swift pointedly recalls Palmerston holding this post "worth near £2,000." Created Baron Temple of Mount Temple, County Sligo, and Viscount Palmerston of Palmerston, County Dublin (1723), Temple then sat in the English House of Commons as a placeman representing sequentially three different districts (1727–47). A strong supporter of Sir Robert WALPOLE, who was in effect the prime minister (1721–42), Temple with his WHIG sympathies was welcomed in successive administrations, where he was known as "Little Broadbottom Palmerston." He did secure the services of the Weekly Miscellany as a ministerial organ for a hefty payment.

Swift quarreled with Temple, whom he had known since his days at Moor Park, when Temple refused to grant the dean a favor. Swift's feelings toward the Temple family were complex and often ambivalent, and in this instance he answered Temple harshly, reminding him of the value of gratitude in their actions toward each other. The three letters in the *Correspondence* reflect the full exchange between the two men, although Swift wrote as well to John Temple, the younger brother.

**Parnell, Thomas** (1679–1718) Poet. Born in Ireland of English parents, supporters of Cromwell, who had moved there after the restoration of CHARLES II in 1660, Parnell entered Trinity College, Dublin, at the age of 13. After taking clerical orders in 1704, he married Anne Minchin in 1706, soon became the archdeacon of Clogher, and gained his Doctor of Divinity in 1712. Traveling to England frequently and writing poetry, Parnell with the help of his friend Swift came into contact with the London literary world and was introduced to Robert HARLEY and Henry BOLINGBROKE. He enjoyed the company of Joseph ADDISON and Richard STEELE and later, the members of the Tory-affiliated Scriblerus Club of which he, along with Swift, John ARBUTHNOT, John GAY, and Alexander POPE, formed the central core. While in England from 1712 to 1714, Parnell lived with Pope for a summer helping him translate Homer's *Iliad*. His excellent classical training and poetic instincts combined to produce pieces that supported Pope's Homeric enterprise, but when the Tories left office, Parnell returned to Ireland.

Without the urging of Pope and Swift, Parnell would likely have not published any of his poetry, especially since he was prone to depression and alcoholism after the death of his young wife and their children. His early death left only nine pieces available to the public, but he had entrusted Pope with his manuscripts, and from these, his friend selected 20 poems and published *Poems on Several Occasions* (1722). In "SCRIBLERIAN VERSES," Swift describes Parnell as a member of the SCRIBLERUS CLUB (founded in 1714 to satirize false tastes in learning). The *Correspondence* and *The JOURNAL TO*

*STELLA* show Swift serving as his unofficial patron, always seeking to help this young man reach his potential.

**Partridge, John** (1644–1715)   Also known as John Hewson, an almanac maker and astrologer who had been trained as a shoemaker. He became the leading member of a pack of false prophets who pretended to know the future, and his annual publication, *Merlinus Liberatus* (beginning in 1680), was well known and had an annual circulation of more than 20,000 copies. It was infamous for its anti–High Church rhetoric and lowbrow fortune-telling. Swift despised those who would attack the Established Church, or true religion, as he referred to it, and Partridge's efforts in defending nonconformity (along with his hubris at foretelling the deaths of various public figures) outraged the dean.

Swift, who was living with Sir Andrew Fountaine in England (1707–09), decided the Church of England could best be served if he would satirize Partridge and his predictions as a moderate churchman who is trying to rescue a much maligned science from a bad practitioner. "PREDICTIONS FOR THE YEAR 1708" by Isaac Bickerstaff, Esq., appeared in January 1708 and immediately elicited strong reaction, and Swift predicted Partridge's death in "The ACCOMPLISHMENT OF THE FIRST OF MR. BICKERSTAFF'S PREDICTIONS." In 1709 Partridge complained that he was not dead and could prove it, and with this ammunition, Swift gleefully wrote "A VINDICATION OF ISAAC BICKERSTAFF, ESQ." with evidence of Partridge's certain death. At the same time he followed with "A FAMOUS PREDICTION OF MERLIN," parodying the political prophecy and using the appearance of a 16th-century translation to add to its credibility. Later, Swift assisted Richard STEELE in adopting the mask of Isaac Bickerstaff for the *Tatler*, which began April 1709. During 1708 Swift also published the poem, "AN ELEGY ON THE SUPPOSED DEATH OF MR. PARTRIDGE, THE ALMANAC MAKER" and referred to the former cobbler in "The PROGRESS OF BEAUTY."

**Parvisol, Isaiah** (d. 1718)   Swift's land agent (steward) at Laracor and chief tithe collector. He was possibly a French Huguenot, and worked for the dean from 1702 until he was dismissed in 1714. He reported directly to Thomas WALLS, Swift's financial manager, and was rehired in 1717 but died in November of the following year. Though *The JOURNAL TO STELLA* and the *Correspondence* contain numerous references to him from 1708, Swift seems to have been generally dissatisfied with his efforts, accusing him of one sin or another and calling him a knave. Apparently, the "puppy" Parvisol did not adequately collect the income Swift was owed as dean through tithes and rents, and left numerous deanery debts and fees unpaid. Obsessive about his income, Swift needed a good agent and sent numerous notes complaining about Parvisol's "scurvy" inefficiency and expressing the need for him to improve his collection methods. Swift mentions him in "HORACE, EPISTLE VII, BOOK I: IMITATED AND ADDRESSED TO THE EARL OF OXFORD."

**Patrick**   Swift's famous Irish manservant (last name unknown) who was hired in Dublin and accompanied him to London in February 1710 and was dismissed in April 1712. Patrick plays a comic character in *The JOURNAL TO STELLA*, where he introduces anarchy to the orderly life Swift plans for himself. Drunk, unreliable, prone to forgetting his master's keys and breaking or losing various items, Patrick represents another dimension of the human comedy Swift finds both amusing and repellant. Quite conscious of his status in London as a clergyman with ambition who lives at the fringe of the court, Swift had certain expectations of his servants. Patrick punctures Swift's unsteady pride, leaving the poet with an understanding of the servant's psychology.

This insight reveals itself in Swift's late treatise, "DIRECTIONS TO SERVANTS," "a handbook," David Nokes calls it, "for domestic guerrilla warfare" (402). Patrick and his fellow servants reveal the power of self-love, and their desperate efforts at maintaining their own individuality and dignity forces the long-suffering master into his own dark despair. The supposed order of society shows itself collapsing, and Swift finds himself in sympathy with both sides.

**Pembroke, Thomas Herbert, eighth earl of** (c. 1656–1733)   Lord lieutenant of Ireland (1707–08).

As a nobleman from a large family of ancient lineage, he succeeded to the title in 1683 and was given many important offices of state: first plenipotentiary at the Treaty of Ryswick (1697) and president of the Privy Council (1702). Pembroke seemed less interested in WHIG or TORY party issues but instead adhered to the needs of the monarchy and supported the constitution above all else, voting to protect its integrity. The Junto (a group of Whig leaders) wanted to give his presidency to one of their own, but Queen ANNE refused, and Pembroke found himself with both of the top positions in Ireland.

Swift's opinion of Pembroke was immediately favorable, since this aristocrat combined the strengths of intellect, wit, and taste. As a collector of objets d'art and other curious items and with a passion for good conversation, Pembroke found a most engaging companion in Swift, even though the men held opposite political viewpoints. Pembroke also included in this coterie a distinguished young man, Sir Andrew FOUNTAINE, accomplished in numerous fields who also loved collecting. Swift found him irresistible, and they met often at Dublin Castle for entertainment. During this encouraging period, Swift wrote several short essays for sheer enjoyment, such as "A MEDITATION ON A BROOMSTICK" and "A Tritical Essay upon the Faculties of the Mind" (written for Fountaine). The three men loved puns and riddles, and Swift also wrote "A DIALOGUE IN THE CASTILIAN LANGUAGE" (1707) as an entertaining conversation piece for them. When Pembroke was recalled to England that winter, Swift accompanied him and stayed with Fountaine, continuing their friendship and his attendance on the lord lieutenant. Swift had come to use his contacts and the influence of his powerful friends to obtain the remission of the First Fruits for the Irish church. Though Pembroke did not directly influence the result, Swift believed his presence added to the eventual remission, and their friendship remained strong. See also the "DYING SPEECH OF TOM ASHE."

**Pendarves, Mary (née Granville) (later Delany)** (1700–1788) Wife of A. Pendarves (1718) and later Patrick DELANY (1744), and a talented bluestocking who joined the dean's Dublin circle in the 1730s. Mrs. Pendarves was related to John CARTERET and the statesman George GRANVILLE. Her first marriage had been a disappointment when her family arranged a safe and convenient situation in marrying her to a "disgusting" clergyman whose advanced age and excessive drinking ruined the relationship. With his death, the young widow joined friends in Dublin (1731) and immediately was invited into the best social circles in the capital. Dr. Delany, who would become her second husband, invited her to dinner, where she met Swift and many of his closest friends. Though she returned to England in a few months (while considering Dublin more agreeable than London), Swift valued her as an excellent companion, and the two kept up a lively correspondence. Certain letters from Swift border on the seductive to this young lady, and she willingly flattered him. See the *Correspondence* for their nearly 20 letters.

**Penn, William** (1644–1718) Quaker reformer and colonialist, the founder of Pennsylvania. Born in London, Penn was the son of one of Oliver Cromwell's admirals and disappointed his father by joining the Society of Friends in 1666. Penn had joined the society while living on his father's Irish estate in County Cork. In 1688 he was imprisoned in the Tower of London because of his writings, and while a prisoner wrote his most famous devotional work, *No Cross, No Crown*, explaining the Quaker-Puritan morality. At the death of his father, he inherited a valuable estate and a large debt the Crown owed to his father, which was discharged in 1681 by a grant of land in North America that he named Pennsylvania in honor of his father. He sailed in 1682 and governed the colony for two years, drawing up—with the help of Algernon Sydney—a constitution (the first to contain an amendment clause) and a code of laws. He also designed the city of Philadelphia. He returned and supported JAMES II, working for religious toleration, but with the arrival of WILLIAM and Mary, suspicion descended on him. Since his colony had problems, he returned in 1699 to rewrite the constitution, and with the granting of a permanent charter (1701), he returned to England to face financial difficulties at home.

Swift met Penn at Robert HARLEY's London home in October 1710. Later, in *The* JOURNAL TO STELLA Swift describes a meeting between Penn and a group of Quakers with the duke of ORMONDE to thank this former lord lieutenant of Ireland for his kindness to Irish Friends. The dean suggests his general dislike for these nonconformists: "to see a dozen scoundrels with their hats on, and the duke complimenting with his off, was a good sight enough" (January 15, 1712). In "MR. COLLINS'S DISCOURSE OF FREE-THINKING" Swift satirizes freethinkers like Penn and his Quakers who disturb the Established Church. His marginalia, however, suggest his contradictory feelings toward Penn: "he spoke very agreeably and with much spirit."

**Percival, John** (d. 1718)    Irish M.P. for Granard, later Trim and Swift's friend and neighbor. Percival lived across the river from Laracor, often playing cards with Swift beginning in 1702, and visited him in London in 1712. Swift considered him an intelligent, good-humored man, but Percival's ambition for increasing his landholdings annoyed him, though this Irish squire was one of Swift's wealthiest parishioners in a heavily Catholic area. When Swift intended to expand the land (the *glebe*) around his church in 1716 and improve the living for those who would follow, he found negotiations for purchasing the land difficult, even when he had complained about Percival's encroaching on his land. Friendship notwithstanding, Percival expected the best price for his land and sold it only when Swift and the trustees accepted this fact. Later, after Percival's death, Swift had a vigorous argument with the squire's son, who demanded payment of rent on a piece of land and refused to pay his tithe until the dean met this supposed obligation. Swift found this attack impossible and responded with the strongest language pointing to his legal position and condemning the young man's rudeness and stupidity. See *Prose Works* 5.196.

**Percival, William, dean of Emly**    Clergyman of contentious TORY principles; served as archdeacon of Cashel, elected prolocutor of Irish Lower House of Convocation (a post Swift had hoped to secure); later dean of Emly. Percival was a graduate of Christ Church, Oxford, and was considered the principal agent in Ireland of the Anglican Church and its convocation. Swift considered him a difficult and stubborn extremist when it came to his interpretation of High Church issues, and the two men were not friends. Percival knew of Swift's long-standing WHIG sympathies and did not trust his conversion to Tory beliefs.

Swift's "The PART OF A SUMMER" superficially deals with rural life and its supposed quiet order, while inverting the tranquility in the second half of the poem. One example of this inversion is the attack on Percival and his wife, satirizing their supposed pedantry, snobbery, and poor housekeeping. Percival responded with "A Description in Answer to the Journal" (1722), in which he ridicules Swift's housekeeping at the deanery.

**Perrault, Charles** (1628–1703)    French author, famous for his *Contes de ma mère l'oye* (*Tales of Mother Goose*; 1697). In "The BATTLE OF THE BOOKS," Homer unhorses Perrault and hurls him at Bernard le Bovier de FONTENELLE, "with the same blow dashing out both their brains." As a member of the Académie Française, he was deeply engaged in the ancients-and-moderns controversy that led to Swift's "Battle of the Books." Perrault's support of the Moderns was based on his view that, since literature evolves along with society, ancient writings are naturally more primitive and less sophisticated than more modern works. His poem *Le Siècle de Louis le Grand* ("The Age of Louis the Great"; 1687) made clear his belief that modern authors such as Molière were far superior to ancient Greek and Roman authors. Perrault was bitterly opposed by Nicolas Boileau, a fellow member of the Académie.

**Peterborough, Charles Mordaunt, third earl of (Charles Mourdaunt Peterborow)** (1658–1735) General, diplomat, and patron to literary artists. His critics called him brilliant, heroic, and erratic; he became earl of Peterborough in 1697, having first succeeded to his father's title, Viscount Mordaunt, in 1675. Although he commanded a Dutch squadron in the West Indies in 1687, his first major command was in Spain as joint commander with

Admiral Sir Cloudesley Shovell in 1705 but was recalled in two years to explain his conduct. His efforts in Spain resulted in the surrender of Barcelona and Valencia, while enabling Archduke Charles of Austria to claim the Spanish throne. Nonetheless, the House of Lords began an investigation into his activities, which was nothing more than a battle between the two parties in which the TORIES supported Peterborough, a WHIG, and the Whigs vigorously denounced him. The charges were dropped, and with the ascendancy of the Tories, he became their answer to Marlborough. His skill in diplomatic intrigue even as a soldier added to his fame during his service first for WILLIAM III, later as privy councillor and first lord of the Treasury. Queen ANNE created him Knight of the Garter (1713) and continued sending him on diplomatic missions while remaining concerned that his presence in England created parliamentary furor. With the arrival of the Hanoverians, he found himself cast aside and returned to England and his home at Peterborough House, Fulham, which Swift visited, finding the gardens magnificent.

Swift had great respect for Peterborough, and the two promised to be "mighty constant correspondents" maintaining contact from 1711 to 1733. This nobleman had made the acquaintance of many of the writers in Swift's circle, including Alexander POPE, John ARBUTHNOT, and John GAY. In his later years, Peterborough developed a spacious hillside retreat, called Bevis Mount, near Southhampton, where Pope would visit and consult on developing the gardens, which had one section known as "Pope's Walk." Swift had first consulted Peterborough during the disorderly parliamentary session of 1701 and alluded to the nobleman's views in "The DISCOURSE OF THE CONTESTS AND DISSENSIONS IN ATHENS AND ROME." In *The JOURNAL TO STELLA* Swift mentions him fondly as a fellow with more spirit than anyone he knows. Later, "TO THE EARL OF PETERBOROUGH" celebrated this nobleman as the last of the knight errants riding across Europe with speed and grace "shin[ing] in all climates like a star." Though Swift understood him, Pope's modern biographer, Maynard Mack, conveys the man accurately: He possessed "both a theatri-

Charles Mordaunt, earl of Peterborough, by Michael Dahl

cality of . . . imagination and . . . invincible high spirits."

A character representing Peterborough appears in Part 3 of GULLIVER'S TRAVELS during Lemuel Gulliver's visit to Glubbdubdrib. When Gulliver asks the Governor to call up from the dead some individuals who have done "great Services to Princes and States," an unnamed "Person" appears among them with "a Youth of about eighteen Years old standing by his side." He tells Gulliver that despite his brave fighting as a ship's commander during the Battle of Actium (as well as the loss of his son, who now accompanies him), he was denied preferment when he returned to Rome. Agrippa, who was one of the two fleet commanders at Actium, appears and confirms the unnamed man's story. In addition to recalling the death of Peterborough's son and the earl's own unsuccessful search for preferment following his service in the War of the Spanish Succession, this episode affirms Swift's view—and Gulliver's conclusion—that those who do great service to "Princes and States" are not only neglected and left to die "in Poverty and Disgrace" (if not by execution) but are consistently forgotten or misrepresented as "Rogues and Traitors" in history.

**Philip V, king of Spain** (1683–1746)   Also known as duke d'Anjou, king of Spain (1700–46), and creator of the Bourbon dynasty in Spain. He was a grandson of LOUIS XIV of France, whose designation as the successor to the Habsburg king of Spain, Charles II, precipitated the War of the Spanish Succession in 1701–14. With the conclusion of the war, Philip was on the throne of a greatly weakened Spain, having lost the symbolic Gibraltar, among other possessions, to Britain. His wife, Queen Elizabeth Farnese, and her cardinal ran the government during the second half of the period.

Swift, in "The HISTORY OF THE FOUR LAST YEARS OF THE QUEEN," refers to Philip as a pawn of France and England who would not negotiate a peace with any Spanish representatives present. "The CONDUCT OF THE ALLIES" recommends keeping Philip on the Spanish throne, something MARLBOROUGH and the WHIGS opposed, so as to end the war as quickly as possible and secure a lasting peace. Six months later, Swift published "SOME REMARKS ON THE BARRIER TREATY," insinuating how the Dutch wished to give up Spain in order to end the war, and the British felt that one more year of war might compel France to sue for a generous peace. Further references to Philip's actions appear in "The Public Spirit of the Whigs" and "An ENQUIRY INTO THE BEHAVIOUR OF THE QUEEN'S LAST MINISTRY."

**Philips, Ambrose** (1674–1749)   English poet who was born in Leicestershire, served as a Fellow of St. John's, Cambridge, from 1699 to 1708 and began writing verse there. Philips was known as a member of Joseph ADDISON's "little senate." He wrote the *Pastorals* (1709), which made Alexander POPE jealous and inspired John GAY's *Shepherd's Week* (1714), and also poems in praise of childhood, which earned him the nickname "Namby Pamby," for their cloying sentimentality. In the *Guardian* (number 31), Thomas Tickell praised Philips as a pastoral writer of nearly the same caliber as Virgil and Spenser. Pope, whose *Pastorals* formed his first published work (1709) and appeared in the same volume of Tonson's *Miscellany* as those

of Philips, was disappointed at being overlooked, and created a comparison in the next number of the periodical between his poems in this genre and those of Philips, covertly preferring his, while quoting the worst of Philips's passages. Though Pope prompted the writing of Gay's six burlesque pastorals as an attack on Philips, the reading public enjoyed both Gay's and Philips's poems and ignored issues of literary rivalry. Philips was probably the editor of a pioneer collection of old ballads (1723–25), and he adapted Racine's *Andromaque* under the title of *The Distressed Mother* (1712). He had begun a short-lived periodical in imitation of the *Spectator*, entitled the *Freethinker* (1718).

Swift had already broken off his friendship with Philips when the latter had held an official post in Ireland as secretary to Archbishop Boulter (1724), then as Irish M.P. (1727), and as judge of the Prerogative Court (1733). Before arriving in Dublin, Philips had played a brief but active role as a military officer, seeing combat at Barcelona and Almanza, as well as being held as a prisoner of war who finally escaped from the French. Swift liked both his pastorals and him on first meeting him in London in 1704, but not the young man's strong WHIG sympathies. From 1708 to 1709 Swift and Philips carried on a lively correspondence when both thought preferment from the Whigs might be forthcoming. When Addison asked Swift for help securing a minor diplomatic post in Switzerland for his protégé Philips (1710), the dean immediately agreed to speak to Robert HARLEY or BOLINGBROKE. Nothing came of this effort, but when asked again for assistance a year later, Swift refused to help this "puppy," and political disagreements destroyed this friendship. See also *The JOURNAL TO STELLA*, "The FIRST ODE OF THE SECOND BOOK OF HORACE PARAPHRASED AND ADDRESSED TO RICHARD STEELE, ESQ.," "APOLLO'S EDICT," "A COPY OF VERSES UPON TWO CELEBRATED MODERN POETS," and "A LIBEL ON THE REVEREND DR. DELANY AND HIS EXCELLENCY JOHN, LORD CARTERET."

**Phipps, Sir Constantine** (1656–1723)   Lord chancellor of Ireland. He was trained as a lawyer and called to the bar in 1684, becoming a member of the inner or higher bar who acted as a governor of Gray's Inn in 1706. His excellent management of the Henry SACHEVERELL defense brought him further praise and notice with the new TORY government. Knighted in 1710, he was appointed to the distinguished post of lord justice of the kingdom. Swift mentions him in "A VINDICATION OF HIS EXCELLENCY JOHN, LORD CARTERET" in connection with his friend, Patrick DELANY, as "a certain Person, then in a very high station here" who was especially kind to Delany (Phipps made Delany one of his chaplains). Phipps apparently was also loud, belligerent, and bigoted—a man who seemed singularly unsuited to hold his position in Ireland at this time, especially as he was a Jacobite, and to advocate the political philosophies of an extreme Tory when the Irish House of Commons was held by the WHIG majority. His actions brought trouble to the new lord lieutenant of Ireland, the duke of SHREWSBURY. Phipps was removed from office in 1714 and returned to England. Swift, who sought moderation in Ireland, found Phipps's efforts very troublesome.

Swift and Phipps corresponded briefly, having met each other for the first time in August 1713 in Dublin. But by the time GEORGE I had come to power in October 1714, all the principal officers of state, including in the royal household, army, navy, law, and local government, were replaced with their political opponents. Though Phipps's departure was long sought after, Swift believed the political situation in Ireland was ripe for Jacobite revolt. Nonetheless, Oxford University showed its support for the Hanoverians and their Whig ministry with an invitation to Phipps, who would receive an honorary degree.

**Pilkington, Laetitia** (1712–50) Author, Dublin bluestocking, and friend of Swift. Mrs. Pilkington and her husband Matthew PILKINGTON, a Trinity College clergyman and minor poet, first met Swift when she was newly married and 17 years old (1729). Her vivaciousness, energy, imagination, and pleasure at being in the dean's company were immediately appealing to Swift, who complained of loneliness and ill health in the 1730s. Her *Memoirs of Mrs. Laetitia Pilkington . . . with Anecdotes of Dean Swift, 1712–50* in three volumes (1748–54) contains excellent details of Swift's late middle age and his circle. Frequent comments by modern scholars allude to her shortness of height and deficient morals; apparently her husband finally divorced her on grounds of adultery. Her relationship with Swift describes scenes that Victoria Glendinning calls "sadistic silliness" (214). Swift eventually found reasons to regret his association with the Pilkingtons. In 1733 Swift had sent a poem, "TO A LADY," to London for publication, and Pilkington acted as an agent in this effort, but when the printer was arrested for publishing a libel against Robert WALPOLE and questioned, he incriminated another person who gave up the young clergyman. Pilkington, it was reported, was involved in naming Swift as the author of the poem. Now, in 1738, Swift denounced the pair—one for his supposed conduct in London and the other for being immoral: "the falsest rogue, and the most profligate whore" in either kingdom.

**Pilkington, Matthew** (c. 1701–c. 1774) Clergyman and minor poet. Pilkington graduated from Trinity College, Dublin, in 1722 and married Laetitia Van Lewen in 1729 (the year he met Swift). Swift befriended the couple, having him preach in St. Patrick's Cathedral, lending him money, and advising him on his poetry. Pilkington published *Poems on Several Occasions* (Dublin, 1730) with the assistance of George FAULKNER, Swift's most valuable Dublin printer. Various poems in the collection praise Swift, as does the preface, but the overall volume was certainly weak.

Swift expected Pilkington to do him the favor of carrying material for another volume of miscellaneous works to London. Alexander POPE had served as editor for the first three volumes, but the young clergyman who agreed to serve as agent was sent to arrange for a separate publication of this volume, apart from the original group. Apparently, Swift wanted the profits of this volume to go to Pilkington, though not intending to anger or disappoint Pope. Certainly, Swift's willingness to act as the young man's patron seems remarkable, continuing in 1732 when he obtained the position of a year's chaplaincy for him with his friend, the lord mayor of London, John BARBER. Having divorced his wife in 1737 and earlier failed to protect Swift from a threat of involvement in a charge of libel, Pilkington became persona non grata with the dean. This nine-year friendship ended abruptly.

**Pope, Alexander** (1688–1744)   Poet, friend, and correspondent of Swift. Both men were members of the Scriblerian Club, along with John GAY, Robert HARLEY, Thomas PARNELL, and John ARBUTHNOT. Pope's early years exhibited both frustrations and the first signs of an astonishingly mature poetic gift. His frustration was the result of severe physical disability (spinal tuberculosis) and the oppression suffered because of his Roman Catholic upbringing (this forced his family to move a prescribed distance from London and denied him a university education). Yet his precocious intellect and innate

Alexander Pope, laureated, by Jonathan Richardson, c. 1738  *(Library of Congress)*

social skills brought him into contact with those who would recognize his talents and advise him. Tonson published his polished *Pastorals* in 1709, and later, his *Essay on Criticism* was both praised and attacked as a major contribution to literary culture. Adopting political neutrality, Pope made friends with John ADDISON and Richard STEELE and their WHIG circle, yet the TORY wits of the Scriblerus Club also found his favor.

With the demise of the Tory ministry and the dispersal of his literary friends, Pope was under severe pressure from Robert WALPOLE and the new Whigs, and only freedom from political and royal patronage would secure his future. His translations of the *Iliad* and the *Odyssey*, published by subscription in the 1720s, brought him a fortune. Always skilled at marketing his works and developing new projects, Pope continued producing significant poems: *The Rape of the Lock, Eloisa and Abelard,* and *Windsor-Forest.* His satiric mock epic *The Dunciad* (1728) marked an even more serious effort at defending cultural values against the growing commercialization of the age. With the first *Dunciad,* Pope embarked on an impressive new phase in his writing with the *Imitations of Horace, the Moral Essays* (1731–35), and *An Essay on Man* (1733–34). In the 1730s he became increasingly involved in attacks on the Walpole administration, led by his friend Henry BOLINGBROKE, often from Pope's Twickenham villa on the Thames. His *Epistle to Dr. Arbuthnot* (1735) and the *Epilogue to the Satires* (1738) reflect the power of his satire when used to name the villains of his time. *The Dunciad* was completed in 1743, and he worked with William Warburton on a new edition of his *Works* (1751), even as his health rapidly deteriorated.

Swift met Pope in early 1713. Pope had been living in London with the painter Charles JERVAS, whom Swift had known well in Ireland. Victoria Glendinning remarks that Swift and Pope took to each other immediately: "Pope was a hero-worshipper, and Swift became one of his idols" (111). Pope, who needed to earn a living as a writer, depended on his friendships for literary capital—constant allusions to his friends added to the currency of his letters and occasional poems. In 1714 Swift and his friends were satirizing the usual targets in an active culture: critics, quackery, false wit (learned fools), and bad writing. With the queen dying and the ministry dismissed, Swift retreated to the English countryside, depressed by the turn of events. The remarkable correspondence between the two men begins during this period; nearly 90 letters are extant (1713–41) and many others lost. Their letters were written with sincerity, art, and sense of a future audience. Both intended to gather, edit, and publish the correspondence, and Pope did so in 1741. On June 18, 1714, he wrote, "you [Swift] are like the sun, while men . . . are hourly exerting your indulgence, and bringing things to maturity for their advantage." And on June 30, 1716, he asserted that "A Protestant divine cannot take it amiss that I treat him in the same manner with my patron-saint." Swift, always seeking a method for bringing his views before the public, wrote Pope a pamphlet masquerading as a letter (January 10, 1721) with this closing bit of irony: "I am too much a politician to expose my own safety by offensive words." Pope appears in a number of Swift's prose works, including "HOLYHEAD JOURNAL," COMPLETE COLLECTION OF GENTEEL AND INGENIOUS CONVERSATION, "A Modest Defence of Punning," and "The HISTORY OF POETRY." Pope was involved in helping publish some of Swift's later poems and appears in "SCRIBLERIAN VERSES," "A PASTORAL DIALOGUE BETWEEN RICHMOND LODGE AND MARBLE HILL," "DR. SWIFT TO MR. POPE," and "The LIFE AND GENUINE CHARACTER OF DR. SWIFT." Swift often found inspiration from one of Pope's poems or prose pieces. During April 1727, Swift made his last visit to England and stayed with Pope at Twickenham while working on the second edition of GULLIVER'S TRAVELS. Finding himself ill and knowing Stella (Esther JOHNSON) was near death, Swift left Pope's home without notice and returned to Ireland. Later that year, he agreed to a literary project that would offer a selection of both their writings, trusting Pope to collect and edit material for a set of Miscellanies. Though expecting the work would be authoritative, Swift was disappointed. He maintained his friendship with Pope but delayed sending the younger poet a number of manuscripts because he now intended to care for his literary reputation himself. Swift's Correspondence and JOURNAL TO STELLA contain numerous references to Pope.

**Portland, Hans Willem Bentinck, first earl of** (1649–1709) Dutch courtier, diplomat, later duke of Portland who served WILLIAM III, accompanied him to England, and became an important asset in exercising the king's foreign policy. As groom of the stole, he had access to the king at all times and ultimately became wealthy. Swift knew him but did not respect his abilities. In 1693 Portland took counsel with Sir William TEMPLE at Moor Park on a constitutional matter before Parliament. Temple assured the king's agent that the bill was harmless and sent Swift as his personal emissary (armed with letters) to convince the king and Portland of the same. These meetings failed, yet Swift became well known to the WHIG leaders: John SOMERS, Portland, Robert HARLEY, and Charles HALIFAX. In 1700 Portland married Jane Martha Temple BERKELEY, niece of Sir William Temple. Swift calls him "Phocion" in "The CONTESTS AND DISSENSIONS IN ATHENS AND ROME," celebrating his warrior spirit and renown as a negotiator.

**Portland, William Henry Bentinck, second earl** (1682–1726) Politician. Bentinck was the son of first earl of PORTLAND, William Bentinck, whom Swift knew but found weak and vacillating, though "a very good-natured man, but somewhat too expensive." The son served as a WHIG M.P. (1705), but he had no electoral influence within his home district. When the SOUTH SEA COMPANY stock collapsed, he was forced to apply for a governorship in the West Indies and made was governor of Jamaica in absentia (1721–26) in order to meet expenses. Earlier, he had been a gentleman of the bedchamber, and GEORGE I created him first duke of Portland in 1716, mainly because of his father's efforts in the Hanoverian cause. He married Lord Edward HARLEY's only surviving child and heir, the Lady Margaret Cavendish Holley Harley (1715–85).

Matthew PRIOR celebrated Margaret as "my noble, lovely little Peggy" in "A Letter to the Honorable Lady Mrs. Margaret Cavendish Harley" (1720). Lady Margaret's dowry included Welbeck Abbey, Nottinghamshire, inherited from the family of Cavendish. In an August 8, 1734, letter to Swift, Harley calls Bentinck "the fairest and unexceptionable character . . . as he is free from . . . gaming, sharping, pilfering, lying. . . . [H]e is endowed with qualifications . . . such as justice, honor, excellent temper both of mind and body, affability, living well with his own family" (*Corr.* IV. 244). Harley later wrote (in an April 7, 1737 letter to Swift) that "the Duke of Portland so far answers our expectations that indeed he exceeds them for he makes the best husband, the best father, and the best son, these qualities are I assure you very rare in this age" (*Corr.* V.27).

**Pratt, Dr. Benjamin** (c. 1669–1721)   Provost of Trinity College, Dublin, later dean of Down. He was Swift's classmate at Trinity, and both were students of St. George ASHE; Pratt remained Swift's friend and collaborated with him in church politics, visiting him in London in 1713. Their comradeship, often tested by the ambition of both men, survived the rumors of Pratt's efforts to gain an Irish bishopric. Earlier, in 1708, Swift learned of Pratt's imminent appointment to the deanship or the provostship of St. Patrick and made the current dean immediately aware of the fact (see Swift to Dean STEARNE, April 15, 1708). When the government in Ireland changed and the TORIES were out in 1714, Pratt lost his post as provost, held since 1710, but managed through some difficult negotiations to secure the deanship at Down in 1717. Pratt had become wealthy and his cultivated tastes brought him into the best social circles; his late marriage to the daughter of the earl of Abercorn, Philippa Hamilton, added to his modest fame.

Swift found the whole effort absurd, saying "what a ridiculous thing is man." Writing a poem to satirize his friend and the marriage (lasting only 12 months), Swift finished it shortly after the man's death: "The PROGRESS OF MARRIAGE." Pratt's death surprised and upset Swift, who once again was forced into contemplating the nearness of death in the middle of life's fullness. Both The JOURNAL TO STELLA and Swift's *Correspondence* contain numerous references to Pratt.

**Pratt, John** (b. c. 1670)   Deputy vice-treasurer of Ireland and constable of Dublin Castle, younger brother of Dr. Benjamin PRATT, and an army captain (1703). Meeting Swift as a college classmate, John graduated from Trinity College, Dublin, in 1689 with a B.A. He later became Swift's financial adviser, investing substantial amounts of income for him. Swift enjoyed his company, as well as that of his wife, Henrietta Pratt, née Brookes (1676–1769), who was related to Sir William Petty, the founder of the Dublin Philosophical Society. Her relations were the Shelburnes (brother and sister), who joined the Pratts when they visited him in London in 1710–11. Swift enjoyed the company of the sister (Lady Kerry), who suffered from his same illness—Ménière's syndrome. They discussed how they each coped with the disease.

The duke of ORMONDE had assisted Pratt in securing his government post, but in June of 1725 he was found guilty of embezzling public funds and imprisoned. Apparently Pratt's mishandling of funds did not result in any losses for Swift (thanks to the quick action of Thomas STAUNTON, Swift's lawyer and agent, and John WORRALL, his vicar at St. Patrick's), nor did he seem disturbed at the possibility of losing money at the treasurer's hands and worried more about Pratt's arrest. Swift alluded to Pratt in "MAD MULLINIX AND TIMOTHY," "VERSES FROM QUILCA," and the verse "Trifle," not recognized by Rogers but available in Williams: "Musa Clonshoghiana." After prison, Pratt became involved in the coal industry and glass manufacture. Some evidence exists that Pratt wrote the pamphlet *Relation of Several Facts, Exactly as They Were Transmitted to Me from Ireland,* which followed upon Swift's "SHORT CHARACTER OF HIS EXCELLENCY OF IRELAND" (1710), a very successful attack on a thoroughly corrupt politician. Swift, who was supplied by the deputy treasurer with facts and other information about Wharton, encouraged Pratt in writing this second essay.

**Prendergast, Sir Thomas** (c. 1700–1760)   Second baronet who succeeded to the title after his father's death at the Battle of Malplaquet (1709), became an Irish and English M.P. and postmaster general of Ireland. His uncle, General William CADOGAN, whom Swift lampoons in the EXAMINER, annoyed the TORIES, and his mother, Penelope Cadogan Prendergast, whom Swift called the litigious Widow Blackacre (a character in Wycherley's

*The Plain Dealer*), sued his friend Theobald Butler. Swift lampooned Prendergast in two poems, "ON NOISY TOM" and "A CHARACTER, PANEGYRIC, AND DESCRIPTION OF THE LEGION CLUB," calling him, among other slanderous names, "that rampant ass." Prendergast's involvement in George FAULKNER's imprisonment and general contempt for the Church of Ireland clergy over tithing earned Swift's dislike.

**Pretender**   See STUART, James Francis Edward.

**pride, Swift's view of**   Throughout his prose and poetry, Swift presents pride as an intensely vexing but remarkably widespread evil. For example, in "ON THE DAY OF JUDGMENT" Jove characterizes the "offending race of human kind" as "by nature, reason, learning, blind," including those "who thro' frailty stepped aside" and those "who never fell—*thro' pride*." Swift rails against pride in "VERSES ON THE DEATH OF DR. SWIFT," listing pride among several related vices that hold dominion in human hearts: "Vain humankind! Fantastic race! / Thy various follies, who can trace? / Self-love, ambition, envy, pride, / Their empire in our hearts divide" (39–42). He makes a similar point (if more ironically) in what is probably Gulliver's best-known comment on pride in GULLIVER'S TRAVELS. Near the end of Part 4, Gulliver cites pride as an evil utterly unknown among the Houyhnhnms but the characteristic vice of the Yahoos, among whom he finds himself after his return home. He finds it particularly ironic that Yahoos, who have the least reason to be prideful, are especially prone to that vice. He explains that it was only with much difficulty that he was finally able to reconcile himself "to the Yahoo kind in general," and he admits that, "when I behold a Lump of Deformity, and Diseases both in Body and Mind, smitten with *Pride*, it immediately breaks all the Measures of my Patience; neither shall I ever be able to comprehend how such an Animal and such a Vice could tally together" (271).

While Gulliver's final comments illustrate the remarkable levels of pride and hypocrisy to be found among men, Swift portrays women as equally guilty of giving themselves over to pride. His exclamation in "DEATH AND DAPHNE" that "What pride a female heart inflames!" sums up his contention that too many women (like "haughty Celia" in "The LADY'S DRESSING ROOM" and "The PROGRESS OF BEAUTY") are devoted to the false pride that comes from hiding their blemishes behind more attractive "artificial face[s]" to present to the world. He cites this misdevotion as an economic issue in his "LETTER TO THE ARCHBISHOP OF DUBLIN CONCERNING THE WEAVERS." There he suggests that many men are guilty of "cowardly slavish indulgence" of "the intolerable pride, arrogance, vanity, and Luxury of the Women, who strictly adhering to the rules of modern education seem to employ their whole stock of Invention in contriving new arts of profusion, faster than the most parsimonious husband can afford" (IV.67).

As Swift attacked what he saw as the overwhelming pride that typified humankind, many of his acquaintances and friends found him quite guilty of the same sin. Victoria Glendinning has pointed this out in her biography of Swift: "Swift's ruling passion may be his pride. All those who knew him commented on his pride. 'His pride, his spirit, or his ambition, call it what you please, was boundless, says Lord [John Boyle, fifth earl of] ORRERY. His pride was 'not to be conquered' " (277). In "Thoughts on Various Subjects," however, Swift complicates traditional notions of pride (along with the many accusations of his own devotion to it) when he makes an interesting distinction between pride and vanity. He asserts that, "To be vain, is rather a Mark of Humility than of Pride" since "Vain Men delight in telling what Honours have been done them, what great Company they have kept, and the like" while freely admitting that they deserved none of it. A proud man, on the other hand, "thinks the greatest Honours below his Merit, and consequently scorns to boast." Swift sums this up with a maxim: "whoever desires the Character of a proud Man, ought to conceal his Vanity" (4.245).

**Prior, Matthew** (1664–1721)   Poet and diplomat. Prior was born in Dorset, England; attended Westminster School; and attracted as a patron the earl of Dorset, John DRYDEN's friend, who supported his going to St. John's College, Cambridge.

After securing a fellowship, he focused on writing poetry, some of which was published. He became a diplomat when appointed secretary to the embassy at The Hague, once again thanks to the intervention of the earl of Dorset. His chief service as an ambassador emerged through negotiating the Treaty of Utrecht (1713) for the TORY ministry. Change of national policy with the arrival of the Hanoverians brought about his loss of position and a brief imprisonment, but his poetry, including the philosophic *Solomon on the Vanity of the World* (1718), a disquisition on the vanity of human knowledge, and some of the most direct and coolly elegant love poetry of the period, brought him wide popularity. Lord Edward HARLEY copurchased with him a country mansion in Essex, where he died a bachelor whose critics found his poetry skillful and witty—"an amusement."

Robert HARLEY introduced Swift to Prior in 1710 in London, and the clergyman immediately found him an ideal companion for conversing and walking, but more important for his ideas and knowledge of French culture. Henry BOLINGBROKE formed his club, The Society or "The Brothers Club," inviting Swift, Prior, Joseph Addison, and nine others for the advancement of conversation and friendship. Prior collaborated with Swift on the *EXAMINER* and in later years influenced both Swift and Alexander POPE in their mock-heroic verse (especially Pope's couplets in his *Essay on Man*). Swift complains about the WHIG ministry's harsh treatment of Prior in 1715 in "To CHARLES FORD, ESQ. ON HIS BIRTHDAY." Earlier, in 1711, Swift wrote "An EXCELLENT NEW SONG" haranguing the Whigs for not welcoming the efforts toward peace, especially Prior's diplomatic mission. When writing "The HISTORY OF THE FOUR LAST YEARS OF THE QUEEN," Swift praises Prior's choice as the chief envoy to France.

**Pulteney, Sir William, earl of Bath** (1684–1764) Wealthy English M.P. and WHIG statesman who served as secretary at war (1714) and supported Robert WALPOLE's government. He later broke with his mentor and rejoined Henry BOLINGBROKE in establishing an opposition to the ministry. His support and direction of the *Craftsman*, a leading anti-Walpole journal, added to the intellectual flavor of the ministerial attacks. He formed a group of dissident Whigs, called the Patriots, who worked successfully against the ministry. After Walpole's fall, Pulteney refused further office when he could not overcome the Pelhams' political power, becoming instead the earl of Bath (1742).

Swift met him in 1726 on a visit to England, when Pulteney tried to enlist his help in opposition activities. "ON MR. PULTENEY BEING PUT OUT OF THE COUNCIL" complained of Pulteney's dismissal from the English Privy Council. By then the two men were maintaining an active correspondence, and Swift followed with "To A LADY," which censures Robert Walpole. References to Pulteney exist in "VERSES ON THE DEATH OF DR. SWIFT, D.S.P.D." and in the *EXAMINER*, as well as a controversial essay, "The ANSWER OF THE RIGHT HONORABLE WILLIAM PULTENEY," complaining of the dangers inherent in selecting the country's prime minister.

# Q–R

**Queensberry, Catherine Douglas, duchess of** (c. 1701–77) Wife of Charles Douglas, third duke of Queensberry, and daughter of Henry Hyde, second earl of Rochester. Matthew PRIOR called her, "Kitty, beautiful and young," and she became the patron of John GAY, the correspondent of Swift, and the friend of William CONGREVE, Alexander POPE, and other writers. Swift, who first met her when she was 12, later began a lively correspondence with her, suggesting the two might meet again at her home, to which she had invited him. Their 30 letters were clever and seem to have been well intentioned, but they never met again. Both Swift's *Correspondence* and *The JOURNAL TO STELLA* contain references to Queensberry.

**Radcliffe, John** (1650–1714) Physician to Queen Anne, becoming the principal medical authority in 1686, who declined to attend at her death because he and his chief patient had a falling out after he could do nothing to keep her sickly son, the duke of Gloucester, alive. Nonetheless, the public and the House of Commons found his behavior unacceptable and censured him. Swift requested his medical advice for special diets and various medicines for headaches and other ills. Radcliffe, who is mentioned in "ON THE WORDS 'BROTHER PROTESTANTS AND FELLOW CHRISTIANS'" represents the medical profession, a type of figure on whom Swift often relied but whom he also distrusted.

**Raymond, Rev. Anthony** (c. 1676–1726) Rector of Trim, former fellow of Trinity College, Dublin (1699–1705), and lifelong friend of Swift. Harold Williams calls him eccentric, improvident, and vain, yet capable of keeping his friendship with Swift. Esther JOHNSON (Stella) and Swift were Raymond's and his wife's guests at Trim and Moymet, a small Crown living given him in 1713 through Swift's good offices. Near the end of his life, he wrote a prospectus for a history of Ireland, a work which he never completed. Swift, in *The JOURNAL TO STELLA*, contradicts Stella's good opinion of Raymond: "I'm sure I used him indifferently enough, and we never once dined together, or walked . . . he came sometimes to my lodging, and even there was oftener denied than admitted." When opportunities arose for improving Raymond's salary and position, Swift was more than willing, even considering offering his first post at Laracor to him if the Court would give permission (though guilt at being unable to do much for his friend had more to do with this suggestion as he really needed the Laracor income himself). Swift's "ON THE LITTLE HOUSE BY THE CHURCHYARD OF CASTLEKNOCK" mentions his friend. Extensive reference to him exists in the *Correspondence*, but only one letter to Raymond remains extant.

**Richmond, Charles Lennox, first duke of** (1672–1723) Natural son of CHARLES II and Louise de Keroualle, duchess of Portsmouth. The duchess was a great favorite of Charles, and the king remained an attentive father to his children of which there were 12. Richmond, an agreeable man, lacked the exceptional qualities of either parent.

His social prominence brought him opportunities to make himself useful, serving as aide-de-camp for nine years and lord high admiral under Prince William of Orange (WILLIAM III). He joined the WHIG Kit-Cat Club in 1702, along with a number of noblemen who often supported various artistic venues, like the building of the new Queen's Theater in the Haymarket, which opened in 1705.

Swift did not respect him, calling him a "shallow coxcomb," and refused to speak to him at Court. In "TOLAND'S INVITATION TO DISMAL TO DINE WITH THE CALVES' HEAD CLUB," Swift unites Richmond with a group of well-known Whigs he ridicules in this comic feast.

**Ridgeway, Anne**  See BRENT, ANNE.

**Robinson, John, bishop of Bristol** (1650–1723) Churchman and diplomat. He served as chaplain to the English embassy at the Swedish court for 25 years. With his diplomatic experience, Robinson returned to England, becoming the dean of Windsor (1709), bishop of Bristol (1710), lord privy seal (1711), and bishop of London (1714). He assisted in the negotiations for the Treaty of Utrecht, and was the last ecclesiastic to hold diplomatic and political office.

Swift writes of the bishop's activities in *The JOURNAL TO STELLA* but finds him a person of "not many parts." In "The WINDSOR PROPHECY" Swift attacks the duchess of Somerset, a Whig and close friend of Queen ANNE, and mentions Robinson in the early lines. Clearly, the bishop seems, at least to Swift, too moderate a TORY, often accommodating himself too easily to WHIG intentions.

**Rochester, Laurence Hyde, earl of** (1641–1711) M.P. for the University of Oxford, created Viscount Hyde and earl in 1681, and lord lieutenant of Ireland from 1701 to 1703, but served in Ireland for only four months; described as an intransigent High Church TORY who unwillingly took this post. He was the first lord lieutenant who convinced the sovereign that the viceroy need not be in residence in Ireland except for six months every two years when the Irish Parliament was in session. As uncle to ANNE, he had his wish, though Swift found the

practice another example of bad government. Curiously, Swift had accompanied Rochester from England to Dublin but, having no great liking for him, remained when the lord lieutenant returned to London.

Later, when Rochester succeeded John SOMERS and became lord president of the council (1710), Swift had reason to think well of this Tory and mourned his sudden death in May 1711: "[this] is a great blow to all good men, and even his enemies cannot but do justice to his character. What influence it will have on public affairs, God only knows. . . . I was of opinion that he contributed much to keep things steady" ("To Archbishop KING, May 15, 1711"). Swift also noted the loss in the *EXAMINER* (number 40), worrying that the Tory leadership in the House of Lords (Rochester was the son of the earl of Clarendon) was severely weakened now. Other references to him appear in "DISCOURSES OF THE CONTESTS AND DISSENSIONS." Rochester was a patron of John DRYDEN and figured in his *Absalom and Achitophel* as the character "Husai."

**Rochfort, George** (c. 1682–1730) Irish M.P. for West Meath, elder son of Robert Rochfort, chief baron of the exchequer in Ireland, and friend of Swift. Rochfort was given the Gaulstown country estate on his marriage to Lady Betty MOORE in 1704. Swift, whose enjoyment in working the land—"busy with plantations and ditching"—was limitless, would stay months at his friends' houses. The hospitality at Gaulstown remained lavish, and Swift visited in 1718, 1719, 1721, and 1723.

"The PART OF THE SUMMER" formed part of a series of amusements between Swift and his friends: George, his brother John, the Reverend Daniel JACKSON, the Reverend Thomas SHERIDAN, and the two brothers' wives. Swift's wit remains sharp, and some critics feel he was unnecessarily harsh in his comments here, but their reaction seems an overreaction. Swift also adds "The DEAN TO THOMAS SHERIDAN," one in a series of trifles between these friends, and continues with "GEORGE NIM-DAN-DEAN, ESQ. TO MR. SHERIDAN," "GEORGE NIM-DAN-DEAN'S INVITATION TO MR. THOMAS SHERIDAN," "TO MR. SHERIDAN, UPON HIS VERSES WRITTEN IN

CIRCLES," and other trifles that have no real place in the Rogers edition. Swift's *Correspondence* contains the only two extant letters between the two friends, though a number of references exist throughout.

**Rochfort, John** (1692–1771)  M.P. for Ballyshannon and subsequently for the manor of Mullingar; youngest son of Robert Rochfort, chief baron of the Irish Court of Exchequer; brother of George ROCHFORT; and friend of Swift, who called him Nim or Nimrod (from Genesis 10.9). John Rochfort enjoyed hunting and entertaining and married Deborah, the daughter of a good friend, the lawyer and financial adviser of Swift, Thomas Staunton.

In his biography of Swift, Irvin Ehrenpreis indicates that John was Swift's "particular favorite"— "well-educated and sweet-tempered and an unusual disposition to sobriety and virtue" (III.87). When Swift planned a birthday party for Esther JOHNSON (Stella), the deanery group included Charles, FORD, Thomas SHERIDAN, GRATTAN brothers, and George and John Rochfort. Later, when Stella drew up her will, her executors were Swift's friends, among them John Rochfort. Swift attended the marriage of John and Deborah, and in a critical period in his own personal life as well as theirs, he wrote "A LETTER TO A VERY YOUNG LADY, ON HER MARRIAGE." This essay recognizes the intellectual nature of women and sets aside gender as a qualification for virtue. In May 1740 Swift asked John to witness his last will; ironically, John was selected as a member of the Lunacy Commission in 1742, to inquire into the state of Swift's mind. He is mentioned in "The PART OF A SUMMER," "BILLET TO THE COMPANY OF PLAYERS" and "STELLA'S BIRTHDAY (1723)," as well as those poems associated with his brother.

**Romney, Henry Sidney, earl of** (1641–1704)  Lord lieutenant of Ireland. He held many honorary positions as a court officer, as well as ministry posts and diplomatic assignments. In an eight-year period, he was created viscount, secretary of state, lord lieutenant, an earl, and lord justice. These achievements unfortunately had less to do with his merit and more with King WILLIAM's fondness for him. In

deciding to respond to a rambunctious Irish Parliament while lord lieutenant, Romney simply dismissed them, causing much anger throughout the country.

Swift sought his help in gaining preferment at Canterbury or Westminster after the death of William TEMPLE, but Romney did nothing for him. Later, in "The FAMILY OF SWIFT" (Swift's autobiographical fragment), Swift shows he never forgot this failed promise: "as [Romney] was an old, vicious, illiterate rake, without sense of truth or honour." "The PROBLEM" portrays a disgusting aristocrat whose every function is designed to annoy and repulse. Swift also refers to him in the marginalia, denying him any honesty.

**Roper, Abel** (1665–1726)  Publisher and journalist. Roper started the leading TORY newspaper, the *Post-Boy*, which published three times a week from 1695 to 1714. It was considered the partisan voice of the HARLEY ministry, and Henry BOLINGBROKE approved the contents. Swift wrote infrequently for the paper and in one instance prevented the printing of a particularly scandalous attack on the Dublin bishopric. As the unofficial press agent for the Tory ministry, Swift managed a group of unknown writers and printers who turned out propaganda in support of ministerial projects. He referred to Roper as a "humble slave," who was only too eager to print whatever information was given him and to treat it as a legitimate, newsworthy item. Swift's enemies believed he was in constant league with Roper, producing a stream of invective against the WHIGS and others, although there is no conclusive evidence to back that suspicion. Often when an item appeared in the *Post-Boy*, it also was reprinted in the *London Gazette* and the *Evening Post*. The main purpose of these reports was to hold support for the ministry together and keep the public informed of certain facts and interpretations. Swift's effort, as limited as it may have been, continued from August 1711 to February 1713.

In "The IMPORTANCE OF THE GUARDIAN CONSIDERED," Swift, who is attacking Richard STEELE, comments on the unoriginality of his former friend's ideas, since many others had made the same points, one being Roper. He hopes in criticizing Steele's person to diminish the man and his credibility, and ironically to enhance Roper's position in the public mind. "The FIRST ODE OF THE SECOND BOOK OF HORACE PARAPHRASED AND ADDRESSED TO RICHARD STEELE, ESQ." mentions Roper as "a matchless hero." "UPON THE SOUTH SEA PROJECT" refers to the *Post-Boy* during the period of 1711.

**Rowe, Nicholas** (1674–1718) Dramatist and poet. He was a very successful writer of well-constructed tragedies focusing on patriotism, heroism, constancy, a passion for liberty, and on particular lovers in distress during the Restoration. A graduate of Westminster School, he proceeded to the Middle Temple and then held a number of small government posts as a WHIG. He took a more important post as clerk to the Council of the Prince of Wales, and in 1715 succeeded Nahum Tate as poet laureate. He notably served as the first editor of Shakespeare in 1709 and is responsible for the divisions into acts and scenes, the notations of entrances and exits, and the lists of dramatis personae. His translation of Lucan's *Pharsalia* (1718) is one of the best translations of the century.

Although he did not believe the clergy should attend theater productions, Swift admired Rowe's *Tamerlane* (1701) as an effective celebration of WILLIAM III and an accurate portrayal of LOUIS XIV as a monster of villainy. Swift met Rowe in London in 1710 and dined with him and other literary figures. Rowe (who admired Swift greatly) praised the early poem he wrote and published in the *Tatler* after a few weeks in the city: "A DESCRIPTION OF A CITY SHOWER." When the TORY ministry came into power, Swift urged HARLEY and Henry BOLINGBROKE to recognize some of the Whig writers, especially William CONGREVE, Ambrose PHILLIPS, Joseph ADDISON, and Rowe. With the last, he "got a promise of a place." See The JOURNAL TO STELLA and the *Correspondence* for further information on Rowe, one of Swift's "Amis Vivants et morts."

**Rundle, Thomas, bishop of Derry** (c. 1688–1743) Churchman. Swift had an excellent relationship with Rundle, a WHIG prelate sent from England in 1735. Rundle had been nominated for an English

bishopric but lost the post due to his religious opinions and curiously received the rich Irish preferment instead. He was a good friend of Alexander POPE (which on its own would have brought about Swift's friendship) and had also added an Irish clergyman, Rev. Marmaduke Phillips, as his chaplain—something Swift described as "a very wise and popular action" ("Swift to Alexander Pope" September 3, 1735). Swift visited and dined with the bishop often, and they would discuss Pope's activities and health. Rundle, he wrote to Pope, "is esteemed here as a person of learning and conversation and humanity, but . . . he is a most excessive Whig, but without any appearing rancor . . . besides £3,000 a year is an invincible sweetner" (February 7, 1736).

Before meeting Rundle, Swift had attacked the clergyman in "ON DR. RUNDLE," but the real focus of this satire was the Irish bishops as a group, led by Hugh BOULTER, who annoyed the dean no end for his easy alliance with the WALPOLE ministry. See also "An EPIGRAM."

**Rymer, Thomas** (1641–1713) Critic and historian. Rymer was educated at Cambridge University, proceeded to Gray's Inn, and passed the bar in 1673. His views on neoclassical drama were more in keeping with French dramatists than English. He published two critical studies attacking Elizabethan drama, and became historiographer royal in succession to Thomas Shadwell in 1692. Soon he began working on his major effort, a collection of treaties between England and foreign powers from the year 1101 onward, entitled Foedera [Treaties], of which 15 volumes appeared by 1713. Samuel BUTLER and John DRYDEN objected to his severity and his denigrating comments on Shakespeare, but Rymer practically inaugurated the detailed study of literary texts.

Swift considered even preferment outside the church preferable to having no achievement at all, especially if the opportunity afforded the writing of history. He asked for the assistance of Joseph ADDISON in being named historiographer after Rymer's death, but neither the WHIGS nor the TORIES cooperated in this wish. Once again his friends were unable or unwilling to envision Swift in such a post, though clearly they believed he deserved some place. See "ON POETRY: A RHAPSODY."

# S

**Sacheverell, Rev. Henry** (1674–1724) Clergyman. Sacheverell was the son of a poor parson and became a fellow of Magdalen College, Oxford. He depended on his oratorical skills and impressive looks, rather than his intellect or character. He attacked all Low-Church types from the pulpit, including WHIGS, and his famous 1709 sermon against the Revolution Settlement of 1688 (in which he pointed out Sidney GODOLPHIN and his ministers as enemies of the church) led to his impeachment. The storm produced by this ill-conceived impeachment trial, instead of punishing Sacheverell, resulted in the destruction of the Whig ministry. Though found guilty, Sacheverell's punishment was tantamount to an acquittal. This event encouraged the TORIES, and Robert HARLEY and Henry BOLINGBROKE soon gained a landslide victory.

During Sacheverell's three-year suspension, Swift met him in January 1712 and immediately became his supporter and even requested Harley's help in getting his brother a post. Swift published "MR. COLLINS'S DISCOURSE OF FREE-THINKING" attacking Collins's deistic philosophy and by comparison praising Sacheverell's position. Swift refers to this clergyman's courage in "A Preface to the Bishop of Sarum's Introduction" and in "Some Reasons . . . in a Letter to a Whig-Lord" he mentions Sacheverell's impeachment as an example of outrages perpetrated during the Whig ministry. Sacheverell also figures prominently in two of Swift's better-known essays, "The Public Spirit of the Whigs" and "An ENQUIRY INTO THE BEHAVIOUR OF THE QUEEN'S LAST MINISTRY."

**St. John, Henry** See BOLINGBROKE, HENRY ST. JOHN.

**Sancroft, William** (1617–93) Archbishop of Canterbury. Educated at Cambridge and Fellow of Emmanuel College, he held other posts at the university and then took the distinguished position of dean of St. Paul's Cathedral in 1664. He was revered in Protestant England for his decision to accept imprisonment in the Tower instead of agreeing to JAMES II's damaging edicts concerning the Established Church. Later, he refused to acknowledge WILLIAM III and lost his primacy in 1691.

Swift considered him one of the pillars of the Anglican Church and took every opportunity to defend him, even to his patron William TEMPLE, who severely criticized Sancroft. In the "ODE TO DR. WILLIAM SANCROFT," Swift admires Sancroft's martyrdom and raises the archbishop to the height of other defeated heroes, Robert HARLEY and CHARLES II. In "A Preface to the Bishop of Sarum's Introduction," he mentions Sancroft as a "pious and excellent Prelate." In various references throughout the marginalia, Swift finally refuses Gilbert BURNET's negative characterizations with one overarching comment: "False as hell." Swift repeats the unfortunate treatment of Sancroft in "The Presbyterians' Plea for Merit."

**Saunders** See MCGEE, ALEXANDER.

**Savage, Philip** (d. 1719) Chancellor of the exchequer of Ireland (1695–1717) and father of

Anne Savage ACHESON, an acquaintance of Swift. In "TO A LADY," Swift compliments Lady Anne as a daughter who was raised in a family with much love and attention. Savage had been a friend of Swift's from the dean's early days in London, when they dined together and enjoyed the camaraderie of the Irish Club (The JOURNAL TO STELLA, December 12, 1710). Later, in "A PANEGYRIC ON THE DEAN," Swift comments affectionately on Lady Anne as he puns on her maiden name: "poor I, a savage bred and born, by you instructed every morn." "A Continuation of a Short Character of Thomas, Earl of Wharton" gives particular emphasis to Savage's practicing the duties of his office, much to the disdain of his opponents.

**Sawbridge, Thomas** (1690–1733)  Dean of Ferns and Leighlin (1728). An English clergyman who took his degree at Emmanuel College, Cambridge, in 1709, and then returned to Leicestershire for his first church posting, Sawbridge for unexplained reasons lost this living. He then accepted a chaplaincy in the navy and soon moved to a more lucrative post with the East India Company in Bombay. His arrival in England surprised and upset Swift, especially when Jonathan SMEDLEY, whom Swift despised, was replaced with an English import.

The situation became unexpectedly intolerable when Sawbridge was charged with rape and arraigned in Dublin in February 1730. Swift understood the man had become drunk and "forcibly and feloniously ravish[ed]" a young woman. The trial followed quickly, but no evidence against him was brought forward, and even with the case postponed for a week no one appeared against Sawbridge. With the case dismissed, Sawbridge threatened to sue the woman for perjury. Swift, however, would have none of this explanation and believed the woman's silence had been purchased. This entire case confirmed Swift's opinion of the corruption and bias at the center of the government's ecclesiastic policy. In "An EXCELLENT NEW BALLAD," Swift explored the political ironies in this case as England raping Ireland—power and violence overcoming innocence.

**Scarborough, Richard Lumley, first earl of** (c. 1650–1721)  Aristocrat, army officer, and WHIG M.P. His Anglo-Irish family supported JAMES II, though they had become Protestant, but in 1688 the certainty of WILLIAM's ascendancy convinced Baron Lumley to change sides. His support of William resulted in his becoming viscount (1689) and earl (1690). As a successful army officer, he served in Flanders and Ireland, fighting at the Battle of the Boyne, and retired as a general in 1697. Most scholars believe he was a reliable Whig, though Swift opposes this view.

Swift calls him "a knave and a coward," probably because the dean felt Lumley had left James when the king most needed his support. In "Some Reasons to Prove, That No Person is Obliged by His Principles, as a Whig, to Oppose Her Majesty or her Present Ministry. In a Letter to a Whig-Lord" (1712), Swift tries to restrain the extremists among the Whigs and appeals to all party members concerned about the damage radical change will cause in the country. Though he does not identify the Whig lord as Lumley, many think Swift may be appealing to him. Later, his poem "TOLAND'S INVITATION TO DISMAL TO DINE WITH THE CALVES' HEAD CLUB" satirizes this republican society, which focuses on the imaginary Calves' Head Club as having more to do with the actual Whig dining group, the Kit-Cat Club, of which Lumley was an early member. Also, Lumley plays a minor role in "The HISTORY OF THE FOUR LAST YEARS OF QUEEN ANNE'S REIGN" as a spoiler in Queen ANNE's efforts to end the War of the Spanish Succession.

**Scriblerus Club**  This club was organized in London in 1713, when a friendship developed between Alexander POPE and Jonathan Swift while both were seeking to support the TORIES' efforts toward peace with France and the end of a long war. Pope's introduction of Swift to a group of like-minded writers—Dr. John ARBUTHNOT, John GAY, William CONGREVE, Reverend Thomas PARNELL, and even Henry BOLINGBROKE—led to the club's plan to develop a series of projects attacking false taste in culture. Arbuthnot led the writing of an early mock-biography, The Memoirs of the Extraordinary Life, Works and Discoveries of Martinus Scriblerus, which satirized a fictional intellectual pedant.

With Swift's departure for Ireland in 1714, the club ended its formal meetings, but the associations it fostered remained a strong influence on its members and the friendships were maintained through personal contact and extensive letter writing. Critics recognize that many of the most important works of these club members emerged from their discussion with each other of their ideas and interests, especially GULLIVER'S TRAVELS, Gay's *Beggar's Opera,* and Pope's *Dunciad.*

**Scroggs, Sir William**   (c. 1623–83)   Lord chief justice of England from 1678 to 1681. Scroggs presided over the infamous "Popish Plot" of 1678, involving an alleged attempt to murder King Charles II and replace him with James, duke of York, all in order to reinstate Roman Catholicism as the official religion of England. Swift's interest in Scroggs was based on the latter's dismissal (in 1680) of a Middlesex grand jury before the end of its term in order to prevent the jury from convicting the duke of York as a Roman Catholic sympathizer. Swift alludes to Scroggs in his *DRAPIER'S LETTERS.* In "An Extract of a Book" (part of letter 4), the Drapier argues against the dismissal of a grand jury that refused to condemn one of his letters. As a precedent, he quotes a resolution passed by the English House of Commons in response to Scroggs's dismissal of the jury. The resolution makes it illegal to dismiss a grand jury before the end of term or (among other conditions) "while Matters are under their Consideration." In letter 5, Swift goes into more detail about Scroggs's illegal dismissal of the jury.

**Seymour, Sir Edward** (1633–1708)   TORY Speaker of the House of Commons from 1673 to 1708. In "A TALE OF A TUB" Swift's "Digression Concerning Madness" suggests that Seymour and other Tory M.P.'s should look to Bedlam Hospital as a primary source for recruiting "admirable" candidates "for the several offices in a state, ecclesiastical, civil, and military." In John DRYDEN's *Absalom and Achitophel,* Amiel is based on Seymour, whom Dryden characterizes as "Of ancient race by birth, but nobler yet / In his own worth" (900–901). See also John HOWE and Christopher MUSGRAVE.

**Shaftesbury, Anthony Ashley Cooper, third earl of** (1671–1713)   Moral philosopher and essayist, M.P., and grandson of the first earl, whom John DRYDEN portrayed as Achitophel in his *Absalom and Achitophel* (1681). He was educated under the supervision of John Locke and at Winchester and traveled on the Continent. He served as a member of Parliament from 1695 to 1698, becoming an earl in 1700. His poor health led to his retiring to a life of writing and leisure in Italy, where he died in 1713. His *Characteristicks of Men, Manners, Opinions, and Times* (1711) collects his writings on the perfection of the universe and the naturalness of virtue in man. His view of nature as the teacher of beauty and benevolence was ahead of his time. This idealistic philosophy remained much appreciated during the early 18th century.

Swift believed, rather differently, in man's virtue, finding hope for humankind's moral integrity, yet acknowledging constant backsliding under the attack of sin and ignorance. He doubted the credibility of natural benevolence, distrusting the chaotic passions even under the influence of reason. Swift objects to Shaftesbury's *Letter Concerning Enthusiasm* (1708) as aggressive "free Whiggish thinking," in his pamphlet "Project for the Advancement of Religion" (1709). With the expanded "Apology for a Tale of a Tub" (1710), Swift again refers to this moralist's work in an ironical fashion.

**Shannon, Henry Boyle, earl of** (c. 1686–1764)   WHIG politician, chancellor of the exchequer of Ireland, privy councillor, and Irish commissioner of revenue. The most politically eminent member of the Boyle family during the 18th century, Shannon became an effective "undertaker." This term, used in Ireland during the period, refers to local power brokers who managed the business of government in the Irish Parliament. Shannon was a protégé of Alan MIDDLETON, entering Parliament in 1707 and, by 1733, being accepted as Speaker by the English government.

In his marginalia, Swift comments on Shannon's character: "some very scurvy Qualities particularly avarice." After Shannon ultimately agreed with Swift's concern about William WOOD's patent and signed the "Address to the Privy Council of Ireland," arguing against the Crown's efforts to introduce this coinage, he not unexpectedly signed "A Proclamation against the Drapier," urging the authorities to "discover the author of the said seditious pamphlet ["To the Whole People of Ireland . . ."] so as he be apprehended and convicted thereof." Swift disliked Shannon's cynical manipulation of popular patriotism and the momentum he gained from events and enthusiastic allies. When he accepted a wealthy pension and the title of earl of Shannon in 1756, the public became disillusioned and rejected his role as a champion of Irish interest. Though Swift was long dead, his opinion of Shannon was affirmed in the end.

**Sharp, John archbishop of York** (1645–1714) Educated at Cambridge, Reverend Sharp assumed the usual chaplaincies and postings, in keeping with an intelligent and ambitious young churchman, advancing to chaplain in ordinary to JAMES II. He received his doctor of divinity degree in 1679 and accepted two important deanships in close order: Norwich, 1681, and Canterbury, 1689. Though suspended for preaching against Roman Catholicism, Sharp found support from WILLIAM III and later ANNE, and was soon promoted to the archbishopric of York in 1691.

Scholars often refer to Sharp as Swift's mortal enemy for his efforts in speaking against bestowing an English deanship or bishopric on the deserving Swift. Swift believed the rumors and used that term also, admitting "I have many friends, and many enemies; and the last are more constant in their nature" (The JOURNAL TO STELLA, October 22, 1711). Whether the evidence is conclusive against Sharp seems unclear; Swift certainly had offended many for his effective propaganda in support of the Tory ministry. But some reports suggest Henry BOLINGBROKE assured his friend that his suspicions were wrong, and Robert HARLEY had promoted the story so Swift would willingly accept the deanship of St. Patrick's Cathedral, Dublin. The important poem "The AUTHOR UPON HIMSELF" reflects Swift's anger and resentment at the treatment he received from English ecclesiastical authorities, as well as the queen and her chief lady-in-waiting, the duchess of SOMERSET. He calls Sharp a "crazy prelate" and once again argues that "A TALE OF A TUB" does not attack religion but only the corruptions within religion. In the 1710 Apology to that

work, Swift alludes to Sharp: "the weightiest men in the weightiest stations are pleased to think it a more dangerous point to laugh at those corruptions in religion . . . than to endeavour pulling up those very foundations."

Earlier, in the *Tatler* (number 68), Swift (who either wrote or provided hints) comments on the Sharpers who might sit at his Table of Fame and how he intends to deal with these evil characters. Swift found another opportunity in satirizing and puncturing Sharp's pride in A SHORT CHARACTER OF HIS EX[CELLENCY] T[HOMAS] E[ARL] OF W[HARTON]. He accused the former lord lieutenant of adultery, greed, and avarice, as well as any other associates who were connected even faintly with Wharton, and by association, Sharp, who involves himself in a ludicrous scandal.

**Sheridan, Rev. Thomas** (1687–1738) Clergyman, schoolmaster, and friend of Swift. Sheridan graduated from Trinity College, Dublin, in 1711, and became an Anglican priest in 1712. Swift and Sheridan met in 1717 and their relationship was both entertaining and intellectually stimulating. Always short of money, Sheridan could not live comfortably on a priest's salary and opened a boys' school in Dublin. His marriage remained unhappy, though the couple produced many children. Sheridan's third son, Thomas the Younger, became the father of the playwright Richard Brinsley Sheridan. Swift recommended Sheridan to Lord CARTERET in 1725 and was given a living. Also, the younger man and Esther JOHNSON (Stella), whose apartment was in the same neighborhood as Sheridan's school, liked and respected each other, which pleased Swift.

Reports of why the friendship between Sheridan and Swift lasted for more than 20 years usually focus on the humor and ebullience that the two men shared, as well as the entertaining word-games they played. Swift respected his intelligence and ability as a teacher, but the two also wrote each other mock-panegyrics, poems, riddles, bits of doggerel, and trifles. Though Sheridan was extravagant and even improvident, Swift was able to scold him without ever eroding their appreciation for each other. Visiting Sheridan at his country estate in Quilca, County Cavan, Swift brought Stella and her companion to visit the family. Though the home was in shambles and Swift gave no sympathy to Sheridan's wife, he enjoyed the opportunity to write and completed GULLIVER'S TRAVELS there. Continuing financial difficulties, however, annoyed the practical dean, and the final objection came when Sheridan became ill while visiting at the deanery and was urged to leave. Swift recovered himself after his friend's death and wrote a glowing epitaph, which would be added to other writings concerning their association. These include "THE DEAN OF ST. PATRICK'S TO THOMAS SHERIDAN," "DEAN SWIFT'S ANSWER TO THE REVEREND DR. SHERIDAN," "THE DEAN TO THOMAS SHERIDAN," "DR. SWIFT'S ANSWER TO DR. SHERIDAN," "FROM DR. SWIFT TO DR. SHERIDAN," "GEORGE NIM-DAN-DEAN, ESQ. TO MR. SHERIDAN," "GEORGE NIM-DAN-DEAN'S INVITATION TO MR. THOMAS SHERIDAN," "A LEFT-HANDED LETTER TO DR. SHERIDAN," "A LETTER TO REVEREND DR. SHERIDAN," "MARY THE COOK-MAID'S LETTER TO DR. SHERIDAN," "A POETICAL EPISTLE TO DR. SHERIDAN," "SWIFT TO SHERIDAN," "TO MR. SHERIDAN, UPON HIS VERSES WRITTEN IN CIRCLES," "TO QUILCA," "TO THOMAS SHERIDAN," "VERSES FROM QUILCA," "CHARACTER OF DOCTOR SHERIDAN," "THE BLUNDERS, DEFICIENCIES, DISTRESSES, AND MISFORTUNES OF QUILCA," "THE HISTORY OF THE SECOND SOLOMON," "A Vindication of His Excellency Lord Carteret," "Thoughts on Various Subjects," and "Preface to Sheridan's Sermon." Swift's *Correspondence* contains 60 letters between the two men.

## Shrewsbury, Charles Talbot, first duke of

(1660–1718)  Statesman, courtier, and friend of Swift. Born a Roman Catholic, Talbot converted to Anglicanism in 1679 and held offices in the courts of JAMES II and WILLIAM III. He was created duke of Shrewsbury in 1694, but six years later retired from public life. When ANNE dismissed her WHIG lord chamberlain, she appointed Shrewsbury to the same post in 1710. He then rose rapidly, becoming ambassador extraordinary to France (1712), lord lieutenant of Ireland (1713), and, most unexpectedly, lord treasurer in August 1714. With the death of Anne in the same month, as well as the imminent arrival of GEORGE I, and in light of the clear

understanding that Shrewsbury's appointment as treasurer was meant to forestall Henry BOLINGBROKE's appointment, Shrewsbury had the good sense to resign in favor of a new appointee.

Swift had met the duke and duchess of Shrewsbury at Windsor in 1711, and found the duke (as he wrote in a January 8 letter to Archbishop KING) to be "a very great and excellent person." He adds, "I will wager that your Grace will be an admirer of his Dutchess [sic]" (*Corr.* I.286–87). Adelaide Paleotti, whom the duke married in 1705, was a most entertaining woman and, much to Swift's delight, gave him the name of Presto. As lord lieutenant, Shrewsbury disappointed Swift because of his ignorance of Irish politics and general ineffectiveness with the Irish parliamentarians. Though Shrewsbury was a moderate politician who hoped for compromise between Whig partisans and the TORIES, his administration seemed doomed to failure, and only adjourning Parliament stopped the chaos. Swift believed Shrewsbury was responsible for the disasters, deciding a hidden political agenda caused the problems. See also "ON DR. RUNDLE," *The JOURNAL TO STELLA,*" "An ENQUIRY INTO THE BEHAVIOUR OF THE QUEEN'S LAST MINISTRY," AND "THE History of the FOUR LAST YEARS OF THE QUEEN."

## Sican, John and Mrs. E.

Successful Dublin grocer and his wife who were both friends of Swift, especially Mrs. Sican, whom he regarded as "a very ingenious and well-bred lady." Swift had met her in 1729 and a year later silently dedicated the poem "ON PSYCHE" to Mrs. Sican's good taste, wit, humor, hospitality, and overall kindness to him. She has been called a reader, critic, and poet, but apparently her most important role was as friend to a man who had always enjoyed the company of educated women. He wrote to Alexander POPE in 1730 of how she (with two or three other "shopkeeper's wives") represented Dublin female taste. Such compliments did not come easily for Swift, and he would later recommend her directly to his English friends, as well as to Pope, so she might meet them and be entertained properly on a visit to England.

John Sican was directly involved with Swift's interests, personal and professional. Sican served on the grand jury (1724) that refused to issue a finding of criminal wrongdoing and a charge against the printer, John HARDING, for publishing the fourth of *The DRAPIER'S LETTERS*, ignoring the wishes of the chief Irish prosecutor, William WHITSHED, to prosecute the unnamed author of "Seasonable Advice to the Grand Jury" (contained in that section of the *Letters*). Swift's impulse in writing "WHITSHED'S MOTTO ON HIS COACH" was certainly related to the moral courage of the grand jury that Whitshed dissolved for cause. Later, Sican served on the 1742 committee created to care for Swift's estate and personal affairs when the dean became mentally incapacitated.

**Singleton, Henry** (c. 1682–1759)   Lawyer, chief justice of the Common Pleas in Ireland, and Swift's executor. Singleton graduated from Trinity College, Dublin, in 1703; was appointed to the Irish bar in 1707; and was elected to the Irish House of Commons in 1727. Singleton was Swift's good friend, though not an intimate one, but Swift considered him "one of the first among the worthiest persons in this kingdom." He attained the rank of prime sergeant in the Commons in 1727 and chief justice in 1740.

During the 1733 Irish legislative session, Swift became particularly alarmed when the government, Dissenters, and landlords united against the clergy in proposing a bill for improving the financial benefits available to hemp and flax growers. If this bill had become law, the clergy would have lost income from reducing the tithe requirement on these growers. Swift's pamphlets, "Some Reasons against the Bill for Settling the Tyth of Hemp, Flax, . . . by a Modus" and "Some Further Reasons against the Bill for Settling the Tyth" pleaded that an already poor clergy not be further impoverished. One sergeant-at-laws, Richard BETTESWORTH, a frequent satiric target for Swift, apparently supported the bill and in doing so suggested the other sergeants-at-law were of the same mind. Swift's "ON THE WORDS 'BROTHER PROTESTANTS AND FELLOW CHRISTIANS'" made it abundantly clear that no similarity existed between the two sergeants—one was closer to a piece of dung, and the other a plump apple. In May 1740 Swift completed his last will, and Singleton joined a small group of lawyers and prebendaries as executors.

**Smedley, Jonathan** (c. 1671–c. 1729)   Clergyman and author. Smedley graduated from Trinity College, Dublin, in 1695; served as an army chaplain; and established himself as a WHIG. Lord TOWNSEND became his patron and arranged for Smedley's preferment as the dean of Killala in 1718. Later, he once again succeeded in rising higher to the richer deanery of Clogher in 1724. While writing for a Whig newspaper in the early 1720s, he sought closer association with the duke of GRAFTON, the current lord lieutenant of Ireland. His method of gaining favor included satiric attacks on Swift and Alexander POPE, and the legend exists that he posted a few lines of verses to the door of St. Patrick's Cathedral on the day of Swift's installation as dean (1713) that were cruel and petty. These attacks and others were printed in his miscellanies of Gulliveriana (1728), and Pope responded by inserting Smedley into *The Dunciad*, thoroughly belittling him. Soon after, seeking his fortune, Smedley resigned his deanship and shipped out for India, dying on the voyage.

Though Swift never met Smedley, the two actively disliked each other. Swift refers to Smedley in a number of works, including "HIS GRACE'S ANSWER TO JONATHAN," "A LETTER FROM DEAN SWIFT TO DEAN SMEDLEY," "STELLA'S BIRTHDAY (1723): A GREAT BOTTLE OF WINE, LONG BURIED, BEING THAT DAY DUG UP," "DEAN SMEDLEY GONE TO SEEK HIS FORTUNE," "A PANEGYRIC ON THE DEAN," and "An EXCELLENT NEW BALLAD."

**Smith, John** (1655–1723)   Politician. He served as an English M.P. for various constituencies for 45 years. As a WHIG, he made a trusted friend in Sidney GODOLPHIN, who asked him to become the chancellor of the exchequer for the period 1699–1701 and again in 1708–10. Earlier, he was elected Speaker of the House of Commons (1705–08). His ability in maintaining a balanced relationship with both his own party's leadership and the moderate Tories led by Robert HARLEY earned him the respect of both groups. Swift included him in a list of prominent Whigs in "TOLAND'S INVITATION TO DISMAL TO DINE WITH THE CALVES' HEAD CLUB" without delivering more than a passing blow: "Smith with hopes to keep his place." In his marginalia, Swift is more severe, calling him "a heavy man," objecting to John Macky's comment that he was an "agreeable companion in conversation, a bold orator."

**Smythe, James Moore** (1702–1734)   Author and infamous fop. Smythe (or Moore-Smythe) was the son of the Irish TORY politician Arthur MOORE, who had conspired with Henry BOLINGBROKE in the last days of the Tory ministry in hastening Robert HARLEY's end and encouraging the Jacobites. As the author of "the much expected" *Rival Modes* (1727), Smythe had some success until Alexander POPE accused him of stealing lines for the drama from his birthday verses to Martha Blount. When Pope added him to the list of dunces in his *Dunciad*, Smythe began attacking all the Scriblerians. He wrote "One Epistle to Mr. Pope," abusing Swift, John GAY, Francis ATTERBURY, and John ARBUTHNOT. Swift and Pope both replied to this and the other attacks; Swift's "ON POETRY: A RHAPSODY" and "VERSES ON THE DEATH OF DR. SWIFT, D.S.P.D." mention Smythe. Though Swift probably never met him, Smythe's folly and vanity qualified him for ridicule, especially on the count of false taste.

**Somers, John, baron** (1651–1716)   Lawyer and politician/statesman. He was the son of a rural attorney and attained great rank and prestige due to his own abilities and ambition. He graduated from Oxford and was called to the bar in 1676. His entrance (1689) into Parliament as a WHIG member launched his career when he helped draft the Declaration of Rights (1689). After the Revolution of 1688, he held several posts under WILLIAM III, culminating in his appointment as lord chancellor in 1697, when he was raised to the peerage as Baron Somers of Evesham. As the king's most trusted minister, he was the object of frequent attacks that led to his impeachment, along with that of three other Whig lords, in 1701 for their role in the partition treaties.

Swift's "DISCOURSE OF THE CONTESTS AND DISSENSION IN ATHENS AND ROME" (1701) defended Somers, under the name of Aristides, and gained his acquittal. Yet in the marginalia to John MACKY,

Swift writes "I allow him to have possessed all excellent qualifications except virtue. He had violent passions, and hardly subdued them by his great prudence." As one of the Whig Junto during Queen ANNE's reign, he became president of the Privy Council but was removed in 1710. In a December 19, 1733, letter to Henry BOLINGBROKE (who had gone into exile in France) Swift writes of 10 "great geniuses," adding Somers to the list and praising his work ethic—the "regularity of an alderman or a gentleman-usher" (*Corr.* II.333). "TOLAND'S INVITATION TO DISMAL TO DINE WITH THE CALVES' HEAD CLUB" takes as its target the Kit-Cat Club, the premier Whig political and social club, of which Somers was one of the original founders. "THE FAGGOT" warns the quarreling TORIES against further dissension, as the great Whigs like Somers will quickly unite and replace them.

As a patron of John DRYDEN, Joseph ADDISON, Richard STEELE, William CONGREVE, Alexander POPE, and Swift (in his early career), Somers had the admiration of men of letters from both parties. Swift dedicated "A TALE OF A TUB" to him, and Somers tried to gain Swift an Irish bishopric, even recommending him to Thomas WHARTON, the new lord lieutenant of Ireland, but without success. Swift also mentions Somers in "Memoirs Relating to That Change Which Happened in the Queen's Ministry in the Year 1710," "An ENQUIRY INTO THE BEHAVIOUR OF THE QUEEN'S LAST MINISTRY," *The JOURNAL TO STELLA*, "A LETTER OF THANKS FROM MY LORD WHARTON," "The Public Spirit of the Whigs," "A LETTER FROM DR. SWIFT TO MR. POPE," *The DRAPIER'S LETTERS* (To Lord Chancellor Middleton), and the *INTELLIGENCER*.

**Somerset, Elizabeth Percy, duchess of** (1667–1722)   Only surviving daughter and sole heiress of Josceline Percy, 11th and last earl of Northumberland. Her early life presented particular challenges from the death of her father when she was three and, at age 12, the first of her three marriages between 1679 and 1682. Her second husband, Thomas Thynne, was assassinated by friends of a rival suitor a few months after she left him on their honeymoon. Her third husband, Charles Seymour, sixth duke of Somerset, was a WHIG grandee and a lukewarm supporter of Robert HARLEY's ministry, as well as one of the most arrogant oligarchs of the period. Nicknamed "the Sovereign," legends about his vanity were prolific but as chancellor of the University of Cambridge and a strong patron of the arts, he had his good points. In 1723, soon after Elizabeth's death, he proposed marriage to Sarah Churchill, the duchess of MARLBOROUGH, now a widow, too.

Elizabeth, a highly intelligent and ambitious woman, had ingratiated herself with Queen ANNE, becoming groom of the stole and mistress of the robes, supplanting the powerful duchess of Marlborough. Sarah Churchill disliked her red hair and rivalry (Swift called her "Carrots"), and found her to be obsequious, insinuating, and the greatest liar in the world. Mistrustful and sarcastic, Sarah's comments can be understood in the light of her current insecurity at Court. Swift fiercely satirized Elizabeth in "The WINDSOR PROPHECY," advising Anne to stay loyal to Mrs. MASHAM, whom he liked very much. This advice backfired, as the queen seemed even more fiercely loyal to Elizabeth, and decided to block all efforts at preferment for Swift. He believed this poem and "A TALE OF A TUB" prevented his gaining a bishopric in England or Ireland. *The JOURNAL TO STELLA* provides extensive comment on this active Whig noblewoman, with Swift accusing her of direct negative political influence on the queen. "The AUTHOR UPON HIMSELF" displays the full wrath of Swift's resentment toward Elizabeth Percy—she is clearly his enemy. See also "ADVICE HUMBLY OFFER'D TO THE MEMBERS OF THE OCTOBER CLUB," "THE HISTORY OF THE FOUR LAST YEARS OF THE QUEEN," and "An ENQUIRY INTO THE BEHAVIOUR OF THE QUEEN'S LAST MINISTRY."

**South Sea Company**   Joint stock company, founded in 1711 to engage in trade—mainly in slaves—with Spanish America. In 1720 Parliament allowed the company to take on England's national debt, resulting in a rapid increase in the value of company shares. The subsequent burst of the "South Sea Bubble" (when share values plummeted later that year) bankrupted numerous investors and exposed corruption among company directors and supporters in Parliament. Although he had been an early stockholder, Swift ultimately denounced the company and satirized those who bought into it. See, for example, "RUN UPON THE BANKERS" and "UPON THE SOUTH SEA PROJECT." John Carswell's *The South Sea Bubble* (Stanford, Calif.: Stanford University Press, 1960) provides a full-length account of the panic following the devaluation of the company's stock.

**Stanhope, James, first earl** (1673–1721)   Soldier, statesman, and WHIG politician. Stanhope, who was educated at Oxford, was the grandson of Philip Stanhope, the first earl of Chesterfield, and (after entering the army in 1691) served with MARLBOROUGH in 1705. Since he had the entire confidence of Marlborough and was one of the duke's most trusted informants on Spanish affairs, he was appointed commander-in-chief of British forces in Spain in 1708. Though he had initial success, he was defeated in 1710 and imprisoned there for two years. During this first decade, Stanhope had been developing a political career, had been elected as M.P. in 1701, and played a role in the Henry SACHEVERELL impeachment but was defeated in the 1710 TORY resurgence. With the arrival of the Hanovers, he began a seven-year exhibition of political success, achieving one government posting after another: secretary of state, ambassador, chancellor of the exchequer, and diplomat.

Swift disagreed with Stanhope's politics, but respected him as one of the new Whig post-Junto leaders—one of the notable figures of the age. The modern editors of Swift's poetry disagree on whether the two poems mentioning Stanhope are in fact his work: Kathleen Williams believes one may be and accepts a possible attribution on the other, whereas Pat Rogers argues that neither is Swift's. With prose references in the *Correspondence* and *The JOURNAL TO STELLA*, Stanhope also appears in the *EXAMINER*, "A Modest Defence of Punning," "The CONDUCT OF THE ALLIES," and "The Public Spirit of the Whigs."

**Stannard, Eaton** (c. 1685–1755)   Recorder of Dublin, lawyer, and Irish M.P. for Cork. He was elected as recorder in 1733, mainly due to the helpfulness of Swift, who then chose him as an executor of his will. The dean decided that the majority of his estate should be used for the founding of a hospital for the insane—St. Patrick's Hospital—and (as he indicated in a letter dated April 11, 1735) Stannard would be his "director in the methods I ought to take for rendering my design effectual" (*Corr.* IV.319). Swift liked Stannard, regarding him as responsible and intelligent, but what was more, the dean needed help to realize his hospital, and who better than a highly placed Dublin official could carry out this effort. Later, Stannard had brought the gift of the City of Cork to Swift—a silver box, signifying the freedom of the city, which after certain negotiations Swift accepted. Swift mentions Stannard in "CONSIDERATIONS IN THE CHOICE OF A RECORDER," the *Correspondence,* and other works.

**Stearne, John, bishop of Clogher** (1660–1745) Churchman. He graduated from Trinity College, Dublin, in 1678, becoming rector of Trim in 1688. In 1700 he met Swift, who had the living at Laracor, the adjoining parish. Soon after, both men assumed corollary duties in St. Patrick's Cathedral, Dublin, where Swift served as the prebendary of Dunlavin and Stearne as chancellor. With the death of the dean, Jerome Ryves, Stearne became the new dean of the cathedral (1705–12), immediately preceding Swift. During this period, he had become close friends with Swift and Esther JOHNSON (Stella), who immigrated to Ireland in 1701, dining and entertaining them both at the deanery, which Stearne had built. With the assistance of Swift, he secured a promotion to bishop of Dromore (1713) and then succeeded St. George ASHE, Swift's Trinity College tutor, as bishop of Clogher (1717). Considered intelligent and a man of sincere religious belief, Stearne apparently wrote one letter to Swift, but the dean wrote nine letters to him. Both Kathleen Williams and David Woolley believe other letters were written but no longer are extant. Though their friendship was longstanding, it had been severely tried when Stearne did not present Swift with a post that was within the control of the cathedral chapter. Later Stearne supported two anticlerical bills, which angered Swift.

Swift's "HORACE, EPISTLE VII, BOOK I: IMITATED AND ADDRESSED TO THE EARL OF OXFORD" alludes to the liability he owed Stearne after moving into the deanery. *THE JOURNAL TO STELLA* contains extensive reference to their relationship, especially the recognition for Swift that English preferment and even an Irish bishopric would not occur. He now knew that with Stearne's cooperation he might find a place in Ireland—a deanship. In his sad, sincere essay "ON THE DEATH OF MRS. JOHNSON," Swift mentions Stearne's kindness in visiting her and the welcome he extended to this young woman in Dublin.

**Steele, Sir Richard** (1672–1729) Dramatist, essayist, WHIG politician, school friend of Swift in Dublin and later schoolfellow of Joseph ADDISON at Charterhouse in England. Steele left Merton College, Oxford (1694), without a degree to enlist in the duke of ORMONDE's regiment of horse guards but gave it up to become a writer. He wrote three successful comedies and in 1707 became editor of the London *Gazette.* He initiated the *Tatler* (1709–11) and cofounded the *Spectator* (1711–12) with Addison. Both periodicals are best known for their satirical, political, and moral essays. The political differences between Swift and Steele began emerging when the latter wrote a number of Whig pamphlets attacking the terms of the Peace of Utrecht. Swift quickly responded with his strongest weapons: ad hominem arguments attacking the character of his subject. "The Public Spirit of the Whigs" and "The IMPORTANCE OF THE GUARDIAN CONSIDERED" made clear how foolish, ignorant, and presumptuous were Steele's words.

Earlier, Steele had borrowed the pseudonym of Isaac Bickerstaff, with Swift's blessing, for the narrator/persona of his *Tatler.* But in Swift's poetry, especially "The FIRST ODE OF THE SECOND BOOK OF HORACE PARAPHRASED AND ADDRESSED TO RICHARD STEELE, ESQ.," "A LIBEL ON THE REVEREND DR. DELANY AND HIS EXCELLENCY JOHN, LORD CARTERET," and "An EXCELLENT NEW BALLAD," he toys with or lashes out at Steele, even after the dramatist's death. The political differences and misunderstandings were too deep for Swift to put aside in this charged atmosphere of party wrangling.

**Stella** See JOHNSON, ESTHER.

**Stopford, James, bishop of Cloyne** (c. 1697–1759)    Bishop of Cloyne and a young friend and confidante of Swift. Stopford was a fellow of Trinity College, Dublin (1711), who resigned his fellowship in 1727 for the post of vicar of Finglas. He married his cousin, Anne, sister of James Stopford, first earl of Courtown. After a successful period of service, Stopford was promoted as provost of Tuam (1730) and later dean of Kilmacduagh (1748). He was raised to bishop of Cloyne in 1753.

According to Irvin Ehrenpreis, Stopford represents "the well-endowed filial character that supplied an element of hopefulness to Swift's view of the future" (*Swift* III.335). Swift found him balanced, intelligent, and trustworthy—characteristics he demanded in fellow clergymen. Becoming Stopford's patron, Swift recommended him to John CARTERET, encouraged him in his desire for travel to the Continent, and praised him to Alexander POPE, John ARBUTHNOT, and John GAY. Stopford appreciated his kindness but was too shy and modest in fully exploring all that Swift could have done in furthering his career. Promotions came but not with the rapid rise others may have hoped for him. Later, Swift made Stopford one of the executors of his will, leaving him various bequests (See also "A VINDICATION OF HIS EXCELLENCY LORD CARTERET" and "GEORGE NIM-DAN-DEAN'S INVITATION TO MR. THOMAS SHERIDAN," where Swift refers to him as "Long Shanks Jim." Sixteen letters exchanged between the two men appear in the *Correspondence*.

**Strafford, Thomas Wentworth, third earl of** (1672–1739)    Diplomat, army officer, and TORY government official. Strafford was the son of Sir William Wentworth, and succeeded to the title of Baron Raby with the death of his cousin, the second earl of Strafford in 1695. His long military service reached its apex with WILLIAM III and MARLBOROUGH; he retired as a lieutenant general in 1707. His diplomatic posts included Berlin (1701–05) as envoy and later as the English ambassador there from 1706 to 1711. In June 1711 he was created Viscount Wentworth and earl of Strafford. As the joint plenipotentiary for the peace negotiations in Utrecht, he spent two months in London during 1712 for briefings, before proceed-

ing to establishing agreement between the allies on the cessation of war with France.

Swift, who had only a passing acquaintance with Strafford, comments in *The JOURNAL TO STELLA* that "Strafford has some life and spirit, but is infinitely proud and wholly illiterate." Apparently he was badly educated, for which his enemies, and even Swift at various points, criticize him for showing a lack of humility. Extensive reference to him occurs in The HISTORY OF THE FOUR LAST YEARS OF THE QUEEN, An ENQUIRY INTO THE BEHAVIOUR OF THE QUEEN'S LAST MINISTRY, and the marginalia.

**Stratford, Francis** (born c. 1662)    Merchant, speculator, and Irish friend of Swift. Stratford and Swift had attended Kilkenny Grammar School together and then matriculated to Trinity College, Dublin, in 1682. Stratford became remarkably wealthy in London through various business and mercantile dealings, reportedly amassing more than £100,000. Swift mentions him often in *The JOURNAL TO STELLA*, and in September 1710 Stratford lent money to the new TORY government. This surprised Swift, but the two maintained their friendship, visiting each other frequently during the next three years. Swift was directly responsible for Stratford's becoming a director of the SOUTH SEA COMPANY and purchased £500 worth of stock, using funds provided by Stratford. With the collapse of the South Sea Bubble, Stratford suffered complete financial ruin, though Swift seems to have escaped similar losses. In order to protect himself from creditors, Stratford voluntarily imprisoned himself in the Queen's Bench, one of the eight debtors' prisons in London. Swift provided some assistance when Stratford was paroled so he might secure funds to pay his debts, but he decided to go abroad.

**Strephon**    Stock name in Swift's poems for the young "swain" whose image of his "nymph" (whether CELIA or CHLOE) as a pure, angelic being is shattered by the realities of her humanity. He speaks what is probably the most famous line in "The LADY'S DRESSING ROOM" when, after lifting the lid of Celia's commode, he cries, "Oh! Celia, Celia, Celia shits!" (118). See also "The PROGRESS

OF BEAUTY," "STREPHON AND CHLOE," and "RIDDLES" ("Louisa to Strephon").

**Stuart, James Francis Edward ("Pretender," "Old Pretender," Prince of Wales and Chevalier de St. George)** (1688–1766)  Only son of King JAMES II (the Roman Catholic English monarch who was deposed as a result of the Glorious Revolution of 1688) and his second wife, Mary of Modena. Those who supported the Stuarts' claim to the throne became known as Jacobites. Born in London, James was taken as a small child to Saint-Germain, near Paris, and was announced as his father's successor in 1701. His failed landing in Scotland in 1708 led to his military service in the Low Countries. Finally, he successfully arrived at Peterhead, Scotland, in 1715 during the Jacobite Rising but left after only a few weeks, becoming a resident of Rome. He was known as the "Pretender" because of his own weak efforts (and those of his supporters, the "Jacobites") to assert his claim to the Crown. Swift wrote disparagingly of the Pretender throughout his works, and spent a great deal of time in the "ENQUIRY INTO THE BEHAVIOUR OF THE QUEEN'S LAST MINISTRY" defending Queen ANNE, Henry BOLINGBROKE, and Robert HARLEY against accusations that they sought to alter English succession and establish the Pretender as king. See also "DISCOURSE CONCERNING THE FEARS FROM THE PRETENDER" and "LETTER FROM THE PRETENDER TO A WHIG LORD."

**Sunderland, Charles Spencer, third earl of** (1674–1722)  Politician and statesman. He was a member of the WHIG Junto and secretary of state for the Southern Department but lost the position in 1710. Queen ANNE dismissed this extreme Whig as her first step toward toppling the Sidney GODOLPHIN ministry. Sunderland was well known for his emotional outbursts and uneven temper. He had married Anne, the daughter of the duke of MARLBOROUGH, in 1700. Sunderland had been a widower, and his father, Robert Spencer, the second earl of Sunderland, had been close friends with both Marlboroughs. This marriage between the two families celebrated close personal relations but an important political association. With the arrival of

the Hanovers, Sunderland's fortunes improved as he helped direct the government of King GEORGE I from 1714 to 1721. He soon became lord lieutenant of Ireland (1715) and then lord privy seal. His political power coalesced in the government ministry with James STANHOPE, Robert WALPOLE, and Charles TOWNSEND. He and Stanhope managed to oust the other two leaders, and Sunderland became lord of the treasury until the South Sea Bubble burst and forced his retirement.

Swift included him in his general attack on the Whig grandees in "TOLAND'S INVITATION TO DISMAL TO DINE WITH THE CALVES' HEAD CLUB" and "PEACE AND DUNKIRK." The Tory tracts Swift wrote ridiculing the Whigs use a considerable number of techniques in mocking the central figures of Godolphin, Daniel NOTTINGHAM, and Sunderland. In the EXAMINER and "HUE AND CRY AFTER DISMAL," Swift relies on the use of nicknames, calling Sunderland "Charles." Attacking Sunderland's republican principles as dangerous, he introduces him in "The HISTORY OF THE FOUR LAST YEARS OF THE QUEEN." Sunderland also appears in Swift's "Preface to the Memoirs of Sir William Temple," marginalia, "Some Considerations upon the Consequences Hoped and Feared from the Death of the Queen," Memoirs, "Relating to That Change Which Happened in the Queen's Ministry in the Year 1710," and The DRAPIER'S LETTERS (letter 7—"An Humble Address to Both Houses of Parliament)."

**Swift, Abigail Erick(e)** (1640–1710)  Mother of Jonathan Swift. Her family was from Leicester, and her father was the Rev. James Ericke, vicar of Thornton. Her parents immigrated to Ireland from England in 1634. In "The FAMILY OF SWIFT," Swift indicates that the Erick family traced its roots back to "Erick the Forester, a great Commander" who fought William the Conqueror. He also remarks, however, that since that time, the family has "declin[ed]" with "every age, and are now in the condition of very private Gentlemen" (191). Abigail married Jonathan SWIFT, Sr., in 1664, and their first child (Jane SWIFT, later Fenton) was born in 1666. Her husband died in 1667, seven months before the younger Jonathan's birth. In his biography of Swift, Irvin Ehrenpreis writes that "The relations between Swift and his mother make one of the puzzles in his life" (I.28). See also the biographical entry on Swift in Part I.

**Swift, Deane** (1706–1783) Biographer, editor, son of Swift's first cousin, the elder Deane Swift. His biography, *Essay upon the Life, Writings, Character of Dr. Jonathan Swift* (1755) set the traditional approach to Swift along with Thomas SHERIDAN's *Life of the Rev. Dr. Jonathan Swift* (1784). In *Swift at Moor Park* (1982), A. C. Elias points out Deane Swift's desire for correcting negative impressions left by an earlier biography, the earl of ORRERY's *Remarks on the Life and Writings of Dr. Jonathan Swift* (128) in 1751. Deane Swift had access to essential Swift papers, including "The FAMILY OF SWIFT," but his insistence on praising his uncle often outweighs his objectivity. In 1739 Deane Swift married Martha WHITEWAY's daughter by her first marriage, his cousin Mary Harrison.

**Swift, Elizabeth Dryden** (d. 1609) Paternal grandmother of Jonathan Swift; wife of Rev. Thomas SWIFT. Her father was Nicholas Dryden, and her great-uncle, Erasmus Dryden, was the poet John DRYDEN's grandfather. This connection made Swift and John Dryden distant cousins.

**Swift, Godwin** (1624–95) Highly successful lawyer; eldest uncle of Jonathan Swift. He was the first of Rev. Thomas SWIFT's sons to move to Dublin from England after his father's death. In terms of Swift's biography, Godwin is best known for having provided financial support for Jonathan, his mother, Abigail SWIFT, and his sister, Jane SWIFT, after the death of Jonathan SWIFT, Sr., in 1667. It was Godwin who made it possible for his nephew to attend Kilkenny Grammar School from 1673 to 1682, but Jonathan blamed his subsequent academic struggles at Trinity College, Dublin, on the "ill treatment" he received from Godwin and his other relatives ("The FAMILY OF SWIFT 192).

**Swift, Jane** See FENTON, JANE.

**Swift, Jonathan, Sr.** (1640–67) Father of Jonathan Swift; 10th child of the Rev. Thomas SWIFT. Like all but one of his brothers, he was trained in the law and (two years after the death of

his father) moved to Dublin in an attempt to make a living for himself. He practiced law there and was named steward of the King's Inn in 1665. He died two years later at the age of 27. At the time of his death he and his wife, Abigail SWIFT, had a one-year-old daughter (Jane SWIFT), and Abigail was pregnant with their first son, who would also be named Jonathan and be born seven months later. In "The FAMILY OF SWIFT," Swift writes that his father's "death was much lamented on account of his reputation for integrity with a tolerable good understanding." He adds, however, that his parents' marriage was "very indiscreet" on both their parts, since his mother brought little or no dowry to the match, and his father's sudden death prevented him from having sufficiently provided for his family—a shortcoming that affected the younger Jonathan "not only through the whole course of his education, but during the greatest part of his life" (191–192).

**Swift, Rev. Thomas** (1595–1658) Vicar of Goodrich; paternal grandfather of Jonathan Swift. In addition to being a respected clergyman, he was a staunch supporter of Charles I during the Puritan Revolution, was persecuted by the Cromwellian Roundheads, and ultimately lost his church living because of his Royalist loyalties. He and his wife, Elizabeth Dryden SWIFT, had 14 children. Jonathan Swift's unfinished autobiography, "The FAMILY OF SWIFT," shows that Swift was extremely proud of his grandfather—especially due to his loyalty to King Charles I. He writes, for example, that although "This Thomas" owned a great deal of land in Goodrich, he was best known for his "courage, as well as his loyalty" to the king, "and the Sufferings he underwent for that Prince, more than any person of his condition in England" (188). Swift relates that his grandfather was "plundered" 36 times by the Roundheads, but nonetheless gathered all the money he could muster, sewed it into the quilting of a coat, and arranged for the coat to be sent to the king. He also designed and built an iron-spiked barrier that was hidden beneath the water of a river he knew the Roundheads intended to cross. According to Swift, 200 "Rebels" lost their lives when their horses ran into this contrivance while crossing the river. Swift also claims that King

CHARLES II had once promised to restore the lands and church livings Thomas Swift lost to the Puritans, and even to promote him in the church. These promises were never fulfilled, however, and "Mr Swift's merit dyed with himself" (190–191).

**Synge, Edward, archbishop of Tuam** (1659–1741) Early in his career, he enjoyed steady promotions in the Irish church from chancellor of St. Patrick's Cathedral, Dublin, to bishop of Raphoe. Synge was one of the acknowledged leaders of the Irish interest in Parliament who often came to the support of Archbishop KING of Dublin. Though a firm WHIG in his politics, his allegiance to Ireland's cause led him across party lines, especially when the fear of Jacobitism had ebbed, violent anti-TORY attitudes lessened, and the Whigs became indifferent to Ireland's welfare during the 1720s. Both King and Synge found Swift's "PROPOSAL FOR THE UNIVERSAL USE OF IRISH MANUFACTURE" an excellent summary of how the Irish might retaliate economically against the English government's tyranny.

Synge became one of the chief troublemakers against England's disposition to treat Ireland like a colony. He signed the *Address of the Privy Council of Ireland,* against WOOD's patent for the new copper coinage (which the Crown had granted in 1722). Synge had also joined STEARNE and Swift in opposing the creation of an Irish bank—an issue of great concern given primary focus in the dean's "Wonderful Wonder of Wonders" and "Subscribers to the Bank Plac'd According to their Order and Quality with Notes and Queries."

# T

**Temple, Lady Dorothy Osborne** (1627–1695)
Wife of Sir William TEMPLE from 1654 to 1695, and
letter writer. Lady Dorothy was the daughter of a
gallant and poor royalist and niece of the essayist
Francis Osborn. She was born in Bedfordshire,
England, and raised in the Channel Islands during
the English Civil War. Her family objected to Temple, with whom she maintained a notable correspondence from their meeting in 1648 until their
marriage. The couple spent their honeymoon at
Moor Park in Hertfordshire and would retire to the
renamed Moor Park, Surrey, in 1686.

Her letters were first printed in selections in
1836 and reveal the perfection of the 16th-century
loving and lovable feminine character. Not only are
the letters charming but they also embrace the life
and background of many men and women, both
plebeian and aristocratic, of her time. Swift praised
her as "Mild Dorothea, peaceful, wise and great" in
"OCCASIONED BY SIR WILLIAM TEMPLE'S LATE ILL-
NESS AND RECOVERY." Irvin Ehrenpreis notes the
connection in character and spirit between Temple
and Dorothy Osborne and the king and queen of
Brobdingnag in Part II of GULLIVER'S TRAVELS
(Swift III.457).

**Temple, Sir William, baronet** (1628–1699)
Diplomat, statesman, author, and Swift's early
patron. Temple was a native Londoner, educated at
Cambridge. On his "tour of the continent," he met
the talented Dorothy Osborne in 1648, whom he
married in 1654. He became a diplomat in 1655,
was made ambassador at The Hague, and negotiated the Triple Alliance (1668) against France. He
was made baronet, and in 1677 helped bring about
the marriage of the prince of Orange to the
Princess Mary, daughter of James, duke of York
(later JAMES II). After the Glorious Revolution of
1688, he refused an important ministerial post to
devote himself to literature, though he continued
to advise WILLIAM III. Swift joined Temple as his
personal secretary in 1689 at the ex-diplomat's
small estate, Moor Park, near Farnham in Surrey.
The 10-year relationship between these two men
remains complicated, and Temple's effect on Swift
the man and his work is a continual source for discussion and analysis.

A number of the best writers of the period
praised Temple's prose style for its elegance, charm,
and intellectual depth. He wrote about European
diplomacy in *Observations upon the United Provinces
of the Netherlands* (1673) and *On the Original and
Nature of Government.* In his philosophical works,
especially *Upon Ancient and Modern Learning* and
*Upon the Gardens of Epicurus*, Temple argued
against the idea of progress and appealed to the
notion of a cyclical pattern of physical and historic
change. Swift directly alludes to this position in
"The BATTLE OF THE BOOKS." Later, after Temple's
death, Swift continued editing his patron's memoirs, miscellanea, and letters, publishing them
between 1700 and 1709. Swift's "ODE TO THE HON-
OURABLE SIR WILLIAM TEMPLE" points toward the
imagery in Temple's essays. The familiar poem,
"OCCASIONED BY SIR WILLIAM TEMPLE'S LATE ILL-
NESS AND RECOVERY," discusses the important issues

Sir William Temple, by Sir Peter Lely, c. 1660 *(Library of Congress)*

of Swift's feeling that all his devotion to Temple has been wasted. References to Temple also appear in "TO MR. CONGREVE" and throughout Swift's prose.

**Tenison, Edward, bishop of Ossory** (1673–1735) He was educated at Cambridge, became prebendary of Canterbury (1709) and then first chaplain (1730) to the duke of Dorset, who accepted the post of lord lieutenant of Ireland. As the cousin of Thomas Tenison, archbishop of Canterbury, he had access to church preferment throughout his career. Dorset soon nominated him for the bishopric of Ossory (1731), as he was considered "a man of devotion and high principle." Swift disliked his political leanings, and in the poem "ON THE IRISH BISHOPS," he criticizes Tenison's support of two proposed bills, the Bill of Residence and the Bill of Division, which Swift felt would harm Irish clergy further. His fury goes as far as calling Tenison a "baboon." He later followed up this attack with an essay, "On the Bill for the Clergy's Residing on Their Livings" (1732), complaining of how the

bishops of the Irish House of Lords were showing contempt for the lower clergy while protecting their own financial interests.

**Theobald, Lewis** (1688–1744)  Poet, critic, dramatist, and editor. He was best known as the author of *Shakespeare Restored; or, A Specimen of the Many Errors as Well Committed as Unamended by Mr. Pope, in His Late Edition of This Poet* (1726), a critique of Alexander POPE's edition of Shakespeare, which had been published the previous year, and for this and other examples of pedantry, Pope avenged himself by making Theobald the hero of *The Dunciad* (1728). Theobald provided his own edition of Shakespeare's plays in 1734 and was the first editor to approach the plays with the respect and attention then normally reserved for classic texts. His drama *The Double Falsehood* (1728), though promoted as a new play, owes much of its light to Shakespeare. His other work, writing pantomimes for the theater and doing hack work for printer Edmund Curll, was roundly criticized, yet Colley CIBBER dethroned him as King Dunce in the 1743 edition of *The Dunciad*.

Swift alludes to Theobald and Cibber in "ON POETRY: A RHAPSODY." In a November 19, 1730, letter to John GAY, Swift jokingly mentions Theobald "or some other hero of the *Dunciad*" as the next poet laureate, since Pope "talks like a Philosopher and one wholly retired" (*Corr.* III.421). In *A COMPLETE COLLECTION OF GENTEEL AND INGENIOUS CONVERSATION,* he playfully attacks pedantry and vanity, thanking Theobald and others for supplying so many fine examples of these flaws.

**Thynne, Thomas** (1648–1682)  Wealthy WHIG nobleman, friend of the duke of Monmouth, and Issachar in John DRYDEN's *Absalom and Achitophel.* Swift recalls his strange end in "The WINDSOR PROPHECY." Thynne had married the much younger Elizabeth Percy in 1681, but his new wife almost immediately fled the marriage before it was consummated. In February 1682 Thynne was assassinated by friends of a rival suitor, Count Konigsmark, who was later acquitted at trial. Thynne's widow soon married Charles Seymour and became the confidante of Queen ANNE. Swift despised her Whig sympathies and manipulations, and may have believed as other Tories that certain highly placed government figures had conspired in Thynne's murder.

**Tickell, Thomas** (1686–1740) Poet, bureaucrat, and disciple of Joseph ADDISON. Tickell held a number of minor government posts in England and Ireland and became Addison's biographer and literary executor. In 1707 Tickell published a poem on Robert HARLEY and later one on Kensington Garden in imitation of Denham's *Cooper's Hill,* glorifying the picturesque. He later connived with Addison in denigrating Alexander POPE's translation of Homer. Tickell had issued his own translation of the first book of the *Iliad* at the same time as Pope. He edited Addison's *Works* (1721) with a famous elegy on his patron ("On the Death of Mr. Addison"), admiring him as "the first man of the age." In 1724 he became chief secretary to John CARTERET, the lord lieutenant, with offices in Dublin Castle. Carteret may have met him when he was undersecretary to Addison while he was secretary of state.

Swift became acquainted with Tickell upon the latter's arrival in Ireland, and they exchanged 12 letters as their friendship grew over the next 15 years. He married Clotilda Eustace in 1726, and when Esther JOHNSON (Stella) was in her final illness and the dean was in London, she stayed with Mrs. Eustace at her home and died there. Both Swift and Pope thought Tickell "a fair and worthy man." In "A HISTORY OF POETRY," Swift puns on Tickell's name: "I will therefore only venture to lay down one maxim, that a good poet, if he designs to tickle the world, must be gay and young; but if he proposes to give us rational pleasure, he must be as grave as a pope." Earlier, Swift had mentioned Tickell who "mourned his Addison" in "APOLLO'S EDICT." Tickell is also referenced in THE JOURNAL TO STELLA.

**Tighe, Sir Richard** (c. 1678–1736) WHIG politician, M.P., and member of the Irish Privy Council. Swift attacked him in prose ("A VINDICATION OF LORD CARTERET" and *The JOURNAL TO STELLA*) and in a number of coarse, insulting poems such as

"MAD MULLINIX AND TIMOTHY," "TIM AND THE FABLES," and "DICK, A MAGGOT." Tighe incurred Swift's wrath by ruining Thomas SHERIDAN's career as a clergyman. Soon after Sheridan had received the living of Rincurran, Cork, he preached a sermon on "Sufficient unto the day is the evil thereof" (from Matt. 6:34). In an unfortunate coincidence, the date he chose to preach on that text was Aug. 1, 1725—the anniversary of King GEORGE I's accession. A "self-appointed watchdog for the Whig interest," Tighe immediately reported the sermon to Lord CARTERET, and despite there being "no syllable of politics of any sort" in the sermon, Sheridan's name was removed from the list of chaplains (Ehrenpreis, *Swift* III.658, 363).

**Tindal, Matthew** (1657–1733) Deist. Tindal graduated from All Souls College, Oxford, and then studied law. He converted to Catholicism under JAMES II, and reconverted in 1688. Swift owned a copy of Tindal's famous work, *The Rights of the Christian Church Asserted* (1706), and in "The YAHOO'S OVERTHROW" he lumped Tindal together with other philosophers, freethinkers, and fanatics. In 1708, Swift refuted Tindal's subversive doctrines against state-supported religion and creating a national church in "Remarks upon a Book, Intituled, The Rights of the Christian Church Asserted," though Swift ultimately dropped the project because he could not develop a thoroughly effective attack on his opponent. Later, Tindal's *Christianity as Old as the Creation* (1730), a statement of natural religious doctrine, caused a real furor among orthodox believers who despised his rationalist approach to Christianity.

Swift considered him one of the most effective enemies of established religion and devoted considerable energy in satirizing his ideas, and in the EXAMINER (May 3, 1711) he accuses the Whigs of attempting to destroy the Established Church and introducing fanaticism and freethinking through the words of Tindal and others whom they patronized. His attack on Bishop BURNET in "A Preface to the Bishop of Sarum's Introduction" reviews the bishop's contempt for clergymen, especially Tory clergy. "An ARGUMENT AGAINST ABOLISHING CHRISTIANITY IN ENGLAND" wonders how Tindal's strength as a writer could have emerged without having a subject as various and potent as Christianity. "MR. COLLINS'S DISCOURSE OF FREE-THINKING" heaps ridicule on the deist Anthony COLLINS, whose various works were quite controversial. See also "LETTER FROM A MEMBER OF THE HOUSE OF COMMONS IN IRELAND."

**Tisdall, Rev. William** (1669–1735) Clergyman and early friend of Swift. Tisdall was born and raised in County Meath, Ireland, and educated at Trinity College, Dublin. He entered in 1688 and became a fellow in 1696. He was appointed to cures in the counties of Antrim and Armagh after marrying in 1706, and took his doctor of divinity degree in 1707. Tisdall, who considered himself intelligent and an "outstanding controversialist" on par with Swift, became vicar of Belfast and rector of Drumcree in 1712.

About 1704, while Swift was in England, he learned in a letter from Tisdall that this younger man had proposed marriage to Esther JOHNSON (Stella). Nothing could have brought Swift more immediate emotional distress than such news. In his biography of Swift, Irvin Ehrenpreis makes clear that Tisdall was on intimate terms with Swift who tolerated his poor personal habits and the man's presumption as a literary artist (though he referred to Tisdall as "a puppy") (II.657). However, when it came to supporting the idea of marriage he adopted a passive role. Stella, who apparently did little to dissuade Tisdall, finally broke it off after learning that Swift did not want the marriage to take place. The two had been toying with Tisdall as entertainment for them both, but when the situation changed, Swift had to take his rival seriously. A code of disinterestedness, a focus on what was apparently best for Stella and Tisdall, became Swift's approach but clearly he felt the challenge deeply and for a time "panic[ked]." Swift's poetry reveals a pattern of complex responses to this early friend; see "THE BEAU'S REPLY TO THE FIVE LADIES' ANSWER" and "PROBATUR ALITER."

**Toland, John** (1670–1722) Religious writer and philosopher. He was born into a Catholic Gaelic Irish family in County Donegal and then converted to Presbyterianism, only to become the period's most notorious critic of religious orthodoxy. He studied at Edinburgh, Oxford, Glasgow, and Leyden between 1687 and 1695. His *Christianity Not Mysterious* (1696), the first deist manifesto, was burnt by order of the Irish Parliament, as being "atheistical and subversive." He had to flee Ireland for the Continent, where he resided at the Hanoverian court, in Holland, and with other free-thinking groups across Europe. Toland followed a somewhat precarious literary career, giving voice to extreme political views in editing the prose works and writing the lives of several 17th-century republicans, including John Milton. Denouncing other churchmen, Tories, and Jacobites, he challenged the authority of the Bible and the truth of revelation in a series of miscellaneous writings.

Swift and Toland despised each other, having recognized (through their writings) that they were polar opposites—politically and spiritually. "TOLAND'S INVITATION TO DISMAL TO DINE WITH THE CALVES' HEAD CLUB" attacks the WHIG leaders, but also criticizes the uncontrolled irresponsibility of Toland. "The YAHOO'S OVERTHROW" lists him among all the deists and other freethinkers who are threatening the Established Church and the kingdom as a whole. In a number of pamphlets, Swift reacted strongly against Toland and the threat his writings posed as a guide to freethinkers: "An ARGUMENT AGAINST ABOLISHING CHRISTIANITY IN ENGLAND," the *EXAMINER* (numbers 22, 25, 29, and 39), "MR. COLLINS'S DISCOURSE OF FREE-THINKING," and "Some Arguments against Enlarging the Power of Bishops."

**Torcy, Jean-Baptiste Colbert, marquis de** (1665–1746) French statesman. He was an experienced diplomat serving as the French foreign minister and the son of the great chief minister of finance for LOUIS XIV. As early as 1710 the TORY ministry was secretly in touch with Torcy through the medium of a French priest with experience as a secret agent who was living in London as chaplain to the imperial ambassador. Torcy's master had been seeking a peace since MARLBOROUGH's defeat of the French at Blenheim (1704) but would not accede to absolute defeat, so a long period of negotiation and war proceeded. Torcy even attempted to bring pressure on Marlborough by giving concessions to the Dutch and offering a colossal bribe to win the general's goodwill, but both Louis XIV and the WHIG ministry refused the various offers of peace. Robert HARLEY and Henry BOLINGBROKE sought to negotiate a peace, the latter accompanied by Matthew PRIOR to debate terms in Paris with Torcy in 1712. The Congress of Utrecht dragged on from late 1712 and into the spring of 1713, and the treaty was signed in April 1713.

Swift discussed these issues and the character of Torcy (whom he respected) in "The HISTORY OF THE FOUR LAST YEARS OF THE QUEEN." Other references to Torcy appear in "A New Journey to Paris" and "Some Free Thoughts upon the Present State of Affairs." According to Swift, Torcy treated everyone "of so great a negotiation with the utmost candor and integrity, never once failing in any one promise he made, and always tempering a firm zeal . . . with . . . what was reasonable and just."

**Tory**   See EXAMINER, number 43, May 31, 1711.

**Townshend, Charles, second viscount** (1674–1738)   Statesman and agriculturist. Townshend was born in Raynham, Norfolk, England, and studied at Cambridge. Succeeding his father as viscount (1687) and taking his seat in the House of Lords in 1697, he gained valuable experience as a diplomat and served as member of the British contingent negotiating and signing the Barrier Treaty with the Dutch in 1710. As a WHIG peer and one of the primary diplomats representing the British crown at Utrecht, his entry into public life as a TORY seems all the more unexpected. Under the influence of Baron Somers, he transferred his allegiance to the

Whigs. With the arrival of GEORGE I, he was appointed secretary of state (1714–16; 1721–30), becoming a leading figure in the Whig ministry with his brother-in-law, Robert WALPOLE. After a resignation engineered by Walpole, he acquired his nickname, "Turnip Townshend," for his interest in agricultural improvement and his proposal to use turnips in crop rotation.

Swift despised Townshend, as seen in "TO CHARLES FORD, ESQ. ON HIS BIRTHDAY," in which the dean attacks him for his role in persecuting Bishop ATTERBURY. Also, Swift correctly believed Townshend responsible for the collection of spies, informers, agents, and miscreants who ran interference for the Walpole ministry and assisted in convicting any of its perceived enemies, such as the bishop. He took the lead in harassing the Tories who had signed the Treaty of Utrecht. Pat Rogers calls him the preeminent hatchet man of the Walpole administration. "HIS GRACE'S ANSWER TO JONATHAN" is Swift's answer to Rev. Jonathan SMEDLEY, the dean of Killala, who had been recommended for the position by Townshend. Smedley had opposed, even provoked, Swift on a number of issues. Other references in Swift's prose focus on Townshend's involvement in attacking Robert HARLEY's ministry or securing Whig dominance. These appear in "Some Remarks upon a Pamphlet Entitled A Letter to the Seven Lords," "The HISTORY OF THE FOUR LAST YEARS OF THE QUEEN," "Some Remarks on the Barrier Treaty," "ADVICE HUMBLY OFFER'D TO THE MEMBERS OF THE OCTOBER CLUB," and "The CONDUCT OF THE ALLIES."

**Treaty of Utrecht**   See "HUMBLE ADDRESS OF THE RIGHT HONOURABLE THE LORDS SPIRITUAL AND TEMPORAL IN PARLIAMENT ASSEMBLED, The."

# V

**Vanbrugh, John** (1664–1726) Architect and dramatist. Vanbrugh was born in London of upper-middle-class parents and grew up a gentleman. He never served an apprenticeship but instead joined the army, taking a commission in the earl of Huntingdon's regiment. After leaving the service, he traveled in France and was arrested there in 1690, spending two years in prison on suspicion of being a spy. On release his decision to enter the theater with two comedies of manners, *The Relapse* (1696) and *The Provoked Wife* (1697), proved his wit, intelligence, and sense of perfect pitch in revealing his time. More plays followed, but in 1699 he had already become an architect "without thought or lecture," according to Swift. His design of Castle Howard for the earl of Carlisle placed him in the ranks of the dean of English architecture, Christopher Wren. After receiving further support from the Crown, he was selected by the duke of MARLBOROUGH to design the house that was the gift of the nation to this great general. Beginning Blenheim Palace in 1705, Vanbrugh worked and fought with the militant Sarah, duchess of MARLBOROUGH, finally being dismissed; his working partner and collaborator Nicholas Hawksmoor completed the house. As a WHIG and an original member of the Kit-Kat Club, he was caught up in the collapse of the party but recovered on the arrival of the Hanovers, was knighted, and succeeded Wren as surveyor of Greenwich in 1716.

Reminding Esther JOHNSON in *The JOURNAL TO STELLA* of the two poems he had written criticizing Vanbrugh's houses, Swift mentions how the duchess of Marlborough had teased him repeatedly about these verses, but all in all he finds Vanbrugh a "good-natured fellow." "VANBRUG'S HOUSE" and "The HISTORY OF VANBRUG'S HOUSE" treat the architect harshly and lampoon his abilities.

**Vanessa**  See VANHOMRIGH, ESTHER.

**Vanhomrigh, Esther or Hester (Vanessa)** (1688–1723)  Swift's friend. She was the daughter of Bartholomew Vanhomrigh, lord mayor of Dublin (1697) who had arrived in Ireland as a Dutch merchant. He later became commissary-general to the army in Ireland and a member of the Irish Parliament. His accomplishments were known to the English ministers and the lord lieutenant, but before he could receive further honors, he died (1703). After a considerable period his estate was settled. The family, consisting of his widow, Hester, and four children, were left in more than adequate financial condition. In hopes of improving their social status, Mrs. Vanhomrigh (who apparently was not very thrifty) moved the family to London in December 1707.

Though he may have met the family in Dublin earlier, Swift, who had been out of Ireland since November 1707, certainly met them soon after their arrival in London and became a frequent visitor at their house. He was attracted to Esther from the first, and their correspondence began in December 1711 (though some evidence exists that the earliest letter may have been in 1709), extending to the last surviving letter in August 1722 (45 letters remain extant). Ten months later she died unexpectedly and unhappily.

Though he was attracted to the young woman, Swift—as with Esther JOHNSON (Stella)—wanted the relationship to continue as one of teacher and pupil. In his biography of Swift, David Nokes explains that the dean's renaming of Stella, Varina, and Vanessa allowed him to distance himself and his feelings. The technique made the women seem more like pets (who could be stroked one moment and ignored the next) rather than real women who possessed desires and hopes for themselves. Yet his relationships with them were complex and continue to resist the easy psychological analysis some modern critics are often tempted to provide. Apparently, Vanessa declared her love for Swift in London, but he held her off, arguing against her passion. Nonetheless, he willingly continued to talk with her about their feelings for each other and fur-

Esther Vanhomrigh (Vanessa), by Philip Hussey *(Library of Congress)*

ther encouraged her by accepting her mother's hospitality. Finally he attempted to disentangle himself from this situation through a series of communications including the well-known (and some say brutal) letter of August 12, 1714, urging Vanessa not to follow him to Ireland because "I shall see you very seldom" and "CADENUS AND VANESSA" (*Corr.* II.123). "The ANSWER TO VANESSA'S REBUS" is not part of his warning to her, though the irony of his reference to "the nymph who wrote this in an amorous fit" takes on a sharper meaning in this context. When Vanessa became increasingly impatient with Swift's extended absences and excuses in 1722, he once again detached himself from her. And when she died in June 1723, he immediately left Dublin for the south of Ireland, hoping to escape any hint of scandal.

**Van Lewen, Laetitia**    See PILKINGTON, LAETITIA.

**Varina**    See WARING, JANE.

**Verres, Gaius (Caius Verres)** (c. 120–43 B.C.) Roman quaestor and eventual governor of Sicily (73–71 B.C.). Notorious for his corruption, greed, and thievery, Verres was prosecuted in Rome for his mishandling of Sicilian resources during his time as governor. In the *EXAMINER* (number 17), Swift includes an extract from Cicero's remarkably successful oration condemning Verres as "an Overturner of Law and Justice."

**Victor Amadeus II, duke of Savoy** (1666–1732) King of Sicily (1713–20), king of Sardinia (1720–30). He succeeded his father, Charles Emmanuel II, as duke of Savoy in 1675, and later overthrew his mother's regency in 1683. The pressure placed on Savoy by the French caused him to work continuously in escaping their influence, and in 1690 he joined the League of Augsburg against LOUIS XIV. After further political and foreign policy entanglements, Victor Amadeus found it necessary to side with France in the War of the Spanish Succession (1701–13) but changed sides in 1703. After he assisted in the defeat of the French, the Peace of Utrecht awarded him Sicily and some additional territories. When the Spanish seized Sicily, he later abandoned his claim to the island in exchange for Sardinia and became its king.

Swift mentions him frequently in "The CON-DUCT OF THE ALLIES," "The HISTORY OF THE FOUR LAST YEARS OF THE QUEEN," and "The Public Spirit of the Whigs." In his letters to Bishop KING, Swift writes concerning the English government's participation in negotiations to return lands and titles to Victor Amadeus. Lord PETERBOROUGH, Swift's most admired diplomat, led the English efforts in restoring the duke of Savoy his lands.

## Voltaire (François-Marie Arouet) (1694–1778)

Author and philosopher. Voltaire was a major figure of the Enlightenment, and at an early age he gained fame as a poet and dramatist, and notoriety as a deist and satirist. Two years' exile in England (1726–28) left a deep impression on him. His return to France brought further literary success (*Histoire de Charles XII, Zaïre*) and further scandal (the pro-English *Lettres Philosophiques* of 1734). A period of welcome at Court proved brief, as did his "honeymoon" with Frederick the Great (1750–53). Later, he settled at Geneva (1755) and Ferney (1760), where he dominated the "philosophic" movement, pouring forth liberal and deistic propaganda and intervening in the defense of victims of injustice. He died shortly after a triumphant return to Paris.

In 1727 Swift arrived in London for his final visit and stayed six months, mostly with Alexander POPE at Twickenham. Voltaire had fled to England the preceding spring and quickly gained admittance to the best circles because of his wit, charm, and fluency in English. Voltaire knew Henry BOL-INGBROKE, and with his help corresponded with and

Voltaire *(Library of Congress)*

met Pope at the poet's home. Voltaire was introduced to Swift through Pope or Bolingbroke, and after learning that Swift intended to visit France, willingly wrote him letters of introduction to his friends (see his letter to Swift dated June 16, 1727: *Corr.* III.214–15). Less than six months later, Voltaire found himself in financial difficulty and wrote again to Swift, asking for help in gaining subscriptions for a projected edition of *La Henriade*. Swift agreed, and provided him a list of subscribers.

**Walls, Thomas** (c. 1672–1750) Archdeacon of Achonry, master of St. Patrick's Free School, and friend of Swift. Walls, an Englishman who graduated from Trinity College, Dublin, came to Swift's attention since he was a member of St. Patrick's chapter and its cathedral school since 1698. Walls and his wife, Dorothy, accepted Esther JOHNSON (Stella) and Rebecca DINGLEY into their home in 1714 and provided them with an apartment there through 1717. Walls's career began improving when Archbishop KING, whom Swift had urged to reconsider his initial unfavorable opinion, became convinced of the young cleric's ability. But the opportunity evaporated under various political and religious pressures, and Swift was never able to obtain this post for his friend. Walls remained Swift's factotum and receiver until 1717, and accepted the archdeaconry in 1705. Resigning his schoolmastership in 1710, he became vicar of Castleknock until 1738.

Swift wrote at least 50 letters to Walls from the years 1708 to 1725. *The* JOURNAL TO STELLA contains extensive references to Walls and his wife, suggesting the affection and trust Swift had for this man and his wife. The strength of their relationship shows itself in the humorous "ON THE LITTLE HOUSE BY THE CHURCHYARD OF CASTLEKNOCK." See also "STELLA AT WOODPARK."

**Walmsley, John** (d. 1737) Clergyman. He entered Trinity College, Dublin, in 1696, becoming a Fellow in 1703, and Senior Fellow in 1713. He married in 1723, becoming vicar of Clonfeacle, County Tyrone, but did not live there, though he would frequently officiate at services. Walmsley remained in Dublin, maintaining his friendship with Thomas SHERIDAN and Swift. In "MY LADY'S LAMENTATION AND COMPLAINT AGAINST THE DEAN," he mentions Walmsley as one of the group of friends and colleagues who are associated with MARKET HILL and its pleasant associations. "DR. SWIFT'S ANSWER TO DR. SHERIDAN" responds to a verse letter, "A Letter from Dr. Sheridan to Dr. Swift," which Swift had earlier prompted with his own verse letter. Sheridan refers to Walmsley as one of the close friends both men considered their immediate colleagues. Later, Swift mentions Walmsley again in "GEORGE NIM-DAN-DEAN'S INVITATION TO DR. THOMAS SHERIDAN," recalling an enjoyable holiday in Gaulstown in 1721.

**Walpole, Horace (Horatio Walpole)** (1678–1757) Diplomat, ambassador to France, and brother of Sir Robert WALPOLE. He was educated at Cambridge University and became an M.P. in 1702. After holding a number of minor parliamentary and diplomatic posts, as well as that of secretary to the lord lieutenant of Ireland (1720), he became a privy councillor in 1730, and then assumed two important diplomatic ambassadorships at The Hague and Paris (1722–40). "ON THE WORDS 'BROTHER PROTESTANTS AND FELLOW CHRISTIANS'" takes an opportunity to criticize both Walpoles and their current policies. Swift understood Horace's talents as a diplomat but disliked his interference in Irish politics and willingness to support his brother's policies. Swift alludes to Walpole in a number of works, including "The CONDUCT OF THE ALLIES," "The HISTORY OF THE FOUR LAST YEARS OF THE QUEEN," the *INTELLIGENCER,* and the "Proposal That All the Ladies Should Appear Constantly in Irish Manufactures."

**Walpole, Sir Robert** (1676–1745) WHIG first lord of the treasury from 1715–17 and again from 1721–42. He was the younger son of a prominent Whig family of Norfolk; with the death of his father and elder brothers, he was returned (1701) as an M.P. from the family's borough, Castle Rising, and later took his regular seat from King's Lynn. The prevalent image of Walpole as Britain's first prime minister is of an uncouth, foxy squire (at least one writer compares him to Sir Pitt Crawley in Thackeray's *Vanity Fair*) who managed the country using a combination of bribery and sly tricks for more than 20 years. He began his rise as a hardworking administrator with assignments as secretary of war (1708) and treasurer of the navy (1710–11). Soon, promoted to leading the opposition against the TORY administration (1710–14), he suffered through a conviction of corruption in office and was falsely sent to the Tower under an imprisonment order for months. Walpole attacked the ministry's policy toward France, and intelligently responded to Swift's "The CONDUCT OF THE ALLIES," which made the argument that England had betrayed Holland and Austria. His *Short History of Parliament* (1713) remains a good companion piece to Swift's pamphlet.

On the accession of GEORGE I in 1714, this stolidly Low-Church magnate of Hanoverian Britain served in one important post after another: paymaster general of the forces, first lord of treasury, and chancellor of the exchequer. Working with his brother-in-law, Viscount Charles TOWNSHEND, Walpole found himself on the opposite side of the more powerful Whig faction of STANHOPE and SUNDERLAND. Townshend was fired and Walpole resigned, but the Whigs began adopting his plans for managing the national debt. The two returned to office in 1720, in time to salvage the nation from financial ruin in the aftermath of the South Sea Bubble. Walpole's reward came quickly with his appointment as first lord of the treasury, and in 1722 George I named him chief minister, a post he retained for 20 years. His innovative policies regarding taxes, trade, and foreign policy brought stability to the country, though by 1739 the Tories forced him into the War of Jenkins' Ear (1739–41). Compelled to resign in 1742, he was created earl of Orford and remained active in politics until his death.

Swift considered Walpole his greatest enemy, who had managed to screen important players, protect the established order, and secure a seat of power for himself. Though both acted civilly toward each other when in public, their mistrust was mutual—especially considering their opposing views on political ideology and ethics. The dean objected to Walpole's monopoly of power and his contempt for Ireland and the myriad of Irish problems. Certainly, the "great man" remembered Swift's derisive portrait of him in the Drapier's "Letter to the Whole People of Ireland" (see *The DRAPIER'S LETTERS*) and received all his comments with one argument after another. Swift satirized Walpole in a series of poems, including "TOLAND'S INVITATION TO DISMAL TO DINE WITH THE CALVES' HEAD CLUB," "The AUTHOR UPON HIMSELF," "A SIMILE," "VERSES ON THE REVIVAL OF THE ORDER OF THE BATH," "TO MR. GAY," "ON MR. PULTENEY BEING PUT OUT OF THE COUNCIL," "The CHARACTER OF SIR ROBERT WALPOLE," "VERSES ON THE DEATH OF DR. SWIFT, D.S.P.D.," "UPON THE HORRID PLOT DISCOVERED BY HARLEQUIN THE BISHOP OF ROCHESTER'S FRENCH DOG," "WOOD, AN INSECT," "ON READING DR. YOUNG'S SATIRES," "TO DR. DELANY, ON THE LIBELS WRIT AGAINST HIM," and "TO A LADY." References to the minister also appear in *The JOURNAL TO STELLA,* the EXAMINER, "A LETTER TO THE WRITER OF THE OCCASIONAL PAPER," "An ACCOUNT OF THE COURT AND EMPIRE OF JAPAN," "The ANSWER OF WILLIAM PULTENEY TO SIR ROBERT WALPOLE," marginalia, "The HISTORY OF THE FOUR LAST YEARS OF THE QUEEN," *The Drapier's Letters,* and the INTELLIGENCER.

On a tangential point, Swift's friend Alexander POPE's portrait of Timon's Villa in *Moral Essays* (1731) is a satirical analogue to Walpole's palatial home at Houghton in Norfolk. Walpole visited Pope at Twickenham in 1725, but the two men were never friends. Just as Swift and Pope attacked Walpole in print, so did John GAY, Dr. John ARBUTHNOT, Thomson, Fielding, and Samuel JOHNSON.

**Walter, Sir John** (1673–1722) Politician who succeeded to the baronetcy in 1694, and became the third baronet of Sardsen, Oxfordshire. He was twice elected as M.P. to a small district and then changed districts and was M.P. for Oxford in six Parliaments from 1706 to 1722. Walter was also a clerk comptroller of the Green Cloth. Swift had a running argument with him in London, when the drunken Walter criticized Swift in public (see *The JOURNAL TO STELLA*). Swift at first described him as an honest drunken fellow, and four days later as a "brute" who railed at him and uttered a variety of lies about Swift and the noble company with whom both were having dinner. There is a minor reference to Walter in "A TALE OF A TUB."

**Walter, Peter** (c. 1664–1746) Attorney, land steward of the duke of Newcastle, and according to Pat Rogers, "the archetypal villain of Augustan satire." He was considered a miser, dishonest lawyer, usurer, and a symbol of hucksterism who amassed more than £200,000 from making loans at extortionate rates of interest. He was frequently satirized by Alexander POPE and Henry FIELDING (who in 1742 caricatured him in *Joseph Fielding* as "Peter Pounce"). Swift, who inherited his dislike of Walter from Pope, refers to him in his *Correspondence* and "The ANSWER OF WILLIAM PULTENEY TO SIR ROBERT WALPOLE" as an example of corruption without a conscience or "the grasping New Man of aristocratic household finance, who left many a nobleman whose estates he looked after in straitened circumstances."

**Warburton, Rev. Thomas** (1679–1736) Clergyman. He graduated from Trinity College, Dublin, in 1703. Warburton served as Swift's curate at Laracor from before 1709 until 1717, running a school at Trim for £60 annually. Swift hoped he might help this conscientious clergyman gain a better living and post. His letters in 1713 to Bishop William KING show his efforts, but nothing came of these

requests for this "gentleman of very good learning and sense." However, Warburton was granted a living at the rectory of Magherafelt (1717), in the diocese of Armagh, thanks to Swift's recommendation to the archbishop of Armagh, Thomas LINDSAY. See "ON THE LITTLE HOUSE BY THE CHURCHYARD OF CASTLEKNOCK" and *The JOURNAL TO STELLA*.

**Waring, Jane (Varina)** (1674–1720) Swift's friend. An Irishwoman and daughter of the former archdeacon of Dromore, Roger Waring, who had died in 1692, Jane's relatives, especially her cousins who had attended Trinity College, Dublin, were first introduced to Swift. Jane lived with her widowed mother in Belfast, where her family had been successful merchants. Having met her during his posting to the diocese of Down and Connor (January 1695–June 1696), Swift became part friend, father, and lover to this fatherless girl, giving her the Latinized name "Varina." As David Nokes has explained, Swift renames Waring, "Stella," and "Vanessa" as a way of distancing himself and his feelings and avoiding the challenge of having to confront them as women.

In his April 29, 1696, letter before leaving Kilroot, Swift proposed marriage to Waring in a manner both peremptory and inviting: If she would take him as he was, then marriage was possible—otherwise they had no future. Jane was clearly surprised by his tone, and feeling bullied and uncertain, turned him away. He returned to Moor Park and William TEMPLE's cold commands. This strange story seems to have had as much to do with her material needs as it did with his unwillingness to marry, especially as he realized Stella would leave England and move to Ireland without requiring marriage.

**Waters, Edward** See WHITSHED, WILLIAM, and "A PROPOSAL FOR THE UNIVERSAL USE OF IRISH MANUFACTURE."

**Welsted, Leonard** (1688–1747) Poet. Welsted was educated at Westminster and then at Trinity College, Cambridge, and moved on to hold a few minor government posts. His friends were Joseph ADDISON, Richard STEELE, and Ambrose PHILIPS, and he was a client of the duke of Newcastle. He published *Epistles, Odes etc.* (1724) and translated Longinus in 1712 among other occasional pieces. The critic John DENNIS attacked him for ignoring "the rules of poetry." From 1730 to 1733, Welsted leveled memorable attacks at Alexander POPE, publicly dismissing all of his poetry as plagiarized and pieced together from stolen lines. These accusations, however, seemed less significant when Welsted became caught in his own invective in praising the anonymous poet of Pope's *Essay on Man.* Earlier, he had joined Lady Mary Wortley MONTAGU in writing another attack on Pope, *One Epistle to Mr. Pope* (1730). Pope returned the favor, including him in *Peri Bathous* and *The Dunciad* (Pat Rogers calls Welsted one of Pope's most savage opponents among the dunces). Swift, who apparently never met him, became sufficiently annoyed with this obnoxious writer who seemed bent on slandering the Scriblerians and added him to a list of defectives in "ON POETRY: A RHAPSODY."

**Wesley, Samuel the elder** (1662–1736)    Rector of Epworth in Lincolnshire. He was the father of John Wesley (the evangelist and founder of the Methodist Church) and Charles Wesley (the famous hymn writer and poet of the Methodist movement). In "The BATTLE OF THE BOOKS," Homer kills Samuel Wesley "with a kick of his horse's heel." Wesley was notorious for his poetry, particularly *The Life of Our Blessed Lord and Saviour Jesus Christ: An Heroic Poem* (1693) and *History of the Old and New Testament in Verse* (1701–04). In his biography of Swift, Irvin Ehrenpreis lists Wesley (along with Richard BENTLEY and others) among the "self-advertising poetasters" whom Swift regarded as "the true enemies of the proponents of good taste" (I.194).

**Whaley, Rev. Nathaniel** (c. 1677–1738)    Chaplain to Archbishop Thomas LINDSAY. Whaley, who had graduated with his M.A. from Wadham College, Oxford University (1701) with Lindsay, held two diocesan posts under the control of the archbishop in Ireland: Loughgilly, County Armagh (1722), and Donoughmore, County Tyrone. The appointment to the Armagh rectory was hotly con-

tested, as the government and the church wrestled over who had the right to nominate new candidates to these open posts. With the conclusion of a lawsuit in the English House of Lords, Whaley was finally confirmed. Swift argued strongly in his favor in a September 21, 1728, letter to Robert HARLEY: "Mr. Whaley is so worthy a person that I could not refuse his request of recommending him to your Lordship's favor," especially since his rival for the post was "the greatest puppy and the vilest poet alive" (*Corr.* III.300). In "MY LADY'S LAMENTATION AND COMPLAINT AGAINST THE DEAN" (one of his earliest MARKET HILL poems), Swift commends Whaley's character and damns that of his opponent. There are references to Whaley throughout Swift's *Correspondence.*

**Wharton, Thomas, first earl of** (1648–1715) WHIG politician. Raised in a strongly puritanical family, Wharton (though accused of dissolute behavior) became an able administrator, an effective party man, and an efficient political organizer. As an M.P. beginning in 1673, he led the activities of the Whig Junto after the rise of the TORIES. He had become a baron in 1698, succeeding his father, and was later created earl of Wharton in 1706. Before losing his position in this change of governments, he had become lord lieutenant of Ireland (1708–10) with the express purpose of removing the Test Act from Ireland. His choice of a chaplain, Rev. Ralph LAMBERT, would help accomplish this. Joseph ADDISON served as Wharton's secretary in Ireland. Swift had been recommended to Wharton as his chaplain, but neither man seemed to suit the other. Besides, Swift was obsessed with protecting the Test Act, which he felt preserved the Anglican Church in Ireland from the Presbyterians, and decided Wharton would serve as the focal point for a series of attacks on the Whigs, English, nonconformists, and Wharton's character in general. His most famous attack is in the *EXAMINER* (November 30, 1710), where Wharton is called "a robber of the public treasure; an overturner of law and justice, and the disgrace." Swift assigned the pseudonym "Verres" to Wharton, and was contemptuous of his government.

Swift refers to Wharton in a number of works, including "A LETTER FROM A MEMBER OF THE

House of Commons in Ireland," "A Short Character of his Excellency Thomas Earl of Wharton," the *Examiner*, "The Conduct of the Allies," "A Letter from the Pretender to a Whig Lord," "The History of the Four Last Years of the Queen," "An Enquiry into the Behaviour of the Queen's Last Ministry," "A Proposal for the Universal Use of Irish Manufacture," "A Letter from Dr. Swift to Mr. Pope," *The Journal to Stella*, and throughout his *Correspondence*. Swift's poems that reflect an interest in Wharton include "Toland's Invitation to Dismal to Dine with the Calves' Head Club," "Peace and Dunkirk," "Horace, Epistle VII, Book I: Imitated and Addressed to the Earl of Oxford," and "The Storm"—a satire directed against Wharton's second chaplain, Josiah Hort.

**Whig**   See *Examiner*, number 43, May 31, 1711.

**Whiteway, Martha Swift** (1690–1768)   Cousin and friend of Swift. Mrs. Whiteway was the younger daughter of his father's youngest brother, Adam Swift (1641–1704), who was a solicitor practicing in Dublin. She was married twice: first to the Rev. Theophilus Harrison and as a widow to Edward Whiteway in 1716. Although she apparently lived in Dublin, she saw little of the dean until the latter part of his life. Mrs. Whiteway's daughter, Molly Harrison, married Deane Swift, Jonathan Swift's great-nephew and biographer. Beginning in 1730, Mrs. Whiteway and Swift began corresponding, and her second husband died during 1732.

Apparently intelligent, kind-natured, and generous, she became critical to Swift's daily life in his last 10 years, preventing him from suffering further from loneliness as his friends or longtime servants died one after the other. Helping keep his household in order soon became more exacting as her education and intelligence gave her the capability of assisting him with his correspondence, especially as his health and memory declined. He also enjoyed caring for and supporting her children as if he were their father—it gave him pleasure and they prospered from his devotion. The deanery became her unofficial home, though she maintained her own residence, and with her and the youngest children about the place, he had the sense of a family he had never been able to create for himself.

Nearly an independent correspondent for Swift, she began injecting her own opinions and voice into letters to his friends. As Alexander Pope continued his practice of collecting his letters to Swift and those of the dean to him, by 1738 she had been receiving under her care and protection many of Swift's letters and other materials. She objected to the publication of the Pope-Swift letters as possibly connected, at least through the printer, to a "dishonorable intrigue." Ultimately, she acceded to the ongoing plan and delivered some of Swift's letters to an agent acting for John Boyle, fifth earl of Orrery. Swift's will, completed in 1740, left substantial money or property to the Whiteways, especially Mrs. Whiteway, who became a substitute for Esther Johnson (Stella). And as his memory declined, Mrs. Whiteway was the only person he recognized and would let near him in his final days. Like *The Journal to Stella*, Swift's correspondence contains numerous references to Whiteway.

**Whitshed, William** (1679–1727)   Lawyer. Whitshed, a competent Whig, held a number of important judicial posts in Ireland: solicitor general (1709), chief justice of King's Bench (1714), and chief justice of the Common Pleas (1726). He pursued Edward Waters, the printer of Swift's "Proposal for the Universal Use of Irish Manufacture," in 1720 in order to impress the British government with his willingness to root out traitorous behavior and disloyalty in Ireland. After Whitshed arranged the trial jury so as to provide the guilty verdict, the jury instead found Waters not guilty, and Whitshed sent them back nine times until the matter was left "to the mercy of the judge." Ultimately, Swift called upon various Irish and English dignitaries who agreed to help, and Waters was finally released with no punishment.

In 1724, the Dublin printer John Harding, who had printed letter 4: "To the Whole People of Ireland" of *The Drapier's Letters*, became the central focus in the government's effort to quell unrest and dissension in Ireland. Charged with having printed a seditious pamphlet, Harding remained in prison while Swift attacked Whitshed in letter 5: "To Viscount Molesworth." Alluding to Whitshed's lack of integrity and his uncontrolled ambition for Molesworth's lord chancellorship, Swift shows how and why the chief justice directed his venom toward Waters and Harding. Though Whitshed's "zealous exhortation" to the grand jury in the Harding case should have intimidated these Dubliners, the jury instead refused to provide a finding, and they were dismissed after an effort to have them reconsider their decision. He proceeded to impanel another jury, though his legal standing on this approach was highly suspect. The new jury also refused a finding against Harding, and their courage added an unexpected boldness to the Irish public on the more important matter of William WOOD's patent—so much so that the government was brought to a standstill on implementation. Swift's confidence was brimming as he wrote to Ford on November 27, 1724: "The government and judges are all at their Witts end" (*Corr.* III.43). Other references to Whitshed appear in "A Continuation of a Short Character of Thomas, Earl of Wharton," "A LETTER FROM DR. SWIFT TO MR. POPE," "Two Letters to the Chief Justice Whitshed," "ANSWER TO SEVERAL LETTERS FROM UNKNOWN HANDS," "Proposal That All Ladies Should Appear Constantly in Irish Manufactures," "The Substance of What Was Said by the Dean," "A Short View of the State of Ireland," "An Answer to a Paper Called a Memorial," and throughout Swift's *Correspondence.* A number of Swift's poems also reflect his attitude toward Whitshed: "An EXCELLENT NEW SONG ON A SEDITIOUS PAMPHLET," "WHITSHED'S MOTTO ON HIS COACH," "VERSES ON THE UPRIGHT JUDGE," and "VERSES ON THE DEATH OF DR. SWIFT, D.S.P.D."

**Wild, Jonathan** (1682?–1725) A notorious criminal and thief-taker, executed at Tyburn in May of 1725. A thief-taker was an official responsible for "the detection and arrest of thieves" (*OED*). Wild abused the post as a means for advancing his own criminal career. His illustrious career as a gang boss was outlined in a number of writings, including a biography by Daniel DEFOE and a satiric novel by Henry FIELDING. See Gerald Howson, *Thief-Taker General* (London: Hutchinson, 1970) for a modern account. Swift would have known of Wild's infamy in Ireland. See also "CLEVER TOM CLINCH GOING TO BE HANGED."

**Wilkins, John** (1614–1672) One of the founders of the Royal Society of London; later bishop of Chester. In "The BATTLE OF THE BOOKS," he and Johann Mueller (Regiomontanus) command the Moderns' engineers. In "Thoughts on Reviewing the Essay," Sir William TEMPLE makes fun of Wilkins's *The Discovery of a World in the Moon . . . that . . . there may be another habitable World in the Planet* (1638–40) and his *Essay towards a Real Character and Philosophic Language* (1668). In the *Essay,* Wilkins proposes a universal language—an idea Swift lampoons in GULLIVER'S TRAVELS III.5 when Lemuel Gulliver visits the projectors at the Academy of Lagado. Wilkins was a liberal theologian who, in his widely popular *Ecclesiastes* (1646), instructed preachers to speak plainly and to exercise "meekness and lenity in differences not fundamental."

**William III, king of Great Britain** (1650–1702) Known as William of Orange; stadtholder of the United Provinces (1672–1702), and king of Great Britain (1689–1702). He was born in The Hague, the son of William II of Orange and Mary, the eldest daughter of CHARLES I of England. He married his cousin Mary (1662–94), the daughter of JAMES II and Anne Hyde. Invited to redress the various ills of England, he landed at Torbay in 1688 with an English and Dutch army, forcing James II to flee. William and Mary were proclaimed rulers early in 1689, and William led his army against James's supporters at Killiecrankie and at the Boyne (1690). Having achieved relative calm in the British Isles, he then concentrated on the War of the League of Augsburg against France (1689–97), where he once again was successful. His experience on the throne found him dealing with frequent parliamentary opposition to his proposals, and a series of troubling assassination plots. He died in London without an heir to the English crown, so Mary's sister, ANNE, became regent.

Swift petitioned William early in 1699 for "a Prebend of Canterbury or Westminster," which the king had promised Sir William TEMPLE for Swift. When no posting became available, Swift blamed the earl of ROMNEY, his seconder at Court, for negligence. Later, in "DIRECTIONS FOR A BIRTHDAY SONG," "A CHARACTER, PANEGYRIC, AND DESCRIPTION OF THE LEGION CLUB," and "MAD MULLINIX AND TIMOTHY," Swift harries William, not with his early phrase, "our happy prince," but with ambivalence and doubt. In 1690 his "ODE TO THE KING," he imagined William single-handedly defeating his enemies on the battlefield. But William would not have seen this verse, and it pleased only Temple. Swift's prose reflects continued interest in William from the earliest pieces throughout his writing career: "Prefaces to Temple's Works," "SENTIMENTS OF A CHURCH-OF-ENGLAND MAN," "REMARKS UPON A BOOK INTITULED, THE RIGHTS OF THE CHRISTIAN CHURCH ASSERTED," "A LETTER FROM A MEMBER OF THE HOUSE OF COMMONS IN IRELAND," "PREDICTIONS FOR THE YEAR 1708," the EXAMINER, "A NEW JOURNEY TO PARIS," "A Proposal for Correcting the English Tongue," "OF MEAN AND GREAT FIGURES," "The FAMILY OF SWIFT," marginalia, "The CONDUCT OF THE ALLIES," "Some Remarks on the Barrier Treaty," "The HISTORY OF THE FOUR LAST YEARS OF THE QUEEN" "An ENQUIRY INTO THE BEHAVIOUR OF THE QUEEN'S LAST MINISTRY," "The Public Spirit of the Whigs," "A LETTER FROM DR. SWIFT TO MR. POPE," "Some Arguments against Enlarging the Power of Bishops," "ON BROTHERLY LOVE," "A SERMON UPON THE MARTYRDOM OF KING CHARLES I," *The DRAPIER'S LETTERS, GULLIVER'S TRAVELS*, the *INTELLIGENCER*, "An EXAMINATION OF CERTAIN ABUSES," "The Presbyterians' Plea of Merit," *The JOURNAL TO STELLA*, and many letters throughout the *Correspondence*.

**Winchelsea, Anne Finch, countess of**  See FINCH, ANNE.

**Winder, Rev. John** (d. 1717)  Friend of Swift; vicar of Carnmoney and Swift's successor as prebend of Kilroot. Swift's friendship with Winder was one of the few things he enjoyed during his time at Kilroot, and the two appear to have had great respect for each other. After Swift returned to William TEMPLE's home in Moor Park in 1696, he succeeded in arranging for the prebendary of Kilroot to be assigned to Winder.

**Wogan, Charles** (1698–1752)  Soldier known as the Chevalier Wogans, an Irish-born Jacobite who was captured by English troops at Preston during the 1715 Rising. After being charged with high treason and imprisoned in Newgate in London, Wogan joined with six other Jacobites in a successful escape to France. He served with the exiled James Edward Stuart, and for various exploits on the Continent, James conferred upon him a baronetcy. After further military adventures, General Wogan wrote to Swift, whom he called "the mentor and champion of the Irish nation," sending him in 1732 a volume of his writings, including psalms, poems, and letters. Along with the packet, Wogan sent Swift a cask of Spanish wine, and they exchanged at least three letters, all of which express respect for each other. Adding to this exchange was the fact that Wogan apparently was one of the few men of about his own age whom Alexander POPE knew in his early days and with whom he had lived for two or three summers "in perfect union and familiarity" and whom Wogan had had "the honor to bring up to London, to dress a la mode, and introduce at Will's coffee-house." Swift mentions Wogan in a number of letters in the *Correspondence*.

**Wood, William** (1671–1730)  Wolverhampton, West Midlands, ironmaster and financial speculator. Wood provided the copper coinage for Ireland's halfpence and farthings, awarded through a series of corrupt practices carried out during Robert WALPOLE's government in 1722, including Wood's payment of bribes. Using opportunities to advance his own businesses and take an increased share of the profits, Wood became increasingly rich and ambitious. He purchased the patent for the Irish coinage from the king's influential German mistress, the duchess of KENDAL, for £10,000. This action has been called, after the Declaratory Act, the most disruptive event in Anglo-Irish relations since the Revolution of 1689. The outrageousness of this entire enterprise finally roused the Irish Parliament and the commissioners of revenue to protest to the English authorities, but to no avail, until Swift became involved.

Using *The Drapier's Letters* as his forum in the spring of 1724, Swift attacked the English government's greed, mismanagement, and contempt for the Irish economy. Wood intended to flood Ireland with low-quality copper coins amounting to a sizable proportion of the nation's currency. His entire approach to the project contained a multitude of abuses, from manufacturing Irish coins in England to exceeding the terms of his patent. His insolence was legendary, and he wrote letters to an English newspaper insisting on the legitimacy of his project. After enduring months of a highly effective pamphlet war conducted by Swift, Wood surrendered his patent in August 1725. Though Swift won this conflict, Wood was compensated for losing the patent with a handsome (but secret) pension. See also "Doing Good: A Sermon on the Occasion of Wood's Project," "Letter on Maculla's Project about Halfpence," "Answer to the Craftsman," "Letter on the Fishery," "A Serious Poem upon William Wood," "An Epigram on Wood's Brass Money," "A Letter from Dean Swift to Dean Smedley," "Verses on the Death of Dr. Swift, D.S.P.D.," "Aye and No: A Tale from Dublin," "Horace, Book I, Ode XIV," and "Verses Occasioned by the Sudden Drying Up of St. Patrick's Well near Trinity College, Dublin."

**Woolston, Thomas** (1670–1733) Clergyman. As a fellow of Sidney Sussex College, Cambridge, he became a clergyman and wrote numerous tracts on deism. His *Old Apology for the Truth of the Christian Religion* (1705) and *Discourses on the Miracles of Our Saviour* (1727–29) attack the historical interpretation of the Scriptures. He was charged with blasphemy, tried, and imprisoned in the King's Bench (1729) until he died. His books were burned by the common hangman. Woolston's extreme form of deistic thought was considered particularly damaging and regarded as a direct assault on established religion. Alexander Pope added him to *The Dunciad* as "an impious madman." References to Woolston appear in Swift's *Correspondence* and in "A Dialogue between an Eminent Lawyer and Dr. Swift, Dean of St. Patrick's," "Verses on

the Death of Dr. Swift, D.S.P.D.," "On Poetry: A Rhapsody," and "The Yahoo's Overthrow."

**Worrall, Rev. John** (d. 1751) Clergyman and friend of Swift. Worrall served as a minor canon of St. Patrick's and was appointed by William King (later archbishop of Dublin) in 1690. His promotion to the dean's vicar in 1695 had followed an earlier posting as Christ Church vicar from 1694. Swift and Worrall began an extensive correspondence, of which 15 letters survive, in December 1713, nearly six months after Swift had become dean of St. Patrick's. In an apparent revolt, the Vicars Choral, a corporation endowed with lands and with the presumed power of making leases, decided to negotiate a lease without consulting the dean. Worrall was the head of the vicars, and Swift dealt quickly with this rebelliousness. It ultimately took years of patient effort to bring the vicars into line with the dean's authority. Worrall served St. Patrick's even longer than Swift, and they became fast friends. Worrall kept a watchful eye on Esther Johnson (Stella) and also gave Swift assurance on the dean's finances. References to Worrall appear in *The Drapier's Letters*, and in his will Swift poignantly left Worrall his best beaver hat.

**Worsley, Lady Frances (Thynne)** (c. 1673–1750) Wife of Sir Robert Worsley, Baronet, and mother of Lady Frances Carteret, wife of the three times lord-lieutenant of Ireland, John Lord Carteret. She became a friend and correspondent of Swift. In 1732 Lady Worsley presented Swift with an escritoire (writing desk) japanned (decorated with a black enamel finish) by her. She responded with this gift after he suggested humorously that her daughter had outdone her with a gift to him: "For you know, I always expect presents and advances from ladies." He presented the desk to Mary Harrison Swift (Deane Swift's wife), and it is now in St. Patrick's Cathedral. References to Worsley appear in *The Journal to Stella* and in a number of letters in Swift's *Correspondence*.

**Wotton, William** (1666–1727) Clergyman and scholar who opposed Swift's patron Sir William Temple (who advocated the Ancients) in the ongo-

ing controversy over whether or not ancient learning was superior to modern. Wotton became a
member of the Royal Society of London in 1687.
He entered the Ancients versus Moderns fray in
1694 with his *Reflections upon Ancient and Modern
Learning*. In that work he refuted Temple's assertion
of the Ancients' superiority in the 1690 *Essay upon
Ancient and Modern Learning*. Wotton produced a
second edition of his *Reflections* in 1697, which
included (as further evidence against Temple's
arguments) Richard BENTLEY's less diplomatic *Dissertation upon the Epistles of Phalaris, Themistocles,
Socrates, Euripides, and Others; and the Fables of
Aesop*.

In defense of Temple, Swift attacked Wotton and
Bentley in "The BATTLE OF THE BOOKS" and "A
TALE OF A TUB." As the favorite son of the evil goddess Criticism in "Battle," Wotton dies an ignominious death at the hands of Charles Boyle, who kills
Bentley at the same time. In the "Tale," the narrator
refers to Wotton as his "worthy and ingenious
friend" whose "incomparable treatise of *Ancient and
Modern Learning*" is a volume "never to be sufficiently valued, whether we consider the happy turns

and flowings of the author's wit, the great usefulness
of his sublime discoveries upon the subject of *flies*
and *spittle*, or the laborious eloquence of his style."
In 1705 Wotton's popular *Observations upon the Tale
of a Tub* provided meticulous explanations of various allusions in the "Tale." Wotton explained that
his primary goal in the *Observations* was to show
those who pretended to see no harm in the "Tale"
the "Mischief of its ludicrous Allegory," which made
a "May-Game" of such serious topics as "God and
Religion, Truth and Moral Honesty," along with
"Learning and Industry" (Williams, *Critical Heritage*
38). Swift made fun of Wotton's effort by including
the *Observations* piecemeal as footnotes in the fifth
edition of the "Tale," which appeared in 1710. The
notes were also published separately in 1711 as *An
Apology for the Tale of a Tub. With Explanatory Notes
by W. W[o]tt[o]n, B.D. and Others*. As Ross and
Woolley point out in their edition of the "Tale," this
separate publication of Wotton's "commentary"
(which Swift used to "satirize" Wotton as "the
learned commentator") was probably intended to
accommodate readers who had purchased earlier
editions of the "Tale."

# Z

**Zinzendorf, Philip Louis, (Philip Louis Sinzendorf) Count** (1671–1742) Austrian diplomat, Imperial ambassador to The Hague, and chancellor of the Holy Roman Empire. In early 1712 Swift was writing "Some Remarks on the Barrier Treaty," which contains objections to the treaty negotiated with the Dutch and the Sidney GODOLPHIN ministry. Many felt that the ministry had gone too far in its efforts to keep the Dutch in the war. The Imperialist negotiator Zinzendorf had worked with some success in limiting the Dutch, both in territory and in trading privileges, which matched the TORY agenda. The WHIGS, however, were vindicated in the meantime when a positive reply pointed out that the treaty had secured the Protestant Succession, providing a sufficient barrier against the power of France. References to Zinzendorf appear in "The HISTORY OF THE FOUR LAST YEARS OF THE QUEEN."

# PART IV

# *Appendices*

# CHRONOLOGY OF SWIFT'S LIFE

**1658**
Death of Rev. Thomas Swift. Godwin Swift, the eldest of Thomas Swift's sons, migrates to Ireland to practice law after his father's death.

**1660**
Godwin Swift's brother Jonathan (Sr.) moves to Ireland.

**1664**
Abigail Erick and the elder Jonathan Swift are married.

**1666**
Jane Swift (Fenton) born in Dublin.

**1667**
Jonathan Swift, Sr., dies at age 27; Jonathan Swift born November 30 at 7 Hoey's Court in Dublin.

**1669**
Abigail Swift returns to her family's home in Leicester, taking Jane with her and leaving Jonathan with a nurse. The nurse travels to White-haven to visit an ill relative. She and Jonathan remain there for three years.

**1673–1682**
Financed by his uncle Godwin, Swift attends Kilkenny Grammar School in Dublin.

**1682**
Swift begins his studies at Trinity College, Dublin.

**1685**
(February) Death of King Charles II. Roman Catholic James II crowned.

**1686**
(February) Swift receives his B.A. *speciali gratia* ("by special grace").

**1689**
After beginning work on his M.A., Swift leaves for England amid the turmoil leading up to the Glorious Revolution, in which King James II would be deposed and replaced by the Protestant William of Orange (William III) and Mary II. Swift visits his mother in Leicester, and moves to Moor Park in Surrey to become secretary to Sir William Temple. His duties include tutoring eight-year-old Esther Johnson (whom he later called "Stella"). Within six months of taking up residence at Moor Park, Swift develops the first symptoms of Ménière's disease.

**1690**
Based on the advice of physicians, Swift returns to Ireland in an attempt to regain his health. In July, William defeats James II in Ireland at the Battle of the Boyne, and James flees to France.

**1691**
Hoping for preferment in the form of an appointed position in the church or government, Swift returns to Moor Park and resumes his duties as Temple's secretary.

**1692**

Swift receives his M.A. from Oxford.

**1691–1694**

Swift writes a number of odes including his first surviving poem ("Ode to the King"), the first poem he published ("Ode to the Athenian Society," which appeared in the *Athenian Mercury*), and three others. Death of Queen Mary II.

**1694**

(October) Swift becomes a deacon of the Anglican Church.

**1695**

Swift is ordained as a Church of Ireland priest and is assigned to the small parish of Kilroot (near Belfast).

**1696**

(May) After a disappointing year in Kilroot, Swift accepts Sir William Temple's invitation to return to Moor Park. He proposes marriage to Jane Waring ("Varina") that same month. Swift begins work on "A Tale of a Tub" and "The Battle of the Books."

**1699**

(January) Death of Sir William Temple. In August, Swift leaves for Dublin as chaplain to the earl of Berkeley, lord justice of Ireland.

**1700**

(February) Swift becomes vicar of Laracor and eight months later is appointed prebend of St. Patrick's Cathedral in Dublin.

**1701**

(April) Swift travels to England with the earl of Berkeley (who has been dismissed from his post). In August, Esther Johnson and her companion Rebecca Dingley move to Dublin in order to be closer to Swift. He returns there himself in September. Swift publishes his edition of volume 3 of Temple's *Miscellanea* along with his own "Discourse of the Contests and Dissensions in Athens and Rome." James II dies in September; King Louis XIV of France declares James Francis Edward Stuart (the "Pretender") king of Great Britain and Ireland.

**1702**

(February) Swift receives his doctor of divinity degree from Trinity College, Dublin. King William III dies on March 8. Queen Anne (daughter of James II) is crowned. War of the Spanish Succession begins in May.

**1703**

(November) Swift returns to England and publishes "A Tale of a Tub" and "The Battle of the Books."

**1706–1709**

Swift is in London working as a representative of the Church of Ireland, lobbying to have Irish clergymen—like their brethren in England—exempted from having to pay the "First Fruits and Twentieth Parts" (a tax normally levied on clergymen). He meets 20-year-old Esther Vanhomrigh (whom he later calls "Vanessa"), along with Joseph Addison and Richard Steele. Swift publishes the "Bickerstaff Papers" (1708) and begins writing for Steele's *Tatler* (the periodical in which "A Description of the Morning" was first printed in 1709). He returns to Laracor at the end of 1709.

**1710**

(April) Death of Abigail Erick Swift. Swift travels to England in September. Early on in his work as a Church of Ireland commissioner, Swift had found himself aligned with the Whigs, but by late 1710 he becomes more closely associated with the Tories. While in England, he begins writing the letters that would eventually become *The Journal to Stella*. The fall of the Whig ministry led by lord treasurer Sidney Godolphin paved the way for the Tories' rapid rise to power under Robert Harley, and Swift began writing in support of that party in the pro-Tory *Examiner* (which he edited from late 1710 through June of 1711).

## 1711

Swift's *Miscellanies in Prose and Verse*, the first authorized collection of his works, is published, along with his "Conduct of the Allies."

## 1712

Swift's "Proposal for Correcting, Improving and Ascertaining the English Tongue," in which he argues for establishing an academy dedicated to that purpose, is published.

## 1713

(June) Swift is made dean of St. Patrick's Cathedral, Dublin, during a visit to Ireland. He returns to London in September to continue lobbying for Irish clergy to be exempt from the First Fruits tax. Treaty of Utrecht is signed in April, ending the War of the Spanish Succession.

## 1714

Publication of Swift's controversial "Public Spirit of the Whigs." In June he retires to the rectory at Letcombe Bassett, Berkshire. After Queen Anne's death on August 1, Swift reluctantly returns to Dublin to assume his post as dean of St. Patrick's Cathedral. Vanessa follows him there and takes up residence in nearby Celbridge—having ignored his attempt to dismiss her quietly before leaving London and still clinging to the hope that they might one day be married. Hanoverian king George I crowned.

## 1716

Swift's alleged "secret marriage" to Stella.

## 1718

Swift cultivates friendships with Thomas Sheridan and Patrick Delany and begins to view Ireland as something more than a place of temporary exile.

## 1720

Swift suffers more frequent and pronounced onsets of dizziness and deafness. He publishes "Proposal for the Universal Use of Irish Manufacture," in which he urges the Irish to resist English trade policies.

William Whitshed seeks to have printer Edward Waters prosecuted for distributing the tract.

## 1721

Swift begins writing *Gulliver's Travels*.

## 1722

William Wood receives a patent to introduce copper coinage in Ireland.

## 1724

Swift anonymously publishes the first of his *Drapier's Letters* in opposition to Wood's patent. After letter 4 ("To the Whole People of Ireland") appears on October 22, Lord Carteret prosecutes John Harding for having printed it and offers a reward for divulging the author. Swift's "Seasonable Advice to the Grand Jury" causes the case against Harding to be dropped. Wood's patent is revoked.

## 1726

(March) Swift returns to England, where he visits Alexander Pope at his villa near Twickenham. They prepare *Gulliver's Travels* for publication. The first edition is printed in London on October 28 and gains immediate popularity. "Cadenus and Vanessa" is published in Dublin without Swift's approval.

## 1727

(April) Swift travels to England, where he and Pope work for several months on compiling materials for more volumes of *Miscellanies*. Death of King George I; his son George II is crowned.

## 1728

Stella dies on January 28. Swift collaborates with Sheridan on several issues of the *Intelligencer*.

## 1729

"A Modest Proposal" published.

## 1730–1731

Publication of "Answer to the *Craftsman*" (1730), and "Considerations upon Two Bills . . . Relating to the Clergy of Ireland" (1731). Swift writes some of his most famous poetry, including "Verses on the Death of Dr. Swift," "The Lady's Dressing Room," "A Beautiful Young Nymph Going to Bed," and "Strephon and Chloe."

## 1732

"Advantages Proposed by Repealing the Sacramental Test Act" is published, in which Swift opposes granting Dissenters the right to hold office. Another volume of *Miscellanies* (a joint effort with Pope) appears the same year.

## 1733

"On Poetry: A Rhapsody" published.

## 1734–1735

Dublin printer George Faulkner issues four volumes of Swift's collected *Works*, including a revised version of *Gulliver's Travels* in volume 3.

## 1736

"Character, Panegyric, and Description of the Legion Club" is published, in which Swift opposes an effort by Irish landowners to seek exemption from paying tithes to the church.

## 1738

Symptoms of Ménière's disease become more debilitating for Swift. *Complete Collection of Genteel and Ingenious Conversation* (also known as *Polite Conversation*) is published.

## 1742

Rev. Francis Wilson calls for a commission of lunacy to assess Swift's mental state. At the age of 75, he is declared to be of "unsound mind and memory" and "incapable of transacting any business" or caring for himself.

## 1745

Swift dies on October 19 and is buried next to Stella in St. Patrick's Cathedral.

# BIBLIOGRAPHY

## Modern Editions of Swift's Works

*The Account Books of Jonathan Swift*. Edited by Paul V. Thompson and Dorothy Jay Thompson. Newark and London: University of Delaware Press, 1984.

*The Annotated Gulliver's Travels*. Edited by Isaac Asimov. New York: Clarkson N. Potter, 1980.

*Basic Writings*. Edited by Claude Rawson. New York: Modern Library, 2002.

*Collected Poems*. Edited by Joseph Horrell. 2 vols. Cambridge, Mass.: Harvard University Press, 1958.

*The Complete Poems*. Edited by Pat Rogers. London: Penguin, 1983.

*Correspondence*. Edited by Harold Williams. 5 vols. Oxford: Clarendon Press, 1963–65. (Referenced as "Corr." throughout the text.)

*Correspondence of Jonathan Swift, D.D.* Edited by David Woolley. 4 vols. Frankfurt am Main: Peter Lang, 1999–   .

*Directions to Servants*. Foreword by Colm Tóibín. London: Hesperus, 2004.

*A Discourse of the Contests and Dissensions between the Nobles and the Commons in Athens and Rome*. Edited by Frank H. Ellis. Oxford: Clarendon Press, 1967.

*The Drapier's Letters to the People of Ireland Against Receiving Wood's Halfpence*. Edited by Herbert Davis. Oxford: Clarendon Press, 1935.

*Gulliver's Travels*. Edited by Robert DeMaria. Rev. ed. New York: Penguin, 2003.

*Gulliver's Travels*. Edited by Ian Higgins and Claude Rawson. London: Oxford University Press, 2005.

*Gulliver's Travels*. Edited by Albert J. Rivero. New York and London: Norton, 2002.

*Gulliver's Travels*. Edited by Paul Turner. 2d ed. London: Oxford University Press, 1986.

*Gulliver's Travels: A Facsimile Reproduction of a Large-Paper Copy of the First Edition, 1726, Containing the Author's Annotations*. Edited by Harry Shefter. Delmar, N.Y.: Scholars Facsimiles and Reprints, 1981.

*Gulliver's Travels: Case Studies in Contemporary Criticism*. Edited by Christopher Fox. Boston: Bedford Books of St. Martin's Press, 1995.

*The Intelligencer*. Edited by James Woolley. Oxford: Clarendon Press, 1992.

*Jonathan Swift: A Critical Anthology*. Edited by Denis Donoghue. Cambridge: Cambridge University Press, 1971.

*Journal to Stella*. Edited by Harold Williams. Reprint. Oxford: Clarendon Press, 1975.

*Major Works*. Edited by Angus Ross and David Woolley. Oxford World's Classics Series. London: Oxford University Press, 2003.

*Memoirs of the Extraordinary Life, Works, and Discoveries of Martin Scriblerus*. Edited by Charles Kerby-Miller. Reprint. Oxford: Oxford University Press, 1988.

*On Poetry: A Rapsody: A Critical Edition with a Historical Introduction and Commentary*. Edited by Melanie Maria Just. Frankfurt am Main: Peter Lang, 2004.

*Poems*. Edited by Harold Williams. 3 vols. Oxford: Clarendon Press, 1958.

*Polite Conversation*. Edited by Eric Partridge. London: Deutsch, 1963.

*Prose Works*. Edited by Herbert Davis et al. 14 vols. Oxford: Blackwell/Shakespeare Head, 1939–74.

*Swift vs. Mainwaring: The Examiner and the Medley.* Edited by Frank H. Ellis. Oxford: Clarendon Press, 1985.

*A Tale of a Tub.* Edited by A. C. Guthkelch and D. Nichol Smith. 2d ed. Oxford: Clarendon Press, 1958.

*A Tale of a Tub and Other Works.* Edited by Angus Ross and David Woolley. Oxford: Oxford University Press, 1984.

## Bibliographic Works

Landa, Louis A., and J. E. Tobin. *Jonathan Swift: A List of Critical Studies Published from 1895–1945.* New York: Cosmopolitan Science and Art Service, 1945.

LeFanu, William R. *A Catalogue of Books Belonging to Dr. Jonathan Swift: Dean of St. Patrick's.* Cambridge: Cambridge Bibliographic Society, 1988.

Rodino, Richard H. *Swift Studies, 1965–1980: An Annotated Bibliography.* New York: Garland, 1984.

———— et al. "A Supplemental Bibliography of Swift Studies, 1965–1980." *Swift Studies* 2 (1987): 77–96.

Stathis, James J. *A Bibliography of Swift Studies, 1946–1965.* Nashville, Tenn.: Vanderbilt University Press, 1967.

Teerink, Herman. *A Bibliography of the Writings of Jonathan Swift.* 2d ed. Edited by Arthur H. Scouten. Philadelphia: University of Pennsylvania Press, 1963.

Vieth, David M. *Swift's Poetry 1900–1980: An Annotated Bibliography of Studies.* New York and London: Garland, 1982.

Voigt, Milton. *Swift and the Twentieth Century.* Detroit: Wayne State University Press, 1964.

Williams, Harold. *Dean Swift's Library.* Cambridge: Cambridge University Press, 1932.

## Biography

Downie, J. A. *Jonathan Swift: Political Writer.* London: Routledge & Kegan Paul, 1984.

Ehrenpreis, Irvin. *Swift: The Man, His Works and the Age.* 3 vols. Cambridge, Mass.: Harvard University Press, 1962–83.

Foot, Michael. *The Pen & the Sword.* London: MacGibbon and Kee, 1957.

Fróes, João, ed. *Remarks on the Life and Writings of Dr. Jonathan Swift.* By John Boyle, Fifth Earl of Cork

and Orrery. Newark: University of Delaware Press, 2000.

Glendinning, Victoria. *Jonathan Swift: A Portrait.* New York: Henry Holt, 1998.

Greenacre, Phyllis. *Swift and Carroll: A Psychoanalytic Study of Two Lives.* 1955. Reprint. New York: International University Press, 1977.

Harrison, Alan. *The Dean's Friend: Anthony Raymond 1675–1726, Jonathan Swift and the Irish Language.* Dublin: Eamonn de Burca, 1999.

Jackson, Robert Wyse. *Jonathan Swift: Dean and Pastor.* Honolulu: University Press of the Pacific, 2003.

Johnston, Denis. *In Search of Swift.* Dublin: Hodges Figgis, 1959.

McMinn, Joseph. *Jonathan Swift: A Literary Life.* New York: St. Martin's Press, 1991.

Murry, John Middleton. *Jonathan Swift: A Critical Biography.* London: Cape, 1954.

Nokes, David. *Jonathan Swift: A Hypocrite Reversed.* Oxford: Oxford University Press, 1987.

Oakleaf, David. *A Political Biography of Jonathan Swift.* London: Pickering and Chatto. [Forthcoming]

Probyn, Clive T. "Swift, Jonathan." *Oxford Dictionary of National Biography.* Vol. 53, Oxford: Oxford University Press, 2004. 465–79.

Rowse, A. L. *Jonathan Swift: Major Prophet.* New York: Thames and Hudson, 1975.

Van Doren, Carl. *Swift.* New York: Viking Press, 1930.

## Criticism

Abbreviations:

*ELH: English Literary History*
*PLL: Papers on Language and Literature*
*PMLA: Publications of the Modern Language Association of America*
*SEL: Studies in English Literature 1500–1900*

### General

Alderson, Simon J. "Swift and the Pun," *Swift Studies* 11 (1996): 47–57.

Beaumont, Charles A. *Swift's Classical Rhetoric.* Athens: University of Georgia Press, 1961.

Berwick, Donald. *The Reputation of Jonathan Swift, 1781–1882.* 1941. Reprint, New York: Haskell, 1965.

Bloom, Harold, ed. *Jonathan Swift.* Modern Critical Views. New York: Chelsea House, 1986.

Boyle, Frank. *Swift as Nemesis: Modernity and Its Satirist.* Stanford, Calif.: Stanford University Press, 2000.

Brantley, Will. "Reading Swift as a Modernist: A Polemical Investigation," *Essays in Literature* 19, 1 (1992): 20–35.

Brown, Norman O. "The Excremental Vision." In *Life against Death: The Psychoanalytical Meaning of History,* 19–201. Middletown, Conn.: Wesleyan University Press, 1959.

Bullitt, John M. *Jonathan Swift and the Anatomy of Satire: A Study of Satiric Technique.* Cambridge. Mass.: Harvard University Press, 1953.

Burrow, R. W. "Swift and Plato's Political Philosophy," *Studies in Philology* 84, 4 (1987): 494–506.

Bywaters, David. "*Gulliver's Travels* and the Mode of Political Parallel during Walpole's Administration," *ELH* 54 (1987): 717–740.

Carey, Daniel. "Swift among the Freethinkers," *Eighteenth-Century Ireland/ Iris an dá Chultúr* 12 (1997): 89–99.

Chalmers, Alan D. *Jonathan Swift and the Burden of the Future.* Newark: University of Delaware Press, 1995.

———. " 'To Curse the Dean, or Bless the Draper': Recent Scholarship on Swift," *Eighteenth-Century Studies* 36 (2002–03): 580–585.

Coleborne, Bryan. "Swift and Yeats: Reading and Misreading from Swift to 'Swift.' " In *Conflicting Identities: Essays on Modern Irish Literature,* edited by Robbie B. H. Goh, 39–75. Singapore: UniPress, Centre for the Arts, National University of Singapore, 1997.

Connery, Brian. "Self-Representation, Authority, and the Fear of Madness in the Works of Swift." In *Studies in Eighteenth-Century Culture,* edited by Leslie Ellen Brown and Patricia B. Craddock. Vol. 20, 165–182. East Lansing, Mich: Colleagues Press, 1990.

———, ed. *Representations of Swift.* Newark and London: University of Delaware Press, 2003.

Craven, Kenneth. *Jonathan Swift and the Millennium of Madness: The Information Age in Swift's "A Tale of a Tub."* Leiden, the Netherlands: Brill, 1992.

Creaser, Wanda J. " 'The Most Mortifying Malady': Jonathan Swift's Dizzying World and Dublin's Mentally Ill," *Swift Studies* 19 (2004): 27–48.

Croghan, Martin J. "Savage Indignation: An Introduction to the Philosophy of Language and Semi-

otics in Jonathan Swift," *Swift Studies* 5 (1990): 11–37.

Crook, Keith. *A Preface to Swift.* London and New York: Longman, 1998.

Davis, Herbert. *Jonathan Swift. Essays on His Satire and Other Studies.* New York: Oxford University Press, 1964.

———. *Stella: A Gentlewoman of the Eighteenth Century.* New York: Macmillan, 1942.

Deane, Seamus. "Swift and the Anglo-Irish Intellect," *Eighteenth-Century Ireland/ Iris an dá Chultúr* 1 (1986): 9–22.

Delasanta, Rodney. "Putting off the Old Man and Putting on the New: Ephesians 4:22–24 in Chaucer, Shakespeare, Swift, and Dostoevsky," *Christianity and Literature* 51, 3 (2002): 339–362.

DePorte, Michael. "Avenging Naboth: Swift and Monarchy," *Philological Quarterly* 69, 4 (1990): 419–433.

———. "From the Womb of Things to Their Grave: Madness and Memory in Swift," *University of Toronto Quarterly* 58, 3 (1989): 376–390.

———. " 'Mere Productions in the Brain': Interpreting Dreams in Swift." In *Literature and Medicine during the Eighteenth Century,* edited by Marie Mulvey Roberts and Roy Porter, 118–135. London: Routledge, 1993.

———. *Nightmares and Hobbyhorses: Swift, Sterne, and Augustan Ideas of Madness.* San Marino, Calif.: Huntington Library, 1974.

Doll, Dan. "The Word and the Thing in Swift's Prose," *Studies in Eighteenth-Century Culture* 15 (1986): 199–210.

Donoghue, Denis. *Jonathan Swift: A Critical Introduction.* Cambridge: Cambridge University Press, 1969.

———. "Swift and the Association of Ideas," *Yearbook of English Studies* 18 (1988): 1–17.

Doody, Margaret Anne. "Swift among the Women," *Yearbook of English Studies* 18 (1988): 69–82.

Douglas, Aileen, Patrick Kelly, and Ian Campbell Ross, eds. *Locating Swift: Essays from Dublin on the 250th Anniversary of the Death of Jonathan Swift, 1667–1745.* Dublin: Four Courts Press, 1998.

Downie, J. A. *Robert Harley and the Press: Propaganda and Public Opinion in the Age of Swift and Defoe.* Cambridge: Cambridge University Press, 1979.

———. Introduction to *Swift, Temple, and the Ducros Affair, Part II.* Augustan Reprint Society. Los Angeles: UCLA, 1987.

Dyson, A. E. "Swift: The Metamorphosis of Irony," *Essays and Studies* 11 (1958): 53–67.

Ehrenpreis, Irvin. *Acts of Implication: Suggestion and Covert Meaning in the Works of Dryden, Swift, Pope, and Austen.* The Beckman Lectures, 1978. Berkeley: University of California Press, 1981.

———. *The Personality of Jonathan Swift.* New York: Barnes and Noble, 1969.

Eilon, Daniel. *Faction's Fictions: Ideological Closure in Swift's Satire.* Newark: University of Delaware Press, 1991.

Elias, A. C., Jr. *Swift at Moor Park: Problems in Biography and Criticism.* Philadelphia: University of Pennsylvania Press, 1982.

Elliott, Robert C. *The Power of Satire: Magic, Ritual, Art.* Princeton, N.J.: Princeton University Press, 1960.

Ewald, William Bragg, Jr. *The Masks of Jonathan Swift.* Cambridge, Mass.: Harvard University Press, 1954.

Fabricant, Carole. "Colonial Sublimities and Sublimations: Swift, Burke, and Ireland," *ELH* 72, 2 (Summer 2005): 309–337.

———. *Swift's Landscape.* Notre Dame, Ind.: University of Notre Dame Press, 1995.

———. "Swift the Irishman." In *The Cambridge Companion to Jonathan Swift,* edited by Christopher Fox, 48–72. Cambridge and New York: Cambridge University Press, 2003.

*Fair Liberty Was All His Cry: A Tercentenary Tribute to Jonathan Swift, 1667–1745,* edited by A. Norman Jeffares. London: Macmillan, 1967.

Fauske, Christopher J. *Jonathan Swift and the Church of Ireland, 1710–1724.* Dublin and Portland: Irish Academic Press, 2002.

Ferguson, Oliver. *Jonathan Swift and Ireland.* Urbana: University of Illinois Press, 1962.

Fischer, John Irwin, Hermann J. Real, and James Woolley, eds. *Swift and His Contexts.* New York: AMS, 1989.

Flynn, Carol Houlihan. *The Body in Swift and Defoe.* Cambridge: Cambridge University Press, 1990.

Forster, Jean-Paul. *Jonathan Swift: The Fictions of the Satirist.* Rev. ed. Frankfurt am Main: Peter Lang, 1998.

Fox, Christopher, ed. *The Cambridge Companion to Jonathan Swift.* Cambridge and New York: Cambridge University Press, 2003.

Fox, Christopher, and Brenda Tooley, eds. *Walking Naboth's Vineyard: New Studies of Swift.* South Bend, Ind.: University of Notre Dame Press, 1995.

Francus, Marilyn. *The Converting Imagination: Linguistic Theory in Swift's Satiric Prose.* Carbondale: Southern Illinois University Press, 1994.

———. "The Monstrous Mother: Reproductive Anxiety in Swift and Pope," *ELH* 61, 4 (1994): 829–851.

Freedman, William. "Dynamic Identity and the Hazards of Satire in Swift," *SEL* 29, 3 (Summer 1989): 473–488.

Freiburg, Rudolf, Arno Löffler, and Zach Wolfgang, eds. *Swift: The Enigmatic Dean. Studies in English and Comparative Literature.* Vol. 12. Tubingen, Germany: Stauffenburg, 1998.

Goldgar, Bertrand A. *The Curse of Party: Swift's Relations with Addison and Steele.* Lincoln: University of Nebraska Press, 1961.

———. *Walpole and the Wits: The Relation of Politics to Literature, 1722–1742.* Lincoln: University of Nebraska Press, 1976.

"Gosford Forest Park: The Swift Connection." Available online. URL: http://www.gosford.co.uk/index.html. Accessed December 19, 2005.

Grundy, Isobel. "Swift and Johnson," *The Age of Johnson* 2 (1989): 154–180.

Gubar, Susan. "The Female Monster in Augustan Satire," *Signs: A Journal of Women in Culture and Society* 3 (1977): 380–394.

Hardy, Evelyn. *The Conjured Spirit, Swift: A Study in the Relationship of Swift, Stella, and Vanessa.* London: Hogarth Press, 1949.

Harth, Phillip. "Swift's Self-Image as a Satirist." *Proceedings of the First Münster Symposium on Jonathan Swift,* edited by Hermann J. Real and Heinz J. Vienken, 113–121. Munich: Wilhelm Fink, 1985.

Higgins, Ian. "Dryden and Swift." In *John Dryden (1631–1700): His Politics, His Plays, and His Poets,* edited by Claude Rawson and Aaron Santesso, 217–234. Newark: University of Delaware Press/London: Associated University Presses, 2004.

———. *Jonathan Swift, Writers and Their Work.* Horndon, Tavistock: Northcote House, 2004.

———. *Swift's Politics: A Study in Disaffection.* Cambridge: Cambridge University Press, 1994.

Hunting, Robert. *Jonathan Swift.* Twayne's English Authors Series. New York: Twayne, 1967.

————. *Jonathan Swift.* Rev. ed. Twayne's English Authors Series. Boston: Twayne/G. K. Hall, 1989.

Jeffares, A. Norman, ed. *Swift: Modern Judgments.* London: Macmillan, 1969.

"Jonathan Swift." "Before Victoria: Selected Authors from the Eighteenth and Nineteenth Centuries." The Victorian Web. Available online. URL: http://www.victorianweb.org/previctorian/swift/swiftov.html. Accessed December 19, 2005.

Kelly, Ann Cline. *Jonathan Swift and Popular Culture: Myth, Media, and the Man.* New York and London: Palgrave, 2002.

————. *Swift and the English Language.* Philadelphia: University of Pennsylvania Press, 1988.

Kelly, Patrick. "Swift on Money and Economics." In *The Cambridge Companion to Jonathan Swift,* edited by Christopher Fox, 128–145. Cambridge and New York: Cambridge University Press, 2003.

Landa, Louis A. *Swift and the Church of Ireland.* 2d ed. Oxford: Clarendon Press, 1965.

Leavis, F. R. "The Irony of Swift." In *Determinations,* 79–108. London: Chatto and Windus, 1934.

Leddy, Annette. "Borges and Swift: Dystopian Reflections," *Comparative Literature Studies* 27, 2 (1990): 113–123.

Lein, Clayton D. "Jonathan Swift and the Population of Ireland," *Eighteenth-Century Studies* 8, 4 (Summer 1975): 431–453.

"Lesson Plans for Gulliver's Travels and 'A Modest Proposal.'" Web English Teacher. Available online. URL: http://www.webenglishteacher.com/swift.html. Accessed December 19, 2005.

Lock, F. P. *Swift's Tory Politics.* London: Duckworth, 1983.

Louis, Frances Deutsch. *Swift's Anatomy of Misunderstanding: A Study of Swift's Epistemological Imagination in* A Tale of a Tub *and* Gulliver's Travels. Totowa, N.J.: Barnes and Noble, 1981.

Lowe, N. F. "Why Swift Killed Partridge," *Swift Studies* 6 (1991): 70–82.

Mahony, Robert. "The Irish Colonial Experience and Swift's Rhetorics of Perception in the 1720s," *Eighteenth-Century Life* 22 (1998): 63–75.

————. *Jonathan Swift: The Irish Identity.* New Haven, Conn. and London: Yale University Press, 1995.

May, James E. "Edward Young's Responses to Jonathan Swift," *Swift Studies* 18 (2003): 63–79.

McHugh, Roger, and Philip Edwards, eds. *Jonathan Swift: A Dublin Tercentenary Tribute.* Dublin: Dolmen Press and Oxford University Press, 1967.

McKeon, Michael. "Parables of the Younger Son (II): Swift and the Containment of Desire." In *The Origins of the English Novel, 1660–1740,* 336–356. Baltimore: Johns Hopkins University Press, 1987.

McLoughlin, T. O. "Jonathan Swift and the Proud Oppressor's Hand." In *Contesting Ireland: Irish Voices against England in the Eighteenth Century,* edited by T. O. McLoughlin, 65–87. Dublin: Four Courts Press, 1999.

McMinn, Joseph. *Jonathan's Travels: Swift and Ireland.* Belfast and New York: Appletree Press and St. Martin's Press, 1994.

————. "A Reluctant Observer: Swift and Architecture," *Irish Architectural and Decorative Studies: The Journal of the Irish Georgian Society* 6 (2003): 91–119.

————. "Swift and Theatre," *Eighteenth-Century Ireland* 16 (2001): 35–46.

Mell, Donald C., ed. *Pope, Swift, and Women Writers.* Newark and London: University of Delaware Press, 1996.

Meyers, Jeffrey. "Swift and Kafka," *PLL* 40, 3 (Summer 2004): 329–336.

Mezciems, Jenny. "Utopia and 'the Thing which is not': More, Swift, and Other Lying Idealists," *University of Toronto Quarterly* 52 (1982): 40–62.

Montag, Warren. *The Unthinkable Swift: The Spontaneous Philosophy of a Church of England Man.* London and New York: Verso, 1994.

Mullan, John. "Swift, Defoe, and Literary Forms." In *The Cambridge Companion to English Literature, 1650–1740,* edited by Steven N. Zwicker, 250–275. Cambridge: Cambridge University Press, 1998.

Nokes, David. "'Hack at Tom Poley's': Swift's Use of Puns." In *The Art of Jonathan Swift,* edited by Clive T. Probyn, 43–56. London: Vision Press, 1978.

Nolan, Emer. "Swift: The Patriot Game," *British Journal for Eighteenth-Century Studies* 21 (1998): 39–53.

Oakleaf, David. "Politics and History." In *The Cambridge Companion to Jonathan Swift,* edited by Christopher Fox, 31–47. Cambridge and New York: Cambridge University Press, 2003.

Palmieri, Frank. "The Satiric Footnotes of Swift and Gibbon," *The Eighteenth Century: Theory and Interpretation* 31, 3 (Autumn 1990): 245–262.

———, ed. *Critical Essays on Jonathan Swift.* New York: G. K. Hall, 1993.

Paulson, Ronald. *The Fictions of Satire.* Baltimore: Johns Hopkins University Press, 1967.

Phiddian, Robert. *Swift's Parody.* Cambridge: Cambridge University Press, 1995.

Philmus, Robert M. "Dryden's 'Cousin Swift' Re-Examined," *Swift Studies* 18 (2003): 99–103.

Price, Martin. *Swift's Rhetorical Art: A Study in Structure and Meaning.* New Haven, Conn.: Yale University Press, 1953.

Probyn, Clive T., ed. *The Art of Jonathan Swift.* London: Vision Press, 1978.

———, ed. *Jonathan Swift: The Contemporary Background.* Manchester, England: Manchester University Press, 1978.

Quinlan, Maurice. "Swift's Use of Literalization as a Rhetorical Device," *PMLA* 82 (1967): 516–521.

Quintana, Ricardo. *The Mind and Art of Jonathan Swift.* 1936. Reprint. Gloucester, Mass.: Peter Smith, 1965.

———. *Swift: An Introduction.* London: Oxford University Press, 1955.

Rankin, Deana. *Between Spenser and Swift: English Writing in Seventeenth-Century Ireland.* Cambridge: Cambridge University Press, 2005.

Rawson, Claude. *Jonathan Swift: A Collection of Critical Essays.* New Century Views. Englewood Cliffs, N.J.: Prentice Hall, 1995.

———, ed. *The Character of Swift's Satire: A Revised Focus.* Newark and London: University of Delaware Press, 1983.

*Reading Swift: Papers from the Second Münster Symposium on Jonathan Swift,* edited by Richard H. Rodino and Hermann J. Real, with the assistance of Helgard Stöver-Leidig. Münich: Wilhelm Fink, 1993.

*Reading Swift: Papers from the Third Münster Symposium on Jonathan Swift,* edited by Hermann J. Real and Helgard Stöver-Leidig. Münich: Wilhelm Fink, 1998.

*Reading Swift: Papers from the Fourth Münster Symposium on Jonathan Swift,* edited by Hermann J. Real

and Helgard Stöver-Leidig. Münich: Wilhelm Fink, 2003.

Real, Hermann J. "Another Epitaph on Dean Swift," *East-Central Intelligencer* 16, 1 (2002): 24–26.

———. "Psychoanalytic Criticism and Swift: The History of a Failure," *Eighteenth-Century Ireland/Iris an dá Chultúr* 1 (1986): 127–141.

———. *Securing Swift: Selected Essays.* Irish Research Series 1. Dublin, Oxford, Bethesda: Maunsel, 2001.

———. "Swift's Non-Reading." In *That Woman! Studies in Irish Bibliography: A Festschrift for Mary 'Paul' Pollard,* edited by Charles Benson and Siobhán Fitzpatrick, 123–138. Dublin: The Lilliput Press, 2005.

———, ed. *The Reception of Jonathan Swift in Europe.* Bristol and London: Thoemmes Continuum, 2005.

Real, Hermann J., Melanie Just, Neil Key, and Helga Scholz, eds. *The Reception and Reputation of Jonathan Swift in Germany: Essays and Investigations.* Irish Research Series 12. Bethesda, Dublin, Oxford, London: Maunsel, 2002.

Rees, Christine. "Gay, Swift, and the Nymphs of Drury-Lane," *Essays in Criticism* 23 (1973): 1–21.

Reilly, Patrick. *Jonathan Swift: The Brave Desponder.* Manchester, England: Manchester University Press, 1982.

Richardson, J. A. "Swift: Personal Satire, Reputation and the Reader," *English Studies* 68, 5 (1987): 433–444.

———. "Swift's Argument: Laughing Us into Religion," *Eighteenth Century Life* 13, 2 (1989): 35–45.

Richardson, John. *Slavery and Augustan Literature: Swift, Pope, and Gay.* London: Routledge, 2003.

———. "Still to Seek: Politics, Irony, Swift," *Essays in Criticism* 49 (1999): 300–318.

Robbins, Christopher. " 'The Most Universal Villain I Ever Knew': Jonathan Swift and the Earl of Wharton," *Eighteenth-Century Ireland/ Iris an dá Chultúr* 18 (2003): 24–38.

Rogers, Pat. "Comic Maid-Servants in Swift and Smollett: The Proverbial Idiom of *Humphry Clinker,*" *PLL* 39, 3 (Summer 2003): 307–315.

———. *Hacks and Dunces: Pope, Swift and Grub Street.* London and New York: Methuen, 1980.

Rosenheim, Edward, Jr. "Swift and the Atterbury Case." *The Augustan Milieu: Essays Presented to*

*Louis A. Landa,* edited by Henry Knight Miller et al., 174–204. Oxford: Clarendon Press, 1970.

———. *Swift and the Satirist's Art.* Chicago: University of Chicago Press, 1963.

Rosslyn, Felicity. "Deliberate Disenchantment: Swift and Pope on the Subject of Women," *Cambridge Quarterly* 23, 4 (1994): 293–302.

Rushdy, Ashraf H. A. "A New Emetics of Interpretation: Swift, His Critics and the Alimentary Canal," *Mosaic* 24, 3–4 (Summer–Fall 1991): 1–32.

Saccamano, Neil. "Authority and Publication: The Works of Swift," *The Eighteenth Century: Theory and Interpretation* 25 (1984): 241–262.

Said, Edward. "Swift's Tory Anarchy" and "Swift as Intellectual." In *The World, the Text, and the Critic.* Cambridge, Mass.: Harvard University Press, 54–89.

Schakel, Peter J. "Jonathan Swift." In *Dictionary of Literary Biography, Vol. 101: British Prose Writers, 1660–1800,* edited by Donald T. Siebert. Bruccoli Clark Layman/Gale Group, 1991. 319–351.

———, ed. *Critical Approaches to Teaching Swift.* AMS Studies in the Eighteenth Century. New York: AMS, 1992.

Steele, Peter. *Jonathan Swift: Preacher and Jester.* Oxford: Clarendon Press, 1978.

*Swift Studies: The Annual of the Ehrenpreis Center.* Münster: W. Fink, 1986–.

Traugott, John, ed. *Discussions of Jonathan Swift.* Boston: D. C. Heath, 1962.

Treadwell, J. M. "Jonathan Swift: The Satirist as Projector," *Texas Studies in Literature and Language* 17 (1975): 439–460.

———. "Swift, William Wood, and the Factual Basis of Satire," *Journal of British Studies* 15 (1976): 76–91.

Tuveson, Ernest, ed. *Swift: A Collection of Critical Essays.* Englewood Cliffs, N.J.: Prentice Hall, 1964.

Viau, Robert O. "Conservatism Expressed Radically: The Zeal of Jonson's and Swift's Attacks on Zeal," *Journal of General Education* 34, 1 (Spring 1982): 69–83.

Vickers, Brian, ed. *The World of Jonathan Swift.* Oxford: Blackwell, 1968.

Vieth, David M., ed. *Essential Articles for the Study of Jonathan Swift.* Hamden, Conn.: Archon, 1984.

Ward, David. *Jonathan Swift: An Introductory Essay.* London: Methuen, 1973.

Weinbrot, Howard D. "Hearts of Darkness: Swift, Johnson, and the Narrative Confrontation with Evil." In *'But Vindicate the Ways of God to Man': Literature and Theodicy,* edited by Rudolf Freiburg and Susanne Gruss, 205–223. Tübingen: Stauffenburg Verlag, 2004.

Weinbrot, Howard D., Peter J. Schakel, and Stephen E. Karian, eds. *Eighteenth-Century Contexts: Historical Inquiries in Honor of Phillip Harth.* Madison: University of Wisconsin Press, 2001.

Williams, Kathleen. *Jonathan Swift.* Profiles in Literature Series. London: Routledge and Kegan Paul, 1968.

———. *Jonathan Swift and the Age of Compromise.* London: Constable, 1959.

———, ed. *Swift: The Critical Heritage.* London: Routledge and Kegan Paul, 1970.

Wood, Nigel. *Swift.* Brighton, England: Harvester, 1986.

———, ed. *Jonathan Swift.* Longman Critical Readers. London: Longman, 1999.

Woolley, David. *Introduction to Swift, Temple, and the Ducros Affair, Part I.* Augustan Reprint Society. Los Angeles: UCLA, 1986.

Wyrick, Deborah B. *Jonathan Swift and the Vested Word.* Chapel Hill: University of North Carolina Press, 1988.

Zach, Wolfgang. "Jonathan Swift and Colonialism," *Canadian Journal of Irish Studies* 26 (2000): 36–46.

Zimmerman, Everett. *Swift's Narrative Satires: Author and Authority.* Ithaca, N.Y.: Cornell University Press, 1983.

### Gulliver's Travels

Barchas, Janine. "Prefiguring Genre: Frontispiece Portraits from *Gulliver's Travels* to *Millennium Hall,*" *Studies in the Novel* 30 (1998): 260–286.

Barry, Kevin. "Exclusion and Inclusion in Swift's *Gulliver's Travels,*" *Irish Review* 30 (2003): 36–47.

Braverman, Richard. "*Robinson Crusoe* and *Gulliver's Travels*: Some Pedagogical Frameworks." In *Approaches to Teaching Defoe's Robinson Crusoe,* edited by Maximilian E. Novak and Carl Fisher, 37–47. New York: Modern Language Association, 2005.

Bentman, Raymond. "Satiric Structure and Tone in the Conclusion of *Gulliver's Travels,*" *SEL* 11 (1971): 535–548.

Bloom, Harold, ed. *Jonathan Swift's Gulliver's Travels.* Modern Critical Interpretations. New York: Chelsea House, 1986.

Boucé, Paul-Gabriel. "Death in *Gulliver's Travels*: The Struldbruggs Revisited," *Qwerty* 11 (2001): 37–46.

———. "The Rape of Gulliver Reconsidered," *Swift Studies* 11 (1996): 98–114.

Bowden, Betsy. "Before the Houyhnhnms: Rational Horses in the Late Seventeenth Century," *Notes and Queries* 39, 1 (March 1992): 38–40.

Brady, Frank, ed. *Twentieth-Century Interpretations of Gulliver's Travels.* Englewood Cliffs, N.J.: Prentice Hall, 1968.

Brown, Laura. "Reading Race and Gender: Jonathan Swift," *Eighteenth Century Studies* 23 (1990): 425–443.

Bruce, Susan. "The Flying Island and Female Anatomy: Gynaecology and Power in *Gulliver's Travels*," *Genders* 2 (1988): 60–76.

Bywaters, David. "*Gulliver's Travels* and the Mode of Political Parallel during Walpole's Administration," *ELH* 4, 3 (1987): 717–740.

Carnochan, W. B. *Lemuel Gulliver's Mirror for Man.* Berkeley and Los Angeles: University of California Press, 1968.

Case, Arthur E. *Four Essays on Gulliver's Travels.* Princeton, N.J.: Princeton University Press, 1945.

Casement, William. "Religion, Satire, and Gulliver's Fourth Voyage," *History of European Ideas* 14, 4 (1992): 531–544.

Castle, Terry. "Why the Houyhnhnms Don't Write: Swift, Satire, and the Fear of the Text," *Essays in Literature* 7 (1980): 31–44.

Chalmers, Alan D. "Film, Censorship, and the 'Corrupt Original' of *Gulliver's Travels*." In *Eighteenth-Century Fiction on Screen*, edited by Robert Mayer, 70–87. Cambridge: Cambridge University Press, 2002.

Champion, Larry S. "Gulliver's Voyages: The Framing Events as a Guide to Interpretation," *Texas Studies in Literature and Language* 10 (1969): 529–536.

Clark, Paul Odell. *A Gulliver Dictionary.* Chapel Hill: University of North Carolina Press, 1953.

Clifford, James L. "Gulliver's Fourth Voyage: 'Hard' and 'Soft' Schools of Interpretation." In *Quick Springs of Sense: Studies in the Eighteenth Century,* edited by Larry Champion, 33–49. Athens: University of Georgia Press, 1974.

Coleborne, Bryan. "An Irish Gaelic Source for Swift's Flying Island?" *Swift Studies* 2 (1987): 114.

Crane, R. S. "The Houyhnhnms, the Yahoos, and the History of Ideas." In *Reason and Imagination: Studies in the History of Ideas, 1600–1800,* edited by J. A. Mazzeo. New York: Columbia University Press, 1962.

Crider, Richard. "Yahoo (Yahu) Notes on the Names of Swift's Yahoos," *Names: Journal of the American Name Society* 41, 2 (June 1993): 103–109.

Cunningham, J. C. "Perversions of the Eucharist in Gulliver's Travels," *Christianity and Literature* 40, 4 (1991): 345–364.

Darby, Robert. "Captivity and Captivation: Gulliver in Brobdingnag," *Eighteenth-Century Life* 27, 3 (2003): 124–139.

DePorte, Michael. "Teaching the Third Voyage." In *Approaches to Teaching Swift's "Gulliver's Travels,"* 57–62. New York: MLA, 1988.

Donnelly, Dorothy F. "*Utopia* and *Gulliver's Travels*: Another Perspective," *Moreana* 25, 97 (1988): 115–124.

Donoghue, Denis. "The Brainwashing of Lemuel Gulliver," *Southern Review* 32 (1996): 128–146.

Doody, Margaret Anne. "Insects, Vermin, and Horses: *Gulliver's Travels* and Virgil's *Georgics*." In *Augustan Studies: Essays in Honor of Irvin Ehrenpreis,* edited by Douglas Lane Patey and Timothy Keegan, 145–174. Newark: University of Delaware Press, 1985.

Downie, J. A. "Political Characterization in *Gulliver's Travels*," *Yearbook of English Studies* 7 (1977): 108–120.

Dussinger, John A. " 'Christian' vs. 'Hollander': Swift's Satire on the Dutch East India Travelers," *Notes and Queries* 211 (1966): 209–212.

———. "Gulliver in Japan: Another Possible Source," *Notes and Queries* 39 (December 1992): 464–467.

Duthie, Elizabeth. "Gulliver Art," *Scriblerian* 10 (1978): 127–131.

Eddy, William A. *Gulliver's Travels: A Critical Study.* Princeton, N.J.: Princeton University Press, 1923.

Ehrenpreis, Irvin. "How to Write *Gulliver's Travels*," *Swift Studies* 18 (2003): 5–19.

———. "The Meaning of Gulliver's Last Voyage," *Review of English Literature* 3, 3 (1962): 18–38.

———. "The Origin of *Gulliver's Travels*," *PMLA* 72, 5 (1957): 880–899.

———. "Show and Tell in *Gulliver's Travels*," Swift Studies 8 (1993): 18–33.

Erskine-Hill, Howard. *Gulliver's Travels*. Cambridge: Cambridge University Press, 1993.

Falzarano, James V. "Adam in Houyhnhnmland: The Presence of *Paradise Lost*," *Milton Studies* 21 (1985): 179–197.

Fitzgerald, Robert P. "Swift's Immortals: The Satiric Point," *SEL* 24 (1984): 483–495.

Fox, Christopher. "The Myth of Narcissus in Swift's *Travels*." *Eighteenth-Century Studies* 20 (1986–87): 17–33.

———. "Of Logic and Lycanthropy: Gulliver and the Faculties of the Mind." In *Literature and Medicine During the Eighteenth Century*, edited by Roy Porter and Marie Mulvey Roberts, 101–117. London: Routledge, 1993.

———, ed. *Gulliver's Travels: Case Studies in Contemporary Criticism*. Boston and New York: Bedford/St. Martin's, 1995.

Franklin, Michael J. "Lemuel Self-Translated; Or, Being an Ass in Houyhnhnmland," *Modern Language Review* 100, 1 (January 2005): 1–19.

Frantz, R. W. "Gulliver's 'Cousin Sympson,' " *Huntington Library Quarterly* 3 (1938): 329–334.

Freedman, William. "Swift's Struldbruggs, Progress, and the Analogy of History," *SEL* 35, 3 (Summer 1995): 457–472.

Frye, Roland M. "Swift's Yahoos and the Christian Symbols for Sin," *Journal of the History of Ideas* 5 (1954): 201–217.

Gardiner, Anne Barbeau. "Licking the Dust in Luggnagg: Swift's Reflections on the Legacy of King William's Conquest of Ireland," *Swift Studies* 8 (1993): 35–44.

———. "Swift Prophet: The Christian Meaning of *Gulliver's Travels*," *Touchstone: A Journal of Mere Christianity* 17, 8 (October 2004): 34–41.

Géracht, Maurice A. "Pedro de Mendez: Marrano Jew and Good Samaritan in Swift's *Voyages*," *Swift Studies* 5 (1990): 39–52.

Gravil, Richard, ed. *Swift: Gulliver's Travels: A Casebook*. London: Macmillan, 1974.

Gill, James E. "Beast over Man: Theriophilic Paradox in Gulliver's 'Voyage to the Country of the Houyhnhnms," *Studies in Philology* 67 (1970): 532–549.

Goldberg, Julia. "Houyhnhnm Subtext: Moral Conclusions and Linguistical Manipulation in *Gulliver's Travels*," *1650–1850: Ideas, Aesthetics, and Inquiries in the Early Modern Era* 4 (1998): 269–284.

Gottlieb, Sidney. "The Emblematic Background of Swift's Flying Island," *Swift Studies* 1 (1986): 24–31.

Gregori, Flavio. "Gulliver's Myopic Reformation: Reason and Evil in Gulliver's Travels." In *'But Vindicate the Ways of God to Man': Literature and Theodicy*, edited by Rudolf Freiburg and Susanne Gruss, 181–203. Tübingen: Stauffenburg Verlag, 2004.

Guilhamet, Leon. "*Gulliver's Travels* I, vi Reconsidered," *English Language Notes* 21, 3 (March 1984): 44–53.

Guskin, Phyllis J. " 'A Very Remarkable Book': Abel Boyer's View of *Gulliver's Travels*," *Studies in Philology* 72 (1975): 439–453.

Halsband, Robert. "Eighteenth-Century Illustrations of *Gulliver's Travels*." *Proceedings of the First Münster Symposium on Jonathan Swift*, edited by Hermann J. Real and Heinz J. Vienken, 83–116. Munich: Wilhelm Fink, 1985.

Hammond, Eugene R. "Nature-Reason-Justice in *Utopia* and *Gulliver's Travels*," *SEL* 22, 3 (1982): 446–468.

Harrison, Bernard. "Houyhnhnm Virtue," *Partial Answers: Journal of Literature and the History of Ideas* 1, 1 (Jan. 2003): 35–64.

Hart, Vaughan. "*Gulliver's Travels* into the 'City of the Sun,' " *Swift Studies* 6 (1991): 111–114.

———. "The Square City-Palace in the State of Lilliput," *PLL* 28, 4 (Fall 1992): 369–373.

Harth, Phillip. "The Problem of Political Allegory in Gulliver's Travels," *Modern Philology* 73 (1976): 540–547.

Hassall, Anthony J. "Discontinuities in *Gulliver's Travels*," *Sydney Studies in English* 5 (1979–80): 3–14.

Hawes, Clement. "Three Times round the Globe: Gulliver and Colonial Discourse," *Cultural Critique* 18 (1991): 187–214.

Higgins, Ian. "Swift and Sparta: The Nostalgia of *Gulliver's Travels*," *Modern Language Review* 78 (1983): 513–531.

Hinnant, Charles H. *Purity and Defilement in Gulliver's Travels*. New York: St. Martin's Press, 1987.

Hunter, J. Paul. "*Gulliver's Travels* and the Novel." In *The Genres of Gulliver's Travels*, edited by Frederik

N. Smith, 56–74. Newark: University of Delaware Press, 1990.

Jaffe, Lee. "*Gulliver's Travels* by Jonathan Swift." Available online. URL: http://www.jaffebros.com/lee/gulliver/. Accessed March 6, 2006.

Jones, Horace Perry. "Swift's *Gulliver's Travels*," *Explicator* 47, 1 (Fall 1988): 11.

Kallich, Martin. *The Other End of the Egg: Religious Satire in "Gulliver's Travels."* Bridgeport, Conn.: Conference on British Studies at the University of Bridgeport, 1970.

Keesey, Donald. "The Distorted Image: Swift's Yahoos and the Critics," *PLL* 15 (1979): 320–332.

Kelly, Ann Cline. "After Eden: Gulliver's (Linguistic) Travels," *ELH* 45, 1 (Spring 1978): 33–54.

———. "Swift's Explorations of Slavery in Houyhnhnmland and Ireland," *PMLA* 91 (1976): 846–855.

Kelly, James William. "A Contemporary Source for the 'Yahoos' in *Gulliver's Travels*," *Notes and Queries* 45, 1 (Mar. 1998): 68–70.

Knowles, Ronald. *"Gulliver's Travels": The Politics of Satire.* New York: Twayne, 1996.

Kupersmith, William. "Swift's Aeolists and the Delphic Oracle," *Modern Philology* 82, 2 (1984): 190–194.

Landa, Louis. "The Dismal Science in Houyhnhnmland," *Novel* 13 (1979): 38–49.

Lenfest, David S. "A Checklist of Illustrated Editions of *Gulliver's Travels*, 1727–1914," *Papers of the Bibliographical Society of America* 62 (1968): 85–123.

Lock, F. P. *The Politics of* Gulliver's Travels. Oxford: Clarendon Press, 1983.

———. "The Text of *Gulliver's Travels*," *Modern Language Review* 76 (1981): 513–533.

Mezciems, Jenny. "Swift's Praise of Gulliver: Some Renaissance Background to the *Travels*." In *The Character of Swift's Satire: A Revised Focus*, edited by Claude Rawson, 245–281. Newark: University of Delaware Press, 1983.

———. "The Unity of Swift's *Voyage to Laputa*: Structure as Meaning in Utopian Fiction," *Modern Language Review* 72 (1977): 1–21.

Monk, Samuel Holt. "The Pride of Lemuel Gulliver," *Sewanee Review* 63 (1955): 48–71.

Morris, John. "Wishes as Horses: A Word for the Houyhnhnms," *Yale Review* 62 (1972–73): 354–371.

Nicholson, Marjorie Hope, and Nora M. Mohler. "The Scientific Background of Swift's *Voyage to Laputa*." In *Science and Imagination*, edited by Marjorie Hope Nicholson, 110–154. Ithaca, N.Y.: Great Seal Books, 1956.

Nuttall, A. D. "Gulliver among the Horses," *Yearbook of English Studies* 18 (1988): 51–67.

O'Sullivan, Maurice J. "Swift's Pedro de Mendez," *American Notes and Queries* 22 (May/June 1984): 131–133.

Passmann, Dirk F. "The Lilliputian Utopia: A Revised Focus," *Swift Studies* 2 (1987): 67–76.

Patey, Douglas Lane. "Swift's Satire on 'Science' and the Structure of *Gulliver's Travels*," *ELH* 58 (1991): 809–839.

Paulson, Ronald. "Putting Out the Fire in Her Imperial Majesty's Apartment: Opposition Politics, Anticlericalism, and Aesthetics," *ELH* 63 (1996): 79–107.

Phiddian, Robert. "A Hopeless Project: Gulliver inside the Language of Science in Book III," *Eighteenth Century Life* 22, 1 (February 1998): 50–62.

Pierre, Gerald J. "Gulliver's Voyage to China and Moor Park: The Influence of Sir William Temple upon *Gulliver's Travels*," *Texas Studies in Literature and Language* 17, 2 (Summer 1975): 427–437.

Piper, William Bowman. "The Sense of *Gulliver's Travels*," *Rice University Studies* 61 (1975): 75–106.

Probyn, Clive T. *Gulliver's Travels.* Penguin Critical Studies. New York: Penguin, 1987.

———. "Man, Horse and Drill: Temple's Essay on Popular Discontents and Gulliver's Fourth Voyage," *English Studies* 55 (1974): 358–360.

———. "Swift and Linguistics: The Context behind Lagado and around the Fourth Voyage," *Neophilologus* 58 (1974): 425–439.

*Proceedings of the First Münster Symposium on Jonathan Swift*, edited by Hermann J. Real and Heinz J. Vienken. Münich: Wilhelm Fink, 1985.

Pyle, Fitzroy. "Yahoo: Swift and the Asses," *Ariel* 3, 2 (1972): 64–69.

Quinlan, Maurice J. "Treason in Lilliput and in England," *Texas Studies in Literature and Language* 11 (1970): 1,317–1,332.

Radner, John B. "The Struldbruggs, the Houyhnhnms, and the Good Life," *SEL* 17 (1977): 419–433.

Rawson, Claude. *God, Gulliver, and Genocide: Barbarism and the European Imagination, 1492–1945.* Oxford: Oxford University Press, 2001.

————. "Gulliver and Others: Reflections on Swift's 'I' Narrators." In *Swift: The Enigmatic Dean: Festschrift for Hermann Josef Real*, edited by Rudolf Freiburg, Arno Löffler, and Wolfgang Zach, 231–246. Tübingen, Germany: Stauffenburg Verlag, 1998.

————. *Gulliver and the Gentle Reader: Studies in Swift and Our Time*. London: Routledge and Kegan Paul, 1973.

Real, Hermann J. "Allegorical Adventure and Adventurous Allegory: Gulliver's 'Several Ridiculous and Troublesome Accidents' in Brobdingnag," *Qwerty* 11 (2001): 81–87.

————. "Archimedes in Laputa, III, v. 9," *East-Central Intelligencer* 17, 3 (2003): 21–24.

————. "Gulliver and the Moons of Mars, Once More," *East-Central Intelligencer* 15, 2 (2001): 7–8.

————. " 'Wise enough to play the fool': Swift's Flappers," *East-Central Intelligencer* 16, 2 (2002): 8–11.

Real, Hermann J., and Heinz J. Vienken. "What's in a Name: Pedro de Mendez Again," *American Notes and Queries* 24 (May/June 1986): 136–140.

Reed, Gail S. "Dr. Greenacre and Captain Gulliver: Notes on Conventions of Interpretation and Reading," *Literature and Psychology* 16 (1976): 185–190.

Reichard, Hugo M. "Gulliver the Pretender," *Papers on English Language and Literature* 1 (1965): 316–326.

————. "Satiric Snobbery: The Houyhnhnms' Man," *Satire Newsletter* 4 (1967): 51–57.

Richardson, John. "Christian and/or Ciceronian: Swift and Gulliver's Fourth Voyage," *Cambridge Quarterly* 30, 1 (2001): 37–49.

Rielly, Edward J. "Irony in *Gulliver's Travels* and *Utopia*," *Utopian Studies* 3, 1 (1992): 70–83.

————, ed. *Approaches to Teaching Swift's "Gulliver's Travels."* New York: MLA, 1988.

Rodino, Richard H. " 'Splendide Mendax': Authors, Characters, and Readers in *Gulliver's Travels*," *PMLA* 106 (1991): 1,054–1,070.

Rogers, Pat. "Gulliver's Glasses." In *The Art of Jonathan Swift*, edited by Clive T. Probyn, 179–188. London: Vision, 1978.

Rosenblum, Joseph. "Gulliver's Dutch Uncle: Another Look at Swift and the Dutch," *British Journal for Eighteenth-Century Studies* 24 (2001): 63–76.

Rothman, Irving N. "The Execution Scene in *Gulliver's Travels*," *Journal of Evolutionary Psychology* 3, 1–2 (1982): 56–75.

Rothstein, Eric. "Gulliver III; or, The Progress of Clio," *Proceedings of the First Münster Symposium on Jonathan Swift*, edited by Hermann J. Real and Heinz J. Vienken. Munich: Wilhelm Fink, 1985. 217–231.

Sayers, William. "Gulliver's Wounded Knee," *Swift Studies* 7 (1992): 106–109.

Seidel, Michael. "*Gulliver's Travels* and the Contracts of Fiction." In *The Cambridge Companion to the Eighteenth-Century Novel*, edited by John Richetti, 72–89. Cambridge: Cambridge University Press, 1996.

Sena, John. "The Language of Gestures in *Gulliver's Travels*," *PLL* 19, 2 (1983): 145–166.

————. "Swift, the Yahoos, and 'The English Malady,'" *PLL* 7 (1971): 300–303.

Sherbo, Arthur. "Swift and Travel Literature," *Modern Language Studies* 9 (Fall 1979): 114–127.

Sherburn, George. "Errors concerning the Houyhnhnms," *Modern Philology* 56 (1958): 92–97.

Simms, Norman. "Childish Anxieties in the Adventures of Lemuel Gulliver," *Qwerty* 11 (2001): 89–96.

Skau, Michael W. "Flimnap, Lilliput's Acrobatic Treasurer," *American Notes and Queries* 8 (1970): 134–135.

Smith, Frederik N. "The Danger of Reading Swift: The Double Binds of *Gulliver's Travels*," *Studies in the Literary Imagination* 17, 1 (1984): 35–47.

————. "Science, Imagination, and Swift's Brobdingnagians," *Eighteenth Century Life* 14 (1990): 100–114.

————. "Vexing Voices: The Telling of Gulliver's Story," *PLL* 21, 4 (1985): 383–398.

————, ed. *The Genres of* Gulliver's Travels. Newark: University of Delaware Press, 1990.

Starkman, Miriam K. "Satirical Onomastics: Lemuel Gulliver and King Solomon," *Philological Quarterly* 60, 1 (1981): 41–52.

Stillman, Peter G. " 'With a Moral View Design'd': *Gulliver's Travels* as a Utopian Text," *Qwerty* 11 (2001): 97–107.

Sullivan, E. E. "Houyhnhnms and Yahoos: From Technique to Meaning," *SEL* 24, 3 (1984): 497–511.

Swearington, James E. "Time and Technique in Gulliver's Third Voyage," *Philosophy and Literature* 6, 1–2 (1982): 45–61.

Taylor, Aline Mackenzie. "Sights and Monsters and Gulliver's *Voyage to Brobdingnag*," *Tulane Studies in English* 7 (1957): 29–82.

Taylor, Dick, Jr. "Gulliver's Pleasing Visions: Self-Deception as a Major Theme in *Gulliver's Travels,*" *Tulane Studies in English* 12 (1962): 7–61.

Thickstun, Margaret Olofson. "The Puritan Origins of Gulliver's Conversion in Houyhnhnmland," *SEL* 37 (1997): 517–534.

Tippett, Brian. *Gulliver's Travels: An Introduction to the Variety of Criticism.* Basingstoke and London: Macmillan, 1989.

Todd, Dennis. "The Hairy Maid at the Harpsichord: Some Speculations on the Meaning of *Gulliver's Travels,*" *Texas Studies in Language and Literature* 34 (1992): 239–283.

Traugott, John. "The Yahoo in the Doll's House: *Gulliver's Travels:* the Children's Classic." In *English Satire and the Satiric Tradition,* edited by Claude Rawson, 127–150. Oxford: Basil Blackwell, 1984.

Treadwell, Michael. "*Swift, Richard Coleire, and the Origins of Gulliver's Travels,*" *Review of English Studies* 34, 135 (August 1983): 304–311.

Varey, Simon. "Exemplary History and the Political Satire of *Gulliver's Travels.*" In *The Genres of Gulliver's Travels,* edited by Frederik N. Smith, 39–55. Newark: University of Delaware Press, 1990.

Washington, Gene. "Natural Horses? The Noble Horse? Houyhnhnms," *Swift Studies* 3 (1988): 91–95.

———. "Swift's Meniere's Syndrome and *Gulliver's Travels,*" *Swift Studies* 10 (1995): 104–107.

———. "Swift's Struldbruggs and Alzheimer's Disease," *Scriblerian* 27 (1994): 93–94.

Webster, Richard. "The Diminutive Insect: *Gulliver's Travels,* Original Sin, and the Imagery of Size." richardwebster.net. Available online. URL: http://www.richardwebster.net/xgulliverstravelsandoriginalsin.html. Accessed September 22, 2005.

Welcher, Jeanne K. *Gulliveriana V: Shorter Imitations of Gulliver's Travels.* Delmar, N.Y.: Scholars' Facsimiles, 1974.

———. "Horace Walpole and *Gulliver's Travels,*" *Studies in Eighteenth Century Culture* 12 (1983): 45–57.

———. *Visual Imitations of Gulliver's Travels, 1726–1830.* Scholars' Facsimiles and Reprints, 2000.

Wiener, Gary, ed. *Readings on Gulliver's Travels.* Literary Companion Series. San Diego, Calif.: Greenhaven Press, 2000.

Williams, Harold. *The Text of Gulliver's Travels.* Cambridge: Cambridge University Press, 1952.

Wintle, Sarah. "If Houyhnhnms Were Horses: Thinking with Animals in Book IV of *Gulliver's Travels,*" *Critical Review* 34 (1994): 3–21.

Woolley, David. "The Stemma of *Gulliver's Travels*: A First Note," *Swift Studies* 1 (1986): 51–54.

———. "Swift's Copy of *Gulliver's Travels*: The Armagh Gulliver, Hyde's Edition, and Swift's Earliest Corrections." In *The Art of Jonathan Swift,* edited by Clive T. Probyn. London: Vision, 1978. 131–178.

Worth, Chris. "Swift's 'Flying Island': Buttons and Bomb-Vessels," *Review of English Studies* 42, 167 (1991): 343–360.

Zimmerman, Everett. "Gulliver the Preacher," *PMLA* 89 (1974): 1,024–1,032.

Zirker, Herbert. "Horse Sense and Sensibility: Some Issues Concerning Utopian Understanding in *Gulliver's Travels,*" *Swift Studies* 12 (1997): 85–98.

## "A Modest Proposal," "A Tale of a Tub," and Other Prose

Adams, Robert M. "The Mood of the Church and *A Tale of a Tub.*" In *England in the Restoration and Early Eighteenth Century,* edited by H. T. Swedenberg, Jr., 71–99. Berkeley and Los Angeles: University of California Press, 1972.

Baltes, Sabine, ed. *Jonathan Swift's Allies: The Wood's Halfpence Controversy in Ireland, 1722–25.* Frankfurt am Main: Peter Lang, 2004.

Boyle, Frank T. "Profane and Debauched Deist: Swift and the Contemporary Response to *A Tale of a Tub,*" *Eighteenth-Century Ireland* 3 (1988): 25–38.

Briggs, Peter M. "John Graunt, Sir William Petty, and Swift's Modest Proposal," *Eighteenth-Century Life* 29, 2 (Spring 2005): 3–24.

Bruce, John. "Plagued by Enthusiasm: Swift's Fear of Infectious Dissent and His Argument against Abolishing Christian Quarantine in *A Tale of a Tub.*" In *Orthodoxy and Heresy in Eighteenth-Century Society: Essays from the DeBartolo Conference. The Bucknell Studies in Eighteenth-Century Literature and Culture,* edited by Regina Hewitt and Pat Rogers, 89–111. Lewisburg and London: Bucknell University Press, 2002.

Canning, Rick G. "'Ignorant, Illiterate Creatures': Gender and Colonial Justification in Swift's *Injured Lady* and *Answer to the Injured Lady,*" *ELH* 64 (1997): 77–98.

Clark, John R. *Form and Frenzy in Swift's "Tale of a Tub."* Ithaca, N.Y.: Cornell University Press, 1970.

Clegg, Jeanne. "Swift on False Witness," *SEL* 44, 3 (Summer 2004): 461–485.

Connery, Brian. "The Persona as Pretender and the Reader as Constitutional Subject in Swift's *Tale*." In *Cutting Edges: Postmodern Critical Essays,* edited by James A. Gill, 159–180. Knoxville: University of Tennessee Press, 1995.

Cook, Richard I. *Jonathan Swift as a Tory Pamphleteer.* Seattle and London: University of Washington Press, 1967.

Curry, Judson B. "Arguing about the Project: Approaches to Swift's 'An Argument against Abolishing Christianity' and 'A Project for the Advancement of Religion,' " *Eighteenth-Century Life* 20, 1 (February 1996): 67–79.

Davidson, Jenny. "Swift's Servant Problem: Livery and Hypocrisy in the *Project for the Advancement of Religion* and the *Directions to Servants*," *Studies in Eighteenth-Century Culture* 30 (2001): 105–125.

Devine, Michael G. "Disputing the 'Original' in Swift's *Tale of a Tub*," *Swift Studies* 18 (2003): 26–33.

Ellis, Frank H., ed. *Swift vs. Mainwaring: "The Examiner" and "The Medley."* Oxford: Clarendon Press, 1985.

Fabricant, Carole. "The Battle of the Ancients and (Post)Moderns: Rethinking Swift through Contemporary Perspectives," *The Eighteenth Century: Theory and Interpretation* 32 (1991): 256–273.

———. "Speaking for the Irish Nation: The Drapier, The Bishop, and The Problems of Colonial Representation," *ELH* 66 (1999): 337–372.

Fanning, Christopher. "The Scriblerian Sublime," *SEL* 45, 3 (Summer 2005): 647–667.

Fischer, John Irwin. "The Government's Response to Swift's *An Epistle to a Lady*," *Philological Quarterly* 65, 1 (Winter 1986): 39–59.

Fróes, João. "Swift's Prayers for Stella: The Other Side of the Satirist," *Swift Studies* 18 (2003): 56–62.

Hammond, Eugene R. "In Praise of Wisdom and the Will of God: Erasmus' *Praise of Folly* and Swift's *A Tale of a Tub*," *Studies in Philology* 80, 3 (1983): 253–276.

Harth, Phillip. *Swift and Anglican Rationalism: The Religious Background of "A Tale of a Tub."* Chicago: University of Chicago Press, 1961.

Kelling, Harold D., and Cathy Lynn Preston. *A Kwic [Keyword in Context] Concordance to Jonathan Swift's "A Tale of a Tub," "The Battle of the Books," and "A Discourse Concerning the Mechanical Operation of the Spirit."* New York: Garland, 1984.

Kelly, James. "Jonathan Swift and the Irish Economy of the 1720s," *Eighteenth-Century Ireland/Iris an dá Chultúr* 6 (1991): 7–36.

Kelly, Veronica. "Following the Stage-Itinerant: Perception, Doubt, and Death in Swift's *Tale of a Tub*," *Studies in Eighteenth Century Culture* 17 (1987): 239–258.

Korkowski, Eugene. "Swift's Tub: Traditional Emblem and Proverbial Enigma," *Eighteenth-Century Life* 4 (1978): 100–103.

Levine, Jay Arnold. "The Design of *A Tale of a Tub* (with a Digression on the Mad Modern Critic)," *ELH* 33 (1966): 198–227.

Levine, Joseph M. *The Battle of the Books: History and Literature in the Augustan Age.* Ithaca, N.Y.: Cornell University Press, 1991.

Lockwood, Thomas. "Swift's *Modest Proposal*: An Interpretation," *PLL* 10, 3 (1975): 254–267.

Lund, Roger D. "Strange Complicities: Atheism and Conspiracy in *A Tale of a Tub*," *Eighteenth-Century Life* 13 (1989): 34–58.

———. "Swift's Sermons, 'Public Conscience,' and the Privatization of Religion," *Prose Studies* 18 (1995): 150–174.

Lynall, Gregory. "Swift's Caricatures of Newton: 'Tailor', 'Conjurer' and 'Workman in the Mint,' " *British Journal for Eighteenth-Century Studies* 28 (2005): 19–32.

Mahoney, Robert. "Protestant Dependence and Consumption in Swift's Irish Writings." In *Political Ideas in Eighteenth-Century Ireland,* edited by S. J. Connoly. Dublin: Four Courts Press, 2000. 83–104.

Mayhew, George P. "Swift's Bickerstaff Hoax as an April Fools' Joke," *Modern Philology* 61 (1964): 270–280.

McCrea, Brian. "The Canon and the Eighteenth Century: A Modest Proposal and a Tale of Two Tubs," *Modern Language Studies* 18, 1 (1988): 58–73.

———. "Surprised by Swift: Entrapment and Escape in *A Tale of a Tub*," *PLL* 18, 3 (1982): 234–244.

Moore, Sean. " 'Our Irish Copper-Farthen Dean': Swift's *Drapier's Letters,* the 'Forging' of a Modernist Anglo-Irish Literature, and the Atlantic World of Paper Credit," *Atlantic Studies* 2, 1 (2005): 65–92.

———. "Satiric Norms, Swift's Financial Satires and the Bank of Ireland Controversy of 1720–21," *Eighteenth-Century Ireland* 17 (2002): 26–56.

Mueller, Judith C. "Writing Under Constraint: Swift's 'Apology' for *A Tale of a Tub*," *ELH* 60 (1993): 101–115.

Nash, Richard. "Entrapment and Ironic Modes in *A Tale of a Tub*," *Eighteenth-Century Studies* 24 (1991): 415–431.

Partridge, Eric, ed. *Swift's "Polite Conversation."* London: Andre Deutsch, 1963.

Paulson, Ronald. *Theme and Structure in Swift's "Tale of a Tub."* New Haven, Conn.: Yale University Press, 1960.

Probyn, Clive T. "Swift and the Ladies: A New Letter," *Swift Studies* 10 (1995): 57–61.

Ramsey, Richard N. "Swift's Strategy in *The Battle of the Books*," *PLL* 20, 4 (1984): 382–389.

Rawson, Claude. "The Injured Lady and the Drapier: A Reading of Swift's Irish Tracts," *Prose Studies* 3 (1980): 15–43.

———. "A Reading of *A Modest Proposal*." In *Augustan Worlds,* edited by J. C. Hilson et al., 29–50. Leicester, England: Leicester University Press, 1978.

Real, Hermann J. "Birth Weight in *A Modest Proposal*," *Scriblerian* 35, 1–2 (2002–03): 106.

———. "A New Letter from Swift: His Answer to the Earl of Strafford, 29 March 1735, Recovered," *Swift Studies* 18 (2003): 20–25.

Richardson, J. A. "Swift's Argument: Laughing Us into Religion," *Eighteenth-Century Life* 13, no. 2 (May 1989): 35–45.

Richardson, John. "Swift, *A Modest Proposal* and Slavery," *Essays in Criticism* 51 (2001): 404–423.

Robertson, Mary F. "Swift's Argument: The Fact and the Fiction of Fighting with Beasts," *Modern Philology* 74, no. 2 (November 1976): 124–141.

Ross, Ian Campbell. "'More to Avoid the Expence Than the Shame': Infanticide in the Modest Proposer's Ireland," *Swift Studies* 1 (1986): 75–76.

Smith, Frederik N. *Language and Reality in Swift's "A Tale of a Tub."* Columbus: Ohio State University Press, 1979.

Smith, Lisa Herb. "'The Livery of Religion': Reconciling Swift's Argument and Project," *English Language Notes* 31, no. 2 (December 1993): 27–33.

Smith, Margarette. "'In the Case of David': Swift's *Drapier's Letters*," *Prose Studies* 9, 2 (1986): 140–159.

Starkman, Miriam K. *Swift's Satire on Learning in "A Tale of a Tub."* Princeton, N.J.: Princeton University Press, 1950.

Sundell, Kirsten Ewart. "'A Savage and Unnatural Taste': Anglo-Irish Imitations of *A Modest Proposal*, 1730–31," *Swift Studies* 18 (2003): 80–98.

Thaddeus, Janice. "Swift's *Directions to Servants* and the Reader as Eavesdropper," *Studies in Eighteenth Century Culture* 16 (1986): 107–123.

Tinkler, John F. "The Splitting of Humanism: Bentley, Swift, and the English Battle of the Books," *Journal of the History of Ideas* 49, 3 (1988): 453–472.

Walsh, Marcus. "Text, 'Text,' and Swift's *Tale of a Tub*," *Modern Language Review* 85 (1990): 290–303.

Wittkowsky, George. "Swift's *Modest Proposal*: The Biography of an Early Georgian Pamphlet," *Journal of the History of Ideas* 4 (1943): 75–104.

Woolley, David. "The Canon of Swift's Prose Pamphleteering, 1710–1714, and the New Way of Selling Places at Court," *Swift Studies* 3 (1988): 96–117.

### Poems

Aden, J. M. "Those Gaudy Tulips: Swift's Unprintables." In *Quick Springs of Sense: Studies in the Eighteenth Century,* edited by Larry S. Champion, 15–32. Athens: University of Georgia Press, 1974.

Barnett, Louise K. *Swift's Poetic Worlds.* Newark and London: University of Delaware Press / London and Toronto: Associated University Press, 1981.

———. "Voyeurism in Swift's Poetry," *Studies in the Literary Imagination* 17, 1 (1984): 17–26.

Bawcutt, N. W. "*News from Hide-Park* and Swift's 'A Beautiful Young Nymph Going to Bed,'" *British Journal for Eighteenth-Century Studies* 23 (2000): 125–134.

Bogel, Frederic V. "The Difference Satire Makes: Reading Swift's Poems." In *Theorizing Satire: Essays in Literary Criticism,* edited by Brian A. Connery and Kirk Combe, 43–43. New York: St. Martin's, 1995.

Burrows, John. "A Strange and Self Abuse? The Authorship of 'A Panegyric on the Reverend Dean Swift.' " In *Imperfect Apprehensions: Essays in English Literature in Honour of G. A. Wilkes*, 115–132. Sydney, Australia: Challis, 1996.

Carnochan, W. B. "Swift's Poetic Gods: Jove, Apollo, Janus." In *Proceedings of the First Munster Symposium on Jonathan Swift*, edited by Hermann J. Real and Heinz J. Vienken, 13–25. Munich: Wilhelm Fink, 1985.

Conlon, Michael J. "Anonymity and Authority in the Poetry of Jonathan Swift." In *Eighteenth-Century Contexts: Historical Inquiries in Honor of Phillip Harth*, edited by Howard D. Weinbrot, Peter J. Schakel, and Stephen Karian. Madison: University of Wisconsin Press, 2001. 133–146.

———. "Singing Beside-Against: Parody and the Example of Swift's 'A Description of a City Shower,' " *Genre* 16 (1983): 219–232.

De Quehen, A. H. "St. Patrick's Verses by Jonathan Swift," *Swift Studies* 9 (1994): 42–50.

DiGaetani, John Louis. "Metrical Experimentation in Swift's Wood's Halfpence Poems." In *Money: Lure, Lore, and Literature*, edited by John Louis DiGaetani, 217–225. Westport, Conn.: Greenwood, 1994.

Djordjevic, Igor. "*Cadenus and Vanessa*: A Rhetoric of Courtship," *Swift Studies* 18 (2003): 104–118.

Elliott, Robert C., and Arthur H. Scouten. *The Poetry of Jonathan Swift*. Los Angeles: William Andrews Clark Memorial Library, 1981.

England, A. B. *Energy and Order in the Poetry of Swift*. Lewisburg, Pa.: Bucknell University Press, 1980.

———. "The Perils of Discontinuous Form: 'A Description of the Morning' and Some of Its Readers," *Studies in the Literary Imagination* 17, 1 (1984): 3–15.

———. "Quests for Order and the Perils of Discontinuity: Some Readings of 'Strephon and Chloe' and 'A Description of the Morning.' In *Reader Entrapment in Eighteenth-Century Literature*, edited by Carl R. Kropf and Victor A. Kramer, 63–87. New York: AMS, 1992.

Evans, Cleveland Kent. "How Vanessa Became a Butterfly: A Psychologist's Adventure in Entomological Etymology," *Names: A Journal of Onomastics* 41, 4 (December 1993): 276–281.

Feingold, Richard. "Swift in His Poems: The Range of His Positive Rhetoric." In *The Character of Swift's Satire: A Revised Focus*, edited by Claude Rawson, 166–202. Newark: University of Delaware Press, 1983.

Fischer, John Irwin. *On Swift's Poetry*. Gainesville: University Press of Florida, 1978.

Fischer, John Irwin, Donald C. Mell, Jr., and David M. Vieth, eds. *Contemporary Studies of Swift's Poetry*. Newark and London: University of Delaware Press, 1981.

Fox, Jeffrey R. "Swift's 'Scatological' Poems: The Hidden Norm," *Thoth: Syracuse Univ. Graduate Studies in English* 15, 3 (1975): 3–13.

Freedman, William. " 'Phillis, or, Progress of Love' and 'The Progress of Beauty': Art, Artifice and Reality in Swift's 'Anti-Poetry,' " *Concerning Poetry* 17, 1 (Spring 1984): 79–92.

———. " 'Verses on the Death of Dr. Swift,' 'The Beasts' Confession to the Priest,' and the Curious Double Dean," *Concerning Poetry* 20 (1987): 19–39.

Fuchs, Jacob. "Ovid and Swift: Cadenus and Vanessa." *Classical and Modern Literature* 17, 3 (Spring 1997): 191–205.

Gill, Pat. " 'Filth of All Hues and Odors': Public Parks, City Showers, and Promiscuous Acquaintance in Rochester and Swift," *Genre* 27, 4 (1994): 333–350.

Gilmore, Thomas B., Jr. "Freud and Swift: A Psychological Reading of 'Strephon and Chloe,' " *PLL* 19 (1978): 147–151.

———. "The Comedy of Swift's Scatological Poems," *PMLA* 91 (1976): 33–43.

Greene, Donald. "On Swift's 'Scatological' Poems," *Sewanee Review* 74 (1967): 672–889.

Greene, Donald, Peter J. Schakel, and Thomas B. Gilmore, Jr. "Swift's Scatological Poems," *PMLA* 91 (1976): 464–467.

Hammond, Brean S. "Corinna's Dream," *The Eighteenth Century* 36, 2 (1995): 99–118.

Horne, J. "Swift's Comic Poetry." In *Augustan Worlds: New Essays in Eighteenth-Century Literature*, edited by J. C. Hilson et al. Lanham, Md.: Rowman and Littlefield, 1978.

Jaffe, Nora Crow. *The Poet Swift*. Hanover, N.H.: University Press of New England, 1977.

Jarrell, Mackie Langham. " 'Ode to the King': Some Contests, Dissensions, and Exchanges among

Jonathan Swift, John Dunton, and Henry Jones," *Texas Studies in Literature and Language* 19, 7 (1965): 145–159.

Johnson, Maurice. *The Sin of Wit: Jonathan Swift as Poet.* Syracuse, N.Y.: Syracuse University Press, 1950.

Karian, Stephen. "Reading the Material Text of Swift's 'Verses on the Death,'" *SEL* (2001): 515–544.

Keegan, Timothy. "Swift's Self-Portraits in Verse." In *Augustan Studies: Essays in Honor of Irvin Ehrenpreis,* edited by Douglas Lane Patey and Timothy Keegan, 127–143. Newark: University of Delaware Press, 1985.

Kulisheck, Clarence L. "Swift's Octosyllabics and the Hudibrastic Tradition," *Journal of English and Germanic Philology* 53 (1954): 361–368.

Manlove, C. N. "Swift's Strictures: 'A Description of the Morning' and Some Others," *SEL* 29, 3 (Summer 1989): 463–472.

Maresca, Thomas E. "Men Imagining Women Imagining Men: Swift's *Cadenus and Vanessa,*" *Studies in Eighteenth-Century Culture* 24 (1995): 243–257.

Mayhew, George P. "Jonathan Swift's 'On the Burning of Whitehall in 1697' Re-examined," *Harvard Library Bulletin* 19 (1971): 399–411.

Mueller, Judith C. "Imperfect Enjoyment at Market Hill: Impotence, Desire, and Reform in Swift's Poems to Lady Acheson," *ELH* 66, 1 (Spring 1999): 51–70.

Nussbaum, Felicity. "The 'Sex's Flight': Women and Time in Swift's Poetry." In *The Brink of All We Hate: English Satires, 1660–1750,* 94–116. Lexington: University Press of Kentucky, 1984.

Oliver, Kathleen M. "Swift's 'Mrs. Harris's Petition,'" *Explicator* 53, 4 (Summer 1994): 216–219.

Parker, Todd. "Swift's 'A Description of a City Shower': The Epistemological Force of Filth." In *Ideas, Aesthetics, and Inquiries in the Early Modern Era, IV,* edited by Kevin L. Cope, Laura Morrow, and Anna Battigelli, 285–304. New York: AMS, 1998.

Parkin, Rebecca P. "Swift's Baucis and Philemon: A Sermon in the Burlesque Mode," *Satire Newsletter* 19, 7 (1970): 109–114.

Peterson, Leland D. "Problems of Authenticity and Text in Three Early Poems Attributed to Swift," *Harvard Library Bulletin* 33, 4 (Fall 1985): 404–424.

———. "Revisions of Swift's 'On the Day of Judgment,'" *Papers of the Bibliographical Society of America* 86, 4 (December 1992): 461–471.

Pollak, Ellen. *The Poetics of Sexual Myth: Gender and Ideology in the Verse of Swift and Pope.* Chicago: University of Chicago Press, 1985.

———. " 'Things, Which Must Not Be Exprest': Teaching Swift's Scatological Poems about Women." In *Teaching Eighteenth Century Poetry,* edited by Christopher Fox, 177–186. New York: AMS, 1990.

Probyn, Clive T. "The Source for Swift's 'Fable of the Bitches,'" *Notes and Queries* 19 (1968): 2.

Rabb, Melinda Alliker. "Remembering in Swift's 'The Lady's Dressing Room,'" *Texas Studies in Language and Literature* 32 (Fall 1990): 375–396.

Rawson, Claude. " 'I the Lofty Stile Decline': Self-Apology and the 'Heroick Strain' in Some of Swift's Poems." In *The English Hero, 1660–1800,* edited by Robert Folkenflik, 79–115. Newark and London: University of Delaware Press, 1982.

———. "The Nightmares of Strephon: Nymphs of the City in the Poem of Swift, Baudelaire, Eliot." In *English Literature in the Age of Disguise,* edited by Maximillian E. Novak, 57–99. Berkeley and Los Angeles: University of California Press, 1977.

Real, Hermann J. "A Swift Conundrum: *The Beasts' Confession to the Priest,* l, 216," *The East-Central Intelligencer* 18, 2 (2004): 8–12.

———. "Swift's *A Description of the Morning* (1709), ll. 11–12 and 14," *The East-Central Intelligencer* 19, 2 (2005): 32–35.

———. "That 'Flower of Swift's Cynicism,' *The Lady's Dressing Room,* Again," *East-Central Intelligencer* 15, 2 (2001): 8–13.

Reynolds, Richard. "Swift's 'Humble Petition' from a Pregnant Frances Harris?" *Scriblerian* 5, 1 (Autumn 1972): 38–39.

Rodino, Richard H. "Blasphemy or Blessing?: Swift's 'Scatological Poems,'" *PLL* 14 (1978): 152–170.

———. "The Private Sense of *Cadenus and Vanessa,*" *Concerning Poetry* 19, 2 (1978): 41–47.

———. " 'Worse Than Swift': 'The Beasts' Confession,' Tradition and Rhetoric," *Swift Studies* 3 (1988): 79–90.

Rogers, Pat. "Plunging in the Southern Waves: Swift's Poem on the Bubble," *Yearbook of English Studies* 18 (1988): 41–50.

Rothstein, Eric. "Jonathan Swift as Jupiter: 'Baucis and Philemon.'" In *The Augustan Milieu: Essays Presented to Louis A. Landa,* edited by Henry K. Miller, Eric Rothstein, and George S. Rousseau, 205–224. Oxford: Clarendon Press, 1970.

Schakel, Peter J. "'Sauce for Flat Meat': The Epigrammatic Context of Swift's Verse," *Swift Studies* 4 (1989): 79–86.

———. *The Poetry of Jonathan Swift: Allusion and the Development of a Poetic Style.* Madison: University of Wisconsin Press, 1978.

———. "Swift's Remedy for Love: The 'Scatological' Poems," *PLL* 19 (1978): 137–147.

Sherbo, Arthur. "Swift's Abuse of Poetic Diction," *College Literature* 15, 3 (1988): 233–248.

Shinagel, Michael. *A Concordance to the Poems of Jonathan Swift.* Ithaca, N.Y., and London: Cornell University Press, 1972.

Siebert, Donald T. "Swift's Fiat Odor: The Excremental Re-Vision," *Eighteenth-Century Studies* 19, 1 (1985): 21–38.

Vieth, David M. "A Symposium on Women in Swift's Poems: Vanessa, Stella, Lady Acheson, and Celia," *PLL* 19, 2 (1978). 115–151.

Weber, Harold. "Comic and Tragic Satire in Swift's Poetry," *SEL* 23, 3 (1983): 447–464.

Williams, Aubrey. "Swift and the Poetry of Allusion: 'The Journal.'" In *Literary Theory and Structure: Essays in Honor of William K. Wimsatt,* edited by Frank Brady, John Palmer, and Martin Price. New Haven, Conn., and London: Yale University Press, 1973. 227–243.

Wimsatt, William K. "Rhetoric and Poems: The Example of Swift." In *The Author in His Work: Essays on a Problem in Criticism,* edited by Louis L. Martz, Aubrey Williams, and Patricia Meyer Spacks. New Haven, Conn., and London: Yale University Press, 1978. 229–244.

Winch, Allison. "'The Nymph Grown Furious, Roar'd': Lady Mary Wortley Montagu's Response to Jonathan Swift's 'The Lady's Dressing Room.'" In *Misogynism in Literature: Any Place, Any Time.* Frankfurt am Main: Peter Lang, 2004.

Woolley, David. *Swift's Later Poems: Studies in Circumstances and Texts.* New York: Garland, 1988.

Zimmerman, Everett. "Swift's Scatological Poetry: A Praise of Folly," *Modern Language Quarterly* 48, 2 (1987): 124–144.

# WORKS CITED

(This list includes only those works specifically referenced in the text. Please see the bibliography for a more comprehensive list of primary and secondary sources.)

*The Account Books of Jonathan Swift,* edited by Paul V. Thompson and Dorothy Jay Thompson. Newark and London: University of Delaware Press, 1984.

Asimov, Isaac. *The Annotated Gulliver's Travels.* New York: Clarkson N. Potter, 1980.

Backsheider, Paula. *Daniel Defoe: His Life.* Baltimore: Johns Hopkins University Press, 1989.

Barnett, Louise K. *Swift's Poetic Worlds.* Newark and London: University of Delaware Press; London and Toronto: Associated University Press, 1981.

Bate, W. Jackson. *Samuel Johnson.* New York: Harcourt, 1977.

Boyle, Frank. *Swift as Nemesis: Modernity and Its Satirist.* Stanford, Calif.: Stanford University Press, 2000.

Bullitt, John M. *Jonathan Swift and the Anatomy of Satire: A Study of Satiric Technique.* Cambridge, Mass.: Harvard University Press, 1953.

Clark, Carlton. " 'Such a Vision of the Street as the Street Hardly Understands': Jonathan Swift, T. S. Eliot, and the Anti-Pastoral." Document server of the Georg-August-Universität Göttingen. Available online. URL: http://webdoc.sub.gwdg.de/edoc/ia/eese/artic20/clark/4_2000.html. Accessed September 22, 2005.

Clark, Paul Odell. *A Gulliver Dictionary.* Chapel Hill: University of North Carolina Press, 1953.

DePorte, Michael. "Teaching the Third Voyage." In *Approaches to Teaching Swift's "Gulliver's Travels,"* 57–62. New York: MLA, 1988.

Downie, J. A. *Jonathan Swift: Political Writer.* London: Routledge & Kegan Paul, 1984.

Ehrenpreis, Irvin. *Swift: The Man, His Works and the Age.* 3 vols. Cambridge, Mass.: Harvard University Press, 1962–83.

Elias, A. C., Jr. *Swift at Moor Park: Problems in Biography and Criticism.* Philadelphia: University of Pennsylvania Press, 1982.

Fabricant, Carole. *Swift's Landscape.* Notre Dame, Ind.: University of Notre Dame Press, 1995.

———. "Swift the Irishman." In *The Cambridge Companion to Jonathan Swift,* edited by Christopher Fox, 48–72. Cambridge and New York: Cambridge University Press, 2003.

Ferguson, Oliver. *Jonathan Swift and Ireland.* Urbana: University of Illinois Press, 1962.

Fischer, John Irwin. *On Swift's Poetry.* Gainesville: University Press of Florida, 1978.

Fox, Christopher, ed. *The Cambridge Companion to Jonathan Swift.* Cambridge and New York: Cambridge University Press, 2003.

Glendinning, Victoria. *Jonathan Swift: A Portrait.* New York: Henry Holt, 1998.

Gubar, Susan. "The Female Monster in Augustan Satire," *Signs: A Journal of Women in Culture and Society* 3 (1977): 380–394.

Higgins, Ian. *Swift's Politics: A Study in Disaffection.* Cambridge: Cambridge University Press, 1994.

Howson, Gerald. *Thief-Taker General.* London: Hutchinson, 1970.

Hunter, J. Paul. "*Gulliver's Travels* and the Novel." In *The Genres of* Gulliver's Travels, edited by Frederik N. Smith, 56–74. Newark: University of Delaware Press, 1990.

Jaffe, Nora Crow. "Jonathan Swift." In *Dictionary of Literary Biography* Vol. 95, *Eighteenth-Century British Poets,* edited by John Sitter, 275–301. Bruccoli Clark Layman/Gale Group, 1990.

———. *The Poet Swift.* Hanover, N.H.: University Press of New England, 1977.

Kelly, Patrick. "Swift on Money and Economics." In *The Cambridge Companion to Jonathan Swift,* edited by Christopher Fox, 128–145. Cambridge and New York: Cambridge University Press, 2003.

Knowles, Ronald. *"Gulliver's Travels": The Politics of Satire.* New York: Twayne, 1996.

Landa, Louis A. *Swift and the Church of Ireland.* 2d ed. Oxford: Clarendon Press, 1965.

*The London Encyclopedia,* edited by Ben Weinreb and Christopher Hibbert, Bethesda, Md.: Adler and Adler, 1983.

Monk, Samuel Holt. "The Pride of Lemuel Gulliver." *Sewanee Review* 63 (1955): 48–71.

Nokes, David. *Jonathan Swift: A Hyprocrite Reversed.* Oxford: Oxford University Press, 1987.

Pope, Alexander. *The Dunciad Variorum.* In *Poems,* edited by John Butt, 317–459. New Haven, Conn.: Yale University Press, 1963.

Price, Martin. *Swift's Rhetorical Art: A Study in Structure and Meaning.* New Haven, Conn.: Yale University Press, 1953.

Quintana, Ricardo. *The Mind and Art of Jonathan Swift.* 1936. Reprint, Gloucester, Mass.: Peter Smith, 1965.

Radner, John B. "The Struldbruggs, the Houyhnhnms, and the Good Life." *SEL* 17 (1977): 419–433.

Rawson, Claude. *Gulliver and the Gentle Reader: Studies in Swift and Our Time.* London: Routledge and Kegan Paul, 1973.

"Reviving the Mayfair May Fair." Available online. URL: http://news.bbc.co.uk/1/hi/uk/1959418.stm. Accessed September 22, 2005.

Rogers, Pat. *Grub Street: Studies in a Subculture.* London: Methuen, 1972.

Schakel, Peter J. "Jonathan Swift." In *Dictionary of Literary Biography.* Vol. 101, *British Prose Writers, 1660–1800,* edited by Donald T. Siebert, 319–351. Bruccoli Clark Layman/Gale Group, 1991.

Skau, Michael W. "Flimnap, Lilliput's Acrobatic Treasures." *American Notes and Queries* 8 (1970): 134–35.

Swift, Jonathan. *Complete Poems,* edited by Pat Rogers. London: Penguin, 1983.

———. *Correspondence,* edited by Harold Williams, 5 vols. Oxford: Clarendon Press, 1963–65. (Referenced as *Corr.* throughout the text.)

———. *Correspondence,* edited by David Woolley, 4 vols. Frankfurt am Main: Peter Lang, 1999–  .

———. *Gulliver's Travels,* edited by Robert DeMaria. Rev. ed. New York: Penguin, 2003.

———. *Gulliver's Travels,* edited by Albert J. Rivero. New York and London: Norton, 2002.

———. *Journal to Stella,* edited by Harold Williams. 1948. Reprint, Oxford, England: Clarendon Press, 1975.

———. *Poems,* edited by Harold Williams. 3 vols. Oxford, England: Clarendon Press, 1958.

———. *Prose Works,* edited by Herbert Davis et al. 14 vols. Oxford, England: Blackwell/Shakespeare Head, 1939–74.

———. *A Tale of a Tub and Other Works,* edited by Angus Ross and David Woolley. Oxford: Oxford University Press, 1984.

*Swift vs. Mainwaring: The Examiner and the Medley,* edited by Frank H. Ellis. Oxford: Clarendon Press, 1985.

Ward, Robert E. *Prince of Dublin Printers: The Letters of George Faulkner.* Lexington: University Press of Kentucky, 1972.

Williams, Kathleen, ed. *Swift: The Critical Heritage.* London: Routledge and Kegan Paul, 1970.

# INDEX